The Child Placement Handbook
Research, policy and practice

The Child Placement Handbook
Research, policy and practice

Edited by Gillian Schofield
and John Simmonds

ADOPTION
& FOSTERING

Published by
British Association for Adoption & Fostering
(BAAF)
Saffron House
6–10 Kirby Street
London EC1N 8TS
www.baaf.org.uk

Charity registration 275689

British Library Cataloguing in Publication Data
A catalogue record for this book is available from the British Library

ISBN 978 1 905664 46 7

Project management by Shaila Shah, Director of Publications, BAAF
Designed by Andrew Haig & Associates
Typeset by Avon DataSet Ltd, Bidford on Avon
Printed in Great Britain by The Athenaeum Press
Trade distribution by Turnaround Publisher Services, Unit 3, Olympia Trading Estate,
Coburg Road, London N22 6TZ

BAAF is the leading UK-wide membership organisation for all those concerned with adoption,
fostering and child care issues.

FSC
Mixed Sources
Product group from well-managed
forests and other controlled sources
Cert no. SGS-COC-2482
www.fsc.org
© 1996 Forest Stewardship Council

Contents

Preface

Having been concerned with issues of child welfare for over 50 years it is unsurprising that I should compare the present with the past. Of course, there have been major changes in both policy and practice; but one of the most impressive changes has been in the range and quality of the research that is available to those grappling with the complex issues that bedevil this field. It was not so long ago that a fairly comprehensive article or chapter could be written without making reference to much more than a dozen or so pieces of relevant research. That situation has changed in a radical fashion, as this collection of essays so clearly demonstrates. Indeed, it becomes increasingly difficult for those who wish to inform themselves to be aware of what relevant and, equally important, what *reliable* and up-to-date research is available, despite the internet and the commendable efforts of a number of individuals and agencies to create channels of easier access. Furthermore, we are now expected to look beyond British studies and the disciplines conventionally associated with children's services. Equally, not only has the classification of topics that clamour for attention altered but their number has multiplied considerably as our social structures have been modified by demographic change, by immigration, by evolving cultural norms and, not least, by the often graphic exposure of shortcomings in what has been done or not done. In this last sense, child care (I use the term that was widely employed until recently) has become increasingly politicised, both locally and nationally.

All that justifies a volume such as this, which is offered as a handbook for those who are now expected to be better informed than ever before – both practitioners and politicians. Nonetheless, it might be noted in passing that the term *handbook* originally referred to a book of reference that was small enough to be held in the hand and small enough to be carried with you. This work is hardly that. What it is, however, is a benchmark and a benchmark for two reasons. First, it brings us up to date with much of the research and practice that bears upon over twenty issues that presently preoccupy those concerned with aspects of child placement. Secondly, in doing this, it provides an interesting contemporary commentary on what we consider these issues to be; that is, it offers a reflection of how, in 2008, we have chosen to divide up the field as researchers, sponsors of research, practitioners and politicians. It would be both interesting and useful to be able to compare the present volume with another such "handbook" of, say, 40 years ago; but, to my knowledge, no such publication exists. However, I did find on my bookshelf *The International Handbook of Child Care and Protection* that appeared in 1924 and which described the measures that had been taken on behalf of children by countries around the world. We tend to forget that, even then, there were those who aspired to see the trial and error method in the care of vulnerable children giving way to, as Grace Abbott put it in her foreword, 'a scientific determination of their needs by means of careful study of accumulated experience and by research in new fields'.

In the light of this one could ask how this present benchmark collection might be seen in 25 or 30 years time. What new issues will have emerged or what new ways of under-standing or conceptualising the old ones will have been developed? In what ways might research and practice have moved on? At least the commentator of, say, 2030, will have this impressive volume to which to refer. But, of more immediate consequence, it provides those wrestling with today's problems of placement policies and practice points of reference on a wide range of current issues.

Roy Parker
Emeritus Professor of Social Policy, University of Bristol
Fellow, Centre for Social Policy, Dartington

Acknowledgements

The pathway to publication of an edited book is a complex affair. The original idea for this collection came about in discussions in BAAF's Research Group Advisory Committee, which brings together members of the research community to identify, discuss and promote the application of research findings to child placement policy and practice. We are very grateful to them for their commitment and for the support they have given as the project has developed.

We are also grateful to each of the contributors to this volume both for their individual expertise and effort in respect of their own chapters and also for the general advice and guidance they have provided as the project has gathered momentum and been brought to a conclusion. It goes without saying that the book is made up of their individual contributions, but their unseen effort needs to be acknowledged as well.

We owe a particular debt of gratitude to Shaila Shah, BAAF's Director of Publications. Sitting in an adjacent office as one of us does (JS), the sheer volume of first the electronic data that Shaila handled, and then the pages of paper proofs was an astonishing sight, especially for a book that is one of the largest that she has ever produced. The attention to detail and the capacity to encompass the different styles, views and working practices of such a large number of contributors is truly remarkable. In this she has been well supported by Jo Francis, editorial assistant at BAAF and Abi Omotoso who has broken herself into the production editorial task on this volume. Our sincere thanks to all three.

We are both also very much aware that the process of writing or editing any book relies on the patience and unfailing support of our families, Gail, Rachel and Adam, Paul, Marianne and Jonathan. So not just for their support during the preparation of this book, but for their tolerance of the many times when we are writing for deadlines and hardly look up from the computer – they deserve our deepest gratitude.

And lastly this is a book primarily about children and young people, birth parents and families, foster carers and adoptive parents who have lived through and, for some, continue to live through the most difficult of circumstances. The research reported on and discussed in this book is about them and is intended to help improve the services they or those in the future receive. Behind the statistics and findings research concerns itself with, there are individual stories of heroic achievement and determination, sometimes unbearable pain and often challenging questions about what happened, why it happened and what the consequences have been. Every one of those stories is important and this book could not have been constructed without those stories being told.

Gillian Schofield and John Simmonds
November 2008

The editors

Dr Gillian Schofield is Professor of Child and Family Social Work and Co-Director of the Centre for Research on the Child and Family at the University of East Anglia. She was Chair of the BAAF Research Group Advisory Committee from 2001–2006. An experienced social worker, she practised for some years as a Guardian ad Litem. Her research and teaching interests are in attachment theory and family placement practice, the impact of maltreatment on children's development, the role of long-term foster care as a positive permanence option and the experiences of parents of children in long-term foster care.

Dr John Simmonds is Director of Policy, Research and Development at the British Association for Adoption and Fostering. Before coming to BAAF, he was head of the social work programmes at Goldsmiths College, University of London. He is a qualified social worker and has substantial experience in child protection, family placement and residential care settings. He has published widely. He is the adoptive father of 2 children.

Introduction

The last thirty years have seen a significant investment by successive Governments in providing a research evidence base for child placement and in making connections between research, policy and practice. As Malcolm Hill points out in the opening chapter of this anthology, the fit is rarely perfect – we do not always get from research all the answers we need to inform policy and practice, and policy and practice do not always respond to and reflect research findings in an accurate and complete way. However, what has emerged over these three decades is a generation of exceptional researchers and writers, committed to producing and disseminating research that follows rigorous methodological principles and that can be systematically applied in practice. These researchers and writers combine their rigour with a passion for the welfare of children, their families and their caregivers in residential care, foster care, and adoption, and with concern and respect for the social workers who undertake one of the most demanding, though also one of the most rewarding, professional tasks in our society. This collection of chapters is designed to capture something of this wealth of knowledge and wisdom.

Research in a time of change – law, policy, and practice

The publication of this book comes at a time when the Children and Young Persons Act 2008 in England is aiming at significantly improving outcomes for children in public care. The Act is just one part of the comprehensive programme arising from the White Paper *Care Matters: Time for change* and the subsequent commitments included in *Care Matters: Time to deliver for children in care* (Department for Children, Schools and Families (DCSF) 2007, 2008). It follows the significant changes in placement practice since the implementation of the Adoption and Children Act 2002 and the Children Act 2004. The addition of Special Guardianship to the range of placement options, for example, has demanded the development of new procedures and practice at local level. In Wales, the Welsh Assembly has passed its Legislative Competence Order, part of its programme focused on all vulnerable children. Scotland is working on the implementation of its Adoption and Children (Scotland) Act 2007 and its kinship and foster care policy. Northern Ireland is considering the format of its new adoption legislation.

Whatever the outcome of these and other legislative and policy developments in the four countries that make up the UK, one thing is certain – they are a part of a continuous process of change reflecting both concern and aspirations for a group of children and young people temporarily or permanently separated from their birth families, and an awareness of the potential short- and long-term consequences for them and for society as a whole of the quality of care they receive. Both concern about and aspirations for these children and young people are also part of a wider political concern that, at a time of unprecedented national wealth, the UK has been identified as one of the worst countries in the developed world to raise a child (UNICEF, 2007) and that social mobility has ground to a halt with a vast gulf between the richest and poorest sections of the community. The focus on improving outcomes for children and young people separated from their birth families is undoubtedly connected to a more general concern about the social, educational and health outcomes for a large section of the population – or when it isn't, it should be.

The certainty of change is a problem facing the publication of any book – it reflects what it is known at that point in time, and some areas will be quickly supplemented by new research, policy and practice that further articulates, develops and maybe changes what is currently accepted as the "best" in research, policy or practice. At the heart of the English Government's set of new initiatives, for example, is a recognition that, although many looked after and adopted children's lives are transformed for the better by the care and support they receive, too many children continue to enter adult life without having resolved their early emotional, behavioural and health difficulties and without having gained the educational, social and relationship skills they need to fulfil their potential in adulthood. Although these outcomes are undoubtedly linked to a range of adverse pre-care experiences, there are legitimate concerns that our policy and practice in providing services to children separted from their birth parents – whether through reunification, foster care, residential care, adoption or other routes – need to be improved.

The problem of translating professional skills and knowledge, activity and effort, structures and procedures into measurable outcomes is a general problem across social, health and educational policy areas and can have significant political consequences, as policy makers attempt to define what works and then promote it. Research in child placement, therefore, can play an essential part in aiding understanding of the complex relationship between systems, professional practice and child outcomes, by describing, analysing and suggesting links between them. This challenging task is clearly recognised in every chapter of this collection, as authors from research and practice set out and evaluate the evidence: its strengths, its limitations and its implications for future policy and practice.

The role of the state as corporate parent

The role of the state in the lives of children, families and caregivers in placements of all kinds raises important questions in policy and practice that are by no means new. For over 200 years, the state has taken some responsibility for the care of children whose safety and well-being are at risk. But the role of the state more explicitly as a "corporate parent" has preoccupied policy makers and researchers since the 1960s and 1970s. The tensions in the relationship between the state and families were summarised by Roy Parker (1980) in a significant review of the UK's system of state care and have been more recently reviewed and debated by a group of distinguished researchers from the UK (several of whom have chapters in this book) and the USA in an article titled 'Can the corporate state parent?' (Bullock *et al*, 2006).

The working party chaired by Roy Parker in the 1970s identified that, where children are 'received into care', there are four principal changes for a child previously cared for by parents at home. First, there is the separation of the actual day-to-day care for children from the formal responsibility for them by the local authority. Connected to this is a second major change, that this responsibility is divided among a number of people, each taking on specific tasks, thus creating a network of people who need to collaborate and work together, but where the difficulties of doing so can be considerable. Third, there is the problem that, although certain parental rights and duties – parental responsibilities as we would now define them – transfer to the local authority when children come into care, there is a lack of clarity about how these are to be defined and shared. Parker (1980, p 65) states:

The transfer of the care of the child is not an exact process. It is not an act of total severance either legally or physically, and never emotionally. Visits are made, letters are written and things are remembered. Feelings of interest, guilt, love, anger and curiosity are not expunged; and when the pattern of daily relationships is drastically changed, new and lasting attachments are inevitably formed.

This then brings us to a fourth major change: the fact that whatever legal and administrative arrangements are made, the child will make new relationships with new caregivers, relationships that may include formation of new attachments, but also the development of new family loyalties. A question is thus raised about how, in spite of the potential benefits of these new relationships, the potential tensions they create for the child, their parents and the new carers are reconciled. As Parker (1980, p 67) goes on to say:

Complexity, diversity and ambiguity are familiar features of substitute care. For the child in particular they accentuate the conflict between the claims of a lost past and a new present; but the adults involved also experience and have to live with that tension.

These changes and the dilemmas they present are also acknowledged by Bullock et al (2006) and remain an ongoing challenge for policy makers to plan for and practitioners to manage in their work with children and families.

The power of this analysis is in its recognition of the often acute – and inevitable – tensions that lie at the centre of the care system, when the authority of the parents and the boundary around the family of origin become fragmented as the state assumes either a voluntary or compulsory role for the children of that family. The boundaries around the child's relationships in foster families and residential placements, however, also require clarification; in particular, the role and relationship expectations that apply within a placement, whether caregivers are providing temporary, long-term or permanent care. The importance of maintaining a sense of continuity, cohesion, involvement and security needs to be recognised from the perspective of the child, the child's parents, residential care staff, foster carers, field social workers and central government. If there is one theme that stands out in this discussion, it is the necessity of creating a shared understanding about what is happening, why it is happening, what is expected to happen and when it is expected to happen by.

Planning for children's welfare in the context of a range of core principles – including taking account of the wishes and feelings of children, working in partnership with parents and consulting and informing multi-disciplinary networks – creates significant challenges for individual practitioners and for the system in which they work. There is great potential to achieve good outcomes for children and families, but also ambiguities and contradictions that cannot be glossed over. If the child is not to suffer from indecision or the constant skirmishing that conflicting demands and principles can produce, then means have to be found to affix responsibility, take decisions and check that things needing be done are done. In this book, chapters provide an analysis of research concerning a range of often finely balanced decisions – reunification with birth families, the placement of siblings, the role of contact, for example. The authors recognise the need to weigh up such factors as the quality of children's family ties and their need for care and safety, and to focus on what evidence is available that can help practitioners make difficult judgements – and defend them.

Thus far the focus of discussion of corporate parenting has been on children in care, but the decision to place a child in care for adoption carries its own weighty, and also often contradictory, set of child and family-focused imperatives. The fact that in adoption there is clarity that parental responsibility in law rests with the adoptive parents does not, of course, remove the complex emotions and loyalties, hopes and fears that may be experienced by children, birth parents, adoptive parents and the social workers involved. Some uncertainties are resolved, but adoption remains the most drastic intervention that the state can make in the life of a child and a family. As Thoburn's chapter explains, adoption from care and without parental consent is not legally or politically acceptable in most countries, and in the UK it is a step taken only after very careful assessment. The role of social work practitioners in adoption could not be more demanding – it is about contributing to the creation of new families on the basis of professional assessments and judgements of children and adopters, including their needs for support. Adoption practice with all its complexities is discussed in a range of chapters in this collection that focus on policy, practice and outcomes. Even though final decisions are made by the courts, making and supporting adoption placements is an extraordinary responsibility for which the very best training and support is needed – as well as access to the very best research evidence.

The role of theory

In exploring the links between research, policy and practice in child placement, it is important to acknowledge the role that theory, especially developmental theory, plays in underpinning how we think about and make sense of children and their families, their strengths and difficulties, and go on to respond to their needs. One goal of bringing together this body of work was also to demonstrate the richness and diversity of the theoretical frameworks and approaches that are currently in use and underpin social work as a discipline and child placement as a skilled and specialist area of practice.

Social work, especially social work with children and families, has always been in effect multi-disciplinary, needing to draw on and engage with psychology, sociology, law, health, education, ethics, psychiatry, counselling, social policy – and more. The balance in the contribution of different disciplines and theoretical frameworks to social work has changed over time (Stevenson, 1998), but all the difficult child placement questions that face policy makers and practitioners require an integration of disciplines – for example, human rights and psychology, professional ethics and social policy – in forms that will be evident in the varied chapters in this book.

Raising the profile and improving the knowledge base of social work as a profession

The need to raise the profile and expectations of social work as a profession in the light of such complex responsibilities has had a major impact on social work training. It has become an all graduate profession and post-qualifying programmes, including some specialising in child placement, have become an established part of the social work scene. The introduction of compulsory registration for social workers with the General Social Care Councils in 2006, with its expectation of continuous learning during a professional career, has also provided support for the principle of a better-read, better-informed workforce.

A major impetus behind this book, therefore, is to provide the full range of qualifying, post qualifying and experienced social workers and social work managers with a book that brings together expertise from a wide range of specialist research that informs child placement practice. Each chapter requires the reader to think carefully about the arguments that are being put, to reflect on the complexity of each issue, and to consider how they can apply this knowledge in the work they undertake.

The value of social work and social workers

This book demonstrates not only the value of research for social work policy and practice, but also demonstrates – and celebrates – the essential value of social work with children and families. Decisions to place a child in one family or another, to move a child or to place siblings together or apart are never made lightly and will require great skill as well as provoking powerful feelings in social workers that need to be managed. Helping a child to express their wishes and feelings or to participate in life story work can be at times difficult, painful but also extremely rewarding. Offering support simultaneously to children, birth parents and caregivers in all settings requires social workers to be flexible, empathic and committed to the welfare of all parties. Birth parents may have harmed children and had children removed and yet are entitled to our concern and support. The personal qualities and professional skills that social workers need to bring to these tasks can be enhanced by confidence that they are working on the best available evidence. Research will play an important part in informing and supporting their difficult decisions and complex roles – and thus increase the likelihood that professional judgements lead to better outcomes for children and families.

Some comments on this collection and its context

This is a large collection, but it has still inevitably had to be selective. There are some regrettable gaps, particularly on private fostering – an issue which is subject to some debate as well as policy initiatives as the number of notifications remain much smaller than the number of children estimated to be in placement. It is the one issue that straddles the boundary between on the one hand, the privacy of family life and the importance of families being able to make their own arrangements for their children, and on the other hand the direct and immediate concern that the State has for children that it is caring for, whether this is through voluntary agreements with parents or through a court order.

Other issues have proved difficult to address. We are very aware that devolution of governments in the four countries that make up the United Kingdom has resulted in a complex picture when looking at research findings. The different legal systems have long produced a different emphasis and interpretation in the way that issues are defined and addressed. Research studies have emanated from the four countries and sometimes these specifically relate to the evaluation of different country specific policy or practice initiatives. Sometimes, it is not clear what the relationship is between the policy and legislative context and the dataset and methodology used in the study. Sometimes, this matters but at other times a study's findings seem to be generic. There is no easy solution to this problem and readers will no doubt be placing what is presented and discussed in the chapters in their own policy and practice contexts where the fit may be less than perfect. It might be expected that the increasing divergence of policy and legislative drivers in future years may make this issue more challenging.

Another issue which has been difficult to fully address is the increasing complexity of a child and family's ethnic, religious, language and cultural background. It is a core issue in legislation, in policy and in practice, and researchers will inevitably be concerned about how it influences their research questions, the methodology they choose and the way they analyse and report their findings. But often, unless the study is specifically exploring minority groups, sample sizes will reflect the fact that these groups are in a significant minority and it will be difficult for researchers to reliably identify the implications in the findings. This may be particularly frustrating when the issues have had and continue to have a prominence in family finding, although often crudely polarising around the trans-racial, "same-race" placement debate.

Finally, an issue that should not be forgotten is the link between those children that do become the responsibility of the state and those that never become so. In terms of needs and outcomes, for many children there may not be so very much difference between these two groups and the policy and practice issues this raises are very important. There is an explicit focus in a number of chapters on movement out of the care system – reunification back home, family and friends care and leaving care. In that sense the fluidity in the system is recognised and the way that it is embedded within a much larger community of children from disadvantaged economic, social, educational and health circumstances. But the wider political and policy perspective on this should not be forgotten.

Outline of the book

The first section sets the scene in relation to the role of research in child placement, child placement policy in an international context, the developmental consequences of abuse and neglect and a key issue for all practice in child placement – listening to children and young people. The second section covers not only a range of placement options, but also some key issues relating to each, such as contact after adoption and fostering adolescents, which extend and complement the core chapters. Because of the overlap in issues around contact in foster care and work with birth families these two topics have been combined within one chapter that is rather longer.

The final section looks at placement issues in relation to meeting the specific needs of children, such as health and education; in relation to certain groups of children, such as disabled children and unaccompanied asylum seeking children; and in relation to specific issues, such as leaving care and access to information.

The length of each chapter creates its own constraints, but the aim is that each chapter will provide not only a research synthesis and an analysis of policy and practice issues, but also references to selected further reading that offer the reader the route to more detailed accounts of the relevant research and theory. We hope that this combination of breadth of subject areas, synthesis of complex material, and opportunities to explore further will meet the varying needs of a wide readership.

References

Bullock R., Courtney M., Parker R., Sinclair I. and Thoburn J. (2006) 'Can the corporate state parent?' *Children and Youth Services Review* 28:11, pp 1344–1358 (reprinted in *Adoption & Fostering*, 30:4, pp 6–19)

Department for Children, Schools and Families (2008) *Care Matters: Time to deliver for children in care*, London: The Stationery Office

Department for Education and Skills (2007) *Care Matters: Time for change*, London: The Stationery Office

Parker R. A. (1980) *Caring for Separated Children*, London: The Macmillan Press

Stevenson O. (1998) 'It was more difficult than we thought: A reflection on 50 years of child welfare practice', *Child and Family Social Work*, 3, pp 153–161

UNICEF (2007) *Child Poverty in Perspective: An overview of child well-being in rich countries*, Innocenti Report Card 7, Florence: UNICEF

Section I
Research, policy and practice in child placement:
setting the scene

1 The place of child placement research in policy and practice

Malcolm Hill

Introduction

The secret of the universe was famously discovered to be Number 42, in the *Hitchhiker's Guide to the Galaxy* by Douglas Adams (1988). Unfortunately, the research guide to the universe of child placement policy and practice is not quite so simple. Choices and decisions that practitioners and caregivers have to make, whether in relation to individual children or service development more generally, are often a matter of balancing up the information available on many matters, of which research evidence is only one. Compared with the experience of individual practitioners, empirical studies are usually based on systematic examination of a more extensive set of circumstances, and so give access to a wider body of knowledge. Yet, as we shall see, this rarely yields lessons that will be true for all cases. At the point of making a decision, a worker or carer will need to exercise judgements about which research evidence might apply to the situation under consideration and how.

In this chapter the aim is to outline some of the key features of relevant research and discuss both the benefits and limitations in applying the lessons of empirical studies. To give a flavour of the issues, let us consider two key research results about placement outcomes that are well substantiated but still need careful examination and application. First is the repeated finding that when children moving to a new placement are over the age of 11 and/or have serious emotional-behavioural difficulties, the placement often ends prematurely (Quinton *et al*, 1998; Wilson *et al*, 2004). Hence, placing older children with serious difficulties is particularly risky. However, the higher risks of poor outcomes for older children apply to all kinds of placements (including return home), yet such children have to be placed somewhere. The most important implication is therefore to build supports and safeguards into the placement plan, including contingency arrangements for when problems arise. Furthermore, some teenagers do well and significantly improve. Research has shown this happens particularly in well-financed, intensively supported placements, when the young person is positive about the proposed move (Walker *et al*, 2002; Farmer *et al*, 2004) or when older children find caregivers who can meet their needs for emotional and family security (Schofield, 2002a, 2002b; Beek and Schofield, 2004). It is important to remember that research identifies probabilities, not certainties, of outcome. The case you are dealing with may be among the exceptions.

A second recurrent and influential research finding is that adoption placements tend to break down less often than foster or residential placements (Sellick and Thoburn, 1996; Triseliotis *et al*, 1997). This has been a major plank in the efforts to place more children for adoption over the last 30 years or so. It means that reasonable confidence is in order about the prospects for most children placed for adoption, but of course not all adoptions do well. Further, for many children, adoption is not possible legally or is unsuitable for other reasons (Lowe and Murch, 2002; Wilson *et al*, 2004). One of the main reasons it is harder for some kinds of placement to succeed is that the children placed tend to be older and more "difficult", so they begin with a greater challenge to success. When researchers take special care to compare children with similar characteristics, the results are not so different. Indeed, a large survey by Fratter *et al* (1991) showed that planned and supported long-term fostering was as successful as adoption for children who had similar ages and difficulty levels when first placed.

Research is not only about outcomes: it can examine other aspects of placements and the associated services. Thus a large body of experimental and observational evidence gives vital insights into children's feelings and behaviour when separated from home and adjusting to a new care context (Howe, 1996). Subtle and detailed research is important here, since some of these reactions may be misleading. A child's friendly smiles towards a visiting birth mother may conceal anxiety, while apparent anger may be a sign of how much the mother is missed rather than a wish to avoid contact (Cairns, 2002; Schofield and Beek, 2006).

At the service level, research can support implementation of more effective policies. For example, recruitment strategies for carers can be, and have been, strengthened by research findings from surveys that motivation is often triggered by word of mouth (having family, friends or neighbours who enjoy fostering) (Triseliotis *et al*, 2000; Sinclair *et al*, 2005). Also, many people perform different kinds of caring at different stages in their lives (e.g. childminding, fostering, residential care), so that careers and services can benefit from transfers across the different sectors (Brannen *et al*, 2007). Residential care has benefited by responding to research evidence about its previous neglect of education (Berridge and Brodie, 1998) and inconsistencies between units, staff and shifts as regards expectations about family contact and degree of encouragement concerning contact (Brown *et al*, 1998; Hill 2000a).

A common criticism of research is that it only tells you what you knew already (or might have guessed). That is not necessarily a problem – it is good that practice wisdom and hunches should be tested against wider evidence. Practice experience and common sense do not always point in a single or correct direction. Common sense might suggest, for example, that it is good for children to be placed in a fostering household where there are others of the same age so they can have playmates and share friends. Repeated studies over nearly 50 years have in fact shown that more placements break down when children in the household are close in age, suggesting rivalry is a more critical consideration than companionship (Trasler, 1960; Wedge and Mantle, 1991). Yet some closely spaced older children do well (Farmer *et al*, 2004), so again this is a matter of risk rather than certainty and requires detailed assessment in each case.

Practice wisdom often suggests that adolescents prefer residential placements because either their family loyalties or the repeated failures of their birth family make them reluctant to engage with a new family. Although many looked after young people in their teens do express a preference for residential care, research suggests that a similar proportion would like a family placement (Triseliotis *et al*, 1995). Some young people are mistrustful of joining a new family, feeling their own has failed them. Then, a family placement may only work if the carers offer warmth but respect a young person's desire for some emotional space, rather than pushing to achieve a close family (Downes, 1992; Triseliotis *et al*, 1995). In other instances, teenagers want and/or are well capable of developing close and rewarding emotional relationships within a new family, which can last well into adulthood (Beek and Schofield, 2004). The important implication is not to jump to conclusions about what is best for young people, but to pay close attention to their wishes and capacities as regards re-engaging with family life, whether closely or at a distance. Research has helped identify some of the skills and approaches to household rules and sanctions that can produce success in foster placements of teenagers with serious multiple difficulties (Walker *et al*, 2002; Lipscombe *et al*, 2003).

Having given some examples of how research yields valuable insights, it is now time to review more generally the relationships between research, policy and practice.

How much should research influence policy and practice?

This chapter is being written for a book promoting the value of research by a former child care practitioner and educator who now specialises in research. Hence it may be taken for granted that I favour a key role to be played by research in both policy and practice. Nevertheless, it is important to recognise that research findings are, and should be, only one of a range of influences on policy choices, case decisions, agency guidance, the rationales for services, treatments and so on. It is necessary for lessons from research to be considered alongside a range of other considerations. These include:

- legislation;
- agency policies;
- values about children and their rights;
- theory;
- practice experience;
- the unique circumstances of each case;
- resources.

Sometimes, these embody research findings. For example, values, theory and research are often interconnected. Over the last decade, it has become increasingly common to emphasise the concept of resilience in child placement (see e.g. Gilligan, 1997; Schofield, 2001). This has been based partly on a shift in perspective to value and conceptualise the strengths of children and other family members, but it is also founded on a body of evidence identifying the kinds of factors that enable children to do well even when their original families are unable to look after them or have neglected/abused them (Daniel and Wassell, 2002; Hill *et al*, 2007).

Undoubtedly, the late 20th century and the first decade of the 21st century witnessed a concerted effort across a broad range of policy areas and professional practices to take more account of research. Two key phrases sum up the thrust of this trend: "evidence-based practice/policy" and "what works" (Trinder and Reynolds, 2000; Davies *et al*, 2000). The former represents a general desire to see practice and policy based on empirical evidence, while the latter is more specific in suggesting that only those interventions or treatments should be used that have been empirically tested and proven to "work". Both approaches are sometimes used to suggest that research should be the almost exclusive or predominant basis for policy and practice decisions. Some prefer the phrase "evidence-informed" rather than "based" (Attree, 2006) to suggest a more balanced and perhaps more realistic approach, where evidence is influential but takes its place alongside other important considerations as noted above. This acknowledges that certain foundations for policy and practice are moral in nature, such as principles in UK legislation and the UN Convention on the Rights of the Child about the centrality of children's welfare, safety and views. Research can help inform the application of such principles by documenting key welfare needs or wishes of children, for instance.

At least four main reasons may be put forward to specify the benefits of research when compared with the experience of service providers and carers:

- greater objectivity;
- wider knowledge base;
- systematic approach;
- identification of gaps in thinking or provision.

The experiences of professionals and others can be subjective and overly affected by their own attitudes and circumstances. With the best will in the world, experience in families and organisations can lead people to build up taken-for-granted assumptions which may be inaccurate, so it is right that they should be checked against information gathered from a more neutral standpoint. Individual practitioners build up vital understandings from their repeated exposure to similar cases or circumstances to produce practice or clinical wisdom, but these may still be based on only limited numbers ("anecdotal" evidence). Moreover, experiences and hence expectations may be skewed, as when staff or carers regard behaviours they see in looked after children as normal when these may be rare in the wider population. In addition, external researchers are often in a better position to obtain honest answers from the users of services than the professionals providing those services.

Researchers can often draw on a wider and sometimes more typical range of instances, both directly (through a large, representative sample) and indirectly (through placing their work within the context of other research on the same topic). Moreover, researchers often have a specific remit to check out hunches or convictions, by gathering information systematically and reviewing evidence for and against. For example, some practitioners hold the view that secure accommodation is usually harmful for children and so should be avoided if at all possible. Studies have shown that it can indeed provide a distressing or unhelpful experience, but some young people welcome admission and make good progress, at least in the short run (Walker *et al*, 2006). As this example illustrates, research often does not provide straightforward answers, but can usefully challenge generalisations and help to identify the specific factors that help a placement go well.

Research not only serves to confirm, qualify or reject existing ideas and practices, but can be innovative by indicating neglected needs or resources and suggesting new approaches. An example of the former would be the way in which research on the sons and daughters of foster carers showed that they could be both adversely affected by and gain satisfaction from the placement of "outsider" children in "their" homes. They were also vital helpers and confidantes to the looked after children (Pugh, 1996; Hojer, 2004). Of course, many carers and some practitioners were already well aware of such issues, but research helped to shift attention away from an exclusive concern with looked after children's relationships and attachments with adults (especially parents and carers) to recognise more consistently the significance to children of their relationships with other children (Brannen *et al*, 2000).

An instance of innovation with regard to intervention was the action research undertaken by Hazel (1981) and colleagues with the Kent Family Placement scheme to show that foster placements could successfully help adolescents with serious behavioural problems if carers were well supported and remunerated. Previously it had been assumed that only residential care could "cope" with such young people. This project pioneered the way for a wide range of specialist fostering schemes for young people in their teens, including those on remand or who would otherwise be placed in secure accommodation. Evaluations of later projects have yielded further insights to help improve such services (Walker *et al*, 2002; Lipscombe, 2006).

How influential is research, really?

When discussing how influential research *should* be, we have already cited some examples of how it has had an impact, but now fuller consideration is given to the question of how much influence research has. In fact, very little systematic research has been carried out on the topic of research impact, so the points made here are more based on experience, impressions and even speculation than on "hard" evidence.

That said, a number of studies have been undertaken across a range of professions, which indicate that most students and experienced practitioners appear to take very little account of research evidence in their everyday work. This applies in social work, teaching and even health, despite the stronger tradition of research in medicine (Hill, 1999; Davies *et al*, 2005)

When it comes to central and local government policy-makers, it is hard to ascertain the part played by research in affecting or altering priorities compared with that of party policy, constituency consultations, the advice of civil servants or local authority officials, the media, and so on. Probably nearly all researchers have carried out at least one study that appeared to make little or no impression. Evidence-based insights regarded as little gems by the author may sink without trace. A doyen of child care research noted a growth in policy-makers' openness to research over the past 50 years, but also a persistent resistance associated with 'political ideology and short-term expediency' (Parker, 2005, p 26).

Usually there are many demands on the time of policy-makers and many change positions after a few years, so it is hard for them to keep up to date with a wide range of research or to find the time to read lengthy reports. Understandably, there is a tendency to prefer research that has simple rather than complex implications and to favour findings that fit with other political considerations. For instance, the impetus to adoption given by the UK government after 1997 was able to cite findings from research studies showing that the great majority of adoptions work out well (Triseliotis *et al*, 1997), but it is also the case that adopters and adoptees tend to have greater skills and resources for lobbying than looked after children or their birth parents, who – as research shows – are mostly poor and lacking in self confidence (Bebbington and Miles, 1989).

As a consequence of multiple influences on policy and approaches to practice, it is hard to demonstrate simple one-to-one connections between research findings and shifts in directions. The impact of empirical evidence does appear to have been crucial in a number of instances, though usually it is important that research chimes with other influences, that the zeitgeist is favourable. A classic instance of this complexity concerns the effects of research showing the negative effects on young children of being placed in large institutions. In the mid-20th century, Bowlby (1944, 1953) reviewed evidence from various studies to crystallise his conclusion that children brought up in the institutions of the time were seriously damaged emotionally and as a result of this exhibited behavioural difficulties. Although Bowlby went on to conceptualise this largely in terms of children's separation, particularly from their mothers (or as he put it, "mother figures"), the findings fitted with a growing sense among professionals and politicians that large institutions were unsatisfactory places for young children (Heywood, 1978; Hill *et al*, 1991). This led to the development of family group homes in residential care, where children lived in small groups with quasi-parental figures, a housemother and housefather.

The move to make residential care less institutional received a boost in the 1970s when Rutter (1981) reassessed Bowlby's ideas in the light of recent evidence and concluded that negative effects were largely due to inconsistent and impersonal caring rather than separation per se. Subsequently, the promotion of foster care for younger children helped make once common residential nurseries for children under five become largely a thing of the past in the UK, though many remained and even proliferated in other parts of the world (Hill, 2000b). Interestingly the "small" units of 30 or 40 children aged five+ that emerged to replace the larger institutions of the first half of the 20th century themselves came to be seen as too big in the 1990s, with a trend towards units with fewer than 10 young people. This trend did not appear to be much affected by research, but the nature and implications were documented by academic study (e.g. Berridge and Brodie, 1998).

Bowlby developed his ideas into attachment theory (1969), which became probably the most influential way of conceptualising the adjustments and problems experienced by children when placed away from home and when facing moves within care (Howe, 2001; see also Chapter 2). A considerable international body of detailed and rigorous research, largely in the field of developmental psychology, has since been carried out to investigate and elaborate on Bowlby's work. This has provided important insights into children's emotional responses to separation, their formation of new attachments and the effects of abuse and neglect on their ways of relating to others, their behaviour and learning. This has, in turn, informed guidance about how carers and practitioners can best respond to children whose behaviour can seem rejecting and self-destructive (Fahlberg, 1994; Cairns, 2002; Schofield and Beek, 2006).

Interpretation of findings and reframing of issues

Not only does the policy or practice context need to be receptive, but the way in which research evidence is presented or interpreted can be as important in producing change as the findings themselves.

In the UK, a classic study undertaken by Rowe and Lambert (1973) prompted a major shift in thinking about children in care and helped kick-start the permanence movement. The title of the work was significant in itself – *Children Who Wait*. The study here analysed the placement plans for a large sample of children in longer-term care (nearly 3,000) and compared the aims with what actually happened. They concluded that many of the children were left in a kind of limbo, "waiting" for their plan to be put into effect. The plan usually involved return to the birth family, but the records suggested that efforts to achieve this were often unfocused and unsuccessful. In cases where a foster or adoptive family was seen as desirable, that was 'not being sought with much persistence' (p. 3). Of course, practitioners were already aware that many children they were responsible for were in placements likely to last indefinitely with infrequent family contact. What Rowe and Lambert did was assert that this was unacceptable and that an alternative approach was possible. The unacceptability was argued in terms of children's need for having a family they definitely belonged to and their sense of time, which meant that periods of even months could seem like an eternity to them (Goldstein *et al*, 1973).

The different approach advocated (permanence) had a new goal, i.e. giving children a family they belonged to for life instead of staying in a foster or residential home for an uncertain period. This aim could involve successful return to the birth family, but if that was not possible within a short period, then it was desirable for children to have different legal parents, ideally through adoption. The Rowe and Lambert study had been prompted and supported by adoption agencies, so its starting point was that adoption had a bigger part to play in child placement. Some have argued that this skewed the interpretation of the study, so that subsequent policies put more effort into pursuing adoption and severing birth family ties than supporting the restoration of children to their home or placements in foster care (Triseliotis, 1991; Kelly, 2000).

Slightly different and more gradual examples of reframing policy agendas have seen advocacy and research go hand in hand, quite often fuelled by an articulate and passionate champion. Holman (1973) first drew attention to the neglected situation of children in private foster care in the early 1970s. He highlighted that most were unknown to the authorities and many experienced poor care and little birth family contact. This work had little immediate impact, but he returned to the issue 30 years later. Despite pockets of good practice, many problems persisted (Holman, 2003). This time his work gained more media and policy attention, aided by attention given to the death of Victoria Climbié in private foster care and the subsequent Inquiry (Laming, 2003).

More definite if belated change in both policy and practice resulted from the research by Stein and colleagues over two decades on leaving care (discussed more fully in Stein, this volume) (Stein and Carey, 1986; Dixon and Stein, 2005). This body of work contributed to changes in legislation extending local authority responsibilities towards young people over school leaving age and also to practice developments such as the creation of dedicated after-care and through-care teams.

In contrast, Sonia Jackson began with advocacy about the importance of highlighted defects in the care system with regard to education, drawing on official figures of very poor educational attainments of young people. She then went on to produce research, which not only demonstrated the tendency to neglect this issue by social workers at that time, but also showed how and why a small number of young people bucked the trend by going to university (Jackson and Martin, 1998; see also Berridge and Saunders, this volume). The work of Jackson and others has prompted initiatives such as *Learning with Care* by the Scottish Executive and the development of designated teachers with special responsibility towards looked after children. Indirectly, it probably also influenced the later attention to health issues, where analogous neglect was apparent (See Hill C, this volume).

The importance of effective dissemination of research findings

Research implications will not be heeded if nobody knows about them. Furthermore, one-off exposure to research findings (at a conference or reading an article) in a context separate from the everyday work base, although occasionally inspirational, is more often not very influential. Studies have shown that many social workers find it hard to specify research that can back what they do and some may persist with practices that evaluations have shown to be ineffective (Smith, 2004; McLaughlin, 2007). Normally, it is desirable for research findings and conclusions to be put in short, accessible documents and if possible to be accompanied by dialogue between the research producers and consumers. However, academic status and departmental income are now very dependent on publishing in peer-reviewed journals using technical language and, to a smaller extent, writing books and chapters (like this one!). This competes with the time needed to communicate more informally with policy-makers and practitioners.

Until the 1980s, research dissemination in the UK had been largely ad hoc, insofar as it occurred at all. Then the Department of Health and Social Security (DHSS) decided to promote knowledge integrated from a number of research projects concerned with the placement of children. This resulted in a summary document, accompanied by practice tools to help assess whether the findings of research applied locally – were they true for us? – and promote dialogue with children (e.g. ecomaps, house charts) (DHSS, 1985). The documents were made available to local authorities and reinforced by a series of events around the country, led by Jane Rowe, one of the key contributors.

During the next decade, the Department of Health (DH) carried on this tradition, but tied in with research programmes on particular placement types. Hence, summary documents were produced on studies funded by the DH (e.g. on residential care in 1998 and adoption in 1999). Similarly its successor, the Department for Education and Science (DfES), supported reviews of messages from research on foster care (Sinclair *et al*, 2005) and parenting support (Quinton, 2004). These had the advantages of drawing on a coherent body of work, with the researchers usually having met to discuss and co-ordinate the planning and management of their studies. A disadvantage was that research funded by bodies other than the sponsoring government department was mentioned only occasionally. Research carried out in Scotland and Northern Ireland was mostly ignored for this reason.

Interweaving policy and research

In the 1990s, an initiative was developed in England and Wales that went beyond the usual one-off and reactive links between research and practice. This concerned what came to be known as the *Looking After Children (LAC) project* (Ward, 1995). This developed a set of documents aimed at systematising assessment, planning and reviews of individual children and organisational supports for the use of these materials. The contents were closely based on psychological and child care research.

A group of academics brought together by the Department of Health devised a set of criteria, grouped into seven dimensions (i.e. health, education, identity, family and social relationships, social presentation, emotional and behavioural development and self-care skills) for monitoring placement progress and outcomes (Parker *et al*, 1991). These provided the framework for information and assessment forms. Subsequently, a community survey was carried out to test how far the features of children's lives fitted with the views of a cross-section of 'ordinary' parents (Ward, 1995). The *Looking After Children* system was adopted by nearly all English local authorities and most in Scotland, as well as parts of Canada, Australia and Europe (Kufeldt *et al*, 2003; Scott and Hill, 2004). It has been regarded as a positive development by the majority of practitioners and many young people, although reservations have been expressed about the time required for comprehensive usage, which means that in many cases not all relevant forms are used or completed. Criticisms have been made from an academic base about bias in the issues covered by *LAC* (Garrett, 2003).

Making research relevant at local level

Whereas the *LAC* project was driven by central government, more local attempts have been made to help practitioners and managers to understand better the lessons of research and to help researchers tailor their dissemination much more closely to agency needs. For many years, links have been made by individual agencies with researchers, research units or academic departments, while child care research has also figured in the work of the Social Services Research Group and its quarterly publication, *Research, Policy and Planning*. The newer Social Care Institute for Excellence (SCIE) has also supported reviews of relevant research on adoption and foster care, with practitioners included in the advisory group (e.g. Wilson *et al*, 2004).

Over the last ten years, two organisations have been established in England to provide for sustained co-operation between researchers and social care agencies including local authorities. One is Research in Practice, which provides research briefings, joint events and on-line resources to partner agencies, including guidance about how to evaluate reports of research (R.i.P. 2006a, b, c, d). The other is Making Research Count, a network of universities providing research consultation and dissemination in different forms to their local agency partners.

Certain agencies have also sought to encourage research-mindedness among their employees and carers (e.g. Nutley *et al*, 2002; Moseley and Tierney, 2005). Measures that can be taken include taking account of research awareness during recruitment; enabling staff to access seminars; holding discussion groups; and allocating time for carrying out small scale studies.

What counts as evidence? Different types of research, their merits and drawbacks

Amidst all the emphasis on evidence-based practice and the mechanisms to promote application of research, practitioners and students are faced with the issue of how much confidence they should have in particular research findings. Here, I consider first of all the different forms that research may take, then more general considerations when judging the quality of individual pieces of research.

It is usual to make a distinction between quantitative and qualitative research. *Quantitative* research produces data expressed largely in numbers, which are analysed using statistical procedures. The most common form of quantitative study in social care is the large-scale survey. Typically, the data cover aspects such as the characteristics, circumstances, expectations, experiences and/or views of many individuals, for example, looked after children, carers or agency representatives. Common means of gathering the information are by questionnaires, from case records or using standardised interviews. One major advantage of this kind of study is that the large numbers give confidence that the findings have general application. This asset is strengthened when the sample has been chosen in a way that should rule out bias (e.g. random selection). The findings enable individuals or teams to compare their local experience with the wider picture, for example, in relation to allocation of expenditure (Beecham and Sinclair, 2007). Large-scale surveys also make possible complex analyses, for instance, to identify which factors are statistically significant in relation to placement outcomes (e.g. Sinclair and Gibbs, 1998; Thoburn *et al*, 2000). It should be noted, though, that any survey – large or small – has to deal with the problem of non-response, which tends to be particularly high when questionnaires are distributed by mail or e-mail, even if reminders are sent. Quite often those who do not respond differ in important ways from those who do. For instance, young people in crisis are less likely to fill in a form or agree to be interviewed than those in a stable situation.

Survey data, along with other information, are used to examine the impact of particular services or programmes (e.g. Shaw, 2005). Such evaluations often assess satisfaction with the service. This is valuable in its own right, but usually insufficient, since people may like something that is not helping or changing them. It is necessary, therefore, also to determine what the desired outcomes should be, usually by garnering the expectations of key stakeholders like the staff and service users. Then *measures* or *indicators* (either standardised or devised for a particular study) are used to assess degrees of positive or negative change on the relevant outcome dimensions (e.g. child behaviour, improvements in relationships, reduction in offending). A number of standard scales are available for measuring certain features of individuals and families, such as mental health, self-esteem, emotional and behavioural development and family functioning (e.g. Goodman, 1999; Fischer and Corcoran, 2007). Video recording may be used to facilitate close coding of behaviour (Green *et al*, 2000, Hodges *et al*, 2003).

21

Among those advocating a "what works" agenda, purists argue that only studies that are experimental or quasi-experimental should be used to judge whether or not a service or programme works (Sheldon, 2001; McNeish *et al*, 2002). These rely on the idea that it is necessary to compare an intervention with non-intervention and/or other kinds of intervention, since it is well known that people often "get better" without any help (the well-known placebo effect). In order to make fair comparisons of the impact of two or more services, it is vital to consider a reasonable number of people who start off with a similar range and severity of difficulties (as otherwise one group may have better outcomes just because they started off in a better position or began from a very low base). To achieve comparability, it is theoretically most desirable to allocate service users on a random basis to the services being compared. This is rarely possible for ethical, legal or practical reasons, though some randomised control trials have been carried out on child care services, mostly in the USA and Canada, but occasionally in the UK (See Biehal and Rushton, this volume). An alternative is to "match" the populations studied, namely compare samples with the same number of males and females, older and younger people, and so on.

Experimental studies have the advantage that they can demonstrate that something works, while ruling out alternative explanations. Also, it is possible to make statistical meta-analyses of a number of studies on the same topic to provide more conclusive findings about effectiveness, for example, on treatment foster care (Chamberlain and Smith, 2005) and residential treatment of young people who offend (Grietens, 2002). On the other hand, not only are such rigorous studies difficult to set up, but their conclusions may simply be that an intervention did or did not work without specifying how or why. Commonly, experimental studies do not give much detail about the service input. Outcome surveys covering a range of service types can overcome this problem to some extent.

Qualitative research usually provides information in the form of text. This is most commonly based on what informants like young people, foster carers, adopters or practitioners have said, often in an individual interview (e.g. Thomas *et al*, 1999; Neil, 2003). Less commonly, group interviews or focus groups have been used (Beek and Schofield, 2001). These can be particularly helpful in obtaining the views of decision-making bodies like adoption panels (Hill *et al*, 1989). Another common source of qualitative data comprises documents, such as case records or agency policies. Such sources tend to be used with samples of modest size because of the time required for data-gathering and analysis, but detailed qualitative data from a large sample can be obtained from questionnaires, as in surveys of foster care (Triseliotis *et al*, 2000; Sinclair *et al*, 2005).

Participant observation has been employed in some studies of residential care (e.g. Emond, 2005). This makes possible analysis of the social interaction and environment. For instance, work by Berridge (1985) and Berridge and Brodie (1998), ten years apart, identified significant changes in children's homes and highlighted the rarity of staff helping children with homework and the absence of books and newspapers in many children's homes (this was in pre-Internet times). Observation has not been used a great deal in family placement research as it would generally be too intrusive. Occasionally, short-term observations have been made in the home (Tizard, 1977, on adoption), while McAuley (1996) saw foster children at a neutral venue.

Advantages of qualitative research include its capacity to examine issues in depth, assess complex meanings, processes and interactions, and pursue matters as they come to light. On the other hand, often the number of instances or informants is small and they are not necessarily representative of a wider population. Hence, while the themes may well be of wider applicability, differences that emerge (e.g. on the basis of age or gender) are often not generalisable.

Research on children's placements has commonly combined quantitative and qualitative data, in order to achieve breadth of context and depth of understanding. This has quite often taken the form of using a mix of open-ended and fixed-choice questions in questionnaires or interview schedules. Then the former are mostly used qualitatively, while the latter are analysed statistically. It is also possible to use different methods, such as a case survey combined with individual or group interviews with key people.

Both quantitative and qualitative research can be enhanced if they are longitudinal; in other words, if information is gathered at different points in time (e.g. Quinton *et al*, 1998; Beek and Schofield, 2004). Such studies are more expensive. Therefore they are not common, usually only cover a few years and, if extended, may lose a proportion of the sample. However, longitudinal prospective studies do make possible some assessment of progress and changes as they happen, without the dangers of retrospective negative or positive reframing of past events. Also, it becomes easier to identify the direction of a statistical relationship or set of issues if the order of events has been clearly documented (e.g. among birth family problems, a young person's behaviour and foster family stress).

Inevitably, research is carried out in particular places at a specific time, so in an ideal world it would be repeated elsewhere and at a later time to check out whether the findings hold good. As research is expensive, it is rare for exact replication to happen, although now and then studies do cover similar or overlapping issues, while evaluations take place of comparable projects. Then the findings can reinforce each other, identify qualifications or cast doubt on the first research.

Who carries out research?

In the main, research is carried out by four types of people:

1. academics;
2. independent consultants;

3. service agency research staff; and
4. practitioner researchers.

Academic research is most often led by professors and lecturers who also teach. Many though not all of these are former practitioners, mainly in social work, although a few are in other fields like health or law (e.g. Minnis *et al*, 1999; Masson, 2000). These principal investigators often supervise individual researchers or teams of researchers, who may well carry out the bulk of the research fieldwork and analysis. More of these research associates are from non-applied disciplines, notably psychology, sociology and anthropology. Some specialist centres dedicated to research have made important contributions. They are normally affiliated to universities (e.g. the Dartington and Thomas Coram Research Units). Most material published in academic journals in the child care field tends to have a university origin, but some journals combine academic and practitioner research while others are more practice-based.

Recent years have seen a proliferation of consultants and small consultancy companies carrying out research. Some are former academics. Unlike university academics, consultants do not have to teach or contribute to university funds. They usually lack the research infrastructure provided by universities.

Larger local authorities and a few big voluntary agencies like Barnardo's and the NSPCC have their own research sections, which tend to concentrate on locally and nationally useful data, often producing findings of wider interest (e.g. Ramsay, 1996; Hughes *et al*, 2000). The organisation Who Cares? Trust has carried out valuable surveys of looked after young people to obtain their experiences and opinions (e.g. Shaw, 1999).

Finally, practitioners and managers increasingly engage in research. For instance, a study of grandparent care was conducted by a local authority worker prompted by awareness of a gap in information to guide his own practice (Pitcher, 2002). Practitioner research may be carried out as part of a programme of further study (e.g. Pugh, 1996) and occasionally a doctorate (Kosonen, 1999). Many organisations are now striving to encourage an ethos that promotes use of existing research and investigations by staff (Miller, 2007). It appears that there is a thirst among many to engage in systematic enquiries (Marsh *et al*, 2005).

Most funding for research conducted by academics and consultants related to child placements derives ultimately from central government,[1] which often prefers to commission research externally rather than in-house in order to access a more independent viewpoint and, arguably, more expertise. Departments responsible for looked after children have provided significant funding over the years, with most of the research initiatives and topics originating from Government itself and reflecting its priorities and concerns

---

[1] Including devolved bodies like the Scottish Government (formerly Scottish Executive)

(e.g. parenting and adoption in recent years). It is difficult, though not impossible, for researchers interested in studying a topic of their own to persuade government departments to fund it. At more arms length is the Economic and Social Research Council, which funds a wide range of academic research mostly by open competition, a very small part of which has been devoted to placement related subjects (e.g. a comparative study of young people in residential care and in the community by Hallett *et al*, 2003). In addition, certain charitable funding bodies have given grants for studies in this area, such as the work on adoption with contact by Neil or on long-term fostering by Schofield and colleagues, both funded by the Nuffield Foundation. Not uncommonly, service agencies also commission external research typically taking the form of evaluations. This is usually on a local scale, but sometimes agencies co-operate to fund research, as the study by Dickens *et al* (2007) of looked after children in 24 authorities demonstrated.

Substantial studies tend to take two to three years from start to finish, though smaller projects can be done in a matter of months. It is normal practice to write a report for the funder, which is nowadays usually made available on-line quite quickly. Good reports include a thorough literature review besides details of the research undertaken. Preparation, acceptance and productions of journal articles and books may well take a further one–two years or even more to reach the public, so that, not uncommonly, the policy agenda has altered significantly since the study started.

Judging the quality of research

When hearing or reading about research, various signs will give an indication of how reliable the conclusions are likely to be, though there are no guarantees. Papers that have been subject to critical peer review and acceptance should be reliable (Iwaniec and Pinkerton, 2000). The experience and reputation of the researchers is worth checking. Use of an expert advisory or steering group will probably have enhanced the study. Consistency between the aims, design and specific questions is important.

Some different considerations apply to quantitative and qualitative research. For investigations with primarily numerical outputs, it is desirable to assess the size and representativeness of the sample, the number of non-responses and missing data, the rigour of the analysis and inferences, and the appropriateness of the statistical tests applied. If comparisons are being made between the progress of two groups or sub samples, it is vital to know whether they were matched and how far, if at all, they differed at the initial point as well as when followed up.

For qualitative data, the depth and authenticity of examples and quotations are crucial. It is valuable to know if computer packages were used in the analysis and whether colleagues helped to identify key themes and checked selection of "typical" instances. Were the research team careful to check for exceptions to general patterns? When

25

practitioners use research in their assessments or reports, ideally they should reference reliable peer-reviewed publications so that those using the evidence can check the originals for themselves.

Conclusions

We live in an era when most politicians and civil servants aspire to make policy evidence-based and when practitioners are exhorted to apply research evidence about the effectiveness of different kinds of intervention. While there is always scope for plenty more research, the UK has built up a substantial empirical basis in relation to child care placements. This has implications not only for choosing different kinds of placement for children, but for understanding how children experience change and continuity in their care, the needs and views of carers and adopters, relationships in family and residential homes, features of social work support and the organisation of services.

It is usual and in many respects desirable that the application of research findings will blend with other considerations. The impact of research has probably been greatest in identifying gaps in services and highlighting the neglect of issues that later came to be seen as vital, such as clear planning and review, education, health and the transition out of care. Studies have also helped to identify examples of good practice and have provided evidence of effectiveness, as with respect to specialist fostering. This chapter has only been able to present a few tasters as an hors d'oeuvre. The full feast of valuable research lessons is to be enjoyed in the rest of this book.

Selected further reading

Hill M. (ed.) (1999) *Effective Ways of Working with Children and Families*, London: Jessica Kingsley Publishers

Iwaniec D. and Pinkerton J. (2000) *Making Research Work*, London: Jessica Kingsley Publishers

McNeish D., Newman T. and Roberts H. (2002) *What Works for Children*, Buckingham: Open University Press (especially Sellick and Thoburn chapter)

Walliman N. (2005) *Your Research Project*, London: Sage

On-line publications by the Social Care Institute of Excellence, Research in Practice, and Making Research Count

References

Adams D. (1988) *The Hitchhiker's Guide to the Galaxy*. London: Heinemann

Attree P. (2006) 'The social costs of child poverty: A systematic review of the qualitative evidence', *Children & Society*, 20:1, pp 54–66

Bebbington A. R. and Miles J. (1989) 'The background of children who enter local authority care', *British Journal of Social Work*, 19, pp 349–368

Beecham J. and Sinclair I. (2007) *Costs and Outcomes in Children's Social Care: Messages from research*, London: Department for Education and Skills

Beek M. and Schofield G. (2001) 'Foster carers' perspectives on permanence: A focus group study', *Adoption & Fostering*, 26:2, pp 14–27

Beek M. and Schofield G. (2004) *Providing a Secure Base in Long-term Foster Care*, London: BAAF

Berridge D. (1985) *Children's Homes*, Oxford: Blackwell

Berridge D. and Brodie I. (1998) *Children's Homes Revisited*, London: Jessica Kingsley Publishers

Bowlby J. (1944) 'Forty-four juvenile thieves: Their characters and home life', *International Journal of Psychoanalysis*, 25, pp 19–52

Bowlby J. (1953) *Child Care and the Growth of Love*, London: Pelican

Bowlby J. (1969) *Attachment*, Harmondsworth: Penguin

Brannen J., Brockman M., Mooney A. and Statham J. (2007) *Coming to Care*, Bristol: Policy Press

Brannen J., Heptinstall E. and Bhopal K. (2000) *Connecting Children*, London: Routledge/Falmer

Brown E., Bullock R., Hobson C. and Little M. (1998) *Making Residential Child Care Work*, Aldershot: Ashgate

Cairns, K. (2002) *Attachment, Trauma and Resilience: Therapeutic caring for children*, London: BAAF

Chamberlain P. and Smith D. K. (2005) 'Multidimensional treatment foster care', in Hibbs E. D. and Jensen P. S. (eds) *Psychological Treatments for Child and Adolescent Disorders*, Washington D. C.: American Psychological Association

Daniel B. and Wassell S. (2002) *Assessing and Promoting Resilience in Vulnerable Children*, London: Jessica Kingsley Publishers (Three volumes on *Early Years*, *Middle Childhood* and *Adolescence*)

Davies J., Ireland P. and Buchan H. (2005) 'Closing the knowing-doing gap', *Evidence-based Healthcare and Public Health*, 9:5, pp 361–364

Davies J., Nutley S. M. and Smith P. C. (eds) (2000) *What Works? Evidence-based policy and practice in public services*, Bristol: Policy Press

Department of Health (1998) *Caring for Children Away from Home*, London: Department of Health

Department of Health (1999) *Adoption Now*, London: Department of Health

Department of Health and Social Security (1985) *Social Work Decisions in Child Care*, London: DHSS

Dickens J., Howell D., Thoburn J., and Schofield G. (2007) 'Children starting to be looked after by local authorities in England: An analysis of inter-authority variation and case-centred decision making,' *British Journal of Social Work*, 37, pp 597–617

Dixon J. and Stein M. (2005) *Leaving Care: Throughcare and aftercare in Scotland*, London: Jessica Kingsley Publishers

Downes C. (1992) *Separation Revisited*, Aldershot: Ashgate

Emond R. (2005) 'Ethnographic research methods with children and young people', in Greene S. and Hogan D., *Researching Children's Experience*, London: Sage

Fahlberg V. (1994) *A Child's Journey Through Placement*, London: BAAF

Farmer E., Moyers S. and Lipscombe J. (2004) *Fostering Adolescents*, London: Jessica Kingsley Publishers

Fischer J. and Corcoran K. (2007) *Measures for Clinical Practice and Research*, New York, NY: Oxford University Press Inc

Fratter J., Rowe J., Sapsford, D. and Thoburn, J. (1991) *Permanent Family Placement: A decade of experience*, London: BAAF

Garrett P. M. (2003) 'Swimming with dolphins: The assessment framework, new Labour and new tools for social work with children and families', *British Journal of Social Work*, 33:4, pp 441–464

Gilligan R. (1997) 'Beyond permanence: The importance of resilience in child placement practice and planning', *Adoption & Fostering*, 21:1, pp 12–20

Goldstein J., Freud A. and Solnit A. J. (1973) *Beyond the Best Interests of the Child*, New York: Free Press

Goodman R. (1999) 'The extended version of the Strengths and Difficulties Questionnaire as a guide to psychiatric caseness and consequent burden', *Journal of Child Psychology and Psychiatry*, 40:5, pp 791–800

Green J. M., Stanley C., Smith V and Goldwyn R. (2000) 'A new method of evaluating attachment representations on young school age children – the Manchester child attachment story task', *Attachment and Human Development*, 2:1, pp 42–64

Grietens H. (2002) 'Evaluating the effects of residential treatment for juvenile offenders: A review of meta-analytic studies', *International Journal of Child and Family Welfare*, 5, pp 129–140

Hallett C., Murray C. and Punch S. (2003) 'Young people and welfare: Negotiating pathways', in Hallett C. and Prout A. (eds) *Hearing the Voices of Children*, London: Routledge/Falmer

Hazel N. (1981) *A Bridge to Independence*, Oxford: Blackwell

Heywood J. (1978) *Children in Care*, London: Routledge & Kegan Paul

Hill M. (ed) (1999) *Effective Ways of Working with Children and Families*, London: Jessica Kingsley

Hill M. (2000a) 'Inclusiveness in residential child care', in Chakrabarti M. and Hill M. (eds) *Residential Child Care: International perspectives on links with families and peers*, London: Jessica Kingsley Publishers

Hill M. (2000b) 'The residential child care context', in Chakrabarti M. and Hill M. (eds) *Residential Child Care: International perspectives on links with families and peers*, London: Jessica Kingsley Publishers

Hill M., Lambert L. and Triseliotis J. (1989) *Achieving Adoption with Love and Money*, London: National Children's Bureau

Hill M., Murray K. and Rankin J. (1991) 'The early history of Scottish child welfare', *Children & Society*, 5, pp 182–195

Hill M., Stafford A., Seaman P., Ross N. and Daniel B. (2007) *Parenting and Resilience*, York: Joseph Rowntree Foundation

Hodges J., Steele M., Hillman S., Henderson K. and Kaniuk J. (2003) 'Changes in attachment representations over the first year of adoptive placement: Narratives of maltreated children', *Clinical Child Psychology and Psychiatry*, 8:3, pp 351–367

Höjer I. (2004) 'What happens in the foster family', *Adoption & Fostering*, 28:1, pp 38–48

Holman B. (1973) *Trading in Children*, London: Routledge & Kegan Paul

Holman B. (2003) 'Private fostering: Old problems, new urgency', *Adoption & Fostering*, 27:1, pp 8–18

Howe D. (1996) *Attachment Theory and Child and Family Social Work*, Aldershot: Avebury

Howe D. (2001) 'Attachment', in Horvath J. (ed) *The Child's World*, London: Jessica Kingsley Publishers

Hughes M., McNeish D., Newman T., Roberts H. and Sachdev D. (eds) (2000) *What Works? Making Connections: Linking research and practice*, Barkingside: Barnardo's

Iwaniec D. and Pinkerton J. (eds) (2000) *Making Research Work*, Chichester: Wiley

Jackson S. and Martin P. Y. (1998) 'Surviving the care system: Education and resilience', *Journal of Adolescence*, 21, pp 569–583

Kelly G. (2000) 'The influence of research on child care policy and practice: The case of 'Children who Wait' and the development of the permanence movement in the United Kingdom', in Iwaniec D. and Pinkerton J. (eds) *Making Research Work*, Chichester: Wiley

Kosonen M. (1999) ' "Core" and "kin" siblings: Foster children's changing families', in Mullender A. (ed) *We are Family: Sibling relationships in placement and beyond*, London: BAAF

Kufeldt K., Simard M., Tite R. and Vachon J. (2003) 'The Looking After Children Project in Canada: Educational outcomes', in Kufeldt K. and McKenzie B. (eds) *Child Welfare: Connecting research, policy and practice*, Waterloo, Ontario: Wilfred Laurier University Press

Laming Lord (2003) *Victoria Climbié Inquiry*, Norwich: HMSO

Lipscombe J. (2006) *Care or Control? Foster care for young people on remand*, London: BAAF

Lipscombe J., Farmer E. and Moyers S. (2003) 'Parenting fostered adolescents: Skills and strategies', *Child and Family Social Work*, 8:4, pp 243–256

Lowe N. and Murch M. (2002) *The Plan for the Child: Adoption or long-term fostering*, London: BAAF

McAuley C. (1996) *Children in Long-term Foster Care*, Aldershot: Avebury

McLaughlin H. (2007) *Understanding Social Work Research*, London: Sage

McNeish D., Newman T. and Roberts H. (2002) *What Works for Children?* Buckingham: Open University Press

Marsh P., Fisher M., Mathers N. and Fish S. (2005) *Developing the Evidence Base for Social Work and Social Care Practice*, London: Social Care Institute for Excellence

Masson J. (2000) 'Researching children's perspectives: Legal issues', in Lewis A. and Lindsay G. (eds) *Researching Children's Perspectives*, Buckingham: Open University Press

Miller K. H. (2007) 'Preliminary report on practice-related research survey', London: Social Care Institute for Excellence

Minnis H., Devine C. and Pelosi T. (1999) 'Foster carers speak about training', *Adoption & Fostering*, 23:2, pp 42–47

Moseley A. and Tierney S. (2005) 'Evidence-based practice in the real world', *Evidence & Policy*, 1:1, pp 113–119

Neil E. (2003) 'Accepting the reality of adoption: Birth relatives' experiences of face-to-face contact', *Adoption & Fostering*, 27:2, pp 32–43

Nutley S., Walter I. and Davies H. (2002) 'From knowing to doing: A framework for understanding the evidence into practice agenda', St Andrews: University of St Andrews Research Unit for Research Utilisation

Parker R. (2005) 'Then and now', in Axford N., Berry V., Little M. and Morpeth L. (eds) *Forty Years of Research, Policy and Practice in Children's Services*, Chichester: Wiley

Parker R., Ward H., Jackson S., Aldgate J. and Wedge P. (1991) *Assessing Outcomes in Child Care*, London: HMSO

Pitcher D. (2002) 'Placement with grandparents: The issues for grandparents who care for their grandchildren', *Adoption & Fostering*, 16:1, pp 6–14

Pugh G. (1996) 'Seen but not heard: Addressing the needs of children who foster', *Adoption & Fostering*, 20:1, pp 35–41

Quinton D. (2004) *Supporting Parents: Messages from Research*, London: Jessica Kingsley Publishers

Quinton D., Rushton A., Dance C. and Mayes D. (1998) *Joining New Families*, Chichester: Wiley

Ramsay D. (1996) 'Recruiting and retaining foster carers: implications of a professional service in Fife', *Adoption & Fostering*, 20:1, pp 42–46

Research in Practice (2006a) *Adoption and Permanence for Children who Cannot Live Safely with Birth Parents or Relatives*, Dartington, Devon: Research in Practice

Research in Practice (2006b) *Firm Foundations: A practical guide to organisational support for the use of research evidence*, Dartington, Devon: Research in Practice

Research in Practice (2006c) *Placement Stability*, Dartington, Devon: Research in Practice

Research in Practice (2006d) *Recruitment and Retention of Social Workers*, Dartington, Devon: Research in Practice

Rowe J. and Lambert L. (1973) *Children Who Wait*, London: ABAA

Rutter M. (1981) *Maternal Deprivation Reassessed*, Harmondsworth: Penguin

Schofield G. (2001) 'Resilience in family placement: A lifespan perspective', *Adoption & Fostering*, 25:3, pp 6–19

Schofield G. (2002a) *Part of the Family: Pathways through foster care*, London: BAAF

Schofield G. (2002b) 'The significance of a secure base: A psychosocial model of long-term foster care', *Child & Family Social Work*, 7:4, pp 259–272

Schofield G. and Beek M. (2006) *Attachment Handbook for Foster Care and Adoption*, London: BAAF

Scott J. and Hill M. (2004) 'The Looking After Children in Scotland materials', *Scottish Journal of Residential Child Care*, 3:1, pp 17–30

Sellick C. and Thoburn J. (1996) *What Works in Family Placement?*, Barkingside: Barnardo's

Shaw C. (1999) *Remember My Messages*, London: The Who Cares? Trust

Shaw C. (2005) *NIFTY Evaluation*, London: Research in Practice/National Children's Bureau

Sheldon B. (2001) 'The validity of evidence-based practice in social work: A reply to Stephen Webb', *British Journal of Social Work*, 31, pp 801–809

Sinclair I. and Gibbs I. (1998) *Children's Homes: A study in diversity*, Chichester: Wiley

Sinclair I., Wilson K. and Gibbs I. (2005) *Foster Placements: Why they succeed and why they fail*, London: Jessica Kingsley Publishers

Smith D. (ed) (2004) *Social Work and Evidence-Based Practice*, London, Jessica Kingsley Publishers

Stein M. and Carey K. (1986) *Leaving Care*, Oxford: Basil Blackwell

Thoburn J., Norford L. and Rashid S. P. (2000) *Permanent Family Placement for Children of Minority Ethnic Origin*, London: Jessica Kingsley Publishers

Thomas C., Beckford V., Lowe N. and Murch M. (1999) *Adopted Children Speaking*, London: BAAF

Tizard B. (1977) *Adoption: A second chance*, London: Open Books

Trasler G. (1960) *In Place of Parents*, London: Routledge & Kegan Paul

Trinder L. and Reynolds S. (eds) (2000) *Evidence-Based Practice*, Oxford: Blackwell

Triseliotis J. (1991) 'Perceptions of permanence', *Adoption & Fostering*, 15:4, pp 6–15

Triseliotis J., Borland M. and Hill M. (2000) *Delivering Foster Care*, London: BAAF

Triseliotis J., Borland M., Hill M. and Lambert L. (1995) *Teenagers and the Social Work Services*, London: HMSO

Triseliotis J., Shireman J. and Hundleby M. (1997) *Adoption: Theory, Policy and Practice*, London: Cassell

Walker M., Barclay A., Hill M., Hunter L., Kendrick A., Malloch M. and McIvor G. (2006) *Secure Accommodation in Scotland*, Edinburgh: The Scottish Executive

Walker M., Hill M. and Triseliotis J. (2002) *Testing the Limits of Foster Care*, London: BAAF

Ward H. (1995) *Looking After Children: Research into practice*, London: HMSO

Wedge P. and Mantle G. (1991) *Sibling Groups and Social Work*, Aldershot: Avebury/Gower

Wilson K., Sinclair I., Taylor C., Pithouse A. and Sellick C. (2004) *Fostering Success*, Bristol: SCIE & Policy Press

2 International contexts and comparisons

June Thoburn

When seeking to improve on the services we provide to children in care, alongside researching what is happening now in our own country, there are gains to be had from looking at how child placement is managed and practiced in other countries. This chapter draws heavily on a data-based study of children in out-of-home care in 14 countries (Thoburn, 2007) but is also influenced by collaborative work with colleagues in the USA and UK that led to the publication of an edited collection of seminal English language articles on child welfare (Courtney and Thoburn, in press) and an overview of the international research on outcomes for children in care (Bullock *et al*, 2006). The design of the cross-national research grew out of a project to compare and contrast the different placement patterns that emerged from a study of looked after children in 24 English local authorities (Dickens *et al*, 2007; Schofield *et al*, 2007).

At the time when the information was being collected for the intercountry study, government departments in England were exploring child welfare practices in other countries, and some are referred to in the White Paper, *Care Matters* (DfES, 2006), as pointing to promising interventions that might be incorporated into practice in England.[1] The emphasis is, however, very much on "practice" and "interventions". This chapter argues that to make wise choices about the lessons we can learn from other countries, we have to understand how and why the services developed the way they did in our own country and in those we want to learn from. Are the history, culture and political ideologies that have shaped policy and practice in these countries broadly congruent with our own? And if they are not, does that matter when we consider how we might import interventions, which appear promising in other countries, to the child placement services in the UK?

This overview of child placement in other parts of the world concentrates on those countries which are broadly similar in the resources they have available to spend on child welfare services and the existence of fairly well developed child welfare services. Although out-of-home care in poor countries is not discussed here in any detail, great care must be exercised when considering the ways in which child placement policies and

---

[1] It is important to record that the four UK nations are increasingly going their different ways in terms of child placement policy and practice. For the intercountry research, data were reported separately. The term "UK" is used in this chapter when differences between the UK nations are slight, and the separate nations are referred to as appropriate.

interventions developed in rich countries can (or should) be adapted to the most impoverished countries of the world.

The dimensions of child placement services

In looking at the child placement services in different countries, the first dimension to explore is that of size. In my study, numbers in the under-18 population varied between less than half a million in Northern Ireland and around a million in Denmark, the Republic of Ireland, New Zealand and Norway to around 11 million in England, nearly 15 million in Germany, 23 million in Japan and 74 million in the USA. In Australia, Canada, and the USA, individual states/provinces operate their own child welfare laws and systems, with federal policy direction being more robust in the USA than in others like Australia and Canada.

More important than population size in determining child placement policies and practice is the political and economic situation. Alberta (in Canada) had the highest rate of children in care (111 per 10,000 were in care in 2004 compared with 66 in the USA as a whole and 58 in the state of Washington, a state not too dissimilar from Alberta). In Scandinavia, the rate was 104 per 10,000 for Denmark compared with 63 for Sweden and 68 for Norway. In other parts of Europe, the rate for France was 102 per 10,000 compared with 38 in Italy. The rate for England in 2005 was 55 per 10,000 and the lowest rate was for Japan (17 per 10,000).

How do we understand differences between countries and states?

To understand differences between countries, a more accurate gauge is to be found by looking at rates of children entering care during a recent 12-month period. This is because rates in care on a given date (those given above) are influenced by the length of time children stay in care, and the related question of their ages when entering care. Rather to my surprise, I found in undertaking this research that a sizeable minority of government departments responsible for child welfare did not collect data on children entering care. Table 1 gives this information for those states for which it was available. When rates of children entering care are considered, the USA (in the middle range for those actually in care) has the highest rate of entrants to care in a 12-month period (42 per 10,000) compared with Japan (6 per 10,000). Norway, with a higher "in care" rate (68 per 10,000) than the USA has the opposite pattern, with one of the lowest rates of entrants (13 per 10,000) after Japan. England is again in the middle range with 23 per 10,000 and Wales is moving to the upper end with 27 per 10,000.

Table 1
Children 0–17, entrants into care in a given year, and rates per 10,000 under-18 (dates are in most cases for 2004–5)

Country/State	CHN 0–17 in population	Entrants into care	Rate per 10,000 <18
Australia	4,803,218	12,531	26
Australia/NSW	1,591,379	3,105	20
Australia/Queensland	969,553	3,198	33
Denmark *	1,210,566	3,578	30
Germany **	14,828,835	44,780**	30**
Japan	23,046,000	12,807	6
New Zealand	1,005,648	2,441	24
Norway *	1,174,489	1,506	13
Spain	7,550,000	13,305	18
Sweden *	1,910,967	6,115	32
UK/England	11,109,000	24,500	23
UK/N.Ireland	451,514	935	21
UK/Scotland	1,066,646	2,525	24
UK/Wales	662,389	1,709	27
USA	74,000,000	311,000	42
USA/Illinois	3,249,654	5,385	16
USA/N.Carolina	2,153,444	5,996	28
USA/Washington State	1,513,360	7,846	52

(From Thoburn, 2007) (Data not available for Alberta and Ontario in Canada, France, Italy and Ireland)

* For purposes of comparability, the figures in this table are for those aged 0–17 on entering care. In Denmark, young people can enter care up to the age of 23; 489 were over the age of 18 at entry. Around 130 young people in Norway entered care when over the age of 18. The upper age for entry into care in Sweden is 20 and for leaving care is 22. Consequently, the actual number entering care in 2004 was 7,194 (including 1,079 who were aged 18 plus). A small number of children enter care in France and USA when aged 18+.
** This total includes those who entered more than once during the year, so the rate is likely to be lower than that shown. It is possible that this also applies to other countries that do not use a 'child as unit of return' reporting system.

Socio-political explanations

The impact of deprivation can be seen both between and within countries. Poor countries, despite their enormous needs, have very low rates in care simply because they can not afford anything other than the most rudimentary care systems. Within the rich countries political decisions rather than poverty were a major determinant of the size and characteristics of the "in care" population. This was the case not only with respect to the proportion of national income spent on welfare generally but also to the position of child placement within the child welfare system. Political decisions about taxation levels and the amount of public expenditure on universal services impact on the number and the way in which services are provided.

Japan is still a fairly egalitarian society and also has high spending on universal services such as health care. The low rates in Japan are also partly reflected in the legacy of the "cradle to grave" large company employment system, and changes in this will no doubt work through into an increase in child welfare problems and numbers in out-of-home care. In contrast, in the USA, the marked inequality between classes and ethnic groups and numbers of parents living in poverty or having to work very long hours for a subsistence wage, together with the low spend on health care for those without private health insurance, probably account for the rate entering care being much higher than in the other countries in my study. If one added to this the infants who are placed for adoption for reasons of poverty without coming into the care system, the difference would be even greater. Voluntary "in-country" placement of infants for adoption is very low in the other countries included in my comparative study.

Before discussing the detail of child placement policy and practice, there are two other important contextual issues. The first can be defined broadly as socio-cultural and includes the relative preponderance of the broad attitudes to welfare identified by Fox-Harding (1991). Attitudes towards the family and the willingness or otherwise to sanction the "intrusion" of the state into family life impact on the numbers in care and the placement patterns in different ways. A particular country, as represented by its government policies and legislation, may tend towards a "child rescue" or "society as parent" approach (which could be associated with a higher rate in care); or the prevailing view characterised by a pro-family, pro-parental rights approach may be associated with lower numbers in care (as, for example, in Italy) or higher numbers because care services are seen as a positive part of family support services (as in France or Denmark).

The extent of stability and the pace of social change are also relevant. Japan is probably the most stable of the countries I included in my research, with a lower rate of births outside marriage than most of the others, and also a strong extended family tradition that is breaking down less quickly than in other countries. Similar considerations also applied in Italy and Spain until recently but this is changing with high rates of immigration and the lessening of the influence of the Catholic Church. Countries with a predominantly Roman Catholic heritage traditionally had strong pro-family policies and are more likely to guard the family from intrusion of the state. As an example, child placement policies and practice in the Republic or Ireland have more in common with Italy and Spain than they have with the other UK nations which tend to be more interventionist.

The second important contextual issue can be broadly defined as a socio-political factor (linked with general views about the role of the state and attitudes towards "dependency"); this is the prevailing ideology in a country about the place and value of child placement within child welfare services. In most of the Anglophone counties, there has been a growing belief that state welfare services should only be used when absolutely necessary, and that entry into care is something to be avoided. This is strongest in the USA with "welfare dependency" being seen as a sign of poor parenting. In countries such as Australia, Canada and the UK, it is more a lack of confidence that being in care can have a positive impact, though, as demonstrated by Bullock *et al* (2006), the data on outcomes are often misinterpreted by politicians and the media to present a more negative picture of outcomes than is justified by research findings. In all these countries a "target culture" has grown up as a way of "justifying" to the taxpayer state spending on welfare (Tilbury, 2004). Although, in England, having a lower rate of children in care is not actually a performance target, inspection reports regularly commend those authorities that have cut their rates in care. The government's policy document, *Care Matters* (DfES, 2006), makes a positive case that more extensive early support services will reduce the numbers needing to come into care. This may be the case, but it is equally possible that there will be a greater awareness of the need for shorter-term care as family support. It is also likely that better preventive services will reveal that more of the children with behavioural problems or neglected in their family homes need to be in care.

As an aside, it is interesting that performance targets have led to the collection of good data. Some European countries have been slower to collect data because, not having a target culture, the drive has not been there to "prove" the value of welfare spending by demonstrating "good outcomes". France, Denmark and Germany are perhaps the clearest examples of countries that hold that being in care has a positive part to play within their child welfare system. This is also related to the use of care as part of a family support service (linked to the importance given to family autonomy), rather than only as part of a more coercive child protection system.

Reasons and legal routes for entering care in different countries

When reading the literature on child welfare services in different countries (for example, Colton and Williams, 2006; Wiklund, 2006) it is clear that the children entering care do so for broadly similar reasons, with child maltreatment, various forms of neglect and parenting issues such as intimate partner violence and addictions being important reasons in all countries. However, the literature also shows important differences, in that European countries tend to frame their approach as one of helping families to overcome difficulties – broadly a child welfare or "family support" approach – while in Australia, Canada and the USA, the primary focus is on child protection. (In these countries "mandatory reporting" of child maltreatment is the norm. The term "report" (of maltreatment) tends to be used rather than "referral" and self referrals with a request for out-of-home care as part of the help needed in difficult family circumstances are not encouraged.)

In the USA, upwards of 95 per cent enter care through a court order. The proportion in Japan is the direct opposite with only around 10 per cent entering through a court order. These data are less readily available for European countries, but around three-quarters entering care in Scandinavian countries do so through voluntary arrangements as a family support service. In this respect, the UK nations are less like the USA and more like the Scandinavian countries (in England in 2004–5, 67 per cent started to be looked after through arrangements agreed with the family; the proportion for Sweden was 85 per cent). Legislation in France and the UK comes somewhere between the two. Proportions in "voluntary" care on a given date are lower in the UK countries than for entrants to care, as the state is more willing to intervene to secure parental rights in respect of those who stay longer. (Only 31 per cent are accommodated under voluntary agreements compared with around 75 per cent in Germany and over 80 per cent in Denmark in voluntary care. France is more like England in that only around 13 per cent are in "voluntary care".) The underlying philosophy is one of child welfare and family support, but once a child enters care, it tends, in the UK nations but not in France, to switch towards the US (more coercive) model.[2]

A major issue thrown into relief by this study has been the differential use of the care system for different ethnic groups and the way in which this shows up in their under- or over-representation in the care statistics. In the UK nations, whilst African-Caribbean children and those of dual African-Caribbean and white British heritage are significantly over-represented in care (as are those of African heritage, but to a lesser extent), children of South and East Asian heritage are far less likely to enter care than are white British children. In countries and states with substantial populations of indigenous children (in this study, Australia, Canada, New Zealand and USA), it is these children who are most likely to enter care.

It is clear that caution is needed when making comparisons of "in care" or "entrants" data, and especially when using such data to imply more or less successful child welfare policies in one country rather than another.

Understanding difference through a study of placement patterns

The dimensions of difference considered in this section are routes out of care (linked to length of stay in care) and the patterns of placement. Comparative data on length of stay in care are difficult to analyse as statistics are reported differently in different countries.

---

[2] At this stage, it is important to note that in the four UK nations children entering care 'under a series of short-term placements' are not included in the figures. If they were, the rates in care and especially the rate entering care would be higher (a rate of 32 per 10,000 English children entering care if these are included compared with 23 if omitted).

Some provide "snapshot" data on the length of time since children currently in care entered care and others report on the length of time those leaving care had been in care. Sometimes, these data are reported as "mean" and sometimes as "median" or "mode" data. The latter is preferable since the "mean" or "average" can be distorted by a minority who stay for very long periods whereas the "mode" gives the length of time in care of the majority of care entrants (and is generally lower than the "mean"). Because those who have a series of short-term placements are excluded from most of the UK data sets and similar care episodes are included in the statistics in other countries, the data show that a greater number of UK children stay for longer than is the case, for example, in other European countries.

Clearly, one factor influencing length of time in care is the age at entry. A country with many children entering when under the age of five is likely to have a larger "in care" ("snapshot") population as these children could potentially be in care for 18 years, whereas if a large proportion of care entrants are teenagers (as with Sweden), the maximum length in care, and the cumulative impact on the "in care" rate, will be lower. These data are not available from all the countries I studied, but where they were, there were marked differences (See Table 2).

The proportion of care entrants under the age of five is much higher in Anglophone countries and Japan than is the case in mainland Europe. (Over half of those entering care in Illinois were aged 0–5 compared to under a quarter in Norway and Sweden. Almost 50 per cent of care entrants in Norway and Sweden in 2004–5 were aged 15 or over (including some who entered care when over 18), compared with only 4 per cent in England and 20 per cent in the USA.) This is largely explained by policy on young offenders, with the majority in Scandinavian countries being considered as young people in need of welfare as opposed to juvenile justice services. Though (for reasons of comparability) the over 18s are not included in the statistics in this paper, it should be noted that, not only can a young person remain in care in France, Norway, Sweden and Denmark until 21 or 22, but they can actually enter "care" until that age. In England, around 3,000 children and young people under the age of 18 are in custody at any one time (around 6,000 if those entering custody during a year are counted) and therefore not included in the "in care" figures. These data on age at entry emphasise that the child placement system is used predominantly for different groups of children in different countries.

The other key factors influencing length of stay, and therefore impacting on the "snapshot" in care rates, are placement policies which, in turn, are linked to routes out of care. Given the large proportion of young children entering care in the USA (and to a lesser extent in the UK nations), one would anticipate a larger "snapshot" rate. This is not found because children in the USA typically have shorter stays in care than those in other countries, linked to the "target culture" and attitudes to care referred to above. States

Table 2
Age at entry to out-of-home care

Country/State	0–4 (<12 mths in brackets)		5–9	10–15	16–17	18+
Australia	38%	(13%)	27%	27%	8%	
Australia/NSW	39%	(14%)	26%	28%	7%	
Australia/Queensland	41%	(15%)	27%	26%	6%	
Canada*	27% (0–3)		12% (4–7)	20% (8–11)	42% (12–15)	
Canada/Alberta**	34%	(15%)	20%	35%	12%	
Denmark	12%	(5%)	12%	31% (10–14)	41% (15–17)	4%
Germany	!5% (0–5)	(4%)	28% (6–11)	23%(12–14)	28%	5%
Japan	49%	(7%)	28%	20%	3%	
New Zealand	34%	(14%)	19%	47% (10–17)		
Norway	23% (0–5)		18% (6–12)		51% (13–17)	8%
Sweden	12% (0–3)		15% (4–9)	24%	34%	15%
UK/England	35%	(17%)	18%	40%	7%	
UK/N. Ireland	27%	(11%)	31%	36%	7%	
UK/Wales	38%	(20%)	19%	40%	2%	
USA	38%	(15%)	20%	23%	20%	
USA/Illinois	54% (0–5)	(24%)	21% (6–10)	20% (11–15)	5% (16–18)	0.1%
USA/N.Carolina	43% (0–4)	(17%)	21% (5–9)	23% (10–14)	13% (15–17)	
USA/Washington	43% (0–5)		20% (6–11)	27% (12–15)	10% (16+)	<1%

(From Thoburn, 2007)
* Figures from 2001 Incidence Study, child protection cases only
** These figures only concern children who had Permanent Guardianship Orders granted in March 2004.

which have successful "permanence policies" (defined in the USA as higher proportions of children exiting care in defined timescales either through family reunification or adoption or guardianship) are rewarded by additional Federal monies. Only in the USA, Canada and the UK nations is adoption as a route out of care used to any extent (other than adoption by foster carers with whom the child is well settled and usually after a period of years in that placement). Thus, a similar child entering care, for example, at the age of two in mainland European countries, Australia, New Zealand or Japan who can not return safely home may remain within the statistics for 15 or more years, whereas he or she is likely to leave care through adoption within two or three years in the USA, Canada or the UK.

Placement patterns in more detail
Different attitudes to the family and the place of out-of-home care in child welfare services impact on the characteristics of children in care, their length of stay, and therefore

the pattern of placements used. As has already been noted, many of the "easiest to parent" and most easily adoptable children (those in the youngest age groups) will leave care in the USA, UK and Canada through adoption (and to a lesser extent, guardianship), with the result that a larger proportion of the "long-stayers" in these countries can be expected to be "harder to parent" or have complex family histories and relationships. In contrast, some of the long-stayers in the other countries referred to in this chapter will be placed early in long-term placements (usually with kinship or non-kin foster families) and more of them will remain in the same placements till adulthood. They are more likely also to have regular contact with parents, who may have requested a care placement or have become reconciled to the need for out-of-home placement, and continue with an agreed pattern of contact. Often, therefore, securing the placement by legal means will not be considered necessary unless the stability of a planned long-term "part of the family" placement becomes threatened by parental actions. There is, however, concern in all countries to improve stability and to reduce unplanned placement changes (both within and outside the care system) and most of the countries discussed in this chapter are looking at ways of improving stability. Mostly this is through family-based policies, but in some countries, there is greater emphasis on the support of the birth family through therapeutic (usually short-term) foster care or residential care which may be a long-term "family supplement" placement. Table 3 shows the pattern of placements for a range of countries with different placement policies.

Group care

Japan is the only one of the countries in this study with a sizeable proportion of its under-fives placed in group care settings, and in that sense it has more in common with the "transition" countries of central and eastern Europe. While in Denmark and Germany, almost half of the children in care at any one time are in group care placements, this has to be seen in the context of 85 per cent of those in care in Denmark being over the age of seven, and almost 70 per cent in Germany being aged 12 or over. France, Italy and Spain also make greater use of group care placements than Anglophone countries. This increased "professionalisation" of care in these countries is linked with the profession of social pedagogue or (in Francophone countries) "educateur specialisé" (Petrie *et al,* 2006).

Kinship care

Differential use of kinship placements for children in care has to be seen in terms of the broader contexts discussed in the earlier part of this chapter. The comparatively low use of this placement option in Sweden and France is linked to the fact that financial and practical support and casework services are more readily available to support family members taking on the care of their young relatives than is the case in some other

Table 3
Placements of children in care at a given date*

Country/State	Kinship care	Non-kin foster family care	Group care	With adopters	Other**
Australia	40%	39%	5%	–	16%
Denmark	***	48%	52%		
France	7%	46%	40%		7%
Germany	9%	38%	54%		
Italy	26%	24%	50%	–	
Japan	0.6%	7%	92%	–	
New Zealand	35%	40%			25%****
Norway	17%	61%	19%	–	3%
Sweden	12%	65%	21%	–	2%
UK/England	18%	47%	13%	5%	17%
USA	23%	46%	19%	5%	7%

* See Thoburn, 2007 for full list of sources
** "other" placements – include independent living, detention/prison, hospital, or are missing. It also includes, for England, 10 per cent "placed with parents". For some countries, those in "other" placements are left out of the total from which the percentage is calculated.
*** Some of those in "foster family care" may be in kin foster care placements.
**** In New Zealand some children are placed by independent sector agencies – some in group care and some in foster family care.

countries. Although the proportion in care placed with relatives has increased in recent years in UK nations, there is a move towards using legal guardianship and family support arrangements to keep children cared for by kin out of care or to discharge them from care fairly early if there are no child welfare-based reasons for the child remaining in care. Australia, Italy, New Zealand and the USA make greatest use of kinship placements for children in care. The 23 per cent in kinship placements in the USA disguises the very large extent to which kinship placements are used there, since many children leave care through adoption by kin, a legal practice rarely used in other countries. (A quarter of the USA children who left care through adoption in 2005 were adopted by relatives.)

The pioneers in the use of kinship care placements are Australia and New Zealand. This is linked with the high proportion of children in care of Maori or indigenous heritage and also, especially in New Zealand, to the use of Family Group Conferences when decisions are being made about out-of-home care (Marsh and Crow, 1998).

Placements with families recruited by the child welfare agencies
As in the UK, the large population in unrelated foster family placements results from a wide range of circumstances. Most of the children who experience this form of care will

do so for comparatively short periods of time, and some foster carers will care for many children during their "foster care careers". However, especially in European countries, Australia and New Zealand, the majority of foster carers at any one time will be caring for one or two children or a sibling group who have been with them for a period of years. They will either return to the family home as teenagers, move into some form of independent living, or "age" out of care as members of the household in which they have been fostered. There are no explicit data on this as the UK countries are unusual in recognising "long-term" or "permanent" foster carers as a distinct group (Beek and Schofield, 2004; see also Schofield, this volume). In some countries, including Australia, New Zealand and Italy, the "task" element of fostering is not recognised and there is no "fee for service" element in the payment system. However, in these as well as most of the other countries referred to in this chapter, there are specialist carers who are recruited, trained and rewarded for undertaking particular tasks, usually with disabled children, teenagers or those with special needs. Although it does not recognise "long-term" or "permanent" foster carers as such, France has two groups of foster carers – "ordinary" foster families (*familles d'accueille*) and salaried foster carers (*assistants maternels*) who are part of the therapeutic team formed around the child and birth family. This system is similar to the multi-systemic treatment foster care programmes currently being evaluated in the UK but has been in existence for much longer than the Oregon model in the USA on which the UK trials are based (Chamberlain, 1990). In France, there are close links between these salaried foster carers and group care settings.

The relevance of ethnicity and the impact of movements of children across national boundaries

An overarching issue which is responded to very differently in different countries is that of ethnicity and heritage. The over-representation in out-of-home care of some groups has already been noted. In the UK nations, the legislation strongly supports a preference for placing children with carers of a similar heritage. This is the case also with respect to indigenous children in Australia, Canada, New Zealand and some states in the USA, but in these countries, the importance of attempts to match the heritage of child and carer of non-indigenous minority ethnic heritage appears to be less of an issue and it is hard to find data. For example, although Australia is a highly ethnically and culturally diverse nation, data on children in care are only analysed in terms of "indigenous" groups and those of "non-indigenous" heritage. In the USA, the legislation specifically precludes consideration of ethnicity as a major factor when deciding about placement matching. In most European countries other than the UK, the legislation tends to be silent on this point, and practitioners tend not to see it as a major consideration (Warman and Roberts, 2003). In these countries, because of the prominence of intercountry adoption, there are, in any case, far greater numbers of transracial placements than in the UK where the numbers placed transnationally and with families of a different ethnic heritage are much smaller.

Conclusion

As this book is being prepared, a Bill is being debated in parliament in England which seeks to improve the quality of the care experienced by English children and similar debates are taking place in Northern Ireland, Scotland and Wales. Whether you are reading this chapter as a student or a relative newcomer to specialist child placement issues, or an experienced policy maker or practitioner, the main message is the same. In order to provide the best possible service to these most vulnerable children who need the state to become involved in providing out-of-home care, it is essential to learn what we can from best practice in other countries. But in the past in the UK, we have been overly narrow in limiting our gaze to the USA (for example, therapeutic foster care and "concurrent planning") and to other English-speaking countries (for example, kinship care and open adoption of infants from New Zealand) and have missed out on learning, for example, from the professional foster carer approach in France, or the way in which France and Scandinavian countries seek to retain challenging adolescents (including those who commit offences) within their child welfare and out-of-home care systems. Perhaps the most promising interventions from the USA that our policy makers have not seriously looked at are the "reunification" programmes – improving practice for the safe return home of children who have been in care for some time has been a low priority in the UK for researchers and practitioners. It is also important not to undervalue the progress that has been made in the UK – the policies that we can recommend to other countries. In particular, we have reason to be proud of the progress we are making in the UK towards finding a range of alternative routes to permanence and alternative family membership without requiring children to give up links with their birth families (see Schofield, this volume, on long-term foster care as a permanence option and Young and Neil, this volume, on post-adoption contact).

But in looking across national (or even local authority) boundaries, it is essential to understand the context in which apparently successful policies and practices in other areas have been developed. Are the characteristics of the children they are caring for and their families similar to those whose services you are seeking to improve? Are the political considerations and the resources needed to "roll out" an intervention similar? Particular care is needed when a promising intervention comes with a label that says 'this programme has been shown to "work" so you must "follow the manual" and not make changes to adapt it to your own context'. The message I draw from my study is that an "off the peg" approach to learning from other countries is likely to lead to some costly experiments or false starts since most interventions will need to be adapted to different cultures and contexts.

Selected further reading

Bullock R., Courtney M., Parker R., Sinclair I. and Thoburn J. (2006) 'Can the corporate state parent?' *Children and Youth Services Review*, 28:11, pp 1344–1358 (reprinted in *Adoption & Fostering*, 30:4, pp 6–19)

Colton M. and Williams M. (eds) (2006) *Global Perspectives on Foster Family Care*, Lyme Regis: Russell House Publishing

Thoburn J. (2007) *Globalisation and Child Welfare: Some lessons from a cross-national study of children in out-of-home care*, Norwich: University of East Anglia, Social Work Monographs

References

Beek M. and Schofield G. (2004) *Providing a Secure Base in Long-Term Foster Care*, London: BAAF

Bullock R., Courtney M., Parker R., Sinclair I. and Thoburn J. (2006) 'Can the corporate state parent?' *Children and Youth Services Review*, 28:11, pp 1344–1358 (reprinted in *Adoption & Fostering*, 30:4, pp 6–19)

Chamberlain P. (1990) 'Comparative evaluation of specialised foster care for seriously delinquent youths', *Community Alternatives*, 2, pp 21–36

Colton M. and Williams M. (eds) (2006) *Global Perspectives on Foster Family Care*, Lyme Regis: Russell House Publishing

Courtney, M. and Thoburn, J. (eds) (in press) *Children in Need of Out-of-Home Care*, Aldershot: Ashgate

Department for Education and Skills (DFES) (2006) *Care Matters*, London: The Stationery Office

Dickens J., Howell D., Thoburn J. and Schofield G. (2007) 'Children starting to be looked after by local authorities in England: An analysis of inter-authority variation and case-centred decision-making', *British Journal of Social Work*, 37, pp 597–617

Fox-Harding L. (1991) *Perspectives in Child Care Policy*, London: Longman

Marsh P. and Crow G. (1998) *Family Group Conferencing in Child Welfare*, Oxford: Blackwell

Petrie P., Boddy J., Cameron C., Simon A. and Wigfall V. (2006) *Working with Children in Residential Care: European perspectives*, Buckingham: Open University Press

Schofield G., Thoburn J., Howell D. and Dickens J. (2007) 'The search for stability and permanence: Modelling the pathways of long-stay looked after children', *British Journal of Social Work*, 37, pp 619–642

Thoburn J. (2007) *Globalisation and Child Welfare: Some lessons from a cross-national study of children in out-of-home care*, East Anglia, Norwich: University of East Anglia, Social Work Monographs

Tilbury C. (2004) 'The influence of performance management on child welfare policy and practice', *British Journal of Social Work*, 34:2, pp 225–241

Warman A. and Roberts C. (2003) *Adoption and Looked After Children: An international comparison*, Oxford: Oxford Centre for Family Law and Policy

Wiklund S. (2006) 'Signs of child maltreatment: The extent and nature of referrals to Swedish child welfare agencies', *European Journal of Social Work*, 9:1, pp 39–58

3 The impact of histories of abuse and neglect on children in placement

David Howe

Introduction

The more children experience extremes of abuse and neglect in their early years, the more likely it is that their neurological and psychosocial development will be impaired. This chapter explores this thesis and considers its implications for children placed with foster carers and adoptive parents. Although the quality of the environment, particularly the social environment generated by parents, family and peers, is of great consequence for children's development, other factors are also in play. Nature and nurture interact in complex and significant ways as children journey along their life course.

Nature and nurture

Increasing evidence suggests that our genetic make-up predicts much of our behaviour, temperament and personality. However, because the interplay between genes and environment, nature and nurture is dynamic, even the claim that genes play a powerful role in our development has to be understood transactionally. For example, a child whose innate temperament tends towards the uninhibited and extrovert is likely to seek out friends and environments that have a more boisterous, risk-taking quality. In turn, these environments will impact on aspects of that child's development. Exciting environments can be encouraged and may lead the girl or boy to star as a downhill skier or hedge-fund manager. Equally exciting environments may be available to children who live in deprived, socially disadvantaged areas, but here the pursuits might not be socially approved: running across railway lines or spraying graffiti on high bridges can get you into trouble.

These are rather simplistic examples, but they hint at the seemingly surprising notion that genes can "cause" environments (Rutter and Rutter, 1993; Rutter, 2006). And having "caused" the environment, the child's personality, cognitive character, temperament, and biology then interact with the environment caused, and so on in a never-ending series of transactional dynamics. To an extent, then, children's genetic make-up not only determines many features of their personality and psychosocial development, it also influences their choice of environment, particularly peers, and how environments react, particularly parents, siblings, peers, and teachers.

So, the key idea in genetics is how genes express themselves in their environmental context. In part, the nature of the expression will depend on the quality and character of the environment. And this is where things not only get interesting, but at first sight might seem paradoxical. The richer and more responsive the environment, the more our full genetic potential is likely to be realised. In dangerous and deprived environments, including families in which children suffer abuse and neglect, children's innate potential is at risk of not being fully realised. Children raised in benign, socially enriched family environments show maximum variety in their development as each child achieves unique expression of their personality, skills and talents. In contrast, abused and neglected children are behaviourally and psychologically more alike in the sense that their energies need to be spent on survival and not on self-realisation.

An example from the plant world may help. Seeds cast on rich soil allow each seed to reach its full genetic character and potential. We see great variety and profusion. In contrast, seeds cast on stony and poor soil struggle. They fail to flourish. They are alike in that few reach their full height and vigour. In human societies, when diet and nutrition are poor, most people are likely to be on the short side. Of course, not everyone will be the same height, but height differences are likely to be restricted as few people reach their genetic growth potential. In societies where people enjoy a good, highly nutritious diet, not only are people on average likely to be taller, height differences among the population are likely to be greater as everyone achieves their maximum genetically programmed height. We see something of this phenomenon when we compare the heights of young well-fed people with older, poorer generations in the West and East.

So although the analogy is by no means exact, children who suffer maltreatment find that their genetic potential, whether neurological, cognitive, social or emotional is at risk of being depressed by poor quality care and parenting. Average, "good enough" environments promote normal development. Good enough environments include sensitive, protective, responsive and psychologically minded parenting. Supportive relationships with family and friends also enrich the experience. However, when care and social experiences fall short of these normal expectations and fail to provide positive opportunities, development is at risk of being seriously impaired.

Child maltreatment

Maltreatment can take many forms including physical abuse, sexual abuse, neglect, exposure to domestic violence, and emotional and psychological maltreatment. Maltreatment types rarely occur in isolation and many children suffer combinations of any two or more of these basic forms of abuse and neglect. Each type of maltreatment presents the child with a particular kind of caregiving in which key nurturing experiences are missing. The kind of developmental impairments suffered in these sub-optimal environments depend on the age of the child, and the intensity, frequency, duration, and type of abuse and neglect experienced. For example, physical abuse places children at risk of behavioural and mental health problems that are likely to have a very different character to those which neglected children are liable. However, it appears that the younger the age at which children are subjected to maltreatment and the longer they are exposed to it, the more likely they are to suffer peer rejection, aggression and maladaptation (e.g. Bolger *et al*, 1998).

Also influencing children's risk of maltreatment and the effect maltreatment has on their development are a wide variety of other ecological factors. Impeded development and psychopathology are more likely when parents do not enjoy their children, complain about the difficulties of parenting, have no interest in their children's thoughts and feelings, show little love and warmth, do not encourage autonomy or live socially isolated lives in poverty under stress in rundown neighbourhoods. Cicchetti and Valentino (2006) summarise the developmental risks faced by maltreated children as follows:

> *An ecological-transactional perspective views child development as a progressive sequence of age- and stage-appropriate tasks in which successful resolution of tasks at each developmental level must be co-ordinated and integrated with the environment, as well as with subsequently emerging issues across the lifespan. These tasks include emotion regulation, the formation of attachment relationships, the development of an autonomous self, symbolic development, moral development, the formation of peer relationships, adaptation to school, and personality organization. Poor resolution of stage-related issues may contribute to maladaptation over time as prior history influences the selection, engagement, and interpretation of subsequent experience ...* (p 143)

The research literature on the impact of maltreatment on children's development is detailed, extensive and stretches well over half a century. An understanding of some of the key messages from this research will be achieved here by collapsing and contrasting two main types of maltreatment: physical and emotional abuse and physical and emotional neglect.

Physical and emotional abuse
Normally, when children feel frightened or have needs, they seek proximity with their primary caregivers for protection, comfort or sustenance. These biologically programmed proximity-seeking behaviours, known as attachment behaviours, are usually triggered when children feel in danger, threatened, unsure, anxious, hurt, or in pain. In their role as protector, primary caregivers become children's attachment figures. Over time, children who trust that at times of need their attachment figures are generally available, caring and responsive, develop secure attachments. As they mature, secure children begin to develop cognitive models (mental representations) of their carers as loving, interested, available, responsive and protective when needs arise. Children also begin to develop complementary models (mental representations) of themselves as loved, safe, effective

and worthy. These positive experiences build up secure children's esteem, confidence, autonomy and resilience. These qualities predict good peer relationships and a positive attitude to school, both major developmental tasks that add further to healthy cognitive, educational and psychosocial development. Secure children are at low risk of behavioural and mental health problems.

But what happens if your attachment figure is not only unavailable at times of need, but is actually the cause of many of your more extreme fears and distresses? This is the fate of children who experience physical abuse and psychological hostility.

If the cause of children's fear happens to be the behaviour and attitude of their primary caregiver (attachment figure), children experience a behavioural and emotional dilemma. Fear in children, however caused, simultaneously activates two incompatible behavioural responses: approach (seek safety) and avoidance (escape danger). Fear triggers attachment behaviour in which children unconsciously are programmed to seek proximity with and *approach* their attachment figure. However, as the attachment figure is the source of fear, and fear activates an escape response in which children desperately seek a place of safety (normally the attachment figure), abused and frightened children find it very difficult to organise a behavioural strategy to deal with their mounting distress. Getting closer to the frightening attachment figure increases fear. But by escaping danger, children increase the distance between themselves and their attachment figure. This runs counter to the biological imperative to seek proximity with primary caregivers at times of need. Moving away from attachment figures at times of distress also increases anxiety. Pulled in opposite emotional and behavioural directions, children feel alone, in danger, and more and more frightened – fear without escape, fright without resolution as Main and Hesse (1990) graphically describe it. These traumatic experiences in relationships with primary caregivers put children at risk of sub-optimal development neurologically, emotionally, cognitively and behaviourally.

Matters are made even worse when it is appreciated that attachment figures normally act not only as "safe havens" but also as regulators of children's emotional upset and distress. In order to help meet children's needs and deal appropriately with their upsets, good enough parents attempt to think about and ponder what the world might be feeling like from their upset children's point of view. Empathy, emotional intelligence, and having in mind the minds of their children help parents to understand and connect with their children, particularly at times of need. As a result, children feel regulated, managed, understood, valued, worthwhile, safe and contained. Good enough parents are excellent at helping children regulate upset emotions in this way, but they also express, name and regulate their own emotions when interacting with their children. Children who feel safe, understood and emotionally regulated thus become good not only at understanding their own but also other people's emotions, behaviours and mental states.

These achievements allow children to develop coherent and highly integrated brains and self-psychologies in which they understand how thoughts, feelings and behaviour all affect each other, both in the self and other people. Such understanding gives children behavioural options as they negotiate the day-to-day challenges of social life with parents, family and friends. These skills lead to emotional intelligence and social competence and significantly reduce the risk of psychopathology.

Physically and psychologically abused children miss out on many of these positive, protective and resilience-building experiences. Those who should keep them safe are the source of danger. Even more damaging, caregivers who frighten their children, causing severe emotional dysregulation, are not available to help their children feel safe, make sense of what is happening, and regulate their extreme distress. As a result, never having been the recipients of love and psychological understanding themselves, abused children are very poor at making sense of their own and other people's emotions, behaviours, intentions and mental states. Hostile carers provide their children with very limited information about what is happening at the psychological, emotional and interpersonal level, for example, failing to offer comprehensible reasons why they might be angry with the child. The only sense of self that abused children develop in such relationships is an unworthy, unloved self under attack and in danger. It is little surprise then that abused and psychologically maltreated children tend to be anxious and aggressive. They can be bullies. Their range of emotional expressions and understandings are typically limited.

Lacking reflective skills, good social cognition and emotional intelligence, abused children are often poor at seeing the world from other people's point of view. Empathy is the basis of morality and without it, children can behave without conscience. Having been controlled by the use of excessive, harsh, critical and undermining discipline, abused children only know how to manage relationships by using threats and aggression themselves.

Abused children have a bias towards recognising and reacting to the more negative emotions (fear, sadness, anger). They are poor at recognising and responding to positive feelings and their expression. More specifically, the emotion that abused children attend to, recognise and react to most speedily is anger. If they are to avoid danger, hurt and rejection, it makes sense that anger is the emotion that looms largest in their limited emotional make-up.

The other major disadvantage of being on the receiving end of hostile relationship experiences is that abused children tend to possess few behavioural options when they have to deal with social problems. Aggression or withdrawal, anger or avoidance tend to be the most common reactions. Maltreated children generally find it difficult to regulate their emotions in demanding social situations. They lack the social skills of secure children and, as a result, are often unpopular with peers.

With maturation, young abused children, even toddlers and pre-schoolers, begin to sense at some unconscious behavioural level that if their carers can't keep them safe, then safety and survival are down to the self. Abused children do not trust carers to keep them safe. They have little confidence that adults are available as a resource at times of need. They learn never to show need, weakness or vulnerability and so as they get older make few demands on teachers or new carers. Indeed, they associate weakness and vulnerability with anxiety and danger. Whenever they sense weakness and helplessness in themselves or others, they deal with it aggressively, often talking in a sarcastic, humiliating, dismissive way to a teacher they perceive as weak or a peer who is in distress.

Perhaps even more importantly, because carers represent danger, hurt and rejection, abused children will resist getting themselves into a dependent, looked after position. They have learned to stay safe, so they believe, by not letting carers get in control. They therefore resist being protected and cared for. Being cared for suggests weakness, vulnerability and potential danger. With adults, many abused children develop a range of controlling behaviours designed to keep the children in charge of their own care and protection. When they do have to deal with adults, they behave in a bossy, directive, derogatory, and even persecutory fashion. This can annoy adults who might try to re-assert their authority by becoming authoritarian and aggressive. This, of course, merely confirms the abused child's assumptions that it is not wise to let down one's defences or not be in control.

Physically and emotionally abused children do not adapt well to the school environment. They are much more likely to be disciplined by teachers (although in passing, it might be noted that sexually abused and some neglected children are more likely to be passive, helpless and excessively dependent in the school context). Many abused children are excluded from school. And looking beyond childhood, abused children approach adolescence and early adulthood at increased risk of developing a range of conduct disorders, antisocial behaviours, and mental health problems.

Physically and emotionally neglected children

We have already considered the emotional dilemma that abused children experience when they are repeatedly frightened by the behaviour and words of hostile parents. However, it is equally frightening for young children to be cared for by parents who are neglectful. Neglect is more than just physical neglect, being dirty, and poorly clothed. Neglect indicates an "abdicated" state of mind on the part of caregivers. These are parents who fail to connect, be interested in, or be concerned by their children's distresses and needs. They do not have their children's mind in mind. They lack mind-mindedness, emotional attunement, and "mentalisation" – defined as the capacity to think about and reflect on your own and other people's mental states and the relationship between them; in short, holding mind in mind (Allen, 2006; also see Meins *et al*, 2001).

Neglectful carers feel helpless, anxious, depressed, even frightened when faced with the needs and demands of their children. Feeling helpless leads to parental anxiety which is handled defensively by carers switching off psychologically and going mentally "off-line" at the very point the child needs them to be physically and psychologically available and fully engaged. Neglected children learn that their own fears and needs not only go unrecognised and unregulated, but that the very expression of anxiety and need leads to helpless, distressed caregiving. In effect, children feel abandoned, alone and frightened.

From an evolutionary perspective, it makes sense for highly vulnerable human infants to feel frightened when they lose contact with their primary caregivers. Babies are incapable of surviving on their own. In the hunter-gatherer world in which we evolved, and where there were very real threats, lost and abandoned infants would be in great danger. Thus, abandonment of any kind, including neglect and psychological abandonment, triggers feelings of fear which in turn leads to strong activation of children's attachment systems. It is at this point that neglected children find themselves in a profound behavioural and emotional dilemma. The cause of their fear and distress (absence of the attachment figure, physically or psychologically) means that they have nowhere to direct their attachment behaviour. The goal of attachment behaviour is physical and psychological proximity with the sensitive, protective caregiver. Having achieved the behavioural goal, the child can once more feel safe. The attachment system eases down and switches to background monitoring mode. But if the cause of the fear is the unavailability of the caregiver, neglected children find themselves without a behavioural strategy to regulate their extreme upset and distress. Psychological abandonment leaves children's emotions highly dysregulated. Chronic emotional trauma impedes both neurological development and sound psychosocial progress.

So, although abusive and hostile parents also lack sensitivity and good mentalisation, nevertheless they are actively engaged with their children albeit via a distorted relationship that lacks reciprocity and love. Abusive parents are feeding psychological, emotional and relationship information back into the minds of their children, although the information is of a very negative kind. Psychologically abused children are told they are hated, that the parent wishes they had never been born, that they are a waste of space. This repeated negative representation of the self becomes incorporated into abused children's own cognitive self-representation. They find it difficult to get this persecuted, unloved, unworthy sense of self out of their heads (Bateman and Fonagy, 2004; Howe, 2005).

However, in the case of neglect (helpless and frightened caregiving), no mental state, relationship-based information of any kind is actively being fed back into the minds of the children. Deprived of information about what is happening to them emotionally and psychologically, and what is happening interpersonally with others, children who suffer neglect risk compromised brain growth and impaired psychosocial development. Without the rich psychological traffic that takes place between carers and secure children, neglected children's minds lack integration and complexity. Even the sense of self lacks coherence and autonomy. Neglected children, along with physically and sexually abused children, are therefore at particular risk of developing symptoms of dissociation. The symptoms of dissociation can include depersonalisation in which the child experiences events, including what is happening to the self (for example, being sexually abused), as if it was happening to someone else. The child might feel disconnected from her body and feelings. The self is experienced as an emotionally uninvolved observer. Amnesia and trance-like behaviours can also be suffered.

Given the lack of emotional attunement and regulation, it is not surprising to learn that neglected children tend to cry and remain distressed for longer periods than non-maltreated children. They show a limited range of emotional expression. Both abused and neglected children are poor at regulating their own emotions. They are not very good at recognising and interpreting emotions in other people. They also talk less about their own thoughts and feelings than non-maltreated children, although shame, lack of pride and self-deprecation are evident, particularly when carrying out tasks at which they feel they are failing. Again, these emotional deficits interfere with the smooth and skilful conduct of peer relationships, including play.

Play is a major development task for children. In play, children learn to negotiate, share, communicate, empathise, plan, role-take and imagine. It has also been observed that mothers of abused children are more controlling and less involved with their children in play situations. The inability to maintain close involvement with a good group of friends puts maltreated children, both abused and neglected, at risk of feeling isolated, of not belonging. Poor peer relationships in childhood are associated with adolescent delinquency and antisocial behaviours. Dodge *et al* (2003) found that social rejection and the lack of positive peer relationships is stressful. Stress increases the risk of maltreated children behaving aggressively. And aggression raises the risk of yet further rejection.

Many neglected children are the victims of bullying. Being victims of their parents' hostility or helplessness, maltreated children can develop mental representations of relationships with others as dangerous and threatening. They see themselves as victims. Maltreated children's poor relationship histories also mean that they tend to have very low self-esteem, a poor self-image, and a belief that they are useless and ineffective. Neglected children in general, and neglected girls in particular, are at high risk of developing internalising psychopathologies. The most common mental health problems include depression, anxiety disorders, and mood disorders.

Severe neglect and institutional care

If the fate of neglected children is not to be in the mind of their caregiver, what is the experience of children who do not even have a selective attachment figure? For example, some intercountry adopted children raised in grossly under-resourced institutional care in which twenty or more infants might have been looked after by rotating shifts of multiple carers often fail to develop selective attachments. Without an attachment figure, there is nowhere for children to direct their attachment behaviour. Their emotional distress therefore goes unregulated. Environments of extreme neglect and deprivation present children with major developmental risks. Evidence suggests that physical, cognitive and psychosocial development are all in danger of being severely compromised. As a rough rule of thumb, the younger infants are when they are placed in the institution and the longer they remain in the deprived environment, the greater the developmental risk and the less likely they are to achieve full developmental catch-up if placed for adoption, as the longitudinal studies of children adopted from Romania have shown (Chisholm, 1998; O'Connor 2002, O'Connor *et al*, 2003).

In the absence of regular or reliable attachment figures, institutionalised children typically develop a range of self-soothing behaviours including rhythmical rocking and head banging. Some institutionalised children who are placed with foster carers and adopters continue to have difficulties forming selective attachments. Or if they do form attachments, they fail to show many of the separation anxieties displayed by children who are securely attached.

Children who suffer early and global deprivation can develop attachment disorders including directing their attachment behaviour indiscriminately to any adult. O'Connor (2002) suggests that these "disinhibited" forms of attachment disorder occur '*only* when and where there has been severely disrupted care; namely, a virtual absence of care in the early months or years of life' (p 786, emphasis original). Disinhibited children are attention-seeking, clingy, socially unaware, and over-friendly. Or they seek out any adult when they are distressed, even if their new, primary carer is present – seemingly anyone will do (Chisholm, 1998). They violate social boundaries and conventions by interacting with strangers at very close quarters and asking personal and inappropriate questions. Nevertheless, social engagement is superficial and shallow, lacking reciprocity. Some children show an alarming willingness to wander off with total strangers (Howe, 1998, pp 190–96; O'Connor *et al*, 2000).

Behaviours associated with disinhibited forms of attachment disorder include: impulsivity; poor relationships; peer rejection; educational problems; hyperactivity, restlessness and attention deficits; delayed language development; cognitive impairments (seriously affecting their academic performance); aggressive and coercive behaviours; and eating problems (usually eating too much in a voracious manner). In later childhood, previously institutionalised children sometimes cope better in environments that are socially and physically structured rather than those which are permissive and relaxed. Peer relationships also tend to be poor.

Maltreatment and brain development

A huge amount of brain development, neuronal "hard-wiring", re-structuring and integration takes place in the first few years of life. It has been increasingly recognised by developmental neuroscientists that the quality of the environment, particularly the social environment and attachment relationships, has a profound impact on brain development, and hence thought, feeling, perception and behaviour. Brain development is basically guided and controlled by genes. However, a great deal of brain organisation, re-organisation, and neural patterning takes place as children (and their brains) interact with the environment, particularly the psychosocial environment of other people including parents, family and peers. Secure, good enough environments encourage rich, dense, integrated brain development. In contrast, abusive, neglectful and traumatic caregiving environments can have profoundly adverse impacts on early brain development, the growing nervous and hormonal systems, and the brain's ability to regulate itself, especially at the emotional level (for example, see Glaser, 2000).

Severely compromised attachment histories, argues Schore (2001, p 16), are 'associated with brain organisations that are inefficient in regulating affective states and coping with stress, and therefore engender maladaptive infant mental health'. As Fonagy (2001, pp xv) notes, 'the average human mind is simply not equipped to assimilate or protect itself from environmental assaults beyond a certain intensity'. He observes that by far the most intolerable of such assaults are those that occur in relationships with the very people who are biologically earmarked to protect you, your caregivers. The brains of seriously abused and neglected children have an impaired capacity to deal with stress, manage impulses and regulate emotions. Children's nervous systems become over-sensitised to stimulation: 'Both lack of critical nurturing experiences and excessive exposure to traumatic violence will alter the developing central nervous system, predisposing to a more impulsive, reactive, and violent individual' (Perry, 1997, p 131).

The impact of child maltreatment on neurological development is a fast growing and specialist subject, but a sense of its importance for abused and neglected children placed with adopters and foster carers is given by Balbernie (2001) who notes the implications of maladaptive neurological development for later social behaviours, including marked hypervigilance, over-sensitivity, and under-regulated emotional reactions when faced with social stress:

> When abuse and neglect persist, so that the baby has time to create a "wired-in" response, the more primitive (in evolutionary terms) brainstem and midbrain become under-modulated. These are areas of the brain which control immediate reactions to perceived danger that are designed to ensure bodily survival by monitoring important environmental information . . . and regulating levels of alertness. This leads to hypervigilance . . . as scanning the surroundings goes on constantly and

unconsciously, and to instant reactions to stimuli others might not notice. (Balbernie, 2001, pp 245–6)

The brain is often described as "plastic" by which is meant that, although much of the brain's major development takes place during the early years, neurological change continues throughout life, particularly if the environment is experienced as intense and prolonged. In the case of emotional and psychosocial experience, the key environment is that of relationships with other people. For children, caregivers represent one of the most significant relationship environments. Improved brain organisation and functioning can therefore continue in the context of any close relationship, including the relationship abused and neglected children have when they are placed with emotionally attuned and psychologically responsive foster carers and adopters.

Initial behaviours when maltreated children are first placed with adopters and foster carers

Children arrive in their placements with established behaviours and psychological characteristics which will interact with and possibly shape their environment. Children bring to their adopters and foster carers their own unique histories, and the mental states and associated behavioural and relationship styles formed with their previous carers. Many of these mental states and adaptive strategies will have been forged in situations of abuse, neglect and rejection (Howe, 2005). Stovall and Dozier (1998) believe that, although these strategies will have helped children survive in very difficult environments, they can mean that children are ill-equipped to take advantage of good quality, loving and responsive substitute care. In particular, many children seem unable to elicit or respond to sensitive care and protective parenting. Not only are children affected by their environment, the social environment is affected by children and their needs and behaviours. Perversely, many placed children, even in late infancy, are in danger of bringing about behaviours, feelings and responses in their new carers that they had experienced in their relationship with their birth parents.

This model helps explain the different behavioural and developmental pathways taken by children in new families. Each child's pathway depends on the type of abuse, neglect and rejection originally suffered and the particular reactions of the adoptive parents and foster carers to the behavioural consequences of that child's abuse, neglect or rejection. For example, abused and rejected children might have developed attachments classified as "avoidant" (for fuller descriptions of attachment patterns see Howe *et al*, 1999; Schofield and Beek, 2006). This manifests itself as self-containment, an over-regulation of emotions and a dismissive attitude towards those who want to care for them, show love, and get emotionally close. Past experience at the hands of abusive parents has taught these children that closeness represents danger and that love and care cannot be trusted.

Some abused children will bring these avoidant survival strategies into their new placements. With their new families, children might behave in an emotionally self-sufficient manner believing that caregivers are not available at times of need and distress. Faced with such children, adoptive parents or foster carers might feel unwanted, not needed. A sense of disappointment can be felt. New carers may back off, deactivate their caregiving or ignore their children. The challenge to adopters and foster carers is not to be drawn into the defensive logic of their children's way of relating and instead understand the roots of this behaviour and behave in a consistent and persistently responsive, caring and protective manner. This allows avoidant children gradually to feel safe and less anxious whenever they feel in need of care and protection.

In contrast, some children will have lived in birth families where they experienced ineffective, insensitive and mildly neglectful parenting. These families live in states of permanently disorganised chaos, crisis, drama and noise. The unpredictable, uncertain caregiving witnesses children developing exaggerated, needy, and attention-seeking behaviours. If the children are placed with new families, when they are distressed the children continue to act with exaggerated need and anger. These children can make carers feel inadequate. No matter what carers do, the children continue to make demands, profess their helplessness, and show an insatiable emotional need to be acknowledged, recognised, loved, and approved. Carers feel unable to soothe or meet their children's needs. It is often only a matter of time before new parents feel exasperated and exhausted. It is at this point that adopters and foster carers might threaten to give up on such a demanding relationship, one which is emotionally charged but low on satisfaction. For these children, carers need to provide a highly predictable environment which reduces the child's anxiety and builds trust in the carers' availability.

Some of the most demanding and puzzling behaviours faced by new carers are those shown by children who have suffered traumatic physical abuse, sexual abuse and neglect. It has to be remembered that many of these children have survived by not trusting carers. Their anxiety may have led to a variety of controlling behaviours, including bossiness, aggressive sarcasm and compulsive caregiving (shown by children who attempt to "care for their carer"). Under stress, these controlling behaviours can quickly break down leading to sudden rage and out-of-control behaviours. These more extreme experiences of maltreatment leave children feeling hypersensitive to their carer's state of mind with respect to attachment. The children's attachment systems are easily aroused when situations are experienced as uncertain or dangerous. These maltreated children react very quickly to attachment-related stimuli, such as separation when going to playgroup or a carer's expectation of a goodnight kiss, switching unconsciously and unpredictably between states of fear, aggression, rage, depression, and helplessness.

When placed with adopters or foster carers, seriously maltreated children will initially remain in defensive self-survival mode. They will avoid being dependent, vulnerable or being cared for. They might even behave as if the new carer is a source of potential neglect, danger, or helpless need. The new carer is seen neither as a source of care nor protection. Children therefore might try to remain in control by being bossy, directive, angry, derogatory, rageful, aggressive, or seductive. Unless carers understand the origins of the children's behaviour and their need to remain defensive and controlling, carers are liable to feel helpless and angry. In extreme cases they may feel like abdicating the role of caregiver. This would confirm to maltreated children that attachment figures are liable to become distressed and out-of-control when they have to respond to children's anxieties (Howe, 2005). They are therefore not to be trusted.

The above descriptions offer only brief sketches of some of the adaptive behaviours and strategies that maltreated children may bring with them to their placements. Fuller descriptions can be found elsewhere, particularly in the work of Schofield and Beek reporting the findings of their long-term research investigations into foster carers and looked after children (Schofield, 2003; Beek and Schofield, 2004; Schofield and Beek, 2006. Also see Howe, 1998).

Developmental recovery

Maltreated children's initial adaptive and defensive strategies make sense in the short term. But what happens over the long term when children are removed from adverse environments of abuse and neglect and remain with warm, nurturing parents? Do they recover their innate potential? Do they achieve optimal development? In the words of psychologists, do they show developmental catch-up? Although the answers to these questions are promising, it has still to be remembered that nature and nurture, including the effects of children's pre-placement experiences, continue to interact dynamically.

Although parenting children who have histories of abuse and neglect requires skilled caregiving, adoption and foster care represent not only the most radical intervention but, from the research evidence, also the most effective one. Many factors contribute to the success of placement outcomes including good support for parents from friends, family, and schools – as well as social workers. However, the key therapeutic input remains high-quality, sensitive caregiving. The more parents understand how abuse and neglect can affect children, the more they are likely to offer nurturing that doesn't become drawn into the child's negative assumptions about the way relationships work. This will help children disconfirm their internal working models (mental representations) of caregivers as hostile or helpless, and the self as unloved, unlovable, unsafe and alone and start to believe that they can be lovable, loved and loving.

Understanding their children can help carers to become more sensitive and more reflective, especially if they enjoy good social and emotional support. Sensitive, emotionally reflective parenting generates rich soils in which children have the best chances of achieving some, if not total, recovery. Of course, it has to be remembered that the more traumatic and extreme children's abuse and neglect, the greater the challenge both to substitute parent and child to create a relationship that is nurturing and reflective. Successful care requires emotional attunement, creativity, and a great willingness to understand what the world must feel and look like from the children's point of view, given their troubled backgrounds.

Characteristic of many successful placements is the belief that carers have in their children. Children sense this and respond. Nevertheless, the developmental impairments and disturbances suffered by children who have experienced relational trauma in their early years can mean that, even with the most sensitive care, some children achieve limited developmental catch-up and only partial recovery. Although physical and cognitive improvements tend to be good, problems often remain in social relationships and the ability to regulate affect, so progress takes time. In cases where carers are able and willing to continue acting as a safe haven and secure base, it is not unusual for children's psychosocial improvement to continue well into early adulthood (Howe, 1996).

Conclusion

Adoption and foster care offer powerful experiences capable of breaking the transmission of adversity and maltreatment across the generations. In general, adoption and foster care represent the most radical, comprehensive and potent therapeutic input in the lives of abused and neglected children. Sensitive, emotionally reflective caregiving is likely to be the key experience that helps maltreated children recover self-esteem, coherence, resilience and trust. If poor family relationships are where things first went wrong, good family relationships are where things are likely to be put right. The most effective therapeutic focus, therefore, will always be to support and work with new carers, helping them to make sense of and understand their children, their histories and their potential.

Selected further reading

Fonagy P. (2003) 'The development of psychopathology from infancy to adulthood: The mysterious unfolding of disturbance in time', *Infant Mental Health Journal*, 24, pp 212–239

Gerhardt S. (2004) *Why Love Matters: How affection shapes a baby's brain*, Hove and New York: Brunner-Routledge

Howe D. (2005) *Child Abuse and Neglect: Attachment, development and intervention*, Basingstoke: Palgrave Macmillan

Sroufe L. A., Egeland B., Carlson E. and Collins W. A. (2005) *The Development of the Person*, New York: Guilford Press

References

Allen J. G. (2006) 'Mentalising in practice', in Allen J. G. and Fonagy P. (eds) *Handbook of Mentalisation-Based Treatment*, Chichester: John Wiley, pp 3–30

Balbernie R. (2001) 'Circuits and circumstances: The early neurobiological consequences of early relationship experiences and how they shape later behaviour', *Journal of Child Psychotherapy*, 27:3, pp 237–55

Bateman A. and Fonagy P. (2004) *Psychotherapy for Borderline Personality Disorder*, Oxford: Oxford University Press

Beek M. and Schofield G. (2004) *Providing a Secure Base in Long-term Foster Care*, London: BAAF

Bolger K. E., Patterson C. J. and Kupersmidt J. B. (1998) 'Peer relationships and self-esteem among children who have been maltreated', *Child Development*, 69, pp 1171–1197

Chisholm K. (1998) 'A three-year follow-up of attachment and indiscriminate friendliness in children adopted from Romanian orphanages', *Child Development*, 69, pp 1092–1106

Cicchetti D. and Valentino K. (2006) 'An ecological-transactional perspective on child maltreatment: Failure of the average expectable environment and its influence on child development', in Cicchetti D. and Cohen D. J. (eds) *Developmental Psychopathology*, 2nd edn, Chichester: John Wiley, pp 129–201

Dodge K. A., Lansford J. E., Burks V. S., Pettit G. S., Fontaine R., Bates J. E. and Price J. M. (2003) 'Peer rejection and social information processing factors in development of aggressive behaviour problems in children', *Child Development*, 74:2, pp 373–393

Fonagy P. (2001) 'Foreword', in Allen J., *Traumatic Relationships and Serious Mental Disorders*, Chichester: John Wiley, pp xv–xvii

Glaser D. (2000) 'Child abuse and neglect and the brain: A review', *Journal of Child Psychology and Psychiatry*, 41:1, pp 97–116

Howe D. (1996) 'Adopters' relationships with their adopted children from adolescence to early adulthood', *Adoption & Fostering*, 20:3, pp 35–43

Howe D. (1998) *Patterns of Adoption: Nature, nurture and psychosocial development*, Oxford: Blackwell Science

Howe D. (2005) *Child Abuse and Neglect: Attachment, development and intervention*, Basingstoke: Palgrave Macmillan

Howe D., Brandon M., Hinings D. and Schofield G. (1999). *Attachment Theory, Child Maltreatment and Family Support*, Basingstoke: Palgrave Macmillan

Main M. and Hesse E. (1990) 'Parents' unresolved traumatic experiences are related to infants' disorganized attachment status: Is frightened and/or frightening parental behavior the linking mechanism?', in Greenberg M., Cicchetti D. and Cummings E. (eds) *Attachment in the Pre-School Years*, Chicago: University of Chicago Press, pp 161–182

Meins E., Fernyhough C., Fradley E. and Tuckey M. (2001) 'Rethinking maternal sensitivity:

Mothers' comments on infants' mental processes predict security of attachment', *Journal of Child Psychology and Psychiatry*, 42, pp 637–48

O'Connor T. (2002) 'Attachment disorders of infancy and childhood', in Rutter M. and Taylor E. (eds) *Child and Adolescent Psychiatry: Modern approaches*, 4th edn, London: Blackwell Scientific Publications

O'Connor T., Marvin R., Rutter M., Olrick J., Britner P. and the ERA Study Team (2003) 'Child–parent attachment following early institutional deprivation', *Development and Psychopathology*, 15, pp 19–38

O'Connor T., Rutter M. and the ERA study team (2000) 'Attachment disorder behavior following early severe deprivation: Extension and longitudinal follow-up', *Journal of the American Academy of Child Adolescent Psychiatry*, 39:6, pp 703–712

Perry B. (1997) 'Incubated in error: Neurodevelopment factors in the "cycle of violence"', in Osofsky J. (ed.) *Children in a Violent Society*, New York: Guilford Press

Rutter M. (2006) *Genes and Behaviour: Nature-nurture interplay explained*, Oxford: Blackwell

Rutter M. and Rutter M. (1993) *Developing Minds: Challenge and continuity across the lifespan*, London: Penguin

Schofield G. (2003) *Part of the Family: Pathways through foster care*, London: BAAF

Schofield G. and Beek M. (2006) *Attachment Handbook for Foster Care and Adoption*, London: BAAF

Schore A. (2001) 'Effects of a secure attachment relationship on right brain development, affect regulation, and infant mental health', *Infant Mental Health Journal*, 22:1–2, pp 7–66

Stovall K., Chase and Dozier M. (1998) 'Infants in foster care: An attachment theory perspective', *Adoption Quarterly*, 2:1 pp 55–88

4 Listening to children and young people[1]

Nigel Thomas

Introduction

Aunt Ada and I were shown into Miss Hayhurst's office at the Ministry and after a short conversation Aunt Ada just turned and went. She didn't say 'good-bye' or even look at me, and I suddenly realised with a hopeless sense of finality that she was gone. I set up a loud wailing that rose and increased on the chance that somehow I could reach Aunt Ada and bring her back. Miss Hayhurst just went on writing as if I and my crying were non-existent. Another woman was shown in. Putting down her shopping-bag, she came straight across to me, ignoring Miss Hayhurst who had risen and was holding out her hand.

'Don't you take on now, my mawther,' said the woman, kissing me. 'You'll be all right along o' me. Do you know what I got back home? Why, three old pussy cats, and look you here.' From her pocket she brought out a little poke-bag of sweets, of the kind known as butter balls. I can still recall the salty sweet taste of them. The salt was from my tears which continued to flow, though quietly.

Then the woman turned her attention to Miss Hayhurst, and together they filled in the indispensable forms, while I studied my new foster-mother. (From *King of the Barbareens*, Hitchman, 1966, p 49)

I have been here about four months, but I didn't have much choice. The very first time I went, they didn't let me visit or anything. They just took me there. (Boy aged nine)

What foster homes . . . like they choose it, but I can say whether I like it or not. That is what every social worker has done . . . Well I have had most say in it really because they won't put me anywhere if I don't like it. (Boy aged twelve, Thomas and O'Kane, 1999b, p 375)

These quotations give contrasting pictures of children's involvement in moves in foster care. Elsie's experience in 1924, as related by her adult self, Janet Hitchman, was probably

---

[1] Adapted from Chapter 3 of *Social Work with Young People in Care* (Thomas, 2005), with kind permission of Palgrave Macmillan.

not untypical of that period. The interviews from which the second and third quotations are drawn took place in 1996, and by then it was much more common for children to be consulted about their placements. However, as the statement by the boy aged nine suggests, it was still by no means universal, particularly for younger children. Even where practice has significantly improved, there remain important questions about children's understanding of the purpose, process and outcome of consultation.

In this chapter I want to look at why it is important to listen to children and young people in care, what research and experience tell us about how it can be done well, what it means in practice in the different contexts in which it takes place – providing care, choosing placements, planning and reviewing, tackling problems, and in children's everyday lives – and at what some of the difficult issues are.

Why listen to children?

Listening to children and young people should be a fundamental part of social work practice with children and families. There are three main arguments underlying this principle.

The first is a *moral* argument – that children and young people are *persons* with a *right* to be heard and to have a say in decisions about their own lives. This is often supported with reference to Article 12 of the United Nations Convention on the Rights of the Child, which says that

> *States Parties shall ensure to the child who is capable of forming his or her own views the right to express those views freely in all matters affecting the child, the views of the child being given due weight in accordance with the age and maturity of the child.*

'All matters affecting the child' clearly includes matters concerning the child's personal life, such as where she or he lives or goes to school.

The second is a *psychological* argument – that it is good for children and young people to have their wishes understood and their views taken into account. There is considerable research evidence that having a sense of control over our lives is associated with other measures of well-being, both for adults and for children as young as babies (see Maccoby, 1980). Many children grow up feeling that they have little control, or that important decisions about their lives are being taken without really consulting them or even explaining to them what is happening. Taking the time to explain things properly to children, giving them a chance to express their own thoughts and feelings, and creating opportunities for them to influence what happens, can give them a feeling of being more in control, and enable them to move on successfully in other areas of their lives.

The third is a *practical* argument – that listening to children and young people actually leads to better decisions. It is generally true that decisions and plans are better if they are based on the knowledge and opinions of those directly involved, and this surely applies equally where children are concerned. There is some research evidence that allowing children to influence decisions that affect them can improve the quality of those decisions. Children, like adults, are experts in their own lives, and it would be foolish to ignore that expertise when making difficult decisions.

Cashmore (2002), in a comprehensive review of the research evidence for children and young people's participation when they are looked after, suggests that 'the reasons for involving them in decision-making that affects them are also arguably more cogent when those children and young people are in state care' (p 838). She suggests this for the following four reasons, which encompass the same moral, psychological and practical considerations as above. First, while decisions for children living at home are usually made by one or two familiar adults, for children in care decisions may be made by a large number of adults, some of whom are unknown to the child. Second, while it is important for children's self-esteem to have their views respected, this is especially important for children who have been abused or neglected, giving them a sense of being agents rather than 'victims of the whims of adults' (p 838). Third, there is some evidence that when children in care have choice about a placement, it tends to be more stable – 'planning and decision-making which take the children's views into account are likely to be both more appropriate and more acceptable to the child' (p 839). Fourth, participating in decisions with support can help to prepare children and young people for future autonomous decision-making – something of which young people leaving care often have little experience, although they usually have to move to independent living much earlier than other young people.

Elsewhere (Thomas, 2008), I have suggested that approaches to this work are strongly influenced by how one sees children and young people. If we see them primarily as *needy* or problematic, then we are likely to work with them in ways that reinforce their dependence and powerlessness. If, on the other hand, we see children as *resourceful*, then we are more likely to be open to the different ways in which they can contribute to the working relationship we have with them. In relation to the care system there are, I suggest, three ways in which to see children and young people: as recipients of care, in which case our aim is to care for them, to meet their needs and ensure their optimal development; as consumers of a service, which means that we are accountable to them (and their parents) for the quality of service we provide; and as citizens, who are participants both in the care system and in their living situation, with the rights that go with that status. Listening to children is implicit in all three perspectives, whether it be to assess their needs, to respond to their wishes, or to respect their rights.

In England and Wales, the Children Act 1989 requires a local authority to ascertain and consider the 'wishes and feelings' of a child whom they propose to look after (the same expression was used earlier in the 1975 Children Act). This suggests that, when we communicate with children about their care, we need to have a dual focus:

- on *what they want* – on their views and thoughts about their situation, and in particular on what they would like to happen;
- on *how they are feeling* – on the impact of their experiences on their happiness, security and sense of self.

In what follows, it will be important to keep this dual focus in mind. We should respond to what children have to say, include them as participants in decision-making processes, and respect their rights. At the same time, we must remember that they are young people in vulnerable situations who may have undergone traumatic experiences, and who may be bewildered, overwhelmed or frightened – we must respond to their needs on a feeling level.

"Listening to children" should not be taken too literally. Children's non-verbal communication can be just as important and revealing as their words, and sometimes more so. Communication is a dialogue, and what workers say to children, especially in terms of giving explanation, is important too. Finally, listening to children is a precursor to action, not a substitute for it. Children and young people expect us to do something about what they tell us, and soon become cynical or disillusioned if this does not happen.

Communicating with children

Communicating with children and young people is not necessarily so very different from communicating with adults. Wherever people are in need, the basic requirements are the same – warmth, empathy, trust, and sensitivity to the person's verbal and non-verbal language and style of communication. However, children and young people in care may bring particular issues to such encounters. They may be relatively uncomfortable with straightforward verbal conversations, perhaps because their verbal skills are limited, because they are distressed, or because they are simply unused to talking about such matters with an adult – especially a stranger. On the other hand, they may be able to communicate through play or drawing – or, indeed, using newer media such as computers – in ways that many adults might find much more difficult. This applies especially to younger children. Older children and young people may have adolescent inhibitions about talking freely with adults, or may have learned not to trust people who say they want to help them.

O'Quigley (2000, pp 28–9) reviewed the research on what makes for successful listening to children. She identified the following principles, among others:

- Confidentiality 'is empowering and allows the child to speak freely'. She also notes that 'if unconditional confidentiality cannot be guaranteed then this should be made clear at the outset so that the child does not feel that confidences have been betrayed'.
- Age 'should be disregarded as far as possible' – children are often more competent than adults expect and, while being aware of developmental and cultural factors, one should not use them to make assumptions about individual children.
- A friendly and non-intrusive style of interviewing, that allows children space to develop their opinions, is more effective than a protective or controlling approach.
- Information is crucial if children are to explore options and express coherent views.
- Reassuring the child that there are no 'right' and 'wrong' answers frees the child to voice her or his own opinions.
- Adults should be non-judgemental and open-minded about children's views, and allow them to explore their own agendas.
- Children's competencies are different from those of adults rather than lesser. Drawing and other practical supports for communication may help to elicit this competence.
- It is important to recognise that some children may not want to participate in decision making.

Although O'Quigley's focus was on children involved in divorce and separation proceedings, who may be interviewed by relative strangers such as lawyers and guardians, her review of the research was careful, and many of the lessons she draws are applicable to other settings such as the care system.

Talking to children and young people is one of the core activities in this area of social work practice. Of course, some practitioners are more confident than others – but we all have to do it, and it is our individual responsibility to become as skilled as we can in this work. Later in the chapter, we look at the role of independent advocates, who have an increasingly important part to play in addressing the needs and rights of children in care. However, it cannot be emphasised enough that *every* practitioner working with children and families should regard communicating with children as a key part of their professional task. It is not something to be 'left to the experts' – we are the experts!

The following checklist offers a way to remember some of the key points about communicating with children and young people. It is based on the findings of research with children in care.

"TRANSACTS" – key points for dialogue with children

Time – it is essential to have enough time to spend with a child; they do not necessarily want to talk by appointment. Time also means working at the child's pace, allowing them to stay in control.

Relationship, trust and honesty – children communicate best with people with whom they have relationships of warmth and trust. It is important to be friendly and open, empathetic and above all "straight" with children.

Active listening – the skills of "active listening" developed in counselling can be helpful in work with children. This means responding to cues, restating and drawing out the meaning of what the child is saying, combined with the expression of warmth, empathy and acceptance.

Non-verbal communication – an adult's tone of voice, facial expression, body language and even style of dress can affect how children communicate.

Support and encouragement – children need support and active encouragement to speak up, especially when they have something difficult or negative to express. An adult may sometimes need to offer to express a child's views for them. Children don't like it when they feel they are being judged or criticised, and they don't like to be put "on the spot".

Activities – many children find it very boring to "just sit and talk". Games, writing, drawing and other activities can be used to make the process more interesting. Life story work can be an excellent way to involve children in reflecting on their situation.

Choice, information and preparation – children must have a choice about whether and how they participate in a decision-making process. They are more able to have their say if they have been prepared for the discussion and given time to think about things beforehand.

The child's agenda – it is important to give children space to talk about issues that concern them, rather than just having to respond to adults' questions.

Serious fun! – the fact that serious matters are being discussed doesn't mean that everyone has to be po-faced. Most children find this alienating; some find it threatening. If decision-making processes can be made more enjoyable, children are more likely to get involved.

(adapted from Thomas and O'Kane, 1998a)

Listening to children in different contexts

The ways in which we engage with children and young people will vary according to the contexts in which this takes place. The child whom we are meeting, perhaps for the first time and in a crisis, to discuss the possibility of admission into care may need a very different response from the child we meet on a regular visit in an established placement. There are a number of key situations where appropriate engagement with children's wishes and feeling is of crucial importance, and it is worth reflecting on each of these in turn.

- **Prior to admission into care** – it is crucial to include children in discussion so that they understand why admission is being considered and so that they have as much control and choice as possible over what happens. This is something that children and young people have emphasised in research and consultation. It may be very difficult to achieve, especially with a family in a crisis or a child at risk where there are pressures from adults to resolve a problem quickly; but it is essential that the child has space to express their views on what is happening and their wishes and feelings about what should happen next.
- **Choosing a placement** – as we saw at the beginning of this chapter, children can sometimes be treated, and left feeling, like parcels. A placement is more likely to succeed if the child is able to play a part in choosing it – and in planning and making the arrangements. The same applies with even more force to planning an adoption placement.
- **Reviews and planning meetings** – there is a growing body of evidence that the greater inclusion of children and young people in these relatively formal meetings to discuss their care has benefits, for them directly and for the quality of decision-making, although there are some indications that the trend has stalled for children under ten. This may be in part because the format of meetings has not adapted sufficiently to children's needs – young people often complain that the process is alienating and boring. The role of social workers and other adult participants is of critical importance in supporting the child to contribute in ways that feel comfortable.
- **Court hearings** – although not directly part of the arrangements for looked after children, court hearings may be a continuing feature of care planning for some children. The same difficulties in respect of the format and structure of the process apply even more, and good communication skills are at a premium.
- **Children's everyday lives** – one area in which children rightly expect to have a powerful say is in their day-to-day lives in foster or residential care. Clearly much of this work will be the direct responsibility of foster carers or residential social workers; but the child's social worker will also need to be a contributor to these discussions, and has a responsibility to ensure that the child is being listened to with respect and sensitivity.

Work in some of these contexts (especially the last) is principally about various kinds of informal engagement through conversation, play or shared activity, while others raise issues of how children can be successfully included in formal processes of decision-making. However, a large part of the work is also to offer children informal support with these formal processes, and good ongoing relationship-based work provides a foundation for children to engage in more formal decision-making settings with greater confidence.

Issues in work with younger children

Although enabling effective participation by adolescents takes skill and commitment, the inclusion of younger children in decisions about their care offers greater challenges. It is often necessary to use methods of communication that are very different from the ways in which adults usually communicate with each other. This should not mean that communicating with young children is a task reserved for the specialist, for which most of us are then excused from taking responsibility. As social workers, if not simply as citizens, we should be prepared to deal with all people, from the oldest to the youngest, in terms of meaningful human engagement. Every encounter carries challenges as well as rewards, and working with small children is certainly no exception. It is part of the job to face the challenges, and sometimes to enjoy the rewards!

Leeson (2007) worked with a small group of young people to reflect on their experiences of involvement in decision-making processes in care. She found that early experiences of not being consulted (at age 5 or 6) still resonated years later. Her research is a sharp warning against complacency, and a reminder that quite small children have a profound need to be given information and included appropriately in decision-making, and that we create problems for the future if we fail to do this.

A further problem experienced by many practitioners is that, even when they are personally committed to "direct work", as it is called, such work often seems to attract a low priority in the allocation of time and resources. Although many agencies are genuinely committed to enabling staff to engage directly with children and young people, in practice this work may be squeezed out by other imperatives – for example, the procedures associated with formal assessments of various kinds.

In addition, there are sometimes difficult issues around younger children's competence and how to assess it. To some extent this is an issue in work with all children, but the younger a child is, the more sharply the question presents itself. When it comes to the crunch, are young children competent to have a view on what should happen to them?

Children's competence

The question of what children are able to understand at different ages is a complex one. For some time it was dominated by Piaget's model, which sees children's understanding as incomplete and as developing through a series of stages. It is now established that this model tends to underestimate children's abilities, in part because it gives insufficient attention to social context. Children's understanding of a concept may be greater if the situation in which it is used makes "human sense" to them – which means that the life experience which a child brings to a situation, and the explanation and support provided, is often crucial, and it is unwise to make assumptions of the type 'children below the age of 11 cannot . . .'

However, the differences in cognitive skills between children, young people and adults are real, whether they derive from experience or from brain maturation. In early and middle childhood, some important conceptual frameworks may be limited, even with support – for example, the ability to think through hypothetical options. Lloyd (1990), looking at the ability of primary-school-age children to communicate complicated instructions, found that they tended to understand ambiguity but not to express it verbally, and that they needed support in dealing with unclarity or misunderstanding. Garbarino *et al* (1992, p 41) put it well:

Recent research indicates that Piaget probably exaggerated the differences in children's thinking at different stages of development. However, there is ample evidence to demonstrate that there are important differences in how children think, know, and understand and that children are not simply ignorant or inexperienced adults. Rather than describing them as stages, it may be more useful to think of developmental differences as reflecting gradual but perceptible shifts in ways of participating in and understanding experience. Thus, it is important for adults to try to understand that a child's interpretation and understanding of a situation may be quite different from their own.

There is also evidence that emotional development affects cognitive skills. On the one hand, emotional turmoil or stress can affect cognitive development adversely; for example, children who have had emotionally upsetting experiences such as separation from a parent appear to do less well at school. On the other hand, children's reasoning ability sometimes appears to advance most in situations which are emotionally charged (Dunn 1988). Dunn's research was conducted in stable and happy families with warm and positive relationships between parents and children, and the situation may be different for children who come into care, who may have had very adverse experiences. However, it would certainly be wrong to assume that children in care are disabled by their experiences from taking part in decisions about their future. Sometimes the experience of dealing with change, perhaps taking responsibility at an early age, can make children better prepared to take part in decisions.

"Competence" then is the product of an interaction between the developmental capacity of the child, their experience (including experiences of harmful or sensitive care) and the support they have from adults who currently care for them and seek their views. A child in middle childhood who has gained self-awareness and perspective-taking skills in the context of sensitive foster care may well be a more flexible thinker than an adolescent who has remained troubled, traumatised or preoccupied by harmful experiences. For instance, a thoughtful nine-year-old may be able to see both the advantages and disadvantages of a proposed contact arrangement, even though they may still have more concrete ways of thinking about things than they will have when they are older.

As well as the psychological understanding of children's competence, there is a sociological discourse in which competence is seen as something that is negotiated in social context. In this view

> ... the social competence of children is to be seen as a practical achievement: that is, it is not something which is accorded to children by adults, like a right, and can thus be redefined or removed ... But it is an achievement that is bounded by structural features of the milieux in which children live their lives. (Hutchby and Moran-Ellis, 1998, p 16)

The implications for policy and practice of taking a different view of competence are important. It means that the basic question is how we can design processes of decision making in such a way as to elicit and enable children's competence. Underlying this must be the recognition of the child's right to take part. As Eugen Verhellen (1992) puts it, 'the recognition of self-determination in children is essential in order to make them more competent and vice versa' (p 81). In other words, social workers have a vitally important job to do in empowering children, especially younger children, to take an engaged, informed and active part in decisions about their own care.

Listening to children and promoting their "best interests"

Is there a conflict between listening to – and taking account of – children and young people's wishes and feelings and promoting their best interests? Both are legal obligations, so it would be helpful if there were no conflict between them. In practice, however, there can be difficult situations where a choice has to be made between giving full weight to a child's own view of things and following adults' views of what is in the child's interests.

In our research (Thomas and O'Kane, 1998b), we found that these conflicts arose in relation to differences of opinion over placement, over family contact, over school and over children's leisure activities. Differences over placement usually involved conflict between a child wishing to return home and the view of social workers or carers that this was against the child's interests. Differences over contact might involve children wanting more family contact, or less. Differences over school included a boy of ten with learning disability who wanted to go to a mainstream school when his carers wanted him to go to a special school, a boy of eleven whose mother wanted him to go to Catholic school when he did not, and a girl of ten who wanted to change schools because she was 'picked on', when adults thought a move would not help. Differences over leisure time mainly concerned children who wanted to go off with friends in circumstances when parents or carers thought this was inappropriate.

Some social workers and carers were very clear about their responsibility on occasion to override the child's wishes in the interests of their welfare. Others were less confident of their own ability to make the right decision, or more willing to allow the child a substantial role in the process. A third group went for a balance between protecting the child from harm and allowing them to learn by taking risks, as parents do in ordinary families.

Some children were assertive about their wishes and feelings and wanted to be heard. A 12-year-old boy said, 'I don't need, well I do need sometimes, but most of the time I don't need people to say what is best for me'. Others were more self-effacing or accepting of adult judgement – for instance the ten-year-old girl who said. '. . . they care about you – they want you to do what is best' (Thomas and O'Kane, 1998b, p 147).

It is easy to say that the answer is to achieve a balance between these two obligations. In practice, finding that balance can be very difficult. Lansdown (1995) argues that the nature of the balance varies according to the perceived competence of the child in relation to a particular decision. She suggests that 'if the child lacks the competence to understand the implications of the decision, a parent should only override the child if to do so is necessary to protect the child or to promote his or her best interests', whereas if the child is competent, her view is that a stronger test should apply, in that a parent should only override a competent child 'if failure to do so would result in serious harm to the child'. Schofield and Thoburn (1996) respond that it is not simply a question of 'balancing' the child's wishes and feelings against her or his best interests, but that good practice consists in bringing the two together. They see the process of decision-making as

. . . a partnership in which it is acknowledged that the young person has some of the power and that a good outcome for the child depends on the child having a major stake in the decision. The role of children here is not simply based on the idea that these are competent children who should therefore have the right to make their own decisions. (p 24)

They are sceptical of Lansdown's (1995) view that a parent should only override a 'competent' child if failure to do so would result in serious harm, and argue instead that 'the role of any individual child in relation to any particular decision has to rely on a sensitive and careful process of negotiation' (p 25). Of course, children's rights to participation cannot be solely dependent on the quality of professional work, which is why 'children should have the right of access to advocates or complaints procedures when they feel that decisions have not taken their views into account' (p 26); and as Lansdown says, 'in all cases where the child's wishes are overridden, the child is entitled to an explanation of the reasons and acknowledgement of their concerns' (p 26). For a fuller discussion of these complex issues, see Thomas (2002).

A voice for young people in care

Much of the demand for action to involve children and young people in decisions about their care came directly from young people, with the establishment of organisations such as The Who Cares? Trust and NAYPIC in the 1970s and 1980s. It became more common for young people to be invited to planning and review meetings, and many of them found it a valuable experience. Fletcher (1993) found that 61 per cent of her respondents felt that people listened to them at meetings, and 84 per cent were asked before plans were made to move them. However, some still felt alienated from the process:

I never really say anything because I am worried about saying the wrong thing. (15-year-old)

They talk about you as if you are not there, so you just shut up and listen without saying a word. (14-year-old)
(Fletcher, 1993, pp 52–53)

By the early 1990s, it was normal for teenagers to be invited to reviews. However, for children aged 12 and under, it was much less common, and only later did social workers and their agencies begin to consider whether those under 10 might be able to participate. In 1996–7, research in South Wales found that 55 per cent of children aged 8–12 were invited to reviews and planning meetings, but this varied markedly with age; from 39 per cent of eight-year-olds to 85 per cent of 12-year-olds, with the sharpest increase at age ten (Thomas and O'Kane, 1999a). The research found that children whose parents were in conflict with the local authority were less likely to attend even when they were invited; likewise Grimshaw and Sinclair (1997) found that attendance was higher for "accommodated" children than for those in care. This points to the need for extra attention to ensure that children in conflictual situations have appropriate opportunities to contribute to care planning.

The reform of child care law through the Children Act 1989 and the Children (Scotland) Act 1995 undoubtedly gave an impetus to young people's participation. The establishment and publicising of systems for responding to complaints, and the development of advocacy services, have continued this process. Practices such as the involvement of young people in the selection of staff, and in arrangements for independent inspection of care services, show how much things have moved on since the 1970s, let alone the 1920s. Nevertheless, many young people are still unaware of their rights, especially some of those in foster care. Shaw (1998) found that children in foster care were more positive about their situation than those in residential care, but less aware of their rights.

Timms and Thoburn (2003) reported a survey of the views of 706 children and young people in public care, based on a questionnaire distributed in The Who Cares? Trust's magazine. The majority of responses were from children and young people aged between 10 and 17 years. The survey asked about experiences of attending court, about care plans and about contact arrangements. When asked if they had helped to write their care plan, 65 per cent said that they had not. Of those who responded to the question 'Do you think your social worker and/or the Court listened to you and respected your rights?', only 43 per cent answered positively. The authors note: 'It is clear from the responses that not being listened to is a problem for some whilst in care and that this is exacerbated by lack of knowledge about the way in which young people can influence the decisions taken about them' (p 13).

In England and Wales, the Green Paper, *Care Matters: Transforming the Lives of Children and Young People in Care*, proposed to address this:

Children in care have told us that having a choice over where they live is very important. It is also important to them that they know in advance some details about the placement. For example, if they are moving to a new foster placement, children want to know things such as whether there are other children in the placement, what religion the family has or whether their foster family has pets or a back garden. Children with physical disabilities told us that the size and layout of a placement is particularly important for them. We want all local authorities to offer children in care a choice of placements, and comprehensive details about the placements in advance, in order that they can be more meaningfully involved in deciding where they will live.
(Department for Education and Skills, 2006, p 43)

As well as having wishes and feeling about their own care arrangements, which mean that they need to be listened to individually, children may also have collective views about how they are treated and what services are provided for them. Some agencies have developed skills in communicating about these issues with children and young people as a group – through questionnaires and surveys, through open forums, or through representative organisations. This is easier to do with some groups than with others, for instance, with teenagers in residential homes rather than with younger children in foster care. It is also easier to include children who are vocal and articulate than children who have communication barriers of one kind or another. However, there are ways of overcoming these difficulties, and when it works the communication can be very rewarding for children and for professionals. The Green Paper, *Care Matters*, also proposed an expectation that every local authority in England will set up a 'Children in Care Council', made up of a 'rotating group of children in care', through which children's views would be collected and passed to the Director of Children's Services, and that every Director of Children's Services will 'develop an annual feedback mechanism . . . to ensure that every child has the opportunity to provide their views' (Department for Education and Skills 2006, p 97). For such mechanisms to work effectively, the support of social workers working directly with children in care will be crucial.

Advocacy, self-advocacy and complaints

The development of advocacy services for children and young people, particularly for those in care or accommodation, has been very substantial in recent years. Usually provided by "third sector" organisations under contract to local authorities or consortia, advocates provide independent support for children in expressing their views and where necessary challenging the local authority. This is distinct from the "independent visitors" provided for some children in England and Wales under the Children Act 1989 and preceding legislation, which *Care Matters* has proposed to extend to a wider group of children.[2]

For a social worker, working with an independent advocate can be challenging. As Dalrymple (1995, p 111) puts it, an advocate does not work from a best interests perspective but from a rights perspective, and 'from the young person's definition of the problem'. The advocate is not there to make life comfortable for the social worker or for the local authority, but to ensure that the child's own views are articulated effectively and to help the child engage in dialogue with the authority and those responsible for providing care.

There are also organisations that support self-advocacy by young people in care, and that are run by young people in care and represent their collective voice – organisations like A National Voice, Voices from Care Cymru and Who Cares? Scotland.

Although children have legal rights to make formal complaints about the care provided for them, it is not easy for a child in care, who may feel very powerless, to bring a complaint, and this is one situation where an advocate is likely to be needed. A formal complaint can also be challenging and uncomfortable for the social worker working with a child. If the child has been listened to carefully and the service provided in a responsive way, then concerns can often be dealt with informally; but it is important to support the child in taking the issue through a more formal channel if that is their wish. When children do not have an effective and accessible outlet for complaints and concerns, the consequences can be appalling, as illustrated by the report into the abuse of children in care in North Wales (Waterhouse, 2000).

---

[2] The original proposal was to rename the "independent visitor" as an "independent advocate", but this was withdrawn in the face of near-universal insistence, by professionals and by young people, that a clear distinction between the two roles should be maintained.

Conclusion

This chapter has offered an introduction to the topic of listening to children in the care system. Some notes on further reading are in the final section below. It is a complex subject, and the quest for greater knowledge and skill is probably endless. Fundamentally, however, the issue is a very simple one: children can tell us much of what we need to know in order to provide good care for them, if we make time and space for them, give them good information, listen to them carefully and attentively, take notice of what they say and act on it. That is what every social worker should do.

Guide to further reading

There are some good resources around to support this work. A particularly useful one is Naomi Richman's book, *Communicating with Children: Helping children in distress* (Richman, 2000), commissioned by Save the Children and written for people working with 'children in situations of social crisis or conflict' – this may include refugee and displaced children, street children, as well as those who are in foster homes or residential care. Clear and straightforward, it has chapters on verbal and non-verbal communication, on establishing trust, on working with children individually, in groups and in families, on barriers to communication and on working with acute distress as well as bereavement. Each chapter ends with some practical exercises, designed to help develop skills in a group.

Many of the contributions to the BAAF *Direct Work* collection (Luckock and Lefevre, 2008) will be very useful, for instance, the chapters by Lefevre (2008b) and Gupta (2008). Other helpful texts are Daniel *et al* (1999), Luxmoore (2000) and Jones (2003) – the last by an expert on communicating with abused children. For work with very young children, Clark and Statham (2005) can be helpful, and also Clark, Kjørholt and Moss (2005). There are a number of good resource packs for agencies and teams, which contain various combinations of training exercises and direct work materials: for instance, National Society for the Prevention of Cruelty to Children (1997) and Thomas, Phillipson, O'Kane and Davies (1999). Readers interested in exploring theoretical issues further may find Thomas (2000) and (2002) of interest. Schofield (2005) shows how an understanding of developmental theory can help practitioners to 'identify children's strengths and difficulties, make sense of children's communications and enable children to feel more valued and effective'. Lefevre (2008a) analyses communication with children in terms of a very helpful threefold model of knowing, being and doing.

Accounts by children and young people themselves of being and not being listened to, and reflections on what they need from practitioners, are of enormous value. Outstanding in this literature is the Blueprint Project (Voice for the Child in Care, 2004). The voices of children going through adoption can be heard in Thomas and Beckford (1999). It can also be helpful to read direct accounts from young people who have experienced the care system, such as *The Cornflake Kid* (Riddell, 1996) or *The Banana Kid* (Mason-John, 2008), which tells a powerful first-person story of growing up black, female and in care. Fictional accounts such as *The Story of Tracy Beaker* (Wilson, 1991) (all these titles seem to have a breakfast-table theme, for some reason) can also illuminate a child's point of view in an accessible way.

References

Cashmore J. (2002) 'Promoting the participation of children and young people in care', *Child Abuse & Neglect*, 26:8, pp 837–847

Clark A., Kjørholt A. and Moss P. (2005) *Beyond Listening: Children's perspectives on early childhood services*, Bristol: Policy Press

Clark A. and Statham J. (2005) 'Listening to young children: Experts in their own lives', *Adoption & Fostering*, 29:1, pp 45–56

Dalrymple J. (1995) 'It's not as easy as you think! Dilemmas and advocacy', in Dalrymple J. and Hough J. (eds) *Having a Voice: An exploration of children's rights and advocacy*, Birmingham: Venture Press

Daniel B., Wassell S. and Gilligan R. (1999) *Child Development for Child Care and Protection Workers*, London: Jessica Kingsley Publishers

Department for Education and Skills (2006) *Care Matters: Transforming the lives of children and young people in care*, London: The Stationery Office

Dunn J. (1988) *The Beginnings of Social Understanding*, Oxford: Blackwell

Fletcher B. (1993) *Not Just a Name: The views of young people in foster and residential care*, London: National Consumer Council

Garbarino J., Stott F. and Faculty of the Erikson Institute (1992) *What Children Can Tell Us*, San Francisco: Jossey-Bass

Grimshaw R. and Sinclair R. (1997) *Planning to Care: Regulation, procedure and practice under the Children Act 1989*, London: National Children's Bureau

Gupta A. (2008) 'Ascertaining the wishes and feelings of children in the children's guardian role', in Luckock B. and Lefevre M. (eds) *Direct Work: Social work with children and young people in care*, London: BAAF

Hitchman J. (1966) *The King of the Barbareens*, Harmondsworth: Penguin

Hutchby I. and Moran-Ellis J. (eds.) (1998) *Children and Social Competence: Arenas of action*, London: Falmer

Jones D. (2003) *Communicating with Vulnerable Children: A guide for practitioners*, London: Gaskell

Lansdown G. (1995) *Taking Part: Children's participation in decision making*, London: IPPR

Leeson C. (2007) 'My life in care: Experiences of non-participation in decision-making processes', *Child and Family Social Work*, 12, pp 268–277

Lefevre M. (2008a) 'Knowing, being and doing: Core qualities and skills for working with children and young people in care', in Luckock B. and Lefevre M. (eds) *Direct Work: Social work with children and young people in care*, London: BAAF

Lefevre M. (2008b) 'Communicating and engaging with children and young people in care through play and the creative arts', in Luckock B. and Lefevre M. (eds) *Direct Work: Social work with children and young people in care*, London: BAAF

Lloyd P. (1990) 'Children's communication', in Grieve R. and Hughes H. (eds) *Understanding Children: Essays in honour of Margaret Donaldson*, Oxford: Blackwell

Luckock B. and Lefevre M. (eds) (2008) *Direct Work: Social work with children and young people in care*, London: BAAF

Luxmoore N. (2000) *Listening to Young People in School, Youth Work and Counselling*, London: Jessica Kingsley Publishers

Maccoby E. (1980) *Social Development: Psychological growth and the parent–child relationship*, New York: Harcourt Brace Jovanovitch

Mason-John V. (2008) *The Banana Kid*, London: BAAF (previously published by Serpent's Tail in 2005 as *Borrowed Body*)

National Society for the Prevention of Cruelty to Children (1997) *Turning Points: A resource pack for communicating with children*, Leicester, NSPCC

O'Quigley A. (2000) *Listening to Children's Views: The findings and recommendations of recent research*, York: Joseph Rowntree Foundation

Richman N. (2000) *Communicating with Children: Helping children in distress*, London: Save the Children

Riddell M. (1996) *The Cornflake Kid*, Chippenham: Partnership Publications/Antony Rowe Ltd

Schofield G. (2005) 'The voice of the child in family placement decision-making: A developmental model', *Adoption & Fostering*, 29:1, pp 29–44

Schofield G. and Thoburn J. (1996) *Child Protection: The voice of the child in decision-making*, London: IPPR

Shaw C. (1998) *Remember My Messages*, London: The Who Cares? Trust

Thomas C. and Beckford V. with Lowe N. and Murch M. (1999) *Adopted Children Speaking*, London: BAAF

Thomas N. (2000) 'Listening to children', in Foley P., Roche J. and Tucker S. (eds) *Children in Society: Contemporary theory, policy and practice*, Basingstoke: Palgrave/Open University

Thomas N. (2002) *Children, Family and the State: Decision-making and child participation*, Bristol: Policy Press

Thomas N. (2005) *Social Work with Young People in Care*, Basingstoke: Palgrave Macmillan

Thomas N. (2008) 'Consultation and advocacy', in Luckock B. and Lefevre M. (eds) *Direct Work: Social work with children and young people in care*, London: BAAF

Thomas N. and O'Kane C. (1998a) *Children and Decision Making: A summary report*, University of Wales Swansea, International Centre for Childhood Studies

Thomas N. and O'Kane C. (1998b) 'When children's wishes and feelings clash with their "best interests" ', *International Journal of Children's Rights*, 6:2, pp 137–54

Thomas N. and O'Kane C. (1999a) 'Children's participation in reviews and planning meetings when they are "looked after" in middle childhood', *Child and Family Social Work*, 4:3, pp 221–30

Thomas N. and O'Kane C. (1999b) 'Children's experiences of decision making in middle childhood', *Childhood*, 6:3, pp 369–87

Thomas N., Phillipson J., O'Kane C. and Davies E. (1999) *Children and Decision Making: A training and resource pack*, University of Wales Swansea, International Centre for Childhood Studies

Timms J. and Thoburn J. (2003) *Your Shout! A survey of the views of 706 children and young people in public care*, London: NSPCC

Verhellen E. (1992) 'Changes in the image of the child', in Freeman M. and Veerman P. (eds) *Ideologies of Children's Rights*, Dordrecht: Martinus Nijhoff

Voice for the Child in Care (2004) *Start with the Child, Stay with the Child: A Blueprint for a child-centred approach to children and young people in public care*, London: Voice for the Child in Care

Waterhouse R. (2000) *Lost in Care: Report of the Tribunal of Inquiry into the abuse of children in care in the former council areas of Gwynedd and Clwyd since 1974*, London: The Stationery Office

Wilson J. (1991) *The Story of Tracy Beaker*, London: Doubleday

Section II
Placement options and issues

5 Reunification with birth families

Elaine Farmer

Why is it that, while we know an increasing amount about admitting children to care and about their placements while looked after, we still have very little information about returning them to their parents? Entry to care excites interest and activity, exit does not. Reunification is an area of practice that is poorly articulated in policy, has been much neglected in research and suffers from a lack of clear guidelines and ideas for practice. As a result, it has been in some ways an invisible area of work. However, this may be changing since the agenda for children in care envisaged by the White Paper, *Care Matters* (DfES, 2007), leading to the Children and Young Persons Bill, emphasises the importance of an increased focus on reunification.

Although the Children Act 1989 heralded a new emphasis on family support and on the reunification of children with their birth parents, there has been limited research evidence about reunion in the UK in the research conducted since its introduction.[1] Studies have shown, however, that the rates of children returning to care after reunification are now twice as high as was the case prior to the Children Act 1989 (Packman and Hall, 1998). The author has recently completed a study of reunification, (Farmer *et al*, 2008), a second study is in progress (Wade *et al*, forthcoming), both funded by the Department for Children, Schools and Families (DCSF) and a project on return has been conducted by The Who Cares? Trust (2006). In addition, recent research on substitute care includes some information about return. There is a much more substantial body of research on reunification in the US although their findings should be used with caution because of the rather different context and child welfare systems in the USA.

In this chapter, some key messages for policy and practice on reunification are drawn out using research from both countries, with particular emphasis on the more recent UK studies. The term "reunification" is used to denote return to birth parent/s from care and the words "return" and "reunion" are also used interchangeably.

---

[1] There are three pre-Children Act studies of a sub-population of returned children, that is, those placed with parents under a care order or "home on trial" as it was then known (Thoburn, 1980; Farmer and Parker, 1991 and in Northern Ireland, Pinkerton, 1994) and one study of all kinds of return (Bullock *et al*, 1993; revised and reprinted 1998) that also used pre-Children Act data. In addition, Trent (1989) conducted an action research project which pointed the way to effective reunification practice.

What circumstances lead to children returning to their families?

Some children enter care only briefly, say when their mothers are hospitalised, and the return occurs quickly and is relatively unproblematic. However, for other children, return is much less certain and will depend on conflictual or ambivalent relationships improving, changes in a child's behaviour or children's social services believing that the safety of an abused or neglected child is now assured. Perhaps it is not surprising then that voluntarily accommodated children (s20 Children Act, 1989) have been found to be three times as likely to be returned to their families as those placed under care orders (Cleaver, 2000).

Recent UK research (Dickens et al, 2007; Sinclair et al, 2007) has shown that there are also local authority differences with some local authorities being more willing to return children to their parents and deal with a higher level of risk in so doing than others (possibly related to having more support services to offer) and that, for those authorities which took these risks, there were more failed returns. In addition, it has been found that there are differences between teams within authorities as to the chances of children returning home (Sinclair et al, 2007).

Research suggests some factors which relate to the likelihood of children being reunified:

Parental problems

Not surprisingly, families with comparatively fewer problems and more personal resources are more likely to be re-unified than those with more complex problems (Fraser et al, 1996). US studies have found a variety of parental problems to be associated with a lower probability of reunion, including poverty, housing problems, parental drug misuse and chronic mental illness (see eg. Goerge, 1990; Rzepnicki et al, 1997).

Contact

Earlier studies suggested that the maintenance of contact between children and their families was the "key to discharge" from care, that is, to return home (Aldgate, 1977; Fanshel and Shinn, 1978; Millham et al, 1986). However, further investigation of these findings has shown that contact significantly predicted return home only during the first six months of placement in the Millham et al study. Indeed, when Quinton and his colleagues (1997) re-examined Fanshel and Shinn's research, frequency of parental contact only accounted for a very small proportion (2–5%) of the variance in return rates at their four follow-up stages.

This issue was taken further in a study of accommodated children where it was found that it was not clear how contact was linked with restoration plans (Packman and Hall, 1998), while Cleaver's study of contact (2000) suggested that contact alone was often insufficient to promote a child's return home. Direct work on existing attachments was often also needed, as indeed is work on the problems which led to care. Assessing if and when a child can return home, working on relationships between parents and children and dealing with the feelings engendered by separation is highly skilled work and recent evidence in the UK suggests that this work is not consistently undertaken.

Motivation and ambivalence

Parental motivation to care and willingness to change contribute to return and its success (Cleaver, 2000; Sinclair *et al*, 2005). Some parents are motivated to take their children back by the view that their children are behaving better or have matured but other returns occur because parents or children decide on reunion and take matters into their own hands – often because of parental concern about the lack of boundaries around children's behaviour (especially in children's homes), because children have been harmed or abused in care or because the parent and child cannot manage the separation (Fisher *et al*, 1986; Farmer *et al*, 2008). Earlier UK studies (Thoburn, 1980; Farmer and Parker, 1991) highlighted that parent or child determination often provoked reunification, especially in the absence of clear plans by social workers. Parent or child insistence on reunion then sometimes does, and at other times does not, signal positive motivation to make return work.

A few other studies have found parental ambivalence or lack of motivation to be related both to a failure to reunify families (see eg. Bullock *et al*, 1998; Harwin *et al*, 2001) and to increased disruption if children are returned to ambivalent parents (Farmer *et al*, 2008).

In whatever circumstances children are returned, our study shows (Farmer *et al*, 2008) that parents are often uncertain as to whether they will be able to cope with behaviourally difficult children or rebuild relationships with a child with whom they have not bonded. Little has been written about children's attitudes to return. We found that children may harbour uncertainty about a return to parents who have abused, neglected or rejected them and may feel fearful or angry. The young people consulted in the The Who Cares? Trust project (2006) often felt that their views had not influenced the decision for return and would sometimes have preferred a more "incremental" approach to reunion, involving increasing contact with their parent/s, more consultation with themselves and contingency planning which would allow them to return to care if the return home did not work out. Similarly, only a minority of the children in our recent study were recorded as having been consulted about the timing and manner in which they were to return home. The complex feelings that are stirred up by return need to be discussed, understood and worked with.

Testing reality

There are a few children who cannot live at home but who need to return so that their idealised picture of a parent can be tested against the reality (see, e.g. Farmer and Parker, 1991). Fein and her colleagues (1983) found that, for children "stuck" in the care system, those for whom reunification was tried, settled more successfully even if they were eventually placed with permanent substitute families. Thoburn (2003) refers to this as the 'willing to cut your losses' factor which appears to be associated with successful substitute family placement.

Caregivers

Caregivers play a largely unsung role in the return process. On the one hand, Vernon and Fruin (1986) showed the part which placement caregivers played in returning children home when a foster placement broke down or when residential staff demanded a child's removal. Thoburn (1980) also noted that social workers were sometimes influenced by the views of residential workers or foster carers about whether children should go home.

In other situations, caregivers, rather than precipitating returns, may work closely with parents to encourage return and parents may feel more able to trust them than social workers who hold the power to remove their children (Farmer and Parker, 1991). Research in both the UK and USA shows the importance of foster carers mentoring parents, supporting contact and playing a supportive role after reunification (Child Welfare Information Gateway, 2006; Farmer *et al*, 2008). Unfortunately, caregivers sometimes find that planning for reunification happens outside the review process, so that they do not have sufficient opportunity to help children prepare for returning home and some see themselves as an untapped resource (The Who Cares? Trust, 2006). It would therefore be helpful if children's services gave consideration to how the role of caregivers can be enhanced to provide more support for reunification.

Return to parents from kinship care

Research from the USA suggests that reunification with birth parents happens less frequently from placements with family or friends than from unrelated carers (see eg. Wulczyn and Goerge, 1992; Scannapieco and Jackson, 1996). This finding was also shown in our study of kin care (Farmer and Moyers, 2008) and in the study by Rowe and her colleagues (1989) where only a third of children returned to parents from kinship placements as compared with over half (55%) from other kinds of substitute care. It may be that placement with kin is used where the prospects of return are remote or it could be that sometimes the intra-family dynamics involved in placements with family and friends actually militate against children returning to their parents. Our study of kinship care (Farmer and Moyers, 2008) suggests that, while both situations occur, the first of these is particularly relevant at present in the UK.

The timing of return

Studies in both the UK and USA have consistently found that the probability of reunification is greatest immediately following placement in care and that the likelihood of return to parents declines as time in care increases. This has commonly been known as the "leaving care curve". For example, Sinclair and his colleagues (2007) found that 61 per cent of children who returned home did so within six months. Of course, the length of time children spend in care before return is due to a variety of factors so these findings do not mean that remaining in care for longer than six months in and of itself reduces the chances of return, as Biehal (2006) emphasises in her review of research on reunification.

In addition, many studies do not separate out the different groups of children in care and evidence from a major study in the USA of children entering care for the first time suggests that the "leaving care curve" may be true only for children placed for reasons of abuse or neglect and not for those placed as a result of their emotional or behavioural problems or because their parents were unable to care for them (Goerge, 1990).

Research has also suggested that shorter stays in care may be associated with rapid return breakdown (see eg. Wulczyn, 1991; Davis *et al*, 1993), possibly because insufficient change took place before return was attempted and in some cases such short stays are due to adolescents or parents taking things into their own hands and forcing the return for reasons related to dissatisfaction with care rather than improvements in parent–child relationships (Farmer *et al*, 2008).

Maltreatment

When we look at children placed because of abuse or neglect, we find that they are likely to remain in care longer than those placed for other reasons (Davis *et al*, 1996; Cleaver, 2000). Unpicking this further, US research suggests that children placed as a result of physical or sexual abuse are likely to return home more quickly than those placed for neglect. Indeed, sexually abused children may return relatively quickly if the perpetrator leaves the home (Courtney, 1994).

However, while some abused children never return home due to the continuing risk of re-abuse, children placed due to neglect, although likely to remain longer in care, do generally eventually return to their parent/s (Goerge, 1990). As would be expected, children who are more severely physically abused are less likely to return home than those whose abuse is less severe (Barth *et al*, 1987).

Children's characteristics

In terms of children's characteristics, some US studies have found that children with physical health problems tend to remain in care longer than those without (see eg. Grogan-Kaylor, 2001; Harris and Courtney, 2003). There is also some evidence from the UK and the USA that children with disabilities are more likely to remain in care (McMurtry and Lie, 1992; Cleaver, 2000) and that children with a learning disability are especially likely to remain longer in care (Berridge and Cleaver, 1987; Davis *et al*, 1997).

Studies have also found that children who experienced several placement moves are likely to remain longer in care (eg. Goerge, 1990, Webster *et al*, 2005). Of course, placement instability may in some cases be an indicator of emotional and behavioural difficulties, which may make reunion harder to achieve.

Family characteristics

Several US studies have also found that children from lone parent (mostly lone mother) families, are likely to return home at a slower rate than those with two parent figures (Landsverk *et al*, 1996; Harris and Courtney, 2003). Other US research has found that longer stays in care before return are associated with problems in the mother–child relationship, maternal mental illness, and the financial hardship of parents (Finch *et al*, 1986; Lawder *et al*, 1986; Milner, 1987).

Initial care plans

Our recent study on reunification shows four distinct groups of children in terms of the relationship between their initial care plans and the time it took before they returned home. At one extreme were young people who absconded to their families or were removed by their parents from care after only a few days or weeks and before any plan had been made for them. A second group of children whose initial plan was return home were mostly voluntarily accommodated adolescents who returned within an average of six months. In contrast, younger children whose initial plan was time-limited assessment were generally on care orders, considered at risk and took twice this long to get home. A final small group returned to their parents after on average three years in care because the permanence plans made for them outside the family had not been fulfilled.

Pressures for return

Much research assumes that reunification is in the gift of local authorities, but often it is not. UK studies have shown that, in reality, planned reunifications unaffected by pressure from the child, the parents or the substitute care placement, are very much the exception rather than the rule (Thoburn, 1980; Farmer, 1996). In our recent study, whether or not returns were planned, there were pressures in the background for children to return home in the vast majority of the cases. Such pressures need to be acknowledged as an important part of the context in which reunification work takes place.

Planning and purposeful work towards return

In our study, by the time the children returned to a parent, reunification was planned in the majority of cases. Improvements in the family situation (including a violent or abusing partner moving out) – or, more rarely, improved child behaviour – were only noted as having been the primary reason for the return in under half of the cases. Other reasons for reunification included that only a temporary period of care had ever been envisaged, that there were placement difficulties or that the court had ordered the return.

Where the returns had not been planned, children returned home because (when older) they absconded there, or they had been removed from voluntary accommodation by their parents or because of placement breakdown, sometimes accompanied by a lack of suitable alternative placements in care. Similarly, a recent study of children in foster care found that the return of children to their families was frequently poorly planned and supported and often occurred as a result of a series of placement breakdowns (Sinclair *et al*, 2005).

Our recent study echoes US research which suggests that too frequently reunification occurs without resolution of the problems that led to initial placement in care (Barth and Berry, 1987; Fraser *et al*, 1996; Farmer *et al*, 2008).

In the USA, two experimental studies of specialist reunification projects have reported that focused case planning is an important means of achieving reunification. The Alameda study concluded that social workers need to take an active role in planning for children's future as soon as they enter care. Practitioners need to outline options for the future and facilitate early decision-making. This project used written contracts to agree clear goals with parents (Stein and Gambrill, 1977, 1979). The authors concluded that the focus on purposeful case planning was the key difference which distinguished the specialist service from the less successful usual service. The Family Reunion Service study also found that the involvement of parents in joint planning and the setting of objectives were vital ingredients of the project (Walton *et al*, 1993).

In the UK, Trent's action research project (1989) which used permanence with adoptive families as the model for reunification work had promising results and again showed the importance of providing focused work within specified timescales combined with clarity about the consequences if goals were not achieved. Other researchers have provided valuable research-based models of reunification practice (Maluccio *et al*, 1986; Thoburn, 1994).

Harwin *et al* (2001) in the UK found that planning the return of children is particularly difficult in cases where mothers misused drugs or alcohol, as in other respects these parents were often viewed positively. In a subsequent study, Forrester and Harwin (2004) point to the need for improved access to treatment resources and much more training for social workers in the recognition of substance misuse and in making realistic assessments about prognosis that will not be overwhelmed by "misplaced optimism".

Promising results with substance misusing parents in the USA have been shown by three types of service: intensive case management including "recovery coaches" to help with assessment and access to treatment; treatment services designed to meet the needs of women with children; and harnessing strong social support in aid of recovery, including partners, and support from social workers and treatment providers (Child Welfare Gateway, 2006).

Indeed, Maluccio and Ainsworth (2003) suggest that family reunification practice needs to be reshaped to address the issue of parental drug misuse. Parents with substance misuse problems are more likely than other parents to maltreat their children (Famularo *et al*, 1992; Kelleher *et al*, 1994; Farmer *et al*, 2008) and maternal substance misuse is associated with an increased likelihood of return breakdown (Frame *et al*, 2000). Maluccio and Ainsworth (2003) describe a number of relevant US projects, including initiatives where alcohol and drugs specialists are co-located within children's services and a three-stage model of practice to encourage compliance by drug-using parents, with increasing levels of coercion at each stage, since without imposition of requirements to become involved in treatment, many parents are unlikely to do so. Parental peer groups are also used as a device for achieving parental behaviour change. Moreover, this model introduces time limits for reunification when the time needed for parental recovery does not keep pace with children's developmental needs and with the requirement to safeguard them.

Outcomes of reunification

Re-abuse

Evidence from both the UK and the USA shows that children who return home may suffer re-abuse or neglect. In our earlier study (Farmer and Parker, 1991), we found that a quarter of all the "protected" children were neglected or abused during their placement at home. This re-abuse rate was in line with those found in other studies of children in high risk situations at that time (Barth and Berry, 1987; Farmer and Owen, 1995; Gibbons *et al*, 1995; Brandon *et al*, 2005).

In our recent study, the re-abuse rate was almost twice as high as in these earlier studies, with concerns that almost half (46%) the children had been maltreated. While there was a substantial reduction in the overall number of children who were abused or neglected after reunification as compared with the number who had been maltreated before entry to care, *recurrence* rates for some forms of abuse remained fairly high. It is also important to note the close link between parental substance misuse and maltreatment of children during return. It is possible that increases in substance misuse – as well as the increased rates of return – account in part for the apparent rise in maltreatment rates during reunification.

A recent three-year follow-up of 596 children in foster care in England found (as might be expected) that children who were returned home were significantly more likely to be abused than those who were not returned (Sinclair *et al*, 2005). There was strong evidence of re-abuse for 11 per cent of those reunified with their families and some evidence in a further 31 per cent of cases. These figures are similar to those in our recent study.

A UK study which followed up a cohort of 49 babies under one year old, who returned home after placement in care, found that 15 of them (31%) were re-abused or suffered neglect during the three-year follow-up period. Twelve were returned home again after the subsequent abuse and three of these were re-abused yet again (Ellaway *et al*, 2004).

In a useful study from the USA, 120 children for whom there were substantiated reports of maltreatment within 60 days of returning home were compared to 92 for whom no such reports were made during this period (Fuller, 2005). Children under 12 years old were more likely to experience re-abuse than older children, with those under one year old at the greatest risk. Children who had experienced high placement instability (whom we might assume were more likely to be those with significant emotional and behavioural problems) were 11 times more likely to be abused or neglected after return. Children returned to caregivers suffering from mental illness were nine times more likely to be re-abused, and re-abuse was also eight times more likely for those who had been in care for three years or more and five times more likely for those returned together with siblings to a lone parent. These findings suggest that past instability and current stress may trigger re-abuse and that young children are particularly at risk, indicating that more intensive follow-up support and monitoring is likely to be needed for these children to increase the chance of a safe return home.

Psychosocial outcomes

Evidence from both UK and US studies suggests that children reunited with their families are likely to experience worse psychosocial outcomes than those who remain in long-term care or are adopted. Quinton and Rutter (1988) compared scores for psychosocial functioning for 7–13-year-old girls in residential care with their scores 14 years later. Those who had returned to homes with pervasive quarrelling and disharmony were significantly more likely to have poor outcomes in early adulthood in terms of their social functioning, than those who remained in care.

For children in Sinclair and colleagues' study of foster care (2005), rejection following reunion was associated with deteriorating mental health by follow-up. Children aged 11 and over who returned home from placements in foster care were found to have emotional and behavioural problems as serious as those of children entering residential care, including running away, self-harm, substance abuse, and aggression. These problems were significantly less common among children in long-term foster care or adoptive homes. Thus, overall, return home was associated with worse emotional and behavioural outcomes.

A six-year follow-up of a cohort of 149 children in the USA also used standardised measures to compare the emotional and behavioural outcomes for 63 young people who were reunified with their families with those for 86 who remained in care. It found significantly more emotional problems, self-harming behaviour, substance misuse, risk behaviours and total behavioural problems among those who were reunified than among those who were not (Taussig et al, 2001). This echoes the findings of an earlier study by Lahti (1982).

Children reunified with their families have also been found to experience more problems at school than those remaining in care. In Sinclair and colleagues' study (2005), educational performance and participation showed no improvement for children who returned home, in contrast to those who remained in care or were adopted. Similarly, Taussig and colleagues (2001) in the USA found that 21 per cent of the reunified children in his cohort dropped out of school, compared to only nine per cent of those who remained in care. This study found that reunified young people were significantly more likely to have been arrested (49%) than those who remained in care (30%), as did Sinclair and his colleagues.

While it might be argued that children who return to parents who are known to have difficulties might not be expected to do as well as children placed with specially recruited and trained foster or adoptive parents, these studies raise difficult questions about what standards are acceptable when children are returned home, how far services can offset some of the disadvantages of poor parental care, and whether children's services are intervening soon enough when standards fall unacceptably low (see Farmer *et al*, 2008; Sinclair *et al*, 2005). The Who Cares? Trust project (2006) notes the importance of holding a review before children go home when return occurs as a result of a change in the care plan and recommends that a multi-disciplinary panel is needed to approve return decisions and determine the support needed, with accountability at a senior level. Such changes in procedures might assist practitioners and managers and also help to ensure that children's returns are not being driven principally by pressures such as the desire to keep the numbers of children in care down rather than by careful consideration of what is in a child's best interests.

Return breakdown

One UK study, which focused on children admitted to care under voluntary arrangements, found a breakdown rate of half (52%) of all returns, with 24% of the children experiencing more than one reunion (Packman and Hall, 1998). Our recent study of reunification which included children on care orders and those in voluntary care, found fairly similar rates of return breakdown with 47 per cent of the returns breaking down over the two-year follow-up period.

Other UK evidence comes from a study of a sample of new entrants to care, of whom 15 per cent of the 133 children discharged home returned to care within two years (Dickens *et al*, 2007) and from a study of a cross-sectional sample of children in foster care, of whom 37 per cent of the 162 children who returned home re-entered care within three years (Sinclair *et al*, 2005). Our earlier and recent studies show that previous failed returns are strongly related to later return breakdown (Farmer and Parker, 1991; Farmer *et al*, 2008). When returning a child who has been unsuccessfully returned before, the question that needs to be answered is: 'What has changed to make this return work when the last one/s did not?' This is especially important as our recent study shows the deleterious impact on children of "oscillating" in and out of care.

Factors associated with return breakdown

In the US, social and environmental factors have been shown to be associated with return breakdown, including: poverty, receipt of public assistance, exposure to drugs and inadequate housing (Jones, 1998; Schuerman *et al*, 1994) and return disruption has also been shown to occur more often with lone parent families, where isolation and poverty may lower parental effectiveness.

In the USA, African-American children have been found to be more likely than white children to experience disrupted returns (and to have spent longer in care beforehand) (National Black Child Development Institute, 1993). In the UK, Barn (1993) considered that the differential treatment of black and minority ethnic (BME) children and their parent/s affected return patterns and in line with this, in our recent research we found that BME children were more likely than non-BME children to be on care orders and less likely to be accommodated. It may be that agencies are quicker to perceive risk when "dealing with the unfamiliar" or that such families were only drawn into contact with children's services when problems had escalated (Packman and Hall, 1998) or that more BME young people had been drawn into the youth justice system.

There is plenty of evidence that return breakdown is associated with older age at return (see for example Rowe *et al*, 1989; Farmer *et al*, 2008), longer periods in care (Fein *et al*, 1983; Farmer, 1992) and with poor prior planning (Block and Libowitz, 1983). These factors are similar to those associated with foster care and adoption breakdown (Berridge, 1997; Sinclair, 2005).

It appears too that the extent of movement experienced by children during separation can compromise the chances of the return lasting, especially changes of placement (Block and Libowitz, 1983; Packman and Hall, 1998). Children's services have been effective in reducing the need for changes of school, so that only a quarter (26%) of children changed school on return in our recent study. In the past, changes in the composition of the child's birth family in the child's absence have also been found to have a disruptive effect (Packman and Hall, 1998), especially changes in the presence of other children in the household to which they returned (Farmer, 1996). However, our recent research suggests that the issue is not one simply about change per se but whether changes have a positive or negative impact on individual children. It is therefore important that social workers assess the likely impact of new step-parents and other new partnerships on family functioning and ask children, when return is being considered, about their relationship with a parent's new partner. In addition, since many of the children in our recent study experienced changes in the members of their household (parent figures and other children) when they returned, preparation for reunion is important.

In a review of reunification research by Farmer (2001), a number of practice implications from the research are drawn out. For example, where there have been changes in the family, children need to retain their sense of place and belonging and their space and possessions need to remain untouched while they are away. The review also notes that Bullock and his colleagues (1993) emphasised that the return of children to their families is a process that is at least as complex and stressful as that of separation and intimately connected to it. Reconciliation involves facing up to the failures on either side which led to separation and after a period there is often a major row where all of the hurt feelings are expressed. Overcoming this apparent crisis, when children need reassurance that they will not be sent away again, can lay the foundation for a successful return.

Packman and Hall (1998) and our recent study found that return breakdown was more likely when the initial separation was because of parental mental illness or alcohol or drug misuse, no doubt because these problems often recur during reunification (see also Schuerman et al, 1994). Limited parental skill is also associated with disrupted returns (Hess et al, 1992; Davis et al, 1993; Courtney, 1995; Farmer et al, 2008) as is neglect as the presenting problem (Hess et al, 1992; Davis et al, 1993; Courtney, 1995). Packman and Hall (1998) also found that tensions between siblings and concerns about safeguarding were associated with further separation. In their study of accommodated children, difficulties during reunification were related to children with a tendency to violence or self-harm. Problems with schooling, including truancy and school exclusion, also affect the success of reunion (see also Lahti, 1982; Farmer and Parker, 1991; Farmer et al, 2008).

In addition, there is some evidence that return breakdown is associated with lack of support from the extended family, friends and neighbours (Festinger, 1994; Farmer et al, 2008). However, it also appears that high levels of formal support and service are not in themselves sufficient to maintain reunions. Much depends on the content and mix of services provided (Block and Libowitz, 1983). Similarly, research in the UK has highlighted the important contribution that proactive social work, decisive planning and continuous social work involvement can make to successful reunification (Trent, 1989; Farmer, 1996; Farmer et al, 2008).

A US study based on a review of 62 case files of children, whose returns disrupted, highlighted problems arising from failure to allocate cases, lack of social work time to work with families, as well as poor social work assessment (Hess et al, 1992). In this study, Hess and her colleagues found that social work plans were poorly implemented or children were returned where parents did not comply with substance abuse treatments. Even where parents did comply with requirements, for example, through attending parenting classes, this did not always result in behavioural change. There was widespread over-optimism about the degree of parental change and an assumption that reunification was best for children. Both this study and others have found that children were returned home without sufficient resolution of the family problems that had led to their placement and consequently re-entered care (Fraser et al, 1996; Turner, 1984; Farmer et al, 2008).

Sinclair et al's recent study (2005) of children in foster placements found that repeated efforts were sometimes made to return children home, even when this was not in their best interests. Once they returned, the children rarely received further social work intervention or support.

Much research on return considers all children together, yet the issues for younger at risk children (the "protected" group in our 1991 study) and "disaffected" teenagers are often rather different. Indeed, our recent research again shows that somewhat different factors are related to return breakdown for older as opposed to younger children (see Farmer *et al*, 2008).

These findings suggest a range of ways in which greater return stability might be achieved, for example, by ensuring that thorough assessments are conducted when children enter care; proactive planning combined with setting conditions (allied to timescales for these to be met) and providing targeted services to address parents' and children's difficulties; involving caregivers in assisting returns and their aftermath; marshalling parents' informal support systems; and involving schools and other agencies in monitoring and assisting children during reunification.

Specialist reunification projects in the USA

Biehal (2006) analysed the evidence from specialist reunification services in the USA and found that key features of the successful projects were intensity of services, purposeful case planning, goal-setting with parents and, in some cases, the use of behavioural interventions and/or contracts. However, there was little evidence as to which specific features of the service, or combination of features, were associated with their effectiveness, with the exception that the Alameda study found that parents who signed written contracts were more likely to have their children restored.

Other US projects suggest that treatment models with low caseloads, short duration and intensive services and 24-hours-a-day availability may work best, with more intensive services achieving higher success rates. However, it should be noted that Jones and colleagues (1976 and Jones, 1985) found, in contrast, that services of longer duration and lower intensity did better at keeping children out of care and successfully reuniting them with their families. In addition, it is noted that it is crucial to assess parental ambivalence to return and the family's readiness for reunification in terms of the resolution of their original and other emerging needs (National Family Preservation Network, 2003). These findings give further pointers as to how reunification work can be made more effective.

What is needed

The research base to assist practitioners and policy makers with reunification is still thin in the UK, although the findings from the small number of studies are remarkably consistent, including emphasising the need for authoritative but empathic relationship-based practice and monitoring. There is, in particular, a need for research into which interventions in which circumstances are most effective in reducing risk and supporting return; studies of what appear to be promising types of reunification practice (in terms of social work practice methods, organisational structures and practice innovations); and research showing children's longer-term outcomes, in order to develop a deeper understanding of when return should not occur. Over and above this, there is a need for recognition that reunification practice involves serious dilemmas about what standards of care by parents are good enough. This requires careful social work judgement assisted by good supervision and assistance from other professionals at reviews and other children's services meetings.

This view is backed up by what parents said they needed in our recent study, which included: earlier recognition of their difficulties with their children; assistance to build up their self-confidence and skills as parents; monitoring of their progress that is combined with emotional warmth; treatment for substance misuse combined with clarity about the consequences of their taking no action about their addiction; direct help for their children (such as mental health assistance, anger management and mentoring) and respite care.

The White Paper, which led to the Children and Young Persons Bill, promised revised guidance addressing the need for effective care planning to ensure that work is undertaken while children are in care and that appropriate services are provided for children and parents when the children return home. In addition, all children who return home from care will, in future, be required to have a Child in Need Plan identifying the areas in which parental capacity needs to be strengthened, which will be regularly reviewed. Clearly, it is also very important that resources are more consistently available to help parents and children to resolve their difficulties before reunion and to support them during return. In high risk cases, intensive help over a defined period combined with written agreements may help to identify those parents who are able to make changes within the timescales needed by their children and those who cannot. There is a need for much greater recognition that reunification work is highly skilled, demanding and time-consuming. If these initiatives are to make return practice more effective, then reunification also needs to "come in from the cold" by being made a clear strategic priority backed up by protocols informed by research and linked to multi-disciplinary training (The Who Cares? Trust, 2006).

Selected further reading

Biehal N. (2006) *Reuniting Looked After Children with their Families: A review of the research*, London: National Children's Bureau.

Farmer E. (2001) 'Children reunited with their parents: A review of research findings', in Broad B. (ed.) *Kinship Care: The placement choice for children and young people*, Lyme Regis: Russell House Publishing.

The Who Cares? Trust (2006) *The Journey Home: How children's services can support the reunification of children with their families*, London: The Who Cares? Trust

References

Aldgate J. (1977) 'The identification of factors influencing children's length of stay in care', PhD thesis, University of Edinburgh

Barn R. (1993) *Black Children in the Public Care System*, London: BAAF/Batsford

Barth R. P. and Berry M. (1987) 'Outcomes of child welfare services since permanency planning', *Social Service Review*, 61, pp 71–90

Barth R. P., Snowden L. R., Ten Broek E., Clancy T., Jordan C. and Barusch A. (1987) 'Contributors to reunification or permanent out-of-home care for physically abused children', *Journal of Social Service Research*, 9:2/3, pp 31–45

Berridge D. (1997) *Foster Care: A research review*, London: The Stationery Office

Berridge D. A. and Cleaver H. (1987) *Foster Home Breakdown*, Oxford: Blackwell

Biehal N. (2006) *Reuniting Looked After Children with Their Families: A review of the research*, London: National Children's Bureau

Block N. M. and Libowitz A. S. (1983) *Recidivism in Foster Care*, New York: Child Welfare League of America

Brandon M., Thoburn J., Rose S. and Belderson P. (2005) *Living with Significant Harm: A follow-up study*, Final report for NSPCC, Norwich: University of East Anglia, Centre for Research on the Child and Family

Bullock R., Gooch D. and Little M. (1998) *Children Going Home: The re-unification of families*, Aldershot: Ashgate

Bullock R., Little M. and Millham S. (1993) *Going Home: The return of children separated from their families*, Aldershot: Dartmouth

Child Welfare Information Gateway (2006) *Family Reunification: What the evidence shows*, Washington DC: U.S. Department of Health and Human Services

Cleaver H. (2000) *Fostering Family Contact*, London: The Stationery Office

Courtney M. E. (1994) 'Factors associated with the reunification of foster children with their families', *Social Service Review*, 68:1, pp 81–108

Courtney M. E. (1995) 'Re-entry to foster care of children returned to their families', *Social Service Review*, 69:2, pp 226–41

Courtney M. E., Piliavin I. and Wright B. (1997) 'Note on research: Transitions from and returns to out of home care', *Social Service Review*, 71, pp 652–667

Davis I. P., English D. J. and Landsverk J. A. (1993) *Going Home – and Returning to Care: A study of foster care reunification*, San Diego, CA: San Diego State University, College of Health and Human Services, School of Social Work and the Child and Family Research Group

Davis I. P., Landsverk J. A. and Newton R. R. (1997) 'Duration of foster care for children reunified within the first year of care', in Berrick J. D., Barth R. P., and Gilbert N. (eds) *Child Welfare Research Review*, Vol 2, New York: Columbia University Press

Davis I. P., Landsverk J. A., Newton R. R. and Ganger W. (1996) 'Parental visiting and foster care reunification', *Children and Youth Services Review*, 18:4/5, pp 363–382

Department for Education and Skills (June 2007) *Care Matters: Time for Change*, Cm. 7137, Secretary of State for Education and Skills

Dickens J., Howell D., Thoburn J. and Schofield G. (2007) 'Children starting to be looked after by local authorities in England: An analysis of inter-authority variation and case-centred decision making', *British Journal of Social Work*, 37:4, pp 597–617

Ellaway B. A., Payne E. H., Rolfe K., Dunstan F. D., Kemp A. M., Butler I. and Sibert J. R. (2004) 'Are abused babies protected from further abuse?' *Archive of Diseases of Childhood*, 89, pp 845–846

Famularo R., Kincherff R. and Fenton T. (1992) 'Parental substance abuse and the nature of child maltreatment', *Child Abuse and Neglect*, 61:4, pp 475–483

Fanshel D. and Shinn E. (1978) *Children in Foster Care*, New York: Columbia University Press

Farmer E. (1992) 'Restoring children on court orders to their families: Lessons for practice', *Adoption & Fostering*, 16:1, pp 7–15

Farmer E. (1996) 'Family reunification with high risk children: Lessons from research', *Children and Youth Services Review*, 18:4/5, pp 403–424

Farmer E. (2001) 'Children reunited with their parents: A review of research findings', in Broad B. (ed.), *Kinship Care: The placement choice for children and young people*, Lyme Regis: Russell House Publishing

Farmer E. and Moyers S. (2008) *Kinship Care: Fostering effective family and friends placements*, London: Jessica Kingsley Publishers

Farmer, E. and Owen M. (1995) *Child Protection Practice: Private risks and public remedies*, London: HMSO

Farmer E. and Parker R. (1991) *Trials and Tribulations: Returning children from local authority care to their families*, London: HMSO

Farmer E., Sturgess W. and O'Neill T. (2008) *The Reunification of Looked After Children with their Parents: Patterns, interventions and outcomes*, Report to the Department for Children, Schools and Families, School for Policy Studies, University of Bristol

Fein E., Maluccio A., Hamilton V. and Ward D. (1983) 'After foster care: Outcomes of permanency planning for children', *Child Welfare*, LXII, pp 485–558

Festinger T. (1994) *Returning to Care: Discharge and re-entry into foster care*, Washington DC: Child Welfare League of America

Finch S., Fanshel D. and Grundy J. (1986) 'Factors associated with the discharge of children from foster care', *Social Work Research and Abstracts*, 22:1, pp 10–18

Fisher M., Marsh P. and Phillips D. (1986) *In and Out of Care*, London: Batsford/BAAF

Forrester D. and Harwin J. (2004) 'Social work and parental substance misuse', in Phillips R. (ed.) *Children Exposed to Parental Substance Misuse: Implications for family placement*, London: BAAF

Frame L., Berrick J. D. and Brodowski M. L. (2000) 'Understanding re-entry to out-of-home care for reunified infants', *Child Welfare*, 79:4, pp. 339–72

Fraser M. W., Walton E., Lewis R. E., Pecora P. J. and Walton W. K. (1996) 'An experiment in family reunification: Correlates of outcomes at one-year follow-up', *Children and Youth Services Review*, 18:4/5, pp 335–361

Fuller T. (2005) 'Child safety at reunification: A case-control study of maltreatment recurrence following return home from substitute care', *Children and Youth Services Review*, 24:12, pp 1293–1306

Gibbons J., Conroy S. and Bell C. (1995) *Operating the Child Protection System: A study of child protection practices in English local authorities*, London: HMSO

Goerge R. (1990) 'The reunification process in substitute care', *Social Services Review*, LXIV, pp 422–457

Grogan-Kaylor A. (2001) 'The effect of initial placement into kinship foster care on reunification from foster care: A bivariate probit analysis', *Journal of Social Service Research*, 27:4, pp 1–31

Harris M. A. and Courtney M. E. (2003) 'The interaction of race, ethnicity and family structure with respect to the timing of family reunification', *Children and Youth Services Review*, 25:5/6, pp 409–429

Harwin J., Owen M., Locke R. and Forrester D. (2001) *Making Care Orders Work: A study of care plans and their implementation*, London: The Stationery Office

Hess P. M., Folaron G. and Jefferson A. B. (1992) 'Effectiveness of family reunification services: An innovative evaluative model', *Social Work*, 37:4, pp 304–311

Jones L. (1998) 'The social and family correlates of successful reunification of children in foster care', *Children and Youth Services Review*, 20:4, pp 305–323

Jones M. A. (1985) *A Second Chance for Families: Five Years Later: Follow-up of a program to prevent foster care*, New York: Child Welfare League of America

Jones M. A., Neuman R. and Shyne A. W. (1976) *A Second Chance for Families: Evaluation of a program to reduce foster care*, New York: Child Welfare League of America

Kelleher K., Chaffin M., Hollenberg J. and Fischer E. (1994) 'Alcohol and drug disorders among physically abusive and neglectful parents in a community based sample', *American Journal of Public Health*, 84:10, pp 1586–1590

Lahti J. (1982). 'A follow-up study of foster children in permanent placements', *Social Service Review*, 56, pp 556–71

Landsverk, J. A., Davis, I. P., Ganger, W. and Newton, R. R. (1996) 'Impact of child psychosocial functioning on reunification from out-of-home placement', *Children and Youth Services Review*, 18:4/5, pp 447–62

Lawder E., Poulin J. E. and Andrews R. (1986) 'A study of 185 foster children five years after placement', *Child Welfare*, 65, pp 241–245

Maluccio A. N. and Ainsworth F. (2003) 'Drug use by parents: A challenge for family reunification practice', *Children and Youth Services Review*, 25:7, pp 511–533

Maluccio A. N., Fein E. and Olmstead K. A. (1986) *Permanency Planning for Children: Concepts and methods*, London: Tavistock

McMurtry, S. and Lie, G. Y. (1992) 'Differential exit rates of minority children in foster care', *Social Work Research and Abstracts*, 28:1, pp 42–48

Millham S., Bullock R., Hosie K. and Little M. (1986) *Lost in Care: The problems of maintaining links between children in care and their families*, Aldershot: Gower

Milner J. (1987) 'An ecological perspective on duration of foster care', *Child Welfare*, 66, pp 113–123

National Black Child Development Institute (1993) *Parental Drug Abuse and African-American Children in Foster Care: Issues and findings*, Washington DC: NBCDI

National Family Preservation Network (2003) *Intensive Family Reunification Services Protocol*, Buhl, ID: National Family Preservation Network

Packman J. and Hall C. (1998) *From Care to Accommodation: Support, protection and control in child care services*, London: The Stationery Office

Pinkerton J. (1994) *In Care at Home*, Aldershot: Avebury

Quinton D., Rushton A., Dance C. and Mayes D. (1997) 'Contact between children placed away from home and their birth parents: Research issues and evidence', *Clinical Child Psychology and Psychiatry*, 2:3, pp 393–413

Quinton D. and Rutter M. (1988) *Parenting Breakdown: The making and breaking of inter-generational links*, Aldershot: Avebury

Rowe J., Hundleby M. and Garnett L. (1989) *Child Care Now: A survey of placement patterns*, London: BAAF

Rzepnicki T. L., Schuerman J. R. and Johnson P. (1997) 'Facing uncertainty: Reuniting high-risk families', in Berrick J. D., Barth R.P. and Gilbert N. (eds) *Child Welfare Research Review*, 2, New York: Columbia University Press

Scannapieco M. and Jackson S. (1996) 'Kinship care: The African-American response to family preservation', *Social Work*, 41:2, pp 190–196

Schuerman J. R., Rzepnicki T. L. and Johnson P. R. (1994) *Outcomes in Evaluation of the 'Family First' Reunification Program of the Department of Children and Family Services*, Final Report, Chicago: Chapin Hall Centre for Children at the University of Chicago

Sinclair I. (2005) *Fostering Now: Messages from research*, London: Jessica Kingsley Publishers

Sinclair I., Baker C., Lee J. and Gibbs I. (2007) *The Pursuit of Permanence: A study of the English care system*, London: Jessica Kingsley Publishers

Sinclair I., Baker C., Wilson K. and Gibbs I. (2005) *Foster Children: Where they go and how they get on*, London: Jessica Kingsley Publishers

Stein, T. J. and Gambrill, E. D. (1977) 'Facilitating decision-making in foster care: The Alameda Project', *Social Service Review*, September 1977, pp 502–513

Stein T. J. and Gambrill E. D. (1979) 'The Alameda project: A two-year report and one-year follow-up', *Child Abuse and Neglect*, 3, pp 521–528

Taussig H. N., Clyman R. B. and Landsverk J. (2001) 'Children who return home from foster care: a 6-year prospective study of behavioral health outcomes in adolescence', *Pediatrics*, 108:1, p 10

Thoburn J. (1980) *Captive Clients: Social work with families of children home on trial*, London: Routledge and Kegan Paul

Thoburn J. (1994) *Child Placement: Principles and practice*, Aldershot: Arena

Thoburn, J. (2003) 'The risks and rewards in adoption for children in the public care', *Family Law Quarterly*, 15:4, pp 391–402

Trent J. (1989) *Homeward Bound: The rehabilitation of children to their birth parents*, Ilford: Barnardo's

Turner, J. (1984) 'Predictors of recidivism in foster care: Exploratory models', *Social Work Research and Abstracts*, 20–2, pp 15–20

Vernon J. and Fruin D. (1986) *In Care: A study of social work decision making*, London: National Children's Bureau

Wade J., Biehal N., Sinclair I. and Farrelly N. (forthcoming) *Outcomes for Children Placed for Reasons of Abuse or Neglect: The consequences of staying in care or returning home*, Report to the Department for Children, Schools and Families, University of York

Walton E., Fraser M. W., Lewis R. E. and Pecora P. J. (1993) 'In-home family-focused reunification: An experimental study', *Child Welfare*, 72:5, pp 473–87

Webster D., Shlonsky A., Shaw T. and Brookhart M. A. (2005) 'The ties that bind II: Reunification for siblings in out-of-home care using a statistical technique for examining non-independent observations', *Children and Youth Services Review*, 27:7, pp 765–782

The Who Cares? Trust (2006) *The Journey Home: How children's services can support the reunification of children with their families*, London: The Who Cares? Trust

Wulczyn F. (1991) 'Caseload dynamics and foster care re-entry', *Social Service Review*, 65, pp 133–156

Wulczyn F. H. and Goerge R. M. (1992) 'Foster care in New York and Illinois: The challenge of rapid change', *Social Service Review*, 66, pp 278–294

6   Family and friends care

Joan Hunt

Introduction

The White Paper, *Care Matters: Time for Change* (DfES, 2007), and the Children and Young Persons Bill currently going through Parliament, are likely to give a substantial boost to the placement of children, who cannot remain with their birth parents, with members of their extended families or social networks. The Scottish government's National Fostering and Kinship Care Strategy is intended to have a similar impact. The officially preferred term for this placement option is family and friends care, although it is also often referred to as relative or kinship care.

Although the use of this form of care by child welfare agencies is not new, in the years leading up to the Children Act 1989 it had substantially declined. In the wake of research evidence (Rowe *et al*, 1984; Millham *et al*, 1986; Berridge and Cleaver, 1987; Rowe *et al*, 1989; Farmer and Parker, 1991; Malos and Bullard, 1991) highlighting the good outcomes from these placements, the Act sought to reverse this trend, stipulating that when substitute care is required, the local authority:

> . . . *shall make arrangements to enable him to live with a relative, friend or other person connected with him, unless that would not be reasonably practical or consistent with his welfare.* (Children Act, 1989, section 23(6))

This statutory endorsement was reinforced in guidance issued to accompany the Act:

> *Possibilities for a child to be cared for within the extended family should have been investigated and considered as an alternative to the provision of accommodation by the responsible authority. However, even when it has become necessary for the responsible authority to arrange provision of accommodation, placement with a relative will often provide the best opportunities for promoting and maintaining family links in a familiar setting.* (Department of Health, 1991, p 27)

In the years after the Act was implemented, however, progress was slow and patchy. Government initiatives such as the "Quality Protects" and "Choice Protects" programmes had some effect but there was a widespread view among academics, practitioners and voluntary agencies that much more needed to be done to give effect to the principles of the legislation. The same conclusion was reached by two government working groups, (Laming,

2006; Narey, 2006), and endorsed in the White Paper, *Care Matters: Time for Change* which promises a "new framework" for family and friends care, as summarised below.

> The White Paper *Care Matters: Time for Change*.
> Proposals for family and friends care.
> The government's intention is to provide 'a new framework for family and friends care . . . which will set out the expectations of an effective service'. This is intended to address concerns about:
> * variation across the country in the extent to which family and friends placements are used;
> * absence of policy frameworks to underpin services to these families and, where they are in place, inconsistent application of the policy;
> * lack of transparency of entitlements and services available and inequitable treatment of carers; and,
> * suitability of the approval process for family and friends carers.
>
> Revised Children Act guidance will set out details of the "gateway approach" which will be put in place to 'make sure that family and friends care is considered as an option at the first and every subsequent stage of decision-making', and is included in the initial care plans put to the court in care proceedings. Local authorities will be required to have transparent policies on supporting family and friends carers and this will be monitored through Ofsted inspections.

Some local authorities, of course, will be ahead of the game. Others may have to do a lot of work to put in place policies, structures and mechanisms to ensure that they are making the fullest possible use of this placement option and supporting it effectively. Some practitioners may have to examine their attitudes and beliefs and check how far they are supported by the evidence. Others may already be convinced of the potential value of this form of care, but will feel the need to extend their knowledge base and/or improve their skills in working with a distinctive form of placement.

Whatever the particular circumstances, it is important that policy and practice are developed, as far as possible, in the light of what is known about this form of care. The purpose of this chapter, therefore, is to summarise the present state of research on the topic, highlighting what we do know with a reasonable degree of confidence, identifying the areas of uncertainty, and outlining the key issues. It will largely focus on UK studies. Until recently much of the thinking about kinship care has been, necessarily, based on international research, most of it undertaken in the USA. While this is often highly relevant, there are substantial differences in cultures and social systems. The UK knowledge base is still pitifully small, not only compared with international research but with home-grown research on other placement options. However, there are now sufficient studies, with a variety of samples and approaches, to make it feasible to use them to develop policy and practice. Readers interested in the broader literature will find references in overviews (Hunt, 2003; Hunt, 2006; Nixon, 2008) and in the UK literature mentioned.

Social workers' ambivalence about kinship care

Social workers will encounter kinship care in a great range of circumstances. At one extreme there will be families with whom they only ever have minimal involvement, perhaps facilitating an informal placement which the family then manages themselves. Some placements will be receiving support under the "children in need" provisions in section 17 of the Children Act, 1989. At the other end of the spectrum social workers will be responsible for assessing and then supervising the placement of a looked after child, either accommodated under section 20 of the Children Act 1989, or on a care order made by the courts. They will be responsible for providing reports to the courts in applications by kinship carers for special guardianship or adoption orders and may be asked to report on applications for residence orders.

Whatever their legal status, many of the children whom social workers encounter in kinship placements will be very similar to those in unrelated foster care, with both groups exposed to multiple adversities prior to placement and the majority already manifesting emotional and behavioural difficulties (Farmer and Moyers, 2008; Hunt *et al*, 2008).

Social workers recognise many positives in family and friends placements. They see it as affording greater stability and continuity, preserving family ties, facilitating contact, enhancing children's identity and sense of belonging, and lessening the stigma of living away from parents (Doolan *et al*, 2004; Farmer and Moyers, 2008; Hunt *et al*, 2008). Indeed, one study (Doolan *et al*, 2004) reports that all those interviewed expressed support for kinship care, with a large majority seeing it as the best option and first choice and the rest as valid, or a consideration. However, it goes on:

> . . . as the consultation probed attitudes more deeply . . . it was clear that support was more ambiguous. Nearly all said their support was conditional. Most saw it requiring checks and assessment to ensure safety and needed to be convinced that the placement could meet the child's needs adequately and that the right level of support and services could be put in place. (p 74)

Many concerns are voiced: a poorer quality of care than expected of non-related place-ments; greater safety risks; doubts about the ability of carers to meet the child's emotional needs and cope with behavioural problems; complicated family dynamics; family conflict and/or collusion; problems with contact; the difficulties of working with carers. Some workers also still appear to subscribe to the ideas expressed in the phrase "the apple does not fall far from the tree" i.e. the parental problems which have resulted in substitute care being required are attributable in large part to the care they themselves received from their parents (Flynn, 2002; Doolan *et al*, 2004; Aldgate and McIntosh, 2006; Sinclair *et al*, 2007; Farmer and Moyers, 2008; Hunt *et al*, 2008).

The following section examines the extent to which research supports social workers' views about the advantages and disadvantages of family and friends care.

The advantages and disadvantages of family and friends care

Placement stability

Placement stability is usually considered to be one of the key advantages of family and friends placements, protecting children from the risks of the multiple moves which can be so disruptive. It is true that placements tend to be lengthy and last longer than those with non-related carers: Farmer and Moyers (2008), for example, found the average duration of continuing placements in family and friends care to be four years and nine months, compared to three years and 11 months in "non-related" foster care. Broad *et al* (2001) report a mean of four years for placements of non-looked after children known to the local authority. Children are also likely to have fewer moves before entering placement (Rowe *et al*, 1984; Kosenen, 1993).

The evidence in terms of disruption, however, is less clear. UK studies report very different rates, from less than 10 per cent to a third or more. Even the highest of these still appears to be lower than the 43 per cent reported for long-term foster care (Triseliotis, 2002). However, Farmer and Moyers (2008) report very similar disruption rates in both family and friends (18%) and non-kin (17%) foster placements. A study which followed up children placed through care proceedings (Hunt *et al*, 2008) reports that, although the overall disruption rate (28%) looked positive, this was largely accounted for by placements of children under five (11% disruption rate). Forty-three per cent of placements of children aged between five and 12 foundered (compared to the average of 35% in long-term foster care reported by Triseliotis, 2002), while the rates for older children (50%) were the same. Disruption figures were also higher than for adoption for both the under-fives (11% compared to 5%) and the 5–12-year-olds (43% compared to 15%). The authors suggest a number of reasons, however, why the comparisons may be less stark than they seem. First, all the children in their sample had been placed through care proceedings and therefore represented a 'heavy end group in terms of adverse life experiences', while other research samples may be diluted with children who have been somewhat less unfortunate. A previous study of children placed in stranger foster care after care proceedings reported an overall disruption rate of 52 per cent (Hunt and Macleod, 1999). Second, that the follow-up period, of between three and nine years, is likely to be longer than in most other studies. Fifty per cent of the placement disruptions occurred two or more years after the proceedings had ended. Nonetheless, it does seem that blanket claims that kinship care is more stable, in the sense that it carries a lower risk of disruption than non-related care, are not supportable.

Continuity

Placement in family and friends care is likely to be a less disruptive experience for children than moving into stranger care. Its distinguishing feature is that children are going to people with whom they already have some connection. Sometimes this may be tenuous, occasionally it will be no more than a blood relationship – some children are placed with carers whom they have never met before. Typically, however, there will be a pre-existing bond and a shared culture. Many will be placed with siblings, although there is contradictory evidence as to whether this is more likely than for children placed in non-kin care; others will have contact with siblings placed elsewhere, sometimes with other family members. Contact with at least one parent is more likely than in non-kin care although this is rarely with both parents and tends to reduce over time. Children also tend to be in touch with members of their extended families other than their carers, although typically not with both maternal and paternal sides of the family. Many are able to remain in the same neighbourhood and in the same school – although some will be moving many miles away and even out of the country. Finally, there is some evidence that when placements disrupt a substantial proportion of children either go back to their parents or move to another relative and their original carer is likely to stay in touch and offer support (Rowe *et al*, 1984; Kosenen, 1993; Hunt and Macleod, 1999; Tan, 2000; Harwin *et al*, 2003; Aldgate and McIntosh, 2006; Farmer and Moyers, 2008; Hunt *et al*, 2008).

Security, belonging and stigma

It is unfortunate that almost all the children who have been interviewed about kinship care have been in ongoing placements. The very positive picture presented may, therefore, be somewhat rose-tinted. Nonetheless, it seems clear that when placements do survive, most children feel secure, settled, safe, happy, and loved and enjoy close and positive relationships with at least one carer (Rowe *et al*, 1984; Broad *et al*, 2001; Doolan *et al*, 2004; Aldgate and McIntosh, 2006; Farmer and Moyers, 2008; Hunt *et al*, 2008). Farmer and Moyers (2008) report that kin-placed children were more likely than those placed with strangers to feel close to the carers' children and there was less likely to be tension in relationships with either carers or children. Consistent with this picture, some studies also report that children see themselves remaining with their carers into adulthood – and often beyond (Doolan *et al*, 2004; Hunt *et al*, 2008) although Aldgate and McIntosh (2006) caution that half the children interviewed felt uncertain about their future, even though their carers were certain it was permanent.

It is not yet clear to what extent placement with relatives minimises the stigma children placed away from their parents feel or experience. Although there is one piece of US research (Messing, 2005) which concluded that it did, UK studies indicate that at least some children feel "different" or are vulnerable to being bullied and teased (Broad *et al*, 2001; Aldgate and McIntosh, 2006; Farmer and Moyers, 2008; Hunt *et al*, 2008).

Quality of care, safety and child well-being

Concerns about the quality of care and capacity to protect children from abuse tend to feature prominently in social workers' reservations about family and friends placements (Doolan *et al*, 2004; Sinclair *et al*, 2007; Farmer and Moyers, 2008; Hunt *et al*, 2008). In terms of safety, research indicates that while concerns about risk of harm are borne out in a few cases, the proportion is low (between 2% and 10% of placements) and no higher than in non-kin placements, although kin carers may be more vulnerable to unsubstantiated allegations (Nixon, 1999; Farmer and Moyers, 2008; Hunt *et al*, 2008). Children can also be exposed to risk through parental contact, but the incidence appears to be low: Farmer and Moyers (2008) report cause for concern in only six per cent of cases; Hunt *et al* (2008) report the same proportion in which contact restrictions were breached, none resulting in actual harm to the child.

There is more substance to concerns about the quality of care, although still in only a minority of cases. Thus Hunt *et al* (2008) found that, while there were some concerns in 64 per cent of placements, only 20 per cent appeared to present major issues. In 14 per cent of cases there were concerns about the carer's ability to meet the child's emotional needs and in 26 per cent about managing behaviour. Farmer and Moyers (2008) report concerns about quality in 34 per cent of placements (compared with 27% of unrelated placements), with family and friends carers being more likely than stranger carers to have poor parenting skills and substantially more of them struggling to cope.

The outcome data in terms of child functioning are fairly positive, particularly given the multiple pre-placement adversities to which most children had been exposed and the emotional and behavioural difficulties they were already manifesting on placement. Thus Hunt *et al* (2008) report that 47 per cent of the children had no problems at all, with only 19 per cent presenting problems in more than two areas of functioning. Children generally seem to do as well as those in non-kin care: Farmer and Moyers (2008) report the same proportions (52%) displaying emotional and behavioural problems; 78 per cent showing improvement since placement (77% non-kin placements); and 68% having a positive view of themselves (63%). Health was slightly better (91% being normally well, compared to 86%); the proportion under-performing at school about the same (36% and 35%) and school attendance slightly worse (78% and 86% regularly attending).

There is as yet no UK evidence on how these children fare as adults. There is also a pressing need for a longitudinal comparative study of children placed in non-kin care and family and friends care, assessing the two groups at the point of placement and then tracking their progress. Although there is mounting evidence that the two groups of children are very similar in terms of prior adversities and level of difficulties presented, as yet there is no UK study which can demonstrate this conclusively.

Problematic contact and family conflict

This is the area in which social worker concerns are most strongly supported by research (Rowe *et al*, 1984; Malos and Bullard, 1991; Russell, 1995; Hunt and Macleod, 1999; Cleaver, 2000; Laws, 2001; Richards, 2001; Farmer and Moyers, 2008; Hunt *et al*, 2008). Hunt *et al* (2008) note seriously strained or conflicted adult relationships between carers and at least one parent in 41 per cent of cases, while Farmer and Moyers (2008) report difficult relationships with either the parents or other family members in 54 per cent of cases, more than three times the rate in non-kin foster care (16%):

> *Some parents were resentful that a relative had taken over the care of their children, other parents were actively hostile to the kin carers and a few made threats or actually attacked them, while others made false allegations against the carers or undermined the placement in other ways. Occasionally, two sides of the family were in conflict about who should be caring for the children.* (p 223)

Somewhat surprisingly, however, this research found that contact which was seriously detrimental to the child was more likely in non-kin care (31% compared with 45%), although the researchers suggest this may simply reflect closer monitoring of non-kin placements. Hunt *et al* (2008) calculated that for 63 per cent of children parental contact was either entirely negative (21%) or had some negative elements, and that in almost half the ongoing placements problematic contact, particularly maternal contact, continued. This suggests that while, of course, attention needs to be paid to physical risk, contact planning and intervention need to focus primarily on positively managing relationships and reducing conflict.

Relationships with social services

A key theme in the research is the challenge that working with kinship placements presents to social workers more used to dealing with non-kin foster carers and often with little training in this area of work (Doolan *et al*, 2004; Farmer and Moyers, 2008; Hunt *et al*, 2008). Placements can be more difficult to supervise because of role uncertainty on the part of both workers and carers and sometimes even resistance to agency requirements. Working with the whole family is needed but the dynamics are complex. Some placements require more support than non-kin placements; other carers may be unwilling to accept support. A third of the social workers interviewed in one study saw the key problem in working with kinship placements lying with the families themselves having the wrong attitude, being obstructive, not wanting to work with social services and being unable to work in partnership (Doolan *et al*, 2004).

The research findings on carers' attitudes to social workers are mixed, as one might expect, given the wide range of circumstances in which placements are made and inevitable variations in competence and personality "fit". One study, for example, concluded that 'the role of the social worker is highly valued . . . it is the delivery that causes problems' (Doolan *et al*, 2004, p 112), while the most another could report was that 'not all (carers) rejected social services involvement' (Waldman and Wheal, 1999). Farmer and Moyers (2008) refer to "a few cases" where relatives were unco-operative, hostile or colluded with the parents to keep the social worker on the periphery and carers who resented the restrictions which came with being an approved and regulated local authority foster carer.

Clearly, however, many carers do accept social work involvement and value the support they receive and at least some would like more (Rowe *et al*, 1984; Russell, 1995; Pitcher, 1999; Laws, 2001). Hunt *et al* (2008) comment that carers often differentiated between different social workers, indicating that it was not always simply a question of their general attitude to local authority involvement. Moreover, 63 per cent of the carers interviewed found something positive to say about social workers and 26 per cent were wholly positive.

Factors associated with better/poorer outcomes

Family and friends care is clearly a viable placement option for many children, but it does not work for all. Are there any factors which might help to identify which placements are most likely to succeed and which are likely to be more vulnerable?

It has to be said that research on this, even internationally, is in its infancy. Hunt *et al* (2008) identify seven statistically significant characteristics of the child or the placement which were independently related to outcome. Positive outcomes were more likely when the child was relatively young at placement; was presenting few difficulties; had lived with the carer before; when the carer had instigated the placement; when the carer was a grandparent; a sole carer; and when there were no non-sibling children in the household. Some of these factors are also supported by other research, notably age, prior difficulties and being a grandparent carer (Hunt and Macleod, 1999; Harwin *et al*, 2003; Farmer and Moyers, 2008). Farmer and Moyers (2008) additionally found that having a sibling in placement was a protective factor, as was the presence of other children. They also found poorer outcomes where a parent had abused drugs (which is also cited in some international research) or had a history of multiple partners or prostitution, or where the child had long-term health difficulties or disabilities. This study found that the combination of factors which best predicted disruption was: the child being 10 or older at placement; low carer commitment; the child being beyond control and contact not being supervised.

The child's perspective

Although a number of recent UK studies of kinship care have included interviews with children and young people (Broad *et al*, 2001; Doolan *et al*, 2004; Aldgate and Macintosh,

2006; Farmer and Moyers, 2008; Hunt *et al*, 2008), the research is not extensive and, as indicated earlier, almost entirely focuses on children in ongoing placements. Research is clearly needed with children whose placements have ended, particularly those where placements have not worked out, and with young adults brought up in kinship care. It would also be useful for research to investigate, near to the point at which it happens, how children manage the transition into kinship care. It is likely this will be experienced as less traumatic than going into non-kin care, particularly if relationships are well established, but it is unlikely to be entirely stress free and may bring its own unique difficulties (Aldgate and MacIntosh, 2006). Similarly, it appears that when placements break down a good proportion of children move to other relatives (Farmer and Moyers, 2008; Hunt *et al*, 2008). Is this easier than moving to strangers? What impact does it have on children when the carer who has given up on them is also a relative?

Despite these limitations and gaps, it is clear that kinship care is a very positive experience for many children, who enjoy close, reciprocal, loving relationships with carers they can trust and who make them feel safe, secure, wanted and part of the family. Whether they are more likely to express these views than those placed long-term with non-related carers has not been conclusively demonstrated since there is no UK comparative research, although one US study reports that 94 per cent of kin-placed children said they "always" felt loved, compared to 82 per cent of children placed with non-related carers. Broad *et al* (2001) report that young people who had come into kinship care from non-kin placements were more positive about being with relatives. However, since many had had traumatic experiences in care, this finding is probably not generalisable. The young people in Broad's study identified the positive features of kinship care as feeling loved, valued, cared for and nurtured; belonging and feeling settled; sustaining a sense of identity, including their cultural/racial heritage, through maintaining contact with family and friends; being listened to; and being supported in their education and life plans.

Children and young people generally report few negative features about kinship care with even the generation gap only appearing to be occasionally problematic for adolescents living alone with elderly grandparents. Studies, however, highlight the fact that, while living with relatives may be a less stigmatising experience than living in a children's home or with non-kin carers, children are still aware of being "different" and may need help to deal with their peers' curiosity or even bullying. It is also important not to assume that, because children are with their families and usually have contact with at least one parent, they will understand why they are there or that these matters are readily discussed with their carers. As reported earlier, Aldgate and Macintosh (2006) also found that some children were not at all sure about their future, even though their carers were confident they would be remaining with them long-term, while Doolan *et al* (2004) similarly comment on children's lack of involvement in planning and decision-making.

Children's reported views of social workers are generally positive. Aldgate and Macintosh, for instance, found that two-thirds of children saw their social workers as helpful while Farmer and Moyers (2008) describe most children as 'enthusiastic' about their social workers. The children interviewed by Doolan *et al* (2004), however, were more negative, not because they did not value what social workers did (on the contrary, they wanted more contact with them), the problem was the difficulty they experienced in developing a constructive relationship when workers changed so frequently: 'they wanted a more consistent relationship with a social worker who took an interest in them, knew them and would work with them. Many of them had never had a good relationship with a social worker' (p 39).

Making effective use of family and friends care

Tapping the potential of the child's family and social networks

One of the objectives of the "new framework" promised in the White Paper, *Care Matters: Time for Change* (DfES, 2007), is to address the issue of 'variation across the country in the extent to which family and friends placements are used'. This has been a clear theme in research, with one recent large scale study reporting that the proportion of family and friends foster placements varied between six per cent and 32 per cent and concluding that councils with low rates could safely aim to increase their use (Sinclair *et al*, 2007).

It is important to be realistic about the extent to which kinship care can be expanded. Sadly some children do not have relatives able and willing to care for them (Hunt *et al*, 2008) and for others it will not be appropriate. Nonetheless, there is evidence that social workers could be more pro-active in searching out potential carers. One study, for instance, found that only four per cent of placements were instigated by social workers and that in 57 per cent of non-kin placements it had not even been considered (Farmer and Moyers, 2008). The new requirement under the Public Law Outline, that initial care plans presented to the court in care proceedings must identify what efforts have been made to find and assess relative carers, should help to ensure that fewer cases reach court before the extended family has been properly explored and that they are positively involved in decision-making (Hunt and Macleod, 1999; Hunt *et al*, 2008).

Care proceedings, however, tend to come at a late stage in local authority involvement and do not apply to all children. Other changes will therefore be needed, such as the use of network mapping at an early stage in a family's contact with children's services and greater use of decision-making processes which involve the wider network, such as family group conferences, which are more likely to divert children from non-kin placements (Marsh and Crow, 1998; Lupton and Nixon, 1999). These are specifically endorsed in the White Paper. Systems need to be in place to ensure that the possibility of care within the extended family is explicitly considered, not only for children on the threshold of being looked after but at reviews for children who are already being looked after.

Assessment and approval

The suitability of the approval process for family and friends care is another thorny issue, which the proposed new framework for family and friends care is intended to address (DfES, 2007).

The importance of assessment in family and friends care has been highlighted in two recent studies. Farmer and Moyers (2008) found that placements were more stable where carers had been assessed as foster carers while Hunt *et al* (2008) report better quality placements where there had been a pre-placement assessment (not necessarily a full assessment). They also caution social workers and courts not to become preoccupied with specific concerns (such as carer age, contact, or child protection issues) since prac-titioners were quite poor at predicting the cases in which problems would materialise. The key factor to focus on, they argue, is parenting capacity – about which predictions were much more accurate – since this was linked to better quality placements.

Assessment for family and friends care, however, which is very different from assessment for non-kin care, is an extremely complex area of practice which can be difficult for both worker and family. Research indicates that carers usually accept the need for assessment but dislike the process – Doolan *et al* (2004) for example, report that carers resented the concentration on risk and wanted a more inclusive process that respected their skills and knowledge. Practitioners, too, appear to want an assessment format specifically designed for this form of care. A number of assessment tools have been developed (Pitcher, 2001; Talbot and Calder, 2006) but as yet there does not appear to be any research into their effectiveness and acceptability to local authorities and carers, although material developed by the Family Rights Group is currently being piloted. There are also issues about the assessment and approval process, which at times may be too long and drawn out but at others, especially in emergencies or court proceedings, may be too rushed. Other questions arise about who should carry out the assessment – the child's social worker? A family placement worker? Both of these working together? Or a specialist kinship practitioner possibly independent of the local authority? Should there be separate standards for family and friends foster care, as happens in some other countries? Does it help to have distinct approval processes, such as a separate placement panel, which have been established in some local authorities? Information about what is happening in different local authorities about this and the evaluation of different practice models are badly needed.

Supporting placements

A central and consistent theme in the research on kinship care has been the need to provide better support to family and friends placements. There is, perhaps, still an assumption that because kinship care is "natural" it is also unproblematic. In fact, it presents unique challenges from the outset. Unlike non-kin carers, however, who offer

their services out of free choice, have time to consider and go through a careful assessment and preparation process, kinship carers usually make their decisions at a time of
family crisis and have to make significant and rapid changes to their lives which often
entails considerable sacrifices. Farmer and Moyers (2008), after reporting on the many
positive aspects of caring identified by carers, go on to say:

The positives in caring for these children were bought at a high cost for many carers.
Some were living in very overcrowded conditions . . . a few carers had moved house to
accommodate the children, sometimes leaving behind places where they had been
happy. Most struggled on low incomes to care for the new arrivals. Almost a third had
health conditions, which made caring for the children more difficult. Several relatives
gave up their jobs to look after the children (which) reduced their income . . . and
would have an effect on their pension entitlement later on. (p 177)

Some of the benefits of kinship care – such as sibling placements and parental contact –
make additional demands, while relationships with parents and other family members
may be strained. The circumstances which led to the need for care may also require carers
to cope with a maelstrom of conflicting emotions. Above all, the children have difficulties
far in excess of those in the general population and those placed by local authorities
appear to have very similar levels of need to children in non-kin care (Sinclair *et al*, 2007;
Farmer and Moyers, 2008; Hunt *et al*, 2008). Two recent research studies have used a
standardised test (The Strengths and Difficulties Questionnaire, Goodman, 1997) to
assess children's emotional and behavioural difficulties. Both report that 35 per cent of
the children had abnormal scores on the questionnaires completed by carers, more than
three times that found in the general child population (10%) (Farmer and Moyers, 2008;
Hunt *et al*, 2008).

It is clear from the evidence that relative carers are taking on challenging children in
challenging circumstances. It should not, therefore, be surprising that many experience
significant levels of stress. Indeed one US study suggests that the psychological stress
experienced by kinship carers is greater than for any other form of caring (Strawbridge *et
al*, 1997). In the UK, Hunt *et al* (2008) report that, in 45 per cent of continuing kinship
placements, scores on a standardised test indicated that at least one carer had abnormal
stress levels – more than twice the proportion expected in the general population.

There are good reasons to believe, therefore, that kinship carers are likely to need as
least as much support as non-kin carers, and possibly more, particularly in the early stages
of placement. In fact, the research evidence suggests that they get less, even those who are
approved foster carers, and that across the whole spectrum of kinship care arrangements,
from informal private arrangements to foster care under a care order, there are service
gaps (Farmer and Pollock, 1998; Flynn, 1999; Macleod, 1999; Laws, 2001; Richards,
2001; Doolan *et al*, 2004; Hunt and Hunt *et al*, 2008). Farmer and Moyers (2008), noting

that many of the gaps were in cases which had an allocated social worker, suggest that this may reflect an attitude that kin should be able to look after children without help, or that the perceived strengths of kinship placements may fuel ideas that they can do so. They cite a telling case where the carer was unwell and struggling to cope with a child with multiple problems, who had been suspended from school. The file note read:

> As the child is "in family" [the placement] meets all of his physical, emotional and cultural needs . . . He presents no problems in the home except when the police are called. (p 174)

Interviews with carers indicate that they are uncertain about what help is available and how to access it (Richards, 2001; Doolan et al, 2004; Hunt et al, 2008). Hence the White Paper commitment to address the issue of lack of transparency about entitlements and services is much needed. Information about sources of help may be particularly important for carers living outside the placing authority or those whose involvement with Social Services has ended (Hunt, 2001; Richards, 2001; Hunt et al, 2008). Carers, however, may also need encouragement to seek help, to feel confident that by doing so they will not be seen as failing, and that they will receive a positive and consistent response (Malos and Bullard, 1991; Russell, 1995; Pitcher, 1999; Bourne and Porter, 2001; Hunt et al, 2008). Again, in cases where the local authority is no longer actively involved, carers may be particularly anxious about this. Hunt et al (2008) cite a case where the carers had had a very positive relationship with Social Services at the time of the care proceedings, in which they obtained a residence order. Five years on they were really struggling to cope with a child with multiple problems but were reluctant to go back to the department because of how they might be viewed and their fear that the child would be removed.

In terms of the help carers would like or need, the research gives a fairly clear picture. The need for financial assistance is a major theme. Farmer and Moyers (2008), for example, found evidence of financial difficulty in 75 per cent of cases. Grants need to be immediately available to enable carers to meet the sudden increased demand on their resources, followed by regular adequate payments which meet the cost of caring, allowing for expenditure on activities for children, holidays and baby-sitting. Some carers will need help with the costs of larger accommodation or a car; some with the costs of court proceedings.

How these needs should be met and by whom is a matter of debate. It may be reasonable to expect local authorities to meet immediate needs out of s17 (children in need) funds; in the longer term, however, there would seem to be a good argument for a national allowance or tax credit, which would be available, as of right, to all kinship carers. This would address the variation between local authorities in the payment of residence and special guardianship order allowances and s17 funds (Morgan, 2003; Hall, 2007), and, since there is evidence that some children remain looked after purely because of financial considerations, might enable more children to be discharged from care. Where there are welfare reasons for children being in care, the question of the parity of foster care allowances then arises, not just the basic costs of caring but eligibility for additional allowances.

Another key theme is the need for information, advice and possibly advocacy to navigate legal, benefits, education and social services systems. Some local authorities have produced information packs for potential carers and for many years one local authority has been running a monthly advice surgery with an independent lawyer, a benefits specialist, a social worker, a manager, and a grandparent carer (Pitcher, 1999).

A range of practical help is required: from initial assistance with equipment and clothes, to transport and accommodation. Child care is a common theme: child-minding, baby-sitting, holiday clubs and perhaps above all, respite care, to which even kin carers who are approved foster carers rarely appear to have access (Farmer and Moyers, 2008) but which could offer much needed relief from the stress of caring (Aldgate and McIntosh, 2006; Hunt et al, 2008).

Access is needed to a variety of services, both broadly based ones such as Sure Start and more specialised ones such as therapy and counselling for carers and/or the children. Farmer and Moyers report that 47 per cent of kin-placed children with the most serious behavioural/emotional difficulties were not receiving any intervention (compared with 38% in non-kin care). Carers would like help to enable them to help the child both with everyday matters such as unfamiliar homework to more problematic areas such as coming to terms with their situation. Help with managing behaviour and dealing with contact would seem particularly important (Doolan et al, 2004; Aldgate and McIntosh, 2006; Farmer and Moyers, 2008; Hunt et al, 2008).

Carers need to have access to both professional social work help and peer group support. In terms of social work input, what is needed may be as little as the occasional call and access to a named person in a crisis or substantial input with not only a social worker for the child but their own worker (Sykes et al, 2002; Farmer and Moyers, 2008; Hunt et al, 2008). While many carers would probably shy away from anything specifically designated as "training", some might find it invaluable. This might be most acceptably delivered by tapping into carers' expressed need for opportunities to meet with others in their position (Doolan et al, 2004; Grandparents Plus, 2006; Farmer and Moyers, 2008; Hunt et al, 2008). This could take the form of a support group and/or mentoring.

In theory, the introduction of special guardianship orders could help meet the needs of at least one category of kinship placements since there is provision for an assessment of needs and local authorities are required to provide a special guardianship support service. It could also provide a spur to the development of services for the wider range of kinship placements. While there is only limited research evidence on the use of special guardianship and, in particular, on the support packages kinship carers have been able to obtain

(Hall, 2007), the emerging picture suggests that it is not, in fact, having either of those effects. At the time of writing, there is a campaign to introduce amendments to the Children and Young Persons Bill requiring local authorities to meet the support needs of all kinship placements, irrespective of their legal status. Whether or not this is successful, it points to the most pressing issue in kinship care: how to provide support to placements.

Conclusion

Kinship care is now at a very exciting stage in the UK. The Children Act 1989, in the event, proved something of a false dawn, in that while the legislation itself signalled an official sea change in the way the extended family was viewed, this was not consistently and effectively translated into local authority policies and practices. Gradually, however, there has been movement and the White Paper and ensuing legislation, it is to be hoped, represents a significant step forward. There is also, now, a more extensive body of UK research to inform the development of policy and practice, a growing practitioner literature, and more opportunities for training and the exchange of ideas about this unique area of work. Kinship care has not yet assumed its rightful place as the important and distinctive placement option it undoubtedly is, worthy of at least the same amount of policy attention as adoption, residential care and non-kin foster care. However, the auguries, at this point, would seem to be more favourable.

Selected further reading

Aldgate J. and McIntosh M. (2006) *Looking after the Family: A study of children looked after in kinship care in Scotland*, Edinburgh: The Scottish Executive

Broad B. and Skinner A. (2005) *Relative Benefits: Placing children in kinship care*, London: BAAF

Farmer E. and Moyers S. (2008) *Kinship Care: Fostering effective family and friends placements*, London: Jessica Kingsley Publishers

Hunt J. (2006) 'Substitute care of children by members of their extended families and social networks: An overview', in Ebtehaj F., Lindley B. and Richards M. (eds), *Kinship Matters*, Oxford: Hart Publishing

Hunt J., Waterhouse S. and Lutman E. (2008) *Keeping Them in the Family: Outcomes for children placed in kinship care through care proceedings*, London: BAAF

Nixon P. (2008) *Relatively Speaking: Themes and patterns in family and friends care research and implications for policy and practice*, Dartington: Research in Practice

References

Aldgate J. and McIntosh M. (2006) *Looking After the Family: A study of children looked after in kinship care in Scotland*, Edinburgh: The Scottish Executive

Berridge D. and Cleaver H. (1987) *Foster Home Breakdown*, Oxford: Blackwell

Bourne J. and Porter D. (2001) *Life Changes When You Take On Grandchildren: The experiences of a group for grandparent carers*, Unpublished, Barnardo's Peepul Family Resource Centre, Croydon

Broad B., Hayes R. and Rushforth C. (2001) *Kith and Kin: Kinship care for vulnerable young people*, London: National Children's Bureau

Cleaver H. (2000) *Fostering Family Contact*, London: The Stationery Office

Department for Education and Skills (2007) *Care Matters: Time for change*, London: Department for Education and Skills

Department of Health (1991) *The Children Act 1989 Guidance and Regulations, Volume 3: Family Placement*, London: HMSO

Department of Health (2001) *Children Act Report 2000*, London: Department of Health

Doolan P., Nixon P. and Lawrence P. (2004) *Growing up in the Care of Relatives or Friends: Delivering best practice in family and friends care*, London: Family Rights Group

Farmer E. and Moyers S. (2008) *Kinship Care: Fostering effective family and friends placements*, Jessica Kingsley Publishers

Farmer E. and Parker R. (1991) *Trials and Tribulations: Returning children from care to their families*, London: HMSO

Farmer E. and Pollock S. (1998) *Sexually Abused and Abusing Children in Substitute Care*, Chichester: Wiley

Flynn R. (1999) *Kinship Foster Care: The forgotten face of kinship care. Making research count*, University of Luton: Unpublished

Flynn R. (2002) 'Kinship foster care: Research review', *Child and Family Social Work*, 7, pp 311–322

Goodman R. (1997) 'The strengths and difficulties questionnaire: A research note', *Journal of Child Psychology and Psychiatry*, 38, pp 581–586

Grandparents Plus and Adfam (2006) *Forgotten Families: The needs and experiences of grandparents who care for children whose parents misuse drugs and alcohol*, London: Grandparents Plus and Adfam

Hall A. (2007) *Special Guardianship and Permanency Planning: A missed opportunity?* MA Dissertation, King's College London

Harwin J., Owen M., Locke R. and Forrester D. (2003) *Making Care Orders Work: A study of care plans and their implementation*, London: The Stationery Office

Hunt J. (2003) *Family and Friends Carers: Scoping paper prepared for the Department of Health*, London: Department of Health

Hunt J. (2006) 'Substitute care of children by members of their extended families and social networks', in Ebterhaj F., Lindley B., Richards M. (eds) *Kinship Matters*, Oxford: Hart Publishing

Hunt J. and Macleod A. (1999) *The Best-Laid Plans: Outcomes of judicial decisions in child protection cases*, London: The Stationery Office

Hunt J., Waterhouse S. and Lutman E. (2008) *Keeping Them in the Family: Outcomes for children placed in kinship care through care proceedings*, London: BAAF

Kosenen M. (1993): 'Descriptive study of foster and adoptive care services in a Scottish agency', *Community Alternative*, 5:2, pp 126–128

Laming Lord (2006) *Care Matters: Placements working group report*, London: Department for Education and Skills

Laws S. (2001) 'Looking after children within the extended family: Carer's views', in Broad B. (ed) (2001) *Kinship Care: The placement choice for children and young people*, Lyme Regis: Russell House Publishing

Lupton C. and Nixon P. (1999) *Empowering Practice? A critical appraisal of the family group conference approach*, Bristol: Policy Press

Malos E. and Bullard E. (1991) *Custodianship: The care of other people's children*, London: HMSO

Marsh P. and Crow G. (1998) *Family Group Conferences in Child Welfare*, Oxford: Blackwell Science

Messing J. T. (2005) *From the Child's Perspective: A qualitative analysis of kinship care placements*, National Abandoned Infants Assistance Resource Center, School of Social Welfare, University of California at Berkeley.

Millham, S., Bullock R., Hosie K. and Haak M. (1986) *Lost in Care*, Aldershot: Gower

Morgan A. (2003) *Survey of Local Authorities in England: Policy and practice in family and friends care*, London: Family Rights Group, Unpublished

Narey (2006) *Beyond Care Matters: The future of the care population working group report*, London: Department for Education and Skills

Nixon P. (2008) *Relatively Speaking: Themes and patterns in family and friends care research and implications for policy and practice*, Dartington: Research in Practice

Nixon S. (1999) 'Safe care, abuse and allegations of abuse in foster care', in Kelly G. and Gilligan R. (eds) *Issues in Foster Care: Policy, practice and research*, London: Jessica Kingsley Publishers

Nixon S. and Verity P. (1996) 'Allegations against foster families', *Foster Care*, January 1996

Pitcher D. (1999) *When Grandparents Care*, Plymouth City Council Social Services Department

Pitcher D. (2001) 'Assessing grandparent carers: A framework', in Broad B. (ed.) *Kinship Care: The placement choice for children and young people*, Lyme Regis: Russell House Publishing

Richards A. (2001) *Second Time Around: A survey of grandparents raising their grandchildren*, London: Family Rights Group

Rowe J., Caine M., Hundleby M. and Keane A. (1984) *Long Term Foster Care*, London: Batsford

Rowe J., Hundleby M. and Garnett L. (1989) *Child Care Now: A survey of placement patterns*, London: BAAF

Russell C. (1995) *Parenting the Second Time Around: Grandparents as carers of young relatives in child protection cases*, Unpublished dissertation, University of East Anglia

Sinclair I., Baker C., Lee J. and Gibbs I. (2007) *The Pursuit of Permanence: A study of the English care system*, London: Jessica Kingsley Publishers

Strawbridge W. J., Wallhagen M. I., Shema S. J. and Kaplan G. A. (1997) 'New burdens or more of the same? Comparing grandparent, spouse and adult child caregivers', *The Gerontologist*, 37, pp 505–510

Sykes J, Sinclair I., Gibbs I. and Wilson K. (2002) 'Kinship and stranger foster carers: How do they compare?' *Adoption & Fostering*, 26:2, pp 38–48

Talbot C. and Calder M. (2006) *Assessment in Kinship Care*, Lyme Regis: Russell House Publishing

Tan S. (2000) *Friends and Relative Care: The neglected carers*, Unpublished dissertation, PQ award in Social Work, Brunel University

Triseliotis J. (2002) 'Long-term foster care or adoption? The evidence examined', *Child and Family Social Work*, 7, pp 23–33

Waldman J. and Wheal A. (1999) 'Training needs of friends and families who are foster carers', in Greeff R. (ed.) *Fostering Kinship: An international perspective on kinship foster care*, Aldershot: Ashgate

7 Foster care in England

Ian Sinclair and Kate Wilson

Introduction

At any one time, English local authorities look after about 60,000 children and young people (DCSF, 2007). Around seven out of ten of these children are in foster care. This chapter gives an overview of recent research on these children and the care they receive.

Most of the research we review has been funded by the government. It addresses questions that are of interest to those making and implementing policy. In particular it asks:

- What is the role of foster care? (For example, what kind of children does it cater for and for how long and with what purpose?)
- What do children want from it?
- How does it compare with other possible provision such as adoption or residential care?
- What determines how placements go? (For example, what makes a difference to the outcomes achieved by a placement and whether or not it lasts for as long as it is needed?)
- What are the long-term outcomes?
- What is needed in order to recruit an adequate number of foster carers, support them properly and retain them?

This chapter is organised around these questions. We shall, however, pay particular attention to what foster children want, and what seems to determine their outcomes. In our conclusion, we use this information to make some suggestions for policy and practice.

Inevitably the chapter picks and chooses. We draw mainly on English research, although we do refer to Welsh and Scottish studies. There is no reason to think that English research is not relevant elsewhere in the United Kingdom, but there are differences in the legal background and the definitions of who is "in care" which need to be kept in mind.

What is the role of foster care?

Descriptions of foster care are normally provided within the context of more general studies of the care system (sometimes referred to as the "looked after" system). The

English system has its origins in systems designed to deal with destitution, juvenile crime, and child abuse. Over time, these systems were brought together and, for a while, the care system dealt with children who were removed from their homes for any reason. Some of these children were placed because of legal orders made by the courts while others were "voluntarily accommodated". These broad reasons for care still apply, although their relative importance has greatly changed.

Officially, just under two-thirds (62%) of the children in the system on any one day are looked after because they are at risk of serious emotional, physical or sexual abuse or of neglect. The system also caters for some teenage children who are at serious odds with their families and who are often in trouble with the law and at school (Skuse and Ward, 2003; Farmer *et al*, 2004). A very small number (about 4% at any one point in time) are first looked after primarily for reasons of disability although rather more (around one in six) may be seen by social workers as having problems of disability (Sinclair *et al*, 2005a; Sinclair *et al*, 2007). Around five per cent are (mainly older) young people who are in this country without their parents and seeking asylum. (For recent figures, see DCSF, 2007 and Sinclair *et al*, 2007.)

Many of the children who enter the care system return home quickly – just under half leave within a year of arrival and usually to go home (Sinclair *et al*, 2007). Foster care is equally important for this group. Three-quarters of the children are first placed in foster care (DCSF, 2007). After a year, children may leave for adoption if they are young or to live independently when they reach 18. Almost all those adopted and just over half those who graduate out of the system have been fostered immediately before they leave it. With these exceptions, the chance of leaving the system in any one year is low (about 5%). Around three-quarters of the children who are in the care system at any one point in time have already been there for a year or more. As we have seen, seven out of ten of these are fostered.

These figures illustrate the key role of foster care in the British system. They also suggest a basic distinction between short-, intermediate- and long-term foster care. Further distinctions can then be made according to the purpose of a stay. For example, some short-stay care may be simply to gain a breathing space until a mother returns from hospital whereas other short stay care may be to provide a "remand" placement. A possible general classification would follow Rowe and her colleagues (1989) and distinguish between

- short-term – emergency, assessment, remand, "roof over head";
- shared care – regular "short-breaks";
- intermediate (task-centred) – treatment, bridging placements, preparation for independence or adoption;
- long-term – upbringing.

In general, research has concentrated on the three main forms of foster care (short-term, intermediate and long-term) and particularly on long-term foster care – the form which serves most of the children in the care system at any one time and which is the focus of most of the studies on which we draw.

What do foster children want?

Some people say, 'Yeah, but that sort of thing goes on in all families' and I'm like, 'Well, how am I supposed to know that?' I mean, I've been in care ten years, and it's just not like not a normal family, do you know what I mean . . . it's foster mum and dad and foster kids. It's not normal at all. (Foster child)

I love where I am because they are like my real family. I love them with all my heart. (Foster child)

[Foster care] is lots of moving about – different sets of rules, never knew where I stood . . . no control over my life – everyone making decisions without me. (Foster child)

Foster children differ in ages, gender and ethnicity. They have differing histories, personalities, and abilities. Unsurprisingly, different foster children have different wants. Despite these differences, all foster children face some common issues. They are not living with their families. They are in somebody else's house and are expected to abide by their rules. Their future is not secure: they can be moved against their wishes and their expectations. Their lives are encompassed with regulations. Their friends are unlikely to see their situation as "normal".

Against this background, those studies which have sought children's views (eg Sinclair *et al*, 2005a and b; Skuse and Ward, 2003; Lowe *et al*, 2001) suggest that they have five main requirements:

1. *Normality*. Children want fostering to be as "normal" as possible. They do not want their status to "single them out".
2. *Family care*. Children want to feel that they belong in their foster home, that they are treated the same as other children in their home and, ideally, that they are loved, listened to and encouraged. They resent harsh or inconsistent discipline, and any feeling that their foster carers are "just doing it for the money". They value treats, opportunities for their hobbies and, in most cases, a room of their own.
3. *Respect for their origins*. Children do not want a conflict of loyalty between their foster carer and their birth family. They have differing views about how far they want to belong to their own family or to their foster family and about which members of their family they wish to see. They want these views respected.

4. *Control*. Foster children want some control over their lives. They have differing "wants" (for example, some want to be with other children, some like houses in which there are babies, some want to be with their siblings, and so on). They want social workers to be aware of their feelings on these matters and to take action accordingly. They do not like situations in which it is not clear what plans there are for them or in which they are moved suddenly and with little notice.

5. *Opportunity*. There is no evidence that foster children differ from others in what they want for their futures. Success at school, a good job, a happy family and children are all common aspirations. Carers are praised not only for providing a family environment and making the children feel valued but also for offering opportunities and enabling skills.

Comparing foster care: returning home

Decisions over whether children should return home are usually taken soon after a child arrives "in care". In our view, there is no solid British research on the comparative benefits of returning home early or remaining in the care system. There is, however, some research which compares remaining in care (generally foster care) and returning home after some time.

Children who do not go home quickly are typically more "vulnerable" than those who do. So they are more likely to be young, removed for reasons of abuse or neglect, or disabled (Sinclair *et al*, 2007). Comparisons between those in this group who have returned home at some point and those who have not (Hensey *et al*, 1983; King and Taitz, 1985; Minty, 1989; Sinclair *et al*, 2005b) suggest that those who do not return are safer (less likely to be abused), and may benefit in terms of health, "mental health" and behaviour.

In these comparisons it is hard to ensure that like is being compared with like. It is also true that some "returns" are more likely to succeed than others (see e.g. Sinclair *et al*, 2005b). However, it seems probable that those who do go home are returning to more satisfactory situations than would have been the case with the others. It therefore seems likely that the better outcomes for those who remain in care reflect "cause and effect", i.e. differences in outcome are attributable to the fact that the children have not gone home and not to differences between the children involved.

Comparing foster care: adoption

There's no way I'd have wanted to be adopted. I love my foster mum and dad, but I also love my birth mum, and they're my family as well. (Foster child)

The social worker should not call so much at my home and stop asking the same things over and over again, especially about my past. I want to forget all that. I want my foster carer to adopt me. Nobody talks to me about that. (Foster child)

The UK does not have a tradition of intercountry adoption. Adoptions other than those of family members most commonly involve British children in care. The chance that such children will be adopted drops very rapidly with age. It is quite high for children who enter the care system at birth and negligible for those who first enter over the age of five. One study of adoption, for example, found that the chance of not being adopted increased by 1.8 for every extra year of age at entry to care, and by 1.6 for every subsequent year before the best interest decision was made (Selwyn *et al*, 2003).

After allowing for age at entry, the relevant comparison is with long-stay foster care. In practice, however, very long stay foster care is quite rarely on offer. Only a quarter of the children who enter the care system under the age of 11 and are still there at 17 are in placements of five years or more. A third are in placements that have lasted for less than a year (Sinclair *et al*, 2007).

Once again, it is hard to be sure that like is being compared with like. In general, the comparisons suggest that, while the children are being brought up, there is often very little to distinguish between the outcomes of genuine long-stay foster care and adoption. Where differences are found, however, they seem to favour adoption and to relate in particular to the nature or strength of attachments. Adoptions by foster carers are, if anything, even more successful than stranger ones at the start of placement, although their frequency is reduced by reluctance on the part of some professionals to sanction them and by the reluctance of carers to lose financial and other supports. Moreover, their apparent advantages at the beginning may become less apparent over time (Selwyn *et al*, 2003).

Other comparisons also favour adoption. In comparison with adoptive parents, long-term foster carers often feel hampered in acting as parents by the lack of a clear division of responsibility between themselves and social workers. They also complain of the expectation that young people start to move on between the ages of 16 and 18, seeing this practice as unsettling and unfair to the young people (Selwyn *et al*, 2003).

By contrast children themselves, once they are of an age to express an opinion, have very strong views on whether they wished to be adopted or fostered. Only a minority of foster children (about 10%) wanted to be adopted, almost always by their own carers (Sinclair *et al*, 2005 a and b). In short, there probably could and should be more adoptions. Most looked after children, however, are not going to be adopted and there need to be alternative arrangements that suit them.

Comparing foster care: residential care

In a children's home, it's like staff in and out, isn't it? . . . And I prefer to be in a foster home, because then you've got two parents there for you 24/7. (Young person in foster care)

Residential care is used comparatively rarely in the UK (although its frequency of use varies somewhat between the four countries) and then predominantly for adolescents whose behaviour is thought too challenging for foster care. In England, this form of care provides just over a quarter (28%) of the days that children over 12 spend in the care system (Sinclair et al, 2007).

There are no conclusive comparisons between these foster care placements and residential care for adolescents. The evidence shows that residential care is typically very expensive. Most of those in foster care seem to prefer this to residential care (Colton, 1988; Sinclair et al, 2005a) but some of those in residential care prefer that (Sinclair and Gibbs, 1998), perhaps finding it difficult to deal with families that seem competitive with their own or valuing the company of their peers. Despite such preferences, very well supported foster care is capable of containing some very difficult adolescents without losing foster carers (Walker et al, 2004). This form of care is cheaper and in some ways more benign. There is as yet no evidence that it has better outcomes.

Concerns about the costs and dubious effectiveness of residential care have led to experiments with 'Multi-dimensional Treatment Foster Care'. This model of care derives from Oregon, USA and has the theoretical advantage that foster carers and parents are trained in the same behavioural approach (see Chamberlain and Reed, 1991, 1998; Fisher and Chamberlain, 2000). This should help to overcome the disadvantage that residential care has strong effects on the behaviour of young people in it but often little or no effect when they enter new environments on leaving (see discussion in Sinclair, 2006). The experiments are being evaluated by researchers at the Universities of Manchester and York but the results are not yet available.

Irrespective of whether this form of foster care proves effective, it is clear that something like this is needed. The decline of residential care has left a gap for those children who are not seeking a new family but who are proving too difficult for their current one. If they cannot be helped to "sort themselves out" they will have no place to be.

Comparing foster care: kinship care

This is my home and this is my family. I think I'll be here until I am 19 or so. (Young person looked after by relatives)

It doesn't matter but sometimes my uncle goes against black people. (Dual heritage young person looked after by relatives)

Some children are fostered with friends or relatives rather than with strangers. Such "kin placements" make up just under a fifth of all foster placements, although there are wide variations in the extent of its use. Recently there have been a number of comparisons between foster care with kin and foster care with strangers. This research is discussed elsewhere in this book. The following brief summary draws mainly on two sources (Sinclair *et al*, 2005a; Sinclair *et al*, 2007).

Kinship care is predominantly used for long-stay placements that are intended to last. From this point of view it has many advantages. It can build on existing relationships. It often allows children to stay in the same geographical area. It should be less threatening to a child's sense of belonging to a family, build on and strengthen a family's ability to offer care, reduce the child's trauma of moving to an unknown family and, perhaps, make it easier to keep siblings together.

Comparisons show that some of these advantages are real. Social workers do tend to see kin placements as more satisfactory than other apparently similar ones. Children recount many of the advantages listed above. The placements also last longer. The advantages, however, are not all one way. In comparison with stranger carers, kin carers are poorer, less well-educated and more likely to have problems with housing. They are also seen as providing placements of lower quality, although their greater commitment may make up for their lack of parenting skills. In some cases these placements persist despite offering a very low standard of care.

In general kin carers put themselves forward for the job. It is not known if the commitment which characterises kin carers would be equally high if social workers became more proactive in recruiting them rather than depending on their volunteering for the task. There are in practice wide variations in the use of kinship care between different local authorities. There is no evidence that authorities that make more use of this form of care do less well with it. This, however, would not necessarily be the case if the use of kin care approached the levels found in some US or Australian cities. So although the evidence suggests an expansion of this form of care, this should be done cautiously and with proper support.

Explaining the course of foster care: children's characteristics

I was too bad for them ... always getting into trouble at school. And my temper, if anything would get on my nerves or I couldn't get what I wanted ... I would go mental. (Foster child)

I am happy. I thought coming into care was a good thing. I am looked after properly here. (Foster child)

I should never have been in care. Social workers should leave kids alone. (Young person who was looked after)

Much research has focused on the question of what makes individual foster placements go well or badly (see for example, Quinton and Rutter, 1998; Thoburn *et al*, 2000; Rushton *et al*, 2001; Farmer *et al*, 2004; Sinclair *et al*, 2005a). Almost all this research has focused on long-stay placements. The most common criterion for "going well" has been "absence of breakdown". Other criteria have included the judgements of social workers and carers, and, less commonly, improvements in scores or ratings. In assessing the effect of particular factors on these outcomes, some attempt is usually made to allow for differences between children. These differences are therefore a useful starting point.

The children's characteristics which seem to have most impact on whether "things go well or badly" seem to be their age, wishes, and behaviour. Older children, children who do not want to be in the placement, and children who show challenging behaviour are all less likely to have placements which last. Behaviour and wishes seem to become more important as determinants of placement breakdown when the child is older and hence better able to influence the course of the placement (Sinclair et al, 2007).

Explaining the course of foster care: placement process

Children should always meet their carers before they move to a new placement. (Foster child)

The course of placements may also be influenced by the way the placement is made. There is some evidence (e.g. Farmer et al, 2004; Sinclair et al, 2005a) that those which are made in a rush, without adequate consultation with child or carer, and without the provision of full information to the carer are all more likely to disrupt. So too are those where the carer's preference (e.g. for a girl) are over-ridden. These findings do not necessarily represent cause and effect. For example, carers may well be more likely to complain of lack of information when a child proves to have more difficulties than they expected. However, it is generally held to be good practice to allow time for consultation with carers and children before placement. It therefore does no harm to assume that such practice also helps to ensure good outcomes.

Explaining the course of foster care: family contact

I think all children should see lots of their natural family even if they are in care. (Foster child)

I would like to see Gran and Grandad (mum's side) or speak on the phone with any family. (Foster child)

I would like social services to respect my decision not to see my family. (Foster child)

Contact between foster children and their families is common. Between 40 and 50 per cent of foster children have face-to-face contact with at least one family member who is not living with them, at least once a week. A few (somewhere between one in seven and one in five) have virtually no contact with their families at all (Cleaver, 2000; Farmer *et al*, 2004; Sinclair *et al*, 2005a).

Generally such contact is encouraged. Children want more of it. Professionals believe that it makes it easier for them to go home and benefits their sense of identity and mental health. Research provides rather more equivocal support. Children who are in close contact with their families are more likely to go home (Aldgate, 1980; Bullock *et al*, 1993) but contact itself is not necessarily the reason for their return (Sinclair *et al*, 2005a and 2005b). Many children are upset by irregular contact or troubles at home and while some contacts seem beneficial, others are detrimental and it is quite possible for the same child to have both (Quinton *et al*, 1997; Schofield *et al*, 2000; Farmer *et al*, 2004). One study compared previously abused foster children who had unrestricted contact with others who had at least one relative who was not allowed to see them (Sinclair *et al*, 2005a). The group with unrestricted contact were three times more likely to have a placement breakdown.

For their part foster carers often find these contacts difficult, complaining of unreliable visiting, the effects on the child and sometimes the hostile or threatening behaviour of the visitors. In part, these difficulties may also have to do with the carers' roles. Two linked studies compare contact with young adopted children and children in middle childhood long-term foster care. Face-to-face contact, although less frequent, was found to be more straightforward in the adoptive families, with the adopters being centrally involved in contact meetings and able to act as they saw fit. By contrast, the experience of foster carers was more varied and some felt they could not take the decisions that needed to be made (Neil *et al*, 2003).

Rather similar findings apply to placements with brothers and sisters in the same placement. In general children want to be with their siblings and this is encouraged. Children who have been rejected at home and are placed apart from their siblings are particularly likely to have placement breakdowns (Rushton *et al*, 2001). A possible reason is that the placement increases their sense of rejection. In keeping with this, children who have siblings at home are also more likely to have placement breakdown, although this association is not necessarily causal (Sinclair *et al*, 2005a). More generally, relationships between siblings can be harmonious and a source of strength. However, they can also be very fraught and threaten placements (Rushton *et al*, 2001).

In general, the research discourages "rigid rules" over contact or placement with siblings. Most foster children want contact with their families and want to live with their brothers and sisters. Other things being equal, it is their right to have their wishes respected. That said, children may want contact with one relative (say their mother's mother) but not others and living with siblings is not always best. In these situations a general presumption in favour of family ties should not lead to rules of thumb.

Explaining the course of foster care: carer characteristics

I had a couple of bad foster homes. But when I found Jane and Mike, it all changed. I knew they were the ones for me. They treated me as one of their own. (Foster child)

Theories about parenting suggest that some styles – particularly authoritative parenting, which combines clear boundaries with warmth – work better than others. In keeping with this, there is evidence that some foster carers are consistently less likely to have placement breakdowns than others. Such successful carers are rated as "authoritative" (warm, encouraging, sensitive to their child's needs, willing to listen and clear over expectations etc.). They are also more likely take part with their foster children in enjoyable joint activities (such as reading a bedtime story or going to a football match) and when they are older encourage them in developing needed skills. By contrast, "unsuccessful" carers do not have these attributes and may be rated as "aggressive" and "unresponsive" (Quinton *et al*, 1998; Farmer *et al*, 2004; Sinclair *et al*, 2005a; Sinclair *et al*, 2005b; Sinclair *et al*, 2007).

One study (Sinclair *et al*, 2005a; Wilson, 2006) found that, although foster care was rarely seen as a place where change can take place, skilled, committed foster care could make a difference and some carers were more likely to have placements which were considered successful and which did not break down. The researchers developed a model to demonstrate that foster carers who were "child oriented" and practised a particular kind of responsive parenting experienced fewer placement disruptions and were more likely to have outcomes that were seen as successful.

Irrespective of the merits or otherwise of this model, there seems no doubt that the qualities of the foster carer are key to outcomes. Sadly there is as yet no solid evidence that any form of training enhances these qualities or improves the chances of success.

Explaining the course of foster care: matching and interactions

I think chemistry has got a lot to do with it . . . in all honesty, there's some you bond with and some you don't – James I instantly bonded with . . . he just gave me a look, and I thought – ooh – I've got my hands full here. But I thought I'd jump at the challenge, because I love a challenge. (Foster carer)

Relationships between carers and children show both stability and change over time. Both child and carer play their part in this process. The factors that play a part include:

- "chemistry" – some carers take to particular children and some children take to particular carers;
- commitment – difficult behaviour tends to lead to carer rejection which in turn leads

to placement breakdown – if a carer remains committed despite difficult behaviour, breakdown does not occur;

- "vicious circles" – difficult behaviour on the part of the child can lead to less skilled behaviour by the foster carer and hence to more difficult behaviour;
- relationships with other children or foster children – carers may be prepared to tolerate very difficult behaviour directed at themselves but are much less tolerant of such behaviour directed at their own children (Quinton *et al*, 1998; Sinclair and Wilson, 2003; Farmer *et al*, 2004).

Explaining the course of foster care: support

Much of the support given to foster placements takes the form of individual contacts between the child and an outside professional. In general the evidence suggests that the usual levels of contact with these professionals (commonly low) do not affect outcomes for children (Sinclair *et al*, 2005a). There is some (in our view inconclusive) evidence that contact with an educational psychologist may improve outcomes for children as may contact with a counsellor (Farmer *et al*, 2004; Sinclair *et al*, 2005a).

A rather different approach is to provide support for the foster carer in the belief that this will improve their morale and hence their ability to deal with the child. There is evidence that "stressed carers" are more likely to have placement breakdowns (Farmer *et al*, 2004; Sinclair *et al*, 2005a). However, it is not yet clear whether stress produces the disrupted placement or the other way round. The evidence does suggest that support and training for foster carers can improve their morale (Farmer *et al*, 2004; Sinclair *et al*, 2004). It has yet to be shown that this in turn improves outcomes for the children. Quinton *et al* (1998), for example, found no association between the amount of social work support and the success or otherwise of placements, and the researchers in the York studies concluded that foster carers' 'perceived lack of support from social workers was more probably a consequence of a placement going wrong than a cause of it' (Sinclair, 2006, p 85).

Explaining the course of foster care: school

The way they've handled James, the support I mean, the headmaster himself, he's one in a million. In fact, they've helped make the placement a success . . . If James has had a problem, they've pulled him out, they'll fetch him down home, and they'll work together with James. (Foster carer)

School was a dead loss – I got picked on the whole time 'cos I was in care, so I got into fights and stopped going, and they never bothered about it. (Foster child)

British research suggests that the school performance of children in care is poor (Wilson *et al*, 2004). This probably reflects their experience prior to entry to care. The care system, however, does not improve this performance and could almost certainly do more in this respect. Particular difficulties include the frequency with which children change placements and hence schools and, in the case of foster care, some confusion of responsibilities between foster carers and social workers, and the low educational expectations of some carers (Fletcher-Campbell, 1997).

In practice, school for foster children is much more than a route to academic success or otherwise. It provides a structure to their day (Walker *et al*, 2004), can be a way of keeping in touch with friends from their former lives and provides a source of positive role models. Less positively, it is a place where they must cope with the stigma of "being in care". Generally, schools are important as potential sources of self-esteem and as places where children can try out their social wings and get in with the "right" or "wrong" crowd (Jackson and Martin, 1998).

In general, foster children who are unhappy at school, who truant from it or are excluded, tend to show other difficulties (Farmer *et al*, 2004; Sinclair *et al*, 2005a and b). Young people of school age but not at school place carers under considerable strain (Walker *et al*, 2004). Conversely, young people who are confident about their schoolwork are less likely to have a placement breakdown (Farmer *et al*, 2004). These associations do not necessarily represent cause and effect. However, the pattern of associations tends to suggest that schools do have an impact on placements (Sinclair *et al*, 2005b).

As noted above, one study found that contact with an educational psychologist was associated with the avoidance of placement breakdown (Sinclair *et al*, 2005a). This unpredicted finding was not explained by the characteristics of children seeing the psychologist. There was some evidence that the effects depended on the attitude of the carer and the attitude of the child. Where neither carers nor child had a positive attitude towards school the effect was not apparent. Whatever its explanation, this finding reinforced other evidence that doing well at school is of value for its own sake and because of its contribution to placement success.

The long-term outcomes of foster care

I'm still moving around at 18 years of age and I've been moving since I was a little girl and I've got nobody apart from my dad and he's poorly. Guess that is how it is always going to be. (Former foster child)

With the help of my foster carers I passed all my GCSEs, went to college and achieved a GNVQ in social care. If it hadn't been for my foster carers I would not have passed my GCSEs or been interested in work in a nursing home or doing a college course. I've bought my own house, had a baby son (now four months old), got my own dog. I pay all my bills (with boyfriend) and keep in touch with foster carers and their family. (Former foster child)

A number of British research projects have focused on what happens to children who leave care when 17 or 18. Very few of these, however, have looked specifically at foster care. One that did showed that long-term foster care *could* provide a family for life (Schofield, 2003). This heartening evidence must be seen in the light of the difficulty of finding representative samples. It is easier to find adults who have had successful and happy lives.

Another study which followed up a sample of foster children also found some impressive successes along with many less positive outcomes. There was a relatively high incidence of unemployment, depression, loneliness and difficulties over money and housing (Sinclair *et al*, 2005a). Contact with former foster carers was quite common but not apparently sufficiently intensive to counteract these problems. The foster children themselves fell into three groups. Around a third said that they had left foster care for positive reasons – for example, to go to university or move to a job. A third felt that they had been pushed out before they were ready. A third said they had left because they could not get on with their foster carers.

In many ways the weak point of foster care is not what happens in foster care itself but what happens afterwards.

Recruiting and supporting foster carers

Foster care depends on the successful recruitment of carers and on retaining enough of those who are recruited.

There is only one recent and substantial study of recruitment (Triseliotis *et al*, 2000).This suggested that successful recruitment would largely be based on local media campaigns, supported by foster carers (many carers are recruited by other carers), and the involvement of experienced foster carers, foster children and social workers. It was important that recruitment was efficient (many carers are "lost" after the initial contact) and carried out throughout the year.

Fortunately for retention, most foster carers find their experience life-enhancing (Sinclair *et al*, 2004). Turnover is quite low at around 10 per cent a year (Triseliotis *et al*, 2000; Kirton *et al*, 2004; Sinclair *et al*, 2004). Carers leave either because fostering no longer fits their plans for their family, or because they feel they are offered poor support or because of "events", traumatic incidents such as fostering breakdowns or allegations of abuse that undermine their confidence (Wilson *et al*, 2000). Breakdowns are particularly important. Few carers decide to leave while there are foster children with them. Break-downs upset carers while offering them the chance to cease fostering without breaking their obligation to particular children.

There is evidence that support for foster carers is most effective if it is tailored to their particular family situation; if it combines regular social work visits with relevant training, contact with other carers in training or groups and adequate remuneration; if it pays attention to the particular issues raised by carers such as the need for a good after-hours service; if it is responsive to "events"; and if it makes carers feel they are part of a team. (Pithouse and Parry, 1997; Fisher *et al*, 2000; Triseliotis, 2000; Wilson *et al*, 2000; Sinclair *et al*, 2004).

There is evidence that support can enhance retention and rather more equivocal evidence that it may improve outcomes. Irrespective of whether it achieves these ends, it should, in our view, be seen as a moral duty. Foster care can have a devastating effect on the families that undertake it. It seems essential to do everything possible to reduce its strains. It should be possible to provide such support not least because the independent sector appears able to offer a higher level of support than the local authority one (Kirton *et al*, 2004).

Conclusion

Foster care is in many ways a very impressive form of provision. It looks after a wide variety of children, some of whom display very challenging behaviour. Most foster children speak very highly of their foster carers. Most foster carers are very committed to their foster children.

At the same time foster care faces a basic dilemma. It rarely provides very long stays in the same family and it may fail either to change the situations from which foster children come, to offer them a permanent home or bring about much change in their long-term well-being and behaviour. In the end children leave foster care for adoption, their own homes or independent living. Of these, adoption is virtually only available to children who start to be looked after under the age of five (Sinclair *et al*, 2007) but is the only route out of care that commonly offers the children the secure base that they want and need.

There are, as we see it, three main routes out of this situation.

First, authorities need to be able to provide the choices that children need if they are to grow up happily in a long-term family. This means:

- a "level playing field" between adoption by carers, long-term fostering, fostering with relatives, residence and special guardianship orders so that the choice reflects the wishes of child and carer and is not, as at present, constrained by considerations of loss of support;
- more adoption by strangers – an option which some authorities use much more than others and which could almost certainly be more used in authorities that make little use of it;
- greater use of and support for fostering by relatives which the research suggests can be a particularly useful form of fostering and which is not as much used in some authorities as in others;

- more genuine "permanent" foster care so that carers are able to take more "parental decisions" and encouraged to keep young people who need this beyond the age of 18;
- the development of "treatment foster care" so that young people are enabled to "get their head together" and return to parents who are prepared to receive them rather than as often at present being unable to settle either in care or at home;
- better support packages for the families of those who are not happy away from home and who might safely return if better support was available, and where appropriate, the inclusion in this support of properly supported short breaks with the same carers (Aldgate and Bradley, 1999);
- a general willingness to support the strong relationships which grow in foster care. This might be achieved, for example, by enabling children whose rehabilitation breaks down to return where possible to the same carers, by maintaining contact between carers and their former foster children where a basically good relationship exists despite a placement breakdown and, again where possible, by enabling carers to support their former foster children when these have returned to their homes;
- a wide view of the role of school wherever the child is placed and a perception that qualifications gained at school are unlikely to be of value to the child unless he or she is supported in making use of them when they leave.

These changes would need to be accompanied by skilled social work on the aspects of placement that are crucial to its success. The research reviewed in this chapter suggests that social workers in this field need skills in:

- negotiating placements and ensuring as far as possible that carer and child understand what they are taking on and are happy with it;
- managing contacts so that they are purposeful, controlled if necessary and benign rather than detrimental;
- deciding on the weight to be put on keeping siblings together and negotiating acceptable levels of contact between siblings when this is not possible;
- explaining the children to their carers in such a way that the carers' natural anger or upset at a child's behaviour does not take the form of rejection, an unrealistically poor view of the child or other counterproductive reactions;
- maintaining good communication with the carer and the child in such a way that they have a clear understanding of what is going on and are able to carry out the tasks listed above.

Finally, there is abundant evidence that the key to effective foster care lies in the quality of the foster carers. In the long run, it may be possible to enhance this with support and training. It is essential that we find out how to do this. At present research has failed to find any form of training that improves performance (Minnis and Devine, 2001; Pithouse *et al*, 2002; MacDonald and Kavavelakis, 2004; Sinclair *et al*, 2005a). Social workers are, however, able to pick out "good carers" (Sinclair *et al*, 2005a). Their judgements are not infallible but those they see as warm, clear, empathic and so on do tend to have placements that succeed. Very few carers seem to have the opposite of these qualities but those that do can do damage.

The key to improving the care system must therefore for the moment rest heavily on the ability of authorities to "hang on" to those carers who have the right qualities and ease out the minority who do not. This basic requirement is sadly not the focus of inspections of foster care, which perhaps understandably because of lack of time, focus on matters of organisation and may look in detail at the work of six foster carers at most. A better focus might be the systems that agencies have for assessing the quality of their carers and ensuring that they keep the best and not the worst.

In summary, therefore, and no doubt too imprecisely, we are calling for excellent practice by carers and social workers, supported by appropriate provision and inspection. These requirements are difficult both for the practitioners who must fulfil them and for the authorities who are supposed to ensure them. Perhaps that is why so much effort is focused on organisational change, a costly if outwardly impressive diversion, for the benefits of which we can find no evidence at all.

Selected further reading

Schofield G. (2002) *Part of the Family: Pathways through foster care*, London: BAAF

Sinclair I. (2005) *Fostering Now: Messages from Research*, London: Jessica Kingsley Publishers

Thoburn J. (2007) 'Out of home care for the abused or neglected child: A review of the knowledge base for planning and practice', in Wilson K. and James A., *The Child Protection Handbook*, London: Bailliere Tindall Elsevier, 3rd edition, pp 494–515

For a research-based guide to practice access www.scie.org.uk/practiceguides/fostering/iundex.asp

Similarly for references to relevant fostering literature access: www.scie-socialcareonline.org.uk

References

Aldgate J. (1980) 'Factors influencing children's length of stay in care', in Triseliotis J. (ed.) *New Developments in Foster Care and Adoption*, London: Routledge and Kegan Paul

Aldgate J. and Bradley M. (1999) *Supporting Families Through Short-term Fostering*, London: The Stationery Office

Bullock R., Little M. and Milham S. (1993) *Residential Care for Children: A review of the research*, London: HMSO

Chamberlain P. and Reid J. (1991) 'Using a specialized foster care community treatment model for children and adolescents leaving a state mental hospital', *Journal of Community Psychology*, 19, pp 266–276

Chamberlain P. and Reid J. (1998) 'Comparison of two community alternatives to incarceration for chronic juvenile offenders', *Journal of Consulting and Clinical Psychology*, 66:4, pp 624–633

Cleaver H. (2000) *Fostering Family Contact*, London: The Stationery Office

Colton M. J. (1988) *Dimensions of Substitute Child Care: A comparative study of foster and residential care practices*, Aldershot: Avebury

Department of Children, Schools and Families (2007) http://www.dfes.gov.uk/rsgateway/DB/SFR/s000741/SFR27-2007rev.pdf

Farmer E., Moyers S. and Lipscombe J. (2004) *Fostering Adolescents*, London: Jessica Kingsley Publishers

Fisher P. and Chamberlain P. (2000) 'Multi-dimensional treatment foster care: A program for intensive parenting, family support and skill building', *Journal of Emotional and Behavioural Disorders*, 8:3, pp 155–164

Fisher T., Sinclair I., Gibbs I. and Wilson K. (2000) 'Sharing the care: The qualities sought of social workers by foster carers', *Child and Family Social Work*, 5:3, pp 235–234

Hensey D., Williams J. and Rosenbloom L. (1983) 'Intervention in child abuse: Experience in Liverpool', *Developmental Medicine and Child Neurology*, 25, pp 606–611

Jackson S. and Martin P. Y. (1998) 'Surviving the care system: Education and resilience', *Journal of Adolescence*, 21:5, pp 569–583

King J. and Taitz L. (1985) 'Catch-up growth following abuse', *Archives of Disease in Childhood*, 60, pp 1152–1154

Kirton D., Beecham J. and Ogilvie K. (2004) *Remuneration and Performance in Foster Care. Report to the Department for Education and Skills*, Canterbury: University of Kent

Lowe N., Murch M. with Bader K., Borkowski M., Cooper R., Lisles C. and Shearman J. (2001) *The Plan for the Child: Adoption or long-term fostering*, London: BAAF

Macdonald G. and Kavavelakis I. (2004) *Helping Foster Carers to Manage Challenging Behaviour: An evaluation of a cognitive-behavioural training programme for foster carers*, Exeter: Centre for Evidence-Based Research, University of Exeter

Minnis H. and Devine C. (2001) 'The effect of foster carer training on the emotional and behavioural functioning of looked-after children', *Adoption & Fostering*, 25:1, pp 44–54

Minty B. (1989) 'Annotation: Outcomes in long-term foster family care', *Journal of Child Psychology and Psychiatry*, 40:7, pp 991–999

Neil E., Beek M. and Schofield G. (2003) 'Thinking about and managing contact in permanent placements: The differences and similarities between adoptive parents and foster carers', *Clinical Child Psychology and Psychiatry*, 8:3, pp 401–418

-0.7

Packman J. and Hall C. (1998) *From Care to Accommodation – Support, Protection and Control in Child Care Services*, London: The Stationery Office

Pithouse A., Hill-Tout J. and Lowe K. (2002) 'Training foster carers in challenging behaviour: A case study in disappointment', *Child and Family Social Work*, 7:3, pp 203–215

Pithouse A. and Parry O. (1997) 'Fostering in Wales: The All Wales Review', *Adoption & Fostering*, 21:2, pp 41–49

Quinton D., Rushton A., Dance C. and Mayes D. (1997) 'Contact between children placed away from home and their birth parents: Research issues and evidence', *Clinical Child Psychology and Psychiatry*, 2:3, pp 393–413

Quinton D., Rushton A., Dance C. and Mayes D. (1998) *Joining New Families: Adoption and fostering in middle childhood*, Chichester: Wiley & Sons

Quinton D. and Rutter M. (1988) *Parenting Breakdown: The making and breaking of inter-generational links*, Aldershot: Averbury

Rowe J., Cain H., Hundleby M. and Garnett L. (1989) *Child Care Now: A survey of placement patterns*, London: BAAF

Rushton A. and Dance C. (2000) 'Findings from a UK based study of late permanent placements', *Adoption Quarterly*, 3:3, pp 51–71

Rushton A., Dance C., Quinton D. and Mayes D. (2001) *Siblings in Late Permanent Placements*, London: BAAF

Schofield G. (2003) *Part of the Family: Pathways through foster care*, London: BAAF

Schofield G., Beek M. and Sargent K. (2000) *Growing up in Foster Care*, London: BAAF

Selwyn J., Sturgess W., Quinton D. and Mayes D. (2003) *Care and Outcomes of Non-infant Adoptions: Report to the Department for Education and Skills*, London: DfES

Skuse T. and Ward H. (2003) 'Listening to children's views of care and accommodation', Report to the Department of Health, Loughborough: Centre for Child and Family Research

Sinclair I. (2006) *Fostering Now*, London: Jessica Kingsley Publishers

Sinclair I., Baker C., Lee J. and Gibbs I. (2007) *The Pursuit of Permanence: A study of the English Care System*, London: Jessica Kingsley Publishers

Sinclair I., Baker C., Wilson K. and Gibbs I. (2005b) *Foster Children: Where they go and how they get on*, London: Jessica Kingsley Publishers

Sinclair I. and Gibbs I. (1998) *Children's Homes: A Study in Diversity*, Chichester: Wiley & Sons

Sinclair I., Gibbs I. and Wilson K. (2004) *Foster Carers: Why they stay and why they leave*, London: Jessica Kingsley Publishers

Sinclair I. and Wilson K. (2003) 'Matches and mismatches: The contribution of carers and children to the success of foster placements', *British Journal of Social Work*, 22, pp 871–884

Sinclair I., Wilson K. and Gibbs I. (2005a) *Foster Placements: Why they succeed and why they fail*, London: Jessica Kingsley Publishers

Thoburn J., Norford L. and Rashid S. (2000) *Permanent Family Placement for Children of Minority Ethnic Origin*, London: Jessica Kingsley Publishers

Triseliotis J., Walker M. and Hill M. (2000) *Delivering Foster Care*, London: BAAF

Walker M., Hill M. and Triseliotis J. (2002) *Testing the Limits of Foster Care: Fostering as an alternative to secure accommodation*, London: BAAF

Wilson K. (2006) 'Can foster carers help children resolve their emotional and behavioural difficulties?' *Clinical Child Psychology and Psychiatry*, 11:4, pp 495–511

Wilson K., Sinclair I. and Gibbs I. (2000) 'The trouble with foster care: The impact of stressful events on foster carers,' *British Journal of Social Work*, 30, pp 191–209

Wilson K., Sinclair I., Taylor C., Sellick C. and Pithouse A. (2004) *Fostering Success: An exploration of the research literature on foster care*, SCIE: Knowledge Review 5. Bristol: Policy Press

8   Permanence in foster care

Gillian Schofield

My foster mum looked at me as her son and I looked at her as my mum sort of thing. Even though when you're 18 you officially leave care, we kept in touch. We go round there for dinner, she comes round here. She classes my children as her grandchildren. (Christopher, 29, placed in this foster family at four years old in Schofield, 2003, p 42)

I want for Jessie (15) to be part of our family forever. (Long-term foster carer in Schofield and Beek, 2006, p 265)

The questions posed by this chapter are challenging – is it possible to think about foster care as offering permanence? Can foster carers who do not have biological, legal or socially sanctioned roles as parents offer children a nurturing and inclusive family life through to adulthood?

Policy makers, service providers and practitioners need to establish strategies for achieving stability and permanence for children who come into care from high risk backgrounds and grow to adulthood in foster families. These children require the foster care system to provide them with good quality, and in many cases therapeutic, family care that will help them through childhood to success in adult life. But foster children also need to feel that they belong, to feel part of the foster family, even in the absence of a legal order. It is therefore very important to think carefully about how "permanence" is defined, whether foster care can be a positive permanence option and how care planning procedures and social work practice may increase the likelihood that the long-term foster child will find committed care that lasts into adulthood. This chapter focuses primarily on planned long-term foster placements, where the goal is to achieve permanence for a child in a foster family.

What is permanence?

The concept of "permanence" was originally developed in the United States in the 1980s (Maluccio *et al*, 1986). Concern about children drifting in care had led to the conclusion that children needed the psychological security (attachment and a sense of permanence) that was best achieved in birth families. But where a child's needs could not be met in birth families, permanence was said to be otherwise best achieved in adoption, where new family ties were established by law. This concept of permanence, and the preference for adoption as a permanent route out of care, became established in the UK at around the same time, in part because of similar concerns about children "drifting" in care (Rowe and Lambert, 1973; Thoburn *et al*, 1986), but in part also because the development of good practice in adoption enabled an increasingly wide range of children to be successfully placed in adoptive families (Simmonds, this volume).

Although already well-established in the UK by the late 1980s, the profile of adoption from care received a significant boost in the build up through the 1990s to the Adoption and Children Act 2002 (England and Wales). As preparation for the new legislation highlighted the benefits of adoption, a system of performance indicators also encouraged local authorities to consider adoption for a wider range of children (*Quality Protects*, Department of Health (DH), 1999). Long-term foster care was viewed as a more uncertain placement, and the drive to promote adoption was often accompanied by criticism of a system that otherwise left children "lingering" or "languishing" in care.

Permanence in adoption was defined as 'The security and well-being that comes from being accepted as members of new families' (Performance and Innovation Unit, 2000), capturing that combination of stability, good developmental outcomes and family membership that has remained at the heart of definitions of permanence. Although Government policy did not give the same amount of attention to long-term foster care as a permanence option, the two major policy initiatives affecting care planning since the Adoption and Children Act was passed have appeared to place an equal value on adoption and long-term foster care. *Every Child Matters* (DfES, 2003, p 45) stated that there was a 'need to ensure that different permanence options are equally credible, including long-term fostering'. This position was reinforced by *Care Matters: Time for Change* (DfES, 2007, p 54), which included long-term foster care as one of the permanence options available and went on to say that 'There should be no disincentives attached to any one option or another'.

In spite of these supportive policy statements, the only detailed study that has compared planning for adoption and long-term foster care concluded that 'long-term fostering has become something of a Cinderella option', and commented not only on the lack of resources but also the lack of clarity at that time in definitions and systems:

> There is a need for policy and planning for long-term fostering to be sharpened up – with clear answers as to what it is and positive reasons for its use.
> (Lowe and Murch *et al*, 2002, p 149)

What is long-term foster care?

The lack of clarity about what "long-term foster care" is perhaps has something to do with its long and varied history. Long-term foster care has been a type of fostering placement for centuries (George, 1970; Rowe *et al*, 1984). But the meaning of long-term foster care has varied in accordance with other policies and values, in particular, the extent to which it was seen as a fresh start that excluded the birth family (as it tended to be in the 19th century) or was seen to a greater or lesser extent as working alongside the birth family, as it became during the latter part of the 20th century.

The emphasis in the Children Act 1989 (England and Wales) on partnership with parents, on the importance of the birth family and on contact with birth families (Cleaver, 2000; Schofield and Stevenson, this volume) stands in contrast to the characteristics of permanence through adoption as reflected in the Adoption and Children Act 2002.* Two very different options therefore developed simultaneously in family placement policy and practice – adoption, which was possible in opposition to the wishes of birth parents and where contact was more likely to be limited and indirect, and long-term foster care, which was not treated separately from other types of short-term or task-centred foster care in terms of retaining and prioritising birth family ties. Remarkably little was said in legislation or guidance about the expectations of the role of long-term foster care or the nature of relationships in long-term foster placements. So it has been left unclear, in spite of the policy endorsements mentioned above, as to whether long-term foster care was actually to be promoted as offering permanence. The introduction of special guardianship in the Adoption and Children Act 2002 brought another addition to the range of permanence options, but has tended to push long-term foster care further down the hierarchy of permanence options and may, in some areas, have diverted attention away from clarifying and valuing the role of long-term foster care (Schofield and Ward et al, 2008a) – as Lowe and Murch et al (2002, p 148), with remarkable prescience, predicted that it might.

This lack of clarity about permanence in foster care led to some tensions developing in the 1980s and 1990s in social work practice and in the courts as to what should happen when a care plan for adoption was either not appropriate or not possible and long-term foster care became the only available alternative. Even with active policies to keep children with their birth families, with increasing rates of adoption in the late 1990s and with the development of kinship care, there were still going to be a significant number of children who would be spending a considerable part of their childhood in foster care. As of March 2007 (Department for Children, Schools and Families (DCSF), 2008), as many as 22,400 children in care under the age of 16 (just under one third of the total in care) had been looked after for two-and-a-half years or more, of whom at least two-thirds would be in foster care. But remaining in foster care for a particular length of time is not necessarily an indicator of a defined permanence plan or placement. Given the fact that permanence plans are required at the four month review for all looked after children, the question of care planning for permanence in foster care needs to be explored.

---

* There are similar requirements in law in relation to birth parents and contact in all four countries in the UK. This chapter refers to the law in England and Wales, as this is where most of the research quoted was undertaken, but the policy and practice issues that emerge are very similar throughout.

How do local authorities plan for long-term foster care?

In the absence of official government guidance on what long-term foster is and does, the definition and use of long-term foster care as a permanence option has been shown to vary greatly between local authorities. This has an impact on how permanence is thought about and care plans are developed. Schofield *et al* (2007), in their study of pathways through care in 24 local authorities, found that long-term foster care could mean until 16, until 18, being part of the family into adulthood or a family for life. There was, in particular, a lack of clarity about the expected role of the foster family in the late teenage years and especially after a young person has moved into "independence" at whatever age, a problem also identified by Sinclair *et al* (2005).

In a subsequent and more specific study of planning for permanence in foster care in England and Wales (Schofield and Ward *et al*, 2008a), it was found that not only did definitions of long-term foster care vary across the 93 local authorities which provided information, but that some had developed another classification of foster care called "permanent foster care". Definitions and terminology did not go together in any predictable way, with, for example, different local authorities defining the same terms in different ways but also defining different terms in similar ways e.g. permanent *or* long-term foster care as 'being part of the family through to adulthood'. In addition, local authorities with different terminology and systems were using different procedures and taking the decisions about these placements, especially the making of the match between child and carer, to different panels. Again, the routes are not predictably linked with terminology, with some local authorities taking long-term foster care cases to an adoption and permanence panel, while others were taking permanent foster care placements to a fostering panel.

As well as a range of differences in terminology, definitions and routes, Schofield and Ward *et al* (2008) found that there were some specific models for care planning. The majority (61%) of local authorities had a single route called long-term foster care *or* permanent foster care. But the remainder, a significant number of authorities (39%), had dual systems of permanent *and* long-term foster care. Where there were dual systems, definitions of *permanent* foster care were more likely to include firm commitments to the child remaining in the foster family beyond 18, with long-term foster care being more likely to mean "until independence". But the majority of single route systems also defined long-term foster care as "into adult life" and these local authorities referred to it emphatically as permanence.

According to managers and practitioners, each system has different challenges in meeting the needs of children. Single systems have the challenge of providing a route for a wide range of children from six-year-olds, needing a family through to adulthood, to 14-year-olds, for whom the goal, even in a placement defined as long-term or permanent, may be less predictable in terms of the young person accepting membership of a new family. Dual systems with long-term *and* permanent foster carer options have the rather different challenge of determining *which* children need a permanent foster family, generally defined as more of a commitment through to adulthood, and which children (more commonly teenagers) will be taken down the long-term route, where some doubt arises as to whether the placement is to be promoted and thought of as permanent.

However, undoubtedly some children in long-term foster care in single system authorities would have the same characteristics and expectations for placement as children in permanent foster care placements in dual authorities. In all systems and all authorities, the age of the child, the relative role of the birth family and the foster family in the mind and life of the child, and the expected length of the placement into adulthood would affect the choice of plan and placement. Such factors are discussed in the rest of the chapter. Although recognising that terminology remains a fiercely contested issue, for the sake of clarity the term "long-term foster care" is used here to mean a plan for permanence and therefore includes those placements described as "permanent foster care" in some authorities.

Why are some children in long-term foster care rather than adoption?

Since this is a key decision for many children, it is important to address it here. There are a range of factors that make it more likely that children will have foster care rather than adoption as the permanence plan (Thoburn, 1991; Schofield *et al*, 2000; Lowe and Murch *et al*, 2002; Selwyn *et al*, 2006; Schofield and Ward *et al*, 2008). Significant factors that might lead to a care plan for long-term foster care are age, history of abuse and current emotional and behavioural difficulties. These factors operate separately and in combination, so that a child from a background of neglect or abuse may be more likely to have significant behavioural problems if they come into care at five rather than two years of age and so have been exposed to that type of environment for longer – though even this kind of formula will not apply in a predictable way, since the impact of abusive or neglectful parenting will vary greatly between children, depending on a range of risk and protective characteristics (see Howe, this volume). These factors of age and background will be important, not only in determining the care plan for long-term foster care, but also in making the match with carers who can meet their specific needs (Schofield and Beek, 2008).

The nature of the child's birth family relationships is also extremely important in planning for adoption or long-term foster care. It may be decided that young children are to be placed with older siblings and that this is more likely to be suited to, or possible in, a fostering placement. Often the child's relationship with birth parents is seen as so significant that it will affect the child's capacity to form a new attachment or to commit themselves to a new family. There are some assessment difficulties here, especially where existing relationships with birth parents are described as too "strong" for a child to be adopted or to commit to a planned long-term foster family (Schofield and Beek, 2008).

Often these relationships with birth parents may be "strong", but are actually profoundly insecure, preoccupied or based on fear. There are risks in either prioritising this relationship or concluding that the child will never form another attachment because of it. Whether in adoption or foster care, new and more secure experiences of parenting and attachment will be important for that child's healthy development and progress (Schofield and Beek, 2006).

The child's need for contact with birth family members will form part of the assessment, not only in relation to choosing a long-term fostering plan rather than adoption, but also in determining the appropriate level of contact once the child is in placement. Beek and Schofield (2004a) found that contact arrangements in long-term foster care varied from staying contact every week-end, by agreement between the birth parent and the foster family, to supervised contact twice a year, where there were significant concerns about distress to the children and disruption of the placement by the birth mother. In some exceptional cases, there was no contact with birth parents. Schofield and Beek (2004b) suggest that contact in long-term foster care, as in all placements, needs to be determined by the developmental benefit for the child. There is no psychological reason why children need or should have more contact in foster care than in adoption – although different expectations of adoptive parents and foster carers are a factor to consider. It is important not to assume that, where foster care is the choice of permanent placement, contact should necessarily be any more than in adoption or that, when a foster placement becomes confirmed as permanent, contact should automatically reduce. It is the characteristics and developmental needs of the child and the quality of their relationships in both birth and permanent families that should determine the plan for contact – not legal status or type of placement (Schofield and Stevenson, this volume).

Other important factors relating to the likelihood of a long-term fostering care plan for the child will be ethnicity and culture, which may affect plans in a number of ways. For example, it may be that both birth and substitute families are from a particular ethnic or cultural group who oppose adoption for religious or cultural reasons and so a long-term fostering plan is a positive choice for all parties. Or it may be that difficulties in waiting for a match in adoption cause so much delay and uncertainty that a parallel plan develops for the child to be placed with the first available matching family, which may be a long-term foster family (Selwyn, this volume).

A child's legal status will have some part to play in the adoption or long-term foster care decision. For children who are in care but accommodated on a voluntary basis under section 20 Children Act 1989, birth parents retain full parental responsibility. These children will be placed for long-term foster care rather than adoption, unless birth parents are willing to consent to adoption or the local authority is prepared to take the case back to court for a Care Order (s31 Children Act, 1989) and a Placement Order (s21 and s22 Adoption and Children Act, 2002). In most local authorities a child's accommodated status is no barrier to being formally matched in a long-term foster care placement and social workers would work as far as possible in partnership with birth parents (Schofield and Ward, 2008a). But some authorities, which have a separate system for permanent foster care, are reluctant to use this option for accommodated children, because they anticipate being able to delegate more powers to permanent foster carers than may be possible where birth parents retain full parental responsibility.

One of the most contentious issues in permanence planning is the significance to be given to the fact that a child's existing foster placement may have been stable for some significant length of time, may have lasted through a significant developmental period (e.g. birth to 18 months) and/or may offer continuity of attachment security with the carers. In such circumstances, practitioners and courts struggle with the question of whether this placement should be considered as suitable to become an adoption, special guardianship or long-term foster care placement. Furthermore, if this placement or the legal status on offer in the placement is not seen as in the child's best interests, consideration has to be given to the risk to the child's development of a move in order to achieve a placement that better meets the child's needs in the longer term.

This complex issue is discussed in more detail elsewhere (Schofield and Beek, 2006; Schofield and Beek, 2008), but even the closest examination of social work and developmental research will never provide a simple formula answer. On the one hand, children will grieve and feel a profound sense of loss when leaving familiar family homes where they have felt loved and safe, perhaps for the first time. It is simply not the case that securely attached children move easily because they are secure, nor can secure attachment be "transferred" to new caregivers – it has to be earned in the context of sensitive caregiving. On the other hand, if they have been well-prepared, children do successfully move from stable loving foster placements to new loving adoptive or long-term or permanent foster care placements. There will, of course, be an emotional cost to the child that can only be successfully managed by the foster carer, the social worker and the new adoptive/long-term foster parents working together and supporting each other and the child.

The key is to have long-term goals, but also short-, medium- and long-term strategies to increase the likely benefits of staying or moving for the child. If the child remains in foster care, it may be necessary to ensure that the permanence plan is recognised and respected. If the child is moved to an adoptive family, it may be necessary to manage some ongoing contact with former carers and birth family members. In the early days, continuity with significant figures from the past, who are able to reassure the child that they are well, still thinking about the child and positive about the new placement, are likely to reduce anxiety and promote acceptance of the new family. However, the contact plan will depend very much on the previous new carers and their support for the placement as well as the characteristics of the permanent carers.

Running alongside these different factors that influence the choice of a long-term foster care plan are the wishes and feelings of the child (Schofield, 2005; Thomas, this volume). Sinclair *et al* (2007) have stressed the importance of the child's views; for example, a child's acceptance of being in care influences a number of placement outcomes, including behaviour and school performance. But as Sinclair *et al* also point out, children's views will evolve. As they settle more in placement and at school, they may become reconciled to being in care, which in turn can feed back into closer relationships and further improved behaviour and performance. The message here is twofold. It is important to listen to children when planning long-term placements – but it is also important to review this over time. Children who did not want the commitment of a permanence plan in their foster family at a certain age and stage may later wish to have that commitment. Children who initially rejected adoption by their long-term foster family may wish to review that later – even at the point when they are thinking about leaving care in their late teens. How often does the leaving care team raise the possibility of adoption by the carers? Too often assessments become fixed, so that what was said about and by the child when the child was six is still reverberating without adequate reflection and review 5–10 years later.

Finally, it is important to bear in mind that for many children a long-term foster care plan may be arrived at after a reunification or kinship care plan has been unsuccessful, an adoption plan has been unsuccessful, or a short-term placement is changed into a long-term placement. Unfortunately, such routes to permanence in foster care have led to long-term foster care being talked of disparagingly, even by social workers, as placement "by default" or as "drift". This is illogical – nobody talks of adoption as being by default because reunification was tried first. Most local authorities in fact now have systems in place to ensure that whatever long-term/permanent foster care route is taken, specific assessment and matching occurs before a child's foster placement is confirmed as long-term/permanent (Schofield *et al*, 2008a). This is not to say that these procedures would not benefit from greater clarity and consistency – but it is clear that if social workers wish children, foster carers, birth parents and the general public to respect foster care as a positive permanence choice, they need to be positive about it themselves. This means considering the evidence about whether long-term foster care works and how it can be made to work more effectively for more of the children for whom this is their only and best chance of a family for life.

Does long-term foster care work as a permanence option?

Most recent research and research reviews (Triseliotis, 2002; Schofield, 2003; Beek and Schofield, 2004a; Sellick *et al*, 2004; Wilson *et al*, 2004; Schofield and Beek, 2005a, b; Sinclair, 2005; Sinclair *et al*, 2007) conclude that foster families *can* transform the lives of troubled children and provide a secure and lasting family life. However, research also shows that too many long-stay foster children are at risk of placement moves, may experience care that does not meet their complex needs and may not have the support they need from a family as they move into adult life. Factors in the child, the foster family, the birth family, the social work planning and support, and the quality of input from health and education will interact to affect the outcomes for the child. Research can help us identify which factors make a difference across samples, but the interaction of factors in each child's case will be a matter for professional assessment and judgement.

There have been few specific studies of planned long-term foster care. The largest study of planned permanent placements in the UK, using a sample of 1,100 placements made by voluntary agencies, compared outcomes in long-term foster care and adoption (Thoburn, 1991). Their conclusion was that if age was held constant, long-term foster care had a similar success rate in terms of placement stability – around 75 per cent – as adoption. This has rightly been an influential finding, but it is important to bear in mind that the long-term foster placements in this study were planned and supported as permanent placements. This is not so much a positive finding regarding long-term foster care, as a positive finding regarding *explicitly planned and supported* long-term foster care.

Nevertheless, what this study showed is that it is possible for a foster family to provide loving care, commitment and stability for a child within the care system and without legal parental responsibility (see also Thoburn *et al*, 2000). This finding has been reinforced by the work of Schofield and Beek. A study by Schofield (2002, 2003) of young adults (18–30) who grew up in foster care found that children placed as young as 18 months and as old as 15 years could become full members of their foster families and find security, as well as later establishing themselves in settled and successful adult lives. As adults they were clear about the benefits.

> *The first time I met them, David, my foster dad, sat and talked to me as if I was somebody. They were just brilliant, they turned me right round. If it hadn't have been for them I wouldn't have passed any exams, I wouldn't have been able to read and write. Without them I wouldn't have the life I have now.* (Melanie, placed at 15, now age 25, Schofield, 2003, p 156)

Not all of this adult sample had successful placements or found a family for life, and this had led, for a minority, to downward spirals that led to prison or psychiatric care – although one young man, with the help of his former social worker, went on to university after leaving prison.

This perhaps not surprisingly mixed picture from a retrospective study has been reinforced by a prospective study. Schofield and Beek's longitudinal study of planned long-term foster care placements (Schofield *et al*, 2000; Beek and Schofield, 2004a; Schofield and Beek, in press) found that 75 per cent of the 52 placements lasted at least three years and that some of those placements that ended were replaced by further long-term placements that worked well for children and young people. At Phase 3 (8–9 years later) 30 of the 52 young people (57%) were stable in their original placement from 1997–8 or had moved to independence in a relatively planned way. A further 10 (19%) were stable and thriving in more successful placements they had moved to either between Phase 1 and 2 or since Phase 2 – or had moved in a planned way to independence. This yielded 40 (76%) who were stable and functioning reasonably well (e.g. in peer networks, in mainstream school or college, in employment), although difficulties in managing transitions from school to work were apparent for a number of young people with learning difficulties. The significance of the adolescent years for difficult times and placement breakdown is well-documented (Berridge and Cleaver, 1987; Farmer et al, 2004; Biehal, this volume). But what was striking also is the potential for positive change in adolescence. At a point when too often it is assumed that young people no longer need or would accept a foster family, some young people were benefiting from quite exceptional experiences of parenting and family life.

Selwyn et al (2006) conducted a study of a cohort of children who had a plan for adoption, some of whom were ultimately placed in planned long-term foster care. The fostered sub-sample included some children who had been placed for adoption or had been adopted, but this had broken down. In this context just over half (54%) of subsequent long-term foster placements had lasted. Some very important themes emerged from long-term foster carers in this study. In particular, foster carers felt that they had been entrusted with the care and responsibility for children as part of their family through to adulthood, but had not received the corresponding rights to make a range of simple parenting decisions, such as going on school trips, or to contribute to a range of very important decisions, such as the frequency and nature of birth family contact. Carers were committed but felt vulnerable to social work decisions about the placement.

The large study by Sinclair, Wilson and colleagues of a complete range of foster placements raised some concerns about placement stability, reporting that, after a three-year period, 24 per cent of sample children were still in the same placement, with a further four per cent adopted by the same carer (Sinclair et al, 2005). This study did not report on care plans and did not distinguish between planned long-term foster placements and more short-term, task-centred placements. However, although some of these moves may have been appropriate and planned, the level of movement certainly raises legitimate concerns.

This study, like other studies mentioned here, did find evidence of some highly committed and skilled foster carers (Wilson et al, 2003). It also found evidence of many children who said that they wanted to stay longer in their placements, particularly up to and beyond the age of 18, raising very important issues about how expectations for post-18 family membership are handled and the role of leaving care teams in promoting continuity in family life.

Sinclair (2005, p 32) has outlined a very helpful model of permanence, based on their large foster care study (Sinclair et al, 2005). This model has four dimensions:

- *Objective permanence* occurred if children had a placement, which would last for their childhood, would provide back-up and, if needed, accommodation after the age of 18.
- *Subjective permanence* occurred if the child felt he or she belonged in the family.
- *Enacted permanence* occurred if all concerned behaved as if the child was a family member (e.g. the child was included in family occasions).
- *Uncontested permanence* occurred if the child did not feel a clash of loyalties between foster and birth family.

It is an essential that in any policy for care planning, the concept of permanence in foster care is looked at in this way on a number of different dimensions and from the point of view of a number of different parties Each of these four permanence dimensions would require a different kind of assessment, planning and practice when matching children and carers, supporting a placement or identifying when there are problems and finding solutions. But at the heart of the fit between foster care and permanence, Ian Sinclair (2005, p 123) has argued, we need:

> . . . the development of a form of foster care that more nearly approaches a "family for life", which is not seen as "second best" and in which carers can act as parents.

What are the motivations and roles of long-term foster carers?

The question of whether long-term foster carers are or can act as parents and whether therefore they differ from short-term carers is important. Foster carers who foster children long-term may have set out with this aim from the outset or have come to that role because of their relationship with a particular child placed short-term with them or because they decided at some point in a short-term fostering career that they would like to make a longer-term commitment to children. This move to long-term foster care can sometimes happen when carers start to feel that the coming and going of children in short-term or task-centred care is too upsetting for them or their children, or is just too disruptive to family life (Schofield *et al*, 2000; Sellick *et al*, 2004; Schofield and Ward *et al*, 2008a). Although figures will vary between local authorities, it seems likely that at least half of long-term carers will have been assessed and matched with a child already in their care (Schofield *et al*, 2000; Schofield and Ward *et al*, 2008a).

Policy on recruitment, assessment and preparation of long-term or permanent foster carers reflects these varied pathways. Some local authorities and independent fostering providers recruit foster carers with a view to becoming long-term or permanent foster carers for their first placement, while others (the majority) focus on short-term recruitment, but work with carers who may express an interest in long-term foster care after they have gained experience of short-term care.

This issue divides opinion, with some fostering agencies (both local authority and independent fostering providers) suggesting that it would be impossible to place children long-term with inexperienced foster carers, while others suggest that there are foster carers who know from the outset that they only want to foster long-term and do not wish to "practise"; such agencies often make the comparison with adoption and suggest that new carers *can* foster long-term but need specific preparation and support to do so (Schofield and Ward *et al*, 2008). This debate highlights the similarities and differences between adoption and long-term foster care, with some important questions being raised about whether, although long-term foster carers and adopters may share the same commitment to parent difficult children as part of their family, foster carers need to have very different expectations in terms of an ongoing relationship with the local authority as corporate parent and with birth parents who retain parental responsibility in law.

Research suggests that long-term foster carers have similar motivations in essence as other foster carers in terms of their wish to provide a home for a child from a difficult background in need of a family (Schofield *et al*, 2000; Sellick *et al*, 2004). But for long-term carers, both the longer-term nature of the commitment and the importance of the child becoming part of the family mean that family structures as well as parenting skills through to adulthood may influence the decision. Schofield *et al* (2000) found that long-term foster carers fell into different categories in terms of family structure. There were families who had already parented birth, fostered or adopted children through to adulthood, for whom long-term foster children would create a second family. For some childless couples, long-term fostering a child or sibling group was a way of building a new family. Other families chose to extend their existing young family through fostering. Across these groups there were carers who also saw long-term fostering as an alternative professional career and/or as a career that would allow them to work flexibly and from home.

All foster carers, but especially those who foster long-term, have to manage the task of sharing the parenting role with social workers, on behalf of the local authority, and (to some degree) with birth parents (Beek and Schofield, 2004a; Schofield and Beek, 2008). Carers have day-to-day responsibilities delegated to them by local authorities, who remain the corporate parents. Although there can be tensions in sharing the parenting responsibilities with local authorities, there can also be opportunities and advantages, as many foster carers value the fact that local authorities will offer support, advocate on behalf of the child for education or health resources, and manage any difficulties that may arise for the child in relation to the birth family. Many foster carers also develop positive relationships with birth parents or other birth relatives, such as grandparents, and are able to use these relationships to help the child feel more comfortable with their membership of two families.

However, where there is uncertainty over who is going to make decisions over matters such as having haircuts, school trips and staying over with friends, both carers and children find this difficult and unsettling. Young people have reported that for them it is experiences like this that make them feel not part of a "normal" family (Timms and Thoburn, 2003) and foster carers report that they feel undermined in their necessary role as parents (Schofield and Ward *et al*, 2008). Good practice suggests that at each stage from the point that care plans are developed, to the preparation of placement agreements when placements are first made, to each stage that placements are reviewed, it is important to consider the appropriate degree of delegated parenting responsibility to foster carers, so that daily decisions can be made in the child's best interests as promptly as possible.

What kind of parenting do children need in long-term foster care?

My mum's helped me a lot because she was determined for me to do well. That's a really important thing, people, other people, believing that you can do well.

It was my home, whereas before it was just somewhere I was staying.

It just feels like a normal family now. I don't really look at them as anything different than a mum and dad really. They treat me the same as their normal family, take me on holiday, go shopping.

Most children who are in a planned long-term placement will need parenting that addresses the fact that they are likely to have experienced some combination of abuse and neglect, separation and loss. But they also need someone who believes in their capacity to do well and to promote their achievements, as these comments from teenagers in the *Growing Up in Foster Care* study (Schofield and Beek, in press) suggest. In addition, they need to feel that this is their home, a normal family where ordinary things happen like going shopping or going on holiday together – rather than a "placement". Because children's development, sense of self and trust in family life will have been impaired by negative experiences in the past, achieving ordinary family life will be a challenge (Wilson *et al*, 2003; Schofield and Beek, 2006).

Parenting for most long-term foster children will therefore need to be to some degree *therapeutic*. Children need to be helped to find ways of managing and moving on from the past while building strengths for the future. Attachment theory would suggest that exposure to warm, consistent and reliable caregiving can change children's previous expectations both of close adults and of themselves and there is ample evidence from research and practice to support this (Downes, 1992; Schofield, 2003; Wilson *et al*, 2003; Cairns, 2004; Beek and Schofield, 2004a; Schofield and Beek, 2005a).

The active intervention of foster carers, therefore, is of central importance. They need to parent in ways that demonstrate, implicitly and explicitly to the child, that they are trustworthy and reliable, physically and emotionally available and sensitive to the child's needs. In addition, they must be mindful of the protective strategies that the child has learned in order to feel safe in the past and adjust their approaches so that their parenting feels comfortable and acceptable to the child rather than undermining or threatening. In these circumstances, children can slowly begin to mentally represent their new caregivers as protective and available and themselves as loved and lovable. The ensuing relationships will provide a secure base, from which children can develop and be supported to explore and maximise their potential.

From their research on long-term foster care and from a broader base of research in developmental psychology, Schofield and Beek (2006) have developed a model of parenting based on the attachment concept of "providing a secure base", which has been recommended in *Care Matters* (DCSF, 2007) and is being incorporated in the revised Skills to Foster training programme (The Fostering Network, in press). The model draws on the dimensions of parenting found by Ainsworth *et al* (1971) to be associated with developing a secure attachment in infancy, but promotes parenting designed to make children of all ages more confident, competent and resilient *and* to address the need for the child to feel part of the foster and birth family. Although the model focuses on the development of the child's sense of self and relationships, it fits comfortably alongside other essential aspects of parenting such as promoting physical health and educational achievement.

There are five related dimensions of caregiving, each with an associated developmental benefit for the child.

- **Availability – helping children to trust**
  This dimension focuses on the carer's ability to convey a strong sense of being physically and emotionally available to meet the child's needs, both when the carer and child are together and when they are apart. From this, the child begins to trust that he is safe and that his needs will be met warmly, consistently and reliably. Anxiety is reduced and he gains the confidence to explore the world, safe in the knowledge that care and protection will be available in times of need.

- **Sensitivity – helping children to manage feelings and behaviour**
  Responding sensitively refers to the carer's capacity to "stand in the shoes" of the child, to think flexibly about what the child may be thinking and feeling and to reflect this back to the child. The reflective, "mind-minded" carer also thinks about their own feelings and shares them sensitively with the child. The child thus learns to think about his own ideas and feelings and the thoughts and feelings of others and is helped to reflect on, organise and manage his own feelings and behaviour.

- **Acceptance – building children's self-esteem**
  This dimension defines the extent to which the carer is able to convey that the child is unconditionally accepted and valued for who he is, for his difficulties as well as his strengths. This forms the foundation of positive self-esteem, so that the child can experience himself as worthy of receiving love, help and support and (when linked to self-efficacy) also as robust and able to deal with setbacks and adversity.

- **Co-operation – helping children to feel effective**
  Within this dimension, the carer thinks about the child as an autonomous individual whose wishes, feelings and goals are valid and meaningful and who needs to feel effective. The carer therefore looks for ways of promoting autonomy, but also working together and achieving co-operation with the child wherever possible. This helps the child to feel more effective and competent, to feel confident in turning to others for help, if necessary, and to be able to compromise and co-operate.

- **Family membership – helping children to belong**
  This dimension refers to the capacity of the carer to include the child, socially and personally as a full family member, at a level that is appropriate to the longer-term

Figure 1
Secure Base Star

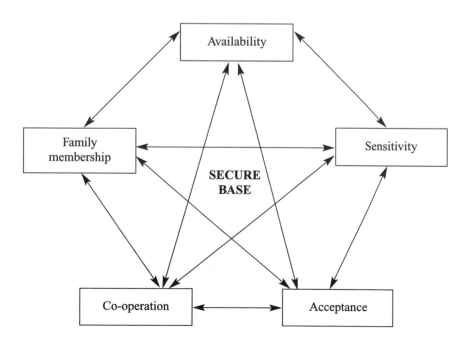

plan for the child. At the same time, the carer is able to help the child to establish an appropriate sense of connectedness and belonging to his birth family. In this way, the child can develop a comfortable sense of belonging to two families.

Each of these parenting dimensions in the Secure Base Star (Figure 1) interacts with and reinforces each other, with self-esteem, for example, underpinning effectiveness, and trust contributing to family membership.

This model can be used for assessing and matching children's needs and parenting in long-term foster care, but it can also be used by social workers to help foster carers to focus their attention on positively promoting the different aspects of the child's current and future developmental well-being, rather than finding themselves focusing only on short-term problem solving.

The social work role in long-term foster care

In long-term foster care, the social work role with children, foster carers, birth families or other agencies such as health and education, is to support the core principles of permanence in terms of promoting well-being and achieving family membership that has the potential to last into adult life (Schofield and Beek, 2008). In summary, there are a number of key tasks that social workers need to undertake.

Work with children
- Work with the child initially for assessment, planning and matching – including establishing their wishes and feelings.
- Life story work, to launch what will be a life-long process of managing their history and their dual family memberships.
- Regular visits through childhood to build and sustain a relationship with the child, which offers support and promotes the child's well-being.
- Work with the child in relation to participating in the six-monthly LAC review process.
- Planning and reviewing contact arrangements to ensure that they promote the child's development, including family membership in the birth and foster family.
- Ensuring that leaving care procedures are sensitively applied to take into account the long-term plan and the aim of continuity and interdependence as well as "independence".

Work with foster carers
- Recruitment, assessment, preparation and approval of foster carers who have the commitment, resilience, qualities and skills to offer a permanent home to a child or young person.

- Matching and placement – helping foster carers to welcome children and enable them gradually to thrive as a member of their family.
- Placement agreements – clarifying the range of parenting decisions and the extent to which these will be delegated to foster carers.
- Promoting the carers' capacity to provide therapeutic care, a secure base which actively promotes well-being and resilience.
- Helping carers to promote the child's membership of their birth family, not only through appropriate levels of contact, but through realistic appraisal and open communication (Brodzinsky, 2005; Young and Neil, this volume).

Work with birth families
- Ensuring that birth parents are involved when child care plans are first being made for permanence in foster care and if revised.
- Ensuring that plans for birth family contact (including with siblings) are carefully thought through to maximise benefit for the child, but also being realistic about what is possible and rewarding for birth relatives and the kind of support they need.
- Involving birth parents in placement agreement meetings that set out clear guidelines regarding their role in parental decision making, from hair cuts to choice of school.
- Keeping parents and other significant family members (e.g. grandparents) informed about the child's progress and involving them in appropriate ways in the LAC review process.

Work with other agencies
- Ensuring that other agencies, especially education and health, are aware that the foster family has a special status as a long-term/permanent placement, which does not change the legal status of the child or the carers but will have implications for the increased parental role of foster carers.
- Managing involvement by other agencies in LAC reviews to take into account the status of the child and the foster family e.g. not all foster children want their head teacher in their living room or meeting their birth parents.
- Engaging other agencies in actively promoting the child's development and well-being for the longer term.

Conclusion

For many children, foster care will be their best if not their only chance to achieve the stability, security, well-being and family membership through to adulthood that is the goal of permanence. The debate must therefore move on from asking *whether* long-term foster care *is* a positive permanence option to *ensuring* that it *becomes* a positive permanence option. We have no choice. If we do not work to this end, we will do a great disservice to the children and foster families who currently too often struggle with inadequate recognition and support, during childhood and at the point of transition to adulthood. There are no easy answers or perfect solutions, but increased activity in local authorities in recent years to build structures that support permanence planning and practice in foster care suggests that perhaps there is now some momentum to provide children and families with the services they need and deserve.

Selected further reading

Beek M. and Schofield G. (2004) *Providing a Secure Base in Long-Term Foster Care*, London: BAAF

Schofield G. and Beek M. (2006) *Handbook of Attachment for Foster Care and Adoption*, London: BAAF

Schofield G. and Beek M. (2008) *Achieving Permanence in Foster Care – A Good Practice Guide*, London: BAAF

Schofield G. and Ward E. with Warman A., Simmonds J. and Butler J. (2008) *Permanence in Foster Care: A study of care planning in England and Wales*, London: BAAF

Sinclair I., Baker C. and Wilson K. (2005) *Foster Children: Where they go and how they get on*, London: Jessica Kingsley Publishers

References

Ainsworth M. D. S., Bell S. and Stayton D. (1971) 'Individual differences in strange-situation behavior of one-year-olds', in Schaffer H. (ed.) *The Origins of Human Social Relations*, New York: Academic Press, pp 17–52

Beek M. and Schofield G. (2004a) *Providing a Secure Base in Long-Term Foster Care*, London: BAAF

Beek M. and Schofield G. (2004b) 'Promoting security and managing risk: Contact in long-term foster care', in Neil E. and Howe D. (eds) *Contact in Adoption and Permanent Foster Care: Research, theory and practice*, London: BAAF

Berridge D. and Cleaver H. (1987) *Foster Home Breakdown*, Oxford: Basil Blackwell

Brodzinsky D. (2005) 'Reconceptualizing openness in adoption: Implications for theory, research and practice', in Brodzinsky D. and Palacios J. (eds) *Psychological Issues in Adoption: Research and practice* (pp 145–166). New York: Greenwood

Cairns B (2004) *Fostering Attachments*, London: BAAF

Cleaver H. (2000) *Fostering Family Contact*, London: The Stationery Office

Department for Children, Schools and Families (2007) *Care Matters: Time for change*, London: The Stationery Office

Department for Children, Schools and Families (2008) *Children Looked After by Local Authorities, Year ending 31 March 2007*, London: The Stationery Office

Department for Education and Skills (2003) *Every Child Matters*, London: The Stationery Office

Department of Health (1999) *Quality Protects: The Government's objectives for children's social services*, London: The Stationery Office

Downes C. (1992) *Separation Revisited: Adolescents in foster family care*, Aldershot: Ashgate

Farmer E., Moyers S. and Lipscombe J. (2004) *Fostering Adolescents*, London: Jessica Kingsley Publishers

The Fostering Network (in press) *Skills to Foster*, London: The Fostering Network

George V. (1970) *Foster Care: Theory and practice*, London: Routledge and Kegan Paul

Lowe N., Murch M., Bader K., Borkowski M., Copner R., Lisles C. and Shearman J. (2002) *The Plan for the Child: Adoption or long-term fostering*, London: BAAF

Maluccio A. N., Fein E. and Olmstead K. A. (1986) *Permanency Planning for Children: Concepts and methods*, London: Batsford

Performance and Innovation Unit (PIU) (2000) *The Prime Minister's Review of Adoption*, London: Cabinet Office

Rowe J., Cain H., Hundleby M. and Keane A. (1984) *Long-term Foster Care*, London: Batsford

Rowe J. and Lambert L. (1973) *Children Who Wait: A study of children needing substitute families*, London: ABAA

Schofield G. (2002) 'The significance of a secure base: A psychosocial model of long-term foster care', *Child and Family Social Work*, 7:4, pp 259–272

Schofield G. (2003) *Part of the Family: Pathways through foster care*, London: BAAF

Schofield G. (2005) 'The voice of the child in family placement decision making: A developmental model', *Adoption & Fostering*, 19:1, pp 29–44

Schofield G. and Beek M. (2005a) 'Providing a secure base: Parenting children in long-term foster family care', *Attachment and Human Development*, 7:1, pp 3–26

Schofield G. and Beek M. (2005b) 'Risk and resilience in long-term foster care', *British Journal of Social Work*, 35:8, pp 1283–1301

Schofield G. and Beek M. (2006) *Attachment Handbook for Foster Care and Adoption*, London: BAAF

Schofield G. and Beek M. (2008) *Achieving Permanence in Foster Care: A Good Practice Guide*, London: BAAF

Schofield G. and Beek M. (in press) 'Growing up in foster care: Providing a secure base through adolescence', *Child and Family Social Work*.

Schofield G., Beek M., Sargent K. and Thoburn J. (2000) *Growing up in Foster Care*, London: BAAF

Schofield G., Thoburn J., Howell D. and Dickens J. (2007) 'The search for stability and permanence: Modelling the pathways of long-stay looked after children', *British Journal of Social Work*, 37, pp 1–24

Schofield G. and Ward E., with Warman A., Simmonds J. and Butler J. (2008) *Permanence in Foster Care: A study of care planning in England and Wales*, London: BAAF

Sellick C., Thoburn J. and Philpot T. (2004) *What Works in Adoption and Foster Care?* London: Barnardo's/BAAF

Selwyn J., Sturgess W., Quinton D. and Baxter C. (2006) *Cost and Outcomes of Non-infant Adoptions*, London: BAAF

Sinclair I. (2005) *Fostering Now: Messages from research*, London: Jessica Kingsley Publishers

Sinclair I., Baker C., Lee J. and Gibbs I. (2007) *The Pursuit of Permanence*, London: Jessica Kingsley Publishers

Sinclair I., Baker C., Wilson K. and Gibbs I. (2005) *Foster Children: Where they go and how they get on*, London, Jessica Kingsley Publishers

Thoburn J. (1991) 'Survey findings and conclusions', in Fratter J., Rowe J., Sapsford D. and Thoburn J. *Permanent Family Placement: A decade of experience*, London: BAAF

Thoburn, J., Murdoch, A. and O'Brien, A. (1986) *Permanence in Child Care*, Oxford: Basil Blackwell

Thoburn J., Norford L. and Rashid P. S. (2000) *Permanent Family Placement for Children of Minority Ethnic Origin*, London: Jessica Kingsley Publishers

Timms J. and Thoburn J. (2003) *Your Shout! A survey of the views of 706 children and young people in care*, London: NSPCC

Triseliotis J. (2002) 'Long-term fostering or adoption: The evidence examined', *Child and Family Social Work*, 7:1, pp 23–34

Wilson K., Sinclair I. and Petrie S. (2003) 'A kind of loving: A model of effective foster care', *British Journal of Social Work*, 33, pp 991–1003

Wilson K., Sinclair I., Taylor C., Pithouse A. and Sellick C. (2004) *Fostering Success: An exploration of the research literature on foster care*, London: Social Care Institute for Excellence

9   Foster care for adolescents

Nina Biehal

Older children and adolescents account for a substantial proportion of children in the care system. Forty per cent of all new entrants to care during the course of a year are 10–15 years old and, at any one time, nearly two-thirds of children who are looked after in England are between 10 and 17 years old. The majority of these children and young people live in foster placements. At any one time, nearly three-quarters of looked after 10–15-year-olds and nearly half of 16–17-year-olds are placed in foster care (Department for Children, Schools and Families, 2007). Foster care for adolescents is therefore a key issue for policy and practice in relation to children both in and on the edge of care.

Foster care has always been used for adolescents, both for those who are placed when younger and subsequently grow up in foster care and, at least since the 1950s, for those who enter care during adolescence (Trasler, 1960; Parker, 1966). Today, however, it is likely that the population of looked after adolescents will include a higher proportion with complex needs than in the past, for a variety of reasons.

First, the emphasis on family support in the Children Act 1989, together with the financial pressures on local authorities, has raised the threshold for entry to public care. Those with less serious difficulties, who might previously have entered foster care, may today be supported at home. As a result, a higher proportion of those who do enter foster care are likely to have serious difficulties. Second, the massive decline in the use of residential care since the 1980s has meant that children's homes are mainly used to provide short-term care for a much smaller proportion of the care population (currently only 11 per cent at any point in time). Many young people with challenging behaviour, who in the past might have been cared for in children's homes, are now placed in foster care. Third, the last three decades have seen the development of specialist fostering schemes, which have in many cases been used principally for adolescents with complex needs who might in the past have entered residential care.

Finally, in recent years, social services have begun to look after a new, albeit small, group of adolescents, namely unaccompanied asylum-seeking children, who have often experienced traumatic events prior to their entry to the UK. This group accounts for nearly one-fifth of all 16–18-year-olds who are looked after at any one time and many of them are placed in foster care. Their circumstances are discussed elsewhere in this volume in the chapter by Jim Wade.

Patterns of entry

It is important to distinguish between the different groups of adolescents in foster care. These have recently been conceptualised as:

- **Adolescent graduates**, who enter care when under the age of 11 and remain there through to adolescence.
- **Adolescent entrants**, who enter the care system at the age of 11 or over, though not necessarily for the first time, principally because their relationships with their parents have broken down. A smaller group of abused adolescents are admitted at 11 or over for reasons of abuse or neglect (Sinclair *et al*, 2007).

Adolescent graduates

Since the mid-1990s, the trend has been for younger children to enter care, often for reasons of abuse and neglect, and to remain longer due to the seriousness of their difficulties. Many of this group have quite serious emotional, behavioural and attachment difficulties which may persist into adolescence. The recent Pursuit of Permanence study (Sinclair *et al*, 2007) of 7,399 looked after children found that "adolescent graduates" accounted for over a quarter of all children looked after during the course of a year by 13 English local authorities. They had entered the system as younger children, generally due to abuse or neglect, and often had difficulties at home, at school and with their behaviour.

Adolescent graduates fall into two groups, each with quite different experiences of foster care. Some live in stable, long-term foster placements while others have more unsettled care careers. Over the years, the accumulation of children who become looked after in early or middle childhood means that the system contains a substantial minority of adolescents who have been continuously looked after for many years (although not necessarily in a single placement). National statistics show that, among young people who left care at the age of 16 or over during 2005/6, nearly one-third had been looked after for at least six years and over one-fifth had been looked after for eight years or more. It is possible that growing up in foster care may become more common. Despite the recent policy emphasis on increasing adoption from care and the introduction of the new provision for Special Guardianship (in England and Wales), these provisions are currently used for relatively few children and it remains likely that the majority of children unable to return to their birth families will continue to grow up in foster care.

Adolescent entrants

Other young people may enter care at the age of 11 or over. Some of these young people may be "teenage erupters", who enter care for the first time in their lives while others, with previous experience of care, may re-enter one or more times during adolescence. In the *Fostering Adolescents* (Farmer *et al*, 2004) study of 68 new foster placements, 62 per cent of the young people had entered care for the first time when 11 years old or over. Adolescent entries to care are often re-admissions and this was the case for 61 per cent of the adolescent entrants in the *Fostering Adolescents* study and for half of all children entering at age 11 or over in the *Pursuit of Permanence* study. It is not uncommon for these young people to experience multiple episodes of care during their lives, punctuated by repeated attempts at reunion with their families.

The *Working with Adolescents* study (Biehal, 2005) followed up 209 young people "on the edge of care" who were referred for family support services and found that, during the subsequent six months, a quarter of them had been accommodated. This study found that previous admission to care was the strongest predictor of admission on this occasion, and this has also been a finding of a number of large studies of family support services in the USA. In these circumstances, the experience of previous placement is likely to be an indicator of persistent child and family difficulties. This study found that the likelihood of admission to care was also influenced by the local authority in which the young people lived, as thresholds both for the provision of family support services and for admission to care varied across authorities.

Even where adolescents are experiencing their first admission, they have often been known to social services for a number of years (Millham *et al*, 1986; Rowe *et al*, 1989; Farmer and Parker, 1991; Triseliotis *et al*, 1995; Packman and Hall, 1998; Farmer *et al*, 2004; Biehal, 2005). Several of these studies also noted that adolescent entrants often stay with a number of relatives and friends immediately prior to admission, becoming looked after once these informal arrangements have broken down. In addition, a small number enter care in adolescence following the disruption of an adoption.

Reasons for entry to care during adolescence

The principal reasons for which adolescent entrants become looked after are the break-down of relationships with families, abuse or neglect and the young person's behaviour, but these often overlap. National statistics show that, in England, one-third of those who become looked after between the ages of 10 and 15 years do so due to abuse or neglect (Department for Education and Skills, 2007). The *Pursuit of Permanence* study found that adolescent entrants admitted for reasons of abuse or neglect tended to have more challenging behaviour and were doing much worse at school than adolescents who had entered the system as younger children.

Although abuse is less likely to be the principal reason for admitting children during adolescence than at a younger age, nevertheless, many of those admitted for other reasons have experienced abuse or neglect, either recently or earlier in their lives (Triseliotis *et al*, 1995; Packman and Hall, 1998; Farmer *et al*, 2004; Biehal, 2005). For example, the *From Care to Accommodation* study (Packman and Hall, 1998) found that there were suspicions of abuse and neglect in relation to over half of a sample of 51 newly-accommodated "difficult adolescents". Furthermore, for some of this group, one aim of admission was the protection of the young people from actual or threatened violence that often accompanied (or constituted) the crisis that led to admission.

Older children are particularly likely to display challenging behaviour and, although it is relatively unusual for young people's behaviour to be recorded as the principal reason for entry, research suggests that this is often a precipitating factor (Selwyn *et al*, 2003; Biehal, 2005; Sinclair, 2005; Sinclair *et al*, 2005b). The majority of the "difficult adolescents" in both the *From Care to Accommodation* and the *Working with Adolescents* studies had demonstrated difficult behaviour at home and nearly half were described as aggressive. Behaviour in the community may also cause concern. One-fifth of the young people in the *From Care to Accommodation* study were persistent offenders and many more had had occasional brushes with the law. However, this was a vulnerable group whose behaviour was often harmful to themselves as well as troublesome to others.

In the *Fostering Adolescents* study (Farmer *et al*, 2004), over a third of the young people entering new foster placements did so as the result of a breakdown in relationships with parents and over a quarter had moved due to a breakdown in relationships with their previous foster carers. Among the young people "on the edge of care" at the start of the *Working with Adolescents* study who subsequently became looked after, admission occurred as a result of the breakdown in their relationships with their families. The *Pursuit of Permanence* study also found that adolescent entrants, who had been admitted primarily because their relationships with their families had broken down, frequently displayed challenging behaviour and were often found to be doing badly at school. In all of these studies, the breakdown in relationships was frequently reported to be a consequence of the young people's difficult behaviour. However, this difficult behaviour had, in many cases, emerged in a context of abuse, neglect, rejection, domestic violence or parental mental health difficulties.

Preparation and admission

Researchers have found that the families of adolescent entrants frequently report long histories of difficulty and complain that they have made repeated requests for help, often to no avail, until family relationships reach crisis point and the parent demands accommodation or, less commonly, the young person refuses to remain at home. As a result, researchers have noted a predominance of crisis admissions among placements for teenagers, which typically take place shortly after referral (Fisher *et al*, 1986; Sinclair *et al*, 1995; Packman and Hall, 1998; Farmer *et al*, 2004; Biehal, 2005).

Two-thirds of the admissions in the *Fostering Adolescents* study and around 60 per cent of admissions in the *From Care to Accommodation* study were unplanned, as they often took place rapidly after the precipitating episode. As a result, there was rarely time to consider a choice of placements or to allow young people and foster carers to meet prior to placement. In these circumstances, there is rarely time to consult with young people, share information with foster carers or ensure that young people and carers have compatible expectations of the placement.

Some studies have suggested that the lack of opportunity to plan, consult and to match young people to placements, and to ensure that they and their prospective carers have congruent expectations about the placement, might reduce that placement's chance of success (Farmer *et al*, 2004; Triseliotis *et al*, 1995). For example, the *Fostering Adolescents* study found that placements were more likely to be successful if they were planned, if the young people had been consulted, and if they had been given information about the foster family. Emergency placements were more likely to disrupt than planned placements, usually for reasons connected to behaviour, although it is possible that the behaviour precipitating emergency admissions may also contribute to the disruption of placements.

Types and duration of foster placements for adolescents

The duration of foster placements for teenagers is closely connected to the purpose of the placements and these, in turn, may vary according to whether young people are adolescent graduates of the care system or adolescent entrants to it. This section outlines the evidence on short-term and long-term foster care. The next section, on specialist fostering, discusses medium-term and respite care.

Short-term foster care

Adolescent entrants to care rarely stay for very long. Nearly half of those entering care when aged 10–15 years old stay for less than eight weeks and two-thirds leave within six months. Indeed, almost one-third remain in care for under two weeks (Department for Education and Skills, 2007). Among those young people in the *Working with Adolescents* study who entered care (in most cases foster care), one-third of admissions lasted less than one week and 46 per cent lasted for one month or less. A further 46 per cent of admissions lasted for one to six months, often to allow time for a fuller assessment to be made or to allow time for work on family relationships or therapeutic work with the child to take place. The *Pursuit of Permanence* study found that the duration of care episodes was related to the reasons for admission. In that study, adolescents admitted due to a breakdown in relationships with parents were more likely to leave care within six months (60%) than those admitted for reasons of abuse or neglect (49%). This is consistent with the international research on family reunification, which indicates that time in care is closely associated both with reasons for entry to care and age at entry (Biehal, 2006).

Adolescent entrants to care are often placed in short-term foster care with the aim of defusing a crisis and preventing a longer-term rupture in family relationships (Packman and Hall, 1998; Biehal, 2005). Although such brief episodes are often unplanned, they may serve not only as a means of relieving tension but also as an opportunity for social workers to help families rebuild relationships. The *Working with Adolescents* study found that, in some cases, short-term admissions provided a breathing space and an opportunity to work on problems, but in others there was a serious breakdown in family relationships which led to a longer period of care.

It was clear from this study that, in some circumstances, short-term foster care could be a helpful ingredient in family support services for adolescents. However, it found, as others have done, that social workers were extremely reluctant to use short-term accommodation in this way and tried to avoid admission at all costs. Social workers and parents often had different perspectives on whether the family or the state should take responsibility for difficult adolescents. Social workers' views were strongly influenced by local policies on avoiding accommodation and by a lack of resources, particularly for teenagers not thought to be at risk of significant harm. Social workers often complained that it was particularly difficult to find placements for teenagers and decisions about placement often appeared to be resource-driven rather than needs-led. Their reluctance to accommodate young people even in extreme circumstances also derived from a sense of pessimism about the impact of placement and a genuine concern that it might result in psychological harm to the young person. The consequence of this reluctance to plan short-term admissions, in circumstances where these might make a useful contribution to family support work, was that such admissions as did occur tended to be emergency admissions made in crisis.

Long-term foster care

The sample in the *Pursuit of Permanence* (Sinclair *et al*, 2007) study included a large number of children who had been placed for several years, which offered an opportunity to investigate patterns for children placed long-term. Although the *Pursuit of Permanence* study is referring here to all types of placements, we can assume that the vast majority of the long-term placements were in foster care since very few children are today placed in residential care and only a tiny minority of those who are stay there for two years or more. This study found that adolescents who last entered care before the age of 11 were more likely to be placed 'for care and upbringing' (60% of adolescent graduates) than those placed when age 11 or over (27% of adolescent entrants). By definition, placements whose purpose is the provision of care and upbringing are intended to be long-term. Adolescent graduates were therefore more than twice as likely to be living in placements which were intended to be long-term than adolescent entrants. These adolescent graduates had been looked after for an average of five-and-a-half years since their last admission. The average length of their last placement was just under three years, although there were wide variations in this.

A study (Beek and Schofield, 2004) of 52 children who entered long-term foster placements at the age of 11 or under found that nearly three-quarters of these planned long-term foster placements were still intact three to four years later. This is encouraging, but as only half of these children were teenagers by this stage, it is difficult to draw firm conclusions about how well such placements endure through adolescence (see also Schofield, this volume). The most stable groups appeared to be the rather closed, defended and emotionally cool children and those described as "rewarding", who were generally easier to manage. Children described as "on the edge", who were wary, distrustful, fearful and controlling, experienced a higher rate of disruption.

The much smaller proportion of adolescent entrants placed long-term for the purpose of care and upbringing is unsurprising since, as we have seen, the placements of adolescent entrants are frequently made with the express purpose of preventing the need for long-term care. Evidence from the *Working with Adolescents* study (Biehal, 2005) gives some indication of the circumstances in which, in a small number of cases, long-term placements are made for those entering care during adolescence. Eight per cent of the young people in that study had entered care by follow-up and were expected (by all concerned) to remain long-term. This group gave higher ratings on self-completed measures of the severity of difficulties and family functioning than others in the sample. They were also more likely to be living with neither birth parent at referral and to be admitted as the result either of an adoption breakdown or the breakdown of relationships with the relatives or friends they had been staying with. Alternative options, such as informal care by family and friends, had already been tried and long-term care was now the last resort. In a few cases, the severity of young people's mental health difficulties had led to their long-term placement away from home.

A key question in relation to long-term foster placements is whether they had been planned as such. Had foster carers and children always thought of these arrangements as permanent, or had they become long-term by default, as the years passed? Crucially, did young people view these foster homes as offering them a family for life? The challenge, in relation to children and young people for whom placement is intended to provide care and upbringing, is to ensure stability, emotional security and a sense of permanence (Schofield *et al*, 2000; Sinclair *et al*, 2005). Yet, limits to the decision-making powers and level of responsibility of long-term foster carers, alongside well-intentioned social work interventions with 14–15-year-olds to discuss the option of moving to independence at the age of 18, may undermine any sense of stability and permanence (Selwyn and Quinton, 2004).

Specialist fostering for adolescents

Specialist fostering schemes first appeared in the UK in the 1970s and typically provide medium-term care for adolescents. The earliest scheme was the Kent Family Placement project, which placed young people aged 14 years and over with specially trained foster carers, who received a fee as well as maintenance payments. Foster carers undertook task-centred work with the young people, underpinned by written agreements. Evaluations at the time indicated that this specialist scheme was able to contain and work successfully with many difficult teenagers in foster care, although it is difficult to reach any conclusions as to whether the scheme was any more effective than alternative placements, as these studies lacked control groups (Yelloly, 1979; Hazel, 1981). Disruption rates were lower for placements with experienced foster carers, but behaviour problems and truancy increased the risk of placement breakdown (Fenyo *et al*, 1989).

The Kent scheme was very influential. Surveys conducted during the 1980s found that the number of specialist fostering schemes for teenagers had expanded rapidly and that their aims were now wider. Although these schemes initially targeted teenagers with difficult or delinquent behaviour and offered time-limited, task-centred placements, as the number of schemes increased, foster placements were increasingly offered to a wider variety of young people for more flexible periods of time (Shaw and Hipgrave, 1983; Lowe, 1990). However, a major survey of child care placements found that the outcomes of these specialist placements were mixed, as over half ended sooner than planned (Rowe *et al*, 1989).

Evaluations of more recent specialist fostering schemes in the UK which, unlike the evaluations of earlier schemes, compared young people receiving the specialist service to a control group, have had disappointing results. Two randomised controlled trials of specialist fostering schemes, which trained carers in managing behaviour, found that these schemes did not have a significant impact on outcomes (Minnis *et al*, 2001; Macdonald and Turner, 2005).

Today, there are a variety of forms of specialist foster care, which normally offer foster carers enhanced training, support and payment to provide time-limited placements, usually for older children and adolescents with complex needs. Specialist fostering schemes may offer treatment, an alternative to custody, respite care or more than one of these.

Treatment foster care

Various models of treatment foster care exist, which have for the most part been developed in the USA, and these are underpinned by a variety of theoretical approaches (Reddy and Pfeiffer, 1997). Probably the best known model is Multidimensional Treatment Foster Care (MTFC), a model based on social learning theory which was developed in the USA during the 1980s. It was initially developed for work with boys with serious and chronic criminal behaviour and was later extended to girls. It has also been developed and tested as an alternative to hospitalisation for adolescents with mental health problems and as an early intervention with very young children at risk of long-term care. The use of MTFC with these populations has been positively evaluated in a number of controlled studies in the USA (Chamberlain and Reid, 1991; Chamberlain and Reid, 1998; Fisher *et al*, 2000).

The DCSF is currently piloting MTFC with 10–16-year-olds in 18 English local authorities by targeting older children and adolescents with complex needs and histories of placement instability. As MTFC has not previously been offered to a group of this kind, no research evidence is currently available as to its effectiveness with this population (a national evaluation is currently being conducted by the Universities of York and Manchester). MTFC carers are trained in a standardised and manualised model of treatment and are intensively supported. They work alongside case managers, individual therapists, skills workers, birth family therapists and education workers (Roberts, 2006).

Alternatives to custody

Specialist foster care has also been used as an alternative to custody. The Youth Justice Board is currently piloting the use of MTFC in England through its Intensive Fostering Scheme for young offenders at risk of custody. Controlled studies in the USA have indicated that young offenders placed in MTFC were incarcerated less frequently, and for shorter periods of time. MTFC was found to be significantly more effective at reducing officially recorded criminal activity than alternative disposals (Chamberlain, 1990; Chamberlain and Moore, 1998).

In Scotland, the CAPS scheme offered time-limited placements to 12–16-year-olds with exceptional emotional and behavioural difficulties who were on the brink of admission to secure accommodation. Twenty young people on the CAPS scheme were compared with 20 others who were currently or recently admitted to secure accommodation. All but five of these young people had been charged with offences at the time. Carers were well-supported but were not trained in a specific treatment model and saw their role as using their relationships with the young people to help them to change. The study found that the scheme was often successful in containing young people who would otherwise be in secure accommodation but nevertheless only a minority of placements were thought to have lasted as long as needed. It was difficult to motivate the young people and outcomes such as a reduction in the level of offending and an increase in participation in school were similar or worse for the CAPS group than the control group (Walker *et al*, 2002).

Another scheme, remand fostering, offers short-term placements as an alternative to custody for young offenders remanded by the courts to await reports or sentence. In one study (Lipscombe, 2006), placements were typically short, lasting on average for 37 days. The young people were a high risk group and, like those on the CAPS scheme, the majority had very troubled family relationships. Over half had previously been in care and 20 per cent had experienced physical abuse. Half of the placements broke down before the young person was sentenced and one-fifth of the young people re-offended while on remand. However, the experience of remand foster care was highly valued by many of the young people who felt that the support and care they received from their carers showed them 'another side of life'.

Follow-on placements and follow-up support are key issues for time-limited specialist fostering schemes. Such schemes often experience difficulties in identifying appropriate move-on accommodation when placements end. Returning children to the environment in which their problems emerged may be unhelpful, especially if work in the family environment is not undertaken during the placement and then continued once the child returns home. Work of this kind is an integral part of the MTFC model and is undertaken by birth family therapists. Where children are unable to return home, this work may be undertaken with move-on foster carers instead to ensure that the young people continue to receive consistent care once they leave the scheme.

Support care

Support foster care has developed in a few areas to support adolescents and parents experiencing severe relationship problems. Such schemes operate as a form of family support, offering placements for one or two nights a week over a period of several months, often to pre-teenage and teenage children in conflict with parents (Aldgate and Bradley, 1999; Greenfields and Statham, 2004). Such schemes involve work with parents, partnership between parents and carers and continuity of carers.

Parenting fostered adolescents

Relationships with birth families

Although in the past foster "parents", as they were then called, often cared for children on an exclusive, quasi-adoptive basis, today birth parents have continuing responsibility for their children and there is an expectation that in many cases they will maintain regular contact with them. Furthermore, foster carers, along with social workers, are expected to work in partnership with birth parents whenever possible.

Fostered children may therefore find themselves in a triangular set of relationships, which may sometimes be characterised by ambivalence and may engender conflicting loyalties for children, irrespective of whether they are actually in contact with their parents. Young people may have to make sense of the differing roles of two sets of parenting figures, so there is a need for clarity about the authority and responsibilities of each in relation to the care and control of the child.

This may be a particular problem during adolescence, an age when it is normal for young people to be testing boundaries and striving for greater autonomy and when consistency on the part of parental figures is perhaps more important than ever. Equally, foster carers may have to work in partnership with parents and manage contact, which can be problematic or unsettling for young people. Young people's relationships with their birth parents, and foster carers' understanding and support of this, are key issues. For many young people, relationships with their birth families will endure once they have left the care system, so it is important for social workers and foster carers to support and encourage the young person make best use of these relationships including, where necessary, keeping themselves safe.

Relationships with foster carers

The nature of the relationship between young people and foster carers that is desirable, or possible, is likely to be linked to the purpose and planned duration of the placement. Children in long-term foster placements need to establish a secure base that can offer them long-term emotional security. On the other hand, many adolescents enter foster care for only brief periods of time and would not wish, or need, their carers to act as quasi-parental figures, although they nevertheless wish to feel valued and cared for.

Carers may therefore need to respond differently to young people's differing desires for attachment or detachment (Downes, 1988). Many, despite feeling wary or ambivalent, may nevertheless wish for a close relationship with a carer even if this is something they find difficult to manage without giving out the opposite signals. Others may prefer to maintain greater emotional distance, perhaps as a result of their past experiences of parenting in their families or the care system, their loyalty to birth parents or, alternatively, if the placement is intended to be short-term.

Relationships with foster carers may also be affected by the nature of children's relationships with their own families, although the *Fostering Adolescents* study (Farmer *et al*, 2004) found that nearly one-third of the newly-placed adolescents in that study expressed little or no strong feeling towards any adult when their placement began. The York studies of 595 children in foster placements found that the nature of attachment difficulties were strongly related to age, with children aged 11 or over more likely than younger children to be rated as 'aloof' on a measure of attachment behaviour. Young people's ability and readiness to form new positive relationships to carers will therefore be influenced both by their earlier experience of parenting and by how far they have managed to resolve their feelings about their families, for example, by accepting that they will remain in care (Sinclair *et al*, 2005a).

Young people's characteristics and behaviour may have a significant influence on the parenting style of foster carers and the interaction between these may affect outcomes. The *Fostering Adolescents* study found that carers were less likely to respond warmly to young people who had been scapegoated or rejected by their own families. Relationships were particularly likely to be poor, or to deteriorate, where young people displayed greater emotional or behavioural difficulties. Outcomes were less positive where carers became less warm in response to the challenges posed by young people and relationships deteriorated, or where carers reduced their efforts at control. These findings echo those of an earlier study of permanent placements, which found that the more problems the children presented, the harder carers found it to be responsive. In many cases, relation-ships worsened as children's behaviour deteriorated (Quinton *et al*, 1998).

For young people entering new foster placements during adolescence, engagement is likely to be a key issue. The readiness of young people to engage in relationships with their foster carers may be related both to whether children want to be in a particular placement, or indeed looked after at all, their feelings about their birth families and, related to both of these, their readiness to form new relationships. Relationships between recently placed young people and foster carers may be volatile. The majority of the young people in the *Fostering Adolescents* study (Farmer *et al*, 2004) said they felt close to their carers shortly after placement but by one-year follow-up, relationships had deteriorated markedly for nearly a third of these young people. Some studies have found that whether or not children want to be in their foster placement is strongly related to outcome (Sinclair, 2005).

Balancing autonomy, care and control

As we have seen, for many adolescent entrants to foster care, difficult behaviour is often a precipitating factor in admission and many of those who enter foster care at this point may have quite serious emotional and behavioural difficulties (Biehal, 2005). Even settled adolescent graduates of the care system may continue to display emotional and behavioural problems but for some, these may intensify during adolescence since mental health problems, which are uncommon among younger children, typically emerge and become identified as such during adolescence. Adolescence is also a time at which young people are at increased risk of involvement in substance misuse and offending (Meltzer *et al*, 2000; Wilson *et al*, 2006).

Carers of adolescents therefore have to manage behaviour that is often difficult and sometimes extremely risky and need to set appropriate boundaries. This may be a particular challenge in relation to adolescent entrants, who may be unused to reasonable boundary setting and unwilling to accept it. Unlike younger children, teenagers who are unsettled in foster placements may "vote with their feet". Some may go missing from foster placements, typically because they find it hard to accept that they need to be looked after, because they wish to be with their families or friends, or because they are unhappy about the particular placement. Adolescents may return home contrary to their social workers' intentions or take actions themselves which initiate their discharge from care (Sinclair *et al*, 1995; Biehal and Wade, 2000).

Different approaches have been taken in response to this difficult challenge of balancing care, control and autonomy for young people with serious emotional and behavioural problems. MTFC offers a highly-structured model which sets very firm boundaries at the outset and gradually allows young people greater autonomy as they learn to positively manage their own behaviour. In contrast, some carers in the *Fostering Adolescents* study, recognising that teenagers unused to consistent, authoritative parenting would resist too many restrictions on their behaviour, began by imposing a few loose boundaries and then gradually established more as time progressed. Other studies suggest that the quality of relationships with foster carers may often affect young people's willingness to accept attempts at boundary-setting. It is sometimes only within the context of a relationship with a particular carer that young people begin to respond to attempts to set boundaries (Triseliotis *et al*, 1995; Wade *et al*, 1998).

Outcomes of foster care

Success in foster care has often been measured in terms of stability, assessed in terms of placement disruption rates. More recently, researchers have taken a broader view of success, turning their attention to measuring child well-being as well as stability. Although stability is generally positive, it cannot be regarded as a measure of success in cases where children continue to live in placements in which they are unhappy or which do not meet their needs. Equally, it may sometimes be beneficial for an unsettled young person with serious emotional or behavioural difficulties to move temporarily to a specialist placement which offers treatment.

Disruption

Age, emotional disturbance, difficult behaviour and a placement the child feels unhappy about have commonly been found to be predictors of placement disruption. Researchers have consistently found that disruption rates for foster placements are higher for adolescents. For those aged 11 and over, difficult behaviour is particularly likely to threaten the stability of foster placements. Studies have indicated that for 11–15-year-olds, around 40 per cent of placements break down in the first year and around 50 per cent over longer follow-up periods, and national statistics show that 10–15-year-olds are more likely than other children to have three or more placements during the course of a year (Sinclair, 2005; Department for Education and Skills, 2007; Sinclair *et al*, 2007). Furthermore, among children of any age, those who display emotional and behavioural difficulties at the start of placement are more likely to experience disruption (Sinclair, 2005).

In the *Fostering Adolescents* study (Farmer *et al*, 2004), 40 per cent of the new foster placements disrupted within one year. For these young people, disruption was associated with behavioural problems prior to this placement, a high number of past adversities in the young person's life, being older (over 14.5 years) and having been admitted from home rather than from another placement. Difficulties with contact with birth families were also associated with higher disruption rates.

In this study, young people who felt able to confide in an adult were less likely to experience placement disruption. It is possible that young people such as these may have a greater ability to engage in interpersonal relationships and, through their care-seeking behaviour, may reinforce the care-giving behaviour of their foster carers, setting up a mutually reinforcing positive cycle. Those who settled early in the placement, confided in their carers and participated in activities with them tended to do well. However, place-ments were *also* less likely to disrupt where young people excluded themselves from relationships with their foster carers. These young people were often depressed and bullied by others. The behaviour of carers also had an effect on outcomes, as these were likely to be worse where carers became less warm or responsive when young people's behaviour deteriorated, or who reduced their efforts at control.

Interestingly, this study found that psychological distress and difficulty in peer relationships made placement disruption *less* likely. Young people who experienced psychological distress were often those who also had close ties with at least one adult, and it may be this capacity for forming relationships which reduced the risk of disruption. In contrast, not having good relationships with peers, distressing though this may have been for the young people concerned, may have prevented some of them from being led astray.

In the York fostering studies (Sinclair *et al*, 2005a; Sinclair *et al*, 2005b), 595 children living in foster care were initially followed up after one year. During this period, it was found, that the placements of 10–15-year-olds were more than twice as likely to disrupt (33% of placements) as those of 5–10-year-olds (15%). The disruption rate was slightly lower than in the previously mentioned study, since Farmer *et al*'s study (2004) focused on new foster placements, whereas the Sinclair and colleagues' study included a cross-section of foster placements of varying duration and therefore included a number of children in settled, long-term placements. Nevertheless, over a period of three years, nearly half (48%) of the 11–14-year-olds in the York study experienced at least one disrupted placement. This study found that being 11 years old or over was one of a cluster of factors which together predicted placement breakdown. The other predictors of disruption (for children of all ages) were having a placement of less than two years' duration, being unhappy at school, not wanting to be in the placement, having a childlike attachment style and having foster carers with poor parenting skills.

Well-being

Evidence on well-being comes primarily from studies of adolescent entrants to care. The *Pursuit of Permanence* study (Sinclair *et al*, 2007) found that children who were doing poorly on indicators of well-being tended to be older, male, to have spent relatively little time looked after since their last admission and to have had a relatively large number of placement moves. They were likely to have experienced abuse or to come from families marked by domestic violence or substance abuse. They were also more likely not to want to be in care. A study of social work services for teenagers in Scotland (Triseliotis *et al*, 1995) measured the success of interventions on a range of measures, including emotional and behavioural difficulties, self-esteem and participation in education or work. On this composite measure of success, one-third of those placed in foster care during the course of the study were thought to have very successful outcomes, but for another third, outcomes were rated as unsuccessful. Nevertheless, a higher proportion of those who entered foster care were deemed to have positive outcomes on this measure compared to those placed in residential institutions or remaining with their families.

Similarly, the *Fostering Adolescents* study assessed whether the young people's well-being had improved one year after they entered their new foster placement. Placements were more likely to be successful if they were planned, if the young person was under 14½ years old at placement, their emotional and behavioural difficulties were less severe, they were not hyperactive, they had fewer past adversities in their lives and had not had previous placement breakdowns.

Finally, there has been much concern about educational outcomes for looked after young people as they are far more likely to have no, or fewer, qualifications than the wider population. However, in considering the potential impact of being looked after on educational outcomes, it is important to take account of individual circumstances of adolescents, particularly their care careers and, for adolescent entrants to care, their baseline level of educational participation and achievement. Young people who enter care in their mid-teens with low levels of educational achievement may make substantial progress while they are looked after but may nevertheless fail to achieve the same level of qualifications by the age of 16 as others starting from a higher baseline. This is borne out by a recent study of care leavers which found that educational performance tended to be higher for those who had entered care younger and stayed longer, particularly those in stable foster placements (Dixon *et al*, 2006).

Leaving foster care

Nearly three-quarters (72%) of young people who enter care between the ages of 10 and 15 years subsequently return home (Department for Education and Skills, 2007). The *Working with Adolescents* study compared young people who returned home within a few weeks or months with others thought likely to remain looked after in the longer term. It was clear from this that a key ingredient in the rapid rehabilitation of young people with their families was quite simply the fact that their parents were prepared to have them back and the young people agreed to return home. Some parents had simply wanted a brief respite from their child's extremely difficult behaviour. Others were reluctant to have their children back, but a combination a steadfast refusal by workers to allow them to remain in placement and the provision of support and advice persuaded these parents to accept their children back. The availability of staff to undertake the necessary work to rehabilitate the young people with their parents as quickly as possible was vital.

Research on young people leaving care at the age of 16 or over indicates that continuing support from foster carers may be crucial to successful transitions to independence, yet formal and informal support from carers tends to decline following discharge from care (Wade, 1997). A recent study of leaving care found that one-third of the young people continued to live with their foster carer for some time after their formal discharge at the age of 18. These stays were relatively brief, however, and the majority had moved on within nine months. Within two to three months of leaving care, 42 per cent of those who had been in foster care were still in at least monthly contact with their carers, but nine months after discharge, only 14 per cent maintained this level of contact. Evidence from this study suggests that contact with foster carers helps to ameliorate the risk of social isolation, as over half of those in continuing contact with carers had weak links with their birth families. However, none of the authorities in this study had formal policies to resource continuing support by former foster carers and the support that was provided was offered on an informal basis (Dixon *et al*, 2006).

Conclusions

Foster care for adolescents is immensely varied, catering as it does for young people who have entered care at any time from infancy to adolescence, for a variety of reasons, and who remain for periods of time ranging from a few days to many years. Young people's experience of foster care may be influenced by the age at which they enter care and their feelings about their birth families, which, in turn, are likely to be related to the reasons for which they are admitted and the particular emotional and behavioural difficulties they may experience. All of these factors may have an impact on their capacity to build positive relationships with their foster carers, to accept being looked after by them and to achieve positive outcomes in the different domains of their lives.

Since the purpose, nature and intended duration of foster placements is normally related to the histories and circumstances of young people, the experience of a young person fostered in a settled placement from an early age is likely to be very different to that of an adolescent entrant to short-term care. It follows from this that positive outcomes may be easier to achieve for some young people, in some types of placements, than for others. For example, disruption rates may be particularly high for some kinds of specialist foster placements, as these often target young people who are particularly challenging to care for. Research has shown that outcomes tend to be more positive for adolescents who enter foster placements at a younger age, have fewer emotional and behavioural difficulties, and display a greater capacity to form attached relationships to adults.

Foster care for adolescents, as for younger children, should be viewed as an essential element in a continuum of services. At one end of the continuum, foster care has a role to play in family support through providing short-term care, while at the other it can offer a secure base for young people who require care and upbringing, as well as offering short- to medium-term specialist care or treatment to young people with particular difficulties. In some cases, foster carers may also have a role to play in young people's lives once they move to independence and this has become subject to a programme of change by the government to enable this to happen.

Selected further reading

Biehal N. (2005) *Working with Adolescents: Supporting families, preventing breakdowns*, London: BAAF

Farmer E., Moyers S. and Lipscombe S. (2004) *Fostering Adolescents*, London: Jessica Kingsley Publishers

Packman J. and Hall C. (1998) *From Care to Accommodation*, London: The Stationery Office

Sinclair I., Baker C., Lee J. and Gibbs I. (2007) *The Pursuit of Permanence: A study of the English care system*, London: Jessica Kingsley Publishers

Sinclair I., Baker C., Wilson K. and Gibbs I. (2005) *Foster Children: Where they go and how they get on*, London: Jessica Kingsley Publishers

References

Aldgate J. and Bradley M. (1999) *Supporting Families Through Short-term Fostering*, London: The Stationery Office

Beek M. and Schofield G. (2004) *Providing a Secure Base in Long-term Foster Care*, London: BAAF

Biehal N. (2005) *Working with Adolescents: Supporting families, preventing breakdown*, London: BAAF

Biehal N. (2006) *Reuniting Looked After Children with Their Families*, London: National Children's Bureau

Biehal N. and Wade J. (2000) 'Going missing from residential and foster care: Linking biographies and contexts', *British Journal of Social Work*, 30, pp 211–225

Chamberlain P. (1990) 'Comparative evaluation of specialized foster care for seriously delinquent youths: A first step', *International Journal of Family Care*, 2, pp 21–36

Chamberlain P. and Moore K. (1998) 'A clinical model for parenting juvenile offenders: A comparison of group care versus family care', *Clinical Child Psychology and Psychiatry*, 3, pp 375–386

Chamberlain P. and Reid J. (1991) 'Using a specialized foster care community treatment model for children and adolescents leaving the state mental hospital', *Journal of Community Psychology*, 19, pp 266–276

Chamberlain P. and Reid J. (1998) 'Comparison of two community alternatives to incarceration for chronic juvenile offenders', *Journal of Consulting and Clinical Psychology*, 66, pp 624–633

Department for Children, Schools and Families (2007) *First Release. Children Looked After in England Year Ending 31 March 2007*, London: Department for Children, Schools and Families

Department for Education and Skills (2007) *Children Looked After by Local Authorities Year Ending 31 March 2006*, London: Department for Education and Skills

Dixon J., Lee J., Wade J., Byford S. and Weatherly H. (2006) *Young People Leaving Care: A study of costs and outcomes*, York: University of York

Downes C. (1988) 'Foster families for adolescents: The healing potential of time-limited placements', *British Journal of Social Work*, 18, pp 473–487

Farmer E., Moyers S. and Lipscombe S. (2004) *Fostering Adolescents*, London: Jessica Kingsley Publishers

Farmer E. and Parker R. (1991) *Trials and Tribulations*, Norwich: The Stationery Office

Fenyo A., Knapp M. and Baines B. (1989) *Foster Care Breakdown: A study of the Kent Family Placement Scheme*, Canterbury: University of Kent Personal Social Services Research Unit

Fisher M., Marsh P. and Phillips D. (1986) *In and Out of Care*, London: Batsford/BAAF

Fisher P., Gunnar M., Chamberlain P. and Reid J. (2000) 'Preventative intervention for maltreated preschool children: Impact on children's behavior, neuroendocrine activity, and foster parent functioning', *Child Adolescent Psychiatry*, 39

Greenfields M. and Statham J. (2004) *Support Foster Care: Developing a short-break service for children in need*, London: Thomas Coram Research Unit

Hazel N. (1981) *A Bridge to Independence*, Oxford: Blackwell

Lipscombe J. (2006) *Care or Control? Foster care for young people on remand*, London: BAAF

Lowe K. (1990) *Teenagers in Foster Care: A survey by the National Foster Care Association*, London: National Foster Care Association

Macdonald G. and Turner W. (2005) 'An experiment in helping foster carers manage challenging behaviour', *British Journal of Social Work*, 35, p 18

Meltzer H., Gatward R., Goodman R. and Ford T. (2000) *The Mental Health of Children and Adolescents in Great Britain*, Summary Report, London: National Statistics

Millham S., Bullock R., Hosie K. and Little M. (1986) *Lost in Care: The problem of maintaining links between children in care and their families*, Aldershot: Gower

Minnis H., Pelosi A. J., Knapp M. and Dunn J. (2001) 'Mental health and foster carer training', *Archive of Diseases of Childhood*, 84:5, pp 302–306

Packman J. and Hall C. (1998) *From Care to Accommodation*, London: The Stationery Office

Parker R. (1966) *Decisions in Child Care*, London: Allen and Unwin

Quinton D., Rushton A., Dance C. and Mayes D. (1998) *Joining New Families: A study of adoption and fostering in middle childhood*, Chichester: Wiley

Reddy L. and Pfeiffer S. (1997) 'Effectiveness of treatment foster care with children and adolescents: A review of outcome studies', *Journal of the American Academy of Child and Adolescent Psychiatry*, 36, pp 581–588

Roberts R. (2006) *Multidimensional Treatment Foster Care in England (MTFCE)*, London: Department for Education and Skills

Rowe J., Hundleby M. and Garnett L. (1989) *Child Care Now*, London: Batsford/BAAF

Schofield G., Beek M., Sargent K. and Thoburn J. (2000) *Growing up in Foster Care*, London: BAAF

Selwyn J. and Quinton D. (2004) 'Stability, permanence, outcomes and support: Foster care and adoption compared', *Adoption & Fostering*, 28:4, pp 6–15

Selwyn J., Sturgess W., Quinton D. and Baxter C. (2003) *Costs and Outcomes of Non-Infant Adoptions*, Bristol: Hadley Centre for Adoption and Foster care Studies, University of Bristol

Shaw M. and Hipgrave T. (1983) *Specialist Fostering*, London: Batsford

Sinclair I. (2005) *Fostering Now: Messages from research*, London: Jessica Kinglsey Publishers

Sinclair I., Baker C., Lee J. and Gibbs I. (2007) *The Pursuit of Permanence: A study of the English care system*, London: Jessica Kingsley Publishers

Sinclair I., Baker C., Wilson K. and Gibbs I. (2005a) *Foster Children: Where they go and how they get on*, London: Jessica Kingsley Publishers

Sinclair I., Wilson K. and Gibbs I. (2005b) *Foster Placements: Why they succeed and why they fail*, London: Jessica Kingsley Publishers

Sinclair R., Garnett L. and Berridge D. (1995) *Social Work and Assessment with Adolescents*, London: National Children's Bureau

Trasler G. (1960) *In Place of Parents*, London: Routledge and Kegan Paul

Triseliotis J., Borland M., Hill M. and Lambert L. (1995) *Teenagers and the Social Work Services*, London: HMSO

Wade J. (1997) 'Developing leaving care services: Tapping the potential of foster carers', *Adoption & Fostering*, 21:3, p 40–49

Wade J., Biehal N., Clayden J. and Stein M. (1998) *Going Missing: Young people absent from care*, Chichester: Wiley

Walker M., Hill M. and Triseliotis J. (2002) *Testing the Limits of Foster Care: Fostering as an alternative to secure accommodation*, London: BAAF

Wilson D., Sharp C. and Patterson A. (2006) *Young People and Crime: Findings from the 2005 Offending, Crime and Justice Survey*, London: Home Office

Yellowly M. (1979) *Independent Evaluation of Twenty-Five Placements*, Maidstone: Kent County Council

10 Contact and relationships between fostered children and their birth families

Gillian Schofield and Olive Stevenson

Whatever the quality of relationships between children and their birth families before they come into care, fostered children continue to think about and need to manage and resolve complex feelings about their birth parents, siblings and other relatives. Family member-ship and family loyalties are built into our society and into our psychological make-up in ways that separation and court orders do not sever. Birth relatives, and in particular birth parents, also continue to have diverse roles and complex feelings in relation to their children who are now being cared for in somebody else's home. This chapter explores children's relationships with their birth families when they are in foster care. It includes detailed discussion of contact. However, since the meanings of these relationships to children are much more than what is usually meant by "contact", we need to explore and highlight the importance of interventions that aim to achieve a workable and sustainable pattern of relationships that promote the child's healthy development.

The nature of relationships between foster children and their birth families raises some of the most important and challenging issues for child care planning and practice. It goes to the heart of what being a member of a family, or several families, means to children. Clarity is therefore needed about what each foster family placement is trying to achieve for each child. An understanding is required not only of the developmental needs of children and young people, but also how different families work and how, in the interests of the child, birth and foster family networks, they can be helped to work together. There are no simple answers to even the most obvious contact questions, such as with whom, where and how often. There are no easy "rules of thumb", as Sinclair and Wilson (this volume) have put it, that can be applied. Careful professional judgments are required in each case.

The chapter begins by identifying some key issues from law, research and practice which arise in relation to the various forms of birth family contact (see also Lord and Borthwick, this volume, for discussion of siblings). We then focus on the social work role, particularly the work with birth parents, which is too often neglected in research and practice (Alpert, 2005).

The legal context

The Children Act 1989 (England and Wales) and the Children (Scotland) Act 1995 set out a number of key principles that recognised the importance of the birth family in the lives of foster children. These included local authorities being expected to work in partnership with birth parents and to offer family support to enable children to be brought up, where possible, in their birth families. This principle of partnership was to continue where children became looked after by the local authority. Law and guidance relating to birth family contact for all looked after children must therefore be seen in this policy and statutory context.

However, these legal requirements frequently raise complex dilemmas in which there may be controversy as to what is best for children. Even if the legal requirement is that the child's interests are paramount, there may be tensions in relation to the interests of parents, who are themselves often vulnerable adults. The concept of partnership with parents has undoubtedly helped to produce a constructive focus, and yet also contributed to some uncertainty about the objectives of the work, especially when children are in care because of neglect or ill treatment by their parents.

Schedule 2 (para 15, 16) of the Children Act (CA) 1989 states that the local authority has a duty to promote contact between looked after children and their parents, relatives and other people connected with them, as far as is practicable and consistent with their welfare. (There is a similar requirement, in law, in Scotland.) For those foster children under care orders, section 34(1) states that the local authority shall allow the child "reasonable contact" with his parents or guardians. This is now thought of as a statutory "presumption of reasonable contact". Because of the general duty under Schedule 2, the principle tends to be applied also to children accommodated on a voluntary basis (section 20).

It is important to note that provisions in the Act are worded as a *right of the child*, not as a right of parents or other relatives. However, it is expected that parents' views and feelings will be taken into account in court and other decision-making forums. This is for good reason, as parents' feelings and children's rights can interact. If parents find that the level of contact or information about the child's progress does not enable them to sustain their sense of parenthood and commitment, nor to feel that they know the child well enough to send the appropriate birthday presents or to have a meaningful conversation when they meet, and this leads to failure to maintain contact, the child's right to contact may be compromised. It is not clear whether the Human Rights Act, in particular implementing Article 8 of the European Convention, the right to respect for family life, will be used by parents seeking contact with their children – or indeed children seeking contact with their parents – but the debate on human rights has become more central in recent years.

When considering the making of a care order, the court is required to consider arrangements for contact. Under section 34 (2) and (3) (CA 1989), the court can make specific orders for contact, whether there is an application for contact orders or not. The frequency of contact, the venue and whether it is supervised or not can be the subject of an order, although these arrangements are often negotiated and agreed more informally and flexibly as part of the care plan presented to and sanctioned by the court. It is important for social workers to be mindful of this negotiation process outside of the court room (Dickens, 2006) and to instruct the local authority solicitor explicitly regarding their assessment of the child's contact needs. As with other decisions under the Children Act 1989, care plans and contact orders are subject to section 1, known as the "Welfare Checklist", which includes the child's developmental well-being and also the child's wishes and feelings.

Under section 34 (CA 1989), there is not the same "presumption of reasonable contact" with other family members, such as grandparents or siblings. But they are included in the Guidance under Schedule 2 and can be the subject of a section 34 order or included in the care plan. If, over time, the arrangements for contact made by the local authority are not seen as satisfactory by family members, then parents can apply under section 34 for an order or for an existing order to be varied, while other relatives can also apply for an order but need leave of the court to do so.

In an emergency, if the local authority believes existing arrangements to be putting the child at risk, the local authority has the right to suspend contact immediately, but must present their case for continued refusal of contact to the court within seven days. The Children Act 1989 also sets out the court's role where a local authority is considering it necessary and in the child's best interests to refuse contact to named individuals as part of the care plan. On application from the local authority, the court can make an order under section 34(4) giving the local authority permission to refuse contact to a parent, guardian or previous carer, which they may or may not choose to exercise straight away.

Where children are accommodated (section 20, CA 1989), the decisions about contact are not made in court and the situation is less straightforward. Birth parents are the only "parents" with parental responsibility, but the local authority is nevertheless bound by section 22, the duty to safeguard the welfare of all looked after children. Local authorities are therefore, in this sense, corporate parents for accommodated children. Social workers and foster carers need, as far as possible, to work collaboratively regarding contact with birth parents of accommodated children, but if this is not possible, then the local authority may make an application for a care order or, exceptionally, a private law application under section 8 for a defined contact order. Birth parents (with parental responsibility) also have the right to remove the child from foster care or to make an application for a section 8 order for contact.

In summary, the legal framework is intended to establish a presumption of reasonable contact, to give birth parents (and other relatives with leave) the right to challenge contact arrangements in the courts – but also to give local authorities powers to act in the interests of the child. The definition of what kind or frequency of contact is "reasonable" remains an area of considerable dispute in some cases.

The case for keeping the link with birth families

It is important to understand the foundations upon which the policy of maintaining links between children and birth families is based. There are three fundamental arguments which arise from our understanding of child development and the significance of family membership.

First, it is widely accepted that *there is a profound need to know about and come to terms with our origins, the basis for our sense of identity.* Recognition of such a need does not presume that there has to be an ongoing relationship, as distinct from knowledge about parents; these choices will be made according to circumstances and may in the end be made by the individual child, as they grow older. Nor does a general principle mean there can be no exceptions and there will be cases where it is rightly judged not to be in the child's best interests to have contact with certain family members. But the importance of the general presumption of contact is that it places on workers the responsibility, in every case, to consider what kind of links with parents (or other relatives) there should be, and to justify the nature of the contact or its absence.

Secondly, children and birth parents *need to face the reality of their past feelings and behaviour towards each other so that they may come to terms with what has happened to them and move forwards.* Relevant here for both children and birth parents, psycho-analytic theory suggests that emotional maturity includes the ability to hold an internal image of "significant others" and the self which is realistic and can balance and integrate positive and negative thoughts and feelings (Winnicott, 1964). It is not helpful for foster children to idealise or denigrate their birth parents (or their foster carers), as this leaves some doubt about where they as children fit in a polarised "all good" or "all bad" view of human nature. Skilled life story work can help with resolving these dilemmas, but carefully managed contact can make this integration more likely to be achieved. Distorted and exaggerated pictures, whether positive or negative, are strengthened by the absence of actual contact.

Where there is no contact, for whatever reason, additional work with children is necessary to explore and reconcile uncertain memories, fantasies and mixed feelings about family members they no longer see. But even where there is contact, children need help to talk about and make sense of the experience in order to resolve feelings about confusing and often disturbing experiences from the past that may well be mixed in with some positive memories. To varying degrees, children may move between blame and for-giveness, love and hate, anger and understanding, preoccupation with and rejection of birth parents through childhood and into adult life (Schofield, 2003). They need to understand that mixed feelings are normal. Birth parents and foster carers also often need to manage the same range of mixed feelings about each other and the child.

This is a complex picture of what has to be achieved in order to enable the family networks to work together and the child to move forwards and become a more secure, autonomous adult. But when contact – its presence, its absence and its quality – is worked at with understanding and patience, it will make a difference to the processing of past experiences into a coherent story and to achieving forward movement for all parties.

Thirdly, *many children in care will in fact return to live with birth parents* – whether within a few months or after many years in care. This may be well planned, poorly planned or unplanned (Farmer, this volume). In one study of 180 children and young people who were reunited within two years, it was noted that 27 per cent of the returns were unplanned (Farmer *et al*, 2008). The quality of children's experiences of links with their birth family – both through actual contact and by the way in which birth families are thought about, talked about and treated during a placement by social workers and carers – must always have this future possibility in mind, even in foster placements planned to be permanent.

Before looking at the research and practice issues in more detail, we are conscious of a further dilemma in referring to the case for links with birth "parents". The reality is that for the majority of fostered children, the primary link is with the mother, either because they were born into a lone parent family, because the parents have separated and they have had little contact with their father, or their contact with fathers is experienced as less significant. In contrast, there are a smaller number of cases in which fathers have assumed a primary role. The lack of attention paid to fathers of children in foster care is unfortunate but may not be surprising, since the population of children in care includes a sizeable proportion where children's fathers are unknown or untraced.

Acknowledging these contexts as a reality for many fostered children does not, however, mean that workers should accept the absence of fathers from children's lives or that the possibility of maintaining links with fathers should not be diligently pursued whenever possible (Daniel and Taylor, 2001). However, for the purposes of this discussion, the current position has to be faced: the social worker is likely to be involved with a far larger proportion of mothers than fathers in relation to plans for, and contact with, children.

Clearly, underlying this issue there are complex and troubling factors concerning not only gender roles but family structures in modern Britain. Research studies have also found that children who "go home" rarely go back to the same family constellation from which they came – partners change as do the children in the household. For these reasons, the use of the words "birth family" or "parents" in this chapter is a kind of shorthand for a range of widely different family patterns, changing over time, to which the child in care has to make some emotional adjustments, whether in terms of actual contact or of what is in their minds.

Research on outcomes

The Children Act 1989, with its emphasis on the value of birth family links and contact, built on a body of research that suggested that contact was associated with a number of key outcomes – in particular reunification, placement stability and children's well-being (Fanshel and Shinn, 1978; Aldgate, 1980; Thoburn *et al*, 1986; Berridge and Cleaver, 1987; Fratter *et al*, 1991) – and needed to be promoted more actively by social workers than it often was at that time (Rowe *et al*, 1984; Milham *et al*, 1986).

Subsequent research and research reviews (Quinton *et al*, 1997; Barber and Delfabbro, 2004; Wilson *et al*, 2004; Sinclair, 2005) conclude that research evidence has not been able to show that the relationship between contact and these outcomes was *causal*. It seems possible that the correlation between contact and these outcomes found in some studies is caused by other factors that affect both. It is also suggested that it is not the *existence of contact* per se that makes the difference, for better or for worse, but the *quality of the contact experience* (Cleaver, 2000; Beek and Schofield, 2004b; Sinclair *et al*, 2005; Moyers *et al*, 2006).

Research on what children say they want from contact may help us clarify what is valuable from their perspective, but this, too, is rarely straightforward as a basis for decision making. As Sinclair (2005, p 91) put it: 'Children usually look forward to contact, commonly want more contact than they get, but are nevertheless commonly upset by it'. Contact is therefore a potent and often contradictory part of foster children's lives and we need subtle ways of listening to children and young people and making sense of these mixed feelings in order to make judgments and contribute to desired outcomes for each child.

Contact and reunification

Contact will inevitably play a role both in the assessment of whether return home will be safe and meet the child's needs and in the process of actively proceeding once that plan has been agreed. Whether reunification is just a possibility during a period of assessment or whether it is an active plan that is being put into effect, observation, analysis and review of contact are likely to play an important part.

Research on the impact of contact on reunification needs close examination. On the one hand, there is a strong association between quantity of contact and return home (Sinclair, 2005). But on the other hand, there is no clear evidence that contact in itself causes or even contributes to reunification (Farmer, this volume). Where it exists, a correlation between contact and reunification could be explained by factors common to both that make successful contact *and* return home more likely – such as a warm relationship between the child and the parents, or a co-operative relationship between the birth family and the social worker, or a foster carer who assists in facilitating contact and reunification.

Cleaver (2000) found that certain factors associated with contact appeared to increase the likelihood of successful return home, in particular, where contact was well-planned and resourced, where both parent and child responded well to the increased contact, and where the attachment was positive. Quality of relationships accompanied by purposeful, good quality professional practice around contact can be seen as making a contribution at least to good outcomes of reunification. Contact will always be relevant to reunification planning and practice, but will interact with other factors – notably, and not surprisingly, the quality of relationships and of social work practice.

Contact and placement stability

The picture regarding the links between contact and placement stability is also complicated – and for the same reasons as the link to reunification. Factors in the child, the birth family, the placement and the professional practice will all play a part in placement stability. Evidence that contact can contribute to placement stability was reported by Berridge and Cleaver (1987) and Thoburn (1991). Thoburn and her colleagues in their study of 1,165 children found a statistically significant association between face-to-face contact and the placement lasting five years, with age and behavioural difficulties held constant.

Although contact may statistically be associated with stability in some large samples, it is also recognised that contact can do harm in certain cases and may contribute to placement instability. The study by Sinclair *et al* (2005) showed that poor quality contact for children who had spent less than a year in placement predicted disruption, but also that in cases of prior abuse, refusal of contact to specific individuals may be protective. Moyers *et al* (2006) found that only five of their sample of 68 adolescents had contact that was without difficulty and that 63 per cent had contact that was detrimental. Although contact in this study was only thought to have led directly to placement breakdown in five cases, it contributed, alongside other factors, in many others. A study of 52 planned, long-term foster placements (Schofield *et al*, 2000; Beek and Schofield, 2004a and b) also found that few children had unproblematic contact. Foster carers in this study were helping most children to make the best of even rather difficult contact, and were generally advocates for contact, as (on balance) valuable. But unsupervised contact in cases where there had been physical or emotional abuse, appeared at least to contribute to placement breakdown.

Although there remain questions about the exact degree and nature of the link between contact and placement stability, the message from the research, as with reunification, will be that contact, its quality and the way it is experienced by children, birth relatives and foster carers, is relevant to achieving placement stability in individual cases. Social workers need an in-depth understanding of the complexity of contact that draws on detailed assessment and good understanding of children's behaviour and emotional development to help determine how contact impacts on and interacts with other factors to affect stability.

Contact and child well-being

Successful reunification and placement stability can perhaps more easily be measured than the range of dimensions that make up well-being, so that making sense of the link between contact and well-being is even more complicated. Contact can be thought of as one strand in the overall strategy for the placement to promote the child's healthy growth and development (Cleaver, 2000; Schofield and Beek, 2006). Contact in principle should not, therefore, be seen as separate from but must be integrated within the overall plan for the child's development in the placement.

Research has made some links between contact and the promotion of certain areas of developmental well-being. For example, studies have suggested that contact is associated with increased self-esteem and sense of identity (Weinstein, 1960; Fanshel and Shinn, 1978; Aldgate, 1980; Thoburn *et al*, 1986). But the impact of particular contact on any individual child will still require a careful assessment. Browne and Moloney (2002) found that 53 per cent of their sample reacted negatively to contact. As Howe and Steele (2004) have suggested, there will be children for whom certain kinds of contact with certain individuals will be a traumatic and unsettling experience which can leave children frightened, distressed and dissociated and may damage their development in the short, medium and longer term. Forsberg and Pösö (2008) suggest that children experience supervised meetings with parents who present a risk, for example, very differently, with emotions varying from happiness to fear, anger and confusion. Very careful assessment and review are needed, as there are no short-cuts to identifying where on a continuum of developmental impact, from most constructive to most damaging, contact may be for each child.

When planning and reviewing contact, questions need to be asked that link contact plans and arrangements with a range of developmental goals (Beek and Schofield, 2004b). These might include questions such as does contact with this person in the context of this quality of relationship, with this frequency, at this venue and in the presence or absence of supervision enhance or diminish any or all of the following: the child's self-concept; identity; self-esteem; self-efficacy; capacity to come to terms with the past; opportunities to meet up with friends or play football for the school? The emphasis on contact as a basis for promoting "roots and identity", often the focus among lawyers in court proceedings, is only one part of understanding the contribution it can make to developmental well-being.

Research evidence concerning the measurable, relatively short-term outcomes of specific contact arrangements must be considered alongside the importance of helping children to manage their *conscious awareness* of their birth parents and other family members – something we should take as a given. But research needs to be taken seriously, since some assumptions, e.g., that more contact must inevitably increase the likelihood of certain outcomes, are unhelpful in planning for children.

Current issues in practice

Thus far we have considered the legal context, underlying issues and research on outcomes for contact. We move now to discuss some more specific practice issues involved in keeping the links between fostered children and their birth families – and the importance of work with birth parents.

The range, purpose and frequency of contact arrangements

Given the significance of the legal framework in relation to contact, it is not surprising that almost all fostered children at placement have care plans that include contact with one or more family members. But these plans will vary in their detail (Cleaver, 2000; Beek and Schofield, 2004b; Sinclair *et al*, 2005; Moyers *et al*, 2006). The term "contact" may, in practice, refer to opportunities provided to children and young people to see birth family members (or significant others) in person, to speak to them over the telephone or to send and receive letters, cards and presents – in various combinations in each case.

Depending on age and circumstances, contact may be anything from almost daily (for young infants) to once a year, and may be with one family member, several family members or with the whole family. Sinclair (2005) reports recent studies as showing that 40–50 per cent of foster children have at least weekly contact with at least one family member (citing Cleaver, 2000; Farmer *et al*, 2004; Sinclair *et al*, 2004). This is a significant increase from pre-Children Act 1989 days, when Berridge and Cleaver (1987) reported that only 11 per cent had weekly contact. The current overall frequency of contact probably reflects the fact that the majority of children who come into care will return home (Dickens *et al*, 2007).

Frequency, of course, needs also to be considered in terms of the regularity and predictability of the contact. Contact may be planned for or offered to parents at a particular frequency, but parents may not keep to arrangements. At times, the arrangements may be more flexible. Whatever the reason for unreliable or irregular contact, and whether expected to be frequent or infrequent, Browne and Maloney (2002) report that uncertainty contributes to what they describe as "ambiguous" placements, in which children and carers both feel unsettled.

Contact with siblings, grandparents, aunts and uncles is often part of a care plan. With increasingly complex families, children can have very complex contact arrangements, sometimes seeing large extended family groups on each occasion or having annual, monthly, weekly and fortnightly cycles of contact with different family members (Cleaver, 2000; Beek and Schofield, 2004b). Such multiple contacts can be difficult to manage for everyone, including the child. Foster carers, who often bear the brunt of the practical arrangements and emotional consequences, are too often not adequately consulted on what is right for the child or practically possible. Often contact frequency and arrangements can put pressure on birth relatives too. So the notion that more is better needs to be challenged in preference to what works and is appropriate for all, especially the child (Cleaver, 2000; Sinclair, 2005). Contact with a sibling in an adoptive placement is often seen as a significant part of both children's plans, but is rarely subject of a court order, relying on the adoptive parents and the foster carers to promote it. It often fails to happen as planned, much to the concern of the children (Schofield and Ward *et al*, 2008; Lord and Borthwick, this volume).

Frequency of contact may be affected by a number of factors in the child, the placement and the birth family, but research has shown that disabled children in particular have lower levels of contact on average and are, for example, less likely to have weekly contact (Baker, 2006). Baker suggests that this may be, in part, because they are placed further away, in part because they are less able to get their views heard, but also because their experience of contact is complex and the value of contact to disabled children is underestimated (see also Cousins, this volume). For these children in particular, work with the child, with the foster family and the birth family is crucial in maintaining the safe and high quality contact to which disabled children, like other children, are entitled.

Venue

Contact may take place in the foster home, the birth family home or at social services venues, such as family centres or designated contact centres. Cleaver (2000) found that, where it was possible, contact in the birth family home was on the whole preferred by children and birth parents. Her study found that in the first three months of placement, 23.7 per cent of contact was at home with 33.9 per cent in social services venues. But as time went by, this changed to 40.6 per cent at home and 27.1 per cent in social services venues. Complex transport arrangements to social services venues may be necessary, but can add an extra layer of potential anxiety for the child (and foster carers and birth parents). It is not unusual for children to be taken to contact by drivers and escorts who are different each time, unfamiliar to the child and may not be able to give feedback to the foster carers on how the contact went (Cleaver, 2000; Beek and Schofield, 2004a).

Contact in social services venues is generally being assessed, facilitated and/or supervised by children's services staff, some of whom are unqualified. Here, too, changing and inadequately prepared staff may add to anxieties and risks, for example, allowing a relative who is also a child's former abuser to join the family contact (Beek and Schofield, 2004a). The role of staff involved needs to be clear, as although the welfare of the child is a given priority, the point at which a supervisor may move from the role of observer and intervene to facilitate or regulate the behaviour of a child or contact relative may not be explicit (Forsberg and Pösö, 2008). Where parents are in prison or in a psychiatric hospital, visiting contact has to be very carefully planned and managed for children, but can still be valuable and necessary (Cleaver, 2000; Schofield *et al*, 2000).

Age of the child

The age of the child is a very significant factor in the varied purposes and arrangements for contact. Whereas for older children the focus of contact will be around assessing, preserving or developing existing relationships, for newborn or young infants the contact plan may be designed to build a first attachment relationship with a birth mother, as well as for teaching and then assessing the practical aspects of parenting (Schofield and Beek, 2006). This may occur where mothers have been substance misusers during pregnancy or have mental health problems or learning difficulties or have lost previous children. Contact in infancy is commonly several hours a day, for three to five or more days a week. Infants may spend this time in the foster home, but frequently spend it with birth parents, usually mothers, in a family centre setting away from the foster home. In the absence of research data on this practice, it is not clear exactly what proportion of infants have this very extended contact and in what circumstances, although we know courts tend to expect it. There is also a worrying lack of research on the value or impact of this level or pattern or quality of contact on the infant's development. These infants are often already very vulnerable at birth and need extra degrees of sensitivity and continuity in order to thrive physically and psychologically (Hill C., this volume).

For young children where the decision has been made to reduce contact prior to permanent placement for adoption, social workers often have a particularly challenging task. The court and the adoption panel may have their eye on the ultimate goal of a settled and successful adoption placement. However, it is social workers and foster carers who have to manage and cope with the practicalities of reducing contact and the feelings of all concerned (including other children in the foster and birth families) during the months of waiting for a placement to be identified, for the move to happen, and for the adoption order to be made. This is part of a gradual process of separation that requires maximum support to all involved – including the foster carers, who are managing the feelings of the children in relation to both the diminishing role of their birth relatives and the loss of the foster family, while coping with their own mixed feelings about the child's move to a new adoptive family. Although face-to-face contact in adoption is now more common (Neil, 2004; Young and Neil, 2004; Simmonds, this volume), there will still be cases when there is a point at which there may be a final contact visit, to parents or siblings or other relatives, prior to placement. Contact during these transitions is both a challenge and an opportunity, as it will be at the point of contact that full realisation of the changes ahead must be faced and feelings processed and managed.

For children in middle childhood, contact will tend to be less frequent than in infancy, often for practical reasons, and may take very different forms. It might be an activity-based outing as an alternative to a family home visit or social services venue (Cleaver, 2000; Beek and Schofield, 2004a, b). Where the plan is for assessment or reunification, this contact may be fairly clear in focus, but where the child is, say, six or seven years old and the subject of a long-term foster care plan till 18 and beyond, the role of contact and the nature of birth family relationships need to be carefully negotiated (Schofield, this volume). All parties need to understand that the child may have multiple attachments to birth and foster family caregivers who will play different, but hopefully complementary, roles over the coming years. The notion that children in this age group can have multiple attachments, albeit in a hierarchy of importance to the child (Kearns and Richardson, 2004), is often not well understood and this will affect how professionals think about and plan contact.

The study of adolescents by Farmer *et al* (2004) produced some rather concerning findings about the difficulties of contact for adolescents (Moyers *et al*, 2006). Although there may be an expectation that teenagers want to and should be allowed or even encouraged to start making their own contact arrangements, adolescents often need more help than they may get in managing their relationships with their birth families and therefore contact. The availability of mobile phones and e-mail has complicated the picture still further, but there are risks in simply leaving control in the hands of the teenager as if this was inevitable. For some young people the shift to a degree of flexibility and responsibility for contact may be straightforward and may indeed feel like a big step forward towards a more "normal" dual family life, rather like after divorce. But for other young people, "freedom" can place them back in the role some may have left years ago, when they first came into care, of being at risk of sexual or physical abuse or of meeting the needs of mentally ill or substance dependent birth parents (Schofield and Beek, 2008) or simply feeling confused and unsafe (Moyers *et al*, 2006).

Absence of contact

Although contact features in almost all care plans at the point of placement, a minority (approximately 15 per cent, Sinclair, 2005) have been found not to have contact with anyone in their family network. There are a number of very different reasons why a child may not have birth family contact. For a small group of children the local authority may have been given the right to refuse contact to one or more specific family members by a court order under section 34(4) Children Act 1989. It is one of the most taxing and problematic of decisions to terminate all contact or face-to-face meetings and must clearly only be taken when in the child's best interests. This would most commonly be where a family member represents a risk of significant harm to the child, possibly through sexual abuse, but also through physical or emotional harm, or if there is a high risk of abduction. Less obvious but always troubling are cases in which the child has become enmeshed with a parent who is so severely disturbed emotionally, often associated with mental illness, that he or she can no longer see themselves as a separate individual and contact can be very troubling or traumatic for the child. This enmeshed relationship is often harder for children to manage and move on from than rejection (Schofield, 2003).

Another group of children will not be having contact because birth family members feel unable or have made the decision not to visit or maintain the relationship. This withdrawal by a birth family may happen gradually over time or may be an instant abandonment at the point the child first comes into care, which may itself have been at the family's request. In extreme cases, parents may also ban other members of the extended family from making any contact with the child (Beek and Schofield, 2004a). It is important also to remember that some adopted children will be coming into care after placements have broken down. Many of these children will have lost contact with their birth family at the point of placement for adoption; some, though not all, will have the ongoing support of adoptive parents through contact.

There will also be children whose parents cannot be found. Here it is important to bear in mind that, although both mother and father may have disappeared from the child's life before or since admission to care, the absence of fathers is often not remarked upon or challenged to quite the same degree as mothers. This, in part, reflects the fact that a significant proportion (77% in Moyers *et al*, 2004) were not living with their fathers at the time they came into care. In a US study of long-term foster care, 80 per cent saw their birth father either infrequently or not at all (Pecora *et al*, 1998). Most practitioners do give some thought to the possible benefits and risks of reviving or creating a relationship through contact with previously absent fathers. At best, the father and the father's family may be enabled to fulfill a significant role in the child's life, including in some cases offering the child a home (Sinclair *et al*, 2007). At worst, the father may appear in a flurry of presents and apparent good intentions only to disappear again two weeks later. But in the middle are a range of negotiated relationships that, with the support of a social worker and a positive approach from the foster carer, may contribute to the child's self-esteem and sense of self through contact in some form.

A further group of children will not be having birth family contact with one or more family members because they have indicated that they do not wish for contact. This is more likely in adolescence and /or after a period of time in care and is often when there has been a long-standing troubled relationship (Beek and Schofield, 2004a). However, it is very common for children to want a wide range of contact, including no contact, with different people, as Sinclair concludes.

It was possible to want unrestricted contact with a grandmother, never to see a step-father again, have supervised contact with a mother and talk to siblings on the phone. (Sinclair, 2005, p 93)

The importance of the general principle of "reasonable contact" is that it places on workers the responsibility, in every case, to consider what kind of links with parents or other relatives there should be, and, as discussed above, to justify the exceptions. However, it should be possible in all cases for the plan to specify the anticipated *positive* purpose or *benefits* of contact in order to make sure the arrangements work in the interests of the child. As Moyers *et al* (2006, p 557) say in their study of adolescents, there needs to be clarity about the purpose of contact.

> *Was it a step towards reunification and/or to maintain the young person's sense of identity and their place within their family network; was it to improve relationships between young people and their parents and resolve attachment issues or to reassure young people that they had not been rejected; or was it for a combination of some or all of these reasons? The purposes of contact need to be considered carefully so that the way in which it is managed matches those aims.*

The role of the social worker

Social workers play a key role in the lives of fostered children and, in the context of this chapter, they have two critical responsibilities. The first is to enable children to manage their multiple family relationships and to make sense of their past in relation to their present, so that each child has a coherent narrative. The second is to work with birth parents to facilitate the best available relationship between them and their children.

These areas of practice were described many years ago by Clare Winnicott, whose work was influential in the years following the 1948 Children Act. She argued that the social worker has a crucial part to play as a bridge between a child's past, present and future and as holding together the different parts of the child's life. Thoburn (2007, p 512) refers to Winnicott's work as 'classic, and still the best statement of the principles and values that must underpin social work'. Winnicott (1964) established the importance of work with the child and the birth parent, but also acknowledged that 'some of the most difficult interviews that the child care worker has to conduct are with the parents of the children who are in care' (Kanter, 2004, p 163). Social workers nevertheless need to be a repository of knowledge about the child's parents and other family members, past and present, and bring reality to the child – 'she knows my mother' – as well as helping the child with the feelings arising from their relationship history.

The challenge is how to apply Winnicott's insights to contemporary child welfare in a radically different organisational context. Social work practice is always affected by the organisational context and the structures in which it is practised. In British child welfare today, there is often a disjunction between what children need and what they receive. While in theory, for example, we place great store on life story work as part of a process to help children make sense of their lives, past and present, the reality is that the fragmentation of their relationships is often increased by the processes of "being in care". In some circumstances, social workers find themselves contributing to fragmentation instead of acting as a bridge for the child. For the contemporary social worker, Winnicott's conception of the social work role with children in care and their parents poses a problem. It seems to assume that one individual worker will be holding everything together for the child. Yet our current organisational arrangements rarely facilitate this. Within a particular local authority, a "case" may well fall between several teams, with parents, children and carers being the responsibility of different workers. Instability in the work force and use of agency staff exacerbate the problem. This varies in extent from one authority to another, but at its worst, it has resulted in parents (and children) having frequent changes of social worker, which does nothing to promote stability and a sense of long-term professional responsibility for particular children. This lack of continuity is a major complaint of parents (Schofield *et al*, 2000, p 251–2).

> *I have lost count of how many social workers I've had. I can remember at least half a dozen, and there is probably another half a dozen I don't remember.*

> *You confide in them and then they leave . . It's constant.*

Thus, to translate theory into practice, it is essential that organisational arrangements do not increase the sense of fragmentation which children and parents inevitably experience. Ways must be found, at a minimum, of ensuring that social workers and others who are in touch with parents communicate effectively with the child, the carers and others involved in the life of the child.

Working with birth parents
The critical and unique task of the social worker is to put knowledge into action which is helpful to the parents in a particular situation while keeping a hold on the best interests of the child. This is the point at which the thinking *and* feeling of the worker must come together if the parents and child are to be well served. Both are essential to understanding and the social worker must use the impact of the case on her/himself as part of the evidence. Feelings are facts.

Crucial to the effective management of these links between separated children and their families is an appreciation of the intensity of the emotions which some or all of the parties experience, including the professional workers involved. It is not unusual for professionals to disagree, sometimes intensely, over plans for contact or reunification; indeed, there have been examples in some Serious Case Reviews, such as that of Jasmine Beckford (Blom-Cooper, 1985). These arguments will usually be ostensibly about what is in the child's best interests and may indeed arise from genuinely held different theoretical frameworks. But it is equally possible that they arise from difficulties in holding the tensions which such situations may create and which may trigger complex emotional reactions in the workers, particularly in relation to the parents. However, there is always a dynamic interplay between child, parents, foster carers, and a range of others, such as relatives who may be in the background but still be influential. This is why efforts have to be made to avoid fragmentation of the role of the social worker.

Issues may arise when a social worker working with the parents was also responsible for the case leading up to the removal of a child from home. In such circumstances, it is sometimes suggested that continuing work with parents may be best undertaken by a different worker, because of the likely anger and antagonism which the situation has generated. Indeed, a recurring theme in Serious Case Reviews has been the difficulty social workers have experienced with the hostility and false compliance with parents. There will be some circumstances in which such a change of worker should be considered. However, we should always be careful about a split between "good cop" and "bad cop". Not only is it important to help parents understand that an individual social worker alone does not make the decision that a child has to leave home, but receiving support from a social worker who demonstrates concern for the child *and* the parent following separation can help both of them to resolve angry feelings and feel connected. One social worker whose court report had recommended the removal of four children from a mother with learning difficulties went to the trouble subsequently of taking her to the dentist for urgently needed treatment that she had been too anxious to seek out alone. Small kindnesses of this sort for a mother who no longer had her children with her were much valued. This mother was still in regular contact with her children ten years later.

Decisions about a change of worker will have to be made on the basis of an assessment of the parents' capacity to engage with a particular practitioner and the capacity of the practitioner to empathise with the parents and to manage the intense emotions which may be generated.

Assessing risk

Since many children in care have been subjected to abuse and neglect by parents, there are often fundamental questions of risk from birth parents to be addressed in the management of contact (Cleaver, 2000; Beek and Schofield, 2004b; Sinclair, 2005). In such cases, the extent and type of risk also have to be assessed in relation to the age and general capacity of the child. Past events will have to be considered, but the current situation is critical. This may be in relation to changes, for better or for worse, in the parents' capacities to parent but there are also often changes, as mentioned above, in the structure of families after a child comes into care. There is, in addition, the possibility that a vulnerable mother whose child has been sexually or physically abused by her partner is unable to maintain the separation from him which she had initially accepted as necessary for the child's sake. In such circumstances, it is not surprising if the mother is not open with the worker.

In working with parents where there are child protection issues, social workers are faced with a difficult balancing act. Establishing trust and confidence are key elements in establishing a relationship, but where the safety of the child is involved, a degree of caution and scepticism is necessary. It is possible for the worker to have deep sympathy for a parent who may be guilty and angry and desperate not to acknowledge failure as a parent. But a parent in denial of the past may represent a real risk in the future.

Various Serious Case Reviews of children who have died, have found that failure by social workers adequately to understand the dynamics of the household and the "dangerousness" of one of the parents or a parent's partner has contributed to the tragedy. This has usually occurred before the child comes into care, but it is important to recognise that levels of risk may ebb and flow during the years after a child has gone into foster care. There are particular issues in relation to children who have been seriously neglected by parents who have problems with drug addiction and/or alcoholism (Stevenson, 2007). It is well understood that these parents may relapse and that their optimism about their capacity to take responsibility for their children, even for "outings" or weekends, may not be well founded. In such cases, supervised contact may be the only realistic option, even if it can be problematic.

Assessing the benefits of maintaining links

Although for the child's safety such assessments of risk are essential, subtle and more nuanced questions must also be asked to address the fundamental issues: in what ways are the current arrangements for contact beneficial to the child? What are perceived to be the main benefits of future contact and/or reunification? What are the emotional costs? Is some degree of current upset to the child manageable in the interests of his/her longer-term well-being? These are profound and difficult questions which often cannot be answered with certainty. They are matters of judgement in which the social workers play a critical role. Even if a social worker is working exclusively with parents, they have an obligation to put at centre stage the impact of these arrangements on the child and the implication for future plans.

The work to be done directly with parents has two components. The first is, in all cases, a specific assessment of parental capacity in the here and now to give the child "good-enough" experiences, either through contact or, where appropriate, to take her/him back into the family. The second is to intervene, directly or indirectly, to provide help to parents in ways which will support or increase their parenting capacity. In both spheres of activity, there is a significant body of relevant government guidance, literature and research, but it is more about assessment and intervention and it does not focus upon the particular situation of parents with fostered children. Rather, it deals with the parents of children who need protection and safeguarding with their families before they enter care. There seem to be few significant studies of detailed ongoing work from the onset of the care episode, either towards reunification or towards more satisfactory contact, or even to limit contact in certain circumstances.

Social workers will need to consider the factors which led to a child's entry to care, especially those relating to parental characteristics and behaviour, and ask two questions. Have the parents' and family characteristics changed and, if so, how? Are the children or young people less vulnerable to harm than they were? Age may or may not be a critical factor; for example, where a child has been physically neglected, this may be less important when they are older, whereas emotional abuse may be very destructive to an adolescent. If the intention is to maintain or to increase contact or to pursue reunification, it is essential to have defined goals for intervention. These should arise naturally from the assessment and from the theoretical framework which underpins it.

In cases in which children have been seriously neglected, for example, there is a body of research and literature which suggests that it is best understood through an "ecological" model. By this is meant the interaction and interdependence of factors in such cases. 'You can never do just one thing' (Harbin, 1980) to change a situation in seriously neglectful families. However, there can be priorities – those changes which are perceived to be essential before others can be made. In the present context in the UK, this might well be when a parent is seriously dependent on drugs or alcohol. To reduce or eliminate that dependence may be crucial but, if achieved, there will be other issues to tackle – for example, poverty or extreme debt.

A second example of "work to be done" may derive from the application of attachment theory to a particular parent–child interaction. Almost by definition, there are issues in "attachment" and "bonding" when children have entered care, either because of problems which pre-date the admission or as a result of it. There needs to be a very subtle use of attachment theory when observing and assessing children and parents in relation to contact (see Schofield and Beek, 2006, Chapter 14).

Working with parents' own histories

Work with the parents will have to make connections with their own past experiences and present behaviour. All parents bring into current relationships with their children elements of their own childhood experiences. This is not to say that current behaviours are determined by the past, but the quality of their past experiences can affect their current behaviour, for better and for worse. Past/present connections always need to be explored and they frequently throw light on parents' behaviour towards their children and to other key people, such as the foster carers and social workers.

There are some instances of parents who have been so deeply deprived of the essential early bonding and attachment relationships, that they cannot form lasting relationships with their own children or with adults. It is likely that parents of children in care will have had troubled and insecure attachments in childhood. In such cases, the social worker may have an opportunity to make a relationship with a parent which is remedial and restorative and goes some way to enabling a parent to be a better parent, even if only through a contact relationship.

At its most basic level, this potential for a therapeutic role is bound up with the social worker's qualities. A parent who experiences a social worker as a *reliable* person, a secure base who has *time* for them, may act as a corrective to previous experiences in childhood.

Sometimes, but not always, the worker may be able to help a parent to understand better the complex connections between their feelings about their own childhood and those towards their own child. This may decrease some of the tensions and enable more constructive patterns of contact to be developed.

The feelings of parents about their situation

Most parents whose children come into care experience sadness, grief and anger, and it is important for social workers to understand these feelings.

It's like a death, except there isn't a funeral.

It's like a grieving that just goes on and on. I can't believe how long it has been.

I felt lost. One day I was a mother of three children, and then a mother with no children. There was nothing to do. I was lost, no children to look after.

(All quotations above and below from Schofield *et al*, 2000).

Some parents acknowledge that they did not have the "right" feelings or the ability to parent the child and express indirectly relief that the child is now safe and well.

I just didn't feel motherly towards her.

Some of the things I done were dreadful. They certainly weren't the way you should look after a child. I wasn't feeding her properly – just throwing a bag of crisps at her.

She didn't stand a chance really, what with me being ill and not knowing what the matter was and in and out of hospital right from when she was born.

Certain types of complex feelings need special attention. It is often said, for example, that parents feel "guilty" about the loss of the child or about their own behaviour. This assertion requires further analysis. We need to ask whether a parent experiences feelings of guilt at a conscious level which can be discussed, in which responsibility for failure is acknowledged. There are some parents whose own upbringing has been so deprived or damaged that they have not reached this stage. They may feel shame and experience stigma because they realise that others criticise what they do. But that is a social construct and may not spring from internalised guilt or remorse. Guilt may also be deeply repressed, beneath layers of powerful denial of personal responsibility; everyone else is blamed. It may be that the time when they failed as a parent was one of turmoil and instability (for example, if alcohol or drugs were misused) and they have inadequate recall of events which precipitated a child's removal from home. Thus, although there may be generalised guilt, it is not pinned to a particular sequence of events.

There may also be parents who do not comprehend why their children were taken away. This may often be in cases of serious neglect but also physical harm.

They kept saying he was neglected, but I was looking after them all right. I only ever smacked them lightly.

Thus, the important question for social workers is whether guilt is available as a basis for work with parents. Guilt can lead to emotional paralysis, depression which leads to inactivity or to running away from the child who has been hurt. Or it can lead to reparations, sometimes seen in exaggerated gifts or promises. Both manifestations of guilt can give a worker an opportunity to discuss the pain and the most effective and practical ways of making reparation to the child. Good practice with parents already feeling deeply guilty does not reinforce this feeling but "holds" it and uses it constructively, for the benefit of the parents and also their relationship with the child.

There are also some parents who have, for many reasons to do with their personal histories, never felt a strong connection with or responsibility for their children and who abandon them, emotionally or practically, when they come into foster care. This may happen gradually or suddenly and without warning at any stage. The social work then has to be done with the child and the carers to come to terms with the parents' behaviour. However, in that bleak situation, there may still be a door left open for the child who, as an adolescent and adult, may go on to form a different kind of relationship later with parents or other relatives, adult to adult.

Parents' views of social workers and foster carers

Social workers may variously be seen by parents as unhelpful or as an essential and reliable empathic resource.

I didn't feel they helped in any way.

I hate them all, all social workers.

I felt I could build up a relationship with her. I phoned her up and just burst into tears and she came over within half an hour.

Mike was really there. He was friendly, he was warm. He was everything you didn't think a social worker was.

She [social worker] was marvellous. She used to come and see me every two to three weeks and have a cup of tea. I had a Christmas card from her after she left too, just wishing us well. When she was the one on the case, we always knew what was happening.

It often surprises new social workers to find that not all birth parents of children in foster care are angry and hostile towards them or towards carers – though often the fear that birth parents will react negatively leads to social workers keeping their distance or enforcing distance between birth parents and foster carers. It is important to distinguish between parents who do indeed remain angry and potentially destructive to placements and those who actually could manage a more open and collaborative relationship with carers than is often encouraged, as these comments from birth parents suggest:

> *We [parent and carer] have become good friends over the years. I feel I can talk things through with them.*

> *We [parent and carers] have really fought to keep him in mainstream school, and he is. We did that together.*

> *I get together with her [carers] once a month on the first Wednesday. We have a coffee and a chat. That's nice.*

When one birth parent, whose four children were growing up in foster care as a result of her drug and mental health problems, was asked what advice she would give to social workers, she said:

> *If they can remember what the person is going through, through losing their kids and the pain that causes. We are not made of stone, none of us are.*

The social worker's feelings
Work with parents of a fostered child necessitates awareness of the impact that these complex and varied situations of separation and loss are having on oneself and other professionals, and of the task of managing these emotions constructively. It is not possible to be an effective social worker without being "involved"; that is the essence of empathy. But often there are complex and painful mixtures of feelings. For example, there may be aspects of the parents' past behaviour towards the child which were particularly distressing. There may be cases in which the social worker is defensive because she knows that the child has not been served well while in care and has been subject to changes and foster home breakdowns. (It is not unknown for parental contact to be increased or re-established as a kind of measure of last resort when this happens.) There may be times when the social worker feels sympathy and compassion for a vulnerable and deprived parent, perhaps with limited intellectual capacity. There may also be times when workers have had particular experiences in their own family life which trigger a more extreme reaction than may be appropriate.

It is therefore essential that models of consultation and supervision are available which encourage workers, as individuals or in groups, to reflect upon the impact of their cases on themselves as well as others. Conventional "line management" supervision has an important part to play, especially in relation to risk, but it does not itself provide a safe place for the exploration of underlying tensions and ambivalence about these extra-ordinarily difficult situations.

Unfortunately, however, it seems that, too often, work with parents is not underpinned by arrangements designed to support the workers. Regular visits before the reviews of long-term fostered children, in particular, may be somewhat perfunctory, because seen as low priority by the organisation, and may not make ongoing assessments of what parental contact or knowledge about parents means to the child now or may mean in future. When this happens, the "connecting" role of the social worker is lost. Social work with separated children and their parents needs the very best kind of thoughtful and reflective supervision to ensure that practitioners feel confident, competent and sensitive to the sometimes conflicting needs of both children and parents.

Conclusions

Children, foster carers and birth parents all have their own needs to be met within the relationships that are woven into the placement. Contact is the point at which this complex network of needs, feelings, meanings and experiences come together. There is a job of emotional management to be done alongside the practical arrangements.

The key messages for practice are simple but require thoughtful application.

- Promoting as constructive a relationship as possible between fostered children and their birth families, including all aspects of contact, needs to be based on a careful, developmentally-informed assessment of each child and family member.
- Although it is tempting for agencies to adopt a formula for the frequency and arrangements for contact, each case needs to be judged on its own merits in relation to the risk and benefits to the child.
- However "permanent" the plan is for the child in a foster placement, and whether contact is frequent or non-existent, the birth family will continue to be important in the mind of the child. This needs to be taken into account in work with the child, in work with foster families and in work with birth families.
- Social workers need good training and regular sensitive supervision if they are going to be able to remain empathic, active, creative, flexible and open-minded in their work with the child, the foster family and the birth family.

Selected further reading

Cleaver H. (2000) *Fostering Family Contact*, London: The Stationery Office

Neil E. and Howe D. (eds) (2004) *Contact in Adoption and Permanent Foster Care: Research, theory and practice*, London: BAAF

Schofield G., Beek M., Sargent K. and Thoburn J. (2000) *Growing up in Foster Care*, London: BAAF

Winnicott C (1964) *Child Care and Social Work*, Hitchin: Codicote Press

References

Aldgate J. (1980) 'Identification of factors which influence length of stay in care', in Triseliotis J. P. (ed) *New Developments in Foster Care and Adoption*, London: Routledge

Alpert L. T. (2005) 'Research review: Parents' services experience – a missing element in research on foster care case outcomes', *Child and Family Social Work*, 10:4, pp 353–360

Baker C. (2006) 'Disabled foster children and contacts with their birth families', *Adoption & Fostering*, 30:2, pp 18–28

Barber J. G. and Delfabbro P. H. (2004) *Children in Foster Care*, London: Routledge

Beek M. and Schofield (2004a) *Providing a Secure Base in Long-term Foster Care*, London: BAAF

Beek and Schofield (2004b) 'Promoting security and managing risk: Contact in long-term foster care', in Neil E. and Howe D. (eds) *Contact in Adoption and Permanent Foster Care: Research, theory and practice*, London: BAAF

Berridge D. and Cleaver H. (1987) *Foster Home Breakdown*, Oxford: Basil Blackwell

Blom-Cooper L. (1985) (Chair) *A Child in Trust (Jasmine Beckford)*, London Borough of Brent

Browne D. and Maloney A. (2002) 'Contact irregular: A qualitative analysis of the impact of visiting patterns of natural parents on foster placements', *Child and Family Social Work*, 7, pp 35–45

Cleaver H. (2000) *Fostering Family Contact*, London: The Stationery Office

Daniel B. and Taylor T. (2001) *Engaging with Fathers*, London: Jessica Kingsley Publishers

Department for Education and Skills (2007) *Care Matters: Time for change*, Cm 7137. Crown Copyright

Dickens J. (2006) 'Care, control and change in child care proceedings: Dilemmas for social workers, managers and lawyers,' *Child and Family Social Work*, 11:1, pp 23–32

Dickens J., Howell D., Thoburn J. and Schofield G. (2007) 'Children starting to be looked after by local authorities in England: An analysis of inter-authority variation and case-centred decision making', *British Journal of Social Work*, 37, pp 597–617

Fanshel V. and Shinn E. B. (1978) *Children in Foster Care: A longitudinal study*, New York: Columbia University Press

Farmer E., Moyers S. and Lipscombe J. (2004) *Fostering Adolescents*, London: Jessica Kingsley Publishers

Farmer E., Sturgess W. and O'Neill T. (2008) *Reunification of Looked After Children with their Parents: Patterns, interventions and outcomes*, Report to the Department for Children, Schools and Families, Bristol: School for Policy Studies, University of Bristol

Forsberg H. and Pösö T. (2008) 'Ambiguous position of the child in supervised meetings', *Child and Family Social Work*, 13:1, p 52–60

Fratter J., Rowe J., Sapsford D. and Thoburn J. (1991) *Permanent Family Placement: A decade of experience*, London: BAAF

Harbin G. (1980) 'The Tragedy of the Commons', in Daly H. (ed.) *Economics, Ecology and Ethics*, New York, NY: Freeman, pp 100–114

Howe D. and Steele M. (2004) 'Contact in cases in which children have been traumatically abused or neglected by their birth parents', in Neil E. and Howe D. (eds) *Contact in Adoption and Permanent Foster Care: Research, theory and practice*, London: BAAF

Kanter J. (ed) (2004) *Face to Face with Children: The life and work of Clare Winnicott*, London: Karnac

Kearns K. A. and Richardson R. A. (2005) *Attachment in Middle Childhood*, New York NY: Guilford Press

Milham S., Bullock R., Hosie K. and Haak M. (1986) *Children Lost in Care: The family contacts of children in care*, Aldershot: Gower

Moyers S., Farmer and Lipscombe J. (2006) 'Contact with family members and its impact on adolescents and their foster placements', *British Journal of Social Work*, 36, pp 541–559

Neil E. (2004) 'The "Contact after Adoption" study: Face-to-face contact', in Neil E. and Howe D. (eds) *Contact in Adoption and Permanent Foster Care: Research, theory and practice*, London: BAAF

Pecora P. J., Le Prohn N. C., Nollan K., Downs A. C., Wolf M., Lamont E., Horn M., Paddock G., Adams W. and Kingry K. (1998) *How are the Children Doing? Assessing your outcomes in family foster care*, Seattle, WA: The Casey Family Program

Quinton D., Rushton A., Dance C. and Mayes D. (1997) 'Contact between children placed away from their home and their birth parents: Research issues and evidence', *Clinical Child Psychology and Psychiatry*, 2:3, pp 393–413

Rowe J., Cain H., Hundleby M. and Keane A. (1984) *Long-term Foster Care*, London: Batsford

Schofield G. (2003) *Part of the Family: Pathways through foster care*, London: BAAF

Schofield G. and Beek M. (2006) *Attachment Handbook for Foster Care and Adoption*, London: BAAF

Schofield G. and Beek M. (2008) *Achieving Permanence in Foster Care: A good practice guide*, London: BAAF

Schofield G., Beek M., Sargent K. and Thoburn J. (2000) *Growing up in Foster Care*, London: BAAF

Schofield G. and Ward E., with Warman A., Simmonds J. and Butler J. (2008) *Permanence in Foster Care: A study of care planning in England and Wales*, London: BAAF

Sinclair I. (2005) *Fostering Now: Messages from research*, London: Jessica Kingsley Publishers

Sinclair I., Baker C., Lee J. and Gibbs I. (2007) *The Pursuit of Permanence: A study of the English care system*, London: Jessica Kingsley Publishers

Sinclair I., Baker C., Wilson K. and Gibbs I. (2005) *Foster Children: Where they go and how they get on*, London: Jessica Kingsley Publishers

Stevenson O. (2007) *Neglected Children and Their Families* (2nd ed), Oxford: Blackwell

Thoburn J. (1991) 'Survey findings and conclusions', in Fratter J., Rowe J., Sapsford D. and Thoburn J, *Permanent Family Placement: A decade of experience*, London: BAAF

Thoburn J. (2007) 'Out of home care for the abused or neglected child,' in Wilson K. and James A. (eds) *The Child Protection Handbook* (3rd edition), pp 494–515, Edinburgh: Balliere Tindall

Thoburn J., Murdoch A. and O'Brien A. (1986) *Permanence in Child Care*, Oxford: Basil Blackwell

Weinstein E. A. (1960) *The Self-image of the Foster Child*, New York: Russell Sage Foundation

Wilson K., Sinclair I., Taylor C., Pithouse A. and Sellick C. (2004) *Fostering Success: Exploration of the research literature in foster care*, SCIE. Bristol: Nottingham University Policy Press

Winnicott C. (1964) *Child Care and Social Work*, Hitchin: Codicote Press

Young J. and Neil E. (2004) 'The "Contact after Adoption" Study: The perspective of birth relatives after non-voluntary adoption', in Neil E. and Howe D. (eds) *Contact in Adoption and Permanent Foster Care: Research, theory and practice*, London: BAAF

11 Residential care

Roger Bullock

Introduction

There are several reasons why those involved in caring for children away from home – managers, professionals, parents and young people – will be interested in residential child care. First, it is a part of a system of services designed to promote children's welfare. Quite a lot is known about this as national statistics indicate the numbers, characteristics and lengths of stay of those in residence, making it possible to discern the role and function of residential care in the broad spectrum of provision. Such concerns generate an interest in the origin of admissions and destination of leavers and relationships to other interventions, especially foster care, support at home and prison custody.

A different view focuses more on the child and the contribution that residential care makes to meeting his or her needs. So young people who have been in care through their middle childhood might be placed in residential care in adolescence to protect themselves and others from the consequences of what has become seriously disruptive behaviour. As an intervention, it is important to know something of the child's situation before and after their residential placement and identify whether the evidence for the "hoped for" or "intended change" is sufficient: in short, was the "treatment effective"?

A third perspective focuses on the residential settings themselves and their culture and the quality of care that they provide. In selecting a placement for a child, professionals will seek an establishment that suits the young person and meets their needs and, hopefully, where he or she will be happy.

Many other frameworks for understanding residential services are possible, such as the relationship between costs and outcomes or marrying societal expectations of control and welfare, but the three identified above are sufficient for the purposes of this chapter.

Defining residential care

Having described various perspectives on residential care, the next task is to identify what the service comprises. This is by no means easy as all of the features usually cited as characteristic can be challenged. For example, an emphasis on group living might be expected but many children's homes only accommodate one or two children, fewer than found in some foster homes. It may be thought that staff stay longer than the children, but this may not be so in establishments such as boarding schools and therapeutic communities. Control over children's behaviour might be a specified aim of the establishment but many children go home at weekends and school holidays when they might have far less supervision. Similarly, keeping children safe from harm might be thwarted by abuse, bullying by other children or sometimes staff in the establishment. Giving children a chance to catch up on their education might be obstructed by poorly trained staff where education is a lower priority than managing challenging behaviour. The age of the children in residential care might be a significant factor, given that it is not usually the placement of choice for pre-adolescent children, but this is not the case for disabled children in respite care. A key difference could be in the role of the staff in that much of their work is conducted in a public arena. They are also in "loco parentis" as a group but not expected as individuals to undertake parenting tasks; yet, children frequently report that residential workers are experienced as caring, supportive parental figures.

So what can be concluded? Initially, it is clear that residential care is a setting in which children are placed with other children for at least one night with the aim of meeting a welfare need and, hopefully, improving their health and development. Children spend the majority of time outside school or work in this context and there are usually no adult family members present. In addition, the number of children will usually exceed the number of staff on duty at any one time.

There are a large number of different residential care settings run by different organisations that fit this set of criteria. At one extreme, there are the prestigious boarding schools favoured by the British upper middle classes seeking long-term education for their children. There are about 80,000 boarders of this kind at any one time in the UK, enjoying excellent facilities now far removed from the public schools of old. Few looked after children attend such establishments, although recently it has become an option that is being explored. The main residential facilities for looked after children are children's homes, hostels, boarding schools for children with special needs, therapeutic treatment establishments and respite care. Some providers, usually independent agencies, operate a network of facilities that includes residence as one option among other services, such as independent living and family placements, so enabling children to move easily between settings depending on their needs. There are about 25,000 children in these types of "welfare" residential provision at any one time in the UK, although the figure increases if establishments such as refuges, temporary family accommodation, supported lodgings, immigration centres and prison custody are included. About 9,000 of the 70,000 children in care or accommodation in the United Kingdom are placed residentially at any one time but more, around another 6,000, will have had such an experience at some point in their care career.

But overall figures can give a misleading picture because although some 14 per cent of the looked after population are placed residentially at any one time, they are mostly adolescents and the proportion for the 16–18 age group is much higher, nearer 30 per cent, compared with only two per cent for those aged under 11. In addition, there are now 4,000 young people under 18 in prison department custody and many others in bed and breakfast accommodation, some of whom in former years would have been in residential homes and schools. So, while there has been an apparent big decline in the use of residential care for looked after children – as much as 75 per cent in the last 30 years – the increasing use of prison custody and lodgings somewhat bucks this trend.

There is a further complication in that each of the four countries that make up the UK has its own legislation and tradition regarding the use of residential care. England shows similarities to Wales and Northern Ireland but Scotland is noticeably different. When children's homes were provided in Scotland, they often reflected religious affiliation and tended to be funded by local groups. As a result, homes opened and closed with some regularity. It was the industrial and reform schools founded in the nineteenth and twentieth centuries that most closely resembled the rest of the UK, largely because they were funded centrally. These different histories urge caution when generalising about residential care in the UK.

Classifying residential care

There have been several attempts to classify the plethora of provision into discrete categories. One, made by Beedell in 1970, identified at least eleven distinct functions – physical care, safety, control, education, relationships, stability, relief to the wider child care system, shelter, containment, assessment and group work. Another, by Berridge (1985), found that the main functions of the children's homes he studied in the 1980s were aiding reception to care, controlling difficult adolescents, caring for groups of siblings, rehabilitating long-stay children and dealing with the aftermath of placement breakdowns.

The most rigorous classification of British and US establishments for children is that by the Chapin Hall Center for Children in the University of Chicago (Chipenda-Dansokho et al, 2003). From a review of evidence, it identified three dimensions that, independent of one another, appeared to differentiate residential provision most sharply. (Other dimensions were significant but were closely related to the three identified.)

They conclude that residential provision can be divided according to:

- the needs of the children being met;
- the organisational structure used to make the provision; and
- the extent and nature of parental involvement and autonomy.

A five-fold typology of establishments emerged:

1. Facilities that are primarily focused on providing high-quality education and less preoccupied with students' health and behavioural needs.
2. Facilities that provide an enriched educational experience but also address children's psychological and behavioural needs to meet these ends.
3. Facilities focused on meeting an identified cognitive or educational deficit in

children's development. Since such deficits frequently have their origins in family dysfunction and/or are manifest in poor behaviour of the child, the placement demands considerable specialist resources.

4. Facilities for children with a mixture of social, psychological and behavioural needs and who are generally educated in ordinary schools. The placement tends to be short and part of a range of provision focused on several family members, not just the child.

5. Facilities for children with serious psychological needs and behavioural problems that overshadow other developmental goals, including education. Some of these placements are secure.

Using this classification, it is clear from what has been said so far that residential care for looked after children in the UK falls mostly in categories 3–5 although there is current interest in the use of the first two types of establishment.

Trends in residential care

In addition to the considerable decline in the use of residential care for looked after children in the UK over the past 30 years, other trends have been identified within the residential sector (Gooch, 1996). These are:

- the replacement of single-sex establishments by ones that are co-educational but which, in practice, are dominated by boys
- the increasing age of residents at entry
- more young people with health problems, behavioural disorders and disabilities
- greater racial and ethnic mix
- larger catchments areas, raising problems for educational continuity and contact with home
- more provision by private agencies
- less specialisation by sector with a resulting mix of needs in each establishment
- assessment by need criteria rather than social role categories, such as disabled or special educational needs
- a more generalist service
- shorter stays
- rising costs
- more concerns about rights and protection; and
- further reductions in the size of units and in the numbers accommodated by the system but a larger proportion of the total places in secure accommodation or other specialist centres.

Naturally, the factors that explain changes in the use of private boarding schools, establishments for children with special educational needs or penal institutions may be different from those that affect child care establishments but in all of these sectors the important point is that viable alternatives have been created. Even in those primarily concerned with delinquent and disruptive adolescents, the emergence of a coherent youth offending service in the late 1990s has been significant, although there is still considerable reliance on the use of residential care as a last resort.

Having set the context, it is now possible to return to the three perspectives important to those placing children residentially and to consider each of them in turn.

1. Residential care as part of the wider child care system

In a study of 193 randomly selected children who were in care on a selected day and looked after for more than three months by two British local authorities (Dartington-I, 2003), it was found that 15 of the 193 children were living in residential care and another 14 had been in such placements at some point.

All but one of the 15 residents (5 girls and 10 boys) were aged between 13 and 18 and all but three were over the age of 11 when they entered care. The 14 (5 girls and 9 boys) who had been so placed in the past were also teenagers aged 13–16, but some had come into care at a younger age, four of them before the age of five. Thus, for children aged ten or more, the proportion in residence more than doubles to 18 per cent.

This evidence suggests that residence is used differently for different children. It is a first placement for many adolescents coming into care because of family tensions and difficult behaviour but a later choice for children whose foster care placements have disrupted or who present increasingly severe needs, often associated with earlier trauma and abuse.

The role of residential care in different areas of a child's life at different times is demonstrated in the diagram published in the Department of Health's research overview (see overleaf), *Caring for Children away from Home* (1998). As can be seen, the girl concerned had four residential placements. Although these involve only a small proportion of her life, they fulfilled important functions at different times and contributed, along with other services – including foster care – to a full outcome in young adulthood.

These studies of looked after children reveal two seeming contrasts. The first is that the majority of young people in residence are difficult adolescents in terms of their challenging behaviour at home, school and in the community. The second is that only a small proportion of all looked after adolescents who display challenging behaviour are placed residentially. In the sample of 193 children previously discussed, there were 68 who presented with behavioural problems but only 29 of them were or had ever been in residential care. Similarly, residential placements were being used for only five young people without behavioural problems. Thus, 39 of the 68 young people displaying

Figure 11.1
One child's experience of residence

Age	Living	Family relationships	Social behaviour	Health	Education
	hospital				
	with mum and dad				
	residence				
			friends mainly from home area		
	with dad and stepmum				
Age 5					primary school
	with mum and stepdad	contact with dad and oldest brother ceases			special education support
	residence				
	with mum	social work and psychiatric support for mother and brother			
10	foster home				secondary school
	with mum and stepdad				educated in therapeutic community
	children's home		friends mainly from residence		
				hospital	
15	**therapeutic community**	separated from younger brother		overdoses	
	foster home	intermittent contact with home	friends mainly from school	hospital	mainstream school
	foster home				
	foster home	regular contact with home	friends mainly from university		
20	own home and foster home				university

Reproduced with kind permission from Archer L *et al* (1998) *Caring for Children Away from Home: Messages from research*, Chichester: Wiley & Sons behavioural problems had never been placed residentially, despite the fact that difficult behaviour is the overwhelming characteristic of those living in residential establishments.

When the needs of the resident children are scrutinised, it is clear that the main reason for choosing residential care nowadays is to control or improve difficult or disturbed behaviour and that most of the other functions suggested by Beedell and Berridge, such as aiding admissions or keeping siblings together, no longer apply. Behaviour that is difficult to manage or understand is the main predictive factor for a residential placement, showing a multiplier effect of 12 over those without such problems. These difficulties do not occur in isolation, however, and affect other areas of children's lives, such as poor peer relationships or suspicion of professionals, and may be associated with special educational needs, making the residential task wider than just ensuring control.

Compared with other looked after children, however, the aforementioned studies found that the harm inflicted by parents on the children placed residentially is, with some notable exceptions, less of an issue than in foster care and, when it has occurred, tends to be emotional and sexual rather than physical. Levels of neglect are also lower and in a third of cases it was parents at the end of their tether who first approached Social Services. However, other family difficulties prevail, for example, the majority of the young people studied came from single parent families and a sizeable minority had parents with a chronic mental health problem.

Out of area placements

An issue facing professionals placing children residentially is whether to use the local authority's own facilities or purchase places from voluntary or independent providers. This latter group are known as "out of area" placements, which is a misleading term because purchased placements can often be local. It is more accurate to perceive them as externally purchased. As these add an extra cost to budgets, they are a highly visible item of expenditure and thus subject to considerable scrutiny.

Studies of "out of area" placements indicate that they are used for four different groups of looked after children, namely: children presenting severe and complex behavioural problems which have exhausted in-house services; children displaying behavioural difficulties and who are at continuing risk of harm; children in need of specialist therapy, especially for sexual abuse; and disabled children whose needs cannot be met locally. As local authority policies vary widely, generalisation is difficult, but studies in eight British local authorities (Dartington-I 2002, 2005) found that there were about 1.6 externally purchased residential placements to every one provided "in house" but that as lengths of stay in the former were much longer, a lower proportion of children were involved. The distribution between the four groups mentioned above was fairly even, being of the order of 23%:37%:22%:18%.

A comparison between children placed internally and externally revealed considerable variation between authorities but the main points are that external placements are used for boys and girls (although the ratio differs across the four groups) and that the reasons for choosing this option are the need for greater protection, therapy following abuse and neglect and highly specialised provision for specific problems, especially for a small number of children of primary school age. Surprisingly, the behaviour of the children and their educational history are not discriminating factors and certain high profile problems, such as alcohol and drug misuse, are found in both groups.

The benefits of external placements have to be balanced against the secondary problems they create for children and families and the risk of "drift". Just over half of the external placements in the surveys were more than 50 miles away from the child's home and 20 per cent were over 100. Moreover, a third of the children had limited contact with their birth relatives. While the future plans for the children included imminent return home (8%), moves to foster care (26%) and independent living (22%), for nearly half of them there was no clear expectation other than to stay put. Naturally, as the young people are mostly adolescents, they often form new friendships and emotional relationships in their new area, making return home difficult. While this experience is common for students going to college at 18, there is a danger that a changing perception of "home area" will affect looked after young people at an earlier age, without the supports and status that student life brings.

2. Effects of residential care

A good care plan for a child should specify expectations about what a residential placement is likely to achieve. But as the young people being admitted are often unsettled and distressed, because of turbulence at home or disruption to foster care, some initial expectations might have to be pragmatic, such as to provide stability in situations marked by limited options and status deterioration. The aims of the placement will, therefore, be a mixture of immediate benefits and, hopefully, improvement in the child's long-term situation.

Because of this complexity, it is difficult to identify any general effects of residential care as the intervention covers such a wide range of approaches and the evidence that would be necessary to show this, namely a set of randomised controlled trials, is scant (Little et al, 2005). Nevertheless, claims are made in the literature but these are often based on case studies and tend to generalise from one type of provision or particular group of children to the whole child care field. Moreover, there is a further danger of attributing to residential care defects of the care system as a whole.

To clarify the situation, it is useful to differentiate "procedural" from "treatment" approaches (Clough et al, 2006). The first stresses good child care practice at the expense of aims and so focuses on making the establishments nice places to live. While this provision does not offer specialist therapy and, as has been shown, control is often the over-riding concern, it should nevertheless provide an auspicious context for the work required to meet children's needs, such as improving their behaviour and family relationships, encouraging positive peer interaction and boosting self-esteem.

Second are "treatment" approaches, for example, those based on special education, behaviour modification or psycho-social models, that fashion regimes and structures to "treat" assessed problems, such as attachment, conduct and emotional disorders, anti-social behaviour and learning difficulties. While therapies will differ for individual children, the important feature is that the whole regime is conducive to their application and is staffed and structured to that end.

Many other opportunities are offered by residential care, for instance, the use of residential groups for therapeutic work, rehabilitative work with children rejected by their families and, of course, the imposition of control, such as for those in secure units.

So what might be expected from a residential experience? Traditionally, it has been suggested, but it has to be said without evidence that attains the status of a clinical trial, that residential care can offer several benefits. These are: to provide stability and a stimulating environment, to widen cultural and educational horizons, to create a framework for emotionally secure relationships with adults and to provide a setting for intensive therapeutic work. But these gains have to be set against difficulties of providing unconditional love, constraints on children's emotional development, poor staff continuity and marginalisation of children's families and other welfare services. While much is known about the dangers of placing young children in residential care and the neurological and emotional damage it can inflict (Browne *et al*, 2005), much less is known about the effects of such placements on the development of older children (Little *et al*, 2005).

But two outcomes are more certain, namely, that residential care can have a profound effect, for good or bad, on children while they are there and that regimes based on child welfare principles achieve better results than those that are not. Numerous studies have compared changes in the lives of children placed in different types of establishment and found that the incidence of such things as running away and of violent behaviour varies and that these contrasts are not explained by young people's background characteristics, although it is usually uncertain that similar gains would have been made without residential placement. The problem is, however, that benefits rarely carry over or are much reduced after leaving and the long-term effects of residential care have proved difficult to identify (Fonagy, 2002). Nevertheless, while there is much less difference in young people's difficult behaviour after leaving, the pattern of good and bad homes is usually maintained, whatever the type of establishment, suggesting that the influence on young people's potentially damaging behaviour while they are resident is mirrored by a smaller but still significant effect on behaviour after departure (Sinclair and Gibbs, 1998).

While long-term outcomes are easy to describe, they are more difficult to explain. For example, follow-up research suggests that some children who are challenging and

211

unsettled while in residential care do quite well in the longer term – some acting out girls for example – while others who are more quiescent, such as withdrawn institutionalised boys, generally fare badly, drifting into homelessness and recidivism (Bullock *et al*, 1998). Whether this is due to the long-term nature of the children's problems or the differential impact of a residential experience, it is hard to say.

Given these uncertainties, any conclusions about the benefits of residential care will be contentious but some establishments claim success in overcoming its alleged weaknesses (Rose, 1990, 1997; Ward *et al*, 2003). This occurs, for example, in response to the criticism of failing to provide unconditional love. Follow-up studies of leavers from long-stay residential treatment units, particularly therapeutic communities and those which provide for learning-disabled adults, indicate a model of "quasi-institutional adoption" and although only a minority of leavers receive such enduring support, the long-term outcomes for those who do are encouraging (Little and Kelly, 1995; Bullock *et al*, 1998). However, critics argue that the numbers of children benefiting is probably smaller than claimed and the high costs of such provision are making this option increasingly unrealistic (Bullock *et al*, 2006).

Of the various studies of residential care undertaken in the last decade, Whitaker and colleagues (1998) are the most optimistic about residential care. They conclude that, although there is no list of circumstances under which residential care should be a preferred option, there are occasions when it can be helpful. These are:

- when the young person has difficulties in allowing any one adult to get close to them and they can benefit from having available a range of carers;
- when a young person has a history of having abused other children;
- when a young person feels threatened by the prospect of living in a family or needs respite from it;
- when multiple potential adult attachment figures might forestall a young person from emotionally abandoning his or her own parents;
- when the emotional load of caring for a very disturbed or chaotic young person is best distributed among a number of carers; and
- when the young person prefers residential care to any form of family care, and would sabotage the latter if it were provided.

In a later research review, however, Rushton and Minnis (2002) are less convinced. They express concern that staff in residential homes have no training or contact with child and adolescent mental health services (CAMHS) to help them deal with the problems they face. They suggest, as does Sinclair (2005), that all of the treatments offered to troubled and troublesome teenagers can be delivered in foster care where there is less likelihood of bullying, sexual harassment and delinquent cultures. In contrast to Whitaker, they argue that when children have attachment difficulties, therapeutic foster care seems preferable.

But given the control difficulties that some young people present, there is probably a need for a small number of high-quality residential establishments for children who cannot be accommodated any other way or for whom there is a policy to keep them out of prison.

The views of children are also important in thinking this through. Much of the discussion in children's accounts of being looked after focuses on relationships, whether between children and staff or among peers and how important and empowered they feel when their views are taken seriously (Morris, 2000). A novel attempt to combine the child's view of residential life with statistical research evidence on outcomes is found in *A Life without Problems: The achievements of a therapeutic community* (Little and Kelly, 1995) in which the findings are informed by a juxtaposition of quantitative evidence on children's care careers and qualitative material from a teenage girl's diary.

When asked for their views, children are often complimentary about residential care, at least in its modern version, stressing the care and attention they receive. But, again, there is a problem of interpretation in that Sinclair and colleagues (1998) found that life after a favourable experience was often wretched and its poor quality meant that there was only a weak correlation between a good residential experience and happiness thereafter. Some young people find the contrast between the caring home and the uncaring community too much to handle. Obviously, a child needs to feel safe and be happy while looked after, but this must not be at the expense of longer-term misery and isolation.

3. Residential establishments as organisations

When the child's needs have been assessed and a residential placement identified, how can professionals decide whether the establishment is any good?

When looking at residential establishments for children, the immediate reference points are the surface features, such as the style of leadership, the physical surroundings and resources. Judgements about quality are often reached from the immediate impact of the establishment, initial conversations with staff or the visible responses of the children. It is easy to assume that the most important aspects are either the people or the regime and that, if these elements are right, all will be well. But a stream of research into this area has revealed a more complicated situation.

Certainly, individuals, whether an efficient manager or an unruly adolescent, are important in affecting what happens in a home or school but they are not enough to explain everything. Successful managers in one context often fail elsewhere and establishments vary in their capability to help young people (Hicks *et al*, 2007). Some features that common sense might associate with a good home have been found to be relatively insignificant – the quality of buildings, the proportion of trained staff, the characteristics of the children, for example, are not sufficient *on their own* to produce good results.

What aspects of residential settings have been found to be associated with good quality care and optimal outcomes for children and families?

While residential homes have many aspects that can be easily differentiated, such as buildings or staff roles, there is something more than the sum of the parts that seems to be important in determining what happens therein. Many writers have used terms such as "culture" or "ethos" to describe this. It is precisely these feelings and messages that a visitor picks up. They may be long standing, such as when there is a traditional way of doing things or may be a product of stress or boredom. These cultures have been shown directly to affect the behaviour of children and staff, not just in terms of conformity or deviance but also in shaping attitudes. However, as the precise nature and direction of the association has been difficult to determine, the principal message for managers has been to ensure that cultures did not cohere in a negative and destructive way. But, even then, homes seemingly well planned from the start have failed to succeed.

Several studies have help us understand better how residential establishments work: *Working in Children's Homes: Challenges and complexities* (Whitaker *et al*, 1998); *Children's Homes: A study in diversity* (Sinclair and Gibbs, 1998) and *Making Residential Care Work: Structure and culture in children's homes* (Brown *et al*, 1998) The first takes a relatively unusual starting point of the experiences of staff, the second analyses the factors that predict optimal outcomes, and the third looks at the relationship between staff and child cultures to unravel precisely what causes what.

All three studies reach similar conclusions although they express them in different ways. In general terms, there has to be a complementary relationship between: the needs and wishes of the children, what the home or school tries to do and how it is resourced and structured to do this, a belief among staff that the aims are feasible and that they have been given sufficient responsibility to undertake the work. Moreover, all of these have to be pursued in a child welfare context and a wider ethos of corporate parenting in the responsible agencies.

Naturally, many factors generate these conditions and among those identified are: the rate of turnover; admissions policy; mix of children with regard to needs; ethnicity and gender. There are also indications of what leads to good outcomes. Sinclair and Gibbs (1998), for example, concluded that homes did best if they were small; the head of the home felt that his or her role was clear, mutually compatible, not disturbed by reorganisation and that he or she had autonomy; and, that staff agreed on how the home should be run. Other researchers have emphasised the quality of staff–child relationships, stressing listening, informality, availability, sensitivity, being informed, respect and an ability to offer practical help.

Although the importance of individual factors, for example, the size of home, might be argued (Chipenda-Donsokho *et al*, 2003), there is little doubt that, if these conditions are in place, the establishments are not only likely to achieve better outcomes but are also more likely to satisfy children's wishes. Sinclair and colleagues found that young people judged homes according to whether they wanted to be there, whether there was a purpose to their stay, whether they moved on at the right time and the quality of life on leaving. Even though a third of them wanted to be somewhere else, they appreciated homes if they were not bullied, sexually harassed or led into trouble, if staff listened, the regime was benign and the other children friendly, and if they showed some tangible improvement, such as in education. Most wanted contact with their families but not necessarily to live with them. Individual misery was associated with sexual harassment, bullying, missing family and friends, poor relations with other residents and lack of success in esteemed roles such as sport.

Conclusions

The studies discussed all emphasise that, when children are looked after, there is a danger that deficiencies in the care placements will exacerbate the deprivation and harm that necessitated the initial separation from family. Residential care is no exception. A child doing badly in residential care needs a good quality intervention, not transfer to another poor quality home. System neglect, whereby the needs of children remain unmet, is less obvious than physical or sexual abuse but is no less dangerous. So, what messages do researchers offer to those placing children?

Three general messages are indicated.

- There is limited value in looking at residential establishments in isolation. There might be organisational changes to improve situations, such as better record keeping or more effective communication, but these are unlikely to be sufficient to guarantee high standards.
- There has to be an initial understanding of the needs of the children being looked after. This is not always the case, resulting in opinionated generalisations about children's situations and limited action in areas such as health, education and work with families.
- There has to be awareness that residence is only one of several means of meeting the child's needs and an understanding of how it contributes to meeting the needs of a particular child. These two points should be reflected in the services provided and the care plans fashioned.

In addition, some shifts in thinking would be helpful. For service managers, two mind-sets need to be challenged. First is the tendency to view residential care as a last resort, as something to fall back on when other interventions fail. The second is to provide residential facilities but then put in place services to keep children out of it. Residence is a method of social care and should be used as such, so arguments "for" or "against" it are absurd. In some instances it is needed, in others it is irrelevant.

For practitioners, two aspects of matching interventions to children's needs are important. First is what actually happens in residential care and, second, what a residential experience adds to a child's welfare. There are few interventions specific to particular care settings, although opportunities may be greater in some contexts than others. In this respect residential care is no different to foster care or living at home.

For the reasons explained, specific effects of residence are claimed but not proven but it does seem to be helpful in two situations. The first is for adolescents whose challenging behaviour at home, school and in the community requires placement in a supportive but emotionally undemanding setting, staffed by experienced people. This should encourage continuities in the young person's social life, education and employment and those family and peer relationships that he or she wishes to pursue. Stays should be short and there should a clear exit strategy. The difference between this and a foster home is in the roles of staff, the relationship demands made on the young person, the availability of a peer group and the capacity of the establishment to contain the effects of difficult behaviour and prevent status deterioration. From the point of view of the child's living experience, however, it may not be obviously different from a large foster family.

The second is when there is a need for specialised treatment, either within the residential setting or outside of a living situation whose style and ethos complement it. For those seeking such placements, the aspects to consider are: the value of the group of residents; the availability of a number of adults and freedom to choose with whom to make relationships; the undemanding emotional nature of the ambience that gives the young person choice and power; an environment that ensures safety, supervision and control and an active stimulating programme. It might be possible to achieve equally good outcomes in foster care or with support at home, but for some individuals and in some situations it is not.

The responsibility of those managing residential establishments is to ensure that the "culture" of the unit is positive. Congregating difficult adolescents creates a potential for disaster and the surveys of children's homes have all found places dominated by crime, bullying, drugs and prostitution, and practice that turned a blind eye to such behaviour.

Finally, service managers cannot ignore the wider population of children in need as the amount and type of residential provision will be affected by broader policies, such as sending young offenders to prison and willingness to accommodate troubled and troublesome teenagers. Good quality residential care can exist within a system of poor adolescent services, and may unwittingly support it.

The future of residential care in the UK

The future thrust in children's services in the UK will be on prevention and early intervention and not residential care. Initiatives are being introduced to identify children at risk and act accordingly, preferably by providing help in family and home community settings. For those in out of home care, there is also a move to speedier permanency. This most certainly means quicker family reunions for some and more adoptions for younger children unable to return home. Neither is there a group of young children who need to be taken out of residential care, as is the case in some other developed countries (Browne *et al*, 2005), or was the case in the UK 50 years ago when residential nurseries and other accommodation were closed.

In such a context, residential care is likely to continue to play a small but significant role in children's services. But, because of expense, alleged ineffectiveness and difficulties of staffing, it will continually be replaced by foster care that is increasingly able to provide for children who are difficult to place. However, there will be a limit to what is possible, and there is a risk that difficult cases will be diverted more readily to the criminal justice system or turned away altogether rather than offered a residential placement. There may be some growth in private residential facilities as local authorities find it difficult to make their own provision. Similarly, some specialist fostering arrangements may become more quasi-residential groups than traditional family settings, thus breaking down traditional boundaries between different types of service.

The main criteria for entry to residential care will remain difficult behaviour, especially dangers to self and others and a need for specialised services. There is no reason to believe that the size of this population will decline as psychological disturbance among juveniles is growing in the UK (Maughan, 2005); so new provision may struggle to maintain the status quo. But financial constraints will mean little growth in expensive psycho-therapeutic facilities. If there are to be regime changes, they are likely to emphasise flexibility with other living arrangements, education, social skills and employment. Neither should the pragmatic constraints on reducing residential provision be underestimated. It may prove just as difficult to recruit specialist foster carers as it is residential workers.

The starting point of any planning, whether for systems or for individual children, is the needs of the young person and what is deemed necessary to meet them. The first question to be asked, therefore, is what does the young person and his or her family need? Does he or she need residential care, and if so what for, of what type, for how long and with what else? For those qualifying, the next question is what regime and treatment approaches are shown by research to be the most effective for meeting those needs? To answer this properly, we need a yet undeveloped validated taxonomy of need and robust evidence on the outcomes of interventions for children with similar needs. However, the research that has been discussed offers some pointers. While considerable effort may be needed to implement its suggestions, the benefits of providing residential care as part of a comprehensive service for children in need should be apparent in improved outcomes for children and enhanced job satisfaction among staff.

Selected further reading

Brown E., Bullock R., Hobson C. and Little M. (1998) *Making Residential Care Work: Structure and culture in children's homes*, Aldershot: Ashgate

Bullock R., Little M. and Millham S. (1998) *Secure Treatment Outcomes: The care careers of very difficult adolescents*, Aldershot: Ashgate

Clough, R., Bullock R. and Burton J. (2006) *What Works in Residential Child Care: A review of research evidence and practical considerations*, London: National Children's Bureau

Department of Health (1998) *Caring for Children away from Home: Messages from research*, Chichester: John Wiley and Sons

Little M. and Kelly S. (1995) *A Life without Problems? The achievements of a therapeutic community*, Aldershot: Arena

Sinclair I. and Gibbs I. (1998) *Children's Homes: A study in diversity*, Chichester: John Wiley and sons

Whitaker D., Archer L. and Hicks L. (1998) *Working in Children's Homes: Challenges and complexities*, Chichester: John Wiley and Sons

References

Beedell C. (1970) *Residential Life with Children*, London: Routledge and Kegan Paul

Berridge D. (1985) *Children's Homes*, Oxford: Blackwell

Brown E., Bullock R., Hobson C. and Little M. (1998) *Making Residential Care Work: Structure and culture in children's homes*, Aldershot: Ashgate

Browne K., Hamilton-Giachritsis C., Johnson R., Chow S., Ostergren M., Leth I., Agathonos-Georgopoulou H., Anaut M., Herczog M., Keller-Hamela M., Klimackova A., Stan V. and Zeytinoglu S. (2005) 'A European survey of the number and characteristics of children less than three years old in residential care', *Adoption & Fostering*, 29:4, pp 23–33

Bullock R., Courtney M., Parker R., Sinclair I. and Thoburn J. (2006) 'Can the corporate state parent?', *Children and Youth Services Review*, XXVIII, pp 1344–58

Bullock R., Little M. and Millham S. (1998) *Secure Treatment Outcomes: The care careers of very difficult adolescents*, Aldershot: Ashgate

Chipenda-Dansokho S. and the Centre for Social Policy (2003) 'The determinants and influence of size on residential settings for children', *International Journal of Child and Family Welfare*, VI, pp 66–76

Chipenda-Dansokho S., Little M. and Thomas B. (2003) *Residential Services for Children: Definitions, numbers and classifications*, Chicago: Chapin Hall Center for Children, University of Chicago

Clough, R., Bullock R. and Burton J. (2006) *What Works in Residential Child Care: A review of research evidence and practical considerations*, London: National Children's Bureau

Dartington-I (2002, 2005) *Looked After Children Placed out of Area*, Dartington: Dartington Social Research Unit

Dartington-I (2003) *The Needs and Care Careers of Looked After Children in Two Local Authorities*, Dartington: Dartington Social Research Unit

Department of Health (1998) *Caring for Children away from Home: Messages from research*, Chichester: John Wiley and Sons

Fonagy P. (2002) *What Works for Whom? A critical view of treatments for children and adolescents*, New York: Guilford Press

Gooch D. (1996) 'Home and away: The residential care, education and control of children in historical and political context', *Child and Family Social Work*, I, pp 19–32

Hicks L., Gibbs I., Byford S. and Weatherley H. (2007) *Managing Children's Homes: Developing effective leadership in small organisations*, London: Jessica Kingsley Publishers

Little M. and Kelly S. (1995) *A Life without Problems? The achievements of a therapeutic community*, Aldershot: Arena

Little M., Kohm A. and Thompson R. (2005) 'The impact of residential placement on child development: research and policy implications', *International Journal of Social Welfare*, XIV, pp 200–209

Maughan B. (2005) *Time Trends in Adolescent Well-Being*, London: Nuffield Foundation

Morris J. (2000) *Having Someone who Cares: Barriers to change in the public care of children*, London: National Children's Bureau

Rose M. (1990) *Healing Hurt Minds: The Peper Harow experience*, London: Tavistock/Routledge

Rose M. (1997) *Transforming Hate to Love*, London: Routledge

Rushton A. and Minnis H. (2002) 'Residential and foster family care', in Rutter M. and Taylor E. (eds) *Child and Adolescent Psychiatry*, 4th edn, Oxford: Blackwell, pp 359–372

Sinclair I. (2005) *Fostering Now: Messages from research*, London: Jessica Kingsley Publishers

Sinclair I. and Gibbs I. (1998) *Children's Homes: A study in diversity*, Chichester: John Wiley and Sons

Ward A., Kasinski K., Pooley J. and Worthington, A. (eds) (2003) *Therapeutic Communities for Young People*, London: Jessica Kingsley Publishers

Whitaker D., Archer L. and Hicks L. (1998) *Working in Children's Homes: Challenges and complexities*, Chichester: John Wiley and Sons

12 Adoption: developmental perspectives within an ethical, legal and policy framework

John Simmonds

Adoption is one of the most radical interventions it is possible to make in the life of a child. When an Adoption Order is made, it legally terminates a child's relationship with his or birth parents and establishes a new legal relationship with the adopter/s. Other than in very unusual circumstances, the effects of this are lifelong and this will fundamentally change the course of the child's life – their primary relationships with parents and other family members, their life opportunities in education and employment, their health and well-being and their access to practical, emotional and social resources. It may also create a profound curiosity for the child about their origins, why they were "given up" for adoption and this may include a deep sense of loss as well as gratitude. The impact on birth parents and adoptive parents can be equally profound as the course of their lives will also be radically changed.

Adoption is not a new arrangement and the story of Moses in the Bible is one indication of how far back in history the idea can be traced (Burguiere *et al*, 1996). But over that time, it has changed as society has changed, and in the modern world it is a highly regulated activity by the State because of the known risks of exploitation of vulnerable birth parents and children and the immense lifelong consequences that the making of an Adoption Order has for all concerned. It has also raised questions about whether removing a child from one set of family circumstances and placing them in another family can actually work. Can new relationships form? Will the child develop to their full potential? Or does the impact of moving the child leave such an indelible mark on them that they are held back in their growth forever? Are adopted children more vulnerable to educational under-achievement, poor self-esteem and mental health problems so that adoption should be considered to be a risk factor? These ethical, legal and policy questions are the backbone to this chapter. However, the question that is core to considering them all is the question of development. What does research tell us about the developmental outcomes for adopted children? And here the answer, as so often is the case in research, is 'It depends!'.

The current legal and policy context

The placement of children for adoption has been undergoing a period of major change brought about by a policy initiative outlined in the Prime Minister's Review of Adoption

(Performance and Innovation Unit, 2000). While many aspects of that change are well underway, many are still to be implemented. This is particularly marked in the differences between the four UK countries. New primary legislation, the Adoption and Children Act 2002, was implemented in December 2005 in England and Wales. The Adoption and Children (Scotland) Act 2007 is about to see consultation on its draft regulations and guidance (2008). A new Act is yet to be placed on the statute books in Northern Ireland. While new laws in the four countries are similar in their intention and objectives – to modernise adoption practice to reflect its changed focus on children in public care – each country has also taken its own route to achieving this. It is also important to acknowledge that, while there has been explicit policy concern to ensure that adoption is available for children in public care, adoption continues to be available for "relinquished babies", for children adopted from abroad and for step-parent adoptions. Legislation in England, Wales and Scotland also introduces other permanency options such as Special Guardianship in England and Wales and the Permanence Order in Scotland.

As with all placement options, these changes in the legal framework of adoption reflect the fact that as society changes, national policy either reflects or drives this, ideas about family life change and so do views about children's development and what best enables and promotes that (Marsh and Thoburn, 2002; Selwyn and Sturgess, 2002; Triseliotis, 2003; Lewis, 2004). Adoption is one part of many years of policy and practice debate about the ability of the public care system to create and provide the necessary conditions that enable children who cannot live with their birth parents to develop into healthy, well-educated and confident adults ready and able to fully participate in society and benefit from as well as contribute to it (Rushton, 2004).

The changing role of adoption

In exploring adoption as a placement choice, it is important to bear in mind the different functions that it has had over the last 80 years or so. For much of its history, adoption has been seen primarily as a solution to the problem of illegitimacy, unwanted pregnancy and the social stigma and shame attached to both of these issues. These were individual and societal problems that lacked effective solution through contraception or abortion or social acceptance and practical support. Similarly, the problem of infertility and childlessness in marriage lacked the solutions that medical science currently provides. The coming together of these two problems at both a societal and individual level generated adoption as a solution, with its notion of a "new start" for the child and the infertile couple, reinforced by the severing of the legal tie between the child and his or her birth parents and family. The assumption was that the child would develop as any other child, with this new start allowing them to become a part of an "ordinary" family with the loving care of their new, adoptive parents. Over 30 years or so, this problem/solution set has radically changed, as contraception and abortion have become available, the social stigma of single parenthood and pregnancy outside of wedlock has largely disappeared in many communities and society has made available a range of practical welfare services to support single mothers and their children.

The exploration of adoption as a solution for "hard to place babies" – those for whom there were health concerns or they were disabled, children from minority ethnic groups or those who were more than a few months old – started in the 1960s and 1970s. There were real concerns that prospective adopters would not come forward to adopt children who were other than "perfect" and some anxiety among professionals that, even if placed, a bond would not be formed and the placement would break down. The commitment of both agencies and adopters to addressing the then new adoption challenge and their success has resulted in this form of adoption becoming mainstream, with additional categories of children being added – those in middle childhood and children placed with their brothers and sisters.

Adoption has therefore evolved into a solution to a new problem set, that of the child in public care who cannot return to their birth family because of the risk of maltreatment or neglect resulting from serious parental problems, such as alcohol or substance abuse or mental health problems. The State has a primary responsibility to plan and organise a stable and permanent solution for these children. Adoption is one possible option and the most radical. The concern of adoption agencies has moved from finding solutions to the problems of illegitimacy and infertility to the problems of maltreated children. It is the immediate and long-term welfare of these children that has become the primary concern in policy and practice.

Adoption has become primarily child-centred and this has resulted in questions being asked about its capacity to enable developmental catch-up for children who have often had a very poor start in life. What is it about adopters and adoptive family life that is most likely to enable this? What action can agencies take both prior to and post the adoption placement of a child that will enable the primary welfare and child development objectives to be achieved?

Ethical issues in adoption

The need for answers to these challenging questions about adoption practice and outcomes must not obscure the fact that adoption is a highly controversial subject from an ethical and human rights perspective. While the adoption of children from care is well established in legislation and practice in the UK, even a brief look at international comparisons will demonstrate that this approach is not shared by most of the countries in Europe, where long-term foster care and/or residential care are the placement of choice. Dispensing with the consent of parents and severing the legal tie of children to their birth parents through adoption is seen as an infringement of human rights in many countries of Europe and therefore not an option that is available. Adoption in Europe usually means intercountry adoption and the numbers of children so adopted are far above what is found in the UK (Selman, this volume).

The only other countries which are broadly similar in approach to the UK are Canada and the USA. Across the United States there is a strong focus on adoption of children from care where the numbers are typically above 50,000 children in any one year. The USA also has very high rates of intercountry adoption and there are large numbers of relinquished infants placed for adoption, as well as children adopted by foster carers and relatives. Understanding why and how countries reach their own position about the use of adoption is a complex issue (see Thoburn, this volume). It is a subject that can evoke the strongest of views and it is a responsibility of anybody involved in adoption to ensure that they are familiar with the complex ethical and policy questions that underpin it and the arguments that are brought to bear on it (Freundlich and Phillips, 2000; van Ijzendoorn and Juffer, 2006).

The question of the capacity of adoption to promote good child development outcomes and enable developmental catch-up for children who have had a very poor start in life is very important, but it is not sufficient in itself as a justification for pursuing an adoption plan. Most parents, whatever health, psychological or social state they are in or whatever conditions they live in, want to care for their children. Even where babies are relinquished for adoption, this is rarely a decision taken without considerable emotional turmoil and most birth parents are genuinely struggling to take a decision that will be best for their child in the long run. For children adopted from care, the situation is more complex. For most, the plan to adopt arises out of the maltreatment or neglect they have suffered or that older siblings have suffered. Sometimes this may be brought about by intent on the part of parents to harm their children, sometimes it may result from the intense and chronic experience of serious mental health difficulties or, increasingly, drug and alcohol misuse (Forrester and Harwin, 2007).

However serious the harm to the child may have been, it is very likely that the parents will have expressed and wanted and maybe still want to care for their child. While services or interventions may have been provided to address whatever problems they faced in doing this, the lack of evidence that they have sufficiently changed will have resulted in the plan for adoption. But even so, this cannot easily be interpreted as a lack of desire to change by parents or a lack of keen interest in the child's welfare. For most parents, it is their own adverse life experiences and current circumstances that cause such serious limitations in their capacity to care and to change. This should not be confused with an expectation that this decreases the desire to parent successfully. The exception to this are those children that have been selectively and actively rejected by their birth parents (Reder and Lucey, 1995; Rushton and Dance, 2003) and the consequences for them when placed can be very serious indeed.

In any of these circumstances, adoption cannot be justified as a course of action simply on the basis of good or better child development outcomes than if the child had remained in the circumstances they were born into. Adoption requires that *either* birth parents give consent to adoption after being fully informed of the consequences of doing so or it must be demonstrated, on the balance of probabilities, that consent should be dispensed with because of the significant risk to the child's development resulting from the parents' inability to adequately parent. It is important then to know that adoption, especially as it is such a radical intervention, works for children in improving their development, but this is not sufficient in itself to establish adoption as an intervention. Adoption is not acceptable if it is conceived of as a form of social engineering – moving children from one set of adverse social circumstances to a more advantageous set of social circumstances even if it is of benefit to the child and society as a whole. The 'right to a family life' in human rights discourse and legislation is established as a powerful principle and adoption has had to ensure that it is fully compliant with this right. Children cannot be removed from their parents just because it might be advantageous to do so in terms of their development or because it might provide them with greater opportunity. Even so, the point at which adoption becomes necessary for the child and ethically defensible is something that continues to exercise policy makers, legislators and practitioners in both domestic and intercountry adoption.

Research on outcomes of adoption

Meta-analytic evidence
Within this broader ethical and legal framework, it remains important to know whether, as an intervention, it works to move children from one set of family and social circumstances to another in the context of adoption. Is there evidence which indicates that children do well enough to justify the pain, disruption and risk involved? As with many questions like this, it is a very difficult question to answer, because adoption is a lifelong issue and so it depends at what point in the life of an adopted child, adolescent, or adult the question is asked. It is also dependent on identifying what counts as evidence for success. For some young children adopted from institutional care or where their parents seriously abused or neglected them, their lives may have been at risk if they had stayed where they were. But is it sufficient to know that they did not die? Or do we want to know whether they caught up with what is generally expected of children of their age in terms of physical, emotional, educational or behavioural development? And how much does this depend on the degree of adversity experienced prior to placement, as for some this will require enormous catch-up to be made and others much less so. And what about the influence of the placement itself – the characteristics of the adoptive parents and their circumstances, and the quality of their parenting and the wider benefits or indeed problems that this might bring?

Van Ijzendoorn and Juffer (2006) have reviewed 270 well-conducted studies of over 230,000 adopted children and parents, comparing them with children who remained in institutional care and children who remained with their birth families. For this meta-analysis, they use five developmental outcome criteria – physical growth, attachment, cognitive development, self-esteem and adjustment (emotional and behavioural). When children are placed in institutional* care at an early age, this has been shown to have a dramatic negative impact on physical development as measured by height, weight and head circumference. The longer the child remains in the institution, the more severe this is. Placing these children in an adoptive home leads to very significant physical development in weight and height, the extent of which is dependent on the age at placement. The earlier the placement of the child (ideally before they are six months old), the more complete the catch-up to developmental norms. Head circumference is something of an exception to this, with longer catch-up times and less complete catch-up, which may indicate a narrower window of developmental opportunity for this factor (van Ijzendoorn *et al*, 2007).

Attachment has become a central concept in family placement with particular concerns about insecure, disorganised patterns of attachment. Across ten studies (Van den Dries, in preparation) of 400 adopted children, the comparisons are as follows:

Table 12.1
Distribution of attachment classifications (children)

	Secure (B)	Insecure avoidant (A)	Insecure ambivalent (C)	Disorganised (D)
Adopted children	45%	13%	10%	33%
Non-adopted children	62%	15%	9%	15%
Children in institutions	23%	3%	4%	70%

There is a significant difference between adopted and non-adopted children for secure and disorganised classifications. As with head circumference, this may indicate that the window of developmental opportunity in relation to attachment is age dependent. Indeed, age at placement continues to be important in distinguishing children's subsequent attachment classification. However, although these figures sound a warning bell about the increased risk to adopted children resulting from early unsatisfactory care, it is also important to compare these figures with children who remain in institutions, and two studies (Vorria *et al*, 2003; Zeanah *et al*, 2005) have done this. The extent of disorganised attachment for institutionalised children is stark at 70 per cent, so although "catch-up" may not be up to community samples for children adopted from institutions, it is significantly better than it is for children that remain in them.

---

* "Institutional" – a term that can cover a wide range in the quality of care a child receives.

In relation to cognitive development (van Ijzendoorn *et al*, 2005), six studies of 253 adopted children compared them with peers and siblings who were not adopted. The analysis shows that those adopted exceed those not adopted on IQ measures and school performance. However, in eight other studies of 13,000 children in the same analysis, 12.8 per cent of adopted children were identified as having special educational needs compared to 5.5 per cent of those from broader community samples. Lastly, another group of 42 studies of 6,000 adopted children showed no significant difference in IQ but those children did less well at school and their language abilities were less good. This suggests something of a discrepancy between cognitive ability and actual school performance, especially for those from extremely deprived backgrounds. This may be explained by either preoccupations with adoption-related matters, such as loss and identity, or the influence of genetic factors or the lasting effects of malnourishment on concentration and application, especially for those adopted after 12 months.

Given the enormity of the experience, it is not surprising that the self-esteem of adopted children should have been raised as a risk factor, with shorter stature compared to non-adopted classmates identified as one factor, especially in adolescence. It is an essential part of the adoption task to build a sense of positive identity that incorporates the past, however difficult that might be, with current experience and opportunity. It has become commonplace in adoption literature to raise questions about how possible this is and how enduring the losses are and how compromised the possibility of positive self-esteem becomes. Surprisingly this is not borne out in 88 studies comparing 10,977 adoptees with 33,862 non-adopted persons (Juffer and van Ijzendoorn, 2007). They say, 'Their overall combined effect size . . . was not significant. We showed that adoptees' self-esteem did not differ from the self-esteem of their peers' (p 1072). This is perhaps not so surprising when we consider that self-esteem is far more dependent on current environmental factors than other areas of development, so that supportive adoptive parents can make more of an impact on self-esteem than on school and learning difficulties.

Lastly, the evidence on children's emotional and behavioural adjustment was explored using the data from 101 studies of 25,000 adopted and 80,000 non-adopted children (Juffer and van Ijzendoorn, 2005). Adoptees did show more behavioural problems, but the differences were small. They were also significantly over-represented in referrals to mental health services. Children adopted from abroad showed lower rates of both problems and referrals than in-country adoptions. As with self-esteem, there is a different picture presented here than is often available about the problematic nature of adopted children and the severe problems they present in adoptive families. Indeed, the authors conclude with a powerful statement about adoption as an intervention in terms of the best available evidence from this comprehensive data set: 'Adoption is a successful intervention that leads to remarkable catch-up in all domains of child development . . . Adoption documents the astonishing plasticity of human development in the face of serious adversity and subsequent drastic change in child-rearing circumstances' (p. 37).

If one were looking for a "good news story" in family placement, this might indeed be it. However, it is important to explore this further because it is puzzling that such a profoundly positive conclusion can be drawn from a meta-analysis of research, when there is concern in the UK about the number of adoption placements that disrupt and evidence about the lack of close and rewarding relationships between some adopters and their adopted children. Here it is essential to consider the role of age and to bear in mind that the majority of studies included by Juffer and van Ijzendoorn were of children removed from adverse environments in infancy, whereas many UK children adopted from care will be older at removal and at placement and will have suffered a range of abusive and/or neglectful experiences.

Children adopted from care aged 5–11

In a UK study (Rushton and Dance, 2006) of 99 children adopted in middle childhood – aged 5 to 11 – evidence was collected on adopters' views on children's development as well as evidence on the stability of the placement about six years after the child had joined the family. All the children, as would be expected, had lived with foster carers prior to placement and on average this amounted to four years. Almost half had experienced one attempt to return them home and the prevalence of physical, emotional and sexual abuse and neglect was very high. Figure 12.1 summarises the outcomes from the study and indeed shows quite a different picture from that presented in the meta-analysis above. The good news is that, despite a very difficult start in life, about half of these older children and their adoptive parent/s had formed a strong and positive relationship. However, just over a quarter were experiencing real stress although the family was still intact. Just under a quarter of the placements had resulted in the child becoming too challenging for the adopters and the placement disrupting. Although it is important not to underestimate the seriousness of the difficulties for half of these families, given the enormity of the task in making a family life for a child whose life has been marked by instability, trauma and loss, a 50 per cent success rate might be considered to be good. On the other hand, there cannot be any sense of complacency in this and such findings should increase the effort made to find ways of ensuring that children and carers have better than a 50:50 chance of making adoption work when children are placed over five years old.

The data available to Rushton and Dance enabled them to identify a cluster of factors that increased the risk of whether any of these placements were likely to end up in one of the three groups. These factors are shown on the right side of Figure 12.1.

Each of these factors will be familiar to family placement practitioners as indicative of potential risk factors in both identifying a suitable adoptive family for a child and then in creating difficulties in the placement itself. The one exception to this may be 'preferential rejection' (Rushton and Dance, 2003), where a child in the family has been singled out from other siblings by birth parents as the child that they cannot live with and who needs

Figure 12.1
Children placed during middle childhood

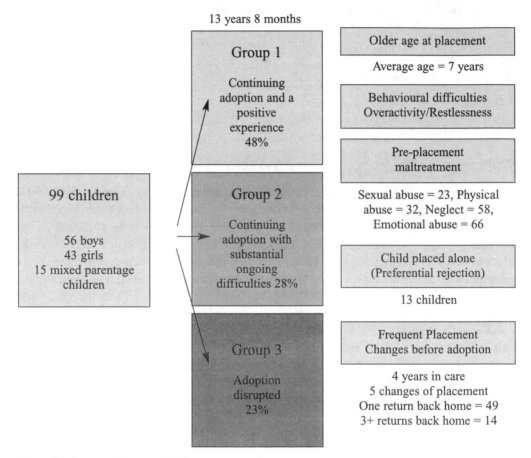

(From Rushton and Dance, 2006)

to be adopted. When these factors are taken together, Rushton shows that being older when placed, having been preferentially rejected by the birth family and having been longer in local authority care prior to placement, and after a year in placement exhibiting difficult behaviour, overactivity and lack of attachment to the adoptive mother predicted 83 per cent of the disruptions.

A second analysis of the data was undertaken to identify the difference between positive and difficult ongoing placements. This showed that a high number of placements in care, repeatedly being returned home prior to being placed for adoption combined with behavioural and over-activity problems reported shortly after placement, and adoptive mother's reported lack of attachment at the end of the first year, identified 87 per cent of the positive experiences and 69 per cent of those reporting substantial difficulties.

This important study raises some significant questions. The first concerns the nature of adoption and adoptive family life. The demands placed on adopters and what is essentially "ordinary family life" to bring about substantial change in the development of children who have had such a poor start in life is substantial. It is testament to the power of ordinary human beings that so much seems to be possible despite the real difficulties encountered in so many "late" placements. The second concerns the numerous adversities heaped on children whose early life is marked by abuse and neglect – uncertainty, anxiety, loss and distrust. Added to this are questions about what turns this around – is family life enough or does it need to be supplemented by specific interventions that attempt to address a child's development that has been knocked so much off course. The third are questions about the operation of the systems that manage care planning for children at risk, when repeated failed attempts to return children home are a significant risk factor together with numerous moves in care and then the length of time it takes for children to be placed. Each of these questions are the subject of discussion in the rest of this chapter.

Children adopted from care aged 4–8 and infant adoptions

Another major study, *Attachment Representations and Adoption Outcome* (Steele *et al*, 2007; Steele *et al*, 2008) gives further insight into the complex psychological processes at work for adopters and older children adopted from care. This study explored the attachment classification of 40 adoptive mothers and 34 adoptive fathers who had between them adopted 58 children between the ages of four and eight all of whom had been seriously maltreated. The research study used the Adult Attachment Interview (George *et al*, 1996) to classify both the adoptive mothers and fathers into one of the four identified patterns. The autonomous/secure group show a capacity for open, reflective, coherent discourse and appropriate affect when responding to questions about their experiences of significant caring relationships as a child. The dismissing/insecure group show marked evidence of denial and dismissal of the importance of such relationships with significant defensiveness and inappropriate affect in the interview. The preoccupied/insecure group also demonstrate defensiveness in the interview. This is characterised by intense feelings of hurt and injustice when talking about their memories of caring relationships. Both of the insecure groups show organisation and coherence in their patterns, despite the defensive quality of their accounts. The last group is classified as unresolved, which is marked by a breakdown in coherence of the story given in the interview when discussing questions of separation and loss or other upsetting experiences. This may suggest that the respondent has not come to terms with these experiences and they still intrude in an active and unresolved way on their mind. The consequences of these patterns on the availability, sensitivity and responsiveness of mothers and fathers to the child's distress and need for comfort have been shown to be significant in determining the child's emotional development in a wide range of families from different community and cultural situations. The question that this study attempted to answer was what impact did different secure and insecure attachment patterns in adoptive mothers and fathers have on the emotional development of adopted children who had previously experienced significant loss and maltreatment.

The first two rows of Table 12.2 show the distribution from a number of samples representing 1,494 Adult Attachment Interviews of both non-clinical and clinical populations (van Ijzendoorn and Bakermans-Kranenburg, 2008) (see also – van Ijzendoorn and Bakermans-Kranenburg, 1996). The third row shows the adoptive mothers from Steele *et al*'s adoption study and the fourth row the adoptive fathers from their sample. The first important thing to note is the fact that only just over half of the non-clinical population are classified as autonomous/secure. In clinical samples the rate of "unclassified" or "cannot classify" at 41 per cent is very high but even there, 26 per cent are classified as autonomous/secure. The second important factor is the high rate of autonomous/secure patterns in the adoptive mother sample, an indication of both the quality of adoptive mothers and the quality of the adoption home study assessment process. Adoptive fathers in this sample are closer to the distribution found in non-clinical mothers (Steele *et al*, 2008).

Table 12.2
Distribution of attachment classifications (adults)

	Autonomous/ Secure	Dismissing/ Insecure	Preoccupied/ Insecure	Unclassified or Cannot classify
Non clinical mothers n = 889	55.2%	19.6%	10.4%	14.9%
Clinical populations n = 605	26%	21%	13%	41%
Adoptive mothers n = 40	68%	12%	0%	Unresolved concerning past loss or trauma 20%
Adoptive fathers n = 34	53%	35%	6%	Unresolved concerning past loss or trauma 6%

Within the adoptive mother sample, the researchers note that eight of the mothers were identified as being unresolved in relation to earlier experiences of relational loss and trauma. Of these mothers, two were also classified within the autonomous/secure group, four within the insecure/dismissing group and two within the insecure/preoccupied group.

With the two adoptive fathers in the unresolved group, one was also classified as dismissing and the other as preoccupied. When the mother's and father's AAIs were combined, 17 of the couples were both rated as secure, 12 where only the mother was secure, five where only the father was secure and five where neither were secure. The consequences of this are identified in the discussion below.

In addition to the AAI assessment of the adoptive mother's and father's attachment pattern, the adopted children were assessed using the Story Stem Assessment Profile (Hodges *et al*, 2000; Hodges *et al*, 2003). This method presents children with the beginnings of an everyday family scenario using doll figures. These scenarios present the child with situations that are typically anxiety-provoking, such as spilling juice at the table or falling off when riding a bike too fast. Children are invited to show and tell the interviewer what happens next. Children continue the stories by drawing on their own experience or understanding of the ways that problems are typically dealt with in families. This might range from sensitive, caring responses on the part of parents, to a sense of the child being able to master the problem by finding everyday solutions, and finally to stories that escalate into dangerous or bizarre endings with high levels of aggression, death, self-blame and particularly the reversal of the child–parent role. In this last group, the story may never end in the sense of the problem being resolved. For some children their anxiety may be such that they cannot engage in the task at all.

The weight of evidence from this study demonstrates that, compared to non maltreated children, abused children typically respond to these everyday stories with the latter set of problematic narratives. In this sample, two themes were found to be particularly significant. The first was "disorganisation" including catastrophic fantasy, the inclusion of bizarre material, figures in the story alternating between "bad" and "good", extreme aggression, magical omnipotence and finally the reversal of the child–adult role. The second theme was "insecurity" with children in the story being endangered, injured or dead, adults being unaware or rejecting, or injured or dead, excessive compliance, aggression, neutralisation or throwing away. These themes are all indicative of the kinds of powerful defences a child might develop in order to survive the threats to their physical and psychological well-being that maltreatment brings about. When a child has developed such powerful negative expectations about the resolution or lack of resolution of everyday events, these are likely to pose a major challenge to adopters whose own experiences and expectations have led them to expect very different kinds of resolutions or endings. Part of the parenting task will be to change these expectations so the child develops a more helpful and realistic view of the way that problems and anxieties are resolved, and in particular to convey the comforting, sensitive and positive role that parents normally play in their children's lives.

By linking the AAI scores with another measure developed from it, the Parent Development Interview (Aber *et al*, 1985), the researchers were able to establish how an adopter's attachment classification became expressed in their relationship with and feelings about the child placed with them. The sample was split into two – those families where at least one of the adopters was classified as secure and the second where neither was classified as secure. In the first group, after two years in placement, insecure themes in the child's stories were significantly less likely and in the second group, 86 per cent of the children had the highest scores for disorganisation. Where an adopter was classified as autonomous/secure, they were less likely to be overwhelmed by anxiety and more likely to be satisfied by their experience of the child. Where this was not the case, and the child's aggression, attempt to control the relationship and their expectation that things always ended badly, the adopters felt overwhelmed by despair and dissatisfaction. Further, there was evidence that children were highly sensitive to the small group of adopters who had unresolved feelings of sadness and loss. This reinforced the defensive strategy the child demonstrated in the story stems of turning parent figures into needy, sad, or injured child-like figures.

Research findings like this, coupled with those discussed above, indicate the complex psychological processes at work in children adopted from care. The messages from Rushton's study indicate a concerning picture of the risks inherent in adoptive placements. Steele *et al*'s study gives insight into some of the complex dynamics at work in establishing a more benign set of relationships for the child. But given the high proportion of adoptive mothers in their study with an autonomous/secure classification, how did this group of maltreated children do over the first two years of placement and how does that compare with another group of 48 children who were not maltreated and placed for adoption as infants?

In a further analysis of the sample (Hodges *et al*, 2005), the children's development was coded into four scales – security, insecurity, disorganisation and defensive avoidance. Each of these was measured shortly after placement (T1) and then at one (T2) and two years (T3) after placement. At T1, the maltreated children had far lower indicators of security than children placed during infancy. Images of parents who are helpful, able to comfort children, manage domestic life realistically and be aware when children are likely to be upset were not well established in their story stems. Children blamed themselves when things went wrong and often a picture of events ended up in a nightmarish catastrophe. Figure 12.2 below shows the change over time at the three points of assessment and compares the maltreated children with the comparison adopted group. The security score, while higher than the other scores, only indicates that there were more ratings in this scale and not that the children's security outweighed their insecurity. Over the three time periods, there was a marked increase in the security rating for the maltreated group and a decrease in their defensive avoidance. However, their insecurity and disorganisation scores remained much the same and significantly higher than infancy-adopted children. Not only then had these children developed an early internal model of an unhelpful and frightening world, but significant elements of this persisted despite the fact that they had grown to develop an alternative picture of a far more benign world where adults were predictably helpful and caring and adults could be relied upon to respond to their everyday worries and difficulties – positive and reassuring endings to their lived experience.

The adoptive parent's state of mind where this was secure–autonomous was shown to be very significant in bringing this about, both in the strength of their own expectations about how stories end and the fact that whatever anxieties and insecurities the child had and however they might be expressed, they did not evoke memories of their own unresolved losses and trauma and threaten whatever defences were in place to manage this. The research contains a very hopeful message about psychological and emotional change brought about by adoptive family life after just two years. It also identifies the persistence of the child's earlier learning about adult carers who cannot create good endings in routine family events. Identifying what happens to these internal models as the child gains more experience in their adoptive families will be very important and is subject to current research.

Figure 12.2
Construct scores after two years in placement

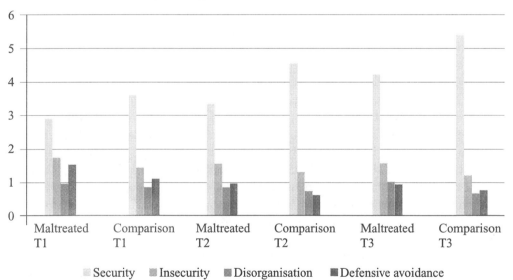

The author is very grateful to Dr Jill Hodges for permission to reproduce her graph.

The outcomes for a sample of 130 children who had a plan for adoption

The last study (Selwyn *et al*, 2006) to be discussed in detail focuses not just on the developmental outcomes for children in adoptive families, but for children where the plan was for them to be adopted but where this did not over time turn out to be the case. The research adds to our understanding of the importance of the planning and decision-making processes of the care system as well as the outcomes for the child. The study focused on 130 children (78 boys and 52 girls) who were between the ages of 3 and 11 when the best interest decision for adoption was made in the period 1991–1996. Their average age when they first came to the attention of social services was six months. However, 63 per cent of the families had been involved with social services prior to the child's birth. The families had a high incidence of domestic violence, serious mental health, substance and alcohol problems and the associated poverty that goes along with this. Many children had a large number of carers in their early life, either other family members or foster carers. Their early life was marked by serious adversity and instability. Yet despite the consequences of such experiences on children's development, and the level of input from services, the seriousness and complexity of the problems were rarely addressed comprehensively. The consequences of this were that many children were referred a number of times before the child entered care for a longer term, at an average age of three and that seemed to be despite the fact that it was clear that the family circumstances had not improved and that the child was continuing to be abused and neglected. Delay was seen to be a combination of drift caused by the absence of assessment, planning and decision making, legal and court delays and the difficulty in productively and positively engaging the family in the process.

The consequences of this were that by the time the child entered long-term care, their development had fallen significantly behind across the board – physical health, social presentation, education, emotional and behavioural development and social and family relationships. It is a disturbing picture, but one that is further compounded by the difficulties in establishing a permanent placement. The initial plan for 42 per cent of the children was return to the birth family, with a further 31 per cent where this was the plan but with a parallel plan for the child to be placed in a new permanent family. By the very nature of this as an adoption sample, these reunification plans failed, although 25 per cent of the children did return home temporarily. For some, this had happened a number of times. For others they were re-abused in the process and for four children, they were sexually abused for the first time.

The children might have had a long-term plan but that did not mean they did not move while they were waiting for an adoptive placement, with only 39 of them remaining with the same carer until they moved to their new home. For 59 per cent of the children, it was quickly established that a new family needed to be found for them although that did not mean that the placement type was quickly agreed. For the rest, the average wait time before a plan was in place was 2.7 years with proactive planning falling away, long legal delays and professional disagreements. An average delay of 1.9 years was then added to this in getting an agreement from the panel that adoption was in the child's best interests. In terms of special needs at the point where the children were approved for adoption, out of the seven dimensions identified in the Assessment of Children Framework, 52 per cent had four or more and only five children had none. However, only seven per cent of the children had regular therapy from mental health services. If these children had suffered in the families of origin, there is much in this study to suggest that that they also suffered from the serious delays in professionals agreeing a permanence plan and in that plan being put into action. Indeed, these kinds of serious delays were the focus of the English and Welsh adoption reforms (Performance and Innovation Unit, 2000) with a clear intention of reducing them, increasing the number of children adopted and establishing a comprehensive framework of adoption support.

Selwyn followed up the children some 6–11 years after the decision that they should be placed for adoption. Three groups were identified. Of the 130 children in the sample, 80 (62%) were still living in their adoptive homes. There were 34 children (26%) in long-term foster care or family and friends care, having never been placed for adoption or having been unsuccessfully placed for adoption. Finally, there were 16 children (12%) who were living in very unstable circumstances. Several factors stand out – the adopted group were younger at entry to care and had shorter times between entry and the best interest decision. The odds of not being adopted increased by 1.8 for each additional year of age and was not much less for the permanently fostered group at 1.6. Other factors also differentiate the groups. Children who had learning difficulties or long-term health problems and black and mixed ethnicity children were more likely to be found in the permanently fostered or family and friends care group. Children in the unstable care group had mothers with significantly more serious mental health disorders. They had also been multiply abused, shown higher levels of emotional and behavioural problems including violence to people and animals and experienced more rehabilitation attempts and more disruptions.

However, although the distinctions between these three groups are very important indeed, across all three groups the level of need for most of these children was very high; 95 per cent of them had one identified special need and more than 50 per cent more than four. Yet the provision of assessments and services was patchy, both before they were permanently placed and following it. It is not surprising with these levels of need that finding adoptive placements for 27 of these children turned out not to be possible at all and of the 104 who were placed for adoption, 15 placements did not proceed during the introductory stages and there was a 50:50 chance that the next match would not either. Of the original 130 children in the study 96 were placed for adoption and 80 continued at follow up. But as the Rushton study points out, placing the child does not indicate the end of the story. In fact, only seven per cent of the families seemed to have had found the child easy and rewarding to care for in the first year, although 45 per cent perhaps more realistically, thought the placement had gone as well as could be expected, and this was particularly and maybe unsurprisingly so for children adopted by previous foster carers. At the point these families were followed up, 28 per cent of them had settled, rewarding children, another one-third were reporting ongoing problems as well as real satisfaction, while another third were highly stressed and vulnerable. Although there were a number of factors that contributed to make up this complex picture, the one that stands out is the behavioural challenges that many of these children posed and the very great difficulty adopters and foster carers had in finding services or solutions that helped on a practical level.

With the other two groups, those in foster and kinship care were more similar to the adopted group. Although 46 per cent of these placements had disrupted, 20 per cent of these had actually had a disrupted adoption placement and all had experienced a change of plan from adoption to foster care. However, many of the well known problems experienced by long-term foster carers were apparent – the problem of exercising day-to-day parental authority when legal parental responsibility was held by the local authority and the problem of the requirement and expectation that children leave care at 18 and the need to plan and implement this from mid-adolescence. For the 16 young people in the unstable placement group, the severity of the difficulties they and the agencies responsible for them faced were enormous. Selwyn notes that the greater majority of these children had come to the attention of the local authority at birth, but there was much evidence to suggest that poor assessments, drift and a failure to get to grips with the increasing severity of their problems produced deeply unhappy young people for which the future was bleak. It is not unreasonable to draw the conclusion that if these children were abused or neglected at home, in its own way the care system created serious secondary neglect which only compounded the original set of problems the child was born into. It is clear that, although this study reports on some generally positive outcomes for the majority of the original high-risk sample, there are a group of particularly troubled and challenging children where earlier decision making and placement may have provided a more secure future and more positive outcomes.

Conclusion

The four studies reviewed in this chapter create something of a puzzle but a necessarily complex picture of outcomes from adoption. It is important in family placement practice to know that moving children from their family of origin to a new unrelated family can have significant beneficial effects in terms of child development outcomes. If the National Institute for Health and Clinical Excellence were to conduct an appraisal of the evidence of the intervention – moving a child from one family to another – and adoption in particular, in the same way they do with drug treatments, then they might conclude with something very like the van Ijzendoorn meta-analysis. The evidence is convincing for identifying adoption's efficacy and positive outcomes. Of course bringing evidence together in this way must not obscure the differences between relinquished infants, intercountry adoptions, older children and children who have been maltreated. Although the literature has often presented adoption as posing inevitable risks, the meta-analysis suggests that for most children these issues work themselves out satisfactorily over time. With any drug treatment, the success rate is never 100 per cent and there are differential rates depending on a whole host of individual factors. Prescribing doctors look for "best possible" from "best available" and it is important that, in finding solutions for children in need of permanent placements, similar criteria are used (see Schofield, this volume).

At the same time we cannot ignore the messages from the three UK studies discussed above. With Rushton (2006) and Selwyn *et al*'s (2006) studies there is a far more complex picture, because while there are good child development outcomes for many of the children, for a significant number there were serious ongoing struggles for them and their adoptive parents, and for others the placement broke down or they did not make it into an adoptive placement at all. Here a number of issues are important but there is one that stands out: *adoption works best the younger the child is and the quicker it is arranged.* This is directly related to the fact that children's development is time sensitive. This is not to deny that there is remarkable catch-up in children adopted from the most depriving of institutional care or from the most serious of maltreating families, but the longer this goes on, the balance for developmental recovery is weighted more and more in the opposite direction. Some children may make it against all the odds, as a couple of the young people did in the unstable care group in Selwyn's study, but as Steele's study suggests, the vulnerabilities may still live on despite the gains made in security and the decrease in defensive avoidance. And this may then point us in a somewhat different direction to the question of what the intervention of "ordinary" family life may be capable of achieving in terms of children's developmental recovery. Child-centred, flexible and mature adults and children cared for by such adults can achieve remarkable things. But the system that enables this must be set up to maximise this potential and Selwyn's study suggests that there is still more scope for making proactive alternative permanence plans for some children when there is clear evidence that the child is suffering ongoing significant harm.

Assessments, planning, decision-making and support services need to reflect the developmental timescales of the child and while this has been the focus of recent reforms across the four countries, it is still not clear whether this has been sufficient. The evidence about this is still to be evaluated. The arguments, therefore, are not so much about what works for children – they need stable, ordinary family life where they feel that they belong and that they are loved – but the ethical and legal framework that drives this and the complex bureaucratic and service framework that supports this may still not be up to the challenge of ensuring that this is so for every child. The issue is about translating the "what works" messages into equitably distributed, real world, everyday practice.

Selected further reading

Department of Health (1999) *Adoption Now: Messages from research*, Chichester: John Wiley and Sons

Fahlberg V. (2004) *A Child's Journey through Placement*, London: BAAF

Harris P. (2006) *In Search of Belonging: Reflections by transracially adopted people*, London: BAAF

Javier R., Baden A., Frank A., Biafora F., Camacho-Gingerich A. (2007) *Handbook of Adoption: Implications for researchers, practitioners, and families*, London: Sage Publications

Lord J. (2008) *The Adoption Process in England: A guide for children's social workers*, London: BAAF

Lowe N., Murch M., Borkowski M., Weaver A., Beckford V. and Thomas C. (1999) *Supporting Adoption: Reframing the approach*, London: BAAF

Thomas C., Beckford V. with Lowe N., and Murch M. (1999) *Adopted Children Speaking*, London: BAAF

References

Aber L., Slade A., Berger B., Bresgi I. and Kaplan M. (1985) *The Parent Development Interview*, The City University of New York: Unpublished Protocol

Burguiere A., Klapisch-Zuber C., Segalen M. and Zonabend F. (1996) *A History of the Family, Volume 1: Distant worlds, ancient worlds*, Cambridge: Polity Press

Department of Health (2000) *Adoption: A new approach*, London: Department of Health

Forrester D. and Harwin J. (2007) 'Parental substance misuse and child welfare: Outcomes for children two years after referral', *British Journal of Social Work*, bcm051

Freundlich M. and Phillips R. (2000) 'Ethical issues in adoption', *Adoption & Fostering*, 24:4, pp 7–17

George C., Kaplan N. and Main M. (1996) *The Adult Attachment Interview*, Department of Psychology, University of California at Berkeley: Unpublished Protocol (3rd edition)

Hodges J., Steele M., Hillman S. and Henderson K. (2003) 'Mental representations and defences in severely maltreated children: A story stem battery and rating system for clinical assessment and research applications', in Emde R., Wolf C. and Oppenheim D. (eds) *Revealing the Inner Worlds of Young Children: The MacArthur story stem battery*, New York: Oxford University Press Inc.

Hodges J., Steele M., Hillman S., Henderson K. and Kaniuk J. (2005) 'Change and continuity in mental representations of attachment after adoption', in Brodzinsky D. and Palacios J. (eds) *Psychological Issues in Adoption: Research and practice*, pp 93–116, Westport, CT: Praeger Publishers

Hodges J., Steele M., Hillman S., Henderson K. and Neil M. (2000) 'Effects of abuse on attachment representations: Narrative assessments of abused children', *Journal of Child Psychotherapy*, 26, pp 433–455

Juffer F. and van Ijzendoorn M. H. (2005) 'Behavior problems and mental health referrals of international adoptees: A meta-analysis', *Journal of the American Medical Association*, 293, pp 2501–2515

Juffer F. and van IJzendoorn M. H. (2007) 'Adoptees do not lack self-esteem: A meta-analysis of studies on self-esteem of transracial, international, and domestic adoptees', *Psychology Bulletin*, 133, pp 1067–1083

Lewis J. (2004) 'Adoption: The nature of policy shifts in England and Wales, 1972–2002', *International Journal of Law Policy Family*, 18, pp 235–255

Marsh P. and Thoburn J. (2002) 'The adoption and permanence debate in England and Wales', *Child & Family Social Work*, 7, pp 131–132

Performance and Innovation Unit (PIU) (2000) *The Prime Minister's Review of Adoption*, London: Cabinet Office

Reder P. and Lucey C. (1995) *Assessment of Parenting: Psychiatric and psychological contributions*, London, New York: Routledge

Rushton A. (2004) 'A scoping and scanning review of research on the adoption of children placed from public care', *Clinical Child Psychology and Psychiatry*, 9, pp 89–106

Rushton A. and Dance C. (2003) 'Preferentially rejected children and their development in permanent family placements', *Child & Family Social Work*, 8, pp 257–267

Rushton A. and Dance C. (2006) 'The adoption of children from public care: A prospective study of outcome in adolescence', *Journal of the American Academy of Child and Adolescent Psychiatry*, 45, pp 877–883

Selwyn J. and Sturgess W. (2002) 'Achieving permanency through adoption: Following in US footsteps?' *Adoption & Fostering*, 26:3, pp 40–49

Selwyn J., Sturgess W., Quinton D. and Baxter C. (2006) *Costs and Outcomes of Non-infant Adoptions*, London: BAAF

Steele M., Henderson K., Hodges J., Kaniuk J., Hillman S. and Steele H. (2007) 'In the best interests of the late-placed child: A report from the Attachment Representations and Adoption Outcome study', in Mayes L., Fonagy P. and Target M (eds) *Developmental Science and Psychoanalysis: Integration and innovation*, London: Karnac Books, pp 159–191

Steele M., Hodges J., Kaniuk J., Steele H., Hillman S. and Asquith K. (2008) 'Forecasting outcomes in previously maltreated children: The use of the AAI in a longitudinal adoption study', in Steele H. and Steele M. (eds) *Clinical Applications of the Adult Attachment Interview*, New York: The Guilford Press

Triseliotis J. (2003) 'Long-term foster care or adoption', in Duncan S., Lucey C. and Reder P. (eds) *Studies in the Assessment of Parenting*, Hove: Brunner-Routledge

Van den Dries, L. (in prep.) *Attachment of Adoptees and Foster Children: A meta-analysis*, The Netherlands: Leiden University van Ijzendoorn M. and Bakermans-Krenenburg M. (1996) 'Attachment representations in mothers, fathers, adolescents and clinical groups: A meta-analytic search for normative data', *Journal of Consulting and Clinical Psychology*, 64:1, pp 8–21

van IJzendoorn M. and Bakermans-Kranenburg M. (2008) 'The distribution of adult attachment representations in clinical groups', in Steele H. and Steele M. (eds) *Clinical Applications of the Adult Attachment Interview*, New York: The Guilford Press, pp 69–96

Van Ijzendoorn M. H., Bakermans-Kranenburg M. J. and Juffer F. (2007) 'Plasticity of growth in height, weight, and head circumference: Meta-analytic evidence of massive catch-up after international adoption', *Journal of Developmental and Behavioural Pediatrics*, 28, pp 334–343

van Ijzendoorn M. H. and Juffer F. (2006) 'The Emanuel Miller Memorial Lecture 2006: Adoption as intervention: Meta-analytic evidence for massive catch-up and plasticity in physical, socio-emotional, and cognitive development', *Journal of Child Psychology and Psychiatry*, 47, pp 1228–1245

van Ijzendoorn M. H., Juffer F. and Poelhuis C. W. (2005) 'Adoption and cognitive development: A meta-analytic comparison of adopted and non-adopted children's IQ and school performance', *Psychology Bulletin*, 131, pp 301–316

Vorria P., Papaligoura Z., Dunn J., van Ijzendoorn M. H., Steele H., Kontopoulou A. and Sarafidou Y. (2003) 'Early experiences and attachment relationships of Greek infants raised in residential group care', *Journal of Child Psychology and Psychiatry*, 44, pp 1208–1220

Zeanah C. H., Smyke A. T., Koga S. F. and Carlson E. (2005) 'Attachment in institutionalized and community children in Romania', *Child Development*, 76, pp 1015–1028

13 Contact after adoption

Julie Young and Elsbeth Neil

Continued contact with birth family members after a decision has been made for the child to live permanently with new legally established parents is a challenging and complex area in the lives of adopted children, adoptive parents and birth family members. This chapter provides an overview of research findings and theory to date, suggesting factors that should be taken into account when making decisions about contact.

The background to current practice

From the 1980s onwards there has been a sustained movement towards more open adoption arrangements in the UK. For many years before this, a "secrecy is best" philosophy had dominated in the belief that this would protect the child and birth mother from the stigma of illegitimacy, and allow the child and adoptive parents the freedom and security to develop their family relationships without undue interference (either actual or psychological) from the child's birth family. Moves towards openness have been fuelled by two main forces. The first of these was concern that the "benefits" of closed adoption were not so helpful after all; birth mothers could be left with unresolved grief and anxiety about their child, adopted people had unanswered questions about their past and their identity, and adoptive parents were hampered in helping children address these issues. The second reason behind an increase in openness has been the changing nature of adoption, from the placement of babies by unmarried mothers to the adoption of older children from care, many of whom had *established* relationships with birth family members (Triseliotis *et al*, 1997; Neil, 2003a).

Contact plans for adopted children have not been centrally recorded, so only estimates of the prevalence and types of post adoption contact are possible. The Prime Minister's Review (Performance and Innovation Unit, 2000) quoted an estimate that 70 per cent of adopted children are expected to have ongoing indirect (letterbox) or direct (face-to-face) contact post adoption. Neil's (2002b) survey of 168 children placed under four years found that only 11 per cent had no plan for any sort of contact with their birth family. However, the majority of plans were for ongoing letterbox contact, with only 17 per cent due to have at least annual face-to-face contact with adult birth family members. Face-to-face contact with birth family may be more commonly planned for older adopted children or between siblings; in Lowe and Murch *et al*'s (1999) study, 39 per cent of children were having direct contact with an adult birth family member, and 55 per cent of placements in one recent study had contact with a sibling (Selwyn *et al*, 2006). The Adoption and Children Act (2002) does not include any presumption of contact for adopted children, as is the case in foster care, but did introduce a new requirement that contact must be considered and proposed arrangements must be set out in the child's placement plan. Decisions about contact should take account of the principle that the child's welfare throughout his or her life should be the paramount consideration.

The label "contact" covers wide variations in current practice (Neil, 2002). Letterbox contact, usually mediated by an adoption agency, can be one-way (from the birth parents/other relatives or the adoptive family) or two-way (with both parties involved in sending and receiving). In some cases the child may be unaware of the contact. The exchange may consist simply of signed cards, basic information or detailed personal letters, and in some cases gifts, photos or videos. It can involve any number of birth relatives from the immediate or extended family. Face-to-face meetings may occur at the time of placement in addition to ongoing letterbox contact and sometimes be planned to occur periodically throughout the adoption, taking place in neutral venues under supervision or with parties having direct access to each other and meeting in their own homes. Plans vary according to what is considered appropriate in a particular case, as well as being influenced by agency rules and traditions.

Debates and theories about contact after adoption

Debates about contact focus on whether it helps or hinders children, adoptive parents and birth parents, to deal with the unique challenges and issues that adoption brings into their lives.

Children

The development of a secure attachment is a priority need for all children. Children integrating into a family through adoption need to form an attachment to new carers, while often coping with the loss of previous attachment figures and in many cases an insecure attachment history. A key issue in the contact debate has therefore centred on the impact of contact upon the formation of the new attachment. There have also been concerns that open adoption may interfere with a child's sense of belonging and permanency in their adoptive family (e.g. Kraft *et al*, 1985c). For children with established birth family relationships, however, it has been argued that the "disappearance" of significant others and pain of loss may interfere with attachment to adoptive parents, as the child is encouraged to accept the severance of ties which may drive their feelings underground (Triseliotis, 1991).

Many theorists have spoken of the sense of loss that may be experienced as children become aware of their adoptive status and its meaning. Even for those adopted as infants a (perhaps covert) sense of loss may arise. They may feel loss of their birth family, loss of self and of genealogical continuity; regret about not being biologically related to the adoptive family; feel rejected or unwanted; and/or a status loss to do with feeling different (Triseliotis, 1973; Brodzinsky, 1990). A healthy sense of self-esteem and identity needs to be achieved by adopted children, incorporating knowledge of their background and answers to questions such as 'why was I adopted?'. Continued contact may provide benefits in relation to children's self-esteem and identity and help reduce their sense of rejection and loss through the development of a deeper understanding of the circumstances of their relinquishment or removal. Contact may also provide children with evidence that their birth family still cares and is interested in their subsequent life. However, where it is not maintained or is experienced negatively, it could be argued that there is a risk that contact may lead to further rejection and emotional (or even physical) harm.

Adoptive parents

For the adoptive parent, a key task will be relationship building with a child who, in most cases, will start out as a stranger and who may be insecure and lack trust in relationships. Adoptive parents need to feel entitled to parent a child born and perhaps partly raised by another. Initial anxieties around contact in relation to adoptive parents were that adoptive parents' sense of control and entitlement to their child would be undermined (Kraft *et al*, 1985b). In contrast, others consider that even without contact the birth parents are psychologically present (Fravel, 1995). Hence, there is a counter argument that contact allows adoptive parents to engage constructively with this reality, allowing them to develop a more realistic and empathic view of the birth family and actually *reducing* fears and insecurity.

Another key task for the adoptive parent is to help the child explore questions, confusion and feelings about their history and identity. Kirk (1964) proposed that adoptive parents who openly acknowledge the difference that adoption makes to their family life are likely to facilitate a healthier psychological environment than those who deny this difference (although, equally, problems can arise with *insistence* on difference). More recently, Brodzinsky's (2005, 2006) theory about *adoption communication openness*, proposes that the open expression and empathic support of adoption-related emotion in the adoptive family are critical for children's healthy psychological adjustment. Schofield and Beek (2006) similarly explain how the child needs to be enabled to retain a sense of their birth family connection while integrating as a member of the adoptive family. Where contact works well, it may aid the process of adoption communication, supporting the child's exploration of adoption issues and helping adoptive parents to feel comfortable with and promote the child's connection to their birth family.

Birth relatives

Following adoption, birth parents and other relatives are left to deal with the loss of a child and with concern about their welfare. Birth relatives, especially parents, also undergo changes to their role and identity; they are no longer the psychological or legal parent of the child. It has been argued that regular reminders of loss through contact could cause birth relatives a continuation of pain, role ambiguity and discomfort, and prevent the completion of the mourning process (Kraft *et al*, 1985a). Alternatively, it could be argued that, without contact, feelings of loss may always remain and be fuelled by anxieties about the child's well-being and happiness, or by unrealistic fantasies about reunion. Contact can, in the right circumstances, provide the parent with reassuring information about how their child is doing, and help them face the reality of their changed role and relationship with him or her.

Research into contact after adoption

When considering research findings, it is vital to remember the diversity covered by the term "contact" and the range of situations (with cases differing according to age of placement, reason for adoption, child background, relatives included in the contact plan etc.) in which contact can occur. Research findings obtained in one kind of situation cannot be seen to apply universally across all others. Certain findings may also only be revealed over a long period of time. Studies which do not include families of black and minority ethnicity may not pick up on cultural issues (for example, a greater comfort with complex family forms, or conversely a greater desire for confidentiality and avoidance of stigma) which may lead to different outcomes.

Research focused on relinquished infants

Our understanding of contact in this group has greatly benefited from Grotevant and colleagues' longitudinal study of 190 adopted children in the United States (Grotevant and McRoy, 1998; Grotevant *et al*, 2004, 2005; Henney *et al*, 2004, 2007); there is no equivalent study in the UK. This research studied in detail the experiences of adoptive parents, birth mothers, and children placed in infancy, following up the sample in middle childhood and adolescence. Outcomes for children were compared across three types of openness: confidential adoptions (no contact after placement), mediated or semi-open adoptions (usually these involved letterbox contact); and fully disclosed adoptions (most of these included face-to-face contact). Across all three groups, adopted adolescents reported high degrees of satisfaction with openness. Just over half of adolescents wanted contact to stay at the same level (55.8%), but 41.9 per cent desired more contact with their birth mothers, and only one person wanted less. Satisfaction with contact type was highest among those adolescents having most contact (Grotevant *et al*, 2005).

There was no evidence from this study that contact after adoption was detrimental to adoptees' relationships with their adoptive parents, or to their overall emotional and behavioural adjustment. Outcomes for birth mothers were also considered, and at the second follow-up, mothers involved in fully disclosed adoptions tended to have lower levels of grief than mothers in confidential adoptions (Henney *et al*, 2007). Overall, this study concluded that fears about openness are unsupported. The authors argue that the level of openness in an adoption needs to be made on a case by case basis, and that what is the right level at one point in time may differ, as the needs of children, adoptive parents and birth parents change over time. This study provides an excellent account of how openness works out in voluntary infant adoptions, but questions remain about whether these findings are applicable to either babies and toddlers or to older children adopted from care.

Research focused on mainly younger placed children

A broader sample has been the focus of research conducted by the current authors. We studied a group of children who were placed for adoption when under the age of four years (mean age at placement was 21 months), following them up two and seven years after placement. Most children were placed from care, and many had experienced neglect and abuse. Over 60 adoptive parents, over 60 birth relatives and 45 children having either letterbox or face-to-face contact plans, took part in interviews at the seven year post-placement follow-up. Face-to-face contact was, more often than not, very much liked by all parties. Most adopters and birth relatives got to know each other quite well and developed a trust in each other, enjoyed meetings and felt better informed about each other (Neil, 2003a and b; Neil, 2004a; Young and Neil, 2004). Children generally did not show negative responses to contact meetings, possibly because in most cases they did not have an established relationship with birth relatives; contact meetings tended to be described as low key, like seeing a distant relative or friend of the family.

Indirect contact could also work very well, but in many cases people found this a difficult way to communicate (Neil, 2004b; Young and Neil, 2004) and seven years after placement, fewer than half of the children having only indirect contact were getting *any* information about birth relatives. More open-minded adoptive parents seemed to opt into face-to-face contact arrangements, but direct meetings also seemed to help adoptive parents become more open as they facilitated empathy for birth relatives, communication with the child and comfort with the birth family connection (Neil, 2007a). Children generally accepted whatever contact they had as "normal", though they tended to express dissatisfaction when planned contact did not happen. Contact (especially that involving at least one face-to-face meeting with adoptive parents) appeared to have a positive impact on birth parents, helping them to accept and feel positive about the adoption (Neil, 2007b). As with the US study, fears about openness harming children were not supported. Adoptive parents did not feel that either type of contact stopped children forming an attachment, and the type of contact children had also did not relate to their broad emotional and behavioural outcomes (Neil, 2007a).

A similar UK sample focused on a sample of children having face-to-face contact (Smith and Logan 2004; Logan and Smith, 2005). This sample included 96 children in 61 adoptive families. Around three-quarters of these children had been placed under the age of five and most had some kind of special need such as a background of neglect or abuse, experience of multiple moves or the need for placement with siblings. The children were aged between two and 18 at the time of the study and interviews were carried out with 51 adopted children, adoptive parents from 60 families, eight birth parents and 35 other birth relatives (grandparents, aunts, uncles or siblings).

Several years into the adoption, Smith and Logan found that most of the direct contact was working well, although it was not always problem free. Almost all adoptive parents felt their family had gained something from having contact and over two-thirds were comfortable and happy with contact. A minority (13%) of adoptive parents experienced discomfort and considered contact to be without benefits or harmful (e.g. because it distressed children). Significant problems were caused if the birth relative opposed the adoption or contact was too frequent. Concerns also arose when sibling contact caused children to worry about brothers and sisters not settled into a family, or presented children with unsavoury role models. All birth relatives were satisfied with contact and could note advantages for themselves or their children, particularly in terms of enabling them to see their child develop, providing them with reassurance as to their children's welfare or enabling them to express love to their children. However, contact was by no means easy and personal discomfort and discomfort about their role was felt by the majority.

Research focused on mainly older placed children

In this category, one longitudinal study worth noting for its large sample of 1,165 children most of whom were placed when over five years (and which included those in permanent foster care placements as well as adoption) is that by Fratter *et al* (1991). Using one main outcome measure, it was found that placements where there was at least some face-to-face contact with a birth parent were less likely to have disrupted.

From this sample, a long-term follow-up interview study with adoptive parents and foster carers of 51 children and 28 young people of black and minority ethnicity (Thoburn *et al*, 2000; Thoburn, 2004) revealed that many young people and parents would have liked or considered contact in the placement, but it was not presented as an option. For those having direct contact, although there were difficult times (including sometimes the experience of further rejection), contact was seen to help the young people understand the problems of their birth parents and why they were adopted and to contribute to a positive sense of ethnic and cultural identity. Those without contact were reported to have more difficulties dealing with their adoption history.

Although based on a small sample, Fratter (1996) conducted an in-depth study of 22 adoptive families with face-to-face contact which also had the benefit of a long-term perspective (most had reached their late teens at the time of interview). The children were from a range of ethnic and cultural backgrounds and had been placed at varying ages from infancy to 14 years (approximately two-thirds were placed aged six and over). This study also revealed mainly positive findings in relation to contact, with adoptive parents, birth relatives and children generally feeling that contact had been beneficial in some way. For children, benefits included less anxiety about birth parents and a contribution to self-esteem. Birth parents felt more comfortable with the adoption, more reassured about how their child was getting on, and less helpless. Some adoptive parents spoke of contact as contributing to their satisfaction with the adoption and enhancing their identity as adoptive parents. For most families, even frequent contact was not thought to interfere with the child's attachment. However, one adoptive parent felt that contact had been an almost entirely negative experience and may have caused attachment issues early in placement.

Macaskill (2002) carried out a cross-sectional interview study looking at the experiences of 76 families of adopted (and some permanently fostered) children, placed when over four years old, who were having face-to-face contact with birth family members. She found that most children with established relationships wanted to see their birth relatives and could experience a great sense of loss or concern if denied this. Unfortunately, the children's views were sometimes not known or not taken into account in decision making. Macaskill's findings, six months to nine years into placement, show that there can be many benefits from contact, including having a confidence-building, reassuring and calming effect on children, but that it is a complex experience. Meetings often stirred up intense emotions, and some problems for children were reported, including feelings of divided loyalty, continued abuse, emotional suffering and progress setbacks. Poor quality interaction sometimes occurred, with birth relatives showing rejecting or hostile behaviour towards the child, and distorted roles re-enacted in contact meetings. Five placements were thought to have disrupted as a result of contact.

Similar mixed findings were shown by Selwyn et al (2004, 2006) from interviews with 64 adoptive parents of children placed when over three years old, most of whom were having face-to-face contact at the beginning of the placement (90% with siblings, 31% with a birth parent and 34% with another adult relative). On average, seven years into placement, although some contact had stopped, most adoptive parents were supportive of contact, and sibling or other non-parent contact was often seen as particularly enjoyable for children. There was some evidence of negative experiences, such as behavioural and anxiety problems shown by children before and after contact. There had also been some incidents of abuse during unsupervised contact. Interestingly, few adoptive parents were positive about letterbox arrangements. Although, for some, letters became part of their normal routine or fundamental to the child's understanding of their history, they could be stressful to write, remind children of a painful past, or cause upset if they did not arrive when expected.

Overall the research into outcomes for older placed children has presented diverse findings. Contact clearly can be very much needed and desired by children who have established birth family relationships, and such contact can work well and reap benefits. But contact for the older placed child can also be problematic, raising difficult issues and memories for children and can involve problematic dynamics between the birth family (who may have parented for many years) and the child's new family.

Research studies – conclusions

Research undertaken in the last couple of decades has shown the potential benefits for all those involved that can be gained from contact. However, the research also highlights the risk of negative consequences which, in certain circumstances, may result. We are left with no simple answer to the question of whether contact will be beneficial within any specific adoption placement. Each study reveals differences between children and families according to whether contact is appreciated and experienced in a positive way and also shows patterns and changes over time. Each adoptive placement is unique and there cannot be one path for all or even one plan for all time within a placement. The developmental stage, attachment and parenting history, personal qualities, and personalities and context of the child and adults involved will no doubt have a part to play in how contact is experienced. It is this level of detail that now needs to be explored.

Research findings: When does contact work or not work?

We can clearly not view contact as "good" or "bad" in itself; it is the *quality* of contact that is the vital consideration. Looking back over the research studies, key themes emerge which inform our understanding of the conditions under which contact is likely to work.

Which contact plan?

Each study found differences between families as to which type of contact was seen as appropriate by adoptive parents, children and birth relatives. Comparing the two main types of contact, letterbox contact and face-to-face contact, it is clear that different advantages and disadvantages might apply to each.

The advantages of face-to-face contact seem to be that this type of contact provides a direct and immediate medium for communication between all parties, allowing children, adoptive parents and birth relatives the opportunity to exchange information and see for themselves what the other person is like (Neil, 2004a; Smith and Logan, 2004). This can build empathy and understanding between people. But this type of contact may not be appropriate in cases where the child does not desire such contact, or where it might expose him or her to the risk of future abuse or extreme anxiety, or where birth relatives may threaten the physical or psychological security of the adoptive family.

Letterbox contact seems to be seen by agencies to be more straightforward (Neil, 2002b) and, when it works, there is no doubt that this type of contact can meet some of the needs of the child and adults involved. But this type of contact should not be thought of as an "easy" option. In the Contact after Adoption study (Neil, 2004b), more barriers to achieving good information exchange arose in letterbox contact where non- (or very limited) response of birth relatives was common. Both adoptive parents and birth relatives found it hard to write to people they did not know and recipients were often left to rely on limited and easily misinterpreted written words. Birth relatives often spoke of their inability to trust the written word, having felt let down and deceived by professionals and the system around them. Photographs were almost unanimously seen as more real and honest than brief written updates, although for some relatives, newsy, friendly and hand-written letters were appreciated. Grotevant and McRoy (1998) also found that participants in letterbox contact often made incorrect assumptions about each other, and in some cases letters could be cold and uninformative. If letterbox is deemed appropriate, then support and mediation to promote communication and quality information exchange that meets each party's needs is essential (Neil, 2004b; Selwyn et al, 2006).

Practical arrangements

All the research reviewed reports that contact arrangements, be they by letter or face-to-face, can vary enormously from case to case in terms of how they are set up and managed, and that what works for one family may not be right for another. Looking first at face-to-face contact, in studies by Neil (2002a, 2004a) and Macaskill (2002), ideal contact venues for some families were safe enclosed family centres. Others preferred neutral everyday settings, such as parks, where there was less pressure on making conversation or no associations with previously poor experiences of being watched and assessed. The presence of a supervisor could be a vital support in some cases and/or unnecessary and restrictive in others. Frequent and open contact (such as fortnightly at weekends, or shared holidays and meetings in each other's houses) were appropriate in some situations but annual, time-restricted meetings with undisclosed personal details vital in others. Macaskill notes that, for older children who have a highly emotional response to contact, meetings should neither be too frequent (as the child needs time to recover) nor too infrequent (such that the relationship appears to have to be made afresh each time) and she suggests that starting slowly and building up to more frequent contact as relationships developed was usually best. She concludes that venues need to be of high quality, relaxed and comfortable. Clear boundaries and written (but flexible and dynamic) arrangements for many may be essential.

When it comes to letterbox contact there are many considerations to be made about when, how and between whom letters should be exchanged, and about the inclusion or otherwise of cards, photographs, video material, vouchers or presents. How people are to address each other is another potential area for discussion. Research does not suggest a "best way" with regard to these issues, but studies do suggest that clarity and agreement about these issues are important (e.g. Neil, 2004b; Selwyn *et al*, 2006). It is clear that agencies mediating contact can have an impact on how plans progress. For example, Dunbar *et al* (2000) found that a lack of efficiency in organising exchanges between the parties can create or exacerbate misunderstandings about the other person's needs and wishes, sometimes leading to a cessation of contact.

Which birth relatives should be included in contact?

Even within the same family, while continued contact may be important and positive with certain birth family members it could be damaging with others. Children do discriminate between different relatives and sometimes do not want contact with particular individuals (Thomas *et al*, 1999; Macaskill, 2002). Caution, however, must be exercised, as children with traumatic backgrounds are not always able to accurately understand or communicate their feelings. Although not based on a sample of adopted children, research by Wilson and Sinclair (2004) showed that outcomes for previously abused foster children were better when one person was forbidden from having contact. Strong feelings in favour of sibling contact were commonly expressed by children in research by both Macaskill (2002) and Thomas *et al* (1999). However, it should not be assumed that all sibling contact will be straightforward and positive as siblings themselves may be perpetrators of bullying or abuse, and negative hierarchies may exist. Neil (2004a and b) found that the vast majority of grandparent contact arrangements were working well (most of these had face-to-face rather than letterbox contact). Grandparents often had fewer life problems than parents, greater resources (e.g. stable address, letter writing skills), and less complex feelings about adoption, all of these meaning they were more likely than birth parents to accept and support the child's adoption (Neil, 2007a).

Individual characteristics of the child involved

We have seen how very young placed children typically have fairly benign reactions to contact. The situation is more complicated with older children. Some of these will desperately want and need to see or hear from members of their birth family, and will benefit from doing so, even if meetings or letters raise difficult feelings. But for other children, especially those who have experienced trauma and associate this with either the relative concerned, or with other features of contact such as the venue, contact may be unwanted or disturbing (Howe and Steele 2004). In attempting to predict which children will enjoy and benefit from seeing their birth family and which others may be negatively affected, factors connected to background, personality differences and age will all need to be considered. Again, it is essential to take into account children's views as well as ensure close and continual observation of behaviour and other visual signs (Schofield and Beek, 2006). There will be particular concern in cases where a child has suffered severe maltreatment at the hands of a birth relative. Howe and Steele (2004, p 213) note how contact in such circumstances 'can trigger old unresolved memories of the traumatic character of the relationship' and may lead the child to re-experience extreme states of emotional deregulation and experience the placement as unable to consistently provide safety and security.

Individual characteristics of adults involved

Consistently shown to be related to the success of contact, regardless of individual circumstances, are the *feelings, relationship skills and attitudes of the adults* involved. Earlier reference was made to the importance of communicatively open attitudes and approaches to adoption (Brodzinsky, 2005), and this comes to the fore in and around contact situations; 'the point at which the two families overlap in the child's life, and their dual membership is made real' (Beek and Schofield, 2004, p 124). Fratter (1996) found adoptive parents' 'openness of attitude' to be important in contact success. Schofield and Beek (2006) explain that secure and comfortable contact is more likely if the adoptive parents are able to show the child that they *are there with them* in their dual connection rather than leaving their child on their own (physically and emotionally) to deal with the issues and feelings that may arise. Ideally, adoptive parents need to be actively present in and comfortable with contact. Grotevant (forthcoming) has also highlighted the contribution of 'relationship skills', such as empathy and perspective taking abilities.

Neil (2007a), applying Brodzinsky's concept of communicative openness, found a wide variation between adoptive parents in their attitudes and behaviour towards contact and birth relatives and towards communicating within the adoptive family about adoption. The degree of communicative openness in adoptive parents influenced how they approached and participated in contact. Some adoptive parents could manage well, feel positive about, and maintain over time, contact situations that were complex or difficult. If contact raised worries or questions for their children, perhaps about the birth family or the past, these parents saw this as an opportunity to keep communication open and facilitate discussion rather than as a problem to be avoided. Adoptive parents who felt that contact was imposed upon them and who struggled with its value found it difficult to deal with issues (Neil, 2003c, 2007a, forthcoming; Smith and Logan, 2004).

It is equally important that the birth relative promotes the child's dual connection in contact and does not undermine the adoptive placement. Birth relatives need to support the child's need to form new relationships and be fully part of the adoptive family (which can include reference to the adopters as 'your mum and dad'), alongside showing interest in and care towards the child (Festinger, 1986; Neil, 2003b, 2007b; Smith and Logan,

251

2004). Both Smith and Logan (2004) and Neil (2007b) report that accepting (or consenting to) the adoption legally is not the same as accepting the adoption emotionally. These authors argue that some birth relatives are likely to need help to deal with their difficult feelings about the adoption and to understand clearly the expectations as to their role in the child's life after adoption.

Relationships between parties

Not only are such individual qualities important, but equally influential is the relationship between the adults. It makes sense that the child will only be able to feel comfortable about contact that unites their two families at the level of feelings and identity if the adults are in some way "united" in contact and comfortable with their relationship.

In Grotevant's study, child adjustment was seen to be positively associated with 'collaboration in relationships' (Grotevant et al, 1999, 2005). He explains how all adults in the 'adoptive kinship network' [need] '. . . to work together effectively on behalf of the child's wellbeing' by showing mutual respect, trust and empathy towards each other, valuing the relationship they have with each other and the child and being committed to working proactively together to ensure that contact works to the benefit of the child (Grotevant, 2005, p 178).

Logan and Smith (2005) analysed 11 cases where the child, adoptive parents and birth relatives were all interviewed. Good relationships between people in these "triangles" were characterised by mutual acceptance, though this was not based on an equality of power, but birth parents expressing gratitude to adoptive parents, and the latter showing sympathy to birth relatives. Similar themes have emerged from Neil's analysis of 30 matched cases where adoptive parents and birth relatives were both interviewed (Neil, forthcoming). Smith and Logan (2004) found that relationship problems were less likely in relationships with the extended birth family, as opposed to birth parents.

The dynamic nature of contact

This consideration of factors necessary for contact success shows that, although practical details must be taken into account, it appears that it is primarily the feelings, behaviour and interactions between the parties involved which will determine whether or not contact is a positive experience. However, individual positions are not fixed (Neil and Howe, 2004a). Brodzinsky (2005) considered communicative openness not to be a stable characteristic but to change according to needs, development and experiences of individuals. It was clear from the interviews in the Contact after Adoption study (Neil, 2003c, 2004, 2007a) that adoptive parents' attitudes, feelings, and understanding could develop over time, with support, education and positive agency attitudes towards contact all having a part to play. Several studies have shown that birth relatives who may have opposed or fought fiercely against the adoption can show support for the adoptive placement as time progresses (Ryburn, 1994; Fratter, 1996; Thoburn *et al*, 2000; Neil, 2007b). Grotevant's longitudinal study showed that trust and mutual respect between parties were gradually established over time. Relationships had to be continually re-negotiated, as roles and needs of participants in contact changed, and the achievement of a comfortable level of closeness between all parties in contact could be difficult and require much 'fine tuning' (Grotevant, forthcoming).

It is clear that the attitudes, feelings, and behaviour of individuals affect contact; however, equally, the *experience of contact* itself and the *interaction* with other parties within the adoption triad can lead to changes in an individual's attitudes, feelings, and behaviour. For example, in the Contact after Adoption study, we found that the initial meetings between adoptive parents and birth relatives could have a profound effect on how each party saw the other. Adoptive parents often saw the humanity of birth parents, a contrast to an often cold or negative picture they had acquired from paperwork and reports. Likewise, a meeting with adoptive parents could be a huge influencing factor on birth relatives' acceptance of the adoption and their ability to participate positively in contact, particularly meetings with adoptive parents who were skilled in enabling birth relatives to feel included and worthy. Over time, similar changes could continue as a result of interactions via contact letters or meetings, and the analysis of 30 matched cases illustrates many of these dynamics. In some cases, contact had remained static over time, but in many cases either positive or negative spirals of interaction between birth relatives and adoptive parents had taken place (Neil, forthcoming).

Children themselves are also influenced by and influence others in contact. For example, in the Contact after Adoption study, the typically benign reactions to contact of very young placed children often allayed anxieties of adoptive parents around meetings with the birth relative (Neil, 2002b). When children enjoyed contact or were inquisitive about their birth family, this could help both adoptive parents and birth relatives to feel more positive about it and keen for its continuance (Neil, 2004a and b). Children are likely to become more curious about their adoption as they get older (Grotevant *et al*, 2005), and this can drive communication about adoption within the adoptive family and motivate both adoptive parents and birth parents to move openness up a level (Wrobel *et al*, 2003). On the other hand, children's negative or indifferent reactions to contact may affect adoptive parents' comfort with the plans (Macaksill, 2002; Logan and Smith, 2004) or discourage birth parents from keeping in touch.

It is clear that all parties affect other participants in the contact dynamic. In the same way as we have seen that all can *gain* from contact, for these gains to occur it is important that all parties *contribute* to contact. All need to work towards a healthy, open, collaborative relationship that will be beneficial in helping children to interpret and experience their birth family and any level of contact in a positive way.

Planning and supporting the contact system

Taking the above research findings into account, we can make some suggestions to be considered when planning for contact.

- **Be open-minded**. Each contact situation is a unique, dynamic, transactional experience. Past contact case experiences of practitioners should therefore inform but must not prejudice judgements for subsequent case decisions.
- **Consider the contribution that all extended family members can make**. Children may have strong feelings about retaining contact with siblings, grandparents or other relatives, and in some cases contact may be easier with these relatives.
- **When planning and supporting contact, consider the *whole system***: adoptive parents need to be supported in becoming more open and empathic, birth relatives need to be supported in becoming more accepting and supportive of the placement and children need space to voice their wishes, feelings and concerns and be heard in a non-defensive way. All parties should be helped to see their own role in contact, but also to recognise the value of the other parties' contributions and of working in a united way for the benefit of the child. Collaboration between all parties – the key factor for contact success – needs to be fostered, so working jointly with parties may be required. Recognition that there can be *gains* for all can help everyone to be committed to working at difficult relationships and accept compromise – an essential quality of collaboration.
- **Match rules and structure with assessed risk**. Structures or rules around face-to-face or letterbox contact should not be applied inflexibly, uniformly and continually to all cases when they may be unwarranted. Consider, for example, does face-to-face contact need to be supervised in *every* case? Must *all* birth parents be forbidden to sign cards "mummy and daddy?" Does *every* contact letter need to be opened and read? Is it *always* inappropriate for the birth mother to bring a friend or partner to contact? Safety and security of the child are paramount and certain boundaries and restrictions are often necessary. However, a flexible and case sensitive approach to all involved should be taken, striving for a balance between reducing anxiety and promoting security AND the fostering of understanding and collaborative relationships. Henrietta Bond's recent book provides guidance on taking an individualised approach to contact (Bond, 2007).
- **Recognise the challenges of letterbox contact**. Establishing a dialogue through annual letters (especially those which cross over) may not be easy and support can be required. Thinking about contact beyond the boxes of "letterbox" OR "face-to-face with child" may be helpful; video material, phone calls, adult-to-adult meetings, a change of venue or participants etc. may all have their place in any contact plan at any time to foster better communication and collaboration. For

example, adult-to-adult meetings could be used periodically throughout a placement to clear up misunderstandings, resolve conflicts and create an opportunity to voice wishes and needs regarding contact.

- **Accept that in some cases, at some times and with some relatives, it may be that face-to-face and even letterbox contact should not happen**. There will always be contact that is inherently difficult, does not have compensatory gains and which is potentially damaging for children. In these cases, alternative ways of meeting the child's identity needs should not be overlooked and links should always be left open to allow for future changes and needs.

- **Be aware that individuals' positions can change as a result of having contact**. There should be an opportunity for all parties to rethink, challenge and adjust arrangements; no plan for contact should be left to roll its course without review. Plans, rules and practical arrangements may need to be reconsidered according to changing relationships and needs.

Contact is a complex area of work. There is no simple formula to get the right answers to questions about contact after adoption. It requires engaging with the emotional complexity, thinking about the whole contact system, acknowledging everyone's needs and feelings, embracing the concept that people can change, and thinking widely about all the ways in which we can learn from and help adopted children.

Selected further reading

Bond H. (2007) *Ten Top Tips for Managing Contact*, London: BAAF

Macaskill C. (2002) *Safe Contact? Children in permanent placement and contact with their birth relatives*, Lyme Regis: Russell House Publishing

Neil E. (2003) 'Contact after adoption: A research review', in Bainham M., Lindley B., Richards M. and Trinder L. (eds) *Children and their Families: Contact, rights and welfare*, Oxford: Hart Publishing

Neil E. and Howe D (eds) (2004) *Contact in Adoption and Permanent Foster Care: Research, theory and practice*, London: BAAF

References

Beek M. and Schofield G. (2004) 'Promoting security and managing risk: Contact in long-term foster care', in Neil E. and Howe D. (eds) *Contact in Adoption and Permanent Foster Care: Research, theory and practice*, London: BAAF, pp 124–143

Bond H. (2007) *Ten Top Tips for Managing Contact*, London: BAAF

Brodzinsky D. M. (1990) 'A stress and coping model of adoption adjustment', in Brodzinsky D. M. and Schechter M. D. (eds) *The Psychology of Adoption*, New York: Oxford University Press

Brodzinsky D. M. (2005). 'Reconceptualizing openness in adoption: Implications for theory, research and practice', in Brodzinsky D. and Palacios J. (eds) *Psychological Issues in Adoption: Research and practice*, New York: Greenwood, pp 145–166

Brodzinsky D. M. (2006) 'Family structural openness and communication openness as predictors in the adjustment of adopted children', *Adoption Quarterly*, 9, pp 1–18

Dunbar N., van Dulmen M. H. M., Ayers-Lopez S., Berge J. M., Christian C., Fitzgerald N., Gossman G., Henney S., Mendenhall T., Grotevant H. D. and McRoy R. G. (2000) *Openness Changes in Adoptive Kinship Network Connections*, Paper presented at the meeting of the National Council on Family Relations, Minneapolis, MN

Festinger T. (1986) *Necessary Risk: A study of adoptions and disrupted adoptive placements*, Washington DC: The Child Welfare League of America

Fratter J. (1996) *Adoption with Contact: Implications for policy and practice*, London: BAAF

Fratter J., Rowe J., Sapsford D. and Thoburn J. (1991) *Permanent Family Placement: A decade of experience*, London: BAAF

Fravel D. L. (1995) *Boundary Ambiguity Perceptions of Adoptive Parents Experiencing Various Levels of Openness in Adoption*, Unpublished doctoral dissertation, University of Minnesota, St. Paul

Fravel D. L., McRoy R. G. and Grotevant H. D. (2000) 'Birthmother perceptions of the psychologically present adopted child: Adoption openness and boundary ambiguity', *Family Relations*, 49, pp 425–433

Grotevant H. D. (forthcoming 2009) 'Emotional distance regulation over the life course in adoptive kinship networks', in Wrobel G. and Neil E. (eds) *International Advances in Adoption Research for Practice*, Chichester: Wiley

Grotevant H. D. and McRoy R. G. (1998) *Openness in Adoption: Exploring family connections*, Thousand Oaks, CA: Sage

Grotevant H. D., McRoy R. G. and Ayres-Lopez S. (2004). 'Contact after adoption: Outcomes for infant placements in the USA', in Neil E. and Howe D. (eds) *Contact in Adoption and Permanent Foster Care: Research, theory and practice*, London: BAAF, pp 46–64

Grotevant H. D., Perry, Y., and McRoy, R. G. (2005). 'Openness in adoption: Outcomes for adolescents within their adoptive kinship networks', in Brodzinsky D. and Palacios J. (eds) *Psychological Issues in Adoption: Research and practice*, Westport, CT: Praeger, pp 167–186

Grotevant H. D., Ross N. M., Marcel M. A. and McRoy R. G. (1999) 'Adaptive behaviour in adopted children: Predictors from early risk, collaboration in relationships within the adoptive kinship network, and openness arrangements', *Journal of Adolescent Research*, 14:2, pp 231–247

Henney S. M., Ayers-Lopez S., McRoy R. G. and Grotevant H. D. (2004) 'A longitudinal perspective on changes in adoption openness: The birth mother story', in Neil E. and Howe D. (eds) *Contact in Adoption and Permanent Foster Care: Research, theory and practice*, London: BAAF, pp 26–45

Henney S. M., Ayers-Lopez S., McRoy R. G. and Grotevant H. D. (2007) 'Evolution and resolution: Birth mothers' experience of grief and loss at different levels of adoption openness', *Journal of Social and Personal Relationships*, 24, pp 875–889

Howe D. and Steele M. (2004) 'Contact is cases in which children have been traumatically abused or neglected by their birth parents', in Neil E. and Howe D. (eds) *Contact in Adoption and Permanent Foster Care: Research, theory and practice*, London: BAAF, pp 46–64

Kirk H. D. (1964) *Shared Fate: A theory and method of adoptive relationships*, New York, NY: Free Press

Kraft A. D., Palombo J., Mitchell D. L., Woods P. K. and Schmidt A. W. (1985b) 'Some theoretical considerations on confidential adoptions, Part II: The adoptive parents', *Child and Adolescent Social Work*, 2:2, pp 69–82

Kraft A. D., Palombo J., Mitchell D. L., Woods P. K., Schmidt A. W. and Tucker N. G. (1985c) 'Some theoretical considerations on confidential adoptions, Part III: The adopted Child', *Child and Adolescent Social Work*, 2:3, pp 139–153

Kraft A. D., Palombo J., Woods P. K., Mitchell D. L. and Schmidt A. W. (1985a) 'Some theoretical considerations on confidential adoptions, Part I: The birth mother', *Child and Adolescent Social Work*, 2:1, pp 13–21

Logan J. and Smith C. (2005) 'Face-to-face contact: Views from the triangles', *British Journal of Social Work*, 35, pp 3–35

Lowe N, and Murch M., Borkowski M., Weaver A., Beckford V. and Thomas C. (1999) *Supporting Adoption: Reframing the approach*, London: BAAF

Macaskill C. (2002) *Safe Contact? Children in permanent placement and contact with their birth relatives*, Lyme Regis: Russell House Publishing

Neil E. (2002a) 'Managing face-to-face contact for young adopted children', in Argent H. (ed) *Staying Connected: Managing contact arrangements in adoption*, London: BAAF

Neil E. (2002b) 'Contact after Adoption: The role of agencies in making and supporting plans', *Adoption & Fostering*, 26:1, pp 25–38

Neil E. (2003a) 'Contact after adoption: A research review', in Bainham M., Lindley B., Richards M. and Trinder L. (eds) *Children and their Families: Contact, rights and welfare*, Oxford: Hart

Neil E. (2003b) 'Accepting the reality of adoption: Birth relatives' experiences of face-to-face contact', *Adoption & Fostering*, 27:2, pp 32–43

Neil E. (2003c) 'Understanding other people's perspectives: Tasks for adopters in open adoptions', *Adoption Quarterly*, 6:3, pp 3–30

Neil E. (2007a) 'Post adoption contact and openness in adoptive parents' minds: Consequences for children's development', *British Journal of Social Work* – Advance Access: doi: 10.1093/bjsw/bcm087

Neil E. (2007b) 'Coming to terms with the loss of a child: The feelings of birth parents and grandparents about adoption and post-adoption contact', *Adoption Quarterly*, 10:1, pp 1–23

Neil E. (2004a) 'The "Contact after Adoption" study: Face-to-face contact, in Neil E. and Howe D. (eds) *Contact in Adoption and Permanent Foster Care: Research, Theory and Practice*, London: BAAF, pp 65–84

Neil E. (2004b) 'The "Contact after Adoption" study: Indirect contact and adoptive parents' communication about adoption', in Neil E. and Howe D. (eds) *Contact in Adoption and Permanent Foster Care: Research, theory and practice*, London: BAAF, pp 46–64

Neil E. (forthcoming 2009) 'The corresponding experiences of adoptive parents and birth relatives in open adoption', in Wrobel G. and Neil E. (eds) *International Advances in Adoption Research for Practice*, Chichester: Wiley

Neil E., Beek M. and Schofield G. (2003) 'Thinking about and managing contact in permanent placements: The differences and similarities between adoptive parents and foster carers', *Journal of Clinical Child Psychology and Psychiatry*, 8:3, pp 401–418

Neil E. and Howe D. (eds) (2004a) *Contact in Adoption and Permanent Foster Care: Research, theory and practice*, London: BAAF

Neil E. and Howe D. (2004b) 'Conclusions: A transactional model for thinking about contact', in Neil E. and Howe D. (eds) *Contact in Adoption and Permanent Foster Care: Research, theory and practice*, London: BAAF, pp 224–254

Parker R. (1999) *Adoption Now: Messages from research*, London: The Stationery Office

Performance and Innovation Unit (PIU) (2000) *The Prime Minister's Review of Adoption*, London: Cabinet Office

Quinton D., Selwyn J., Rushton A. and Dance C. (1999) 'Contact between children placed away from home and their birth parents', *Clinical Child Psychology and Psychiatry*, 4, pp 519–532

Ryburn M. (1994) 'The use of an adversarial process in contested adoptions' in Ryburn (ed) *Contested Adoptions: Research, law, policy and practice*, Aldershot: Arena

Schofield G. and Beek M. (2006) *Attachment Handbook for Foster Care and Adoption*, London: BAAF

Selwyn J. (2004) 'Placing older children in new families: Changing patterns of contact', in Neil E. and Howe D (eds), *Contact in Adoption and Permanent Foster Care: Research, theory and practice*, London: BAAF

Selwyn J.T., Sturgess W., Quinton D. L. and Baxter C. (2006) *Costs and Outcomes of Non-infant Adoptions*, London: BAAF

Smith C. and Logan J. (2004) *After Adoption: Direct contact and relationships*, London: Routledge Taylor & Francis

Thoburn J. (2004) 'Post-placement contact between birth parents and older children', in Neil E. and Howe D. (eds) *Contact in Adoption and Permanent Foster Care: Research, theory and practice*, London: BAAF, pp 184–202

Thoburn J. Norford L. and Rashid S. (2000) *Permanent Family Placement for Children of Minority Ethnic Origin*, London: Jessica Kingsley Publishers

Thomas C. and Beckford V. with Lowe N. and Murch M. (1999) *Adopted Children Speaking*, London: BAAF

Triseliotis J. (1973) *In Search of Origins*, London: Routledge and Kegan Paul

Triseliotis J. (1991) 'Intercountry Adoption', *Adoption & Fostering*, 15:4, pp 46–53

Triseliotis J., Shireman J. and Hundleby M. (1997) *Adoption: Theory, policy and practice*, London: Cassell

Wilson K. and Sinclair I. (2004) 'Contact in foster care: Some dilemmas and opportunities', in Neil E. and Howe D. (eds), *Contact in Adoption and Permanent Foster Care: Research, theory and practice*, London: BAAF, pp 165–183

Wrobel G. M., Kohler J. K., Grotevant H. D. and McRoy R. G. (2003) 'The family adoption communication (FAC) model: Identifying pathways of adoption related communication', *Adoption Quarterly*, 7, pp 53–84

Young J. and Neil E. (2004) 'The "Contact after Adoption" study: The perspective of birth relatives after non-voluntary adoption', in Neil E. and Howe D. (eds) *Contact in Adoption and Permanent Foster Care: Research, theory and practice*, London: BAAF, pp 85–104

14 Adoption support

Alan Rushton

Introduction

Interest in the topic of adoption support has grown considerably in the last thirty years. In the era of infant adoptions, there was a general assumption that, once the healthy baby arrived, the adopters would become like other parents and press on with the job of parenting. The state would withdraw, giving the optimistic message that the new family would thrive without further need of assistance. Since then, the major shift in adoption practice to adopting children from care has given the need for adoption support a much higher profile. However, vestigial elements of the baby adoption system remain and it has taken a considerable time to establish the need for further services through research, legislation and the current adoption support framework.

This chapter concentrates on provisions in England and Wales, as the new Scottish legislation is yet to be implemented and, at present, adoption policy in Northern Ireland is still at the review stage.

Who needs adoption support?

The need for adoption support has arisen mostly because the extent of difficulties of children adopted from care has been often shown to be severe and frequently persistent which then presents the new parent with a considerable challenge (Rushton and Dance, 2006). A complex combination of pre-birth, post birth and in care experiences, including changes of placement, may underlie this. Adoptive parents have therefore to manage and respond to the child's pre-placement development, which may amount to a significant number of years, although this is a period they will have played no part in. The nature of the placements has also become more complex in some cases because of the policy of preserving continuing contact with the birth family (see Young and Neil, Selwyn this volume). The increasing diversity of adopters also calls for more careful matching of services to need: single parent and same sex adopters; adopters parenting children with major disabilities, large sibling groups or children of an ethnicity different to their own; infertile couples with no parenting experience or experienced parents and second time adopters; kinship adopters; black and minority ethnic adopters, adopters of both infants and older children and of ex-orphanage children from overseas. The differing needs of these groups must be recognised as adoption support services develop.

Adoptive parents are not the only people in need of adoption support. In England and

Wales, the *adoption support framework*, arising from the Adoption and Children Act 2002 (England and Wales), has widened the eligibility criteria for assessment to include adopted children, adopted adults, siblings and birth parents. All of these people will have different perspectives, expectations and understanding of adoption e.g. adopted people may need support in searching for their birth parents, in dealing with psychological dilemmas associated with their adoptive status or with the impact of family reunion. Birth parents may need help in resolving the continuing impact of the adoption of their child or in managing contact issues.

Information and advice must be available to prospective adopters, supporting them in their first steps in what may be a life-changing set of decisions and continue through the preparation, assessment and waiting period, and finally the placement and beyond. Adoption support is therefore developing into a far more comprehensive framework, embracing any of the parties to an adoption, and any people on whom adoption may have an impact, at any point, pre-or post adoption order, and in relation to whatever difficulties, from the psychological to the practical, that may arise. Adoption support will also vary depending on whatever point in the adoption life cycle that individuals or the family have reached, some of which are predictable and some of which are not (Hajal and Rosenberg, 1991).

Developments in support services

The voluntary adoption agencies have established a particularly good reputation over many years for developing and providing adoption support services to their adoptive families. Many local authorities had also been developing their support services before the new legislation was enacted. Developments were very dependent on the presence of active champions for adoption support in those authorities and the presence of available resources. Unfortunately, these kinds of drivers for service development can make for great geographical unevenness of provision. The Adoption and Children Act 2002 and associated regulations are intended to make provisions much more uniform and the framework that has been put in place is indeed far reaching. It places a duty on local authorities to assess adoption support needs although it is within their discretion as to whether services will be provided. The right to an assessment of support needs is now extended to cover those wishing to adopt, adopted adults, birth relatives and former guardians. This gives proper recognition to the familial impact of adoption. It also requires the local authority to assist when placements disrupt. The Act also places a duty on local authorities to provide specified adoption support services and to appoint an Adoption Support Services Adviser (ASSA) whose role is to 'ensure best support arrangements, respond quickly to problems and maintain agreements'.

The new legislation and subsequent regulations are exerting more pressure on all local authorities to expand and harmonise their provisions and to conform to required standards. Developments can be seen in local authorities through the setting up of post-adoption teams and post-adoption specialist posts. Initially the staff in these new posts focused on promoting support groups for adopters, and sometimes adopted young people, managing letterbox contact, compiling information and newsletters for adopters 'to keep the doors open' and reminding them of sources of help. These have been the main tasks undertaken. Evidence that points to an increase in the amount of direct, focused intervention with individual families where there are difficulties is much less clear. Usually where more intensive, therapeutic work is required, a referral is made to Child and Adolescent Mental Health Services (CAMHS) or contracted out to independent therapists or to specialist post-adoption centres. So, while statutory frameworks may have been put in place, the reality is that services are probably still subject to a postcode lottery of provision. As critical as adoption support services might be, and as deserving as adopted families and others might be in having easy access to them, this is not enough to eliminate the ever present conflict between recognised need and the desire to provide services with limited resources.

Besides the local authority contribution to adoption support, important service developments have continued to come from voluntary adoption agencies, other charitable organisations, and independent providers. The growth of self-help in this field is particularly well represented by the activities of Adoption UK, which functions as an important source of adopter-to-adopter support. It was originally established in 1971 under the name Parent to Parent Information on Adoption Services (PPIAS). In addition to promoting a self-help network, a helpline and publications on topics like attachment and trauma, it has developed the well known adopter support programme called 'It's a piece of cake?' (a title whose intended meaning is lost without the question mark). Some authorities have bought membership of a post-adoption support organisation for their adopters. Voluntary adoption agencies (VAAs) have specialised in providing direct services (individual, group and family work and telephone helplines) as well as training for professionals. Adoption support agencies have helped to pioneer new services, for example, in managing contact arrangements, in support for birth parents, providing intermediary services and specialist training courses for professionals.

The creation of consortia of adoption agencies (both statutory and voluntary) has helped in sharing preparation and support groups and joint training in practice developments. By pooling resources, more tailored preparation and support groups can be set up, for example, for minority ethnic applicants and adopters. Beyond local services, adopters increasingly make use of expanding international website resources (for example, the Oregon Post Adoption Resource Center www.orparc.org).

Formalising support plans

In order to make the identification of needs and service planning more systematic, local authorities are now required in law to draw up an *adoption support service plan* and to monitor its implementation. The social worker, in having formally to assess the needs of the individual or family, is thereby required comprehensively to explore and identify the nature of the problem, the needs present and the kinds of services that would appropriately and effectively meet those needs. When matching is being considered, the support plan must be drawn up and presented to the adoption panel and the Adoption Support Services Adviser (ASSA) has responsibility for seeking and facilitating access to services. Hart and Luckock (2004) are doubtful about what influence the ASSA might wield in building capacity in a local system that may have few adoption-specific resources. However, the creation of this post has the potential to persuade adopters that the local authority can respond appropriately. This would be a major change from the parlous experience of adopters in the past who tried to obtain help from social services departments used to dealing with rather different, child protection, problems.

It is not yet known how routinely, nor how well this assessment of need is being carried out, nor how well problems and strengths are formulated, nor whether the parties to an adoption are connected to relevant and effective services. Support plans are only likely to be useful if the assessments of children's difficulties and adoptive parents' capacities are made more systematically and reliably by well-trained staff. A study of the fate of support plans, from first recording through to short- and long-term placement outcomes, would give a good indication of the availability and acceptability of services within the new framework. Data on service provision and adopter satisfaction collected in previous adoption support studies could be used as a baseline to investigate whether genuine improvement had been achieved.

This much more inclusive usage of the term adoption support therefore covers a range of people, different levels of intensity as well as different points in time. Conceptualising support as a single continuous process, beginning with matching child and family, may help push practice towards a better connected activity where information as it is gathered is used to formulate interventions and not ignored but built upon. This chapter will have most to say about our current understanding of preparation and support for the adopters, as it is these topics that have been most written about and researched, but the literature on support for other members of the adoption triangle is now growing. For example, Neil and Sellick have researched assistance for birth families and support in complex face-to-face contact arrangements as a part of the adoption research initiative of the Department for Children, Schools and Families (DCSF) (yet to be published). Lightburn and Pine (1996) have researched supporting the adoption of children with disabilities; Triseliotis *et al* (2005) have studied the impact of search and reunion with implications for support for all the parties to adoption; Rushton, Dance *et al* (2001) have examined the need for support for resident children when a new child, or new children, are placed.

Preparation for adopters

When prospective adopters approach an agency, they will initially be given information and advice, and if they decide to apply formally, will be expected to join some form of preparation, normally run on a group basis. The sessions are likely to include information-giving about the legal process of adoption; assessment and matching; and the kinds of children currently awaiting placement, their backgrounds and the common problems of children in care. The sessions may also include possible sources of financial support and post-adoption services. As the child's world involves school and perhaps health concerns, talks by teachers and paediatricians and CAMHS staff are often arranged and could be especially informative for inexperienced parents unfamiliar with children's services. The group is intended to be supportive in its approach to prospective adopters and is expected to provide the beginning of an ongoing relationship with the agency for those who are approved as adopters.

BAAF's eight-session preparation course is one example of a standardised curriculum (Beesley *et al*, 2006). It covers information-giving about children placed from care and is designed to assist applicants to consider the implications of adoption and the criteria for assessment. In addition, it covers child development and attachment, overcoming the effects of abuse and neglect, how children learn to feel secure, and contact with the birth family. Managing behaviour problems is contained in a section explaining the need to reinforce positive behaviour and to promote attachment. The course has been in existence since 2002 and closely follows the recommended curriculum identified in the DfES's *Practice Guidance on Assessing Prospective Adopters* (2006, pp 27–28). Although it is becoming widely used, there is no hard evidence about how well it prepares prospective adopters following the placement of a child.

It has been a source of ongoing debate as to whether participation in group preparation should also be used by the agency as a way of learning about the applicants' personal characteristics, their reactions and behaviour in the group sessions and their level of understanding and skills in relation to children. Some argue that using this information as a part of the process is unduly and unfairly stressful on prospective adopters. As a result, some agencies prefer to demarcate the assessment and preparation processes more clearly. It is generally thought to be helpful for prospective adopters to receive feedback about their participation in the group and, with their agreement, for this to be passed to the assessing social worker. If child protection or other serious concerns become apparent in the group, these would be discussed with the applicant/s and appropriate action taken.

Gradual changes to preparation for adoption have been taking place in many agencies. The more traditional approach of group-based sessions and talks by adoption social workers has moved towards more of a partnership with agency staff, with more open sharing of views and expectations with other applicants, and with more active learning from personal contact with recently formed adoptive families with whom the prospective adopters have been matched. The top-down, predominantly expert information-giving model is being supplemented by approaches that enable applicants to learn about the real life experience of the challenges children from care might present. For applicant/s inexperienced with the kinds of children placed for adoption, links to Family Centres are commonly arranged to provide a better sense of the children to be placed and their backgrounds. Sessions can be also organised for other members of the adoptive family, especially grandparents, so that they too have a realistic sense of the possible challenges and can think about support needs. A well thought out preparation programme can offer adopters an opportunity to examine and adjust their expectations and possible misperceptions before taking a reality-based decision to adopt. The ongoing and life-long impact of adoption is particularly important and the significance of having a supportive network of family friends and services equally so.

Preparation for the placement of matched children

When a proposed link and eventual match between prospective adopters and a child or children has been made, it is important that all the accumulated knowledge from the child's social worker, the family placement social worker, from the previous carers and others is made available to build an accurate picture of the children and their histories. But even when this information is available, a gulf may remain between the expectations of the adopter/s and the reality of a child, or children, moving into their home. It may be hard for potential adopters to grasp the reality of a future life with a child who carries the kinds of experiences that many adopted children have had. Even if they hear that children have major or unknown developmental difficulties, they may hope it will not be true in their case or that their love will be enough to overcome these. It is understandable and important that they should hope for the best, but this may then lead to the shock of the arrival of the child. It is important that social workers are realistic in describing the child's needs, particularly in relation to the consequences of abuse and neglect. Giving this information has to be very carefully handled – an overdose of warnings about the difficulties, and underplaying of the joyful side of adoption, is not advisable and may drive away the adopters, but neither will minimising possible problems be in the long-term interests of the child, the adopters or the agency.

One of the major challenges for organisers of preparation programmes is how much adopters can be taught the relevant parenting skills in advance of the child arriving. Only so much can be achieved in general preparation as each child will present a different combination of difficulties. One child might be endlessly distressed and tearful and prone to, say, stealing and gorging food. Another might be oppositional and defiant and in need of protection from extreme risk taking. Providing the skills, strategies and understanding to manage these particular difficulties may need more concentrated help in the period after meeting the child to be placed and the placement itself. The most useful parenting help may be provided in the crucial period immediately following placement when practitioners can use their greater knowledge of the child, and help the new parents understand why the child is feeling and behaving in the way that they are.

Research on preparation

Little research evidence is available on preparation. Much of it has been conducted in the USA and describes what is on offer in various agencies and how useful or otherwise the adopters found it (Egbert and Lamont, 2004; Wind *et al*, 2006). We know that adopters' experience of preparation can vary a great deal from agency to agency and that some groups of adopters feel the preparation does not meet their needs. In the Maudsley study, Quinton and colleagues (1998) found that parents who had experience of raising birth children were less well provided for, possibly because they were thought to have familiarity with parenting, but the more difficult children were often then placed with them, for which they were not adequately prepared. Lowe and Murch *et al* (1999), in their study of supporting the adoption of older children, also found mixed opinions on the quality of preparation but some adopters found the agencies failed to recognise their previous parenting experiences and imparted information about the child very selectively. Several studies have reported the dissatisfaction of adopters who thought the child's problems had been minimised by social workers. Both of these studies reported that adopters thought there was a lack of information about practical parenting strategies.

It is important to design interventions that are in tune with the needs of adopters, particularly as they have been reported in large scale surveys of opinion about support services. However, consumers' views are not enough by themselves to drive forward services. They don't demonstrate what works, only what consumers think is a good idea. They may be right, but may also be wrong in other ways. Adopters may opt for an approach that, in the light of independent evaluation, turns out to be ineffective and wasteful of resources. More needs to be known not just about what adopters think of preparation but about the consequences of preparation. Do some approaches produce more favourable placement outcomes? Does the level of training of social work staff delivering the preparation make a difference? Can better results be achieved if the preparation is offered at a more carefully judged time? Do the preparation sessions only work if the programme is followed through into the early months of placement? Are positive results achieved without unrealistic staff demands and costs?

Asking what effect preparation has on the subsequent placement has not proved an easy topic to research and may account for the small number of studies. Mailed questionnaires to adopters often have a poor return rate and it is not clear whether the responses are fully representative. Furthermore, as preparation is usually composed of linked and overlapping components, it is not easy to establish what elements are linked with what outcomes. Asking adopters long after the sessions to recall the value of the preparation can be misleading because the way the placement has turned out may colour their judgement.

In the absence of recent UK-based studies of the effects of preparation, it may be helpful to look at the evaluation of a training programme for potential foster carers compared with a no-training control group (Puddy and Jackson, 2003). They found that the experimental group only improved on a minority of the measures and concluded that the programme did not prepare them to manage behaviour problems. The researchers had to reflect on how the training could be improved and made more effective. Clearly more needs to be learned about the feasibility and effectiveness of training people for events as significant and individual as the placement of a child but which have not yet happened.

These studies frequently end with recommendations that preparation should be more tailored to the unique circumstances of the placed child and to the characteristics of the adoptive family. A promising way forward is to create opportunities for more reality-based awareness of the likely difficulties and introduce prospective adopters, pre-placement, to parenting principles, skills and understanding relevant to the child to be placed. A "life appreciation meeting" to review all the information about the child's life, both the positives and negatives, with the prospective adopters can contribute to a much more focused preparation process (Staples, 2005).

The development of post-placement services for adopters

We have come some way in this chapter without pausing to reflect on the term "support". It has been used as a convenient umbrella term, but it is often criticised for being so non-specific as to be of little use. Undefined "support" for adoptive parents can mean an amorphous and largely passive response hardly likely to help in managing severe behavioural problems. On the other hand, we know that adopters can have their confidence dented by a hard-to-manage child and say that simple recognition of their struggles, reminders of small positive changes, and a strong dose of approval when they are full of self-doubt can be very restorative. Genuineness is what matters. False reassurance and empty optimism will be quickly detected and ignored. Getting the basic stance right is fundamental to any therapeutic alliance with adopters. Support can sometimes be a matter of giving hope and persuading the family that they have something to give to the unrewarding child even though they may be feeling defeated.

Which model of support is appropriate has been debated for some time (Rushton, 1989). The range of need can be broad. Not every adoption is highly problematic. Some children arrive in care as part of a sibling group where they may have been differentially treated and been much less exposed to maltreatment and have relatively few problems. Some children have had stable and loving home lives before being deprived of parents, perhaps through bereavement. Others may have been well cared for in loving, stable foster homes and are well-prepared for the move and make a smooth transition into a much desired new family. Such families may need low level support while others require a good deal more. The term support may be more useful if conceived of as a continuum running from basic services, like a point of contact for advice, mutual aid meetings, newsletters and social events through to respite care and to more intensive, therapeutic, professionally delivered interventions.

It has come to be recognised that a longer-term perspective needs to be taken of adoption. We know from studies of late placement adoptions (Rushton *et al*, 1993; Selwyn *et al*, 2006) that problems in children do not hold to a constant pattern, but may abate and then re-emerge afresh or in a different guise at a later developmental stage. This poses a problem for services characterised by the need to open and then close cases, or geared to brief, time-limited interventions. Continuity of service over many years is hard to deliver given inevitable changes of staff and of service organisation and perhaps varying resource levels. From the service providers' point of view, it is difficult to balance carrying responsibility for a continuing group of problematic placements as well as the ongoing business of recruitment, assessment and preparation of potential adopters. But without such continuity, adopters can find it frustrating to have to undertake fresh negotiations each time problems become too pressing to manage. Services need to be available to respond to crises as they arise and when family patterns are not so entrenched that motivation to make fresh efforts has been lost and the placement is heading for disruption. The development of specialist post adoption services in some local authorities is a welcome and necessary solution to this problem.

Evidence on the provision of post-placement support services

Alongside the drive to move more children out of indeterminate care and into adoptive homes, an important part of the Adoption and Children Act 2002 was a recognition of the risk involved to the stability of the placements if a wider range of perhaps older and more challenging children were to be adopted. If increasing the number of children adopted resulted in increased disruption rates, discontented adopters and further distress for the children, the policy would have failed. Evidence was needed on the current state of adoption support services. My colleague Cherilyn Dance and I conducted a mapping of all statutory and voluntary adoption agencies in the UK and came up with a number of findings about support for adoptive families in difficulty. The pattern of services in the UK was found to be unevenly spread, with specialist services much more available in the large cities and inadequate staffing and skill levels a barrier to acquiring accessible therapeutic help. Lack of information about the number of placed children with serious psychosocial problems was also an impediment to planning. Child and Adolescent Mental Health Services (CAMHS) were too often not providing an "adoption sensitive" service and waiting list problems worked against a quick response. Failure to recognise the extent and severity of problems of the placed children appeared to be true in many quarters and the attitudes of some GPs, teachers, and social workers tended to underplay and be dismissive of problems presented by adopters. However, some local authority adoption teams had developed good examples of contracting therapeutic services. Little evidence has been collected about satisfaction levels of black and minority ethnic minority adopters and gay and lesbian adopters with the parenting advice they were offered.

Sturgess and Selwyn (2007) have conducted a survey of the support provided in non-infant adoptions, not just by children's services but also by health, education and CAMHS. This was an interview and questionnaire-based study of 54 families where the adoption was still intact. The study reports on the complexities of help-seeking for adopters. Although a third of these adopters were happy to receive services, others were reluctant to seek help for fear of seeming to have failed or not wanting to feel blamed or because they preferred to struggle alone. The adopters were not satisfied with the behaviour management advice available through the placement team and there were disappointments that CAMHS often failed to provide relevant, sustained and effective help and had poor understanding of the adoption context. These two studies show that, at least during the period that saw the growth of late placements from care, adopters had very mixed experiences of services and some looked in vain for genuine understanding of their needs and for effective support.

Two recent US-based studies have provided useful contemporary feedback from adopters. The US context is different in many ways but these studies report on responses to services that have been in place and developing for some time. The survey by Zosky *et al* (2005) based in Illinois gathered adopters' views of 'adoption preservation services'. Over 800 adopters completed feedback forms following receipt of a service. They were found to favour free, home-based support that was sensitive to the unique and complex needs of the family. They appreciated help in understanding the behaviour and feelings of the child and wanted to develop better parenting strategies for dealing with control problems, anger and lack of trust. Atkinson and Gonet (2007) have conducted lengthy telephone interviews with 500 adoptive families who received post-adoption services through the Adoptive Family Preservation programme in Virginia. Family ratings of placement progress were much higher when the service was more than short term and this appeared to help more in resolving difficulties and coping with challenges. Changes tended to occur more in the parents and their understanding and coping capacities than in the children themselves and the parents valued continuing education as the child passed through various developmental stages. The researchers concluded that ongoing support is the best model offering easily accessed services as and when they are needed.

Approaches to helping adoptive families in difficulty

Many therapeutic approaches are being developed in adoption and they have been recently reviewed by Scott and Lindsey (2003). The model of intervention may be child-focused, family system-focused, parent-focused or group-based and it is hoped that they will bring genuine help to struggling families. However, any novel approaches need evaluation for their suitability for the adoption context, ethical justification and cost effectiveness.

Two concepts tend to dominate the adoption literature: *attachment* and *resilience*. These topics are too large to deal with in any detail here but clearly many adopters are eagerly seeking some means of improving these capacities in their child. Developing a fresh attachment with new carers when the child has a background of distorted and broken relationships is crucial to a satisfactory placement, as is the capacity of the child to surmount life's continuing challenges in spite of early adverse experiences. However, the aim of intervening to promote fresh attachment and resilience lies still in the realm of practice experiment and therapeutic ambition. It is advisable to steer clear of texts that issue therapeutic imperatives and resemble a marketing ploy. More cautious comment-ators have warned of our limited understanding of the elements of effective intervention in this field. Evidence based on rigorous evaluation of reproducible, attachment-based interventions remains hard to come by. Disputes continue as to whether traditional behaviour modification methods and lengthy child psychotherapy work with children with attachment disorders. Some of the more radical approaches have come in for heavy criticism on ethical, theoretical and effectiveness grounds (Pignotti and Mercer, 2007). A secure, loving family environment remains the best means of promoting attachment and there may be no quick fix method. Many adopters may have to adjust and accommodate to the fact that, although hopefully over time, progress will be made in the quality of children's relationships and functioning, some difficulties in social relationships may remain an aspect of the child's personality which may continue to need active support.

A randomised controlled trial of support for adoptive parenting

Despite increasing interest in providing better adoption support services, little has been done to test the effectiveness of interventions in a systematic way (Rushton, 2004). As carefully constructed trials comparing outcomes have not been set up, or not yet reported on, evidence of effectiveness is still mostly at the level of simple before-and-after, uncontrolled evaluations. However, the changes that have been shown in such studies are not necessarily a product of the intervention and could be due to a number of other influences. For example, improvements may have occurred through the positive effects of stable family life and the child's corresponding development. It is sometimes shown that the intervention group does less well than the non-intervention group: a negative effect is possible. This would not be known without a comparison group. Finally, it is possible that other interventions could have achieved the same results, but more cheaply. The closest examples of evaluations of relevance to adoption support are the randomised controlled trials of interventions designed to improve parenting skills in foster carers (Minnis *et al*, 2001; McDonald and Turner, 2005).

A randomised controlled trial designed to investigate the effectiveness of two, 10-

week, home-based interventions to enhance adoptive parenting has recently been undertaken (Rushton, Monck *et al*, 2006; Rushton and Monck, in preparation). The study focused on the early stages of placement (between 3 and 18 months) of children between four and eight years at placement from care and known to have serious difficulties. The families were recruited from local authority adoption agencies in England. The two interventions were selected as potentially helpful to adopters and compared with a control group receiving services as usual. Allocation to the interventions was decided by chance in order that the groups were made equivalent and so any differences in outcome can be reasonably attributed to the type of intervention. The control group received existing adoption agency services and after nine months these adopters were invited to choose one of the interventions. In this way all the adopters received the offer of a service once they had entered the trial.

The parenting interventions were delivered by experienced child and family social workers familiar with adoption. They were trained to use one of the interventions, which had been formalised into a manual, and were provided with supervision from practice consultants. The types of intervention selected for the trial were highly influenced by studies of adopters' views of what they would find helpful. Both interventions were aimed at promoting and sustaining warm, consistent, sensitive and flexible parenting. Severe challenges can mean these qualities can be hard to sustain. The advisers were required to be sensitive to the engagement and help-seeking issues for adopters and had to start by building a trusting relationship and acknowledge existing parenting skills.

Behaviour management advice was compared with an educational programme to aid understanding of the children's problems. As a major challenge to adopters is known to be severe behavioural difficulties, a behaviour management programme was chosen as one arm of the trial. The adoptive parents were shown how to decrease unacceptable and increase acceptable conduct by using praise and rewards, by ignoring unacceptable or inappropriate behaviour, by setting firm limits and using "logical consequences" and problem solving.

The educational programme was designed specifically for the study with the aim of improving the parents' understanding of the *meaning* of the children's current behaviour and to help parents to see how past and present might be connected. The intention was to throw light on the possible origins of problems rather than to attempt to identify very specific causes. The adviser explored with the parent the meanings they had attached to the child's behaviour with a view to arriving at the best-informed interpretation of the child's past experience. If parents can enhance their understanding of the possible reasons for the behaviour, they should be better at anticipating events and increase their ability to manage the behaviour.

Measures were taken prior to the start of the intervention, immediately after the last session and six months later. A battery of child-based and parent-based measures was used to examine whether change could be detected. These were selected to assess the child's psycho-social status; changes in parenting competence and confidence; improvements in parent–child relationships and the parents' satisfaction with the parenting advice.

The final sample consisted of 19 families who received the interventions (9 behaviour management and 8 educational programmes) and 18 "service as usual" families. All the follow-up research interviews were completed with no refusals. In the main analysis the outcomes for the two intervention groups were first of all combined and compared with the "service as usual" (control) group at the post intervention and final follow-up. Preliminary analysis has shown significant differences and modest effect sizes in favour of the interventions over the controls for the adopters' level of satisfaction in parenting their child. Parenting approaches were also shown to have changed more in the intervention group. The increase in satisfaction with parenting was similar in both intervention groups but decreased for the controls. However, significant differences were not found between interventions and controls for any of the child outcome measures, neither at immediate post-intervention, nor at the six month follow-up. It is therefore encouraging that parenting satisfaction increased even though problem levels remained high in the intervention groups. It was perhaps not surprising that rapid change was not shown in the children over this relatively short period of time, given their level of pre-placement adversity (maltreatment, disturbed interpersonal relationships, moves in the care system and late placement) and in relation to a sample only containing those with high difficulties.

Qualitative analysis has been undertaken based on "process" feedback from the adopters and the parent advisers. Very positive feedback came from the adopters in relation to both interventions, especially the opportunity for "working through" problems and strategies rather than simply receiving general advice. The adopters especially valued regular, home-based, interventions tailored to their specific concerns. However, parent advisers found that some adopters' needs extended beyond parenting advice. Also, on the negative side, both manuals were said to be less helpful in dealing with aggressive and dangerous behaviour.

This intervention study focused on parenting skills and understanding early in the placement. Of course, not all problems are specifically about parenting and other complex difficulties may emerge later on. Strong emotions may need to be handled and numerous factors may work against the creation of a harmonious and well integrated family. Expert and more intensive help may be needed to sustain the placement in times of crisis and to ameliorate persistent family relationship difficulties.

Conclusions

After making an unduly late appearance, adoption support is now firmly on the map. Adoption agencies are showing great commitment to making placements work by extending services as far as they are able, although the "framework" of services is just that – and still very short on capacity. Extra government funding has been provided to support the new framework and compliance will be inspected by Ofsted. The overarching question is, how far will all of this go in meeting the main policy objectives? Will services be consistently available wherever parties to the adoption live? Will the services be relevant, adoption sensitive and sufficiently intensive to respond to the need and, above all, be cost effective?

It is still not clear what proportion of adoptive families need a service and at what frequency and intensity. Accurate information needs to be gathered on the numbers of people seeking adoption support and the consequences of their help seeking and the pattern of response. We know that looked after children as a group have high psychosocial problems compared with the not in-care population, but are those placed for adoption the most disturbed? It is possible that the most challenging children are not thought suitable for adoption and are in other forms of care. On the other hand, the push to find homes for children formerly thought hard-to-place might mean they have very high level problems. Even if a more accurate picture of the problem levels is established, it will always be difficult to predict whether a stable placement will become unstable at some later point, especially in adolescence.

Many doubt that mainstream services will provide adequate support and so more capacity has to be developed in permanence teams and in specialist multi-disciplinary services, especially outside the major cities and in smaller authorities with less adoption activity. Staffing levels in family placement teams will need to be increased in order to extend the service and social workers will need more opportunities for in-depth, post-qualifying training which stresses practice skills and encourages a critical approach to new research and theory in life span development. Family placement social workers need to establish themselves with the skills of direct work with a problem-solving focus and may be in the best position to offer relevant support.

The need now is for more equitably distributed, accessible services using methods known to be effective and with growing understanding of the support needs of all those on whom adoption has an impact.

Selected further reading

Beesley P., Hutchinson B., Millar I. and de Sousa S. with Fursland E. (2006) *Preparing to Adopt: A training pack for preparation groups*, London: BAAF

Department for Education and Skills (2006) *Preparing and Assessing Prospective Adopters: Practice guidance*, London: DfES

Hart A. and Luckock B. (2004) *Developing Adoption Support and Therapy: New approaches for practice*, London: Jessica Kingsley Publishers

Rushton A. and Dance C. (2002) *Adoption Support Services for Families in Difficulty: A literature review and UK survey*, London: BAAF

Sturgess W. and Selwyn J. (2007) 'Supporting the placements of children adopted out of care', *Clinical Child Psychology and Psychiatry*, 12:1, pp 13–28

References

Atkinson A. and Gonet P. (2007) 'Strengthening adoption practice, listening to adoptive families', *Child Welfare Journal*, 86:2, pp 87–104

Beesley P., Hutchinson B., Millar I. and de Sousa S. with Fursland E. (2nd edn 2006) *Preparing to Adopt – A training pack for preparation groups*, London: BAAF

Department for Education and Skills (2005) *Adoption Support Services Regulations*, London: DfES

Department for Education and Skills (2006) *Preparing and Assessing Prospective Adopters: Practice guidance*, London: DfES

Egbert S. and Lamont E. (2004) 'Factors contributing to parents' preparation for special needs adoption', *Child and Adolescent Social Work Journal*, 21:6, pp 593–609

Hajal F. and Rosenberg E. G. (1991) 'The family life cycle in adoptive families', *American Journal of Orthopsychiatry*, 61, pp 78–85

Hart A. and Luckock B. (2004) *Developing Adoption Support and Therapy: New approaches for practice*, London: Jessica Kingsley Publishers

Lightburn A. and Pine B. (1996) 'Supporting and enhancing the adoption of children with developmental disabilities', *Children and Youth Services Review*, 18, pp 139–162

Lowe N., Murch M., Borkowski M., Weaver A., Beckford V. and Thomas C. (1999) Chapter 9 'Preparation and training', in *Supporting Adoption: Reframing the approach*, London: BAAF

McDonald G. and Turner W. (2005) 'An experiment in helping foster carers manage challenging behaviour', *British Journal of Social Work*, 35, pp 1265–1282

Minnis H, Pelosi A J, Knapp M. and Dunn J. (2001) 'Mental health and foster care training', *Archives of Disease in Childhood*, 84:4, pp 302–306

Pignotti M. and Mercer J. (2007). 'Holding therapy and dyadic developmental psychotherapy are not supported and acceptable social work interventions: A systematic research synthesis revisited', *Research on Social Work Practice*, 17:4, pp 513–519

Puddy R. and Jackson Y. (2003) 'The development of parenting skills in foster parent training', *Children and Youth Services Review*, 25:12, pp 987–1013

Quinton D., Rushton A., Dance C. and Mayes D. (1998) 'Pre-placement work with new families', Chapter 7 in *Joining New Families: A study of adoption and fostering in middle childhood*, Chichester: Wiley & Sons

Rushton A. (1989) 'Post-placement services for foster and adoptive parents – Support, counselling or therapy?', *Journal of Child Psychology and Psychiatry*, 30:2, pp 197–204

Rushton A. (2004) 'A scoping and scanning review of research on the adoption of children placed from public care', *Clinical Child Psychology and Psychiatry*, 9:1, pp 89–106

Rushton A. and Dance C. (2002) *Adoption Support Services for Families in Difficulty: A literature review and UK survey*, London: BAAF

Rushton A. and Dance C. (2006) 'The adoption of children from public care: A prospective study of outcome in adolescence', *Journal of the American Academy of Child and Adolescent Psychiatry*, 45:7, pp 877–883

Rushton A., Dance C., Quinton D. and Mayes D. (2001) *Siblings in Late Permanent Placements*, London: BAAF

Rushton A. and Monck E. (in preparation) *Enhancing Adoptive Parenting: A randomised controlled trial of parenting programmes in relation to late placed adoptions from care*

Rushton A., Monck E., Upright H. and Davidson M. (2006) 'Enhancing adoptive parenting: Devising promising interventions', *Child and Adolescent Mental Health*, 11:1, pp 25–31

Rushton A., Treseder J. and Quinton D. (1993) 'New parents for older children: Support services during eight years of placement', *Adoption & Fostering*, 17:4, pp 39–45

Scott S. and Lindsey C. (2003) 'Therapeutic approaches in adoption', in Argent H. (ed.) *Models of Adoption Support: What works and what doesn't*, London: BAAF

Selwyn J., Sturgess W., Quinton D. and Baxter C. (2006). *Costs and Outcomes of Non-Infant Adoptions*, London: BAAF

Staples M. (2005) 'Life Appreciation Meetings', *Adoption Today*, October 2005, p 20

Sturgess W. and Selwyn J. (2007) 'Supporting the placements of children adopted out of care', *Clinical Child Psychology and Psychiatry*, 12:1, pp 13–28

Triseliotis J., Feast J. and Kyle F. (2005) *The Adoption Triangle Revisited: A study of adoption search and reunion experiences*, London: BAAF

Wind L., Brooks D. and Barth R. (2006) 'Adoption preparation: Differences between adoptive families of children with and without special needs', *Adoption Quarterly*, 8:4, pp 45–74

Zosky D., Howard J., Livingston-Smith S., Howard A. and Shelvin K. (2005) 'Investing in adoptive families: What adoptive families tell us regarding the benefits of adoption preservation services', *Adoption Quarterly*, 8, pp 1–23

15 Intercountry adoption: Research, policy and practice

Peter Selman

Introduction

Intercountry adoption has seldom been out of the public eye in the past few years since Angelina Jolie adopted her second child from Ethiopia in 2005. Madonna's adoption from Malawi in 2006 caused a justifiable furore and in a much publicised press release based on an article in *Adoption & Fostering* (Chou and Browne, 2008), the director of a survey of residential care in Europe (Browne, 2005) has argued that the "Madonna effect" has encouraged international adoption at the expense of domestic adoption in both sending and receiving countries – a claim weakened by reference to the subsequent rise in adoptions, when the global numbers have fallen sharply in recent years (see Table 15.2 below). A further claim that intercountry adoption is causing a rise in the number of children in orphanages has been challenged in a later edition of *Adoption & Fostering* (Gay y Blasco *et al*, 2008). Less noticed was the first adoption from the United States by Cabinet Minister David Miliband and his wife – a reminder of the continuation of "infant adoption" in that country – although Miliband's absence from the State visit of the Saudi King to be at the birth of his second child did reach the headlines.

More serious have been the continuing reports of irregularities in adoption and of adoption as a cover for child trafficking (Smolin, 2004, 2006, 2007). The arrest in October 2007 of seven French aid workers who were attempting to fly out 103 children from the impoverished country of Chad, which borders on the Darfur region of Sudan, raised again the unacceptability of intercountry adoption as a rescue mission at times of crisis when so many children are separated from their families. The organisation involved, Zoe's Ark, which was set up to help Tsunami victims in 2005, has been condemned by the French Government and the whole episode was reminiscent of a similar crisis over Italian adoptions from Rwanda in 2000 which led to a major crisis between the two countries.

This chapter seeks to put such headlines into an historical and comparative context by looking at the history of intercountry adoption since the Second World War and at the international conventions and national policies which seek to regulate it. The issues for countries which send children are examined through three contrasting "States of origin" – South Korea, India and Ethiopia – and the chapter ends with a review of existing research into outcomes, a look at the growing number of accounts of international adoption by adoptees themselves, and a consideration of the "hidden dimension" of birth mothers in the sending countries.

The history of intercountry adoption

Intercountry adoption as a legal phenomenon involving formal agreements between sending and receiving countries is usually seen as developing in the aftermath of the Second World War as a response to the needs of orphaned children in countries devastated by war. Such adoptions have been identified from Austria, Germany and Japan to the USA but also to European countries such as the Netherlands. These adoptions continued until the 1960s with European countries especially identified as sources of children for families in the United States.

However, the movement of children between countries has a much longer history, notably in the 160,000 "child migrants" sent by the UK to Australia, Canada and New Zealand and the United States between 1618 and 1967 (Bean and Melville, 1989; Parker, 2008), while in the 19th century, American "orphan trains" transported 150–200,000 children across the USA in search of good Christian homes. During the Third Reich, 'a great number of children born to Aryan women in occupied countries and fathered by German soldiers were brought to the "fatherland" and placed in adoptive families' (Altstein and Simon, 1991, p 109).

Intercountry adoption as a practice involving transracial placements became more established during and after the bitter Korean War of 1953–1958. In the 15 years following the war, the number of Korean children sent overseas for adoption rose steadily each year, reaching 1,190 in 1969. By 1970, intercountry adoption was well established in the US and in many European countries and was increasingly motivated by the needs of infertile couples faced with the reality that fewer and fewer babies were available for domestic adoption (Hoksbergen, 2000).

The next decade saw a remarkable increase in intercountry adoption in the US, the Netherlands and Scandinavia (see Table 15.1). In the 1980s, numbers fell back in the Netherlands and Sweden, but the growth continued in the US and intercountry adoptions from Korea rose to 8,837 in 1985. This was also the time when other countries became involved, notably Italy and France, where the number of adoptions rose from 935 in 1980 to 2,956 in 1990.

Global numbers reached 20,000 a year by the late 1980s (Kane, 1993), but by then several countries were experiencing a decline in annual totals as a result of falling demand – e.g. in the Netherlands, where there had been publicity about the problems parents were encountering (Hoksbergen, 1991) – or supply – with major cutbacks in the number of children sent to the US by Korea after 1987. By 1991, Howard Altstein and Rita Simon were predicting an end to growth in intercountry adoption despite a temporary reversal in this trend in 1991 with the surge of adoptions from Romania (Selman, forthcoming, 2009). Initially, Altstein's prediction seemed to be correct, as the number of visas issued in the US fell from 8,481 in 1991 to 6,472 in 1993, the lowest figure for 10 years, but from 1994 totals rose rapidly in most receiving States as China and

Table 15.1

Annual number of intercountry adoptions in USA, Sweden, Netherlands, Denmark, France and Norway, 1970–2005

Receiving country	1970	1975	1980	1987	1993	1999	2005
USA	2,409	5,633	5,139	10,097	7,377	16,363	22,728
Sweden	1,150	1,517	1,704	1,355	934	1,019	1,083
Netherlands	192	1,018	1,559	872	574	993	1,185
Denmark	226	770	766	537	473	697	586
France	n/a	n/a	935	1,723	2,784	3,597	4,136
Norway	115	397	384	465	541	589	582

Source: Selman (2006)

Russia emerged as new sources with a vast number of children potentially available for placement.

By 1998, total annual flow had risen to 32,000 per annum (Selman, 2002) and the next six years saw an increase of 40 per cent as the global total passed 45,000 (Selman, 2006). During this period Spain emerged as a key receiving State and by 2004 was second only to the US in the number of children received and equal to Norway when adoptions are standardised against the annual number of live births. Statistics for the UK show only the applications received by the DCSF but these indicate a low level of intercountry adoptions when standardised against population or births (0.5 per 1,000 live births in 2004 compared to 12.4 in Spain).

In the next two years the global numbers would fall by 12 per cent to under 40,000 a year (see Table 15.2 which shows the growth of intercountry adoptions from 1995 to 2006). Estimates for 2007 suggest a further decline to under 37,000 worldwide.

International controls

Concern over the potential for malpractice and, at worst, child trafficking led in 1984 to 13 Latin American countries agreeing an *Inter-American Convention on Conflict of Laws Concerning the Adoption of Minors*, which came into force in 1988. But the first global initiative was introduced in the 1989 United Nations Convention on the Rights of the Child (UNCRC). Article 21 says that States Parties that recognise and/or permit the system of adoption shall ensure that the best interests of the child shall be the paramount consideration and . . . shall:

'. . . (b) Recognize that intercountry adoption may be considered as an alternative means of child's care, if the child cannot be placed in a foster or an adoptive family or cannot in any suitable manner be cared for in the child's country of origin; (c) Ensure that the child concerned . . . enjoys safeguards and standards equivalent to those

Table 15.2

Intercountry adoption 1995 to 2007: selected receiving States by rank in 1998; totals for 22 States; and proportion going to top 10 States and USA

Country	1995	1998	2001	2003	2004	2006	2007
United States	8,987	**15,774**	19,237	21,616	22,884	20,679	19,613
France	3,034	**3,777**	3,094	3,995	4,079	3,977	3,162
Italy	2,161	**2,233**	2,225	2,772	3,403	3,188	3,420
Canada	2,045	**2,222**	1,874	2,180	1,955	1,535	(1,535)
Spain	815	**1,487**	3,428	3,951	5,541	4,472	3,648
Sweden	895	**928**	1,044	1,046	1,109	879	800
Germany	537	**922**	798	674	650	583	(583)
Netherlands	661	**825**	1,122	1,154	1,307	816	778
Denmark	548	**697**	631	523	528	447	429
Norway	488	**589**	713	714	706	448	426
Sub-total (10)	20,171	29,454	33,738	38,625	42,162	37,024	(34,394)
UK	**154**	**258**	326	301	334	363	356
Ireland	**52**	**147**	179	358	398	313	(313)
Total (22 states)* *	**22,161** (19)	**31,924**	**36,376**	**41,528**	**45,287**	**39,742**	**(37,010)***
% to top 10	91%	92%	93%	93%	93%	93%	93%
% to USA	41%	49%	53%	52%	51%	52%	53%

* At the time of writing, no 2007 data were available for Canada, Germany, Ireland or Israel; (estimate assumes same number as 2006).
** The other countries included in the overall totals are Australia, Belgium, Finland, Iceland, Luxembourg, New Zealand, and Switzerland – with the addition of Cyprus, Israel and Malta from 1998. Children are also adopted from abroad in other countries including Austria, Greece, Japan, Singapore and the UAE, but no data were obtainable for this exercise.

existing in the case of national adoption; (d) Take all appropriate measures to ensure that, in intercountry adoption, the placement does not result in improper financial gain for those involved in it . . .'

Article 21(e) called on members to promote these objectives through 'bilateral or multilateral arrangements', but it was a further five years before this aspiration was made more realistic with the adoption by 66 nations in May 1993 of the Hague Convention on *Protection of Children and Co-operation in Respect of Intercountry Adoption*.

The preamble to the Convention slightly modifies the principles laid down in Article 21(b) by recognising that intercountry adoption 'may offer the advantage of a permanent family to a child for whom a suitable family cannot be found in his or her State of origin'.

Fifteen years later, the Convention is supported by 76 States. The UK ratified the convention in 2002 and the US in 2007 (with effect from April 2008). Of the major receiving countries only Ireland has yet to ratify.

China, as the main sending country today, ratified in 2005 and Russia has signed but not ratified. Of the other major sending countries, Ethiopia, Haiti, Korea and the Ukraine have neither signed nor ratified/acceded and Guatemala's accession has been challenged by several Member States, including the UK which suspended adoptions from the country in January 2008. It is, however, important to remember that the Convention only provides a framework for co-operation which '. . . needs to be brought to life by a wide range of actors from child care workers to health care practitioners to judges who understand its philosophy and objectives and who are given the resources and training necessary to enable them to carry out their duties properly' (Duncan, 2000, p 32).

The success of the Convention depends, therefore, not only on the number of countries contracting but also on the way in which States fulfil their obligations as receiving States or States of origin. Aware of the need to monitor this process, Article 29 of the Convention states that: 'The Secretary General of the Hague Conference . . . shall at regular intervals convene a Special Commission in order to review the practical operation of the Convention'. The most recent such Commission was held in September 2005.

The process of adopting from abroad

Adopting a child from abroad is a long and costly business and one which varies according to the country of residence of the prospective adopters and the child they plan to take into their family. In the early years of intercountry adoption it was for many people an individual "adventure" (Humphreys and Humphreys, 1993) often motivated by humanitarian concerns with the choice of country influenced by the individual's personal experience. Today such adoptions are primarily motivated by infertility and the process is much more regulated, although the rising demand for children from childless couples in rich countries has led to what many regard as a "market" in children. There are a growing number of personal accounts of this process, especially in relation to adoption from China (Shead, 2000; Buchanan, 2005) and a wider picture is provided in recent research in Ireland (Greene et al, 2007) which also shows dramatic variations in the cost of such adoptions.

Central Authorities

One of the key requirements of the Convention [Article 6(1)] is that all States create a Central Authority 'to discharge the duties which are imposed by the Convention'. In many countries this is a Government Ministry, for example, the Ministry of Justice in Netherlands; the Department for Children, Schools and Families in England; the Ministry of Social Affairs in Cambodia. Other countries have established special authorities:

CARA (Central Adoption Resource Authority) in India; CCAA (Chinese Centre for Adoption Affairs) in China; MIA (Swedish Intercountry Adoption Authority) in Sweden. In most there is a single Central Authority, but in some there are many – eight in Australia; seven in Canada; 11 in Germany; 17 in Spain; 26 in Switzerland; 27 in Brazil. There are 5 Central Authorities for the UK – England, Wales, Scotland, Northern Ireland and the Isle of Man. In such cases, one Central Authority must be designated for transmissions of communications from other contracting States. The United States had been under pressure to have a Central Authority for each state within the US but has announced that the Department of State will be the sole Central Authority.

The Central Authority in a receiving State is responsible for transmitting papers to the Central Authority of the State of origin [Article 15(2)] but beyond that may have little further involvement with the applicants if responsibilities are delegated. The report of the 2005 Special Commission (HCCH, 2006) noted much variation in the staffing of Central Authorities and in the extent of work undertaken directly.

Accredited bodies

The Hague Convention allows Central Authorities to delegate tasks to public authorities or to "accredited bodies" [Articles 9–12]. In most receiving countries, there is such delegation for the purpose of home study assessments and in many the Central Authority authorises NGOs – non-governmental organisations – carry out mediating activities. The actual process, however, varies between receiving States. The most extensive and comprehensive use of accredited bodies is found in mainland Europe (Selman, 1993; Selman and White, 1994), especially in the Nordic states and the Netherlands, where most agencies are now members of EurAdopt, an umbrella group, which has established common ethical rules for intercountry adoption (Sterky, 2000).

Information

For most people wishing to adopt from overseas the process starts with a need for information. In the Irish study (Greene *et al*, 2007), respondents noted that the most useful information came from other people who had already adopted and there are now many websites run by parents' organisations around the world. One of the best examples is the Canadian site, *Family Helper* (http://www.familyhelper.net/). In the United States, *Adoption.com* provides excellent information on intercountry adoption from all countries working with the USA. More problematic is the vast amount of information put out by individual agencies in the United States, many of which carry photographs of children available for adoption (Chou *et al*, 2007). In the UK, OASIS (Overseas Adoption Support and Information Service) provides an information service for members (www.adoptionoverseas.org) and the Intercountry Adoption Centre (IAC) has fact sheets for purchase at www.icacentre.org.uk. There is also a growing number of books which explore the intercountry adoption process (Hilborn, 2006; Erichsen, 2007).

Most Central Authorities also have websites which provide details of the process to be followed and often have information about the specific requirements of different sending countries. The US State Department website provides information on over 150 different States of origin (http://travel.state.gov/family/adoption/country/country_369.html). For the UK, the DCSF (website, www.dcsf.gov.uk/intercountryadoption/general.shtml), has information on the process of adoption and information sheets on four countries – Bulgaria, China, India and Peru (as of October 2008). More informative is the website (www.community.nsw.gov.au/adoption) of the New South Wales Department of Community Services.

Home studies

All prospective adopters will need to have a home study assessment. In Ireland, the Netherlands and the Nordic countries, home studies are provide by local social welfare departments and are free of charge. In the UK, local authorities and approved voluntary adoption agencies are responsible and charges are typically around £5,000. Elsewhere, home studies are often provided by "full service" voluntary adoption agencies which also mediate with the sending countries or by "independent" social workers, a practice ended by the UK in 1999.

Preparation courses

In many countries, home studies are linked to attendance at a preparation course. In some, e.g. the Netherlands (Duinkerken and Geerts, 2000) and in Sweden, attendance at such a course is required *before* the home study commences (Swedish Intercountry Adoptions Authority – MIA – 2007). The Swedish course involves seven three-hour sessions. In England, prospective adopters usually attend a three-day preparation course arranged by the local authority or a voluntary adoption agency.

Mediating agencies

The task of linking prospective adoptive parents and a child free for adoption is the responsibility of Central Authorities. In some cases the Central Authority carries out the full function – in New Zealand, Australia and China. But often this task is delegated to voluntary associations accredited by the Central Authority – in Denmark, Finland and Norway adoptions can only be arranged through approved organisations. In November 2008, the Intercountry Adoption Centre (LAC) was registered by Ofsted as a voluntary adoption agency, and plans to seek accreditation in States of origin as the first UK mediating agency.

In his *Report on Intercountry Adoption* (1990), Hans van Loon argued that "agency to agency" adoptions offered the best prospect of avoiding irregularities and that the role of Central Authorities in receiving States should be to ensure that such organisations are regulated and maintain the highest standards. Support was also given by International

Social Services (ISS) in their submission to the Special Commission of 2000 where they stated that they were '. . . in favour of involvement of accredited bodies, particularly in receiving States, since they provide a concrete personalised link, case by case, between States of origin and the receiving State (and) between the child and the adopting family . . .' (ISS, 2000)

There have, however, been concerns over the activities of many US agencies and the careful accreditation of such agencies will be an essential part of the US ratification of the Hague Convention (Hollinger, 2004). The Hague Special Commission of 2005 noted the importance of an ongoing process of re-accreditation.

Post placement and post adoption services

Post-adoption needs can occur at all stages of adoption. Initially, concern may be over physical health, regressive behaviour and attachment difficulties; later, there may be problems of adaptation *outside* the family and especially at school; in adolescence, there may be severe behavioural problems and issues of identity. Most adoptive parents say that support comes mainly from friends and relatives or others who have adopted from abroad, but many countries now have post adoption services provided by the State or voluntary bodies. In the US, the *Center for Family Connections* runs many courses for both adoptive parents and professionals working in adoption (www.kinnect.org/). Parents can also turn to a growing number of books, many by intercountry adopters, exploring post-adoption issues and how to help their children with issues of identity (Rojewski and Rojewski, 2001; Register, 2005; Wolfs, 2008). As adults, adoptees may also have specific service needs in establishing their identity outside the adoptive family; when they become parents themselves; and in their own search and reunion journey (Selman and Wells, 1996).

Support for adoptive families needs to be available at various stages of the post-adoption process, in particular: post-arrival (e.g. early intervention regarding health and promoting attachment); when children are starting school; and in adolescence. As the adopted person grows into adulthood, they will have their own needs, which may again arise at certain key stages: leaving home; becoming a parent; and at any stage in the process of search and reunion.

Search, return and reunion

Many adopted people face problems of identity, but these are especially acute for those children who are adopted transracially. Saetersdal and Dalen (1991; 2000) have talked of adopted children feeling they had a "Norwegian soul in a Vietnamese body". Andersson (1991) has written movingly of the way in which those adopted from overseas cope with being an Indian-Swede or a Korean-Swede and feeling out of place in both countries. For many this will lead to a need to explore their origins and for some to seek out their birth families. However, many international adoptees face difficulties due to lack of information about their background, especially if they are recorded as having been abandoned.

Nevertheless, an increasing number of adopted people return to their birth country at some time in their lives and in many countries, notably the US, organised homeland visits are arranged for groups of adopted adults. In Korea, "gatherings" of adult adoptees are well established and many countries have organisations of adoptees as well as of adoptive parents. Some wish to trace their birth families, but in intercountry adoption the possibility of one side being disappointed by what happens after reunion is very real and there are a growing number of stories of adult adoptees tracking down their birth family and then, curiosity satisfied, returning to their comfortable lives in a rich Western country, while their birth relatives assume that contact will continue for the rest of their lives. For others, the search may fail or lead to birth relatives unwilling to meet or form a relationship with their relinquished child.

What is certain, as in adoption reunions in the domestic UK context (see Feast, this volume), is that there will often be different expectations from those involved in a reunion, that both adoptee and birth relatives will benefit from sensitive counselling before any meeting, and that ideally reunions should be mediated by an experienced support worker who can keep in contact afterwards if needed.

Changes in States of origin

There are few countries that have not been touched by intercountry adoption either as a receiving State or a State of origin and many have experience of both, but in its brief history there have been major changes in the countries which have sent children and the number they have sent. From 1953 to 1979, Korea dominated the intercountry adoption scene. It continued to be the main source of children to the US through to 1990, accounting for over 50 per cent of all visas granted from 1972 to 1987 (Altstein and Simon, 1991, p 35–36). From the late 1960s, children were also being adopted from the Philippines and Vietnam and by the mid 1970s, South American countries featured regularly. Between 1978 and 1987, the top five States of origin for the US – after Korea – were Colombia, the Philippines, India, El Salvador and Mexico with an occasional appearance by other Latin American countries. Korea was the main source of children in the Netherlands until 1980, when Indonesia and later Sri Lanka became more important. Adoptions from India and Latin America also increased from the mid 1970s. In France, South Korea was the main source of children until 1986, after which Brazil was top country through to 1990.

Then for 18 months from January 1990 to July 1991, Romania became the main source of children worldwide, after which a moratorium was imposed. Thereafter, the number of children sent abroad rose again to more than 2,500 by the year 2000, after which Romania reduced the number of intercountry adoptions under pressure from the European Union (Selman, forthcoming, 2009) until there was a final end in 2005.

Since 1995 Russia and China have been the most important source of children worldwide, together accounting for over 50 per cent of all adoptions in 2004 and 2005. Table 15.3 below shows changes in the rank order of States of origin from 1980–9 to 2006: only four of the countries listed in 1980–89 – Colombia, Guatemala, India and Korea – feature in the top ten for 2006. Between 1998 and 2006, Guatemala and Ethiopia have become more important as sources of children and adoptions from Romania have ceased.

Table 15.3
Major sources of children for intercountry adoption 1980–2006

1980–89	1995	1998	2004	2006
Korea	China	China	China	China
India	Korea	Russia	Russia	Russia
Colombia	Russia	Vietnam	Guatemala	Guatemala
Brazil	Vietnam	Korea	Korea	Ethiopia
Sri Lanka	Colombia	Colombia	Ukraine	Korea
Chile	India	India	Colombia	Colombia
Philippines	Brazil	Guatemala	Ethiopia	Vietnam
Guatemala	Guatemala	Romania	Haiti	Haiti
Peru	Romania	Brazil	India	Ukraine
El Salvador	Philippines	Ethiopia	Kazakhstan	India

(Kane, 1993; Selman, 2008)

If we look at the top five receiving countries today, the countries from which children are sent vary. In 2004 and 2005, China was the main source in the US, Spain and Canada, but Italy received no children from China, and Russia has been the main sending country in recent years. In France, Vietnam and Haiti are now the top two countries. Guatemala is of significance only in the US, where the numbers sent increased every year from 1994 to 2006, when 4,136 orphan visas were granted and Guatemala replaced Russia as the country sending most children after China. In the UK, China has been the main source of children since 1995, accounting for over 50 per cent of applications in 2005 and 2006. Since 2004, Ethiopia has become an increasingly important source in the top five countries and Scandinavia but not in the UK.

A tale of three countries

South Korea (hereinafter referred to as Korea) and India have been involved in inter-country adoption for many decades: they were the top two countries in terms of numbers in the 1980s and continued to be amongst the top ten from 1998 to 2006 (see Table 15.2 above). Ethiopia has been involved in intercountry adoption since the 1980s, but has only become a significant source numerically in the past 10 years. Only India has ratified the Hague Convention (in 2003). The three countries provide a striking picture of variations between States of origin in the level of intercountry adoption; the age and gender of children sent; and social and demographic indicators – see Table 15.4 below which also includes details for China and Russia.

Table 15.4
Adoptions from five States of origin in 2005

Country	Number of adoptions 2005[1]	Adoption ratio 2005[2]	Gender[3] female %	Age[3] under 1 %	Age[3] over 5 %	GNI[4] Per capita	Total Fertility Rate[4]
Korea	2,101	4.8	38%	92%	1%	$15,830	1.4
India	867	0.03	73%	8%	20%	$720	3.0
Ethiopia	1,713	0.3	54%	32%	43%	$160	6.1
China	14,493	0.83	95%	35%	3%	$1,740	1.8
Russia	7,471	6.1	50%	20%	29%	$4,460	1.1

[1] Total numbers for Korea and India are provided by those countries; totals for Ethiopia, China and Russia are derived from data from 22 receiving States.
[2] Adoptions per 1,000 births. In 2005 the highest ratio (9.2) was found in Guatemala.
[3] Figures on age and gender are for the USA in 2005 – data from other countries show a lower percentage of girls.
[4] Data from *State of the World's Children 2007*.

South Korea

50 years of intercountry adoption from South Korea
By 2006, the total number of Koreans adopted abroad since 1953 was over 160,000 out of an estimated total intercountry adoptions of 850,000 (Selman, 2007). This makes Korea the most important source of children to date, although it is likely that, by the end of the decade, when total numbers will have reached one million, China will have sent most children. About two-thirds of them went to the US, where the number of Korean "orphans" entering the country peaked at over 6,000 in the mid-1980s. A further 25 per cent have gone to five countries: France, Sweden, Denmark, Norway and the Netherlands. Initially, many of the infants placed were of "mixed race" – the fathers being US military

servicemen – but by the 1990s there were very few mixed race children placed for adoption and in 2004, 3,507 (90%) of a total of nearly 4,000 adoptees (in- and intercountry) were children of single mothers.

Sarri *et al* (2002) argue that reliance on intercountry adoption has discouraged Korea from developing an adequate child welfare programme. Korea has one of the highest rates of institutionalised children in developed countries (Selman, 2007). Thus, the example of South Korea reminds us that the factors influencing intercountry adoption may change over time and that there may also be a factor of inertia which makes it difficult to stop.

Since the Olympic Games of 1988, there has been constant talk in Korea of a reduction in and eventual end of intercountry adoption. In 1989, the Ministry of Social Affairs proposed a schedule which would have reduced the number of intercountry adoptions to 1,700 by 1995 and raised the number of domestic adoptions to 3,500. However, Table 15.5 below shows that, after a steady fall to 2,057 in 1997, numbers have been rising again despite a new 20-year plan, announced in 1997, to phase out intercountry adoptions by the year 2020. Between 1998 and 2005, annual totals fluctuated between 2,250 and 2,500, but in 2006, the number of adoptions from Korea fell below 2,000 for the first time for 40 years. All intercountry adoptions must go through one of the four licensed agencies, most of which now also handle domestic adoption and are developing services for unmarried mothers, but all are dependent on the funds derived from overseas adoption and the agencies have been largely opposed to any ideas for further reductions in the number of intercountry adoptions. In 2007, the number of incountry adoptions exceeded the number of intercountry adoptions for the first time.

South Korea today is a prosperous country with a high level of education and a low birth rate but there is a continuing problem over the stigma of unmarried parenthood and, in the absence of a comprehensive welfare system, it has been impossible for a poor single mother to keep her child. An article in the *Korea Times* in January 2005 noted that in Korea 'a baby born to an unmarried woman often invites discrimination for both mother and child as many people consider having a child in these circumstances to be unacceptable'. Government support remains inadequate and 'society often treats them as second-class citizens, forcing many to give up their babies for adoption'.

Over the past five years, there has been increasing criticism of the Korean government from adoptees themselves and there was much criticism from the local press and academics during the 2007 Adoptee Gathering in Seoul, when adopted Koreans from several countries joined Korean birth mothers in calling for an end to intercountry adoption. Aware of these criticisms, the Korean government has announced increased support for birth mothers and a drive for more domestic adoptions, supported by payments from the state.

Table 15.5
Intercountry and in-country adoptions: India and Korea 1989 to 2006

YEAR	INDIA Adoptions		KOREA Adoptions	
	Intercountry	*In-country*	*Intercountry*	*In-country*
1989	1,213	757	4,191	1,872
1990	1,272	1,075	2,962	1,647
1991	1,190	936	2,197	1,241
1996	990	1,623	2,080	1,229
2001	1,298	2,533	2,436	1,770
2002	1,066	2,740	2,365	1,649
2003	1,024	2,585	2,287	1,564
2004	1,021	2,294	2,258	1,641
2005	867	2,284	2,101	1,461
2006	852	2,409	1,899	1,322
2007	770	2,405	1,265	1,388
Population 2005	1,103 million		47.8 million	
Live births 2005	25,926 thousand		438 thousand	
Ratio (per 1,000 births)	0.034	0.088	4.8	3.3

Source for India: Central Adoption Resource Agency; Damodaran and Mehta, 2000, 2004.
Source for Korea: Ministry of Health & Welfare.

India

Adoption of unrelated children in India dates back to the 1960s, but it was not until the 1970s that child welfare organisations became involved. Intercountry adoption started in the same period and grew rapidly in the next two decades. Concern over abuses led eventually to the historic Supreme Court judgement of 1984, which attempted to regulate intercountry adoption mainly through the Guardians and Wards Act 1890 which deals with non-Hindu adoptions (Damodaran and Mehta, 2000; Bhargava, 2005).

The Central Adoption Resource Agency (CARA) was set up in 1990 and has now become the Central Authority for the country, following India's ratification of the Hague Convention in 2003. Between 1989 and 2004, the annual number of intercountry adoptions recorded by CARA fluctuated between 1,000 and 1,400 per annum, but since 2000 they have been falling and in 2005–2007 were less than 900 a year (Table 15.5).

There have been concerns over "child trafficking" in some Indian States for many years. Krishnakumar (2005) writes that 'intercountry adoption, which began primarily as an ad hoc humanitarian response to children orphaned by the Second World War, who could not find a family to care for them in their own country, is now a complex social phenomenon that has lent itself to serious abuse'. In an investigation for one of India's national magazines, *Frontline*, he claims to expose 'a multi-billion-dollar, countrywide racket in intercountry adoption of children, run by private adoption agencies that exploit the loopholes in the rules', citing the arrest in 2005 of five kidnappers, who had sold over 350 children to an adoption agency in Chennai over many years. Smolin (2005a) talks of the 'two faces of intercountry adoption' and describes and analyses the adoption scandals in Andhra Pradesh, which involved serious charges of abusive adoption practices including baby buying and other illicit means of obtaining children for adoption (see also Rollings, 2008). Scandals continue and there has been growing concern over the activities of Preet Mandir, a leading adoption agency in the city of Pune.

The number of domestic adoptions recorded annually doubled between 1991 and 2000. These were adoptions arranged by Registered Indian Placement Agencies recognised by CARA. Since 2001, the numbers have increased partly due to the inclusion of adoptions arranged by Shishu Grehs (government funded adoption agencies). Whatever the "true" figure, the total adoptions (in- and intercountry) remain very low in a country with an estimated 12 million orphans (www.indianngos.com/issue/child/adoption/statistics) and many thousands of children likely to spend their childhood in large institutions. The ratio is the lowest of any major sending country (Selman, 2006, 2007) and much lower than Korea (see Table 15.5 below, which gives details of in-country and intercountry adoptions in India and Korea from 1989 to 2007, utilising data provided by the countries themselves).

On 22 August 2006, India's President signed into law legislation that set national norms for adoption including: expansion of the definition of "abandoned and surrendered" children to include a juvenile found begging, a street child or a working child; permitting the adoption of a child regardless of religion or marital status; and raising the age limit of adoptive parents. Although the new law encourages domestic adoption, intercountry adoption will continue to be an option and the government is reported to have plans to relax rules governing intercountry adoptions to make it simpler for foreigners to provide a new home to Indian children.

Ethiopia

Few African countries have been involved in intercountry adoption on a large scale. The Nigerian Civil Wars of the 1960s resulted in many thousands of war "orphans", but Nigeria spurned all foreign adoption offers. In Kane's 1993 study, only two countries of sub-Saharan Africa feature in the top 30 sending countries – Madagascar and Ethiopia. Madagascar has sent children to France since the early 1980s – a total of 3,736 by 2006. Adoptions from Ethiopia started later but totalled 3,230 by 2006.

Between 1989 and 2002, there were no African countries in the US top 20, but by 2006 there were three – Ethiopia, Liberia and Nigeria. Table 15.6 below shows the growth of all adoptions from Ethiopia in the period 1998–2007. The total number increased more than five times over this period.

Table 15.6
Ethiopia 1998–2006: with major destinations ranked by number of children sent in 2005

COUNTRY	1998	2002	2003	2004	2005	2006	2007
USA	96	105	135	289	**441**	732	1,255
France	155	209	217	390	**397**	408	417
Spain	0	12	107	220	**227**	304	481
Italy	9	112	47	193	**211**	227	256
Belgium	46	41	52	62	**112**	88	124
Netherlands	18	25	39	72	**72**	48	68
Australia	37	36	39	45	**59**	70	47
Sweden	24	18	21	26	**37**	32	39
Norway	46	44	46	47	**36**	27	33
Canada	–	13	14	34	**31**	61	n/a
Denmark	29	20	40	41	**30**	38	39
TOTAL	481	695	855	1,553	**1,740**	2,128	2,794

By 2006, Ethiopia was sending more children abroad for adoption than any country other than China, Russia and Guatemala. For many years France was the main destination for children, but from 2005 the number going to the US has increased sharply (to 1,255 in 2007), following the adoption of an Ethiopian child by Angelina Jolie. Following China's decision in 2006 to restrict adoptions to married heterosexual couples, Ethiopia has become a favoured destination for single women, especially from the US. In 2007, US figures rose further to 1,255.

With 720,000 AIDS "orphans" it may seem that Ethiopia has a great need for adoption, although most of these are supported by the wider family. However, problems have arisen where such children have themselves been subjected to an HIV test and then been rejected if found to be HIV+, often then ending up in a worse institutional setting than if they had never been considered for adoption.

Responsibility for intercountry adoption in Ethiopia lies with the Ministry of Women's Affairs. Foreigners are normally only allowed to adopt through agencies which have been approved by the Ethiopian Ministry of Justice and each agency is then linked to a specific "orphanage" which they are required to support financially – donations from individual adopters are not permitted. As a consequence, adoptions are not normally possible for UK citizens, although in Australia the Central Authority has made a formal agreement to allow Australian citizens to adopt through their State adoption authorities and a similar agreement has been made with the Irish Adoption Board. By 2007, approval had been given to over 50 agencies from foreign countries – 22 from the US alone. About a third of the 300 orphanages in Ethiopia are said to have indicated an interest in intercountry adoption, but many others remain strongly opposed to the idea. There is currently very little domestic adoption in the country and the fear is that the growth of intercountry adoption will do little to change this and could defer the need for action

Research on intercountry adoption

There is now a substantial body of research into intercountry adoption; there are also a number of published research reviews (Dalen, 1998; Haugaard *et al*, 2000a & b; Swedish Government, 2003).

It is generally agreed that the research shows that most children adopted from overseas do well (Triseliotis, 1991; Thoburn and Charles, 1992; Simon and Altstein, 2000; van Ijzendoorn and Juffer, 2006). There is, however, also evidence of higher continuing rates of behavioural problems and disruption in comparison with native-born children (Hoksbergen, 1991; Rutter *et al*, 2000), especially from adolescence (Verhulst, 2000). Monica Dalen (1998) concluded from her review of Scandinavian research that 'around 75 per cent manage well, without any sign of major problems' but that the remaining 20–23 per cent have 'problems linked to language, learning, identity and ethnicity' and that 'the teenage years are demanding on both adoptees and their families.'

Physical and developmental catch-up

One of the most established findings is the developmental catch-up found in children adopted from institutional care who often arrived in poor physical condition with many functioning in the intellectually impaired range (Irhammar and Cederblad, 2000). In the English Romanian Adoption study (Rutter *et al*, 1998) there had been a virtually complete catch-up for children's weight and height by age six, but head circumference, while catching up, is not complete – even by the later age of 11. A longitudinal study of 83 children adopted from Romania to the Netherlands (Hoksbergen, 2002) found that the delay in physical developmental vanished for the majority of children in the first four years, but emotional and general development lagged for half the group.

Language difficulties

Older children adopted from abroad may arrive in their new country with developed skills in a language they will never use again and have to learn a second language which is to become their primary means of communication. Many younger children have to start language acquisition late, having experienced early (non-verbal) communication in a very different context. All this has to be handled alongside the problems of making new relationships with their adoptive family (Selman and Wells, 1996). In most cases, difficulties of communication appear to be shortlived, but Gardell (1979) reported a persistence of language difficulties in 43 per cent of overseas children adopted in Sweden in the 1970s. Twenty years later, Ryvgold *et al* (1999) found no association between oral language skills or academic skills and a child's age at adoption into Sweden, although there was a suggestion that age at adoption might influence written language, where nearly half of those adopted after the age of two years had a low level of written language skills.

Attachment disorders

Parents usually expect and cope well with problems of health and language in their child, but find it more difficult to deal with emotional problems and, in particular, a lack of responsiveness. In his pioneering study of Thai children adopted in the Netherlands, Hoksbergen (1987) outlined some of the most common problems associated with adaptation to a new family and country: eating and sleeping disorders; lack of emotional response; lying and stealing; lack of concentration; etc. Difficulties were most apparent in older children as was demonstrated earlier in Cederblad's study of 27 children who had been aged three and over when they arrived in Sweden (Cederblad, 1982). In the 20 years following these studies, there has been a huge amount of research into the nature and prevalence of attachment disorders in children adopted from overseas (see e.g. Juffer and van Ijzendoorn, 2009) and many books on how parents can handle these problems (e.g. Keck and Kupecky, 2002). Rutter's study of children adopted from Romania has some striking data reinforcing the relevance of age at adoption to attachment disorders at age six, with the proportion of children with such disorders rising from under 10 per cent of those aged 0–6 months at adoption to over 30 per cent of those aged 25–42 months (Rutter et al, 2000, p 113). Age was also associated with pervasive problems at age six and, in the follow-up at age 11, significant problems continued in a substantial number of the children placed after the age of six months. Age at entry into the UK was taken as an indicator of the duration of institutional deprivation, which was found to be specifically associated with 'disinhibited attachment' (Rutter et al, forthcoming 2009) and quasi-autistic patterns of behaviour. Despite the continuation of problems in many children, the study has found far fewer breakdowns than found in earlier studies of late adoptions. Haugaard et al (2000b) reviewed a number of the early studies of Romanian adoption and found findings similar to those presented by Rutter.

Juffer and van Ijzendoorn (2005) found no risk of disorganised attachment for early-adopted children in their longitudinal study of adoptions from Colombia, Korea and Sri Lanka, but a later meta-analysis (Juffer and van Ijzendoorn, 2009) found that this was less true for children adopted after 12 months of age together with problems at school and more behavioural problems. However, the general conclusion of the meta-analysis is optimistic, finding that intercountry adoptees exhibited fewer behavioural and mental health problems than children who were adopted domestically and concluding that '. . . most international adoptees adapt well to their new families and are well adjusted'. The studies reviewed showed 'massive catch-up in all developmental domains, including self-esteem 'demonstrating that adoption, as an alternative for institutional care, is a very successful intervention in children's lives' (Juffer and Van Ijzendoorn, forthcoming, 2009). Rutter and his team come to a similar conclusion about the potential of adoption and fostering in countering institutional deprivation, while stressing that families who care for such children will need substantial support over a long period (Rutter et al, forthcoming, 2009).

Adoptees into adulthood

There has been considerable publicity for a Swedish study (Hjern et al, 2002; Lindblad et al, 2003) which used national registers for the cohort born in 1970–79 to compare 11,320 intercountry adoptees with 2,343 Swedish-born siblings, 4,006 immigrant children, and a general population of more than 850,000 Swedish-born residents. Indicators used were of severe problems: suicide deaths and suicide attempts; court sentences; discharges for psychiatric illness; and substance abuse. After controls on socio-demographic character-istics, intercountry adoptees were found to be more likely than Swedish-born children to attempt or die from suicide; experience a hospital admission for a psychiatric disorder; commit a crime; or be involved in alcohol or drug abuse. The adopted children fared worse on all measures than their Swedish-born siblings and had similar outcomes to the immigrant group, despite the lower socio-economic status of the latter. Within the adoptees' group, mental health problems and social maladjustment were most common in those placed at older ages. The study concluded that 'adoptees in Sweden have a high risk for severe mental health problems and social adjustment in adolescence and young adulthood' and the authors advised professionals 'to give appropriate consideration to the high risk of suicide in patients who are intercountry adoptees'. However, it must be noted that the measures – especially suicide – are extreme and apply to only a very small minority of the population, and it seems likely that the overall figures are largely influenced by a minority of adoptees with multiple disorders – 80–90 per cent of the adoptees had had no mental health problems.

In a later follow-up to the study (Elmund et al, 2007), adolescent intercountry adoptees were shown to be 'a risk group for placements in out-of-home care' and this was attributed to persistent behaviour problems.

The testimony of adult adoptees

The voice of adult adoptees has been increasingly heard over the past ten years (von Melen, 1998). One of the first published accounts was by Peter Dodds (1997), whose book tells the story of one child "rescued" from a German orphanage in 1957.

Many of the early adoptions from Korea involved older children. These are now adults in their fifties. Susan Soon-Keum Cox was adopted in 1957 and for her and others adopted at the time there is a recognition of the gains made by intercountry adoption, not least for the children of colour who were rejected by their birth country (Cox, 2007). Between 1975–1987, 70,000 Koreans, mainly infants, were adopted abroad, and the voices of these adoptees, now aged 20–40, are increasingly being heard on the internet, in publications and through the adoptee gatherings held over the last decade in the US, Copenhagen and Seoul (Kim, 2005).

In 2007, 500 adopted Koreans from more than 15 receiving countries met in Seoul. Here the view of adoption was less positive, especially as they saw a continuing flow of "pure" Korean infants being sent abroad by a country now ranked as one of the strongest economies in the world. Tobias Hubinette, adopted in to Sweden in the 1980s, provides a detailed critique of intercountry adoption from Korea alongside a fascinating account of media representations of Korean adoption (Hubinette, 2006). The insight and lucidity of other accounts by adoptees (Trenka, 2003; Harris, 2006; Trenka *et al*, 2006) give pause for thought as all would be deemed successful adoptions in terms of conventional research criteria such as educational achievement.

Birth mothers – the hidden dimension

While the voice of adoptive parents has been influential for most of the short history of intercountry adoption, and that of adoptees is increasingly heard, little is known about the views and needs of birth parents, who have been described by Hughes and Logan (1993) as "the hidden dimension" in adoption policy and practice. It has taken a long time to recognise the pain experienced by birth parents in the UK and to acknowledge how little choice many have had in their "decision" to relinquish a child. In the 1960s there was much stigma attached to out-of-wedlock births and little or no support for a mother who wished to keep her child. Many had to go into "mother and baby homes", where they were made to earn their keep. Not surprisingly, about one in four gave up their babies for adoption (Selman, 2004) and in those days adoption was still surrounded in secrecy so that they were told little about the adoptive parents who took their baby.

Very little attention has been paid to the situation of the birth parents in intercountry adoption – partly due to what Gailey (2000) has called the "orphan myth" – but there is much to suggest that many children are "relinquished" by young unmarried mothers in poverty with little support available before or after their decision (see Giberti, 2000). The situation of single mothers in countries like Korea is often related to societal condemnation of such parents, and in this atmosphere, birth mothers who have later married, may face problems if their adopted children return to their birth country and trace them, as it is unlikely that the mother will have told her husband of the shame in her past.

However, the IAPA (Indian Association for the Promotion of Adoption and Child Welfare) has noted that many birth parents secretly experience a strong urge to know about their child although at present scant attention is paid to their needs. Johnson (2004) looks at the stories of 237 Chinese families where the mother had abandoned a child. She found that in all of them an ongoing sense of loss was palpable and that some had suffered 'tangible emotional consequences'.

Dorow (1999) has brought together a collection of letters written by birth mothers who had their babies in Ae Ran Won, a home for unwed mothers in Seoul, and then gave them up for adoption. The book has led to a wide range of reactions from both adoptive parents and adoptees.

A different sort of problem has been revealed in the Marshall Islands where Roby and Matsumara (2002) speak of the 'tragic reality of cultural misunderstanding' whereby many birth mothers believed that adoption did not sever the parent–child relationship and that their children would return to them as adults, having benefited from a better education in the US.

There is, therefore, a tension between a birth mother's right to confidentiality, her adopted child's right to know about his or her origins, and indeed her own right to seek information about a child she has relinquished. In many countries adoption is still stigmatised, closed, and characterised by secrecy and in some contact with birth relatives is prohibited by law. Birth parents or relatives indicating a wish for contact in such a socio-legal environment may be neither encouraged nor supported in pursuing their interest further.

The future of intercountry adoption

The last few years have seen a reduction in the number of intercountry adoptions worldwide. This has been mainly as a result of decisions by sending countries. However, the "demand" for children, especially infants, remains high and most receiving countries report growing waiting lists of largely childless prospective adopters. This could result in competition between such countries for the dwindling number of adoptable children and a further strengthening of the market forces.

The research reviewed earlier demonstrates that, for many individual children, intercountry adoption has resulted in a better life and Bartholet (2005) argues that the negative case put by critics must be countered by the research evidence on outcomes. However, the continuation of reports of irregularities and accusations of child trafficking continue and the adverse publicity has led many sending countries to call at least a temporary halt to adoptions.

The dilemmas over intercountry adoption (Triseliotis, 2000; Masson, 2001) continue and are well expressed by David Smolin in his account of the two faces of India referred to earlier:

> . . . adoption scandals, like those in Andhra Pradesh, illustrate the necessity of building systems of accountability into the global adoption system . . . Without accountability, the pretty face of adoption as a loving act that fills a real need in a child's life will all

> *too often turn out to be no more than a mask covering ugly realities of trafficking, profiteering and needless tragedy.* (Smolin, 2006)

Smolin's words are directed at the practice of intercountry adoption in the US where growing demand for babies and competition between agencies has led to a situation where 'the market forces inherent in international adoption pose a potential threat to the welfare of children as well as their birth parents and prospective adopters' (Freidmutter, 2002). Much will depend on the extent to which the US ratification of the Hague Convention, which came into force on 1 April 2008, leads to a control over the activities of less scrupulous agencies and individuals (Hollinger, 2004), but the increasing competition between receiving countries for a dwindling supply of healthy infants holds out little hope for an end to the "trade" in children (Saclier, 2000; Kapstein, 2003). However, we must not forget the "pretty face of adoption". The research outcomes discussed earlier demonstrate that intercountry adoption can offer new hope to children, including those with special needs, who might otherwise spend all their childhood in an institution. The challenge is to continue this support for individual children while encouraging in-country adoption and foster care and avoiding the negative impact on such provision of the intercountry alternative which has been noted by Dickens (2002), Browne *et al* (2003) and Post (2007). The danger is that intercountry adoption will become a subject for press speculation about the impact of celebrities and irresponsible attack and counter-attack rather than argued consideration of how we can ensure that it is only carried out in the best interests of the child, the position taken by the author of this chapter.

Selected further reading

Readers wishing to expand their reading on intercountry adoption could start with my edited book – *Intercountry Adoption: Developments, trends and perspectives* (BAAF, 2000). A more recent collection of chapters by anthropologists is Toby Volkman's *Cultures of Transnational Adoption* (Duke University Press, 2005) and Wrobel and Neill's *International Advances in Adoption Research* (John Wiley, forthcoming 2009) includes excellent chapters on research by Femmie Juffer and Michael Rutter.

Adoptive parents will enjoy Emily Buchanan's *From China with Love: A long road to motherhood* (John Wiley, 2005) and Cherry Register's *Beyond Good Intentions: A mother reflects on raising internationally adopted children* (Yeong and Yeong Book Company, 2005), and *Adoption Conversations: What, when and how to tell* by Renée Wolfs (BAAF, 2008).

The adoptees' viewpoint is captured by Jane Trenka in her book *The Language of Blood: A memoir* (Minnesota Historical Society Press, 2003) and in *Outsiders Within: Writing on transracial adoption* (South End Press, 2006), a collection of writings by young adopted adults. *In Search of Belonging: Reflections by transracially adopted people*, edited by Perlita Harris, is the first collection of writings by transracially adopted people in the UK (BAAF, 2006) and another forthcoming collection, also edited by Perlita Harris, of writings, poetry and artwork by adopted people is titled *The Colours in Me* (BAAF, 2008).

The feelings of birth mothers can be found in Sara Dorow's *I Wish for you a Beautiful Life: Letters from the Korean birth mothers of Ae Ran Won to their children* (Yeong and Yeong Book Company, 1999) and Kay Johnson's *Wanting a Daughter, Needing a Son: Abandonment, adoption, and Orphanage Care in China* (Yeong and Yeong, Book Company, 2004).

The story of the British "child migrants" is developed in an excellent new study by Roy Parker in *Uprooted: The shipment of poor children to Canada 1867–1917* (Policy Press, 2008). Another very recent book which will be of interest is Julia Rollings' *Love Our Way* (Harper Collins, 2008), which tells the story of parents who discovered that the two youngest of their six adopted children had been stolen from their mother and sold by their father in India.

References

Altstein H. and Simon R. (1991) *Intercountry Adoption: A multinational perspective*, New York: Praeger

Andersson G. (1991) 'To feel or not to feel Swedish', *Adoption & Fostering*, 15:4, pp 91–94

Bagley C. (1993) 'Chinese adoptees in Britain: A twenty-year follow-up of adjustment and social identity', *International Social Work*, 1993, 36, pp 143–157

Bartholet E. (2005) 'International Adoption', in Askeland L. (ed) *Children and Youth in Adoption, Orphanages and Foster Care*, Westport, CT: Greenwood Publishing Group Inc

Bean P. and Melville J. (1989) *Lost Children of the Empire*, London: Unwin Hyman

Bergquist K., Vonk M., Kim D. and Feit M. (eds) (2007) *International Korean Adoption: A fifty-year history of policy and practice*, New York: Haworth Press

Bhargava V. (2005) *Adoption in India: Policies and experiences*, London: Sage

Browne K. *et al* (2005) 'A European survey of the number and characteristics of children less than three years old in residential care', *Adoption & Fostering*, 29:4, pp 22–33

Buchanan E. (2005) *From China with Love: A long road to motherhood*, London: John Wiley

Cederblad M. (1982) *Foreign Adopted Children Arriving in Sweden After Three Years of Age*, Stockholm: NIA

Chou S. and Browne K. (2008) 'The relationship between institutional care and the international adoption of children in Europe', *Adoption & Fostering*, 32:1, pp 40–48

Chou S., Browne K. and Kircaldy M. (2007) 'Intercountry adoption and the internet', *Adoption & Fostering*, 31:2, pp 22–31

Cox S. S. (2007) 'The birth of intercountry adoption', Reprint of 1996 article in *Focal Point*, http://www.holtintl.org/cox.shtml (accessed 15 September 2008)

Dalen M. (1998) *The State of Knowledge of Foreign Adoptions: A summary of the results of key foreign-adoption research projects in Scandinavia*, Oslo: University of Oslo – at http://www.comeunity.com/adoption/adopt/research.html

Damodaran A. and Mehta N. (2000) 'Child adoption in India: An overview', in Selman P. (ed) *Intercountry Adoption: Development, trends and perspectives*, London: BAAF, pp 405–417

Dickens J. (2002) 'The paradox of inter-country adoption: Analysing Romania's experience as a sending country', *International Journal of Social Welfare*, 11, pp 76–83

Dodds P. (1997) *Outer Search/Inner Journey: An orphan and adoptee's quest*, Arizona: Aphrodite Publishing Company

Dorow S. K. (ed) (1999) *I Wish for you a Beautiful Life: Letters from the Korean birth mothers of Ae Ran Won to their children*, Minnesota: Yeong & Yeong Book Company

Dorow S. K. (2006) *Transnational Adoption: A cultural economy of race, gender, and kinship*, New York NY: New York University Press

Duinkerken A. and Geerts H. (2000) 'Awareness required: The information and preparation course on intercountry adoption in the Netherlands', in Selman P. (ed) *Intercountry Adoption: Development, trends and perspectives*, London: BAAF, pp 368–387

Duncan W. (2000) 'The Hague Convention on Protection of Children and Co-operation in Respect of Intercountry Adoption: Its birth and prospects', in Selman P. (ed) *Intercountry Adoption: Development, trends and perspectives*, London: BAAF, pp 40–52

Elmund A., Lindblad F., Vinnerlung B. and Hjern A. (2007) 'Intercountry adoptees in out-of-home care: A national cohort study', *Acta Paediatrica*, 96, pp 437–442

Erichsen J. N. (2007) *Inside the Adoption Agency*, New York NY: iUniverse, Inc

Freidmutter C. (2002) 'International adoptions: Problems and solutions' Testimony before the House Committee on International Relations. 2 May 2002. http://www.adoptioninstitute.org/publications/

Gailey C. W. (2000) 'Race, class and gender in intercountry adoption in the USA', in Selman P. (ed) *Intercountry Adoption: Development, trends and perspectives*, London: BAAF, pp 295–314

Gardell I. (1979) *A Swedish Study on Intercountry Adoption*, Stockholm: Allmanna Barnhuset

Gay y Blasco P., Macrae S., Selman P. and Wardle H. (2008) 'The relationship between institutional care and the international adoption of children in Europe: A response,' *Adoption & Fostering*, 32:2, pp 63–67

Giberti E. (2000) 'Excluded mothers: Birth mothers who relinquish their children', in Selman P. (ed) *Intercountry Adoption: Development, trends and perspectives*, London: BAAF, pp 458–466

Greene S., Kelly R., Nixon E., Kelly G., Borska Z., Murphy S., Daly A., Whyte J. and Murphy C. (2007) *A Study of Intercountry Adoption Outcomes in Ireland, Dublin: Children's Research Centre*, Dublin: Trinity College, The Adoption Board

Harris P. (ed) Haugaard J., Wojslawowicz J. and Palmer M. (2000a) 'International adoption: Children predominantly from Asia and South America', *Adoption Quarterly*, 3:2, pp 83–93

Haugaard J., Wojslawowicz J. and Palmer M. (2000b) 'International adoption: Children from Romania', *Adoption Quarterly*, 3:3, pp 73–84

Hilborn R. (2006) *Canadian Guide to Intercountry Adoption: How to bring your child home from abroad*, 5th edn, Ontario: Family Helper

Hjern A. Lindblad B. and Vinnerlung C. (2002) 'Suicide, psychiatric illness and social maladjustment in intercountry adoptees in Sweden: A cohort study', *The Lancet*, 360, pp 443–48

Hoksbergen R. (1986) *Adoption in Worldwide Perspective*, Lisse: Swets & Zeitliger

Hoksbergen R. (1987) *Adopted Children at Home and at School*, Lisse: Swets & Zeitliger

Hoksbergen R. (1991) 'Intercountry adoption coming of age in the Netherlands: Basic issues, trends and developments', in Altstein H. and Simon R. (eds) *Intercountry Adoption: A multinational perspective*, New York: Praeger

Hoksbergen R. (2000) 'Changes in attitudes in three generations of adoptive parents', in Selman P. (ed) *Intercountry Adoption: Development, trends and perspectives*, London: BAAF, pp 295–314

Hoksbergen R. (2002) 'Experiences of Dutch families who parent an adopted Romanian child', *Journal of Development and Behavioural Pediatrics*, 6, pp 403-9

Hollinger J. F. (2004) 'Intercountry adoption: Forecasts and forebodings', *Adoption Quarterly*, 8:1, pp 41–60

Hubinette T. (2006) *Comforting an Orphaned Nation: Representations of international adoption and adopted Koreans in Korean popular culture*, Seoul: Jimoondang Publishers

Hughes B. and Logan J. (1993) *Birth Parents: The hidden dimension*, Manchester: University of Manchester, Dept of Social Policy & Social Work

Humphreys M. and Humphreys H. (1993) *Intercountry Adoption: Practical experiences*, New York: Routledge

International Social Service (2000) *Evaluation Presented to the Special Commission of November/December 2000 on the Practical Operation of the Hague Convention of 1993*, Geneva: ISS

Irhammar M. and Cederblad M. (2000) 'Outcome of intercountry adoption in Sweden', in Selman P. (ed) *Intercountry Adoption; development, trends and perspectives*, London: BAAF, pp 143–163

Johnson K. A. (2004) *Wanting a Daughter, Needing a Son: Abandonment, adoption, and orphanage care in China*, St Paul, MN: Yeong and Yeong Book Company

Juffer F. and van Ijzendoorn M. H. (2005) 'Behavior problems and mental health referrals of international adoptees: A meta-analytic approach', *Journal of the American Medical Association*, 293, pp 2501–2515

Juffer F. and van Ijzendoorn M. H. (2007) 'Adoptees do not lack self-esteem: A meta-analysis of studies on self-esteem of transracial, international and domestic adoptees', *Psychological Bulletin*, 133:6, pp 1067–1083

Juffer F. and van Ijzendoorn M. H. (forthcoming 2009) 'International adoption comes of age: Development of international adoptees from a longitudinal and meta-analytical perspective', in Wrobel G. and Neil E. (eds) *International Advances in Adoption Research*, London: John Wiley & Sons

Kane S. (1993) 'The movement of children for international adoption: An epidemiological perspective', *The Social Science Journal*, 30:4, pp 323–339

Kapstein (2003) 'The baby trade', *Foreign Affairs*, November/December, pp 115–125

Keck G. and Kupecky R. (2002) *Parenting the Hurt Child: Helping adoptive families heal and grow*, Colorado Springs, CO: Pinon Press

Kim E. (2005) 'Wedding citizenship and culture: Korean adoptees and the global family of Korea', in Volkman T. (ed) (2005) *Cultures of Transnational Adoption*, London: Duke University Press

Klatzkin A. (ed) (1999) *A Passage to the Heart: Writings from families with children from China*, Minnesota: Yeong and Yeong Book Company

Krishnakumar A. (2005) 'The Adoption Market', *Frontline*, 22:11

Lindblad F., Hjern A. and Vinnerjung B. (2003) 'Intercountry adopted children as young adults: A Swedish cohort study', *American Journal of Orthopsychiatry*, 73:2, pp 190–202

Masson J. (2001) 'Intercountry Adoption: A global solution or a global problem', *Journal of International Affairs*, 55:1, pp 141–68

Nelson K. P. E., Kim E. and Petersen M. (eds) (2007) *Proceedings of the First International Korean Adoption Studies Research Symposium*, Seoul: IKAA

Parker R. (2008) *Uprooted: The shipment of poor children to Canada, 1867–1917*, Bristol: Policy Press

Post R. (2007) *Romania – for export only: The untold story of the Romanian "orphans"*, Netherlands: EuroComment Diffusion

Register C. (2005) *Beyond Good Intentions: A mother reflects on raising internationally adopted children*, Minnesota: Yeong & Yeong Book Company

Roby J. and Matsumara S. (2002) 'If I give you my child, aren't we family? A study of birthmothers participating in Marshall Island-U.S. Adoptions', *Adoption Quarterly*, 5:4, pp 7–31

Rojewski J. and Rojewski J. (2001) *Intercountry Adoption from China: Examining cultural heritage and other post adoption issues*, Westport CT; Bergin & Garvey

Rollings J. (2008) *Love Our Way*, Sydney: Harper Collins

Ruggeiro J. A. (2007a) 'Adoptions in and to the United States', in Jagannath P. (ed) *Adoption: Global perspectives and ethical issues*, New Delhi: Concept Publishing Company, pp 102–136

Rutter M. and the English and Romanian Adoptees Study Team (1998). 'Developmental catch-up and deficit following adoption after severe global early privation', *Journal of Child Psychology and Psychiatry*, 39, pp 465–476

Rutter M., Beckett C., Castle J., Colvert E., Kreppner J., Mehta M., Stevens S. and Sonuga-Barke, E. (forthcoming 2009) 'Effects of profound early institutional deprivation: An overview of findings from a UK longitudinal study of Romanian adoption', in Wrobel G. and Neil E. (eds) *International Advances in Adoption Research*, London: John Wiley & Sons

Rutter M., O'Connor T. G., Beckett C., Castle J., Croft C., Groothues C., Kreppner J. and the English and Romanian Adoptees Study Team (2000). 'Recovery and deficit following profound early deprivation', in Selman P. (ed) *Intercountry Adoption: Development, trends and perspectives*, London: BAAF, pp 107–125

Ryvgold A., Dalen M. and Saetersdal B. (eds) (1999) *Mine, Yours and Theirs: Adoption, changing kinship and family patterns*, Oslo: University of Oslo

Saclier C. (2000) 'In the best interests of the child?', in Selman P. (ed) *Intercountry Adoption: Development, trends and perspectives*, London: BAAF, pp 53–65

Saetersdal B. and Dalen M. (1991) 'Norway: Intercountry adoptions in a homogeneous country', in Alstein H. and Simon R. (eds) *Intercountry Adoption: A multinational perspective*, New York: Praeger

Saetersdal B. and Dalen M. (2000) 'Identity formation in a homogeneous country: Norway', in Selman P. (ed) *Intercountry Adoption: Developments, trends & perspectives*, London: BAAF

Sarri R., Baik Y. and Bombyk M. (2002) 'Goal displacement and dependency in South Korean–United States', *Intercountry Adoption Children & Youth Services Review*, 20, pp 87–114

Selman P. (1993) 'Services for intercountry adoption in the UK: Some lessons from Europe', *Adoption & Fostering*, 17:3, pp 14–19

Selman P. (ed) (2000) *Intercountry Adoption: Development, trends and perspectives*, London: BAAF

Selman P. (2002) 'Intercountry adoption in the new millennium: The "quiet migration" revisited', *Population Research & Policy Review*, 21, pp 205–225

Selman P. (2004) 'Adoption – a cure for (too) many ills?', in Bowie F. (ed) *Cross Cultural Approaches to Adoption*, London: Routledge, pp 257-273

Selman P. (2006) 'Trends in intercountry adoption 1998–2004: Analysis of data from 20 receiving countries', *Journal of Population Research*, 23:2, pp 183–204

Selman P. (2007) 'Intercountry adoption in the twenty-first century: An examination of the rise and fall of countries of origin', in Nelson K., Kim E. and Petersen M. (eds) *Proceedings of the First International Korean Adoption Studies Research Symposium*, Seoul: IKAA

Selman P. (forthcoming 2009) 'From Bucharest to Beijing: Changes in countries sending children for international adoption 1990 to 2006', in Wrobel G. and Neil E. (eds) *International Advances in Adoption Research for Practice*, London: John Wiley

Selman P. and Wells S. (1996) 'Post adoption issues in intercountry adoption', in McWilliams E. and Phillips R. (eds) *After Adoption: Working with Adoptive Families*, London: BAAF, pp 192–210

Selman P. and White J. (1994) 'The role of "accredited bodies" in intercountry adoption', *Adoption & Fostering*, 18:2, pp 7–13. (Reprinted in Hill M. and Shaw M., *Signposts in Adoption*, London: BAAF, 1998, pp 216–227).

Shead R. (2000) 'Experiences of adopting from China', in Selman P. (ed) *Intercountry Adoption: Development, trends and perspectives*, London: BAAF, pp 463–484

Simon R. J. and Altstein H. (2000) *Adoption Across Borders*, Lanham: MD Rowman & Littlefield Inc

Smolin D. (2004) 'Intercountry adoption as child trafficking', *Valparaiso Law Review*, 39:2, pp 281–325. Available at: http://works.bepress.com/david_smolin/3

Smolin D. (2005) 'The two faces of intercountry adoption: The significance of the Indian adoption scandals?', *Seton Hall Law Review*, 35, pp 403–493. Available at: http://works.bepress.com/david_smolin/2

Smolin D. (2006) 'How the intercountry adoption system legitimizes and incentivizes the practices of buying, trafficking, kidnapping, and stealing children', *Wayne Law Review*, 52:1, pp 113–200, http://law.bepress.com/david_smolin/1

Smolin D. (2007) 'Child laundering as exploitation: Applying anti-trafficking norms to intercountry adoption under the coming Hague regime', *Vermont Law Review*, 32:1, pp 1–55, http://works.bepress.com/david_smolin/6

Sterky K. (2000) 'Maintaining standards: The role of EurAdopt', in Selman P. (ed) *Intercountry Adoption: Development, trends and perspectives*, London: BAAF, pp 389–404

Swedish Government (2003) 'Adoption – but at what price? Summary of the report of the office (SOU) enquiry into intercountry adoption and compilation of adoption research, Stockholm: SOU, 2003 – report no 49

Textor M. R. (1991) 'International adoptions in West Germany: A private affair', in Altstein H. and Simon R. (eds) *Intercountry Adoption: A multinational perspective*, New York: Praeger

The Hague Conference (2001) *Report on the Special Commission of Nov-Dec 2000*, http://hcch.e-vision.nl/index_en.php?act=publications.details&pid=2273&dtid=2

The Hague Conference (2006) *Conclusions and Recommendations of the Special Commission of September 2005*, The Hague: Permanent Bureau of the Hague Conference

Thoburn J. and Charles M. (1992) 'A review of research which is relevant to intercountry adoption', in *Review of Adoption Law*, Background Paper 3 (Department of Health January 1992) update in *Consultation Paper*, October 1992

Trenka J. (2003) *The Language of Blood: A memoir*, Minneapolis: Minnesota Historical Society Press

Trenka, J. (2007a) 'Fool's gold: International adoption from South Korea', http://jjtrenka.wordpress.com/2007/07/10 (accessed 15 September 2008)

Trenka J., Oparah J. and Shin S. Y. (2006) *Outsiders Within: Writing on transracial adoption*, Cambridge, Mass: South End Press

Triseliotis J. (1991) 'Intercountry adoption: A brief overview of the research evidence', *Adoption & Fostering*, 15:4, pp 46–52

Triseliotis J. (2000) 'Intercountry adoption: Global trade or global gift?' *Adoption & Fostering*, 24:2, pp 45–54

Van Ijzendoorn M. and Juffer F. (2006) 'Adoption as intervention: Meta-analytic evidence for massive catch-up and plasticity in physical, socio-emotional, and cognitive development', *Journal of Child Psychology and Psychiatry*, 47:12, pp 1228–1245

Van Loon H. (1990) *Report on Intercountry Adoption*, The Hague: HCCH

Verhulst F. C. (2000) 'The development of internationally adopted children', in Selman P. (ed) *Intercountry Adoption: Development, trends and perspectives*, London: BAAF

Volkman T. (ed) (2005) *Cultures of Transnational Adoption*, London: Duke University Press

Von Melen (1998) *Strength to Survive and Courage to Live: 18 adoptees on adoption*, Stockholm: Swedish National Board for Intercountry Adoption

Wolfs R. (2008) *Adoption Conversations: What, when and how to tell*, London: BAAF

Wrobel G. and Neill E. (eds) (forthcoming 2009) *International Advances in Adoption Research*, Chichester: John Wiley & Sons

Section III
Meeting the needs of children in placement

16 The health of looked after children

Catherine M Hill

In considering the health of looked after children it is important to understand what is meant by the term "health". For the purposes of this chapter, the 1946 World Health Organisation definition of health will be used: 'a state of complete physical, mental and social well-being and not merely the absence of disease'. This helpful definition moves away from the medical model of health that has formerly dominated child care practice, embodied in its worst guise as the 'freedom from infection medical' to which all children in the past were subject on entry into care.

Children who enter the care system do so for different reasons and at different stages of their developmental course from birth to late adolescence. These two key factors will have a profound impact on the nature of their health problems.

Table 16.1
Percentage of all children looked after England at 31 March 2007: reason for care entry (DCSF, 2007)

Abuse or neglect	Disability	Parental illness or disability	Family in acute stress	Family dysfunction	Problem behaviour	Absent parenting
62	4	5	8	11	2	8

The majority of children looked after in England have experienced parental abuse or neglect (Table 16.1). Such experiences in infancy and young childhood may profoundly influence early brain development and the child's attachment behaviours. Less commonly, children enter the care system having experienced loving attachments disrupted by parental ill health or death. Others have experienced the trauma of war and conflict and arrived in the UK as asylum seekers experiencing cultural bewilderment and isolation. There is clearly no definition that fits all of these children and health and social work practitioners must meet the challenge of promoting health, in its broadest sense, for all children for whom they have a responsibility as corporate parent. It is the duty of the care system wherever possible to redress past health neglect, manage current health difficulties and promote a healthy lifestyle for the present and future. This chapter considers the research evidence for health difficulties for looked after and adopted children and indicates how practice can promote healthier futures for these children and young people.

Health disadvantage in children prior to entry to care

Health through life reflects a complex interaction of genetic and environmental influences. To understand the spectrum of health disadvantage experienced by looked after children, factors operating prior to care entry should be considered, as well as the impact of public care on children's wellbeing.

Pre-birth influences: genetics

Health is powerfully influenced by genetic factors. At the most fundamental level a child's life expectancy is influenced by their genetic make-up. A large Danish case-cohort sample (Petersen *et al*, 2005) studied premature death of adult adoptees between the ages of 16 and 70. Premature death from natural causes and vascular disease was significantly associated with these same causes of death in birth parents, but not in adoptive parents, indicating a powerful genetic rather than environmental effect. Thus, at the most basic level, a child's life expectancy is significantly determined by genetic factors. Consider then the genetic factors that frequently affect birth parents who are unable to care for their children. Parents who struggle to provide appropriate care for their children are more likely than successful parents to have learning difficulties and significant mental health problems, both of which may have genetic implications for the child. In one case series of 80 children in care in the North of England (Stanley *et al*, 2005), half of all mothers were identified as having a mental health disorder. For some conditions, such as schizophrenia, if both birth parents are affected the child has a significant life-time risk – up to 45 per cent – of the same condition (Harper, 2004). While these children may be healthy and thriving in infancy, they live under the shadow of future psychotic illness and many prospective adoptive parents find this risk difficult to countenance, thus leading to delay in finding a permanent placement for the child. Parental learning difficulties may be caused by discrete underlying genetic disorders such as neurofibromatosis. In such situations it is possible to give clear advice about the risk of the child inheriting the same condition. However, in the majority of cases, no discernible genetic cause is identifiable and risk prediction is more circumspect. Nonetheless, a child born of parents with a learning difficulty is likely to embark on life with a genetic learning disadvantage. For many children, genetic information is incomplete, most commonly in respect of their paternal family line. This creates a life-long disadvantage with one half of their "genetic jigsaw" missing.

Pre-birth influences: the intrauterine environment

Seminal work by Barker (1995) shed light on the life-long effects of intra-uterine nutrition. This demonstrated that babies who were light at birth were more likely than better nourished, heavier babies to develop heart disease, diabetes and hypertension in later life. This work generated the concept of "foetal origins of adult disease", namely, that health throughout life is powerfully influenced by foetal health and that an insult at a critical, sensitive period of early life has permanent effects on structure, physiology, and metabolism irrespective of genetic make-up. The hypothalamic-pituitary adrenal (HPA) axis, the major system for regulating physiological responses to stress, is believed to be implicated in this association. Recent research in the Helsinki Birth Cohort (Kajantie *et al*, 2007) demonstrated a persistent association between birth weight and the response of the HPA axis to a psycho-social stress test in old age. Thus the capacity of the body to respond to environmental stress may already be impaired at birth in infants born to mothers whose own health and nutrition were compromised.

This is directly relevant to many children in the care system, particularly if born to young teenage mothers whose own bodies are ill prepared for pregnancy or mothers whose own social circumstances result in poor nutrition. In this way, the cycle of inter-generational deprivation is perpetuated (Webb, 1998). It is salient to consider that 35 per cent of girls become mothers whilst in care or within two years of leaving care (Barn *et al*, 2005) and over 60 per cent of children adopted from care in one study were born to mothers who had themselves been looked after in childhood (Selwyn *et al*, 2006). While nutritional disadvantages may result from poor placental function in otherwise competent mothers, such factors are more common in women who are already at high risk of failure as parents, such as mothers who substance abuse. In such situations poor nutrition is compounded by foetal exposure to toxins such as nicotine metabolites, alcohol, illegal drugs or direct transmission of maternal infections such as hepatitis B, syphilis or HIV. A detailed review of the effects of maternal substance abuse or maternal infections is beyond the scope of this chapter and readers are referred to the reading list for more detail on these topics.

Thus many looked after children have health vulnerability "hard-wired" at birth both through their genetic inheritance and exposure to an adverse intra-uterine environment. It is crucial that such factors are taken into account when assessing a child's health. Social workers have an important role to play in securing information about parental health and maternal antenatal health. Achieving consent from birth parents to share this information for the welfare of their child can present challenges, but is an important goal in order to provide a full understanding of the child's health profile.

Infantile experience – the importance of early nurture and attachment
Young children, particularly infants, are highly vulnerable to environmental influences. This is particularly true of the brain and nervous system which undergo significant development in the first four years of life. This development is underpinned by the concept of "neuroplasticity" – the capacity of the developing brain to functionally organise and sculpt neuronal pathways in response to environmental stimulation. Early brain development relies upon stimulation in order to stabilise the neural systems underpinning cognition, perception, language and emotional regulation (Nelson, 1999).

Extreme deprivation can irreversibly damage neural development. This was first illustrated in experiments with kittens deprived of visual stimulation who failed to develop functional vision in the occluded eye (Hubel and Wiesel, 1970). The fact that this vision was not recoverable with subsequent stimulation generated the concept of developmental "critical periods" – times during which brain development is irreversibly impaired if appropriate stimulation is not achieved. Human examples include those of feral children – the rare examples of children reared by animals who rarely develop the capacity for language and emotion (McCrone, 2003). Happily such extreme deprivation is rare. As neural systems stabilise through childhood, plasticity becomes a less prominent feature of neural functioning although there is evidence that it continues to operate into adulthood. For example, London taxi drivers have increased hippocampal grey matter (an area of the brain responsible for memory) compared to bus drivers running fixed routes due to their need to memorise the "knowledge" of the London street-map (Maguire *et al*, 2006).

Applying these concepts to the infant and young child, the critical importance of early nurturing becomes clear. In order for children to develop the emotional capacity and behavioural repertoire to promote secure positive relationships with adult carers, they need to experience consistent unconditional care from an "attuned" adult. The reciprocal continuous feedback loop of parent–child interaction allows the infant to understand their inner world (Bowlby, 1988). The modelling of neural pathways during this critical period of development creates the basis for future "attachment" behaviours. Furthermore, the HPA axis as the major regulator of stress remains highly plastic in infancy. High infantile stress levels may model a stress response that has implications for emotional wellbeing throughout life. Traumatic experiences in early childhood, such as abuse or loss of a parent, may pre-dispose to depression and anxiety in later life.

While our understanding of the neurobiological mechanisms underpinning these associations is still developing, early brain development is likely, in part, to determine future vulnerability (Nemeroff, 2004). Children who receive consistent, warm parenting become securely attached and have the foundation from which they can develop communication, regulate emotions and safely explore their world. All looked after children by definition have experienced the trauma of separation. However, the quality of early parenting experiences is crucial. Where a parent is inconsistently attuned, for example, through substance abuse, the child develops strategies for securing parental attention – they may be passive and compliant or they may externalise their distress through disruptive behaviours. Either way, they have learnt that adult attention is conditional and they are likely to have poor self-esteem and fear rejection. Such children become insecurely or anxiously attached. Where parenting is consistently unattuned, for example, with the mother having severe mental health problems, children may become avoidant and reject adult relationships. Where children experience aggressive unpredictable parenting, disorganised attachments may ensue, reflecting the child's inner chaos (see Selected Further Reading).

Studies of children reared in institutional settings shed some light on the global impact of sub-optimal stimulation on children's development and on the extent to which deficits in children's functioning can be remedied by subsequent nurture and good parenting. Rutter (1998) studied a group of 165 Romanian children who experienced profound institutional deprivation prior to being adopted into the UK. The study used a comparison group of domestic adoptees, all adopted before the age of six months. On arrival, the Romanian children had significant global developmental delay and were small for their age. At four years, these children had made impressive gains in both physical growth and cognitive development. However, children exposed to institutional deprivation beyond the age of six months failed to achieve the level of gains seen in peers rescued through adoption before six months of age. This difference has persisted in the assessment of language, cognition and scholastic attainment at six and 11 years (Beckett *et al*, 2007; Croft *et al*, 2007). Self-stimulatory behaviour such as rocking and self-injury improved with time but were still persistent in 18 per cent and 13 per cent respectively of the 144 children followed up at six years (Beckett *et al*, 2002). The findings suggest a sensitive period beyond the age of six months where lack of adequate physical and psychological nurture has effects that persist into childhood and adolescence. These data are uniquely informative as they allow a longitudinal perspective.

The nature of the extreme deprivation experienced by these children (mortality rates were high in these institutions) is rarely replicated in UK domestic situations and therefore some caution needs to be exercised in translating the findings to other populations. Nonetheless, data from other institutional settings, where deprivation is less extreme, mirror the baseline findings of the Romanian cohort. A comparison between 25 Guatemalan children (mean age 11 months) adopted from orphanages, who were case matched with 25 children adopted from foster care in the same country, demonstrated that the children in foster care had significantly better physical growth and cognitive abilities than the children in orphanages, therefore confirming the benefits to developing children of a nurturing parent figure (Miller *et al*, 2005). Thus physical growth and early childhood development are dependent on consistent parenting as well as adequate nutrition, opportunities for play (Taneja *et al*, 2005) and attendance to physical health needs. In order to understand the root causes of a child's health in the broadest sense, it is important to know about the quality and consistency of the care they are receiving and to appreciate the importance of sensitive and critical periods of neural development. There is the strongest of arguments for ensuring that the provision of services and intervention are not dependent on meeting high thresholds of risk.

So far this chapter has reviewed some of the key factors in early life that may impact on a child's health before they become looked after. The second part of the chapter reviews the evidence for health problems when children become looked after and adopted. For clarity, this is addressed in three sections – emotional and mental health; physical health; and adolescent and health risk behaviour.

Emotional and mental health of looked after and adopted children

There is little controversy about the high rates of emotional, behavioural and mental health difficulties experienced by looked after children. A UK-based population study of 1,039 looked after children aged 5–17 years was undertaken by the Office of National Statistics (Meltzer *et al*, 2003). Forty-five per cent were identified as having a mental health disorder. This prevalence was four to five times higher than rates reported in an earlier general population survey using the same methodology (Meltzer *et al*, 2000). The response rate was lower in the looked after children sample (with 37% of potential participants excluded) and therefore the sample may have been less representative than the general population. However, in view of the reasons given for non-participation, for example, 26 per cent of carers refused to participate and 13 per cent felt it was not the right time for the child, it is possible that the survey excluded children with more severe problems and hence under-estimated the overall prevalence of mental health problems. Further analysis of these two data sets allowed comparison of the looked after children with a sub-group of the general population who were socially disadvantaged. Compared to children living in disadvantaged family settings, looked after children were nine to ten times more likely to have a conduct disorder, 11 to 12 times more likely to have post-traumatic stress disorder, twice as likely to have an anxiety disorder, two to three times more likely to be depressed and 3 to 4 times more likely to have hyperkinetic disorder (Ford *et al*, 2007). These differences persisted when learning difficulties and neurodevelopmental disorders were accounted for. Furthermore, when ratings of psychosocial adjustment were considered, even having excluded looked after children with evident psychiatric disorder, only 10 per cent compared to 50 per cent of the children living at home were considered to be well adjusted. Good mental health would therefore appear to be not easy to find in the population of looked after children in the UK.

Studies of mental health in looked after children consistently identify conduct disorder as the most prevalent difficulty. The ONS study, for example, reported conduct disorder in 37.7 per cent of the sample compared to a 12.4 per cent prevalence of emotional problems. Aggressive and challenging behaviour typical of conduct disorder can impose a significant burden to carers. Children with conduct disorder are vulnerable to school exclusion (Arcelus *et al*, 1999). Less overt are the problems of children with depression and anxiety, who may carry the burden of their difficulties internally. The potential for professional neglect of the sad, anxious and traumatised child may be compounded by constrained resources and a reluctance of over-burdened child and adolescent mental health services (CAMHS) to engage with children who are not in stable family settings.

It is important to recognise that all looked after children have additional emotional needs by virtue of being separated from their families and in public care. At a minimum, they have experienced loss of continuity of their main carers and will take time to establish therapeutic relationships with substitute carers and professionals. In the worst case, this loss will test the coping mechanism of a child already struggling with experiences of abuse, neglect and deprivation and additional stresses of placement moves. The need to prioritise the mental and emotional health of looked after children is further reinforced by data on long-term wellbeing. A national Swedish cohort study of over 22,000 children who required foster care in their pre-teens between the years 1973 to 1995 demonstrated a significant increase in long-term mental health outcomes compared to children in the general population. Adjusting for socio-economic factors and parental history of mental illness and substance abuse, the relative risk at age 19+ of suicide attempt was approximately doubled and the relative risk of hospitalisation for psychiatric disorder and psychosis was two to three times that of children who had always lived in family care. There was a consistently positive relationship between the time spent in substitute care and risk of adverse outcome (Vinnerljung et al, 2006). The need also to provide post-adoption support to older adopted adolescents is emphasised by data from the National Longitudinal Study of Adolescent Health in the US (Slap et al, 2001). Suicide attempt rates in 214 adolescent adoptees were more than double the rates in young people living with biological parents (7.6% v 3.1%). Similar prospective UK-based data are currently lacking. However, given the high rates of mental health problems in the UK looked after child population, it is reasonable to assume that similar long-term outcomes for those in care and adopted may be expected.

The root causes of emotional and mental health difficulties in children are multi-factorial. Clearly prior experience of abuse, domestic violence and disrupted attachments create an impoverished base from which to develop healthy functional behaviours and relationships. Genetic and environmental influences also play a part. Parents with impulsive, addictive or criminal personalities and genetic risk of serious mental health disorders are more likely to fail in their parenting and leave their children with a legacy of attachment disorder, compounded by increased personal risk of developing such difficulties in their adult lives (Sigvardsson et al, 1982; 1996). Pre-care experiences, however, are not the only cause of mental health and emotional problems for looked after children. The responsibility of the corporate parent needs to be acknowledged. Pre-existing problems may be exacerbated, or indeed problems created by the very system designed to protect children.

Placement instability is a factor consistently associated with increased mental health needs in care. Stanley et al (2005) demonstrated an association between the number of placements and level of mental health need in a sample of 80 looked after children in the North of England. While association does not equate to causation, there is some evidence to support this supposition. The ONS survey demonstrated that children who had experienced longer placements had a lower prevalence of mental health disorder. Furthermore, a study in California showed a strong relationship between the number of placement moves and both internalising and externalising behaviour in children, with initial externalising behaviours being the strongest predictor of placement instability. This is intuitive as the placements of children who are aggressive and disruptive are more likely to fail. However, an important finding of this large prospective study was that for 173 children with normal behaviour scores at the outset of study, the number of placements was a consistent predictor of total behaviour problems 18 months later (Newton *et al*, 2000). Unsurprisingly, placement instability is a cause as well as a consequence of children's behaviour problems. Despite this evidence, placement stability is still difficult to achieve for children looked after in England (Sinclair and Wilson, this volume). Clearly, placement stability as well as quality of placements needs to be a priority in all social care planning.

Another factor in the emotional well-being and mental health of looked after children is their experience within their peer group. Children in care may find themselves stigmatised and vulnerable to bullying at school. Thirty per cent of a clinical sample of children attending a rapid access mental health facility in Birmingham reported bullying in school. One participant in a focus group to research the perspectives of young people in care (Stanley, 2007) reported:

> *It's like you see these people in school, never had a problem, never done anything wrong, been perfect, so perfect families, and they turn round at you and they rip at you, literally go on at you, 'Oh, you're this, you're scum, you're shit' – but they don't understand how hurting it is.*

Many children are acutely aware of living in a home setting that is different to that of their peers, and professionals need to be sensitive to this and work to maintain a child's privacy wherever possible.

One of the most unpalatable and challenging difficulties for professionals working with children in care is where the child experiences further neglect or abuse within the very system designed to protect them. There is no systematic data collection on these incidents and it could be reasonably assumed that many are not disclosed. A UK-based study in Leeds in the early 1990s identified 133 children in foster care or residential care who suffered physical or sexual abuse over a six-year period (Hobbs *et al*, 1999). Perpetrators were reported to be foster carers for 41 per cent, birth parents at contact for 23 per cent, and other children for 20 per cent of incidents. The authors noted that foster children were seven to eight times and children in residential care six times more likely to be assessed by a paediatrician for abuse than a child in the general population. Further evidence comes from a study of children in care in the North of England, purposively sampled due to their presenting mental health and behavioural difficulties: 50 per cent of this selected group had experienced harm or abuse since entering the care system. The majority of incidents related to abuse from peers, nine children reported sexual abuse by another child, five reported abuse by a birth family member and three alleged physical abuse by a residential or foster carer. Clearly where children are presenting mental health, behavioural and emotional problems, the possibility of recent or ongoing abuse should be considered.

Research consistently demonstrates higher levels of mental health difficulties in children and young people living in residential settings. The ONS survey (Meltzer *et al*, 2003) found that 75 per cent of children in residential care were assessed as having a mental health disorder. In part, this will reflect the trend for residential units to accommodate adolescents and also the use of many residential units as a "last resort" for children who struggle to function in a family setting. Nonetheless, it does mean that residential settings have an additional task and challenge to promote good mental health and address difficulties in young people in their care.

For all children in care there is a tension between the public health imperative to provide timely evidence-based therapeutic support (which is often perceived as a responsibility of the child and adolescent mental health services – CAMHS) and the child or young person's need to develop trust and confidence in professionals and to have a sense of control (Davies and Wright, 2008). The latter takes time, resources and continuity, which are often in short supply. Stretched NHS mental health services struggle to provide timely intervention for even the most needy of children (DCSF, 2007). Although the provision of dedicated mental health services for looked after children has proven to be successful (Arcelus *et al*, 1999), this is not yet a universal feature of service provision. In this context, good mental health is everyone's responsibility and needs to be seen holistically rather than the exclusive domain of mental health professionals. Children's mental health is promoted by stable, therapeutic placements, self-esteem promoting activities and educational stability and these outcomes need to be prioritised to provide a setting in which more specialised therapeutic work can take place.

Physical health of looked after and adopted children

In contemporary Britain there is a strong association between poverty and child health. Children from social classes 4 and 5 have higher rates of low birth weight, infant mortality, hospital admission, injuries, asthma, non-accidental injury, special education needs and behavioural problems than children in social classes 1 and 2 (Acheson, 2000). Not surprisingly, many looked after children move into care from situations of disadvantage due to poor housing and inadequate nutrition compounded by parental neglect and abuse. Frequently this neglect will have extended to the child's health care, immunisations may have been overlooked, the child may have lacked basic access to a toothbrush at home, have never seen a dentist, and poor feeding practices with sweet drinks as pacifiers may have resulted in extreme dental caries. Common childhood diseases such as eczema and asthma may be poorly treated and exacerbated by the child's emotional distress or by damp, cold or smoky living conditions. Children may have lacked the structure and stimulation to develop regular toileting patterns and may regress to infantile patterns of soiling and wetting to express their distress.

These conditions will be very familiar to social workers in duty and assessment teams. UK-based studies describing the health of looked after children echo these themes describing neglect of routine immunisations and health screening, inadequate care of chronic health problems and failure to recognise health problems (Mather *et al*, 1997; Rodrigues, 2004). These studies give some insight into the nature of the problem, but are limited by size and lack of controls. A study (Williams *et al*, 2001) in the late 1990s in Wales used the Action and Assessment records as a tool to survey carers' and children's reports of their health problems. Children were aged between four and 17 years and had all been in care for at least six months. The strength of this study was that it matched looked after children with children living at home. Looked after children had more difficulties with interpersonal relationships, more anxieties and worries, were more likely to smoke and use illegal drugs, and had received less advice on healthy living. Interestingly the looked after children reported less physical ill health overall. A weakness of this study is that it did not access health records – absence of evidence cannot be assumed to be evidence of absence – in other words, it is possible that these children had unrecognised health difficulties not appreciated by the child or carer.

Much larger studies have been possible in the USA. One such study (Flaherty and Weiss, 1990) reported the physical examination findings of 5,181 children received into care in Chicago: 44 per cent had an identifiable health problem including acute infections, anaemia and lead poisoning and five per cent of the children examined for physical abuse had an unsuspected fracture. A further study from Baltimore (Chernoff *et al*, 1994) reported on 2,419 children assessed soon after placement in foster care: 92 per cent had an abnormality on physical examination; almost a quarter of the pre-school children had delayed development; and, following assessment, over a half were referred for further medical assessment. While health care utilisation and the practice of medicine differ across the Atlantic, these larger studies provide some indicator of the importance of an initial comprehensive health assessment for children newly looked after.

The challenge for effective care is not only to address these overt problems but to carefully consider those that are not immediately apparent. A good example of this is disease caused by blood borne viruses such as hepatitis. Contrary to popular opinion, children with these diseases may initially appear quite healthy. Neonatal units are generally quite good at identifying newborn babies at risk of these diseases by virtue of their mother's risk behaviours or because of ante-natal screening. However, the risk presented to older infants and children living in intravenous drug-abusing households are not always appreciated. Dirty needles which are not safely disposed of present a risk of needle stick injury and hence infection, particularly to young, inquisitive, mobile children. Such risks need to be actively considered and appropriately screened for.

The benefits to the child of a diagnosis and the opportunity for specialist treatment are considerable. However, the mistaken impression of an inexperienced health care worker who is incompletely informed about the child's prior living situation means that such health risks are all too easily overlooked. Social workers need to actively consider such risks and ensure that health professionals assessing the child have access to information about the child's social background on which to base clinical decisions. Similar arguments apply to the importance of family history. Without knowledge of parental health history, vital opportunities for the child's future health promotion may be missed. For example, a child with a family history of a genetic condition has the right to have this information clearly recorded in their file such that if they lose contact with their birth family they can access this information to inform their future health and life-style decisions. At the most basic they may need additional screening, for example, where there is a family history of cancer. Young people with a family history of psychosis will need additional specific counselling about the particular risks to their mental health if they engage in substance abuse – particularly cannabis and amphetamines which are now well known to precipitate serious mental illness in vulnerable individuals (Thirthalli and Benegal, 2006; Moore *et al*, 2007). Other children may have family histories that will be important when they themselves chose to become parents, conditions that may fundamentally affect their reproductive decisions.

An important challenge to corporate parenting is to both redress the health inequalities experienced by looked after children on care entry and actively promote their health in care. Unfortunately there is evidence that the corporate parent sometimes fails in this responsibility. Data collected during the introduction of the Meningococcal C immunisation campaign in 1999 illustrated the failure of the UK care system (Hill *et al*, 2003). Immunisation rates in 3,028 children looked after by local authorities were compared to those in 501,516 children living at home in nine health districts across England, Scotland and Wales. Children in public care were more than twice as likely as those living at home to have missed out on this immunisation. This failure cannot be attributed to parental neglect as all of these children were in care at the time of study. This health disadvantage continues seven years later when overall only 79.5 per cent of children in England who had been continuously looked after for 12 months were reported as up to date with their immunisations (DCSF, 2007). Immunisations are the most highly regulated, cost effective means of preventing morbidity and mortality in the child population. Failure of the care system to ensure this basic universal health protection is a concern.

Reasons for such health neglect in the system of public care are manifold and present a challenge to practitioners. When children move placement, medical records may not follow in a timely fashion. Primary care records only transfer when children are fully registered with a new GP; temporary registration does not prompt transfer of information. Such difficulties may be overcome with the advent of electronic records but, in the short term, full registration with a local GP is imperative. Children in public care may have had multiple contacts with health services, both hospital and community bases, and may have numerous sets of individual paper health records. While the initial health assessment should attempt to draw these together, this is not always possible, particularly when a child moves outside of their original health provider locality. Foster carers do not have the inherent knowledge of a child enjoyed by a birth parent, so may misinterpret physical symptoms. Furthermore, information about past medical history, allergies or food intolerances may not be passed on. Where children have complex health problems or chronic problems such as diabetes, the advice of specialist health services involved in the care of the child can be invaluable. Where children are accommodated, difficulties in achieving consent may delay treatment. Fundamentally, at the time of writing, health provider organisations have no statutory duty to promote the health of looked after children. It is hoped that this anomaly may be redressed in the near future through the Children and Young Persons Act.

Thus, UK-born children who become looked after are likely to be at risk of physical health problems both through historical neglect and at times through failings of the care system to promote their health. For many children, health disadvantage will be life-long. A US study of adoptees in the 2003 National Survey of Child Health compared 2,903 adopted children with demographically matched children living at home (Bramlett *et al*, 2007). Despite the fact that adoptive parents were accessing more health care for their children, the adoptees were more likely to have special health care needs, moderate or severe health problems, developmental delay and physical impairment. Careful health assessment, healthy care and joined up interagency communication can go some way to improve the health futures of children but inherent health problems may persist.

Adolescence and health risk behaviour

Adolescence is a particularly vulnerable period for children in the care system. During this phase important developmental tasks must take place including renegotiating key adult–child relationships, establishing autonomy as well as developing a greater sense of self and a sexual identity (Christie and Viner, 2005). These tasks are challenging for many children living within stable family settings and are inherently more stressful for looked after children. The natural tendency to resist processes that differentiate adolescents from their peers makes them more likely to reject professional support or statutory processes such as health assessments. A participant in Stanley's focus group study (2007, p 261) articulated this sentiment:

It's, like, I'll get mad if a social worker turned round to me and says 'Right, you've got to talk to this person, you've got to sort your problems out, you've got to do this, you've got to do that'. They wind me up and I'll get mad and then I'll just flip on 'em'.

Rejection of conventional processes can have a real impact on health. Meningococcal C vaccine uptake was poorest in adolescents, the very age group most at risk of the disease (Hill *et al*, 2003). While this trend was true of the general population, the difference was more marked for looked after children. Mental health problems already established in childhood confer increased risks in adolescence for social exclusion and risk behaviours. A survey of 88 adolescents looked after in Oxfordshire identified a psychiatric disorder in 67 per cent compared to 15 per cent of a control group living with their families (McCann *et al*, 1996). Co-morbidity was high in this population, reflecting the complexity of the young people's difficulties. Undeniably, one of the major health threats in adolescence is risk-taking behaviours, in particular, substance abuse. Children in care are four times more likely than their peers to smoke, use alcohol and misuse drugs (DCSF, 2007). Substance abuse, in turn, is associated with poor educational and social outcomes. Initiatives to identify and actively address substance misuse early are a major UK government initiative. Professionals need to use flexible imaginative approaches to engage young people. Nurse-led assessments have been found to be more acceptable to young people, particularly where young people have some choice over venue and timing (Hill *et al*, 2002). Local and national health initiatives such as Positive Futures (see http://drugs. homeoffice.gov.uk/young-people/positive-futures/?version=1), which engage young people through opportunities to participate in arts and sporting activities, can also facilitate positive outcomes.

Sexual health is one issue that needs to be addressed in adolescence. Looked after children initiate sexual activity at a younger age than their peers (McGlone, 2000) and are two-and-a-half times more likely to become pregnant when teenagers (DCSF, 2007). Effective sex and relationships education can reduce the level of teenage pregnancy. Looked after children frequently miss out on this advice due to school moves, learning difficulty and lack of consistent parenting (Corylon and McGuire, 1997; 1999). It is recognised that looked after children need additional services and sex and relationships education (see recommended reading). Reducing teenage pregnancy is an important goal to break the cycle of deprivation and improve the life chances of young women in care.

Health in special circumstances

In this final section, the specific health issues relevant to unaccompanied asylum-seeking children and intercountry adoptees are highlighted.

Asylum-seeking children

Health problems are a particular concern for the increasing numbers of unaccompanied children seeking asylum in the UK (see Wade *et al*, 2006; Wade, this volume). These children – while comprising less than six per cent of the total population of looked after children – nonetheless present quite different physical health needs to children born in the

UK: 58 per cent of unaccompanied asylum seekers in 2006/7 were from Asia or Africa, where infectious diseases such as TB and hepatitis are endemic, and children are likely to have been living in poverty, be malnourished and incompletely immunised. There is currently insufficient research in this area although one study found that one in six refugees (17 per cent) had a physical health problem severe enough to affect their life (Carey *et al*, 1995). Anecdotal evidence suggests that infectious diseases and malnutrition are not uncommon; as many of these conditions are silent they need to be actively screened for.

Specialised health assessment is required by a practitioner with appropriate knowledge about health issues for this group of young people. Professionals working with these children need a sound knowledge of the scientific and ethical limitations of medical age determination investigations (Royal College of Paediatrics and Child Health: policy statement), the diseases endemic in the country of origin, culturally specific practices such as female genital mutilation, and an understanding of the socio-political context of the child's trauma. It is not unusual for unaccompanied children to have experienced torture or witnessed the murder of family members and, for some, trauma may be compounded by physical and sexual abuse during flight from persecution. Coping with the psychological fall out of such experiences within an alien culture is a particular challenge. Post-traumatic stress disorder, depression and anxiety are common (Ehntholt and Yule, 2006) and while many young people show surprising resilience, those younger than 15, who may have fewer coping strategies to call upon, are particularly vulnerable to mental health problems (Sourander, 1998).

Children adopted from abroad

In 2004, 332 children were adopted into the UK from abroad compared to over 3,000 domestic adoptions (Selman, 2006). At present most children adopted into Europe originate from China and countries of the former Eastern bloc. In China the "one child" policy results in many female children abandoned at birth with no family history or information about pre-natal care. Most are cared for in orphanages. A study of 452 Chinese adoptees in the US demonstrated growth delay equivalent to a loss of one month of height age for every 2.86 months spent in orphanage care; 75 per cent of the children had significant developmental delay. Medical problems included: elevated lead levels in 14 per cent, anaemia in 35 per cent, abnormal thyroid function tests in 10 per cent, hepatitis B in 6 per cent, intestinal parasites in 9 per cent, and positive TB test results in 3.5 per cent. Significant medical diagnoses not detected by medical assessment in China were found in 81 children (Miller and Hendrie, 2000).

While care standards in Chinese orphanages are generally adequate, the same is rarely true of Eastern European institutions where physical and emotional neglect is common, particularly when children have pre-existing disabilities. Furthermore, high rates of alcoholism in the former USSR mean that foetal alcohol syndrome is relatively common in children in Russian orphanages (Johnson, 2000). A Swedish study of 76 children adopted from Eastern Europe identified a history of alcoholism in 33 per cent and psychiatric problems in 16 per cent of birth mothers; five years after adoption 46 per cent of the children had at least one neurodevelopmental problem (Landgren *et al*, 2006). There is, however, encouraging evidence from a recent meta-analysis that intercountry adoptees have better behavioural and mental health outcomes than domestic adoptees (Juffer, 2005). This is, perhaps, a surprising finding likely to reflect factors relating to both the adopted children and adopters. It is possible that there are higher rates of mental health problems in birth parents of domestic adoptees, which would predict higher rates of problems in the children irrespective of the quality of parenting in the adoptive family. Intercountry adopters tend to be older and wealthier than domestic adopters and therefore may have access to greater resources to promote the mental health of their adopted children. Another interesting possibility is that the overt ethnic differences between most intercountry adopters and their child necessitates greater honesty and trust in the adoptive family about the child's adoptive status, which may itself promote better adjustment in the child.

While these children represent a small caseload for most local authorities they have unique health issues. With the exception of Northern Ireland, there is no statutory requirement for children arriving in the UK to have a health assessment; nonetheless, these children are known to be at risk of significant health problems and close liaison with the agency health adviser is recommended.

Summary

Promoting the health of looked after children requires a well-founded understanding of the factors likely to constrain optimum health. This chapter has touched upon some of these influences and their likely manifestations. Health professionals have a role in addressing specific health issues in the lives of looked after children. The statutory health assessment process provides an important framework for the identification of health issues unique to each child, but cannot promote health in isolation. Healthy care needs to be a philosophy embedded within corporate parenting that promotes secure attachments, healthy living and self-esteem. The National Children's Bureau Healthy Care Standard (Figure 16.1) provides an excellent standard against which services can be audited and its accompanying programme (see http://www.ncb.org.uk) has successfully translated standards into practice examples. The spirit of healthy care is best summed up by a quote from a 13-year-old boy participating in a National Children's Bureau Health project (Lewis, 1999).

> *What health means to me? Running and playing; being with my friends; on my bike; exercise; eating food, fruit; sleeping at night and good dreams.*

Figure 16.1
The National Healthy Care Standard

Children and young people in a healthy care environment will:

- experience a genuinely caring, consistent, stable and secure relationship with at least one committed, trained, experienced and supported carer
- live in an environment that promotes health and well-being within the wider community
- have opportunities to develop the personal and social skills to care for their health and well-being now and in the future
- receive effective healthcare, assessment, treatment and support.

A child or young person living in a healthy care environment is entitled to:

- feel safe, protected and valued in a strong, sustained and committed relationship with at least one carer
- live in a caring, healthy and learning environment
- feel respected and supported in his/her cultural beliefs and personal identity
- have access to effective healthcare, assessment, treatment and support and have opportunities to develop personal and social skills, talents and abilities and to spend time in freely chosen play, cultural and leisure activities
- be prepared for leaving care by being supported to care and provide for him/herself in the future.

Selected further reading

BAAF (2004) Practice note 46, *Health Screening of Children Adopted from Abroad*, London: BAAF

BAAF (2008) Practice note 53, *Guidelines for the Testing of Looked After Children Who Are at Risk of a Blood-Borne Infection*, London: BAAF

Bowlby J. (1988) *A Secure Base*, London: Tavistock/Routledge

British Medical Association Board of Science and Education (October 2002) *Asylum Seekers: Meeting their healthcare needs*, London: BMA

Phillips R. (2004) *Children Exposed to Parental Substance Misuse: Implications for family placement*, London: BAAF

Teenage Pregnancy Unit (2001) *Guidance for Field Social Workers, Residential Social Workers, and Foster Carers on Providing Information and Referring Young People to Contraceptive and Sexual Health Services*, London: Teenage Pregnancy Unit

References

Acheson D. (2000) *Independent Inquiry into Inequalities in Health Report*, London: The Stationery Office

Arcelus J., Bellerby T. and Vostanis P. (1999) 'A mental health service for young people in the care of the local authority', *Clinical Child Psychology and Psychiatry*, 4:2, pp 233–245

Barker D. J. P. (1995) 'Fetal origins of coronary heart disease', *British Medical Journal*, 311, pp 171–4

Barn R., Andrew L. and Mantovani N. (2005) *Life After Care: The experiences of young people from different ethnic groups*, York: Joseph Rowntree Foundation

Beckett C., Bredenkamp D., Castle J., Groothues C., O'Connor T. G. and Rutter M. and the English and Romanian Adoptees (ERA) Study Team (2002) 'Behavior patterns associated with institutional deprivation: A study of children adopted from Romania', *Journal of Developmental and Behavioral Pediatrics*, October 23:5, pp 297–303

Beckett C., Maughan B., Rutter M., Castle J., Colvert E., Groothues C., Hawkins A., Kreppner J., O'Connor T. G., Stevens S. and Sonuga-Barke E. J. (2007) 'Scholastic attainment following severe early institutional deprivation: A study of children adopted from Romania', *Journal of Abnormal Child Psychology*, 35:6, pp 1063–73

Bowlby J. (1988) *A Secure Base*, London: Tavistock/Routledge

Bramlett M. D., Radel L. F. and Blumberg S. J. (2007) 'The health and well-being of adopted children', *Pediatrics*, 119:1, pp S54–60

Carey Wood J., Duke K., Karn V. and Marshall T. (1995) *The Settlement of Refugees in Britain*, London: HMSO

Chernoff R., Combs-Orme T., Risley-Curtiss C. and Heisler A. (1994) 'Assessing the health status of children entering foster care', *Pediatrics*, 93:4, pp 594–601

Christie D. and Viner R. (2005) 'Adolescent development', *British Medical Journal*, 330:7486, pp 301–4

Corylon J. and McGuire C. (1997). *Young Parents in Public Care: Pregnancy and parenthood among young people looked after by local authorities*, London: National Children's Bureau

Corylon J. and McGuire C. (1999) *Pregnancy and Parenthood. The views and experiences of young people in public care*, London: National Children's Bureau

Croft C., Beckett C., Rutter M., Castle J., Colvert E., Groothues C., Hawkins A., Kreppner J., Stevens S. E. and Sonuga-Barke E. J. (2007) 'Early adolescent outcomes of institutionally-deprived and non-deprived adoptees. II: Language as a protective factor and a vulnerable outcome', *Journal of Child Psychology and Psychiatry*, January 48:1, pp 31–44

Davies J. and Wright J. (2008) 'Children's voices: A review of the literature pertinent to looked-after children's views of mental health services', *Child and Adolescent Mental Health*, 13:1, pp 26–31

Department for Children, Schools and Families website: http://www.dfes.gov.uk/rsgateway/ (accessed 17/12/07)

Department for Education and Skills (2007) *Care Matters: Time for Change*, London: Department for Education and Skills

Ehntholt K. A. and Yule W. (2006) 'Practitioner review: Assessment and treatment of refugee children and adolescents who have experienced war-related trauma', *Journal of Child Psychology and Psychiatry*, 47:12, pp 1197–210

Flaherty E. G. and Weiss H. (1990) 'Medical evaluation of abused and neglected children', *American Journal of Diseases of Children*, 144:3, pp 330–4

Ford T., Vostanis P., Meltzer H. and Goodman R. (2007) 'Psychiatric disorder among British children looked after by local authorities: Comparison with children living in private households', *British Journal of Psychiatry*, 190, pp 319–25

Harper P. S. (2004) *Practical Genetic Counselling*, (6th edn), London: Arnold

Hill C., Wright V., Sampeys C., Dunnett K., Daniel S., O'Dell L. and Watkins J. (2002) 'The emerging role of the specialist nurse promoting the health of looked after children', *Adoption & Fostering*, 26:4, pp 35–43

Hill C. M., Mather M. and Goddard J. (2003) 'Cross-sectional survey of meningococcal C immunisation in children looked after by local authorities and those living at home', *British Medical Journal*, 15:326, 7385, pp 364–5

Hobbs G. F., Hobbs C. J. and Wynne J. M. (1999) 'Abuse of children in foster and residential care', *Child Abuse & Neglect*, 23:12, pp 139–1252

Home Office Positive Futures Programme, www.drugs.homeoffice.gov.uk/young-people/positive-futures/?version=1

Hubel D. H. and Wiesel T. N. (1970) 'The period of susceptibility to the physiological effects of unilateral eye closure in kittens', *Journal of Physiology*, 206:2, pp 419–436

Johnson D. E. (2000) 'Medical and developmental sequelae of early childhood institutionalization in international adoptees from Romania and the Russian Federation', in Nelson C. (ed.) *The Effects of Early Adversity on Neurobehavioral Development*, Mahwah, NJ: Lawrence Erlbaum Associates, Inc

Juffer F. and van Ijzendoorn M. H. (2005) 'Behavior problems and mental health referrals of international adoptees: A meta-analysis', *Journal of the American Medical Association*, 293:20, pp 2501–15

Kajantie E., Feldt K., Räikkönen K., Phillips D. I., Osmond C., Heinonen K., Pesonen A. K., Andersson S., Barker D. J. and Eriksson J. G. (2007) 'Body size at birth predicts hypothalamic-pituitary-adrenal axis response to psychosocial stress at age 60 to 70 years', *Journal of Clinical Endocrinology and Metabolism*, 92:11, pp 4094–100

Landgren M., Andersson Grönlund M., Elfstrand P. O., Simonsson J. E., Svensson L. and Strömland K. (2006) 'Health before and after adoption from Eastern Europe', *Acta Paediatrica*, 95:6, pp 720–5

Lewis H. (1999) 'Improving health care and health education for looked after young people', Final report, London: National Children's Bureau

Maguire E. A., Woollett K. and Spiers H. J. (2006) 'London taxi drivers and bus drivers: A structural MRI and neuropsychological analysis', *Hippocampus*, 16:12, pp 1091–101

Mather M., Humphrey J. and Robson J. (1997) 'The statutory medical and health needs of looked after children: Time for a radical review?' *Adoption & Fostering*, 21:2, pp 36–40

McCann J., James A., Wilson S. and Dunn G. (1996) 'Prevalence of psychiatric disorders in young people in the care system', *British Medical Journal*, 313, pp 5129–5130

McCrone J. (2003) 'Feral children', *Lancet Neurology*, 2:2, p 132

McGlone F. (2000). 'Families', *Research Matters*, pp 32–34

Meltzer H., Gatward R., Corbin T., Goodman R. and Ford T. (2003). *The mental health of young people looked after by local authorities in England*, London: The Stationery Office

Meltzer H., Gatward R., Goodman R. and Ford T. (2000) 'The mental health of children and adolescents in Great Britain', London: The Stationery Office

Miller L., Chan W., Comfort K. and Tirella L. (2005) 'Health of children adopted from Guatemala: Comparison of orphanage and foster care', *Pediatrics*, 115:6, pp 710–7

Miller L. C. and Hendrie N. W. (2000) 'Health of children adopted from China', *Pediatrics*, 105:6

Moore T. H., Zammit S., Lingford-Hughes A., Barnes T. R., Jones P. B., Burke M. and Lewis G. (2007) 'Cannabis use and risk of psychotic or affective mental health outcomes: A systematic review', *Lancet*, 370:9584, pp 319–28

Nelson C. A. (1999) 'Neural plasticity in human development', *Current Directions in Psychological Science*, 8:2, pp 42–45

Nemeroff C. B. (2004) 'Neurobiological consequences of childhood trauma', *Journal of Clinical Psychiatry*, 65;1, pp 18–28

Newton R. R., Litrowinik A. J. and Landsverk J. A. (2000) 'Children and youth in foster care: Disentangling the relationship between problem behaviours and number of placements', *Child Abuse and Neglect*, 24:10, pp 1363–1374

Petersen L., Andersen P. K. and Sørensen T. I. (2005) 'Premature death of adult adoptees: Analyses of a case-cohort sample', *Genetic Epidemiology*, 28:4, pp 376–82

Rodrigues V. C. (2004) 'Health of children looked after by the local authorities', *Public Health*, 118:5, pp 370–6

Royal College of Paediatrics and Child Health X-Rays and Asylum Seeking Children: Policy Statement on the use of X-rays in age determination. http://www.rcpch.ac.uk/Policy/X-Rays-and-Asylum-Seeking-Children-Policy-Statement

Rutter M. (1998) 'Developmental catch-up and deficit following adoption after severe global early privation', English and Romanian Adoptees (ERA) Study Team, *Journal of Child Psychology and Psychiatry*, 39:4, pp 465–76

Selman P. (2006) 'Trends in intercountry adoption: Analysis of data from 20 receiving countries, 1998–2004', *Journal of Population Research*, 23:2, p 183

Selwyn J., Sturgess W., Quinton D. and Baxter C. (2006) *Costs and Outcomes of Non-infant Adoptions*, London: BAAF

Sigvardsson S., Bohman M. and Cloninger C. R. (1996) 'Replication of the Stockholm adoption study of alcoholism: Confirmatory cross-fostering analysis', *Archives of General Psychiatry*, 53:8, pp 681–7

Sigvardsson S., Cloninger C. R., Bohman M. and von Knorring A. L. (1982) 'Predisposition to petty criminality in Swedish adoptees. III. Sex differences and validation of the male typology', *Archives of General Psychiatry*, 39:11, pp 1248–53

Slap G., Goodman E. and Huang B. (2001) 'Adoption as a risk factor for attempted suicide during adolescence', *Pediatrics*, 108:2, E30

Sourander A. (1998) 'Behavior problems and traumatic events of unaccompanied refugee minors', *Child Abuse & Neglect*, 22:7, pp 719–27

Stanley N. (2007) 'Young people's and carer's perspectives on the mental health needs of looked after adolescents', *Child and Family Social Work*, 12, pp 258–267

Stanley N., Riordan D. and Alaszewski H. (2005) 'The mental health of looked after children: Matching response to need', *Health and Social Care in the Community*, 13:3, pp 239–248

Taneja V., Aggarwal R., Beri R. S. and Puliyel J. M. (2005) 'Not by bread alone project: A 2-year follow-up report', *Child Care Health and Development*, 31:6, pp 703–6

Thirthalli J. and Benegal V. (2006) 'Psychosis among substance users', *Current Opinion in Psychiatry*, 19:3, pp 239–45

Vinnerljung B., Hjern A. and Lindblad F. (2006) 'Suicide attempts and severe psychiatric morbidity among former child welfare clients – a national cohort study', *Journal of Child Psychology and Psychiatry*, 47:7, pp 723–33

Wade J., Mitchell F. and Baylis G. (2006) *Unaccompanied Asylum Seeking Children: The response of social work services*, London: BAAF

Webb E. (1998) 'Children and the inverse care law', *British Medical Journal*, 23:316 (7144), pp 1588–91

Williams J., Jackson S., Maddocks A., Cheung W. Y., Love A. and Hutchings H. (2001) 'Case-control study of the health of those looked after by local authorities', *Archives of Disease in Children*, 85:4, pp 280–5

17 The education of fostered and adopted children

David Berridge and Hilary Saunders

Educational achievement is increasingly a prerequisite in modern society for financial security and accomplishment in later life. David Beckham and Sir Alan Sugar may have achieved fame and riches despite leaving school at 16 but, for most, success leads from skills and qualifications obtained at school, college and university.

Many families assume schooling success, but academic achievement remains a problem in the UK and tens of thousands of pupils leave school each year with no or very limited qualifications. It is a particular problem for boys, especially those living in areas of high unemployment. Disadvantaged pupils are more likely to attend poorly performing secondary schools and to miss out on the best teaching, as resources are directed towards high achievers to meet government targets (Cassen and Kingdon, 2007). Psychosocial disorders have increased among the young, which have educational implications (Rutter and Smith, 1995).

As we shall see, a range of factors are associated with low educational achievement. Early upbringing and family background play important parts. Children living in foster homes or who are adopted often have had the most difficult start in life including abuse or neglect and so, unsurprisingly, can experience educational difficulties. Yet, success *is* possible and so this chapter reviews some of the main policy and practice issues in this area and what research offers to help our understanding. Although there is some commonality between types of family placement, there are also important differences and so we deal separately with fostering and adoption. Our discussion is influenced by the range of available evidence and there has been more interest from psychologists specifically in the field of adoption. The education of fostered and adopted children has received attention in policy in recent years and we discuss this too.

Children living in foster care

The low educational achievement of children looked after by local authorities ("in care") is widely recognised and often seen as a major shortcoming of the system. Figures are quoted, for example, in England (2007), showing that some 64 per cent of pupils in Year 11 (16-year-olds) who had been looked after for more than a year obtained at least one GCSE A*–G or equivalent, compared with nearly all (99%) pupils generally. Thirteen per cent achieved five "good" GCSEs A*–C, in contrast to 59 per cent of the total group. Although the gap has narrowed recently by a few percentage points, the difference is striking and government improvement targets have been missed. Looked after pupils are much more likely to be permanently excluded or to miss days from school. As, nowadays, over two-thirds of looked after children at any one time are living in foster homes, these problems are experienced by the fostered group.

Researchers differ in how they explain the low educational achievement of looked after children. (We generally use the term "low achievement" rather than "underachievement" as it is often unclear with what exactly the level of attainment is being compared [see Berridge, 2007]). Some feel that inadequacies in the care system are largely responsible. Government policy has often taken this critical line, although recent proposals, which we discuss later, are more measured (DfES, 2007). Fostering services could certainly be improved, as could the school experience of looked after children. However, it has been argued that previous explanations of low achievement for this group have been insufficient if not simplistic (Berridge, 2007). Too much reliance has been placed on official statistics ("outcome indicators") which, at a local level, are likely to be unreliable. Half of care leavers who had the opportunity to sit GCSEs had entered care after their 13th birthday and local authorities would have had limited time, in any case, to influence their educational achievement.

Background factors and educational attainment

In addition, children living in foster homes are likely to have considerable difficulties (Wilson *et al*, 2004). They come from families with a range of problems, including poor mental health and substance misuse, and have experienced inconsistent and harmful parenting. Maltreated children are at risk of poor outcomes with greater behavioural, emotional, social and educational problems than the wider population. About a quarter of fostered children have a learning disability compared with some three per cent of the general population and estimates of mental health problems range from between a third and two-thirds. Genetic risks may have been inherited from birth parents (Roy *et al*, 2000). All of this has educational consequences for learning and school behaviour.

Attachment theory provides a framework for understanding how deficiencies in parenting affect children's development. Howe (2005) is one of the most prominent authors. He demonstrates, for example, how physically abused children frequently experience problems in their self-concept and self-esteem. They can be aggressive, poorly socialised and unable to develop trusting relationships with others. They become unhappy, unpopular and withdrawn. At school, physically abused children are more likely to show low motivation, poor problem-solving abilities and their play can lack imagination. Language development may also be delayed. Children resort to violence rather than reason to resolve disagreements: 'Under stress, the predominant emotion of abused children is one of anger' (p 79). Abused children may in turn become bullies. Not all physically abused foster children will display the full range of these difficulties, depending on the nature and context of the abuse, its onset, severity and duration. But they are predisposed to these problems and their education will suffer.

Alternatively, from a sociological perspective, the socio-economic risk factors associated with family breakdown and entry to care, such as social class and poverty, are also linked with low educational achievement. Social mobility is more limited in the UK compared with many other countries, and so self-improvement will be difficult for care leavers and others in a similar position. Unlike the post-second world war boom, fewer public service professional posts are now being created and the opportunities for advancement are restricted. Looking internationally, the limited evidence that exists suggests that the UK is not alone in the poor educational results of its care population.

Probably the only in-depth research that has investigated the complex interplay between looked after children's disadvantaged backgrounds and their educational achievement was commissioned by the Social Exclusion Unit (Cheesbrough, 2002). This drew on the cohort study of a large sample of children born in the 1970s – obviously much has changed in the educational and care systems since. However, the results suggested that children who had been in care, but had only ever lived in foster homes, had achievements in full-time education comparable to those from a similar socio-economic background who had never been in care. The position was less encouraging but more complex for those who had spent time in residential care, where achievement for the cohort overall was strongly linked with the interest demonstrated by parents.

But it is important to be clear exactly what this means. The above evidence from educational research shows that the socio-economic background and early upbringing of children who are fostered means that they are likely to be educationally disadvantaged and to face challenges in their learning and at school. However, this is no reason to be complacent or accept poor results, quite the opposite. Those in foster care require and should be entitled to a high quality, compensatory experience from social workers, carers and schools. As we shall see, a number of foster children are very successful at school despite their early adversity, and it is important that we learn the lessons from this amelioration.

Other explanations for low educational attainment

Other explanations have been proposed for the schooling problems of looked after children. Sonia Jackson (2007) first identified these 20 years ago and it has taken a very long time for things to change. For example, *inadequate corporate parenting* has been recognised, in which agencies and professionals fail to collaborate effectively (see Harker *et al*, 2004). Structures have changed considerably in recent years, partly in response to this problem, and schools and child welfare services have been brought together both at central and local government levels in England. However, we have little evidence of the impact of these structural reforms on children and families' experiences. Hitherto, there has been a lack of communication and co-ordination between education and social services professionals, who have found information-sharing and joint-working difficult processes. Social services' records of pupils' academic progress have not always been accurate and there have been insufficient contacts between social workers and schools. Foster carers have sometimes been unclear about their role in education alongside social workers and birth parents.

There has also been a *failure to prioritise education* among looked after pupils and schooling has been considered secondary to placement decisions. Social workers in the past have paid greater attention to emotional development and family links rather than education. Looked after children comprise a very small proportion of most schools' populations. Foster carers, generally, have not been selected based on their ability to support young people's education. Inadequate encouragement from social workers, teachers and foster carers will fail to motivate and support pupils.

Low expectations of looked after pupils may become a self-fulfilling prophecy. There is a body of educational research showing how pupils' achievements are influenced by teachers' perceptions and expectations. If we are not careful, realising how early experiences can affect later learning can hold back pupils if we do not hold high aspirations. Without imposing undue pressure, we should hold high expectations about fostered children's potential for development and provide stimulation, encouragement and support.

The care environment itself may also contribute to poor achievement. Foster carers are a varied group, with different experiences of education themselves and some offering more stimulating homes and experiences than others. Potential placements are often in short supply, limiting possibilities. Furthermore, *placement instability* has been a problem which has led to disruption and uncertainty. Some 15 per cent of looked after children experience three or more placements in a year and movement at key times can be especially distracting. *Disrupted schooling* can occur as a result. It has also been reported in the past that looked after pupils are more likely than the general school population to engage in absenteeism and to be permanently excluded.

However, the education of looked after pupils has received more attention recently and it is a changing picture. We discuss later recent policy proposals to address the above and other issues. Although significantly improving the statistical outcome indicators will be difficult, due to the earlier adversities, some progress has occurred and there is greater professional awareness of the educational problems of looked after children.

Empirical studies

There is not much detailed empirical research specifically on the education of fostered children. Therefore, not enough is known about the exact nature of young people's learning difficulties, their educational experiences while in care and the extent to which they make progress. The useful knowledge review on fostering research found little on education (Wilson *et al*, 2004).

One detailed study – the *Taking Care of Education (TCOE) project* (Harker *et al*, 2004) – evaluated a development project in three local authorities to see whether improvements in corporate parenting led to better educational outcomes for looked after children. Each authority employed a lead officer to pursue initiatives, particularly those which might be "mainstreamed" at the end of the work. Activities generally fell within three categories: promoting strategic change; influencing professional practice; and directly supporting young people's educational progress. The majority of the samples of young people (80 at the outset and 56 at follow-up, traced over two years) lived in foster care. Research methods included interviews with managers to chart policy and practice developments, as well as interviews with the sample of young people and a key adult in their lives (parent, carer, teacher or social worker). Some standardised tests were used.

Managers interviewed felt that developing a corporate approach was the most important stage in improving children's achievements. Sharing up-to-date, accurate information was a problem for each of the three authorities. This stemmed not so much from procedural or technical difficulties but more practical complications concerning poor accuracy or delays in inputting data. It was felt that the project had successfully raised awareness of the importance of education, but the urgency with which placements had to be made and the shortage of fostering resources often undermined good practice. Designated teachers had been established in schools in all three areas but there were questions about their exact roles and responsibilities. Personal Education Plans (PEPs) had been introduced.

The research concluded that annual comparisons of Key Stage results in individual authorities were unreliable as groups varied each year and numbers were often small. Young people generally perceived that they had made progress in their care and educational experiences. They reported that a key feature of this was the degree of encouragement and support for education provided by carers. Placement stability and security were closely linked with the quality of relationships between carers and young people, and with the level of support and encouragement provided.

The study reported that promoting better inter-professional working between education and social services professionals was complex. Senior management endorsement, in itself, was only a start. Additional financial resources and staff redeployment were required. Other barriers were: lack of understanding of respective roles and responsibilities; resistance to change; staff turnover or insufficient staff; and the effects of restructuring. However, improvements occurred in inter-professional working during the course of the development project.

At a more individual level, the research revealed that young people valued awards ceremonies to celebrate their academic achievements. Financial incentives for obtaining

GCSEs were welcomed, but it was unclear how much influence they had on actual performance. The three project authorities developed a range of initiatives to enhance young people's strengths and self-esteem, including employing a dedicated educational psychologist, encouraging leisure and sports activities and after-school homework clubs. These appeared to be positive interventions.

The *TCOE* project also found that, though it was complex and time-consuming, schools were generally willing to become partners in raising the educational achievements of looked after pupils. Young people identified teachers as the most important source of academic and pastoral support. Their attitudes towards designated teachers were more mixed. They were more positive about the potential contribution of PEPs but this was hampered by their lack of involvement in the process. Young people's friendship groups – whether pro-academic or more "deviant" – could influence looked after young people's educational experiences.

The *TCOE* follow-up study revealed improvements in the level of educational support provided in care placements. Therefore, positive change can occur if subjected to strategic, focused intervention. Young people interviewed emphasised the importance of having someone showing a genuine interest in their education and who provided them with support and encouragement. This support was often linked to living in a stable environment, especially foster care, but young people did not see placement moves as necessarily detrimental to their education if they received similar or enhanced support in their future foster or residential homes. They were also most likely to mention social workers as the group that hindered their educational progress. This was mainly linked to their perception that education was too often disregarded by social workers when changes of foster or residential placements were being arranged. Young people also criticised the lack of financial support for further and higher education.

Foster carers interviewed in the study were more aware of the complexities and constraints of social workers' roles and were generally complimentary about their efforts. However, carers across the three study authorities raised a series of common issues that impeded their efforts to enhance children's education. The most important was *communication problems* with social workers. They often found it difficult to contact social workers, or have calls returned. In addition, they felt that there was insufficient information and advice. Secondly, foster carers identified *staffing shortages* and the presence of temporary social workers as jeopardising support for care and education. Thirdly, *financial needs* were raised by carers, who were unclear whether additional individual tutoring could be sought. Some carers reiterated the financial uncertainty for care leavers who might go to university. Finally, *ensuring educational provision* was often problematic and the necessary timescales were not always followed in providing school places.

We need to bear in mind that the fieldwork for the *TCOE* study was undertaken between 2001–03 and policy and practice in this high profile area have moved on. And as is often the case in child welfare research, there was some sample loss during the course of the study and those who were difficult to trace were more likely to have had unsuccessful educational and care histories. Nonetheless, many of the study's findings were encouraging. It showed that positive change could occur and, by the end of the project, most foster placements were providing a good level of educational support.

Resilience

Much social research is concerned with analysing social problems. Rather than looking at problems such as educational failure and why it occurs, an alternative approach is to consider instead situations that work well and what can be deduced from them that may have wider relevance. Jackson's work has been influenced by this approach and resilience theory (Jackson and Martin, 1998). In short, this theoretical approach assesses the "risk" factors in a young person's life, such as family breakdown, and contrasts these with "protective" factors which might have a countervailing influence. Jackson's study of care leavers who had been successful educationally found a number of factors that distinguished their careers. These were:

- stability and continuity;
- learning to read early and fluently;
- having a parent or carer who valued education and saw it as important for later life;
- having friends outside care who did well at school;
- developing out-of-school hobbies and interests;
- meeting a significant adult who offered support and encouragement and who could act as a possible role model; and
- attending school regularly (p 578).

There is much overlap between these protective factors and earlier discussion in this chapter. It is interesting to see that reading is also highlighted. Literacy is key to educational success and poor general progress or classroom disruption may have their roots in poor literacy. Reading stories to a child, and helping them to read and write, also entail an intimate relationship with undivided attention, which will have additional emotional benefits. Interestingly, in the *TCOE* study, the proportions of young people living in foster homes at the outset of the study who had access to a local library, key books and newspapers/magazines ranged from 57–72 per cent, not as high as we would wish. But at follow-up this had improved to 77–94 per cent.

Many of the resilient group of high achievers attributed their success to the support they received from their foster families. Some had lived with well-educated carers who shared their knowledge and advice with young people. Interestingly, the benefits of this could still arise even if there were problems in the placement in other respects. Jackson and Martin rightly concluded that the educational background and awareness of foster carers should be given higher priority in carer recruitment.

Higher education

This approach was extended in other research by Sonia Jackson, who investigated care leavers going on to university (Jackson et al, 2005). The study sample consisted of volunteers, mainly nominated by local authorities, and so it is not necessarily representative of the wider group: as we have already seen, there are a number of methodological challenges for researchers in this field. In contrast to what is often perceived, coming into care was mainly considered to have been beneficial, especially for those who were fostered. Interestingly, the quality of the final placement seemed to be more important than the overall level of stability provided. The university group were clearly highly motivated to succeed educationally and this could stem from a number of sources – birth parents, carers, friends, siblings or school. They had been very determined to overcome adversities.

Initial experiences at university were stressful for those without supportive foster carers. Living, initially, in halls of residence helped provide friendship networks. Some missed this opportunity if there was local authority delay about funding, and the chance to obtain early advice or apply for other benefits such as grants of financial help. Average levels of debt were higher than for the general student population, at more than £11,000 over three years. However, the majority were completing their courses successfully and most serious problems concerned emotional or relationship matters. Few universities had special support or procedures in place for care leavers.

Policy development in foster care

The education of fostered and other looked after children has attracted widespread attention and has been seen as something of a litmus test for the care system more generally. Policy has moved on rapidly in recent years, although government proposals have not always been consistent with overall messages from research. Teachers, social workers and carers are more alert to educational issues as a result of this greater attention, including the Quality Protects government initiative to modernise social services.

Thus, at the time of writing, the Children and Young Persons Bill (2007) (England and Wales) contains a range of proposals to improve the educational experiences of fostered and other looked after pupils. For example, if implemented, greater priority will be given to accommodating children nearer to their school and to avoid unintended transfers, especially in the final period of education in Key Stage 4. Schools must nominate a "designated person", whose responsibility is to promote the educational achievements of looked after pupils. Personal advisers will be able to assist care leavers with their employment, education and training up to the age of 25. Payments will be made to care leavers attending university in line with their pathway plan. Greater priority is being given to placements with family and friends, and authorities will need to be alert to the implications for those carers who give low emphasis to learning or are unfamiliar with the educational system. Furthermore, a controversial measure included within the Bill (Part 1) is the power for authorities to discharge to independent agencies certain social services functions relating to looked after children. It is unclear exactly how this will work, including its educational effects, and we await the results of pilots.

It is one matter to set out general aspirations; it is another to provide the required resources, ensure that they are implemented and operate as intended. Whether they are sufficient to bring about a step-change in children's lives and overcome the deeply-rooted adversities also remains to be seen.

Wider educational issues

Developments elsewhere in the education system are relevant to the experiences of fostered children, including the field of *special education*. We saw earlier that a significant minority of looked after pupils have a statement of special educational needs (SEN), mostly concerning "behavioural, emotional and social difficulties" ("BESD"). Special education is an important and developing area, which is being increasingly integrated with social work services for children in need and their families (DfES, 2004). It appears that looked after children are getting better access to SEN support in classrooms but we do not know the effects of this.

A further interesting educational development is *nurture groups* (Nurture Group Network, 2007). This is an initiative which seeks to help retain challenging pupils in mainstream schools. Nurture groups are small classes of between six to eight children, staffed by two adults, with their own specially furnished room and facilities. By addressing "the emotional curriculum" as well as academic learning, nurture groups seek to promote attachment experiences. Pupils spend the majority of the week within this special classroom but integrate with the wider school on occasions, such as assemblies and PE. On average, pupils spend about a year to a year-and-a-half in the nurture group, integrating gradually with the mainstream class before fully returning. Nurture groups operate mainly in primary schools but there are some at secondary level and one in a young offenders institution. Research results from nurture groups are encouraging, showing improvements in behaviour and attainment. In one evaluation, over 80 per cent of nurture group pupils were successfully being educated in the mainstream two years after leaving the group (Nurture Group Network, 2007).

The education of adopted children

As adopted children have also been separated from their birth parents and looked after by the local authority (usually in the care of a foster family), it might be expected that their educational outcomes would be similar to those of fostered children. The cognitive development of adopted children is thought to be at risk because of a number of factors including genetic inheritance, abuse, inadequate early nutrition and lack of stimulation affecting brain development (Chugani *et al*, 2001). Insecure attachments add to these risks by affecting the ability of infants and children to explore their environments, leading to less optimal cognitive growth (Pinderhughes, 1998; Lansford *et al*, 2001).

A government review (PIU, 2000) described children adopted out of care as 'more challenging than the general looked after population' and commented on their previous circumstances as follows:

> *1996 figures suggest that 44 per cent of children adopted from care had started to be looked after because of abuse, neglect or risk, compared to 17 per cent of the overall number of children ceasing to be looked after that year. Some 45 per cent of children adopted were first admitted under Emergency Protection or Care Orders, compared to 17 per cent for the general looked after population.* (p 12)

There have been hundreds of studies of adoption and most of these have focused on how much intercountry adoptees have caught up developmentally in comparison with their peers. A meta-analysis (Ijzendoorn and Juffer, 2006) of over 42 adoption studies involving more than 6,000 intercountry adopted children found that, in relation to cognitive catch-up, adopted children outperformed their birth siblings and previous peers on IQ tests and educational achievements. In new adoptive homes, children also caught up with the adopters' own birth children and their peers with only a negligible difference in IQ. However, they did slightly less well than their new peers in school performance and in their language abilities. For some children there was a gap between IQ (their competence) and their actual performance in school. The meta-analysis confirmed that intercountry adoption made a positive impact on children's cognitive development and the authors concluded that 'adoption is an impressive intervention leading to astonishing catch-up'. However, these studies did not focus specifically on children who had experienced profound institutional deprivation.

Research (Beckett *et al*, 2007) tracking the outcomes of children adopted from Romanian orphanages into generally well-functioning English families has begun to uncover the complexities of developmental catch-up. Children who had been adopted before the age of six months made remarkable gains, but children who had been exposed to 6–12 months of institutional care continued to show persistent effects. While many of these children also made significant gains, it has been hypothesised (Beckett *et al*, 2006) that there is an early sensitive period for neural effects through which enduring changes occur. Further research is needed to understand the mechanisms.

Age at placement has long been known to be associated with risks of disruption but is also associated with incomplete catch-up in school achievement. This is particularly important when the average age at adoption for children placed out of the care system in England is four years old. Studies of adoption in the UK have shown that many adopted children are removed at or very shortly after birth but often have several foster placements before moving into an adoptive home. Reducing delay, making more use of concurrent planning and reducing moves in foster care would improve adoption outcomes.

Educational needs of adopted children

Very little research in the UK has focused on the education of children who have been adopted out of care: this issue is only covered in passing in studies focusing on other aspects of adoption. This may be because, until the Adoption and Children Act 2002 (England Wales), adoptive parents were responsible for arranging their child's education and it was assumed that children would not need additional support.

The Adoption Support Services Regulations 2005 require local authorities to assess the support needs of any child whom they are considering placing with a particular adoptive parent, and this should include educational needs. Good practice requires that the Personal Education Plan is revised once the adoptive placement is identified so that the adopters are supported to meet the child's needs in this area. Practical help may also be needed, as the transition, possibly to a new school, can present many challenges. Lowe and colleagues (1999) suggested that it is important that children are placed in a school where achievement is the norm rather than the exception; that their entry to school is well-timed; that there is good liaison with teachers to ensure appropriate support; and that measures are in place to reduce the potential risk of bullying.

A scoping review of adoption research (Rushton, 2003) gave the following summary of educational problems:

These children will mostly carry their learning problems into their adoptive placements and schools, and new parents may have to cope with a lack of basic skills, slow educational progress, communication and concentration problems and to have to negotiate with schools over reports of difficult behaviour, poor relationships with peers and teachers. New parents may have to battle with the education system over obtaining psychological assessments and appropriate school placements, finding socially inclusive schools and educational help and advice. (p 23)

A study of children aged 5 – 9 at the time they were placed for adoption or in permanent foster care (Quinton *et al*, 1998) found that 80 per cent of the new parents considered that their child's level of ability was at least average, but most thought the child was under-achieving. Some children had difficulty in grasping particular concepts (for example, time or money), while others did not have age-appropriate basic skills such as reading and writing. Some parents felt their child was afraid of failing and tried to avoid challenging tasks. Disruptive behaviour and lack of concentration in class were also mentioned, and boys displayed significantly more problems at school than did girls. The following table shows how children's difficulties, as perceived by the new parents, changed during the first year of the placement: conceptual and reading problems improved but emotional and behavioural difficulties were more intransigent.

Table 17.1
The prevalence of educational difficulties at the start of the placement and 12 months later

Type of problem	1 month (n = 57)	12 months (n = 58)
Conceptual	16%	3%
Reading	32%	17%
Emotional	21%	22%
Behavioural	32%	29%

Source: Quinton *et al* (1998)

Educational difficulties can also be compounded by the common behavioural, emotional and social problems, which later adopted children are likely to show both at home and at school. The scoping review (Rushton, 2003) listed aggression, non-compliance, over-activity, lying and stealing, anxiety and fearfulness, and stated that some adopted children will have 'difficulty in showing warmth, expressing feelings, regulating their emotions and entering into close relationships' (p 22). Such problems may have an impact on the children's ability to form friendships and to enjoy being at school, and may increase their vulnerability to teasing and bullying.

Some factors have also been identified as being particularly predictive of poor outcomes: selective rejection by birth parents, over-activity, attachment difficulties and the extent of behavioural problems (Quinton *et al*, 1998; Selwyn *et al*, 2006).

Effects of children's educational needs on adopters and prospects of being adopted

A study of children adopted at older ages (Selwyn *et al*, 2006) showed how looked after children often have acute educational needs, which may jeopardise their chances of being adopted or present challenges for their adoptive parents. Children with learning difficulties were less likely to be adopted: a finding also reported by Baker (2006). A group of children who had particularly poor outcomes in Selwyn and colleagues' study were children who were described by their teachers as lacking curiosity and having no sense of wonder about the world or natural phenomena, such as storms or volcanoes. These children were not identified by social workers as needing particular help but all developed marked disturbances in their attachment behaviours and none were successfully placed for adoption.

The late-placed children in this study were reported to have multiple and overlapping needs, with speech and language delay a common problem. For a child starting school, the ability to communicate and be understood is vital to classroom learning, making friends and playing. However, prior to adoption, very few of the children received any intervention despite being on waiting lists. Many adoptive parents showed tremendous commitment to the children. Although support services were often difficult to identify and access, adopters spoke of "fighting for" the child to ensure difficulties were addressed. Other adopters wanted to compensate children for experiences they had missed. Consequently, one in eight of the adopters paid for private educational services such as an educational assessment or extra tuition.

Crises in the placement were often triggered by events at school such as an exclusion, and both adoption (Lowe *et al*, 1999) and foster care research (Sinclair, 2005) have shown that exclusion can place enormous pressure on carers and cause disruptions. However, exclusions and suspensions can be managed with good multi-agency support, and a recent practice innovation linking speech and language therapists with looked after children's teams should help to improve educational progress.

Educational outcomes of adopted children

The National Child Development Study (NCDS) tracked the progress of a cohort of over 17,000 children born in one week during 1958. It contains detailed data on the outcomes for these children and interestingly, in this cohort, just under four per cent of the children were illegitimately born, and of these a third (180) were adopted by non-relatives, while most (363) remained with their natural parent(s) (Maughan *et al*, 1998). Three-quarters of the adoptees were adopted under the age of three months, while a few experienced several previous changes of placement. It is important to remember that these infants were being adopted because of the stigma attached to illegitimacy unlike infants adopted today, who are primarily removed because of abuse and neglect.

The educational outcomes for the adoptees were very good when compared with their "birth comparisons" (illegitimate children who remained with their parents) and with a random sample of 2,872 other children in the study. Adopted children out-performed their birth comparisons on tests of maths and reading at age seven and on a measure of general ability at age 11, and their average achievement levels were comparable with those of most of their legitimate peers, and sometimes exceeded them. Their later attainments were also significantly higher than their birth peers and broadly comparable with other members of the cohort. The strongest predictors of attainment were teacher ratings of parental interest in education and assessments of the child's emotional and behavioural problems. Teachers rated 61 per cent of adoptive parents as "very interested" in their child's education, compared with 39 per cent in the general population sample and only 20 per cent in the birth comparison group (Maughan *et al*, 1998). These findings reinforce the likelihood of better outcomes for younger children but also draw our attention to the importance of interested adults who are committed to the child's welfare.

The advantage of "parental investment"

Research (Hamilton *et al*, 2007) based on data from the Early Childhood Longitudinal Study in the USA has found that adoptive parents "invest" in their children as much if not more than do biological parents. In their study, "parental investment" was defined not only in terms of economic resources (e.g. the provision of books, a computer, private education) but also cultural activities (e.g. reading to the child, playing games, out-of-school activities), interaction with the child (e.g. listening to the child, discussions, having meals together), and also social involvement with other parents, the child's school and religious groups. Analyses indicated that in almost all these respects adoptive parents "invested" more in their children than did other family types. This was partly due to their higher levels of income, education and older age, but when these characteristics were controlled for, an adoptive advantage still remained.

It is suggested that adoptive parents enrich their children's lives to compensate for their difficult start in life, their extra needs and the lack of biological ties. The NCDS study (Maughan *et al*, 1998), discussed earlier, has shown that parental interest in their child's education is generally associated with better outcomes. Whatever the reason, such parental commitment is likely to assist children's educational experience, attainment and self-esteem.

Conclusion

Looking at family placements overall in both fostering and adoption, a number of important messages emerge from this brief review of the research literature. Initially, education is clearly important in modern society, both as a passport to success but also to escape from early disadvantage. However, because of pre-care experiences, many fostered and adopted children will find education difficult, particularly those who have experienced neglect or abuse. Learning and behavioural problems may be evident, which will require a sensitive and skilled response from carers and professionals. Measures to prevent bullying should be in place in schools and carers should be alert to this as well.

Educational progress is linked with parental interest; and continuity, stability and predictability are especially important for children whose lives have been unsettled. These factors can increase children's resilience and enable positive change to occur.

Policies for children experiencing family breakdown have progressed in recent years and professionals are better aware of the educational difficulties for looked after children. Education is now a higher priority in social work decisions and there is better communication with schools. Effective communication with social workers and teachers is particularly important for foster carers and adoptive parents. Carers should take advantage of special educational needs (SEN) support and may need to be persistent to obtain assessments and access to resources.

These are some of the main conclusions from this chapter. But what is more striking is not so much the key messages but how little we actually know. Indeed, astonishingly, there appear to have been no major studies in the UK focusing specifically on the education of fostered or adopted children. There is also a lack of research on effective interventions with regard to behavioural problems, especially inattention and over-activity and attachment difficulties – problems which can have very adverse effects on children's experiences at school.

Research evidence is lacking especially on the *schools* dimension – how teachers respond to children's circumstances and to what effect. Most previous work has taken more of a social work perspective, yet much of the responsibility for educational progress lies within schools. Furthermore, we do not know enough about the use and effects of post-adoption support for families and how education fits into this. Given the particular vulnerability of fostered and adopted children, we have an obligation to develop better knowledge to guide our interventions.

Key considerations for practice

Some of the main implications for practice are as follows.

- Accurate assessment of all fostered and adopted children's abilities and developmental needs is essential at an early stage to ensure a) that appropriate services can be provided and b) that adopters and long-term foster carers, in particular, are not given false expectations and are better able to target their support for the child.
- As fostered and adopted children are likely to continue to have educational needs that overlap with a wide range of other health, identity, emotional and social needs, it is essential to arrange high-quality, multidisciplinary support. This support should continue for as long as necessary, even if the child becomes adopted.
- When preparing adopters, include information about the current school placement and arrange for them to meet key staff who know the child. The adoption placement plan should include support for new adopters in identifying pre-school placements and information about how the schools and teachers will liaise.
- Foster carers of children in permanent or long-term foster placements will need support in actively facilitating older children's education through adolescence and into further/higher education where appropriate.
- As well as moving between families, fostered and adopted children have often changed school/pre-school. These experiences should be included in any life appreciation or life story work. It is good practice to take photographs of the child's schools and to collect work produced by the child to be taken into placement.

- Fostered and adopted children sometimes have difficulties at school due to attachment and relationship difficulties, and the behavioural approaches of many schools may not suit these children. For useful information and advice on dealing with attachment-related difficulties in the classroom, see Bomber (2007).
- As parental interest and support are crucial in motivating children to learn and achieve, it may be beneficial for foster carers and adoptive parents to attend training on this. (BAAF and Southwark Children's Services [in London] are currently developing a programme to train foster carers to take a proactive role in meeting children's educational needs and specifically to support children in a home-based literacy scheme suitable for 5–11-year-olds.)
- Adopted and fostered children may need help in deciding how to respond to other children's questions about their family and to manage any experience of stigma or bullying. Teachers should also be aware that some topics (e.g. my family, family trees, genetics) can make these children feel uneasy and different.
- The positive effects on education of achieving permanency through adoption may be limited by the lack of resources for adoption as opposed to foster care. Local authorities need to address this issue when setting budgets – not just for initial adoption support for education, but for when adopted young people reach adolescence.
- The positive effects on education of achieving permanency through foster care can be limited by premature transitions to "independence" for fostered young people, who could benefit from continuing education. Leaving care practice needs to make education a priority.

We would like to thank Andrew Lister, Consultant Clinical Psychologist, and Kate O'Brien, Adoption Planning Manager at Bristol City Council, for contributing to these recommendations.

Selected further reading

Bomber L. (2007) *Inside I'm Hurting: Practical strategies for supporting children with attachment difficulties in school*, New York, NY: Worth Publishers Ltd

Hamilton L., Cheng S. and Powell B. (2007) 'Adoptive parents, adaptive parents: Evaluating the importance of biological ties for parental investment', *American Sociological Review*, 72, pp 95–116

Harker R., Dobel-Ober D., Berridge D. and Sinclair R. (2004) *Taking Care of Education: An evaluation of the education of looked after children*, London: National Children's Bureau

Wilson K., Sinclair I., Taylor C., Pithouse A. and Sellick C. (2004) *Fostering Success: An exploration of the research literature in foster care*, London: SCIE

References

Baker C. (2007) 'Disabled children's experience of permanency in the looked after system', *British Journal of Social Work*, 37, pp 1173–1188

Beckett, C., Maughan, B., Rutter, M., Castle, J., and the ERA team (2006) 'Do the effects of early severe deprivation on cognition persist into early adolescence? Findings from the English and Romanian adoptees study', *Child Development*, 2006, 77:3, pp 696–711

Beckett C., Maughan B., Rutter M., Castle J. and the ERA team (2007) 'Scholastic attainment following severe early institutional deprivation: A study of children adopted from Romania', *Journal of Abnormal Psychology*, 35, pp 1063–1073

Berridge D. (2007) 'Theory and explanation in child welfare: Education and looked after children', *Child & Family Social Work*, 12, pp 1–10

Bomber L. (2007) *Inside I'm Hurting: Practical strategies for supporting children with attachment difficulties in school*, New York, NY: Worth Publishers Ltd

Cassen R. and Kingdon G. (2007) *Tackling Low Educational Achievement*, York: Joseph Rowntree Foundation

Cheesbrough S. (2002) *The Educational Attainment of People Who Have Been in Care*, London: Department of Social Policy, London School of Economics

Chugani H., Behen M., Muzik O., Juhasz C., Nagy F. and Chugani D. (2001) 'Local brain functional activity following early deprivation', *NeuroImage*, 14, pp 1290–1301

Department for Education and Skills (2004) *Removing Barriers to Achievement: The Government's Strategy for SEN*, London: DfES

Hamilton L., Cheng S. and Powell B. (2007) 'Adoptive parents, adaptive parents: Evaluating the importance of biological ties for parental investment', *American Sociological Review*, 72, pp 95–116

Harker R., Dobel-Ober D., Berridge D. and Sinclair R. (2004) *Taking Care of Education: An evaluation of the education of looked after children*, London: National Children's Bureau

Howe D. (2005) *Child Abuse and Neglect: Attachment, development and intervention*, Basingstoke: Palgrave

Ijzendoorn M. and Juffer F. (2006) 'The Emmanuel Miller Memorial Lecture. Adoption as intervention: Meta-analysis evidence for massive catch-up and plasticity in physical, socio-emotional and cognitive development', *Journal of Child Psychology and Psychiatry*, 47, pp 1228–1245

Jackson S. (2007) 'Progress at last?', *Adoption & Fostering*, 31:1, pp 3–5. (There are other interesting articles in this special edition of *Adoption & Fostering* on education.)

Jackson S., Ajayi S. and Quigley M. (2005) *Going to University from Care*, London: Institute of Education

Jackson S. and Martin P. (1998) 'Surviving the care system: Education and resilience', *Journal of Adolescence*, 21, pp 569–583

Lansford J., Ceballo A., Abbey A. and Stewart A. (2001) 'Does family structure matter?' *Journal of Marriage and the Family*, 63, pp 840–851

Lowe N., Murch M., Borkowski M., Weaver A. and Beckford V. with Thomas C. (1999) *Supporting Adoption*, London: BAAF

Maughan B., Collishaw S. and Pickles A. (1998) 'School achievement and adult qualifications among adoptees: A longitudinal study', *Journal of Child Psychology and Psychiatry*, 39:5, pp 669–685

Nurture Group Network (2007) *Introduction to Nurture Groups*, http://www.nurturegroups.org/ Accessed on 6 July 2007

Performance and Innovation Unit (PIU) (2000) *The Prime Minister's Review of Adoption*, London: Cabinet Office

Pinderhughes E. (1998) 'Short term outcomes for children adopted after age five', *Children and Youth Services Review*, 20, pp 223–249

Quinton D., Rushton A., Dance C. and Nayes D. (1998) *Joining New Families: A study of adoption and fostering in middle childhood*, Chichester: John Wiley and Sons Ltd

Roy P., Rutter M. and Pickles A. (2000) 'Institutional care: Risk from family background or pattern of rearing', *Journal of Child Psychology and Psychiatry*, 41:2, pp 73–80

Rushton A. (2003) *The Adoption of Looked After Children: A scoping review of research*, Knowledge Review 2, Social Care Institute for Excellence. Bristol: The Policy Press

Rutter M. and Smith D. (1995) *Psychosocial Disorders in Young People: Time trends and their causes*, Chichester: Wiley

Selwyn J., Sturgess W., Quinton D. and Baxter C. (2006) *Costs and Outcomes of Non-Infant Adoptions*, London: BAAF

Sinclair I. (ed) (2005) *Fostering Now: Messages from research*, London: Jessica Kingsley Publishers

Wilson K., Sinclair I., Taylor C., Pithouse A. and Sellick C. (2004) *Fostering Success: An exploration of the research literature in foster care*, London: SCIE

18 Placing disabled children with permanent new families: Linking and matching

Jennifer Cousins

Who are the children?

There is very little formal consensus about what constitutes "disability" but, nonetheless, family-finders across the UK seem fairly sure that disabled children are "hard to place". However imprecise the term, when social workers talk about disabled children, they seem to know whom they mean.

The lack of definition is both problematic and liberating. On the one hand, service planning requires that numbers be counted and degrees of impairment be estimated; on the other hand, any child whose difference from the physical or intellectual norm prevents their having a permanent family is truly disabled. Certainly the merest mention of the term disability seems to give children a special untouchable status and to prevent many prospective carers from contemplating such a child. The term is generic and taboo-ridden, and people can be so deterred that they never move beyond the label to see something of the real, individual child. When tackling the barriers which prevent finding families for these so called hard to place children, it is the contention of this chapter that therein lies both the main problem – and a solution. Children must not be assigned to a separate category called disability: they must be seen and treated as individuals.

Despite definitional ambiguities, and a serious lack of comprehensive data (Read and Harrison, 2002), some attempt at describing the scale of the issue may be helpful. From the general population, disabled children are nine times more likely to become looked after than their not-disabled peers (Department of Health, 1998, p 11), though disability is only given as the *principal* reason for entering care in four per cent of looked after children (Department for Children, Schools and Families, 2008). In other words, a disproportionately large percentage of disabled children become looked after, but primarily for reasons other than disability (Gordon *et al*, 2000; Department for Education and Skills, 2005). Perhaps not surprisingly, 80 per cent of these children who enter care primarily through disability (probably the most profoundly and multiply disabled) are accommodated under Section 20 of the 1989 Children Act. Unfortunately there are no available data about the legal status of the much larger total number of looked after children who are disabled – that is, disabled children whose reason for entry to care also includes abuse or neglect. If accommodated children with high levels of complexity eventually need permanent new families, the involvement in the process of birth parents, as sole holders of parental responsibility, can be a crucial factor. It would therefore be very useful to know how many disabled children are looked after on a voluntary basis, and how many are on legal orders.

Gordon estimates that about a quarter of looked after children are disabled (Gordon *et al*, 2000), with the most profoundly affected being in foster care. According to Triseliotis *et al* (2000), about one in six short-term foster carers (in Scotland) looks after a disabled child.

Looking now at the smaller group of disabled looked after children who cannot return home and need a permanent placement, reliable data are also difficult to establish and compare. Readers should be alert to whether statistics relate specifically to adoption or fostering or the generic "permanence" (often used to mean both adoption and permanent fostering); waiting for placement, placed or adopted; and what level of impairment is being described. What follows illustrates the problem.

It is thought that between four and seven per cent of children placed for adoption have a "significant disability" (Rushton and Dance, 2002, p 69; Simon and Dance, 2006, p 1), while Ivaldi (2000, p 3) found that of children who had been adopted, 40 per cent had a 'developmental or learning difficulty, medical problem or hereditary risk' (a broader definition). Simon and Dance's local authority study of 479 disabled children needing permanence in 1998/9 found that they represented 11 per cent of all children *placed* for long-term fostering and 11 per cent of all children *awaiting* a "permanent" placement.

Of children referred for permanence to BAAF's family-finding services, 40 per cent were described as having a "learning difficulty, medical problem and/or physical impairment" (Collier *et al*, 2000, p 12); while Cousins (2006, p 58) also reported that 40 per cent of the children whose profiles she examined in *Be My Parent* appeared to have 'some degree of impairment or "special need"' (again, using quite broad definitions).

Generally, the legal status of disabled children who need permanence may reflect the trend already noted. Simon and Dance (2006) show that only 18 per cent were accommodated under Section 20 of the 1989 Children Act.

In trying to understand the general profile of disabled children either placed or waiting for permanent new families, Simon and Dance (2006, p 2) found that many disabled children were under six years old, nearly two-thirds were boys (compared to 55% of all looked after children) and most (83%) were white. Ivaldi's larger survey (which focused specifically on adoptions) found that children under two-and-a-half with developmental difficulties (especially single boys) wait a long time; and children with severe medical problems wait twice as long as others – particularly boys and children over two-and-a-half. Learning-disabled children present the most difficulties to family finders (Ivaldi, 2000; Collier *et al*, 2000). It appears that young children whose development is uncertain may not fit either the expectations of the small number of adults seeking positively to adopt a disabled child, or those who only want a "straightforward" child.

From the adopters' perspective, fewer prospective adoptive families intentionally come forward for children with learning difficulties than for other disabled children. Only 13 per cent of adopters in Ivaldi's study said hypothetically that they could take a child with a "mental disability", 21 per cent said they could take a child with a physical disability, and 47 per cent a medical condition, whereas they were much less deterred by a history of sexual and physical abuse (Ivaldi, 2000). There are no similar data about children and families for whom permanent foster care rather than adoption is the preferred route. This would be very useful to know.

It is frustrating not to have robust information about the disabled children in state care – their legal status, their living arrangements, their trajectory through care and, most importantly, how long they wait for a permanent new family. This represents a huge gap in government statistics. The overall picture which emerges from the few data available is that there seem to be a significant number of disabled children waiting; and that the predominant profile may be young white boys who are mostly on care orders. Sadly, families who positively want to offer a home to these children seem to be few and far between.

Family finding: the current situation

There are many examples of good practice in family finding, but identifying placements for all the children who need them is challenging and, at times, disheartening. Too often the system is over-bureaucratic and dogged by lack of resources and endemic weariness. This needs to be tackled. Even in optimum conditions, sensible planning and imaginative practice on behalf of children can falter, despite the goodwill and commitment of those involved. New strategies need to be developed which energise the workforce and lead to better success in placing children, particularly those disabled children who wait too long for a family.

There is little research available about the processes of matching children with families, although a study commissioned as part of the Adoption Research Initiative is expected soon (Farmer, forthcoming). As has been argued elsewhere (Cousins, 2003), the methods used by agencies in establishing links between children and carers are in need of updating. Research by Selwyn *et al* (2006) shows that, of 130 children aged between three and eleven who had a "best interest" decision for adoption, over a quarter were not placed for adoption and 12 per cent went on to have very disrupted lives. These are compelling statistics. On the one hand, it is encouraging that the majority of children, all with complex backgrounds, were placed; on the other hand, it is of concern that a significant minority were not. It is not known what percentage of these children was disabled. If anyone doubts the need to find additional ways to create the link between children and new families, these data should provide the spur to action.

Linking and matching

In terms of family finding, the words "linking" and "matching" are often used either inter-changeably, or as one process: "linking-and-matching". However, these can be concept-ualised as two distinct stages. Adding the notion of "compatibility" may also be helpful:

The link can be described as the initial step in thinking that this family may be suitable for this child: the point when out of all the families and all the children, the two halves are first placed side by side.

Compatibility is the process of carefully examining whether a particular child's needs could be met by these carers; whether the family's needs could be met by the child; whether the family will be robust enough to remain committed throughout childhood and beyond, and what supports might be needed to ensure this.

The match is the outcome of this considered assessment: the decision that *this* child and *this* family are indeed suited to each other, and that the connection should be formalised.

As will be explored below, social workers' skills and responsibilities may be more appropriately directed at the latter two stages rather than at the point of linking. But social workers do have a huge responsibility in preparing helpful and complete information about the child in order to generate the link, however that link is to be achieved.

THE LINK (i)
Links managed by social workers

The traditional model for family finding has been based on the social worker taking the lead and managing the linking process, assessing compatibility and making the match. For social workers to make the link, children have to be characterised by a shortlist of what are thought to be relevant factors. Similarly, families are identified by the "kind of child" they have expressed an interest in – usually based on some hypothetical construct. The process is almost certain to highlight some characteristics over others and often these are based on stereotypes and commonly available labels. In worst-case scenarios, families are identified as being able to take "a disabled child" (or, more commonly, not); and children become labelled as "vision-impaired", "autistic", "epileptic" and so on. These labels come to dominate the family-finding process, however partial they are in describing the child as a complete person.

This method of the social worker controlling the linking process, though somewhat serendipitous, is commonplace and not without its successes. The differing methodologies are probably determined by the size and structure of the agency, the numbers and ethnicity of children and potential families, and the age of the children. In small agencies this may be a largely informal process (one family finder reported that if he was placing a baby, he would just choose the family he preferred and take the match to panel without involving colleagues). In larger agencies, family finders are sometimes assigned to particular child-care teams and learn which children are likely to need permanence in the near future; these family finders may also personally know a number of prospective carers. This knowledge is then shared with colleagues at linking/matching meetings where several profiles of children and prospective families can be considered. If in-house resources are exhausted, profiles can then be exchanged between agencies, and referred to the Adoption Register, BAAF's *Be My Parent*, and Adoption UK's *Children Who Wait*. It is widely acknowledged that the requirement to pay interagency fees deters some agencies from looking outside their own resources.

What is certain is that the further from the source the child's and family's profiles go, the more important their quality becomes as there is limited opportunity, especially in the crucial early stages, to expand on what can appear as stark and abbreviated facts. This is especially crucial for disabled children.

Social workers who consider families for a particular child often have an idea of the kind of family they are looking for. This should be based on assessment and evidence. The difficulty with this approach is that the identified characteristics, for example, 'it must be a two-parent family', 'the child must be the only child', 'the family must have experience of disability', can both help as well as unnecessarily limit the range of families identified as suitable. It may even deny some children a family altogether. Unless there is evidence to support the legitimate application of such constraints in respect of a particular child, there is a strong argument that they should not be used, especially where very few families are likely to be available to offer the child a home. It is an uncomfortable truth in family placement work that for some children there may be many choices of family, and for some, very few indeed. It is not in the long-term interests of these particularly disadvantaged children to have the chances of a permanent home reduced still further for no good reason. It is essential to be flexible about what different individuals and families may have to offer.

Links generated through the Adoption Register

The Adoption Register has made a significant contribution to finding families for children in recent years. The Register has demonstrated that, with a combination of a well-established computer database and trained Register staff, potential links can and do emerge that lead to children being placed, even some disabled children. Between December 2004 and September 2007, the Register made the initial link between 433 children and their subsequent adopters. In 2006 alone, 33 children who had "developmental delay or uncertainty" were placed – heartening, given the usual difficulties in linking these particular children; but, as the introduction to the 2006 Annual Report says, 'we still need to work harder together to find more adopters who positively want to adopt . . . children with disabilities' (Department for Education and Skills, 2007). Regrettably, the Adoption Register is not designed to accept either children or families who want permanence through foster care – only adoption; nor is it a resource for Scotland and Northern Ireland.

The computer-generated links are only the first stage of this particular method, and what happens next is controlled by the child's social worker once she or he receives potential links from the Register. Occasionally, the worker's own values prevent a subsequent match. Single people, in particular, tend to be screened out at this stage: during 2006, 156 single adopters were referred to the Register, but only 16 children were finally matched with them. It is a common view that children need two parents despite all the evidence that children can fare well with a single carer (Owen, 1999; Betts, 2007) and that waiting in a limbo of uncertainty for some ideal link is hugely damaging. For disabled adults to be seen as suitable adopters is even more difficult, as what they offer is frequently obscured by a stereotyped view of their limitations. Research on disabled approved carers is almost completely lacking.

Summary
A process which relies upon third parties (social workers) acting as brokers between children-who-wait and potential families requires that social workers should know everything about the child and the approved families, have a well developed linking methodology and remain value-neutral. What this method cannot do is access families who are currently outside the system or pin-point those human, interpersonal connections which only the key players recognise.

On a simplistic level, the two distinct processes have been likened to computer dating or arranged marriages, versus falling in love. This does not mean that falling-in-love cannot develop from the former (clearly it does): but with a direct connection between family and child which is not brokered by third parties, unexpected, deep attachments can emerge which are not pre-planned. These direct connections are explored below.

In summary, it is evident that the linking methods controlled by social workers are, to varying degrees, successful in linking children with new families. But if over a quarter of 3–11-year-olds for whom adoption was intended were never placed for adoption (and even though some eventually found permanence through fostering), something more needs to happen. No one method will suffice, and clearly, processes managed by social work staff are not the whole answer. A menu of possibilities should be developed, including those where links are generated by the prospective carers themselves: the direct approach.

THE LINK (ii)
Direct links

The second broad method of linking is where the initial connection between child and family is generated not by social work staff but by the prospective permanent carers and adopters themselves. There are various vehicles which help this to happen: family-finding newspapers, the internet, exchange events, video profiling events, "activity days" and adoption parties or placement parties*. In each instance, the prospective carers are enabled to respond directly to material about the child – or indeed to the child him/herself. The social work role at this point is enabler and supporter rather than broker.

Newspapers and magazines

Since 1980, BAAF has produced the family-finding newspaper *Be My Parent* (BMP). Initially a photo-listing loose-leaf book available in agencies, in 1990 BMP became a newspaper which, with a print-run of 4,300 copies, features between two and three hundred children each month who need permanent families. Approximately 1,300 people subscribe to BMP – mainly prospective families. In 2005–06, BMP was responsible for the permanent placement of 236 children, and found that black and minority ethnic children, in particular, were placed through being featured in this way. Crucially, *Be My Parent* and Adoption UK's magazine *Children Who Wait* reach a wide readership of people who are not necessarily approved as carers or adopters or part of the system.

Newspapers such as this are demonstrably an important tool in the linking process:

> *I saw the girls in Be My Parent and knew these were the ones. They looked like me and my family and it was almost as if I wanted a sign or a signal and my middle name is Emily, and they shouted at me out of the page instantly. I looked at them and thought 'I want them, I want them', and it was really exciting because I knew these were the ones and it felt right. I wanted to be a part of them instantly.* (from Selwyn *et al*, 2006, p 80)

A further family-finding tool is *Be My Parent Online*, which went live in 2007 and currently features approximately 160 children. This online facility gives extended opportunities to feature children not only through the traditional profiles, but also with children's artwork, several photographs in different settings, foster carers' accounts and short film-clips. Many more aspects of the child can be featured than through paper-based methods. In terms of disability, the effects of the impairment can be shown and discussed in the context of the whole child.

---

*"Adoption parties" was a name used in the 1980s in the UK. Re-evaluation of these events suggests that a more appropriate term for current use is "placement parties" (to encompass both adoption and permanent fostering).

Exchange events

Several consortia of agencies have begun to run special exchange events where they feature some of their waiting children and invite all their approved adopters and carers to view the material. Each agency has a stall, staffed with family placement and marketing officers, showing individualised material about each child they are promoting – photographs, posters, artwork and so on. The potential families circulate around the room to view the children's material and talk to staff. Sometimes a small laptop film about a child is available to view on the stall. Staff are available to talk in detail about any child whom the prospective carers feel they respond to.

The Adoption Register also runs these events across the country, with considerable success, particularly the specialised events aimed at placing black and minority ethnic children. In 2006, two such exchange days resulted in the placement of 22 children from the Register. General events run in conjunction with local consortia have also led to children being placed for adoption and as many as 18 children who were not on the Register have been placed by agencies as a result of a single day's event.

Exchange events not only contribute to making placements for children, but also give prospective carers and adopters a taste of the reality of finding a suitable match.

Video / DVD profiling events

These events are similar to exchange days but use a cinema-style presentation to show short film-clips of each child to the whole "audience". They are founded on work developed in the 1980s by Parents for Children and are now embraced enthusiastically by many local authorities. Northamptonshire call them "Parents for Children" evenings, and include prospective permanent foster carers as well as adopters; and Adoption in the Black Country use the term "Meet the Children". However, "video profiling" will be used here as it conveys that video/DVD footage is key to this method.

The film-clips are normally no more than two-to-three minutes long and the most effective have an edited voiceover (often by the foster carer) that talks about the child in as much detail as appropriate. Probably no more than twenty or so films can usefully be shown in one evening, and it seems most effective when a good range of children are featured. If the audience is predominantly from a particular minority ethnic group, children from these communities must be presented.

Potential adopters and carers come to the meeting by invitation only. Some agencies welcome carers who have completed the initial processes; others invite only approved carers. The advantage of inviting people early in the approval process (though not too early) is that, should a possible link emerge, the family's assessment can be fast-tracked. In this case, as the family goes through the home study, much discussion will centre upon the needs of the child in question and the family's emerging views about parenting this particular young person. Specific support needs can also be identified realistically.

However, should it become clear that this is not the child for them, their approval, once finalised, would still stand: they are not tied to this child.

A competitive element may be unavoidable, but with sensitive support from staff, most people are able to cope with a process which must be focused on what is right for each child.

Most agencies that have run these events are keen to continue, and some claim that the method is both successful and cost-effective. A bonus for Gateshead was the feedback showing that not only had 100 per cent of participants enjoyed the evening, but 40 per cent said they would now consider adopting an older child or sibling group because of the event (an additional 40 per cent were already considering such children). Through three meetings run by Adoption in the Black Country, 10 children were placed, a number of whom had some form of disability, and including three sibling groups. Northamptonshire have run these events since 2001 and have placed nearly three-quarters of the children featured (171 out of 235), with an average disruption rate of only three per cent.

Some agencies are sufficiently large to operate solo; some work alongside neighbouring agencies and share the task. The films can be used for a variety of purposes as well as this meeting: a shortened clip can be referred to *Be My Parent Online* and the longer film can be used more reflectively with the prospective family. Finally, the films form an important item in the child's memory box, providing a record of their time in foster care. Specially made videos/DVDs can be commissioned through *See Me Films* (www.bemyparent.org.uk).

Families who see videos of children have said that they "recognise" the right child at first sight: maybe a child who has a tiny mannerism which reminds them of a family member – something so subtle that this would never be noted in a formal process orchestrated by social workers. The power of film in linking children with families is not yet exploited to the full.

Activity days and adoption parties/placement parties
Activity days are where families and children who are each "waiting" all meet each other:

It is possible . . .to organise an outing for a group of children who need families, and to prepare a group of families to join children in a day of activities. These activities may involve nothing more than playing in a soft environment, sharing meals, going for a walk and keeping tired children occupied. (Argent and Kerrane, 1997, p 34)

Argent's former agency, Parents for Children, held these events in the 1980s (Argent, 1986). A variation was the so called adoption parties run co-operatively by three agencies: Voice, BAAF and Adoption UK (all now renamed as given here). As the title suggests, these were real children's parties with games and ice cream – the difference being that the children and young people all needed new families and the adult helpers were hoping to become adopters. These initiatives were very successful in making links and were only phased out when family-finding developments such as *Be My Parent* took off. In the USA, adoption picnics or adoption parties have been widely used for twenty years and, despite a tiny minority being criticised for resembling beauty contests, are in many states a well-managed, well-respected and effective means of achieving a link.

If prospective carers come to any event with an open mind and then just respond to an individual young person whom they meet face to face, an unexpected placement may emerge. With this very direct method, the child becomes known to the prospective carer as a real person who happens to have a specific difficulty.

I'd always wanted to adopt . . . I never thought about disability till I saw the photos of disabled children who needed families . . . then I was invited to an Activity Day to meet some of the children. They said 'When Adam comes we'd like you to sit with him and give him lunch' . . . I wasn't too happy about it.

Adam was the last one to arrive and they brought him over to me in his wheelchair and left him with me . . . Oh my goodness! So I picked him up and put him on my lap and he got hold of my hand and he moved it to the table and I gave him some food. He put it in his mouth and I looked at him and I said: 'Oh he's lovely'. That was it really; I was just gone. (Argent, 1998, p 5)

This adopter had an open mind about what kind of child she wanted and simply responded spontaneously.

It is not impossible that at such events, young people themselves gravitate towards particular adults. Nothing would be more powerful than prospective carers feeling that they were being chosen by the child.

Short-term arrangements which become permanent

The final way in which a direct connection happens is through the serendipitous emergence of permanent relationships from short-term placements. It is known that many temporary fostering arrangements later and with due consideration become adoption, permanent fostering or special guardianship. In fact, one of the unexpected outcomes from the video profiling events is said to be foster carers suddenly realising that they do not wish to lose the child whom they are being asked to prepare for a move.

A study which began in 2003 followed the fortunes of 18 of the most profoundly disabled children who were featured for permanence in *Be My Parent* during one month of that year (Cousins, 2006, pp 58–64). One child subsequently went home. Over the next 18 months, during which enquiries were periodically updated, ten of the 17 remaining children were placed permanently with their existing foster carer/s; this included six who were adopted by them, which was over a third.

Figure 1

Outcomes for 18 profoundly disabled children in the 18 months after being featured in *Be My Parent*. Seventeen were originally featured for adoption, of whom four could alternatively be placed with permanent foster carers

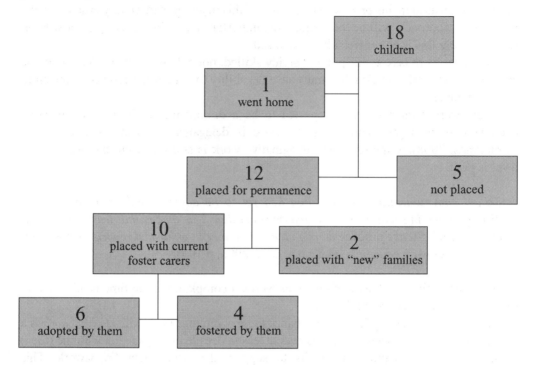

These were largely serendipitous links, often made by chance in a crisis and intended to last mere days or weeks; one or two had been short-break arrangements. It is significant how many became permanent: nearly sixty per cent. Schofield *et al* (2000, p 67) explore this phenomenon in some detail (in relation to all children) and use the term "chemistry". These are not the matches made as a paper exercise in the cold light of adoption panels, but love affairs which spring up unexpectedly, develop over time and become committed relationships. Some of the carers said they would not, if asked in advance, have chosen a disabled child, but came to form a strong and loving bond with the child in spite of all the complexities. The carers and adopters quoted here are acknowledging impairment in the context of a child who is as varied and ordinary as any other: a real child, not a label, a diagnosis or a condition.

If chances are to be maximised for children to have permanent families, this more direct approach, through a variety of means, must be exploited.

The material about the child

Before discussing the next phase of the process, namely the assessment of compatibility (the match), attention is drawn to the vital issue of the child's profile and the other material to be used in this process. The quality of this material, particularly crucial for the more direct approach, will be the single most important factor in achieving permanence. Unfortunately this is not universally recognised.

The social work task at this point is highly skilled: not only must the worker know the child extremely well, but also they must have the ability to convey the essence of the child to other people.

Direct work with children is reported to be a diminishing skill as social workers become case managers, and life story work is delegated to social work assistants (Simmonds, 2008). Some excellent, imaginative work is still done, but the overall skill level is poor.

> *Skilled communication with children has yet to be consolidated as a distinct and discrete topic in social work research or education. This means that frustratingly few examples of effective practice can be identified either in published reports or contemporary social work education.* (Luckock *et al*, 2006, p 105)

Even training fails to solve the problem as workers complain that no time is allocated to this complex and often painful work.

Several tools have been devised to enhance these communication skills. *In My Shoes* is a computer-assisted interview developed over at least a decade in conjunction with the (then) Department for Education and Skills to support the Assessment Framework. This programme enables worker and child to explore together important events and relationships in the child's life. As part of a small research project managed by BAAF, social workers observed their looked after child using the programme with the *In My Shoes* psychologist and were universally impressed by the additional information they gleaned. They said:

> *It's amazing what level of detail I learned about her.*

> *I didn't realise he was that intelligent, but he came across as just a lovely little boy.*

> *I now see that she is very confused about her birth family.*

> *We had been saying "mild autistic" – this put people off. But he was very engaged in the process – articulate and made loads of eye contact.*

Tools such as this enhance the worker's capacity to understand children in a way that feeds directly into the planning and matching process. Again, it is irresponsible to take major life-changing decisions for children who are unknown quantities.

In My Shoes is restricted to practitioners who have completed a two-day training course (Calam *et al*, 2005).

Profiles

The first and most important stage therefore is that the worker should really know and understand their child. The second task is to represent the child in as engaging a way as possible – of particular importance where the link is to be generated by the prospective carers. It has been discussed above that if the profile is heavily prescriptive, many potential families will rule themselves out immediately. Further basic rules for effective profile writing can be found in Cousins (2008, pp 72–75 and Argent (2002)).

Photographs

It is probably not an exaggeration to say that the right photograph can make or break a child's chance of finding a family.

A subscriber survey conducted by *Be My Parent* (2004) showed that 82 per cent of respondents said that the photographs of the children were important when deciding whether to make an enquiry about a child, and a quarter said it made a big difference.

Photographs are so powerful that experts should ideally be involved: but professionals must be given the right brief. There are too many studio shots of children that are so formulaic that all individuality is ironed out.

A professional photographer decided to expand her family by adopting a child from foster care. She was taken aback by the lifeless "mug shots" that the agency used . . . (National Adoption Day 2005)

Videos/films

Film material is arguably the best way to convey a child, and agencies are beginning to use short films to help generate the link (see above). But again the quality is crucial. Indoor film footage shot towards a window when it is impossible to make out the child's features; where there are distracting shots of the floor and the ceiling, and dizzying tracking shots as the child rushes round and the camera tries to keep up; where extraneous noise from the television and front door bell gets in the way of listening to the child or foster carer; or where fancy editing distracts the viewer – all of these detract from the central intention of the film.

Social workers seem to resist using professional photographers and film makers. Apart from the costs, there is a view that professional might mean unnatural, glossy, stilted and child-unfriendly – but a film maker will know how to engage the child so that the final product is a natural portrayal of this individual young person. It may indeed all look so natural that the process is assumed to be easy to replicate, though this is not the case. For agencies which will not use professionals, *Be My Parent* has produced helpful guidelines for video-making (www.bemyparent.org.uk).

Using film footage is vital for the disabled child. The film may draw attention more explicitly than other media to the consequences of a child's impairment and while some viewers will feel they cannot take on the extra issues which this particular impairment brings, others will realise that they could indeed cope with this child.

In a film, disability can be presented as a *part* of a child and not as the whole story. One short film shows a little girl playing happily in a variety of domestic settings. About half way through the film when she runs across the park it suddenly strikes the viewer that she has a slightly lop-sided gait. The voiceover (the foster carer) says that the child's cerebral palsy has very little impact on daily living. Had the child's disability been signalled at the start, or were it mentioned in a profile without the film, it would have dominated the viewers' perception of her and diminished her appeal as an ordinary and lovely little girl.

The argument here is that all material used to portray the child must be of the highest quality. Only then are children being given the best possible chance of finding a family.

The match

It was suggested earlier that linking and matching can be conceptualised as two distinct processes. Adoption outcome research shows that, once the link is made, matches made on the basis of social work assessments lead to reasonably successful long-term relationships (Selwyn *et al*, 2006). However, although it could be argued that the biggest challenge to placing more disabled children is largely located at the linking rather than the matching stage, the fact that prospective families may be drawn into the process through an increasingly wide variety of linking methods would seem to justify strengthening the next stages – the compatibility assessment leading to the recommendation of the match.

Matching methodology in the UK is non-standardised, and agencies have developed their own ways to evaluate the potential fit. Some have a matrix with, on the one hand, a list of the child's needs set against the potential family's ability to meet each need. This can be fine-tuned through grading the importance of each "need" and the degree to which the family is likely to respond satisfactorily. For example, the child may have essential needs around ethnicity, disability, location; and the proposed family might be able to meet these needs completely, adequately or not at all (Byrne, 2000, p 27).

What is largely unexplored is the issue of the prospective carer's motivation and needs. It is known that the best outcomes are where the adults have realistic expectations (McRoy, 1999) and it is thought that the most secure matches are those where adults' expectations (as well as children's needs) are broadly met. Focusing explicitly on the needs of adults and other prospective family members during the assessment process may prove valuable in clarifying to what extent their own needs will affect their ability to respond to the child's needs. For example, a family who have less need for "ownership" may be more relaxed with a child who takes many months to respond to their affection. Developmental psychology shows that parents and children shape each other, so considering what both the new family and the child will be able to *give to* and *take from* the new relationship may be helpful. This attention to reciprocity must not of course detract from professional commitment to foregrounding the needs of children. No one wants a return to the days where adoption was primarily about meeting the needs of adults rather than finding families for children.

Further examples of adults' needs, some of which will be particularly relevant for the placement of disabled children, might be:

- the need for affection to be reciprocated
- the need for the child to fit in with current lifestyle
- the needs of existing children in the family
- the need for developmental certainty in the child
- the need for the child to become independent eventually
- the need for the child to succeed educationally

Issues such as these would emerge as part of the home study, and be weighted for importance, perhaps including the impact of the adult's attachment style (Green, 2003). At the matching stage, a judgement would be made about the extent to which the identified child might be likely to meet each particular need. Whether introducing a scoring system would be helpful is a debate yet to be had.

Support needs

Placing disabled children successfully into a new family who will give a lifetime's commitment requires the promise of resources beyond the comfort zone of most budget-holders. Even if simple finance were the only issue, it must be accepted that it is at least three times more costly to raise a disabled than a not-disabled child (Miller, 2002). Other post-placement supports must also be advertised and delivered. Participants at a recent training session constructed the following lightning list of what "support" really should mean:

Finance – education – health provision – medical information – short breaks – equipment – transport – housing / extensions – "sitting" & overnight service – parents' groups – newsletter – days out – individual mentoring/buddying – after-school clubs – telephone lines for crisis help – domestic help – access to professionals & other carers – help with contact – help for birth children – services into adulthood – support to grandparents – advice and information – training – signposting – relaxation classes – massages – annual fun-days . . .

This list may constitute a counsel of perfection, but if families are to be encouraged to take disabled children, supports such as these must be available, spelled out clearly, and signalled right from the start.

Beyond the match

Much of the process beyond the family-finding stage is little different for disabled children than for the not-disabled. Indeed, any prescription for 'what to do when placing a disabled child' goes against the principle of individuality. Planning the introductions and the move must always be focused on the needs of an individual child – so taking account of communication, mobility, learning or sensory difficulties should be a routine part of any sensitive assessment.

Conclusion

Focusing on the needs of the individual child brings the discussion back to where it started. All children, including those with impairments, have a right to be seen as unique individuals. They also have a right to a family – and to make that more likely, potential families must be shown through every means possible that each child is more than a mere label or diagnosis.

Disabled children are not somehow a separate category of child, to be thought about differently and planned for differently. They need to be included in every aspect of family placement practice. What they also need is imaginative family-finding strategies that push the boundaries and extend opportunities. Policy makers, service managers and practitioners all need to think outside the usual ways of working. This is not always comfortable.

Selected further reading

Cousins J. (2006) *Every Child is Special: Placing disabled children for permanence*, London: BAAF

Phillips R. (1998) 'Disabled children in permanent substitute families', in Robson C. and Stalker K. (eds) *Growing up with Disability*, London: Jessica Kingsley Publishers

References

Argent H. (1986) 'A special programme for special children', *Community Care*, 24 July 1986

Argent H. (1998) *Whatever Happened to Adam? Stories of disabled people who were adopted or fostered*, London: BAAF

Argent H. (2002) *Profiling Children*, Practice Note 41, London: BAAF

Argent H. and Kerrane A. (1997) *Taking Extra Care: Respite, shared and permanent care for children with disabilities*, London: BAAF

Be My Parent (2004) *Be My Parent Subscriber Survey 2004*, London: BAAF

Betts B. (2007) *A Marginalised Resource? Recruiting, assessing and supporting single carers*, Good Practice Guide, London: BAAF

Byrne S. (2000) *Linking and Introductions: Helping children join adoptive families*, Good Practice Guide, London: BAAF

Calam R., Cox A., Glasgow D., Jimmieson P. and Groth Larsen S. (2005) *In My Shoes: A computer assisted interview for communicating with children and vulnerable adults: User guide*, York, Child & Family Training (Available via training course: contact liza.miller@btinternet.com)

Collier F., Hutchinson B. and Pearmain J. (2000) *Linking Children with Adoptive Parents: Messages from a review of BAAF's national family-finding services*, London: BAAF

Cousins J. (2003) 'Are we missing the match? Rethinking adopter assessment and child profiling', *Adoption & Fostering*, 27:4, London: BAAF, pp 7–18

Cousins J. (2006) *Every Child is Special: Placing disabled children for permanence*, London: BAAF

Cousins J. (2008) *Ten Top Tips for Finding Families for Children*, London: BAAF

Department for Children, Schools and Families (2008) *National Statistics First Release* (England) 16 September 2008

Department for Education and Skills (2005) *National Statistics Bulletin: Statistics of education: Children looked after in England (including adoptions and care leavers): 2003–2004*, London: The Stationery Office

Department for Education and Skills (2007) *Adoption Register for England and Wales: Annual Report 2006*, London: Department for Education and Skills

Department of Health (1998) *Disabled Children: Directions for their future care*, London: HMSO

Farmer E., Dance C. and Ouwejan D. (forthcoming) *An Investigation of Linking and Matching in Adoption*, report to the Department for Children, Schools and Families, University of Bristol

Gordon D., Parker R., Loughran F. with Heslop P. (2000) *Disabled Children in Britain: A re-analysis of the OPCS disability surveys*, London: The Stationery Office

Green V. (2003) *Emotional Development in Psychoanalysis, Attachment Theory and Neuroscience: Creating connections*, Hove: Brunner-Routledge

Ivaldi G. (2000) *Surveying Adoption*, London: BAAF

Luckock B., Lefevre M., Orr D., Jones M., Marchant R. and Tanner K. (2006) *Social Work Education Knowledge Review 12: Teaching, learning and assessing communication skills with children and young people in social work education*, Social Care Institute for Excellence, Bristol: The Policy Press. And at www.scie.org.uk

McRoy R. G. (1999) *Special Needs Adoptions: Practice issues*, New York, Garland Publishing Inc

Miller D. (2002) *Disabled Children and Abuse*, NSPCC Information Briefings, February 2002 (www.nspcc.org.uk/inform)

National Adoption Day (2005) *Foster Care Adoption in the United States: An analysis of interest in adoption and a review of state recruitment strategies*, Washington DC: National Adoption Day Coalition

Owen M. (1999) *Novices, Old Hands and Professionals: Adoption by single people*, London: BAAF

Read J. and Harrison C. (2002) 'Disabled children living away from home: recognising hazards and promoting good practice', *Journal of Social Work*, 2:2, pp 211–231, London: Sage Publications

Rushton A. and Dance C. (2002) *Adoption Support Services for Families in Difficulty: A literature review and UK survey*, London: BAAF

Schofield G., Beek M. and Sargent K. (2000) *Growing Up in Foster Care*, London: BAAF

Selwyn J., Sturgess W., Quinton D. and Baxter C. (2006) *Costs and Outcomes of Non-Infant Adoptions*, London: BAAF

Simmonds J. (2008) 'Direct work with children – delusion or reality?', in Luckock B. and Lefevre M. (eds) *Direct Work: Social work with children and young people in care*, London: BAAF

Simon J. and Dance C. (2006) 'Disabled children who are looked after: Local Authority Survey 1999 summarised by Jennifer Cousins', www.baaf.org.uk/about/projects/openingdoors/researchsummary.pdf

Triseliotis J., Borland M. and Hill M. (2000) *Delivering Foster Care*, London: BAAF

19 The placement of looked after minority ethnic children

Julie Selwyn and Dinithi Wijedasa

This chapter examines the research evidence on the placement of looked after minority ethnic children into adoptive families. Ethnicity remains a contested and contentious area of study and debates about definitions, terms and underlying beliefs are fierce. The placement of minority ethnic children has been dominated for the last forty years by competing arguments about the benefits and disadvantages of "transracial" placements. The debate is often polarised with one camp (Gilroy, 1990; Macey, 1995; Hayes, 2003) arguing that placing children according to "race" is a form of apartheid, not supported by the research evidence and deeply divisive. The opposite camp (Maximé, 1993; Small, 2000) argues that research has been Eurocentric, and children's mental health needs are best met in an ethnically matched placement to allow the development of a "Black"[1] identity. Both camps accuse each other of racism and this has limited the willingness of others to become involved and engage with the issues. There are no satisfactory or agreed ways of referring to this group of children. All the current terms have limitations. For ease of reading we will use minority ethnic children although we recognise that in some cities minority ethnic populations will soon be the majority.

In the UK, there has been a striking lack of data on minority ethnic children, how and when they come into care, how decisions are made about their placements and their futures, and what happens to them while in care. One reason for this lack of evidence is the absence, until very recently, of the recording of ethnicity in official statistics and children's records. Local authorities have only been required to collect data on the ethnicity of children receiving services from 2000/1 and are not required to collect data on religion or language. This means that accurate estimates of over-representation or under-representation of minority ethnic children in the care system and studies of their "care careers" have been hard to come by. Several studies (Barn *et al*, 1997; Lowe *et al*, 2002) have highlighted the large gaps in case recording of even basic details of a child's ethnicity, religion and culture, and the impact this has on planning at every level.

Secondly, practice and research cannot keep up with fast-changing demographics. The 2001 Census found that the number of adults in mixed relationships is growing rapidly, as is the number of mixed ethnicity children. Almost four per cent of all children under five

---

[1] In this chapter "Black" with a capital B is used in the political sense to mean all minority ethnic groups. Spelt with a small b, black refers to Black African and African-Caribbean ethnic groups.

Figure 19.1

UK studies which have examined permanence and outcomes for minority ethnic children

Author and title	Sample	Method
Selwyn *et al* (2008) *Pathways to permanence for black, Asian and mixed ethnicity children*	Three local authorities in England were selected with high and contrasting minority ethnic populations. From each of these authorities three samples were drawn: a) 48 white and 54 minority ethnic children under 10 yrs of age who became looked after 2002–2003 b) 120 minority ethnic children with adoption recommendations 2005–2006 c) 50 minority ethnic children with adoption recommendations in 2006–2007	Data were collected from 259 case files, face-to-face interviews with 49 social workers and monthly phone calls tracking the progress of 50 minority ethnic children with adoption recommendations over a 12-month period.
Thoburn *et al* (2000) *Permanent family placement for children of minority ethnic origin*	244 minority ethnic children placed by 24 voluntary adoption agencies in the UK into adoptive/permanent foster families between 1980–1985. Sample boosted in 1991, by addition of a further 53 minority ethnic children placed by the same VAAs.	Data were collected from case files in 1991–1992. Interviews 12–15 years after placement with 38 parents (caring for 51 young people) and with 24 young people themselves.
Bagley and Young (1979) *Transracially adopted children: A review and empirical report*	Initial sample of 30 minority ethnic adopted children placed transracially, 30 white children placed with white adoptive families, 30 minority ethnic children looked after and 24 living with their birth family.	Standardised measures of adjustment.
Bagley (1993) *Transracial adoption in Britain: A follow-up study with policy considerations*	Follow-up sample 12 years later (1991) of 27 minority ethnic children placed with white families and 25 white children with white families.	Measures on self-esteem, self-image, identity and satisfaction in the placement completed by the young people.
Gill and Jackson (1983) *Adoption and Race; Black, Asian and mixed race children in white families*	53 young minority ethnic children placed by the British Adoption Project into 51 families in 1960s. Most of them were placed with white families. Follow-up studies carried out in 1969 and in 1974–1975 with 44 of the original 51 families. This included 36 families with transracial adoptions.	Individual interviews and group discussions with adopters. Individual and group interviews with adopters. Semi-structured interviews with parents and children. Questionnaires for teachers.

years old in England and Wales were of mixed ethnicity in 2001. And of *all* the minority ethnic population under five years old, one quarter were of mixed ethnicity. This is a huge demographic shift in the population. What is most striking is not just the growth of the mixed ethnicity populations as a percentage of the total population but the change within the minority ethnic population. However, the Census is already out of date, as the UK, especially England, has also seen a rapid rise in the number of Eastern Europeans and asylum seekers settling here. The growth in people who consider themselves to be of "mixed ethnicity" raises questions about how identity is conceptualised and challenges boundaries based on identification as "Black" or "White".

Thirdly, although strong statements and claims are often made, there are few studies focusing on looked after minority ethnic children with adoption recommendations (Thoburn *et al*, 2005). Figure 19.1 outlines the only UK studies, where minority ethnic children were specifically sampled to examine questions of permanence and outcomes for this group of children. However, even in these studies, researchers have had to use broad categories (e.g. Asian) to describe children's ethnicity and culture. Consequently, we are at the early stages of understanding issues about permanence for these children. In this chapter, we draw on findings from our study, *Pathways to permanence for black, Asian and mixed ethnicity children* (Selwyn *et al*, 2008). The study was funded by the Department for Children, Schools and Families (DCSF), in the "Adoption Research Initiative", to understand more about minority ethnic children's care careers and to examine whether their placement outcomes were different from those of white children, especially in relation to "permanence". We will refer to the study as the Pathways study throughout this chapter.

"Same race"[2] placements

Evidence on the outcomes of "transracial" placements has been hampered by research studies with biased or very small samples, evidence collected only from the adopter's point of view, samples combining intercountry adoptions with out of care adoptions (from the UK), lack of good longitudinal data and also the assumption that USA research findings hold true in the UK. However, most research has some methodological limitations and it is important to consider what we can reasonably conclude from comparing findings across all the studies.

Overall, studies in the UK and USA have commonly found that 20–25 per cent of "transracially" adopted children have serious problems in adjustment, about the same proportion found in "same race" placements. Levels of self-esteem are also about the

[2] Race is a social construct which rests on the assumption (disproved by scientists) that human populations can be divided into distinct types which are differentiated by genetically transmitted physical and mental characteristics. Although discredited, the term "race" has remained remarkably prevalent in social work.

same. The quality of parenting appears to be the principal influence on outcomes in both "same race" and "transracial" placements. We know of no studies of "transracial" placements within minority ethnic cultures.

The findings on identity are superficially similar to those on other psychosocial outcomes but also point to a greater complexity. The major prospective studies in the US that have compared minority ethnic children in "same race" and "transracial" placements showed no differences in self-concept scores or overall adjustment to school, peers, family and community. However, differences have been found on whether children were proud of their ethnic heritage and identified with it. Broadly speaking, the findings suggest that "transracially" placed children remain generally proud of their heritage but are much less likely to identify themselves as part of that culture. McRoy and Zurcher's study (1983) found that only 30 per cent of "transracially" placed children identified themselves as "black", preferring terms like "mixed" or "human race", and in Vroegh's study (1991), 83 per cent of 17-year-olds in "same-race" adoptions identified themselves as "black" compared with only 33 per cent of those who were "transracially" placed.

The question of whether minority ethnic children *should* have a "black" identity is contentious, as is whether there is a single "black" identity that most minority ethnic people would accept. We all have multiple identities, for example, as a professional, a parent, as someone's child and the development of these are influenced by class, gender and life experiences. Macey (1995, p 482) comments that 'to speak of the need for "black" children to develop a "black" identity begs the question – *which* "black" identity?'

This argument would not matter if it were possible to place all minority ethnic children with stable long-term ethnically matched permanent foster carers or kin. However, Farmer's recent study (2008) showed that, contrary to expectations, minority ethnic children were not more likely than white children to be placed with kin but remained in foster care. The Pathways study also found that when adopters were *not* found, children remained looked after and were less likely to be in matched placements in foster care than they were in adoptive placements. Nearly a quarter of the children with adoption recommendations had disrupted foster or kin placements and, as the number of moves increased, the number of matched foster placements decreased.

Two recent research reviews of "transracial" adoption, one in the US (Evan B. Donaldson Institute, 2008) and one in England (Quinton, 2008), have concluded that the current body of research supports three conclusions: firstly, "transracial" adoption does not produce psychological or behavioural problems in children; secondly, those who do adopt "transracially" face a range of challenges and the way adoptive parents handle these challenges facilitates or hinders child development; and thirdly, that adoptive placements can enable children to develop to their full potential.

Before returning to these contentious issues, it is important to look more closely at the characteristics of minority ethnic children in the looked after population and those being adopted.

Minority ethnic children in the looked after population

Minority ethnic children make up about 23 per cent of the looked after population in England (DCSF, 2008). The situation in Wales and Scotland is different in that their populations are less ethnically diverse and in both these countries less than 230 looked after children are from a minority ethnic group: five per cent and two per cent of their respective LAC populations. The low numbers of minority ethnic children in Wales and Scotland raise particular issues in relation to these children's experiences of care. However, because of limited evidence from these nations, this chapter has to focus mainly on findings from research in England.

Most of the looked after minority ethnic children in England are of mixed ethnicity or are black African or African-Caribbean. There are fewer Asian looked after children (5% looked after compared to 7% of the general child population). The reasons for this are not fully understood but are perhaps connected with a greater perceived stigma attached to the care system, the greater likelihood of being in a two-parent family, and different reasons for Asian children becoming looked after (Selwyn *et al*, 2008).

Table 19.1
Children looked after in England at 31 March 2008 by ethnic origin

	Number	*Percentages*
White	45,920	77
Mixed	5,000	8
African and African-Caribbean	4,500	8
Asian	2,800	5
Other	1,340	2
Totals	59,560	

Children with adoption recommendations

We do not know how many looked after minority ethnic children have an adoption recommendation in the looked after population, but that the age of the child affects whether an adoption recommendation is likely to be made. The younger the age of the child, the easier it is to find an adoptive family and the better the child outcomes. It is unlikely that many looked after black African children will have adoption recommendations, as the majority (80%) are over 10 years of age, probably reflecting the prevalence of older asylum-seeking children among looked after children from this ethnic group. In comparison, looked after mixed ethnicity and Bangladeshi and Pakistani children enter care at younger ages (DCSF, 2007).

Nor do we know how many children with adoption recommendations are never found an adoptive family but minority ethnic children are less likely to be found an adoptive family than white children: 18 per cent adopted compared to 23 per cent in the looked after population. The Pathways study found that, of the 170 minority ethnic children with adoption recommendations, more than a quarter had the plan changed away from adoption and many of these were Asian children. Sometimes, this was because ethnically matched adopters could not be found despite intensive searches and sometimes because the social worker was pessimistic about the chances of finding adopters and consequently, there were reduced or no promotional activities. A small study undertaken by the Adoption Register of children referred during National Adoption Week in 2005 also found that, of the 36 minority ethnic children referred, half were still waiting for a family a year later and therefore would be unlikely to be adopted.

Minority ethnic children are also over-represented in referrals to the Adoption Register, as they comprised nearly a third of all the referrals in 2006. Many of these children were referred with no special placement need other than their ethnicity, and many were of pre-school age. They were also less likely than white children to be referred as a sibling group, maybe because of their very young ages. However, only 17 per cent of adopters on the Register were from a minority ethnic background and, as with many waiting children, there is a mismatch between the characteristics and needs of the children and those of the adopters and the kinds of children adopters feel able to care for.

Adopted children

Most (83%) adopted children are white. There are very few Asian (60) and black African and African-Caribbean children (110) adopted each year in England and these numbers have been fairly steady over the last five years. However, the number of mixed ethnicity children adopted has been increasing, and in 2008 they made up 11 per cent of all those adopted out of care and 63 per cent of all minority ethnic adopted children. These statistics raise questions about why so few Bangladeshi, Pakistani and Indian children are adopted, given their young age profiles. Adoption is a service currently used mainly for white and mixed ethnicity children.

It was evident from the social work interviews in the Pathways study that, although mixed ethnicity children were being placed for adoption, they were seen as "hard to place" and viewed as particularly problematic. It is important for social workers to recognise that being of mixed ethnicity is not inherently problematic, and that children who become looked after and go on to have adoption recommendations are not representative of mixed ethnicity children in general.

Mixed ethnicity children in the general population

In the general population, mixed ethnicity children often live in middle class families, are not faced with daily battles around culture or ethnicity (Caballero *et al*, 2008) and are mainly achieving well educationally (Bradford, 2006). Living in a mixed ethnicity family is just one part of family life and one aspect of their identity. The study by Caballero and colleagues has some important messages for social work practice about the variety of ways parents choose to bring up their children. For example, social class was an important factor in understanding families' lives. The experiences of a working class Jamaican/white family were as different from a middle class Jamaican/white family as they were from a Pakistani/white family. Mixed ethnicity parents used what the authors refer to as 'different but equal approaches' to promote a sense of belonging and to negotiate differences. Parental strategies were chosen to suit the family's own particular circumstances. Some parents wanted their children to see their identity as "open" (letting the young person choose), some focused on a single aspect of their ethnicity and others stressed the mix. There was no evidence that one approach led to better outcomes than another.

These families did share some common experiences and findings confirm earlier research (Katz, 1996; Tizard and Phoenix, 2002). The neighbourhood and wider environment, peers and school were all important in children developing a sense of identity and belonging. Food, too, was important as a means of passing on some elements of cultural heritage.

Mixed ethnicity children who are looked after

Mixed ethnicity children in the looked after population do not have the same kinds of profiles as those in general population studies. In the Pathways study, virtually all mixed ethnicity children had a white mother and a minority ethnic father. Most had none or very little contact with their father or the paternal side of their family. Of all the children in the Pathways samples, mixed ethnicity children's mothers had experienced the most severe of adversities and had high levels of alcohol and drug addiction. Mothers had often been in care themselves, had had abusive childhoods, and had become involved in drug/alcohol abuse, often linked to prostitution. They had fragile partnerships with men, who were also addicts, usually absent and able to offer little or no parenting support. As a result, mixed ethnicity children became looked after at younger ages than children of other minority ethnicities and had speedier adoption recommendations. Also, in the Pathways samples, 75 per cent of mixed ethnicity children with adoption recommendations had siblings of a different ethnicity.

The needs of minority ethnic children being placed for adoption

The circular LAC 98 (20), *Adoption: Achieving the right balance*, stated that all of a child's needs should be taken into consideration when planning for adoption and that simply identifying ethnicity was not sufficient. Language, religion and culture are also important and need to be considered alongside other critical factors. The National Adoption Standards in England set this out in saying:

> *Children's ethnic origin, cultural background, religion and language will be fully recognised and positively valued and promoted when decisions are made.*

This was further developed in Section 1(5), of the Adoption and Children Act (2002) which states:

> *In placing the child for adoption, the adoption agency must give due consideration to the child's religious persuasion, racial origin and cultural and linguistic background.*

The National Standards set out timescales for each stage of the process so that delay is reduced and all those responsible for implementing adoption decisions treat them with greater urgency. However, there is a tension between the need to give due consideration to a child's background and the need not to incur undue delay. The Department of Health circular (LAC 1998 (20)) stated:

> *It is unacceptable for a child to be denied loving adoptive parents solely on the grounds that the child and adopter do not share the same racial or cultural background.*

The Standards reiterate this by stating that best practice is for children to be matched with families who can best meet their needs, but that they must not be kept waiting indefinitely for a "perfect family".

Assessment

All children being placed for adoption should have a thorough assessment. It is the basis on which the match with adopters will be made. A complete assessment also enables adopters to be given a coherent account of the child's early history and the likely impact of this on their child's subsequent development. It is also the basis on which adopters and agencies can think ahead about the child's future needs and plan support. We know that, where children display needs that come as a "shock" to adopters, this can cause placement breakdown (Selwyn *et al*, 2006). In formulating this assessment, it is important to note that ethnicity and culture are not linked to risks of disruption and "transracial" and "same race" placements do not differ in their rates of stability.

The majority of children who are placed for adoption come from backgrounds of abuse and neglect and these early experiences are likely to continue to have an impact on their development and capacity to form relationships. Rushton (2003) has identified the behaviours that are most predictive of placement disruption. These are: oppositional and conduct problems, "acting out", over-activity, restlessness and problems in forming attachments to new parents and families. We know from many studies that these difficulties tend to be persistent (although for some children these problems diminish) and they can wear down adopters' and foster carers' tolerance and ability to cope. However, they are rarely systematically assessed.

Cultural factors can also affect the impact of abuse and neglect on the child and on the way services and support are delivered to the child, birth and adoptive family. For example, some cultures have greater shame attached to sexual abuse, mental illness, and disability (Cohen et al, 2001) and this needs to be taken into account when thinking about the needs of the child, family finding and planning adoption support.

Many of the mixed ethnicity children in the Pathways study were born with neo-natal abstinence symptoms following intrauterine drug exposure or foetal alcohol syndrome. Both present immediate challenges to carers, as symptoms can include loud high-pitched crying, sweating, sleep and gastro-intestinal disturbances. The serious, long-term, negative impact on children's development of alcohol abuse during pregnancy are well documented while the impact of drug abuse is more contentious, partly because of the difficulty in disentangling the impact of inadequate nutrition and combinations of drugs on children's development.

However, minority ethnic children are less likely to have a thorough assessment of their needs. Cleaver and Walker (2004) found in a study of social worker's use of the Assessment Framework that minority ethnic children were less likely to have a core assessment than white children and all children had an inadequate analysis of the domain assessing family and environmental factors. If done well, this domain would provide the description and analysis of the child's cultural background. The Pathways study also found that minority ethnic children, in comparison with white children, had the poorest quality Form E[3] assessments and that quality was not related to the ethnicity of the social worker. Housing, family histories, impact of dislocation, etc. were rarely assessed. "Same race" placements were the dominant and often the only need clearly identified.

It was not possible to know why minority ethnic children's assessments were poorer than those of white children. We hypothesised that it might have been because a) social workers did not know what kinds of questions to ask, and/or b) that the emphasis on all minority ethnic children as simply being "Black" led to gross oversimplification of their needs, and/or c) that social workers lacked an understanding of the ecological systems

---

[3] Form E has been replaced by the Child's Permanence Report.

approach (Aldgate *et al*, 2006) and were therefore not able to make best use of the Assessment Framework.

It is interesting to reflect on what is meant by a "same race" placement. What exactly is being matched? Is it skin colour and ethnic category? Is it the child's birth family culture or the foster carer family culture where a child might have spent most of their life? What is the culture and ethnicity of mixed ethnicity children or siblings with different fathers?

Culture is not easily defined and there is no consensus about what the concept should include. Most definitions emphasise that a family's culture is how they make sense of the world and the meanings they give to situations. Culture includes the religious beliefs, gender relationships, patterns of power and deference, rules of inheritance, ways of dressing, food and social presentation that are shared by groups, and which have some persistence over time and are passed on from one generation to another (Quinton, 1994). However, there are always individuals who do not conform to group norms, and adults and children pick and choose which bits of culture they want to retain. So some of what is taught is lost and therefore culture exists in a constant state of change. Culture is not simply poured in. Children and young people also have their own cultures, for example, the kinds of music enjoyed or football team they support. There is a need to understand culture within an ecological framework and to recognise that it does not work on its own in a vacuum, but is closely linked with social class and gender as well. Culture is not static and fixed and there are as many variations *within* a culture as between cultures. There is not one "Black" culture.

One of the problems for social workers is that, at the time family finding is underway, they are required to identify the child's ethnicity, culture, religion and language so that these factors can be assessed and considered in matching. This process encourages a fixed and static view of culture. In the Pathways study, children's ethnicity and culture were "fixed" in case recording and the term "same race" placement was used to simply describe a child's broad ethnic category (e.g. black or Asian) and rarely included details of culture, except for religion. This led to placements being described on case files as "matched" even when the child's culture was different from that of the adopters, e.g. a Bangladeshi child placed with Indian adopters. Conversely, some workers prioritised the "same race" principle over children's other needs, splitting sibling groups because siblings were of different ethnicity and, as in the case example below, disrupting a stable placement.

Case example

A sibling group, aged 4–10 years (Bengali Muslim) were placed with a Pakistani Muslim foster family. It was recognised at the time of the placement that there were language differences, but the children remained there for two years and they expected to stay.

During this time, no concerns were raised and no additional support offered. However, the local authority decided that the children should be moved, against the children's wishes, to another placement because of their "same race" policy. The guardian later commented, 'It is surprising that the children's emotional needs and attachments have not been identified or prioritised in the plan to move them from their carers'.

Matching based on "same race" principles rarely considered neighbourhoods. So, for example, a Pakistani child from inner London was moved to live with Pakistani adopters in a small Northern town. The cultural differences between North and South, town and inner city were not explored. The adoptive placement was viewed as matched and therefore it was assumed that the needs of the child were met. It is important that the impact of a change in geographical context is also considered in making decisions about matching.

Culture was also associated with something that only became important later in life. An infant begins absorbing the family's culture from the moment of birth (it could be argued from the moment of conception, as for example, infants show preference for foods that their mothers ate during pregnancy). However, some of the mixed ethnicity infants in the Pathways study were placed with white foster carers and there was a view that the cultural needs of infants did not need to be considered. Below is an extract from a social worker's case recording that typifies this view:

> *X is a young baby, two-and-a-half-months old. His foster carers are white UK and not the same race and culture as (child). This does not pose a problem for (child) at the age he is now.*

Some of these infants continued to live with white foster carers for several years. The placements were not given additional support and were only perceived as being problematic when the foster carer applied to adopt. This situation often brought conflict, with workers wanting to remove the child to a "same race" placement and foster carers arguing they loved the child and were the only parents the child had ever known. In the cases we examined, the foster carers were, on the direction of the courts, allowed to keep the child. The research evidence (Rutter, 1989; Black, 2000) on the risks to the child's mental health of breaking a secure attachment outweighed the risks of a transracial placement. Despite concerns about identity, there was no evidence on case files that additional support was made available to these placements after the judgement.

What created the most difficulty for social workers was how to think about the placement of mixed ethnicity children. In particular, there was confusion about whether the adoptive placement was one that should preserve the child's recorded identity and culture before placement or should enable the development of other minority ethnic identities to which the child had some genetic connection. The children were generally viewed by social workers as "Black".

Is it valid to think of all minority ethnic children as "Black"?

In Britain, "Black" has often been used in social work literature to describe everyone from a minority ethnic group. The term has had political impact and has been beneficial in raising awareness of the need to recruit more minority ethnic carers and to pay more attention to the cultural, religious and language needs of the child and the effect of racist attitudes. However, "Black" as a category has functioned both to include and exclude and has been challenged by those of mixed and Asian ethnicity:

> *When Asians are encouraged to think of themselves as black . . . they have to define themselves in a framework that is historically and internationally developed by people in search of African roots* (Modood, 1988, p 5).

Children who are classified as "mixed" include white/Asian, white/Caribbean, white/black African and "mixed other". This latter group contains children with many different cultural links. For example, in the Pathways study, children classified as "mixed other" had parents from the following ethnicities: Vietnamese/white British, Kosovan/white British, African/Caribbean and Chinese/white British. It is clear that to refer to "mixed ethnicity" children as if they comprised a meaningful group or a community with shared values is problematic, when there are so many possible different heritages.

The use of the word "Black" can disguise differences and reproduce stereotypes (Barn and Harman, 2006). It can also lead workers to think literally in "Black" and "white", viewing culture and ethnicity as fixed dyadic categories. Perhaps this dualism provides some certainty for social workers faced with a mass of information and competing demands. In the Pathways study, the use of the term "Black", did little to give any insight into who the children were, what their needs were and what strategies were needed to recruit suitable adopters.

Racism

There has been an emphasis on placing children with minority ethnic adopters because it is thought that they, irrespective of their cultural backgrounds, will be better able to help children deal with racism. Instinctively, one would expect this to hold true but research does not back the assertion.

Racism operates in various ways and is felt at many different levels. It is clear from research that all minority ethnic children will face racism as they grow up and the experience of racism varies according to gender, class, language and the family's culture (Scourfield *et al*, 2002). The little research (Winddance Twine, 1999; Tizard and Phoenix, 2002) that exists suggests that it is simplistic to assume that minority ethnic parents always prepare their children well. First generation immigrants seem to have more difficulty as they are unprepared for the variety of forms that racism takes, lack a vocabulary for discussing racism, and often have a desire to fit in and not complain. Parents (white and minority ethnic) who do provide strategies seem to be more politically aware than those who do not.

Research on children's experiences (Chahal and Julienne, 1999) has found that children do not always tell their parents about racist incidents, but often gain support from friends. We know from other research (O'Connor, 2002) that the influence of peers increases in importance as children grow up. Therefore, when placing minority ethnic children, it is important to consider the future life of the child, including the community and schools that the child will attend, their opportunity for friendships and activities with other minority ethnic children and young people. Thoburn (2000) found that children in "same race" placements were confident about dealing with racism and described how their parents helped them with this. They also thought that living in an ethnically mixed area was a help. Children placed with white families were also positive about the help they got in tackling racism, but emphasised the value of linking up with other Black youngsters.

Importantly, studies have found that white mothers with mixed ethnicity children are also subject to racism. Hays (1996) has described this as 'racism rebounding'. Workers need to help adopters to be prepared and to think through their responses to racist remarks.

Family finding

Many adoption agencies have difficulty in finding an "exact" ethnically matched placement for a child. A number of explanations have been suggested including poor recruitment efforts and preference among potential minority ethnic carers for foster or kinship care due to cultural or financial reasons and institutional racism (Sunmonu, 2000). We do know that agencies which commit resources over a period of time do recruit minority ethnic adopters, and there are several recruitment practice guides available (Hadley Centre, 2005; Rule, 2006).

Less attention has been paid to the size of the adult population from which adopters might be recruited, although the data from the Census in 2001 suggest that this is a very important factor. Most minority ethnic populations are very young, with the bulk of their populations being under four years old. This leaves very few adults who might possibly come forward as potential adopters. If we look at the size of adult populations from which adopters might be drawn, the ratio is seven white British adults to every white British child, but for white/Asian adults and white/Asian children, there are more children than there are adults and the ratio is 0.9:1. The chance of finding an exact ethnic match for a white/Asian child with an adoption recommendation is small. It will take another generation before there are sufficient adult numbers in the population to provide an adequate pool to draw on. The Census also provided information which highlights how

375

difficult it is for some groups to consider adoption. For example, 80 per cent of Bangladeshi and Pakistani families live on half the national average income and 33 per cent of their homes are overcrowded and lack basic amenities such as a bath or hot water.

We also do not know how some minority ethnic communities manage childlessness or fulfil a wish to extend the family. It is interesting to note that, between 2002–2007, there were 155 applications made in the UK to adopt a child from India, 31 from Pakistan and less than five from Bangladesh. Some of these will have been relative adoptions but others might be another response to resolving infertility. Surrogacy is also gaining popularity in some Indian states.

Given the scarcity of minority ethnic adopters and the numbers of waiting children, it was not surprising to find in the Pathways study that minority ethnic adopters were able to be very selective about which children they wanted to adopt. They were able to adopt infants with few special needs. However, even healthy, unproblematic infants had usually only one or two potential minority ethnic adopters expressing interest.

Profiling children is an art and some children were poorly presented, which acted as a deterrent. Below is an example from the Pathways study of an extract from a child's profile promoting a healthy two-year-old girl:

Birth mother is of Ghanaian background (but born in Italy) and a putative father of African-Caribbean background . . . (child) needs a family that will reflect her ethnic background and will also reflect her cultural identity.

No prospective adopters came forward. It would be highly unlikely to find a couple who could meet the Ghanian, Italian and African-Caribbean requirement. In another case, adopters were found who could care for a child with very specific and complicated health needs, but they pulled out because they could not provide the Polish element that was asked for. No other adopters came forward and the child remained in foster care.

Meeting children's cultural needs in other ways did not seem to be considered. For example, in the above case, workers could have considered how the adopters might have been able to link into the local Polish community. In the general population, families look to aunts, uncles, grandparents, friends, etc. to provide experiences that they cannot, but in adoption practice, prospective adopters seem to be expected to meet *all* the child's needs. In many ways, the expectation was that the child's cultural needs would be met by the adoptive mother and that she would be responsible for the transmission of culture. This genderised view annoyed a black birth father who made a complaint that his child was being removed from a settled foster care placement (white) because of "skin colour". He saw it as his duty to teach his child about the family's culture. The extent to which minority ethnic members of the local community can provide additional support and information to adopted or fostered children is under-researched. Some studies of birth families do point to the value of this and the attempts made by white parents to access support (Harman and Barn, 2005).

In the Pathways study, physical appearance played an important role. Children have no control over how others see them, and sometimes, when parentage was unknown or disputed, social workers made decisions about ethnicity on the way a child looked, and sought adopters based on that decision. Skin colour affected where children were placed. Children who were more visibly white were also not always acceptable to minority ethnic adopters. Asian Muslim adopters were keen that an adopted child should not stand out and were anxious that children looked similar and had an Islamic name. For example, a social worker commented in relation to one application from an Asian adopter: 'They would only consider if the child looked like them, meaning they looked Asian and not white . . . They didn't want the child to be rejected by their community.'

There are assumptions that mixed ethnicity children are accepted as "Black" by all minority ethnic communities but they can face hostility from within the Black community and the authenticity of their "Black" identity may be questioned (Alibhai-Brown and Montague, 1992). Banks (1995) has argued that more efforts should be made to recruit adopters who themselves are of mixed parentage or prospective adopters who are in mixed relationships. However, there still seems to be suspicion and questioning of the competence and mental health of white women who already have mixed ethnicity children or the stability of adults in mixed relationships.

Inevitably, children will be placed in families that do not reflect their culture, heritage or ethnic background. These families may well be able to meet children's other needs and it is important for social workers to build into adoption support plans how gaps can be filled, for example, by linking the family with a mentor. These factors are important for *all* children not just those from a minority ethnic group. Most of the work on cultural competency in adoption practice has come from the USA and has mainly concerned the well-being of internationally transracially adopted children. Three critical areas of cultural competence have been identified in the professional literature: racial awareness, multicultural planning and survival skills (Vonk, 2001) and additional adopter education has been developed (Brodzinsky, 2008). We do not know if these models are appropriate for the UK and this is an area that needs urgent attention.

Conclusions

Research and practice in the UK are at the early stages of understanding how best to place looked after minority ethnic children. Social workers have had little to guide their assessment, planning and decision-making and the practice of often describing all minority ethnic children as "Black" has provided a blunt and inadequate matching criterion for choosing a permanent placement for these children.

The population has become so diverse that it is increasingly difficult to have "same race" placements, unless only broad categories are used, such as European, Asian, African etc. This, of course, provides no clue to the culture of the child and prioritises skin colour over all the child's other needs. Even if "matched" by a more precise ethnic category, families may differ culturally because of social class, generation, and neighbourhoods.

However, we do know that adopter commitment; a flexible approach to parenting; an ability to distance themselves from a child's behaviour; willingness to work with the agency; and to understand the information about the child are all related to successful placements (Quinton, 2008). Children's voices suggest that the availability of other children of the same ethnicity and diverse neighbourhoods and schools should be important factors in choosing a placement.

While more efforts need to be made to recruit as wide and diverse a pool of adopters as possible, there also needs to be greater realism about the likelihood of finding a "perfect ethnic match". Most of the children with adoption recommendations are of mixed ethnicity, with complex histories, carrying with them many risk factors for delayed development. Deciding what a "same race" placement is for a mixed ethnicity child is fraught with difficulties. Therefore we suggest that a more sensitive and sophisticated approach to assessment, matching and placement is required.

Adoption brings with it many challenges to adoptive children and their families and there are additional challenges for parents who adopt children who are visibly different from themselves. Families need to receive good preparation and training so that they can help the child positively integrate their heritage into their sense of self. Without good assessment, preparation, training and support, adoptive families and their children are not well served. The challenge for the social workers is to view the children and the adoptive families from a broader ecological perspective, thus enabling the children to flourish in their new families.

Selected further reading

Evan B. Donaldson Institute (2008) *Finding Families for African–American Children: The role of race and law in adoption from foster care*, available at www.adoptioninstitute.org

Thoburn J., Chand A. and Proctor J. (2004) *Child Welfare Services for Minority Ethnic Families, The research reviewed*, London: Jessica Kingsley Publishers

References

Aldgate J., Jones D., Rose W. W. and Jeffrey C. (2006) *The Developing World of the Child*, London: Jessica Kingsley Publishers

Alibhai-Brown Y. and Montague A. (1992) *The Colour of Love*, London: Virago

Bagley C. (1993) 'Transracial adoption in Britain: A follow-up study with policy considerations', *Child Welfare*, 72, pp 285–299

Bagley C. and Young L. (1979) 'The identity, adjustment and achievement of transracially adopted children: A review and empirical report', in Varma G. K. and Bagley C. (eds) *Race, Education and Identity*, London: Macmillan

Banks N. (1995) 'Children of black mixed parentage and their placement needs', *Adoption & Fostering*, 19:2, pp 19–24

Barn R. and Harman V (2006) 'A contested identity: An exploration of the competing social and political discourse concerning the identification and positioning of young people of inter-racial parentage', *British Journal of Social Work*, 36, pp 1309–1324

Barn R., Sinclair R. and Ferdinand D. (1997) *Acting on Principle: An examination of race and ethnicity in social services provision for children and families*, London: BAAF

Black D. (2000) 'The effects of bereavement in childhood', in Gelder M., Lopez-Ibor M. and Andreason N. (eds) *New Oxford Textbook of Psychiatry*, Oxford: Oxford University Press

Bradford, B. (2006) *Who are the 'Mixed' Ethnic Group?* London: ONS, p 34

Brodzinsky D. (2008) 'Adoptive parent preparation project: Meeting the mental health and developmental needs of adopted children', Evan B. Donaldson Institute, available at www.adoption institute.org

Caballero C., Edwards R. and Puthussery S. (2008) *Parenting 'Mixed' Children: Negotiating difference and belonging*, York: Joseph Rowntree Foundation

Chahal K. and Julienne L. (1999) *We Can't all be White! Racist victimisation in the UK*, York: Joseph Rowntree Foundation

Cleaver H. and Walker S. (2004) *Assessing Children's Needs and Circumstances: The impact of the Assessment Framework*, London: Jessica Kingsley Publishers

Cohen J., Deblinger E., Mannarino A. and Arellano M. (2001) 'The importance of culture in treating abused and neglected children: An empirical review', *Child Maltreatment*, 6, pp 148–157

Department for Children, Schools and Families (2007) *Children Looked After by Local Authorities, National Tables, Statistical Volume*, internet only, date released 23/03/07

Department for Children, Schools and Families (2008) *National Statistics First Release: Children looked after in England* SFR23/2008

Department of Health (1998) *Adoption: Achieving the right balance*, Circular LAC (98) 20, London: DoH

Evan B. Donaldson Institute (2008) *Finding Families for African American Children: The role of race and law in adoption from foster care*, available at www.adoptioninstitute.org

Farmer E. and Moyers S. (2008) *Kinship Care: Fostering effective family and friends placements*, London: Jessica Kingsley Publishers

Gill O. and Jackson B. (1983) *Adoption and Race: Black, Asian and Mixed Race Children in White Families*, London: BAAF

Gilroy P. (1990) 'The end of anti-racism', in Ball W. and Solomos J. (eds) *Race and Local Politics*, Basingstoke: Macmillan

Hadley Centre (2005) *Finding Adoptive Families for Black, Asian and Mixed Parentage Children: Best Practice Guide*, available in publications at www.bristol.ac.uk/hadley

Harman V. and Barn R. (2005) 'Exploring the discourse concerning white mothers of mixed parentage children', in Okitikpi T. (ed.) *Working with Children of Mixed Parentage*, Lyme Regis: Russell House Publishing, pp 102–111

Hayes, P. (2003) 'Giving due consideration to ethnicity in adoption placements: A principled approach', *Child and Family Law Quarterly*, 15:3, pp 255–268

Hays, S. (1996) *The Cultural Contradictions of Motherhood*, New Haven: Yale University Press

Katz I. (1996) *The Construction of Racial Identity in Children of Mixed Parentage: Mixed metaphors*, London: Jessica Kingsley Publishers

Korbin J. (1991) 'Cross-cultural perspectives and research directions for the 21st century', *Child Abuse and Neglect*, 15, pp 67–77

Lowe N., Murch M., Borkowski M., Bader K., Copner R., Lisles C. and Shearman J. (2002) *The Plan for the Child: Adoption or long term fostering*, London: BAAF

Macey M. (1995) 'Same race adoption policy: Anti-racism or racism?', *Journal of Social Policy*, 26, pp 473–491

Maximé, J. (1993) 'The importance of racial identity for the psychological well-being of black children', *ACPP Review and Newsletter*, 15:4, pp 173–179

McRoy R. G. and Zurcher L. A. (1983) *Transracial and Inracial Adoptees: The adolescent years*, Springfield, IL: Charles Thomas

Modood T. (1994) 'Political blackness and British Asians', *Journal of the British Sociological Association*, 4, pp 859–876

Modood T., Berthoud R., Lakey J., Nazroo J., Smith P., Virdee S. and Beishon S. (1997) *The Fourth National Survey of Ethnic Minorities: Ethnic Minorities in Britain: diversity and disadvantage*, London: Policy Studies Institute

O'Connor T. (2002) 'Annotation: The "effects" of parenting reconsidered: Findings, challenges, and application', *Journal of Child Psychology and Psychiatry*, 43:5, pp 555–572

Office of National Statistics (2003) *Census 2001: CD supplement to the National Report for England and Wales*, London: ONS

Quinton D. (1994) 'Cultural and community influences', in Rutter M. and Hay D. (eds) *Development Through Life: A handbook for clinicians*, Oxford: Blackwell Scientific Publications, pp 159–184

Quinton D. (2007) *Matching in Adoptions from Care: A conceptual and research review*, Report submitted to the DCSF, Hadley Centre for Adoption and Foster Care Studies

Rule G. (2006) *Recruiting Black and Minority Ethnic Adopters and Foster Carers*, London: BAAF

Rushton A. (2003) *Knowledge Review 2: Adoption of looked after children: A scoping review of research*, London: Social Care Institute of Excellence

Rutter M. (1989) 'Pathways from childhood to adult life', *Journal of Child Psychology and Psychiatry*, 30:1, pp 23–51

Scourfield J., Evans J., Shah W. and Beynon H. (2002) 'Responding to the experiences of minority ethnic children in virtually all-white communities', *Child and Family Social Work*, 7, pp 161–175

Selwyn J., Harris P., Quinton D., Nawaz S., Wijedasa D. and Wood M. (2008) *Pathways to Permanence for Black, Asian and Mixed Ethnicity Children: Dilemmas, decision-making and outcomes*, Report to DCSF, London: DCSF

Selwyn J., Sturgess W., Quinton D. and Baxter C. (2006) *Costs and Outcomes of Non-infant Adoptions*, London: BAAF

Small, J. (2000) 'Ethnicity and placement', *Adoption & Fostering*, 24:1, pp 9–13

Sunmonu Y. (2000) 'Why black carers are deterred from adoption', *Adoption & Fostering*, 24:1, pp 59–60

Thoburn J., Chand A. and Proctor J. (2005) *Child Welfare Services for Minority Ethnic Families*, London: Jessica Kingsley Publishers

Thoburn J., Norford L. and Rashid S. P. (2000) *Permanent Family Placement for Children of Minority Ethnic Origin*, London: Jessica Kingsley Publishers

Tizard B. and Phoenix A. (2002) *Black, White or Mixed Race? Race and racism in the lives of young people of mixed parentage*, London: Routledge

Vonk M. (2001) 'Cultural competence for transracial adoptive parents', *Social Work*, 16:3, pp 246–254

Vroegh K. (1991) *Transracial Adoption: How it is 17 years later*, Chicago: Chicago Child Care Society

Winddance Twine F. (1999) 'Bearing blackness in Britain: The meaning of racial difference for white birth mothers of African-descent children', *Social Identities*, 5:2, pp 185–210

20 Placement of unaccompanied asylum-seeking children

Jim Wade

Introduction

Unaccompanied asylum-seeking children and young people have formed part of the population of forced migrants over many generations (Ressler *et al*, 1988). Despite this being the case, research studies that have attempted to explore the ways in which these children attempt to resettle their lives in unfamiliar surroundings and how social workers (and others) assist their efforts to do so have been, at least until recently, relatively thin on the ground. This chapter provides a focus on placement as a major arena of resettlement; as the place in which children and young people first try to rebuild their lives, find a renewed sense of peace, security and belonging and through which they attempt to develop new networks of support. It reviews what is currently known about factors affecting assessment and making placements, describes the range of placements that are used for different groups of unaccompanied children and young people, the experiences of children in different placement settings and points to what we know (and do not yet know) about how placements can be used, and supported, to assist the resettlement of unaccompanied children. In doing so, it draws on findings from a recent study (to be known as the York study) that investigated social work services for unaccompanied children (Wade *et al*, 2005).

The York study was designed to assess how social services were responding to the needs of unaccompanied children and young people. The study explored how children's needs were assessed, what services were provided as a result, how these varied for different groups within the population and with what consequences for children's lives and progress. A stratified random sample of 212 children were selected from all cases referred to three local authorities between March 2001 and August 2002, taking account of age, sex and length of time since referral (see Wade *et al*, 2005 for further details). The main fieldwork was carried out in 2002–2003. A retrospective analysis of social work case files was conducted for the whole sample and mapped their pathways from arrival in the UK, a period ranging from four to 30 months after initial referral, and semi-structured interviews were conducted with 31 of these young people and their main support workers. The study included children at all stages of the child welfare system, from referral and assessment through to leaving care, and focused on most of the important aspects of children's lives, including placement histories and experiences, education and training, health, well-being and social networks.

The legislative context

The UK Border Agency (UKBA) defines an unaccompanied asylum-seeking child as a person below the age of 18 (or who appears to be if proof is lacking) who is claiming asylum in their own right and who has no adult relative or guardian in this country to provide care (Home Office, 2002). Gaining acceptance as an unaccompanied asylum-seeking child is an important factor in accessing social services. Local authorities' duties are clearly defined for this group and they can then be recompensed for the services they provide through the Home Office Special Grant.

Where a young person claims to be a minor but the UKBA does not accept them as such, they are treated as an adult asylum seeker until evidence is produced to substantiate their claimed age. Age disputes are not uncommon, are a matter of major concern for practitioners working with this group of young people, and may have increased in recent years (Crawley, 2007). Age also affects local authority funding for services, since levels of payment under the Special Grant are significantly lower for those aged 16 or 17 when first applying for asylum – an age group that accounts for over one half of all asylum applications made by unaccompanied minors. Studies have identified this distinction as having been an influential driver of differentiated services for unaccompanied young people, with local authorities having made extensive use of the community support provisions of the Children Act 1989 (s17) to provide accommodation (usually shared housing) to older teenagers in the community (Audit Commission, 2000; Stone, 2000; Stanley, 2001). The regulatory framework for support under these arrangements is considerably weaker than is the case for children formally looked after (s20).

Once an unaccompanied asylum-seeking child's age has been accepted, they have the same rights and entitlements to welfare services as other citizen children. Lacking the presence of their parents or customary caregivers, they should be treated by local authorities as children "in need" (Department of Health, 1995) and receive an assessment in line with the *Framework for the Assessment of Children in Need and their Families* (Department of Health *et al*, 2000). Although most older teenagers have in the past been supported under s17 provisions, thereby lacking the entitlement to allocated social work support, care planning procedures and leaving care support afforded to looked after children, Government guidance issued in 2003 (LAC/2003/13) has brought significant changes to the care pathways of unaccompanied children. This guidance questioned the routine use of s17 accommodation for lone children (defined as those under 18) and advised that there should be a *presumption* for the use of s20 accommodation and support in these cases, unless clear contra-indications were uncovered during assessment (Department of Health, 2003). Reports on the response to this guidance by local authorities suggest that it has led to an increase in the proportion of unaccompanied children formally looked after (and therefore eligible for leaving care services), although significant variations in their care arrangements continue to persist (Free, 2005; Refugee Council, 2005).

However, nothing in the asylum field remains constant for long and further significant reforms to the care and support of unaccompanied children are about to be enacted. Prefaced in the Government's *Care Matters* Green Paper and first detailed in the Home Office's 2007 consultation exercise (the conclusions from which have now been published), the Home Office reform programme for unaccompanied asylum-seeking children proposes to place services for this client group under greater Home Office control (Department for Education and Skills, 2006; Home Office, 2007; 2008). The proposals are premised on a perceived need to contain rising costs (especially leaving care costs), reduce the disproportionate burden placed on a small number of local authorities, tackle inconsistencies in service provision and to speed up asylum decision-making and return procedures for children whose asylum applications fail.

The proposals have far-reaching implications for the care pathways of these children, including the establishment of regional assessment centres (close to ports of entry and asylum screening units) and the subsequent dispersal of children away from London and the South East to a range of specialist local authorities commissioned to provide care and support under the provisions of the Children Act 1989. It is understandable that some of the proposals, especially those surrounding the use of medical procedures (including X-rays) in age assessment and the prospect of the forced return of children (where adequate reception arrangements exist), have created consternation among non-governmental organisations working in this field. Criticisms have also been made about the "one size fits all" approach, paying insufficient attention to the varied experiences and nuanced care needs of these children, and the implications of dispersal for children's ability to connect with settled communities that reflect their cultural, language and religious origins.[1]

Numbers and reasons for arrival

The numbers of unaccompanied children seeking asylum in the UK vary from year to year, ranging from a high point of 6,200 in 2002 to 3,245 in 2006. Around three-quarters of applicants are aged 14–17 years. Over two-thirds (70% in 2006) are granted "discretionary leave to remain", usually until their 18th birthday, and very few (6% in 2006) are granted refugee status.[2]

---

[1] See, for example, the following responses to the Home Office proposals:

BAAF (http://www.baaf.org.uk/res/consultations/consultresponse_asylm.pdf)

Immigration Law Practitioners' Association (ILPA) (http://www.ilpa.org.uk/)

Refugee Council (http://www.refugeecouncil.org.uk/news/press/2008/January/20080131.htm)

[2] The Home Office compiles annual statistics on all new asylum applications in the UK. These are available at: http://www.homeoffice.gov.uk/rds/immigration1.html

Unaccompanied children arrive from a diverse range of countries, although these patterns also change over time as some conflicts diminish and new ones emerge. The York study, for example, involved children from 23 different countries – including from Eastern Europe (32%), the Middle East (26%), Africa (27%) and Asia (15%). The heterogeneity of the overall population is clearly reflected in the diverse origins of the children themselves.

Precise information on the numbers of unaccompanied children supported by local authorities is not available. Government statistics on looked after children based on annual local authority returns do show a steady, if slight, increase in the numbers of unaccompanied children in their care over recent years, from 2,200 in 2001/2 to 3,200 in 2005/6.[3] Furthermore, they consistently show that the majority are supported by London boroughs (63% in 2006) or by other councils in the South East (15% in 2006), although there has been a slight dispersal away from these regions in recent years, and that the majority are male and aged 14 to 17 years. Reflecting this regional pattern, the data suggest that unaccompanied children constitute around five per cent of the population of looked after children nationally, but as much as 17 per cent of children looked after in London. These patterns are likely to change further as the proposed Home Office reforms are rolled out.

The displacement of unaccompanied children to countries near or far from their own occurs for a number of overlapping reasons (Ayotte, 2000; Thomas *et al*, 2004). These are primarily political rather than economic, typically including the need to seek safety from armed conflicts, political upheavals, persecution or natural disasters. However, in some cases there may also be an economic sub-text linked to experiences of deep poverty or limited opportunity, often connected to breakdowns in civil society, or to trafficking for the purposes of exploitation.

Separation from parents and caregivers may have occurred in a variety of circumstances. Parents may be dead, missing, imprisoned or ill and unable to provide care. Children may have been sent away by their parents or close relatives who perceived them to be in danger or who selected them to leave for economic reasons. In these divergent scenarios, young people are often reliant on help from family members, strangers and agencies or are reliant on their own resources for survival for some time before they

---

[3] See: DCSF, Statistics of Education: Children Looked After by Local Authorities, for these year endings. Available: http://www.dfes.gov.uk/rsgateway/DB/VOL/

However, SSDA 903 returns for a given year only identify unaccompanied children if, at some point in that year, they were seeking asylum. Those who may have received an asylum decision in earlier years but remain looked after are not included. These data are therefore likely to underestimate the overall number of unaccompanied asylum-seeking and refugee children in the care of local authorities. Nor, of course, do these data take account of unaccompanied children supported by local authorities in the community under s17 of the Children Act 1989, since they are not formally looked after.

finally arrive in the UK. While these children may therefore arrive with differing experiences and in a variety of circumstances, what unites them is the experience of separation from their families and of being uprooted from their homes, networks and cultures in order to seek shelter in a strange country far removed from their own (Kidane, 2001). Once they do arrive, frequently with only a confused and fragmented understanding of their circumstances, they are confronted by unfamiliar systems of immigration, care and protection and carry an over-riding uncertainty about whether their claims for asylum will be believed and accepted. It is in this context that unaccompanied children generally first come to the attention of social services and in which social workers first attempt to assess and respond to their needs.

Assessment and placement making

Many unaccompanied children present at social services in emergency circumstances and require immediate placement. Almost one half of the young people in the York study (47%) were provided with accommodation on the same day as referral (Wade *et al*, 2005). In keeping with other looked after children, placement making in these circumstances is heavily constrained by available resources and children may then need to wait (perhaps longer than anticipated) for more durable solutions to be found (Farmer *et al*, 2004; Sinclair *et al*, 2004).

Many younger unaccompanied children needing immediate placement have tended to be placed in emergency foster or residential placements, to allow time for further assessment, before moving on to a more durable care placement or to some form of supported accommodation. Many older young people (aged 16 or 17), however, have tended to move straight to supported or independent accommodation with often only a limited initial assessment of their ability to manage. Around one half of the young people in the York study had a first placement in these settings. Where placement resources have been particularly stretched, use has also been made of hotels and bed and breakfast accommodation as a short-term solution for this group, a practice for which local councils have been criticised in the past (Audit Commission, 2000; Stanley, 2001).

Not all unaccompanied children need immediate placement at referral. A proportion of children (around one in nine in the York study) will already be living in informal placements with extended family members, family friends or with adults they have met since arriving in the UK before they approach social services for assistance. In these circumstances, the particular challenge for practitioners is to establish the identities of these adults and to make an assessment of their capacity to provide the child with safe family care.

In all cases, careful assessment is the key to successful placement making. Over the past decade, a range of guidance has been developed to assist local authorities when considering care arrangements for these children. The *Framework for Assessment*, mentioned above, draws particular attention to the needs of unaccompanied children. Official guidance was first issued in 1995 (Department of Health, 1995) and an updated guide, endorsed by Government, was published in 2001 (Kidane, 2001). Guidelines to support good practice have also been issued by the Separated Children in Europe Programmc (2004), the United Nations High Commissioner for Refugees (1994) and by the Council of the European Union (2003). Some training resources for foster carers and social workers have also been made available (Kidane and Amerena, 2004; 2005). Taken as a whole, this body of guidance tends to emphasise the importance of speedy but well-informed responses to children's immediate placement needs, backed up by careful core assessments undertaken over time, of keeping sibling groups together when making placement decisions and emphasises the value of s20 accommodation and support packages. It highlights the importance of listening to children's views about placement, of taking account of their past experiences and of their cultural, linguistic and religious needs. Where children are living with relatives or friends, it emphasises that the need for careful assessment is paramount and highlights the value of ongoing monitoring and support to provide continuity for children and young people, to respond to changing needs and to minimise the need for further movement.

Assessments of unaccompanied children and young people are challenging to conduct. Young people's initial encounters with social services are often marked by confusion and some suspicion about the role of the agency and the reasons for asking questions. While some young people want to talk, to tell their story, some lack information about their pasts and others may appear reticent and questions may be met with silence or with what workers perceive to be formal asylum stories, told to them by adults and committed to memory in the belief that it would strengthen their asylum claim. Many workers understand that silence and the implications that carrying silence may have for children, both as a protective function, to keep past memories under control and allow a focus on the present, and as a burden to be carried alone (Kohli, 2006). Timing, proceeding at the young person's pace and sensitive questioning represent features of good assessment practice. Most social workers tend to be either sympathetic or at least relatively non-judgemental in relation to young people's accounts and tend to focus on the child "in need" (Kohli, 2007). Initial assessments frequently focus on gathering basic information about children's backgrounds, immediate needs for placement, finance, education and health screening. More complex questions about family, past experiences, reasons for exile and the emotional legacy of these are often deferred until the child is more settled in placement (Wade et al, 2005).

Deferring consideration of deeper emotional issues may often be a helpful strategy. However, the York study did find that assessments too often proved to be a one-off truncated event – especially where these concerned older young people or where assessments were not conducted by qualified social workers working in specialist children's teams (see also Mitchell, 2007). Young people frequently needed to re-tell their stories and new needs emerged over time as their confidence in those around them grew. It is important, therefore, that initial assessments are viewed as provisional and that they be subject to a continuing process of review.

Care pathways

At present, not enough is known about the forms of care that work best for unaccompanied children arriving in industrialised countries (Zulfacar, 1987; Tolfree, 2004). Nor, in a UK context, do we know a great deal about how these children fare while they are supported by social services or about how their experiences compare to those of other looked after children. Practitioners tend to report that, despite the adversities faced by these children related to the past, the present and the future, many (though not all) are able to engage with the challenges of resettlement with great purpose, appear resilient and resourceful and are keen to make a success of their personal and educational lives, even though many continue to experience a considerable degree of emotional distress (Kohli, 2007; Chase et al, 2008). In these respects, some differences are noted in comparison to citizen looked after children.

Emerging research findings tend to support this view in relation to looked after unaccompanied children, many of whom appear to fare quite well in comparison to their citizen peers. One large-scale study of patterns of placement stability among 7,399 looked after children found that, in comparison to other looked after children, unaccompanied children were less likely to experience placement instability and, according to reports from social workers, were also significantly less likely to display challenging behaviour or emotional disturbance and were significantly more likely to be doing well at school (Sinclair et al, 2007). These findings are also consistent with those from a recent study on outcomes for young people leaving care, although the numbers of unaccompanied children in this study were very small (Dixon et al, 2006). This study also found that unaccompanied young people were less likely than others to experience a range of troublesome behaviours while being looked after (including running away, truancy and school exclusion, substance misuse or offending) and were less likely to have had involvement in offending after leaving care.

However, the York study also found that those formally looked after (s20) or placed with extended family members tended to fare better than many young people supported in the community under s17 arrangements (Wade et al, 2005). In this study, placement in care or with extended family members was positively associated with young people having a more consistent engagement with education and having stronger networks of social support. The statutory responsibilities associated with being looked after were also influential. These young people were more likely to have had allocated social work support, regular social work contact and more comprehensive packages of support linked to formal care planning and review.

For those following a s17 pathway, support arrangements were more highly variable and the vast majority of those aged 16 or 17 at referral were, at that time, supported in this way. At one extreme, rudimentary assessments led to placements in unsupported shared housing that provided limited (if any) social work contact and support. Placement and support arrangements were routine and resource-led. At the other extreme, where support was provided by children's teams or, to a lesser extent, by dedicated support agencies, the overall package of support for young people was largely indistinguishable from that provided to looked after children. In general terms, however, those supported under s17 fared less well. They were more likely to spend time out of education and training, to experience greater social isolation and, given the lack of formal leaving care responsibilities to this group, were expected to make their own way in the world at age 18.

Although the evidence base is relatively weak, findings do therefore suggest that those who enter the looked after system may do relatively well compared to other looked after children and certainly better than unaccompanied young people supported more independently in the community under s17 arrangements. This is consistent with Government guidance and in line with developing practice in local authorities. The balance of this chapter now briefly reviews evidence about how placements are used for unaccompanied children and about young people's experiences in different placement settings.

Residential care

In an international context, the institutional nature of residential care leads it to be viewed negatively as a long-term care option for separated refugee children (Tolfree, 2004). In a UK context, studies have found that unaccompanied children and young people are relatively unlikely to be placed in residential settings and, where they are, they are most likely to be used for short-term periods of assessment soon after arrival (Williamson, 1998; Stanley, 2001). In the York study, 10 per cent of young people had a first placement in specialist residential settings for unaccompanied children and most were younger looked after males. Residential placements provided a bridge to assist young people's adjustment to life in the UK and allowed a period of time for assessment and preparation before young people moved on to other semi-independent settings.

Studies have found that some young people have valued the time spent in residential care. Comfort could often be found in the companionship of other young people facing similar challenges, in predictable structures and routines at a time of considerable uncertainty, and in the day-to-day support provided by key workers, a relationship that appears pivotal to young people's satisfaction with placement (Stanley, 2001; Chase *et al*, 2008). However, other young people have reported an increasing sense of frustration over time, especially where units are situated in areas remote from the social links and connections that are of increasing importance to young people, and have pointed to tensions and turbulence in peer relationships, sometimes linked to placing young people together from different ethnic or national groups (Stanley, 2001; Wade *et al*, 2005).

Foster care

Around 70 per cent of looked after children now live in foster care settings. It is also the placement of choice for younger unaccompanied children, with around 60 per cent living in foster care for at least a short time before moving on. Given the age profile of unaccompanied children at arrival and the uncertainties generated by the asylum decision-making process, providing young people with a sense of permanence in foster placements is a major challenge. Timescales for achieving positive outcomes are often short.

Foster carers and social workers need particular skills to enable young people to settle, to develop new attachments, to resume their education, to monitor and support their claims for asylum and to help them develop the skills they will need for adulthood, either within the UK or in their countries of origin if they have to return. In addition to these more practical tasks, there is a need to help young people to reconnect the threads of their past and present lives that have been ruptured, by promoting continuities with their homelands (through food, language, culture and religion), by listening to often painful stories of the past as they try to heal emotional wounds and by creating new opportunities for connection in the present with family members (where these come to light), with their communities of origin and through more mainstream youth activities. As such, caring for unaccompanied children incorporates humanitarian activity in the practical domains of life, therapeutic care to address children's psychosocial needs, and dependable companionship along the road towards resettlement (see Kohli, 2007). On balance, existing evidence (limited though it is) suggests that good foster placements try to address children's needs at these different levels (see Hek, 2007). The importance of specific support and training for foster carers, many of whom experience considerable isolation, has therefore been identified (Kidane and Amerena, 2004).

From a research perspective, we have only a limited understanding of what unaccompanied children want from foster placements. From international research we know that children may come with differing cultural notions of what fostering means and that some may be concerned about the risk of exploitation (Tolfree, 2004). Where studies have sought young people's views, responses appear broadly similar to those obtained from citizen children (Sinclair, 2005; Hek, 2007; Chase *et al*, 2008). Children and young people want placements where they feel safe, secure and included as part of the family, where their experiences are recognised, where cultural and religious needs are respected, which are supportive and where they can talk about their needs and experiences at a pace they feel comfortable with. Young people's perceptions of placement are also influenced by their socio-economic backgrounds, their past family circumstances and the degree to which they prioritise familiarisation with the English language and systems (see Hek, 2007).

Although cultural matching is recognised by practitioners as important, all of these factors make it a complex process – one that is best met on a "case by case" basis rather than through a "blanket" approach by agencies, taking account of children's particular experiences, wishes and feelings (Hek, 2007). Limitations in placement supply, often leading to a heavy reliance on independent fostering providers, simply add to the challenge. Placement choice is a perennial problem in child placement, perhaps only available in around 30 per cent of placement decisions (Farmer *et al*, 2004; Sinclair *et al*, 2004). There is evidence of practitioners attempting to broaden the pool of carers available from within refugee communities (Williamson, 1998; Stanley, 2001; Wade *et al*, 2005). However, doing so is not easy and may involve other placement compromises, since many refugee families struggle with low income and may live in poor quality or overcrowded housing where young people lack general privacy or private space for study. Making only a broad cultural match may also bring problems when other dimensions of placement are not fully considered. As one Ugandan female who was placed with a couple of Jamaican and West African descent in the York study reported: 'We had nothing in common, apart from the man being African' (Wade *et al*, 2005, p 82). Although many broadly matched placements lasted well, some, including this one, eventually broke down.

Most unaccompanied children are placed transculturally. Some prioritise living with English families to learn the language and speed their education. Most young people speak fondly of the kindness and support they have received from carers and their families and most placements last and work reasonably well (Stanley, 2001; Kohli, 2007; Chase *et al*, 2008). However, as the York study found, they also often involved considerable sacrifice, as young people found communication difficult, struggled to adjust to new customs, expectations and norms of behaviour and, especially in more isolated locations, to cope with the effects of cultural isolation. Although, in many cases, time aided young people's adjustment, in others a desire for greater freedom or to be closer to their own communities led to young people moving on to supported accommodation elsewhere. Like other young people more generally, some also strained against the boundaries and controls attached to family placements, especially where carers proved inflexible. Where solutions could not be negotiated by social workers, these young people also tended to move on.

Many unaccompanied children (62% in the York study) have no family connections of any kind in the UK and are therefore heavily reliant on carers, friends and social workers for support. The York study found that, while just over one-third were known to have family connections here and 11 per cent overseas, a majority of these links were between siblings. Relationships between siblings were often *the* primary source of family identification, solidarity and emotional support and, as others have also found, social workers were largely successful in keeping sibling groups together (Kohli, 2007). However, larger sibling clusters could not always be placed in foster care and, where an older teenager could act as main carer for the sibling group, placements were found in more independent settings. Staying together was what these family groups tended to want, although the responsibility placed on the main carer was often daunting, assessments were not always undertaken to ensure they could manage and the support provided subsequently was quite variable. In these circumstances, it was not surprising to find that some family groups struggled.

Kinship care

The presence of relatives or adult family friends also opens up the possibility of placing children in kinship settings. Around one in seven (14%) of the young people in the York study had a main placement with relatives or friends. Children may arrive with older siblings or with other adults who may or may not be related. They may arrive with details of a family relative with whom they may never have lived or these connections may come to light while the child is in the care of the local authority. Concerns about trafficked children and the vulnerability of children living in informal care settings makes the assessment of adults laying claim to unaccompanied children challenging for practitioners (Kearney, 2007).

Government endorsed guidance on unaccompanied children emphasises the potential of family and friends care for these young people and, where these informal arrangements exist at referral or come to light subsequently, encourages local authorities to find imaginative ways to support the continuity of these placements, provided assessment reveals that it is safe for the child to do so (Department of Health, 1995; Kidane, 2001). Kearney (2007) also provides a helpful practice description of the work of one kinship assessment team in this regard.

For looked after children generally, evidence about the potential of family and friends care is encouraging, although by no means unproblematic (Sinclair, 2005). Outcomes for children appear to be no better or worse than those for children in other foster settings, but are often achieved in more adverse circumstances. Kinship carers are often more economically disadvantaged, less well educated and less well remunerated than other foster carers. They also tend to receive less training, have fewer parenting skills and lower levels of social work support. In this context, outcomes appear impressive. Familial commitment and loyalty often seem to overcome these disadvantages and children tend to be more closely integrated with family and community – although tensions between family members, management of contact and the ability of carers to protect children from further abuse may be problematic.

With respect to unaccompanied children the assessment tasks are complex. The York study found considerable variability in the quality of assessments that were undertaken, some cases receiving only a perfunctory assessment to ratify a placement where the child was already *in situ*. Assessment has to tackle two sets of issues: first, to "verify" the nature of the relationship between the child and the proposed carer; second, to assess the carer's willingness and ability to care safely for the child. Assessments often take place in circumstances where there is no documentary evidence and no sources outside of the child and carer to whom practitioners can turn for corroboration, where these adults may themselves have only recently arrived in the UK and who may come from cultures where family ties and obligations are strong and who may therefore be reluctant to co-operate with investigations that appear overly intrusive (Mitchell, 2003). Kearney (2007) stresses the importance of timeliness once these relatives become known. Delays can be intensely frustrating for young people waiting to join relatives or family friends and may have consequences for their mental health and emotional wellbeing (Wade *et al*, 2005; Kearney, 2007). However, the subsequent risks that children may face, where careful assessment, monitoring and support are lacking, were also evident in the York study.

Local authorities may support kinship placements for unaccompanied children in a variety of ways – as foster placements (s20), through community support provisions as children "in need" (s17) or as private fostering arrangements. In the York study, the majority of these placements were supported under s17 arrangements. Studies have pointed to the limited statutory framework for monitoring these placements and to a tendency for social work support to withdraw relatively soon after placement (Williamson, 1998). In line with the evidence on family and friends care more generally, this pattern was evident in the York study. Refugee families often have to live in poor-quality accommodation and manage on low incomes. Young people placed with relatives were often therefore living in conditions that were overcrowded and under strain. Undue reliance was also placed on the strength of familial ties and obligations when setting remuneration levels which, for those supported under s17 in particular, were generally lower than those set for other foster carers. Some private fostering arrangements were not supported at all. In some instances, concerned social workers tried hard to improve the conditions of these families, in others, family strains sometimes led to a breakdown in relationships.

Despite these adversities, children placed in family or friends care tended to fare quite well. These placements often provided opportunities for stable and familiar attachments, support for children's education and enabled children to construct stronger networks of social support, especially within their communities of origin. Local authorities may therefore need to consider the extent to which these forms of placement are routinely considered for unaccompanied children, perhaps using the newer provisions for special guardianship where appropriate, and whether effective and imaginative forms of assessment and support can be developed so that the potential in these placements can be realised more consistently.

Supported and independent accommodation

Local authorities have made heavy use of supported and unsupervised accommodation for unaccompanied young people, especially for those aged 15 to 17 years at referral. Studies have consistently expressed concern about the quality of private sector shared housing, the predominant form of provision sourced mainly through private and voluntary housing agencies, with reports of poor physical conditions, overcrowding, limited facilities and variable access to social work support (Audit Commission, 2000; Stanley, 2001; Dennis, 2002; Mitchell, 2003).

Over one in five of young people (22%) in the York study moved straight to supported accommodation at referral and around one quarter (24%) had a main placement of this type over the time they were supported by social services, the majority supported under s17 arrangements. The range of supported accommodation was variable, including use of "host" families (similar to supported lodgings), supported hostels (foyers, YMCA) and floating support schemes (mainly utilising private sector shared housing). Supported accommodation was also used for older looked after teenagers moving on from foster or residential placements. These young people were rarely placed in unsupervised housing, unless their immigration status permitted them access to council or housing association tenancies. Almost one-third of the York sample (29%) moved straight to unsupervised housing at referral. Three-quarters of these young people (74%) were aged 16 or 17 and virtually all were supported through s17.

Floating support schemes varied both in organisation and the degree of support provided. Where young people were placed within the local authority boundary, support was generally provided directly by children's social work teams or through housing support agencies contracted to the local authority. Where they were placed out of authority, greater reliance was placed on bespoke contract arrangements with private housing agencies. The evidence suggested that the former arrangements provided for more effective support, although there was variety within as well as between approaches. Dedicated support services tended to provide clearer lines of responsibility and communication, support appeared more consistent, including more regular patterns of home visiting, and support packages appeared more comprehensive, addressing young people's lives and needs in the round (including attention to education, health and social relationships). Key workers sometimes adopted a quasi-parental role and their support was highly valued by young people (see also Chase *et al*, 2008).

Reliance on private housing agencies to provide key work support was more problematic, especially where young people were placed at some distance from the local authority. This was also the case for young people living in unsupervised shared housing of this kind. The quality of accommodation was highly variable, repairs and equipment were often shoddy, young people were sometimes forced to make sudden moves at the whim of landlords and key workers were often unresponsive or failed to maintain contact or tended to focus only on placement-related issues. Concerned social workers also found it difficult to ensure contract compliance and had to spend considerable time brokering the relationship between young people and housing agencies. Although some of these placements did provide a relatively stable home base for young people, it was not surprising to find that these young people were more likely to struggle in comparison to those in care or kinship placements. They were heavily reliant on their peers for support, were more isolated, were less likely to be fully engaged in education and, since most were then supported under s17, on reaching the age of 18 their cases were routinely closed, leaving them to make their own way in the world as best they could.

Placement out of authority tended to accentuate these difficulties. Distance tended to constrain the relationships between social workers and housing agencies. It also made it much more difficult to build confident relationships with young people, to visit and monitor their progress. Placing unaccompanied children and young people at some distance from the responsible local authority affected all placement making, including those in foster and residential care, and was primarily resource driven. However, the fact that most of these young people were supported through s17 meant that the regulatory framework governing assessment, planning and contact was weaker and probably contributed to the more highly variable support available to them.

It may be the case that these patterns are changing as more unaccompanied children become looked after and eligible for leaving care services. However, subsequent research in this area is lacking. What little there is tends not to offer great encouragement. Chase and colleagues' (2008) research in one local authority also found that those living in independent settings encountered greatest difficulty. They experienced more social isolation and found it difficult to manage on low incomes, with limited skills and support and highlighted the acute tension felt by many young people approaching 18 years of age around the risk of dispersal where their asylum claims had not yet been settled favourably.

The uncertainties generated by the asylum decision-making process are often overwhelming for young people. It may have negative consequences for their mental health and overall wellbeing. In the York study, around one-third of the young people aged 18 or over were still waiting for a final decision on their asylum claim and the majority of these young people (74%) had transferred to the National Asylum Support Service. Not only did this transition raise the spectre of dispersal, although social workers often advocated for them to remain, the quality of accommodation, the level of allowance and the support that was available was generally rated by young people as significantly worse than that provided by social services.

From a practice viewpoint, transition also brings into sharpest relief the tensions that exist between child welfare and immigration policies (Dixon and Wade, 2007). Pathway planning seeks to provide support and continuity for young people through the transition to adulthood. Yet unaccompanied young people often have a significantly foreshortened sense of the future, based on whether or not they will be allowed to remain. Pathway planning is therefore made complex and has to be multi-dimensional, allowing for different outcomes of the asylum process, including the likelihood of young people having to return to their countries of origin. Planning also has to take account of young people's different rights and entitlements linked to their asylum status (for housing, education, benefits and employment). The new Home Office proposals make this form of planning even more pressing, given the emphasis on speedier asylum decision making and the early return of failed asylum applicants.

Conclusions

It is only in recent years that the resettlement experiences of unaccompanied asylum-seeking children and young people have become better understood. The evidence base to support policy and practice with this group of children is therefore relatively weak and there is a need to take forward an agenda of research and evaluation to understand better the ways in which carers, social workers and other support workers can assist their attempts to refashion (and reintegrate) their lives in new and unfamiliar surroundings.

Unaccompanied children are a heterogeneous group. They come from very different parts of the world, from different socio-economic backgrounds and have had different experiences, some highly traumatic and others less so. We know that many are able to rise to the challenges of resettlement and that, given a supportive placement environment and opportunities to resume education and build new networks of support, they are likely to be quite successful. In these regards, they appear to fare rather better than other looked after children. However, many also experience emotional turbulence linked to the past, present and future. Although most will not need psychiatric intervention, many will need therapeutic care, preferably linked to their everyday lives in placement.

Working with unaccompanied children brings uncertainty to the fore. Assessments are made more complicated by uncertainty about children's ordinary lives before leaving, the absence of other sources of information, the understandable suspicions children bring with them to these encounters and the formal asylum stories that are sometimes told. Attention should be given to the timing and pace of assessments, opportunities for revisiting these stories over time and to ensuring that assessments are conducted more consistently across the whole age range.

In line with Government guidance and developing local authority practice, there appear to be advantages in formally looking after these children. They certainly appear to want similar things from their placements as other children, although they also want respect for their language and cultural origins. Placements in foster care or with kin seem to make their transitions easier and make for more supportive environments. The statutory requirements for looked after children also make for more consistent social work support. The potential in family and friends care, wherever it is feasible and safe to provide it, appears to offer another avenue for successful placement making, although attention is needed to the ways in which these placements are supported.

There is likely to be a need to extend the range of options for supported accommodation and to think carefully about how young people are placed together, given the tensions that can arise through mixing residents together inappropriately, and about how these placements are supported. In this regard, much could be learnt from the development of supported housing by specialist leaving care services. Findings also suggest that the use of unsupervised private sector housing should be viewed with the utmost caution. It is unlikely to be avoided, given the scarcity of other placement resources. However, evidence counsels against using it routinely as a first placement option for older teenagers and suggests that, where it is to be considered, young people's needs and capabilities should be carefully assessed beforehand. It would also help for the provision to be near at hand, since this would enable social workers to maintain closer liaison and contact with housing providers and young people.

Finally, however, the world is about to change again. The current Home Office proposals are likely to bring significant changes to the care pathways of unaccompanied children. The focus on specialisation (in assessment and in care arrangements) may bring some benefits by enabling a smaller number of local authorities to develop expertise in working with these children. However, the proposals also raise concerns. They tend to homogenise these children, perhaps failing to recognise their differing and nuanced care needs. They emphasise difference, largely based around their asylum status, when in practice they may have more in common with other looked after children, especially those from minority ethnic backgrounds, than initially meets the eye. They may also underplay the importance of community, in particular whether the dispersal of children to other parts of the country will jeopardise links with their communities of origin. Perhaps, most importantly, they emphasise return for failed child applicants. Very few young people want this, having invested heavily in their futures here, and (if pursued vigorously) this policy will inevitably lead to a significant reshaping of social work practice with these children.

Selected further reading

Chase E., Knight A. and Statham J. (2008) *The Emotional Well-being of Young People Seeking Asylum in the UK*, London: BAAF

Kohli R. (2007) *Social Work with Unaccompanied Asylum Seeking Children*, Basingstoke: Palgrave MacMillan

Kohli R. and Mitchell F. (eds) (2007) *Working with Unaccompanied Asylum Seeking Children: Issues for policy and practice*, Basingstoke: Palgrave MacMillan

Wade J., Mitchell F. and Baylis G. (2005) *Unaccompanied Asylum Seeking Children: The response of social work services*, London: BAAF

References

Audit Commission (2000) *Another Country: Implementing dispersal under the Immigration and Asylum Act*, London: Audit Commission

Ayotte W. (2000) *Separated Children Coming to Western Europe: Why they travel and how they arrive*, London: Save the Children

Chase E., Knight A. and Statham J. (2008) *The Emotional Well-being of Unaccompanied Asylum-Seeking Children and Young People*, London: BAAF

Council of European Union, (2003) *Laying Down Minimum Standards for the Reception of Asylum Seekers*, Council Directive 2003/9/EC. Available: www.ecre.org/eu_developments/reception/recdirfinal.pdf

Crawley H. (2007) *When is a Child Not a Child? Asylum, age disputes and the process of age assessment*, London: Immigration Law Practitioners' Association

Dennis J. (2002) *A Case for Change: How refugee children in England are missing out*, London: The Children's Society/Save the Children/Refugee Council

Department for Education and Skills (2006) *Care Matters: Transforming the lives of children and young people in care*, London: DfES

Department of Health (1995) *Unaccompanied Asylum-Seeking Children: A practice guide*, London: Department of Health

Department of Health (2003) *Guidance on Accommodating Children in Need and Their Families*, LAC (2003) 13, June, London: Department of Health

Department of Health/Department for Education and Employment/Home Office (2000) *Framework for the Assessment of Children in Need and their Families*, London: The Stationery Office

Dixon J. and Wade J. (2007) 'Leaving "care"? Transition planning and support for unaccompanied young people', in Kohli R. and Mitchell F. (eds) *Working with Unaccompanied Asylum-Seeking Children: Issues for Policy and Practice*, Basingstoke: Palgrave MacMillan

Dixon J., Wade J., Byford S., Weatherley H. and Lee J. (2006) *Young People Leaving Care: A study of costs and outcomes*, Final Report to the Department for Education and Skills, York: SPRU, University of York

Farmer E., Moyers S. and Lipscombe J. (2004) *Fostering Adolescents*, London: Jessica Kingsley Publishers

Free E. (2005) *Local Authority Support to Unaccompanied Asylum-Seeking Young People: Changes since the Hillingdon Judgement*, Leeds: Save the Children

Hek R. (2007) 'Using foster placements for the care and resettlement of unaccompanied children', in Kohli R. and Mitchell F. (eds) *Working with Unaccompanied Asylum-Seeking Children: Issues for policy and practice*, Basingstoke: Palgrave MacMillan

Home Office (2002) *Unaccompanied Asylum-Seeking Children: Information note*, London: Immigration and Nationality Directorate, Home Office

Home Office (2007) *Planning Better Outcomes and Support for Unaccompanied Asylum-Seeking Children: Consultation Paper*, London: Home Office

Home Office (2008) *Better Outcomes: The Way Forward: Improving the care of unaccompanied asylum-seeking children*, London: Home Office

Kearney M. (2007) 'Friends and family care of unaccompanied children: Recognising the possible and potential', in Kohli R. and Mitchell F. (eds) *Working with Unaccompanied Asylum-Seeking Children: Issues for policy and practice*, Basingstoke: Palgrave MacMillan

Kidane S. (2001) *Food, Shelter and Half a Chance: Assessing the needs of unaccompanied asylum-seeking and refugee children*, London: BAAF

Kidane S. and Amerena P. (2004) *Fostering Unaccompanied Asylum-Seeking Children: A training course for foster carers*, London: BAAF

Kidane S. and Amerena P. (2005) *Looking After Unaccompanied Asylum-Seeking and Refugee Children: A training course for social care professionals*, London: BAAF

Kohli R. (2006) 'The sound of silence: Listening to what unaccompanied asylum-seeking children say and do not say', *British Journal of Social Work*, 36, pp 707–721

Kohli R. (2007) *Social Work with Unaccompanied Asylum-Seeking Children*, Basingstoke: Palgrave MacMillan

Mitchell F. (2003) 'The social services response to unaccompanied children in England', *Child and Family Social Work*, 8:3, pp 179–189

Mitchell F. (2007) 'Assessing practice with unaccompanied children: Exploring exceptions to the problem', in Kohli R. and Mitchell F. (eds) *Working with Unaccompanied Asylum-Seeking Children: Issues for policy and practice*, Basingstoke: Palgrave MacMillan

Refugee Council (2005) *Ringing the Changes: The impact of guidance on the use of sections 17 and 20 of the Children Act 1989 to support unaccompanied asylum-seeking children*, London: The Refugee Council

Ressler E. M., Boothby N. and Steinbock B. (1988) *Unaccompanied Children: Care and protection in wars, natural disasters and refugee movements*, Oxford: Oxford University Press

Separated Children in Europe Programme, (2004) *Statement of Good Practice* (3rd edn), International Save the Children Alliance in Europe/UNHCR. Available: www.savethechildren.net/separated_children/good_practice/index.html

Sinclair I. (2005) *Fostering Now: Messages from research*, London: Jessica Kingsley Publishers

Sinclair I., Baker C., Lee J. and Gibbs I. (2007) *The Pursuit of Permanence: A study of the English care system*, London: Jessica Kingsley Publishers

Sinclair I., Wilson K. and Gibbs I. (2004) *Foster Placements: Why they succeed and why they fail*, London: Jessica Kingsley Publishers

Stanley K. (2001) *Cold Comfort: Young separated refugees in England*, London: Save the Children

Stone R. (2000) *Children First and Foremost: Meeting the needs of unaccompanied asylum-seeking children*, Barkingside: Barnardo's

Thomas S., Thomas S., Nafees B. and Bhugra D. (2004) 'I was running away from death: The pre-flight experiences of unaccompanied asylum-seeking children in the UK', *Child Care, Health and Development*, 30:2, pp 113–122

Tolfree D. (2004) *Whose Children? Separated children's protection and participation in emergencies*, Stockholm: Save the Children Sweden

United Nations High Commissioner for Refugees (1994) *Refugee Children: Guidelines on protection and care*, Geneva: UNHCR

Wade J., Mitchell F. and Baylis G. (2005) *Unaccompanied Asylum-Seeking Children: The response of social work services*, London: BAAF

Williamson L. (1998) 'Unaccompanied – but not unsupported', in Rutter J. and Jones C. (eds) *Refugee Education: Mapping the field*, Stoke on Trent: Trentham Books

Zulfacar D. (1987) 'Alternative forms of care for unaccompanied refugee minors: A comparison of US and Australian experience', *International Social Work*, 30, pp 61–75

21 Planning and placement for sibling groups

Jenifer Lord and Sarah Borthwick

Brothers and sisters who are brought up together can develop significant lifelong relationships. For many siblings, these may be among the closest relationships they ever experience. They can also change over time, being close and intense in childhood, sometimes more distant in teenage years and young adulthood, and, often, close and supportive in middle and older age (Hegar, 1988). However, it is also recognised that, for some siblings, relationships may be highly conflictual, hurtful, even abusive and these too may last a lifetime.

Who are siblings?

At least 80 per cent of the general population in the UK have one or more brother or sister. Children who are looked after are slightly more likely to have siblings. Estimates (summarised in Rushton, 2001) suggest that the figure for these children could be as high as 87 per cent.

Looked after children often come from very complex and fragmented families and they are unlikely to have lived with all their siblings. They may have lived with full-siblings (with whom they share both biological parents), with half-siblings (with whom they share one parent), with step-siblings (the children of a step-parent to whom they are not biologically related), or with others such as cousins. However, they are likely also to have other full- or half-siblings who live elsewhere, either independently because they are grown up, or with relatives or parents (this will be the case often for half-siblings, particularly on the paternal side, who live with their own mother) or who are looked after but living elsewhere or have been adopted.

This complexity of relationships poses problems for researchers. 'The issue of how to define "siblings" has been identified in the literature as "a sticky research problem" ' (Hegar, 2005, p 721). Research studies have used varied definitions. 'This makes research into looked after siblings very complicated, and wider conclusions often cannot be reached because studies are based on different definitions' (Hadley, 2007, p 2).

We suggest that a useful definition is: 'Children who share at least one birth parent and/or children who live or have lived for a significant period with other children in a family group' (Lord and Borthwick, 2008).

There has been very little research into who looked after children themselves see as their siblings. Practice experience suggests that the above definition is likely to encompass their views. However, it is important to look at this with each child. Siblings may well still be very important to a child even though they are no longer living together or even have never lived together. This needs to be kept in mind and contact arrangements considered where appropriate. Conversely, there may be siblings, perhaps older half-siblings on the father's side, about whom the child knows nothing. It is important that efforts are made to gather information on all siblings and to record it both for care planning purposes and as a record for the child. Even if only minimal information is available, the child should have it as part of their family tree and may want to follow up contacts later in life.

What do siblings get from living together?

The question of what siblings get from living together is a highly complex one. Many siblings who grow up together will experience positive benefits to their emotional and social development, their self-esteem and their learning. Others, however, will experience difficulties through intense competition, bullying and/or scapegoating. Others will experience a mix of positives and negatives. All will be influenced by a range of factors, including, very significantly, the family context and the emotional climate in which they are living or have lived.

Studies from development psychology, such as Dunn and McGuire (1992), have provided evidence about the importance of sibling relationships and the influence of these on children's development. For example, a number of life skills can be learnt and influenced through sibling interaction. Rivalry and jealousy are common in many families from a range of cultures and through the management of this, siblings can begin to learn how to share and co-operate with others. They can develop understanding of the perspectives and views of others. They can develop friendships. Growing up with siblings provides an arena for play and learning, for handling disagreements and conflict, for comfort and protection, and for development of a shared sense of family identity.

In a survey of children's understanding of sibling relationships, Edwards *et al* (2005) found that, for children, their relationships with their siblings are an important part of their everyday lives: 'There is always someone there' was an important feeling. Some children, however, intensely disliked their siblings. Additionally, children often mentioned older siblings taking care of and protecting younger ones as well as having power over them. The researchers concluded that sibling relationships are complex and diverse and that children are active in shaping these relationships.

A range of often very intense feelings towards their siblings is described by many adults and children. These include feelings of love, hate, jealousy, rivalry, competition, joy, protection, sharing and support. Researchers (Furman and Buhrmester, 1985) highlight four key factors that are central to a sibling relationship. These are the degree of warmth, the degree of conflict, the degree of rivalry and the degree to which one of the siblings nurtures or dominates the other.

It seems clear that living with a sibling or siblings is an individual experience with often both positive and negative qualities. One relationship will vary from another depending on a range of factors such as temperament, personality, gender, ethnicity (if different), ability and position in the family. The family context and experience of parenting will influence how the siblings feel about and interact with each other. Whether the child is the eldest child, a middle child or a younger child and the roles they have within the family will have an impact on the development of their relationships. In many families and in many cultures, older siblings take some or considerable responsibility for their younger siblings. Elgar and Head (1999), in their review of research, found evidence that young children develop strong attachments to siblings especially when the older siblings are involved in the child's care. Older children too become very attached to their younger siblings. Schofield and Beek (2006) argue that, although a close sibling relationship lacks many of the characteristics of a child–caregiver attachment relationship, it can provide some of the secure base characteristics such as reducing anxiety, supporting play and exploration. They reinforce the view that a separation when there is such a relationship is likely to lead to a profound sense of loss and grief.

Many factors influence how siblings relate to each other. Some of these have already been described. Others are listed in Patterns and Outcomes in Child Placement (Department of Health, 1991) and include:

- the child's position in the family;
- their gender;
- cultural and family expectations for each child;
- the emotional age at which each is functioning;
- the extent to which they have a shared history and family experience;
- the role each child is perceived to have played (if any) in the sibling group leaving home and starting to be looked after.

Other important factors are the child's attachment to their primary caregiver and the child's innate temperament and degree of resilience.

Kosonen (1994) describes factors in the birth family which can negatively influence the relationship between siblings. These include:

- poor attachments to parents can result in intense sibling conflict;
- a conflictual relationship between the parents may lead to poor sibling relationships with a tendency for boys to be particularly affected;
- parental favouritism is likely to increase sibling conflict and to be negative for both favoured and non-favoured children; however, if children can perceive differential treatment as "fair", their sibling relationships need not suffer;

403

- neglect and parental unavailability can result in strong compensatory sibling relationships; however, it can also result in unmet needs;
- the impact of abuse which may result in poor or hostile sibling relationships for both abused and non-abused children; children who have been abused may be particularly resentful of those who have not;
- siblings who are close in age and of the same gender can have an emotionally intense relationship with high levels of conflict;
- the impact of the non-shared environment; siblings will have a range of experiences away from their brothers and sisters including school and friendships, all of which will have an impact on their development and individual relationships.

Some research studies have examined sibling relationships in adversity (see Bank and Kahn, 1982). They comment that the sibling bond can be strengthened and brothers and sisters can and do provide comfort and protection towards each other. However, it is increasingly being recognised that, for some, the sibling relationship can be significantly damaged. This is particularly the case where children have experienced abuse, neglect, violence and poor attachments with their birth parents or caregivers (see Burnell *et al*, 2007). Dysfunctional or abusive patterns of behaviour between siblings may be established. In some cases, such patterns can be very difficult to transform depending on the severity of the abuse, the length of time over which it occurred and the ability of parents or caregivers to meet the complex needs of each child.

Sibling relationships are complex and individual. There is no question that there are strengths in living together but there can be significant difficulties for a number of children. Comprehensive and careful assessments are essential.

Why and how do looked after siblings end up living apart?

As has been described in the section on 'Who are siblings?' it is inevitable that many children will live apart from their siblings, given that these siblings may be living independently or may be half-siblings living with their own parent(s). However, almost half of looked after children are placed separately from at least some of their siblings who are also looked after (Rushton *et al*, 2001); this study of 133 children in late permanent placements found that they had a total of 146 siblings living elsewhere, 38 per cent living elsewhere in the care system and 40 per cent remaining with birth parents (usually younger half-siblings); 101 of the children in this study were placed with a sibling, even though 80 per cent of them were separated from others.

It is estimated that over half of children being looked after are placed with at least one sibling. However, many are separated from other siblings, who may be looked after and placed elsewhere or may not be looked after. Of all children adopted in 1998/9, 37 per cent were placed with at least some looked after siblings (Ivaldi, 2000). (We have no more recent statistics for this. Another comprehensive analysis of all adopted children is needed.) Children in sibling groups represented 52 per cent of children referred to the National Adoption Register in the year to December 2006.

In an international overview of 17 sibling studies, Hegar (2005) found that siblings were more likely to be separated in care if:

- children were older;
- there was a large age gap between siblings;
- children were of different genders;
- children entered care at different times;
- some of them had special needs;
- placement changes had been more frequent and recent.

She found that placement with kin carers meant it was more likely that siblings stayed together. However, in a recent study (Farmer and Moyers, 2005), it was found that siblings were as likely to be together when placed with "stranger" foster carers as with kinship carers.

Kosonen (1996) found that the most frequent reason for separation was that children had started being looked after at different times. She concluded that the points of entering and leaving care were especially likely to be associated with the separation of siblings.

Rushton *et al* (2001) found that the two most important reasons for separation were:

- specific needs which dictated separate placements; and
- entering care at different times.

When children were placed on their own, it was almost always as a result of the assessment of their individual needs. When siblings were separated from some but placed with others, this was, in 46 per cent of cases, because they had come into care at different times. There were frequently large age gaps and the older siblings were often settled in placements where they had been for some years.

The large age gaps between siblings identified in the studies considered by Hegar (2005) often also involve a different permanence plan (e.g. fostering) for older children, but adoption for a much younger child. This need not, but often does, lead to separate placements. It may also involve different contact needs, which can preclude being placed together.

In one study (Rushton *et al*, 2001), social workers considering whether to separate siblings, to place them together or to re-unite already separated siblings were most influenced by the relationship between the children and the child's individual needs. A shared history and the account by carers of how the children were when together were also important factors. The expressed wishes of the children were considered important in just under half of the cases.

The longer children remain in separate placements the harder it will be for them to maintain a relationship and for a clear assessment of this to be made. Attachments will also form and the foster carers may offer permanence to the child for whom they are caring.

A number of studies (Ellison, 1999; Leathers, 2005) indicate that a lack of foster placements able to accommodate larger sibling groups or children with special needs can often lead to the separation of siblings who come into care together. Practice experience suggests that an anticipated inability to find permanent new families for sibling groups of four or more children can sometimes lead to a decision to split children before family finding starts.

With the increasing emphasis on trying to place children with family members and the often complex nature of these family systems, practice experience indicates that it is increasingly common for relatives to offer permanent care to one or two children in a sibling group, but not the others. The relatives may not, for example, see half-siblings as part of their family but the children themselves may not make this distinction, having lived at home together with the parent, often the mother, whom they share.

Working with sibling groups, particularly those separated in two or more foster homes and with their constellation of parents, relatives and foster carers, is complex and demanding for workers. In her description of her assessment work with a number of sibling groups, Hindle (2007, p 89) comments, 'I found myself wondering if one dynamic in these cases was that the children's sibling relationships evoked complicated feelings in those looking after them or working with them'. Workers were so anxious to get it right that this seemed 'to make it more difficult for them to identify and acknowledge the children's distress'. The complexity of issues involved meant that, 'In my opinion, the question about whether to split or maintain a sibling group was often confused with, or overshadowed by, other issues such as care planning, difficulties in their present circumstances or lack of available resources' (Hindle, 2007, p 89).

How are assessments done of the needs of children as members of a sibling group?

When assessing and planning for a sibling group, it is very important to remember that each child is also an individual with his or her own unique needs. It is essential that each child in a sibling group has a full assessment in their own right. The assessment of their relationship with, and attachment to, their siblings is one component of this, but only one. (Lord and Borthwick, 2008, p 19)

Ryan (2002, p 81) states that: 'The quality of the relationship between siblings is incumbent upon the quality of the relationship between the sibling and primary caregiver'. She suggests that, because of this, the assessment of the sibling relationship must be preceded by a consideration of each child's attachment history. This will involve looking at reports and assessments which have already been done. 'When attachment to parental figures has been insufficient, the bond between siblings may be characterised by unhealthy interaction and serve to inhibit the psychological growth and well-being of the siblings involved' (Ryan, 2002). Whether or not the child has formed a healthy bond with the present caregiver will be very relevant too.

The sibling relationship checklist, reproduced in *Together or Apart?* (Lord and Borthwick, 2008) is a useful tool for the children's carers to record in detail how each child relates to each other child in the group. The child's social worker, or an independent worker, should also observe the children together, ideally on several occasions. Researchers (Furman and Buhrmester, 1985) have highlighted four key factors which need to be assessed.

- the degree of warmth
- the degree of conflict
- the degree of rivalry
- the degree to which one of the siblings nurtures or dominates the other.

Burnell *et al* (2007 citing Panksepp, 1998), suggest that the dimensions of aggression, fear, comfort seeking, and play can provide a framework which can be applied to observations of children.

A comprehensive assessment of siblings and whether they should be placed together or apart, undertaken in a CAMHS setting, is described by Hindle (2007). The assessment protocol involved interviews with the children's social worker, the foster carer's supervising social worker and the foster carer or key worker. Child behaviour checklists and sibling questionnaires were completed, the latter focusing on three dimensions in the sibling relationship – relative status/power, warmth/closeness and conflict.

The children were then seen together twice, individually twice and together for a final session. Narrative story stems (Hodges and Steele, 2000) were completed with each child in their first individual session. The other sessions involved observing the children in play, individually and together.

The use of different methods of assessment enabled the complexity of the issues to "come to life". Hindle (2007, p 89) comments that 'throughout the study, there was repeated evidence of the professional networks' difficulties in thinking about the children's shared experience and a tendency to underestimate their meaning for each other. In the majority of cases, I was repeatedly struck by the discrepancy between what I had been told about the children and my experience of being with them.'

Several researchers (for example, Groza *et al*, 2003; Hindle, 2007) point out that even a thorough assessment over several weeks is essentially taking a "snapshot" of a relationship at one time and stage of development. There is general recognition that a sibling relationship can last a lifetime, and is constantly evolving and changing as children progress through their childhood and beyond. Clearly, decisions have to be made about placement together or apart. However, it is important to try to consider the likely benefits and disadvantages for the child throughout his or her life, not just in the immediate future.

Why do siblings sometimes need to be separated?

The significance of sibling relationships is reflected in social work policy, in the legal framework and in practice guidance in all the different nations in the UK. The focus of these is to enable sibling relationships to be maintained or to be developed through placement together, where this is practicable and consistent with their welfare. However, there is also recognition of the need to separate siblings if necessary. Contact between separated siblings is recommended wherever possible.

As has already been described, it is not infrequent for siblings to be separated on entry into the looked after system. A considerable number of children will remain looked after either in long-term foster placements or residential units or will be placed for adoption. For siblings, the decision whether to place them together or apart on a permanent basis is therefore a crucial one. It is also often a painful one. In our view, it should be treated with the same seriousness as the decision to separate children permanently from their birth parents. This is not to say that permanent separation should not happen, but that it should do so only after very careful assessment. Moreover, wherever possible, consideration must be given to whether children can be helped to form healthier relationships and whether their individual needs can be met together in placement before making permanent decisions for separation.

There are a number of factors that may indicate the need for permanent separation. For example, very intense levels of conflict, dominant or abusive patterns may mean that placement together is not viable. Careful consideration needs to take place for siblings who have been sexually abused as to whether they can be placed together permanently. Farmer and Pollock (1998) found that close supervision was often needed when siblings were placed together as there was a very real risk of sexual activity between the siblings. They noted that often carers were unaware of the history of abusive behaviour. They also found that siblings who were sexually abused were slightly more often separated from their brothers and sisters; 40 per cent never saw their siblings following placement.

Burnell *et al* (2007) suggest that children who have experienced very poor attachments need to develop a secure attachment to safe adult caregivers. Achieving this must take primary importance in care planning for the child. In their view, siblings who have been traumatised may need to be separated because, placed together, they will inhibit the formation of this child–adult primary attachment.

Gerrilyn Smith, Clinical Psychologist (see Lord and Borthwick, 2008, p 20) sets out a number of circumstances which indicate that siblings may need to be placed separately. If children are placed in the same family, it may be impossible (within a reasonable timescale) to help them recover from dysfunctional and disruptive patterns of interaction from the family of origin. These patterns include:

- intense rivalry and jealousy, with each child totally preoccupied with and unable to tolerate the attention which their sibling or siblings may be getting;
- exploitation often based on gender, e.g. boys may have been seen in their birth family and see themselves as inherently superior to their sisters, with the right to dominate and exploit them;
- chronic scapegoating of one child; maintaining unhelpful alliances in a sibling group and family of origin conflicts – sibling patterns of behaviour may be strongly entrenched and may prevent re-parenting or learning new cultural norms;
- maintaining unhelpful hierarchical positions e.g: a child many be stuck in the role of victim or bully;
- highly sexualised behaviour with each other;
- acting as triggers to each other's traumatic material and potentially constantly re-traumatising each other. The triggers may well be unconscious, unintentional and mundane.

In our view, there may be other reasons too.

- An older sibling may not be able to invest emotionally in a new family and will hinder the emotional investment of a younger child.
- There can be considerable age difference between siblings placed. Sometimes, the care plan for a much older sibling may be for permanent foster care with regular direct contact with birth family members but for a much younger sibling, adoption in a new family with indirect contact with the birth family may be in their best interest.
- Sometimes a relative of one of the siblings offers a home to that child but not to others and this adult–child relationship is assessed as more important to the child than the sibling one.
- Sometimes a child may have a significant attachment to another carer and it is too damaging to disrupt this in order to unite or reunite the child with other siblings.
- Sometimes, the size and age range of the group means that there are a very limited number of families available. After time-limited family finding, a sibling group may therefore need to be separated but it is important that ongoing contact arrangements are made which can support the maintenance of their relationships.

For some children, the trauma of separation can be profound and the sense of loss may be longstanding. It is vitally important to record decisions and provide explanations to children as to why separation has occurred or will occur (Groze, 1996). Preparing children for such separations and supporting them and their families are vitally important tasks. Decisions about ongoing contact will need careful assessment.

When and by whom are decisions made about the placement of siblings?

The decision about whether or not to separate siblings on a permanent basis or not to unite those who are already separately placed is a crucially important one with lifelong implications for the children.

It is essential that:

- there is a clear and transparent process for arriving at the decision; and
- it is made following a group discussion to which everyone involved, including, of course, the children concerned, have had an opportunity to contribute in some way. (Lord and Borthwick, 2008, p 14)

It is important that the decision is based on the carefully assessed needs of the children concerned. Rushton (2001, p 51) comments that, in his research into sibling placements, 'On the whole we found that there was relatively little use of any sort of structured procedure informing social workers' decisions'. In two-thirds of cases there was no formal assessment of the children's needs or relationships with each other.

As has already been described, decisions about the initial placement of siblings when they start to be looked after are all too often made pragmatically, based on the vacancies in foster homes or the ages and genders of children whom foster carers can accommodate. It is important that consideration is given to whether siblings, separated on starting to be looked after solely because there was no foster family able to taken them all, should be re-united as soon as a suitable vacancy occurs. In one authority, separated siblings were kept "on referral" with a view to re-uniting them if a placement became available, although in practice this was rarely achieved (Tomlinson, 1999). This should certainly be considered at the first review, if not sooner. There will need to be a clear departmental policy about this as it may well involve a more expensive independent fostering provider (IFP) placement and it will also involve a move for at least some, if not all, of the children.

It is essential that the care plan for each child is clear about whether a joint permanent placement for the child with siblings is planned and the reasons why not, if this is the case. Plans for any contact between separated siblings should be detailed. It is good practice, although not required by legislation or guidance, for there to be one independent reviewing officer (IRO), if at all possible, for all the children in a sibling group, whether they are birth siblings in separate placements or children growing up in the same permanent family who may not be related to each other. This enables there to be a clear overview of the needs of the children involved. If siblings are being looked after by different local authorities, there will need to be liaison between workers and IROs. Plans to split children who are currently living together or not to unite siblings who are currently in separate temporary foster homes, should always be confirmed at a review.

Most local authorities have permanency planning meetings, involving the child's worker and manager, the foster carer and/or their supervising social worker and a representative from the adoption and permanence team. The child's guardian, if in care proceedings, may well also be involved in some, at least, of these meetings. This group will discuss and make plans, based on evidence from assessments, for the future placement of children both in terms of the type of placement and also in terms of whether children will be placed together, re-united or placed separately from siblings. Research (Beckett, 1999, p 124) found that 'in the absence of policy or a corporate response to planning for siblings, the values and commitment of individuals appeared to wield considerable influence'. A permanence planning group should provide an important check and balance to the personal beliefs of social workers, foster carers and others. There needs to be an acknowledgment of the strong personal views, often based on their own family experience, which individuals may have about siblings. Some may feel strongly that they should be kept together at all costs while others may find it impossible to believe that anyone could parent a sibling group of four or more looked after children. These strong views should not be an over-riding factor in decision-making. It is important that a group is involved in evaluating and discussing all the evidence for the placement of siblings together or apart (see Lord and Borthwick, 2008).

Adoption panels can have an important role in decision making about the placement of siblings. When considering whether a child should be placed for adoption, panel members need to evaluate all the information presented. This should include information about siblings, about whether a joint placement is planned and the reasons why not, if this is the case. The plan for the youngest sibling in a group is sometimes adoption, even though this will involve separating him or her from older siblings. The panel members will need to weigh up whether the benefits of adoption will outweigh the loss for the child of the chance to grow up with siblings. Panel members may also recommend that children in a sibling group should be placed for adoption but comment that they might be unlikely to recommend a joint match for these children who appear to have needs which could not be met by one family.

Recruitment, assessment, preparation and support of families

Issues in relation to siblings will need to be discussed and addressed with all prospective adopters and foster carers. Even if they are not applying for siblings, they may already have a child or children whose sibling a placed child will become. The child to be placed is likely to have siblings elsewhere, either in the care system or with birth relatives and contact will need to be thought about. A child with no siblings may have a brother or sister born subsequently who may also need care. Families should be asked to agree to be told of the subsequent need for permanent placement of a sibling of "their" child so that consideration can be given to uniting these siblings. It is important that families are also made aware of the fact that a placed child or children is likely to bring patterns of behaviour from their previous experience with siblings into their new family. This will affect their relationship with any children already in the family.

Although in England and Wales there is a legal "usual fostering limit" of three children, without an exemption, foster carers are able to foster larger groups of children if all the children are in the same sibling group (Children Act, 1989, Schedule 7). It may be necessary to consider a retainer fee so that foster carers able to take larger sibling groups do not have single children placed with them. As described earlier, the separation of siblings on starting to be looked after because of a lack of placements able to take them all can all too easily lead to a permanent separation.

Permanent families can be found for even large sibling groups. A national survey by BAAF (Ivaldi, 2000) showed that, of the children adopted in 1998/9, almost all children for whom the plan was placement with siblings were in fact placed together. This included groups of four and five siblings. In the year to 31 March 2007, 34 groups of two siblings, 12 groups of three and one group of six siblings were placed in permanent new families through *Be My Parent*, a family-finding newspaper published by BAAF. In the year to December 2006, five groups of three siblings were placed via the National Adoption Register and 26 groups of two.

'An aggressive and sustained recruitment campaign for foster and adoptive families who can and want to parent siblings is essential' (Groza *et al*, 2003, p 487). There has been no research that we are aware of examining the successful recruitment, assessment and preparation of new permanent families for large sibling groups. However, some successful adopters of groups of four or more siblings have commented (Lord and Borthwick, 2008) that factors which helped included being shown information on larger groups of siblings needing placement, having an assessing social worker who believed that large sibling groups could be placed together, and being put in touch with adopters of large sibling groups and being able to talk to them. Several of the families in this small survey commented that their children supported each other, played well together and kept each other entertained and occupied. They felt that the positives as well as the many potential problems of parenting a number of siblings should be discussed with families. Other suggestions include making this need clear in all recruitment literature and information meetings, having a project worker who concentrates on this for a time and, crucially, having clear and comprehensive support available.

Research (Rushton *et al*, 2001, p 140) indicates the need 'for careful and thorough preparation of all birth children and a mechanism by which they can get help when they wish'. Most of the birth children in this study 'experienced the arrival of the new children as a positive event but there were tensions and jealousies for a minority'. Some of the placements progressed very well even though the placed children were close in age to the existing children and in others there were problems and jealousy even where there was a big age gap and the birth children had left home. However, in line with other research, Rushton et al conclude that 'the policy of placing with a three-year age gap is a useful guide for practitioners' but warn that 'difficulties can occur even when it is followed'.

Support is a crucial issue and families need to be aware of the sorts of support which may be available from early on in the process. It is suggested (Lord and Borthwick, 2008, p 24) that this should include:

- regular financial support;
- a settling-in grant for equipment such as beds, a larger washing machine, etc.;
- domestic help in the early stages;
- financial help for larger transport;
- a loan or other help towards larger housing;
- therapeutic help – one family in the survey had monthly consultations with CAMHS and another had funding for art and music therapy for their children;
- help with sibling relationships issues – research (Rushton et al, 2001) indicates that sibling relationship difficulties are a factor in less stable placements and that 'appropriate support and funding for specialist help need to be available'.

Outcomes for children placed together and apart

Several research studies have focused on the outcomes for siblings placed together or apart. Findings from a range of studies both internationally and in the UK suggest that joint sibling placements are as stable or more stable than placements of single children or separated siblings. In fact, several studies provide evidence that children can do as well or even better when placed together. Hegar's international overview (2005, p 731) reached the tentative conclusion that:

Joint sibling placements are as stable, or more stable, than placements of single children or separated siblings, and several studies suggest that children do as well or better when placed with their brothers and sisters.

Wedge and Mantle (1991) found that older children in a sibling group placed together had a lower disruption rate than singly placed children of that age. However, they also found that younger siblings had a higher disruption rate than singly placed children of their age. This suggests that a sibling group placement may sometimes "protect" an older child, but also may put a younger sibling placement slightly more at risk. They concluded that, although many sibling placements were positive, they can carry additional risk and stress for carers.

413

Rushton *et al* (1989) found that boys placed with siblings 'generally made somewhat better progress than those placed singly. However, this may have been because they had fewer problems to begin with.' Tarren-Sweeney and Hazell (2005) found that girls separated from their siblings were reported to have poorer mental health and socialisation than girls placed with at least one sibling.

Quinton *et al* (1998) in their study of permanent placements for older children, also concluded that outcomes were poorer for singly placed children. This was particularly true when the child's siblings remained in the birth home and the placed child had experienced rejection by the birth parents. Children scapegoated at home by parents but now placed with siblings did as well as their siblings. They also found that there were poorer outcomes for singly placed children when they joined an established family. Difficulties between the placed children and the family's birth children were relatively frequent. This study confirmed the findings of previous ones (Parker, 1966; Wedge and Mantle, 1991) that where the placed child was older or close in age to the youngest child, placements were more prone to poorer outcomes. However, in Quinton *et al*'s study, sibling relationship difficulties occurred with wider age gaps too. They found that significant problems also arose when the birth sibling was an adolescent. However, Beckett *et al* (1999), in their study of children adopted from Romania, found that the problems reported by adopters between children close in age appeared to reduce over the years.

Rushton *et al* (2001) comment that the findings in many studies are complex, 'showing both advantages and problems'. In their study of siblings placed in late permanent placements, they found that sibling placements were associated with greater stability and there were poorer outcomes for singly placed children. However, they also noted that those children who were singly placed had suffered more adverse experiences and so it was not possible to conclude that they would have done better if they had been placed with a sibling.

A child's violent or sexually abusive behaviour to other children was the apparent cause of all placement disruptions in a study carried out by Lowe and Murch *et al* (1999). Poor outcomes were most closely associated with difficulties in the children's interaction with new parents or their siblings, whether placed singly or jointly (Rushton *et al*, 2001).

Contact issues

In a study of contact in the adoption of younger children, Neil (1999) found that, even though many children were separated from siblings for a variety of reasons, there were often no arrangements made for contact between them after adoption. This was particularly the case for paternal siblings. It was unlikely for there to be contact arrangements with siblings who remained within the birth family.

Lowe and Murch (1999), in their study of 226 adoptive families, found that contact with siblings was set up in 49 per cent of cases, mostly involving children placed elsewhere in the care system. They, too, found it unlikely for there to be contact arrangements with siblings who remained within the birth family. They found that some children may not want contact with siblings early on in their new permanent placement but may change their mind when they feel more secure.

Rushton *et al* (2001) found in their study that half the placements were made without any plan for sibling contact. The families however, expressed positive views about contact particularly when children were placed in other permanent families. Contact was also seen as having positive outcomes for singly placed children.

Smith and Logan (2004), in a study of direct contact after adoption, found that a significant number of children were having direct contact with birth siblings living elsewhere. In fact, birth siblings were the birth relatives with whom they were most likely to have direct contact after adoption. In this study, most children expressed satisfaction about the contact arrangements and wanted these to continue. Their feelings about the contact varied depending on the amount of time they had spent together and the nature of their shared experiences. Some adopted children worried about their siblings, particularly if they were not settled with a permanent family. In these cases, adopters too, reported concerns about contact with some siblings who remained looked after in terms of their sexual knowledge and experience, their language, and rough and excitable behaviour when they met their siblings. Those adopters felt contact was not an easy option but continued to consider it to be very important, particularly for the siblings who remained looked after.

Some children who had more tenuous relationships with their brothers and sisters described their birth siblings more like friends than members of their family. Logan and Smith (2004, p 149), however, state that 'sibling contact may provide not only current pleasure and reassurance but is also an investment for the future when relationships may change, develop and become of enduring importance'. All the studies comment on the importance of adults working well together to ensure and encourage positive contact for children.

Macaskill (2002) undertook a study of older children placed for adoption or permanent fostering, all of whom had suffered emotional trauma. She found that, for a number of the children who had experienced abuse within the birth family, patterns of dominance, continuing anger at separation or sexual exploitation could resurface during contact meetings between siblings. She also found that some children wanted less contact as their relationship became more secure in their new family. They wanted to move on from the past whereas another sibling did not or could not. Macaskill found that, where contact worked well, there was good interaction, affection and it enabled siblings to talk about their past traumas helpfully together.

In our view, wherever children are placed apart from siblings, consideration should always be given to the possibility of some form of contact between them. Clearly, however, this needs careful assessment as to the purpose of contact, the form it should take, the care plan for each child and the nature of the relationship between the siblings. This can apply to a wide range of "siblings", including full-, half-, step- and foster siblings. Issues around the behaviour and capacity of birth parents, adult birth relatives as well as foster carers and adopters to support the contact for children will also need consideration.

Sometimes, older siblings are already placed in their adoptive, foster or birth families. It is important to make contact with those families and consider what contact arrangements could be made. It is also important to consider the purpose of contact and whether it is in the best interests of each child for it to take place.

It needs to be considered whether contact will be arranged between the children in their different families by the adults on their own or with social work support. There would certainly need to be social work involvement initially to introduce families and to help them sort out an agreement about arrangements for contact. It would be necessary to consider the number and frequency of different contact arrangements in relation to what children and their new parents can realistically accommodate in their new life together. Support needs for everyone must be assessed with relevant services provided. Moreover, agencies should always be prepared to negotiate or re-negotiate sibling contact if this is requested.

There are different forms of contact that could take place including face-to-face contact, phone, email, texting or indirect arrangements which might include letters or cards via the agency. Spending birthdays or festivals together could be considered. Sleepovers may be appropriate.

When sibling contact is taking place, it is important to recognise that levels of confidentiality may not be possible to maintain. Children should not be expected to keep secrets from one another and cannot be expected to differentiate between what will and will not be an identifying factor for birth relatives. Workers will need to support adopters and foster carers to accept this and think through any possible consequences.

The deciding factor regarding contact between siblings always has to be the needs of individual children. Like the decision to separate siblings, there may be a number of compelling reasons indicating that there should be no direct or even indirect contact in particular cases. This will need to be based on a careful assessment of the children's needs and wishes and on the family history (see Lord and Borthwick, 2008). It could be that the child is clear that they wish to have no contact at all, at least for the time being. It could be that the relationship between the siblings is an abusive one and any form of contact is likely to result in extreme distress, continuing trauma or a return to previous dysfunctional patterns of behaviour. It could be that a birth parent poses a serious threat to the child's permanent placement and so it is not possible for the child to have direct contact with siblings who remain living with the birth family (Bond, 2007).

We do not yet know the outcomes for children of contact between siblings over the long term. More research is needed. However, they would seem promising, given studies to date. But the success of contact in the short and the longer term is likely to depend on good assessments of the contact needs of each child and their siblings, and the right kind of support. The opportunity to know and, wherever possible, to be encouraged to develop positive and enduring relationships with brothers and sisters is a highly important one.

Conclusion

Most looked after children have brothers and sisters. They may be living with some of them but are likely to be separated from others. Siblings can be a very valuable resource for each other, both in childhood and throughout life. It is essential that information on a child's siblings is gathered conscientiously and the possibility of them living together or having contact with each other is carefully assessed and clear decisions are made that are then properly put into effect.

Selected further reading

Burnell A., Vaughan J. and Williams L. (2007) *Family Futures Assessment Handbook: Framework for assessing children who have experienced developmental trauma*, London: Family Futures

Lord J. and Borthwick S. (2008) *Together or Apart? Assessing brothers and sisters for permanent placement* (2nd edn), London: BAAF

Mullender A. (1999) *We are Family: Sibling relationships in placement and beyond*, London: BAAF

Rushton A., Dance C., Quinton D. and Mayes D. (2001) *Siblings in Late Permanent Placements*, London: BAAF

References

Bank S. and Kahn M. D. (1982) *The Sibling Bond*, New York: Basic Books

Beckett S. (1999) 'Local authority planning and decision-making for looked after siblings', in Mullender A. (ed.) *We are Family*, London: BAAF

Beckett C., Groothues C. and O'Connor T. H. (1999) 'The role of sibling group structures on adoption outcomes', in Mullender A. (ed.) *We are Family*, London: BAAF

Bond H. (2007) *Ten Top Tips for Managing Contact*, London: BAAF

Burnell A., Vaughan J. and Williams L. (2007) *Family Futures Assessment Handbook: Framework for assessing children who have experienced developmental trauma*, London: Family Futures

Department of Health (1991) *Patterns and Outcomes in Child Placement: Messages from current research and their implications*, London: HMSO

Dunn J. and McGuire S. (1992) 'Sibling and peer relationships in childhood', *Journal of Child Psychology and Psychiatry*, 33:1, pp 67–105

Edwards R., Hadfield L. and Mauthner M. (2005) *Children's Understanding of their Sibling Relationships*, London: Joseph Rowntree Foundation/NCB

Elgar M. and Head A. (1999) 'An overview of siblings', in Mullender A. (ed.) *We are Family*, London: BAAF

Ellison M. (1999) 'Planning for sibling continuity within permanence: Needs-led or needs unmet?' in Mullender A. (ed.) *We are Family*, London: BAAF

Farmer E. and Moyers S. (2005) *Children Placed with Family and Friends: Placement patterns and outcomes*, Report to the Department for Education and Skills, School for Policy Studies, Bristol: University of Bristol

Farmer E. and Pollock S. (1998) *Sexually Abused and Abusing Children in Substitute Care*, Chichester: Wiley and Sons

Furman W. and Buhrmester D. (1985) 'Children's perceptions of the qualities of sibling relationships', in *Child Development*, 56, pp 448–461

Groza V., Maschmeier C., Jamison C. and Piccola T. (2003) 'Siblings and out-of-home placement: Best practices', in *Families in Society*, 84:4, pp 480–490

Groze V. (1996) *Successful Adoptive Families: A longitudinal study of special needs adoption*, New York: Praegar

Hadley Centre (updated Feb 2007) *Research Briefing on Placing Siblings Permanently*, Bristol: Hadley Centre

Hegar R. (1988) 'Sibling relationships and separations: implications for child placement', *Social Services Review*, 62:3, pp 446–466

Hegar R. (2005) 'Sibling placement in foster care and adoption: an overview of international research', in *Children and Youth Services Review*, 27:7, pp 717–739

Hindle D. (2007) 'Clinical research: a psychotherapeutic assessment model for siblings in care', *Journal of Child Psychotherapy*, 33:1, pp 70–93

Hodges J. and Steele M. (2000) 'Effects of abuse on attachment representations: Narrative assessments of abused children', *Journal of Child Psychotherapy*, 26:3, pp 433–55

Ivaldi G. (2000) *Surveying Adoption: A comprehensive analysis of local authority adoptions 1998–1999*, England, London: BAAF

Kosonen M. (1994) 'Sibling relationships for children in the care system', *Adoption & Fostering*, 18:3, pp 30–35

Kosonen M. (1996) 'Maintaining sibling relationships: Neglected dimension in child care practice', *British Journal of Social Work*, 26, pp 809–822

Leathers S. (2005) 'Separation from siblings: Associations with placement adaption and outcomes among adolescents in long-term foster care', *Children and Youth Services Review*, 27:7, pp 765–782

Lord J. and Borthwick S. (2008) *Together or Apart? Assessing brothers and sisters for permanent placement*, (2nd edn), London: BAAF

Lowe N., Murch M., Borkowski M., Weaver A. and Beckford V. with Thomas C. (1999) *Supporting Adoption: Reframing the approach*, London: BAAF

Macaskill C. (2002) *Safe Contact: Children in permanent placement and contact with their birth relatives*, Lyme Regis: Russell House Publishing

Neil E. (1999) 'The sibling relationship of adopted children and patterns of contact after adoption', in Mullender A. (ed.) *We are Family*, London: BAAF

Parker R. (1966) *Decisions in Child Care: A study of predictions in fostering*, London: Allen and Unwin

Quinton D., Rushton A., Dance C. and Mayes D. (1998) *Joining New Families: Establishing permanent placements in middle childhood*, Chichester: Wiley and Sons

Rushton A., Dance C., Quinton D. and Mayes D. (2001) *Siblings in Late Permanent Placements*, London: BAAF

Rushton A., Treseder J. and Quinton D. (1989) 'Sibling groups in permanent placements', *Adoption & Fostering*, 13:4, pp 5–11

Ryan E. (2002) 'Assessing sibling attachment in the face of placement issues', *Clinical Social Work Journal*, 30:1, pp 77–92

Schofield G. and Beek M. (2006) *Attachment Handbook for Foster Care and Adoption*, London: BAAF

Smith C. R. and Logan J. (2004) *After Adoption: Direct contact and relationships*, London: Routledge

Tarren-Sweeney M. and Hazell P. (2005) 'The mental health and socialisation of siblings in care', *Children and Youth Services Review*, 27:7, pp 821–843

Tomlinson J. (1999) 'Siblings together: Myth or reality?' in Mullender A. (ed.) *We are Family*, London: BAAF

Wedge P. and Mantle G. (1991) *Sibling Groups and Social Work: A study of children referred for permanent substitute family placement*, Aldershot: Avebury

419

22 Young people leaving care

Mike Stein

Introduction

This chapter draws upon research findings and theoretical perspectives in exploring the journey made by young people moving on from care to adulthood. Set in the context of social exclusion and highlighting evidence of the poor life chances of young people leaving care, the empirical and theoretical material is organised around four main themes: instability in care and attachment; young people's transitions from care; leaving care services and outcomes; and promoting the resilience of young people leaving care. Arising out of the latter theme, a resilience framework is introduced to provide coherence to the material discussed in the earlier themes, including a summary of the main implications for policy and practice.

Social exclusion

I just want to make something of my life. I want as normal a life as any other person.

In European social policy discourse, social exclusion has come to mean both material disadvantage and marginalisation. Whereas the former is usually associated with low income and relative poverty, the latter refers to the way groups may be excluded, omitted or stigmatised by the majority, due to characteristics such as gender, age, ethnicity, appearance or behaviour. Also, these two meanings are often linked, merging causes and outcomes, such as unemployment and social isolation.

In this context, international research has shown the high risk of social exclusion for young people leaving care. They are more likely than young people who have not been in care to have poorer educational qualifications, lower levels of participation in post-16 education, be young parents, be homeless, as well as have higher levels of unemployment, offending behaviour and mental health problems. Also, many of these young people experience a cluster of problems both whilst they are in care, including placement instability, stigma and educational difficulties at school, and after they leave care, including disrupted careers, periods of dependency on benefits, getting into trouble, mental health problems and loneliness (see Stein (2004) for a review of research, and Stein and Dixon (2006) and Stein and Munro (2008) for international research findings).

Specific groups of care leavers face additional disadvantages due to their status or characteristics, compounding their exclusion. Black and minority ethnic young people, including those of mixed heritage, face many similar challenges to other young people leaving care. However, they may also experience identity problems derived from a lack of knowledge, or contact with family and community, as well as the impact of racism and discrimination (Barn *et al*, 2005). Unaccompanied refugee and asylum-seeking young people in England may be excluded from services under the Children (Leaving Care) Act 2000 when local authorities decide not to "look after" them but support them under Section 17 of the Children Act 1989. They are also likely to receive poorer services than other looked after young people, especially in respect of support from leaving care teams (Wade *et al*, 2005).

Young disabled people may experience inadequate planning and poor consultation, and their transitions from care may be abrupt or delayed by restricted housing and employment options and poor support aftercare (Priestley *et al*, 2003). Young women who have been in care are more likely to become teenage parents than other young women and many have short-term difficulties in finding suitable accommodation, as well accessing personal and financial support, although for some young people parenthood can be a very positive experience (Chase and Knight, 2006). Also, longer-term, teenage parenthood is associated with reduced employment opportunities, dependency on benefits, social housing, as well as poorer physical and mental health (Hobcraft and Kiernan, 1999).

The findings from a policy survey of leaving care teams in England indicated that the problems of young people leaving care were derived from a mixture of "social justice" issues (structural exclusions and inequalities), "social welfare" issues (poor parenting), and "technical difficulties" (skill deficits). Leaving care workers responding to the survey suggested that young people would benefit from policies to address the former although they are usually offered assistance with the latter, especially after they leave care (Broad, 1999).

The research evidence summarised above, organised within a social exclusion framework, has contributed to a greater awareness of the reduced life chances of care leavers, their links with other excluded groups, as well as providing a focus for international policy and practice interventions. There is also a body of research, discussed in the rest of this chapter, that has contributed to how we can improve outcomes, or promote the resilience, of this vulnerable group of young people.

Instability in care and attachment

I didn't know what was going on inside my head because I was moving around so much.

A consistent finding from research studies of young people leaving care, carried out between 1980–2005, has been their experience of instability and placement disruption, following their initial or later separation from their birth families. In an early empirical study, based upon 76 young people who had been in care during the late 1960s and 1970s, and who left during the early years of the 1980s, just under three-quarters had experienced three or more placements in care, 40 per cent had five or more placements, and six per cent had 10 or more. The average was 4.2 placements per young person (Stein and Carey, 1986). A study of 18 young people referred to a leaving care project at the end of the 1980s found that half of them had between seven and twelve placements by the time they were 16 years of age and the average was six per young person (Stein, 1990).

Studies of young people leaving care in the 1990s reveal similar findings. A survey of 183 young people found that fewer than one in ten young people remained in the same placement throughout their time in care, 40 per cent made four or more moves and ten per cent moved more than ten times. In a follow-up study of 74 young people, a third of the sample made four or more moves during their time in care and only 16 per cent remained in the same placement throughout (Biehal et al, 1992, 1995).

Comparative research, based upon surveys of young people leaving care in England, Northern Ireland and Ireland during the 1990s, revealed that significant numbers of young people experienced placement moves. In Ireland 19 per cent had between five and ten moves, and in England and Northern Ireland, just over 40 per cent had more than three moves. In the Northern Ireland sample, just under three-quarters of young people experienced two or more moves and over a tenth moved more than five times. In the England and Ireland surveys, 10 and 13 per cent respectively had 10 or more placement moves before leaving care (Pinkerton and McCrea, 1999; Stein et al, 2000). A Scottish survey of 107 young people found that 10 per cent had experienced four or more moves and only seven per cent had remained in the same placement (Dixon and Stein, 2005).

In these studies, between 30–40 per cent of young people had four plus moves and within this group between 6–10 per cent had a very large number of moves, as many as ten or more. Qualitative studies have added to this picture. For the young person, "placement movement" often meant an abrupt end to a foster care or children's home placement accompanied by a sense of failure, guilt and blame, as well as changing carers, friends, neighbourhoods and schools on several occasions (Stein, 2005). What are the consequences of these experiences for looked after young people?

Attachment theory provides a framework for exploring young people's separation from their families and the circumstances surrounding it, their patterns of attachment, their care careers including placement disruption or stability, and the legacy of these experiences for their lives after care (Howe, 1995; Schofield, 2001).

In an early study – although still one of very few studies applying an attachment framework to looked after teenagers – Downes (1992) researched the interaction between fostered adolescents and foster family members in 23 time-limited placements, over a two-and-a-half year period. Her findings showed the difficulties many of the young people had in accepting help or committing themselves to close relationships, often because of past difficulties, including rejection in their birth families. Her study reported that young people became either highly dependent on others or highly independent, keeping people who are important to them at arm's length. In her conclusion she suggested that these patterns of relating may continue into adulthood, unless addressed, thus denying young people satisfaction in personal relationships, and the help they made need, especially during their transition to adulthood.

More recently, Sinclair *et al* (2005), in their study of the outcomes of young people leaving foster care, found a strong attachment to at least one adult was associated with "good outcomes" (as defined by foster carers, young people and a measure of well-being). Some young people were able to establish and maintain good relationships with a member of their birth family from whom they could get support, or a sustained relationship with their foster family, or have good relationships with their partner and their partner's family.

What are the main implications of these findings for child care policy and practice?

First, there is the need to provide young people with stable foster placements that can help them overcome their earlier problems and provide them with a strong emotional platform for their journey to adulthood. Young people need to be able to experience their foster carers as a secure base, to provide them with opportunities and active encouragement to explore and become confident in the adult world. There are good examples of formalising longer-term attachments with foster carers, for example, foster carers becoming "supported lodgings", or being paid a retainer while a young person was at university and then full board when they returned.

Second, assisting young people who are unable to remain with their birth parents should begin with a shared process of assessment, exploring attachment behaviour through patterns of interaction with significant adults and peers. The identification of patterns of attachment may guide the work to be undertaken by the foster carers, their social worker and the young person.

Third, knowledge of attachment patterns may also point to more specific aims and interventions (Schofield and Beek, 2006). The aim in interventions with anxiously attached young people may be to increase their confidence in the availability and reliability of attachment figures, as evidenced by young people increasing their distance range from foster parents and other significant adults, but without losing the capacity for closeness. By contrast, the aim of work with emotionally detached young people may be to encourage and enable them to test themselves out in less distanced interactions, to move closer to their foster carers. Foster carers may also support young people's efforts to reappraise their relationships with parents and other significant attachment figures.

Young people's transitions from care

It's being away from my mum, I'm only 16 and still a bairn, and get a bit weepy at times.

A consistent finding from studies of care leavers is that a majority move to independent living at between 16 and 18 years of age, whereas most of their peers remain at home well into their twenties. They are expected to undertake their journey to adulthood, from restricted to full citizenship, far younger and in far less time than their peers. For many of these young people, leaving care is often a final event. There is no option to return in times of difficulty. Also, they often have to cope with major status changes in their lives at the time of leaving care: leaving foster care or their children's home and setting up a new home, often in a different area, and for some young people starting a family as well; leaving school and finding their way into further education, training or employment, or coping with unemployment. In short, their journey to adulthood is both accelerated and compressed.

Drawing on the 'focal model of adolescence' developed by Coleman and Hendry (1999), it is evident that many young people leaving care are denied the psychological opportunity and space to focus, or to deal with these important issues over time. The empirical testing of this model shows that having the opportunity to deal with interpersonal issues, spread over time, is how most young people cope successfully with the challenges of transition. Conversely, those young people who have to face a number of interpersonal issues at the same time, are likely to experience significant problems of adjustment.

Ethnographic research also highlights the significance of transition for young people during their journey to adulthood (Horrocks, 2002). The process of social transition has traditionally included three distinct but related stages: leaving or disengagement; transition itself; and integration into a new or different social state. In post (or late?) modern societies, providing more opportunities but also more risks, this process has become more extended and less structured, although the "activities'" associated with the three stages still remain. But for many young people leaving care, there is the expectation of instant adulthood. They often miss out on the critical preparation stage, transition itself that gives young people an opportunity to "space out", provides a time for freedom, exploration, reflection, risk-taking and identity search.

For a majority of young people today, this is gained through the experience of further and, especially, higher education but many care leavers, as a consequence of their pre-care and care experiences are unable to take advantage of these educational opportunities. Also, in the context of extended transitions, the family plays an increasing role in providing financial, practical and emotional support. But for many care leavers, their family relationships at this important time may be missing or problematic rather than supportive (Biehal and Wade, 1996; Sinclair *et al*, 2005).

What are the main implications for policy and practice arising out of these findings?

First, services should be organised to reflect the nature and timing of young people's transitions from care, more akin to normative transitions. This should include opportunities for young people to remain in placements where they are settled.

Second, the organisation and culture of services should recognise the need young people have for psychological space, in order to cope with changes over time. This should include recognition of the different stages of transitions, especially the significance of the middle stage, transition itself.

Third, young people should be given the emotional and practical support they need during their journey to adulthood.

The development of leaving care services

I've learnt to live out of care – with a back-up team.

In the UK, specialist leaving care schemes have developed, particularly since the mid-1980s, to provide a more focused response to the core needs of care leavers – for accommodation, personal support, assistance with finance and help with careers. The work of these schemes, post 1989 Children Act, has included: contributing to policy development and the co-ordination of leaving-care services within local areas; developing a range of resource options for young people and co-ordinating access to them, especially housing and financial support; developing inter-agency links to ensure a co-ordinated approach; providing advice, information and consultancy services to young people, social workers and carers; and offering direct and group-based support to young people including both those leaving care and those living independently in the community. Although most specialist schemes contribute to these areas of activity, there is considerable diversity in the types of schemes, in terms of service delivery, philosophy and in the range and intensity of services. Also, as detailed below, the Children (Leaving Care) Act 2000, has resulted in significant changes in England and Wales.

> *In the early literature, two main distinctions were made: first, between specialist, or dedicated leaving care services, and non-specialist approaches where supervision was carried out by field social workers; second, between independence and interdependence models: the rationale of the former being to prepare young people in practical survival skills – "domestic combat courses" – in order to manage on their own from the age of 16 plus. In contrast, the latter saw leaving care more as a psychosocial transition and placed a higher priority on interpersonal skills and providing young people with ongoing support at the time of leaving and after care. Networks of support, including the promotion of continuity in both professional support*

and positive relationships with former cares, birth families and peers, are given prominence by the inter-dependence model. (Stein and Carey, 1986)

In their study of four English leaving care projects during the 1990s, Biehal *et al* (1995) proposed a three-dimensional model for classifying the distinctiveness of schemes: how they compared in their approaches to service delivery, in terms of their perspectives, methods of working and the extent to which their work is young person demand led or social work planned; the nature of the providing agency; and in their contributions to the development of local policy.

A survey of English local authorities carried out during 2000 classified models of authority-wide leaving care provision. This identified a non-specialist leaving care service, a centrally organised specialist service, a geographically dispersed specialist service and a centrally organised integrated service for a range of vulnerable young people including the homeless and young offenders. Variations of these models included specialist dual system arrangements, where the young person is assisted by a specialist team but statutory responsibility is retained by the social worker, and looked after adolescent teams (Stein and Wade, 2000).

Research completed since the introduction of the Children (Leaving Care) Act 2000 in England and Wales, suggests the emergence of a "corporate parenting case model". Its main features are twofold. First, case responsibility held by the designated personal adviser whose responsibilities include needs assessment, pathway planning and the provision of advice and ongoing support to "qualifying" young people. The regulations of the Act require the assessment to address health and development, education, employment and training, personal support from family and other relationships, financial needs, practical and other skills necessary for independent living, and young people's need for care support and accommodation. In addition to these areas, the pathway plans require that contingency planning be undertaken. It is also a requirement under the Act for both needs assessments and pathway plans to be recorded, and the young person must be provided with a copy of the pathway plan. Set against the background of the failures of earlier permissive legislation, this could be seen as an extension of legal authority in respect of qualifying young people under the Act. Second, the increased role played by a range of agencies – this represents a shift from more informal inter-agency links to formal agreements, as specified in the needs assessment and pathway planning requirements of the Act (Dixon *et al*, 2004; Hai and Williams, 2004; Broad, 2005).

Research describing the work of leaving care teams in England and Wales during the first two years of the Children (Leaving Care) Act 2000 suggests that the legislation is viewed by staff as contributing to a number of positive changes: the increased take-up of further education and reductions in those not in education, employment and training, directly linked to improvements in financial support for young people provided by local authorities; the increased provision of supported accommodation; a strengthening of leaving care responsibilities, especially through the introduction of needs assessment and pathway planning; more formalised inter-agency work; and improved funding for leaving care teams. However, there is also evidence that divisions between better and poorer funded services before and after the Act were likely to remain. Broad (2005) found that services for young parents, young accompanied asylum-seekers and refugees, and young people remanded to accommodation, were predominantly reported as 'remaining the same' since the introduction of the Act (Broad, 1998; 2005; Dixon et al, 2004; Hai and Williams, 2004).

The development of specialist leaving care schemes has also raised concerns that they have colonised leaving care (Stein, 2005). This in effect means that many young people may move on to accommodation provided by schemes at 15 or 16 years of age. Not only does this build in additional movement and disruption, and accelerate young people's transitions from care, but it also may contribute to the re-definition of foster or residential care – as for young people only up to 15/16 years of age. There is also evidence that preparation for leaving care may be viewed as the responsibility of specialist workers rather than carers, again, separating leaving care from ordinary care. In this context, the development of specialist leaving care schemes may be seen by authorities as "the answer" to meeting the needs of care leavers, shifting the focus from the carers who provide the stability and continuity young people need during their journey to adulthood. It has been argued that the role of specialist schemes should not be to take over from carers but to assist them in preparing and supporting young people during their transition (Stein, 2005). The importance of stability, continuity and gradual transitions from care has been recognised in the Government's White Paper, *Care Matters*, and the Children and Young Persons Bill.

In the United States, Courtney and Terao (2002) provide a descriptive typology which categorises services for young people ageing out of care into life training skills, mentoring programmes, transitional housing, health and behavioural health services, educational services and employment services. However, as Courtney and Hughes (2003) point out, focusing on the range of services may detract from common programme elements including: case management; their underlying philosophy – many adopt a youth development philosophy which emphasises opportunities for young people to contribute to their community, increase their personal confidence, and provide guidance to other young people; and that many schemes are provided as one part of a wider range of services. Courtney and Hughes also point to the limitation in the categorisation of services in excluding the variation in local policies, for example, in allowing young people to remain in care longer or providing financial support for college education.

The outcomes of leaving care services

My advice as a care leaver – stick in at school, go to college, it will pay off in the end.

Although since the mid-1990s there has been more focus on outcome studies, a survey of international leaving care work highlights the wide variation in both research and the collection of statistical outcome data by governments (Munro *et al*, 2005). In the UK, Simon and Owen (2006) have detailed recent reforms in the collection of government data. Whilst they note that the information base for young people in and leaving care has improved since 1998, they identify three shortcomings: the data are for short "follow-up" time periods; they only cover limited dimensions of young people lives; and in the main are only available for England.

What are the implications for policy and practice arising from outcome studies of leaving care services and interventions?
Outcome studies evaluating specialist leaving care services have shown that they can make a positive contribution to specific outcomes for care leavers. They work well in assisting young people in finding and settling in accommodation and in helping young people out of homelessness. Research by Wade and Dixon (2006) provides evidence of the association between stability in accommodation after young people leave care and positive outcomes in terms of an enhanced sense of well-being, to some extent independent of young people's past care careers.

Leaving care services can also assist young people successfully with life skills and there is evidence from Scottish research of a significant association between preparation before leaving care and "coping" after care (Dixon and Stein, 2005). Leaving care services can also help young people to some extent in furthering social networks, developing relationships and building self-esteem, although these dimensions are also closely connected with young people having positive, supportive informal relationships with family members or friends, or former foster carers (Marsh and Peel, 1999).

These studies also suggest that successful educational outcomes are more closely associated with placement stability and being looked after longer, more often although not exclusively achieved in foster care placements, being female, combined with a supportive and encouraging environment for study. Without such stability and encouragement, post-16 employment, education and training outcomes are also likely to be very poor. Generally, these studies found that young people who left care earlier, at 16 or 17, had more unsettled carer careers and challenging behaviours. They were also more likely to be unemployed and have very poor outcomes. Young people with mental health or emotional or behavioural difficulties were particularly vulnerable to poor outcomes (Wade and Dixon, 2006).

Research has shown that young people who go on to higher education are more likely to have had stable care experiences, continuity in their schooling which may compensate for placement movement, been encouraged by their birth parents, even though they were unable to care for them, and have been greatly assisted by their foster carers in their schooling (Jackson *et al*, 2003; Ajayi and Quigley, 2006; Jackson and Simon, 2006).

Research by Sinclair *et al* (2005) into the outcomes for young people leaving foster care has identified key variables that distinguished those doing well from those who were less successful: a strong attachment with a family member, partner or partner's family or foster carer was associated with a good outcome. Conversely, those young people who were assessed as "disturbed" at first contact – and this correlated with other key variables including performance at school, placement disruption and attachment disorder – had poorer outcomes. Another variable, involvement in work, although identified by foster carers as an indication of success, was seen by young people as problematic, especially low-paid, unfulfilling work. Young people being seen as ready and willing to leave care was also associated with the "doing well" outcome measure.

In the United States, young people placed with Casey foster carers who did well as adults, were likely to have completed their high school education, attended college or job training, acquired life skills and independent living training, participated in youth clubs or organisations while in care and were less likely to be homeless within one year of leaving care. As well as providing stability, Casey families were also able to offer a comprehensive package of practical, financial emotional and social support, which contributed to positive educational outcomes (Pecora *et al*, 2004, 2006). There is also evidence from a French study that adults who grew up in care who had stability and counselling to assist had better mental health outcomes than those with unstable care careers (Dumaret *et al*, 1997).

Ethnographic research using life course theory to explore the transitions of young people leaving care reminds us of the complexities in evaluating outcomes (Horrocks, 2002). These include: the need to recognise the different starting points of young people, given the diversity of their family backgrounds and care experiences; the dynamic nature of "outcomes" for young people – they often change between "official" measurement periods; the separation of outcome measures from each other, even though they are often closely inter-connected; and the normative assumptions held by social services about young people, whose lives have not been easy, achieving independence by 18 years of age.

It is evident from the research findings discussed above that specialist leaving care schemes and projects cannot, by themselves, improve outcomes for care leavers. Their contribution in promoting the resilience of these young people during their journey to adulthood will have to build upon the foundation stones of good quality care – attachment, stability, continuity, maintaining positive social networks, and gradual transitions from care.

Resilience and leaving care

As suggested at the beginning of this chapter, adopting a social exclusion framework may mask differences between different groups of care leavers, especially in relation to their outcomes. By definition, social exclusion is about "risk" factors and poor life chances. However, there is also a growing literature on "looked after" young people, adopting resilience as a central organising concept (Gilligan, 2001; Schofield, 2001; Newman, 2004; Schofield and Beek, 2005; Pinkerton and Dolan, 2007).

Resilience can be defined as the quality that enables some young people to find fulfilment in their lives despite their disadvantaged backgrounds, the problems or adversity they may have undergone or the pressures they may experience. Resilience is about overcoming the odds, coping and recovery. But it is only relative to different ages and cultures, and risk experiences – relative resistance as distinct from invulnerability – and is likely to develop over time (Rutter, 1999; Masten, 2001; Master and Powell, 2003).

The resilience of young people from very disadvantaged family backgrounds has been found to be associated with a redeeming and warm relationship with at least one person in the family – or secure attachment to at least one unconditionally supportive parent or parent substitute; positive school experiences; feeling able to plan and be in control; being given the chance of a "turning point", such as a new opportunity or break from a high-risk area; higher childhood IQ scores and lower rates of temperamental risk; and having positive peer influences (Rutter *et al*, 1998).

A research review of the international literature on resilience factors in relation to the key transitions made by children and young people during their whole life cycle has added to this picture. As well as the first three factors identified above, the authors conclude that children and young people who are best equipped to overcome adversities, will have: strong social support networks; a committed mentor or person from outside the family; a range of extra-curricular activities that promote the learning of competencies and emotional maturity; the capacity to re-frame adversities so that the beneficial as well as the damaging effects are recognised; the ability – or opportunity – to make a difference, for example, by helping others through volunteering, or undertaking part-time work; and exposure to challenging situations which provide opportunities to develop both problem-solving abilities and emotional coping skills (Newman and Blackburn, 2002a,b).

What are the links between empirical research on care leavers and the resilience promoting factors identified above? Why do some young people leaving care, against all odds, cope well and what are the implications for policy and practice?

Promoting resilience: improving outcomes for young people leaving care

Care, it's given me great opportunities. Before, I didn't have a clue what I wanted to do, now I know what direction I am going. At home my parents didn't care what I did.

In addressing these questions, resilience provides a framework to give coherence to the main themes discussed within this chapter, including stability and attachment, transitions from care and what we know about the outcomes of leaving care services.

Young people who experience stable placements providing good quality care are more likely to have positive outcomes than those who have experienced further movement and disruption during their time in care. Stability has the potential to promote resilience in two respects: first, by providing the young person with a warm and redeeming relationship with a carer – or as discussed above, a compensatory secure attachment which may in itself reduce the likelihood of placement breakdown; second, and not necessarily dependent on the first, stability may provide continuity of care in young people's lives, which may give them security and contribute to positive educational and career outcomes.

Helping young people develop a positive sense of identity, including their self-knowledge, their self-esteem and self-efficacy, may also promote their resilience. And although not explicitly recognised as a variable in the research literature on resilience, identity could be seen as connected to, as well as a component of, key associations with resilience: feeling able to plan and be in control; the capacity to re-frame adversities so that the beneficial as well as the damaging effects are recognised; personality – or lower rates of temperamental risk.

Helping care leavers develop a positive identity is linked to first, the quality of care and attachments experienced by looked-after young people – a significant resilience promoting factor discussed above; second, to their knowledge and understanding of their background and personal history; third, to their experience of how other people perceive and respond to them; and finally, how they see themselves and the opportunities they have to influence and shape their own biography.

Having a positive experience of school, including achieving educational success, is associated with resilience among young people from disadvantaged family backgrounds and young people living in care. Research studies, completed on young people leaving care from the beginning of the 1970s, show low levels of attainment and participation beyond the minimum school leaving age. However, as detailed above, good outcomes are associated with placement stability, gender (young women do better than young men, as reflected in national data), a carer committed to helping the young person, and a supportive and encouraging environment for study. This may also include the foster family's own children providing help and acting as role models.

There is also evidence that young people who have had several placements can achieve educational success if they remain in the same school – and this also meant that they were able to maintain friendships and contacts with helpful teachers. Also, late-placed young people, who may have experienced a lot of earlier placement disruption, can succeed in foster care. Although some young people and their foster carers see this as more of a service relationship than a substitute family, other young people placed in families as late as 14 or 15 have found a family for life (Schofield, 2002). School or care itself may also provide turning points and open the door for participation in a range of leisure or extra-curricular activities that may lead to new friends and opportunities, including the learning of competencies and the development of emotional maturity – and thus promote their resilience. Indeed, resilient young people have often been able to turn their negative experiences at home, or in care, into opportunities, with the help of others.

Preparation for leaving care may also provide young people with opportunities for planning, problem-solving and the learning of new competencies – all resilience promoting factors. This may include the development of self-care skills – personal hygiene, diet and health, including sexual health; practical skills – budgeting, shopping cooking and cleaning; and inter-personal skills – managing a range of formal and informal relationships. Preparation should be holistic in approach, attaching equal importance to practical, emotional and interpersonal skills for young people.

As the discussion of transitions and the focal model suggests, many young people leaving care have compressed and accelerated transitions to adulthood, which represents a barrier to promoting their resilience. They are denied the psychological opportunity to focus to deal with changes over time – which is how most young people are able to deal with problems and challenges. Also, as discussed above, they may often be lacking the range and depth of family support of their peers and they may be denied the opportunity to "space out" – a period of risk-taking reflection and identity search.

Drawing on the research findings discussed above, including studies carried out between 1980 and 2007, suggests that young people may broadly fall into one of three outcome groups: those "moving on" from care, those "surviving", and those who are "strugglers". Identifying these groups provides one way of connecting the generality of the research findings discussed above to young people's lives, including the implications for promoting their resilience.

Moving on

I think I am special because I tried and finished college.

The first group, those young people "moving on" successfully, are likely to have had stability and continuity in their lives, including a secure attachment relationship; made sense of their difficult birth family relationships so they could psychologically move on from them; and have achieved some educational success before leaving care. Their preparation had been gradual, they had left care later, and their moving on was likely to have been planned. Participating in further or higher education, having a job they liked or being a parent themselves, played a significant part in "feeling normal". The "moving on" group welcomed the challenge of independent living and gaining more control over their lives. They saw this as improving their confidence and self-esteem. In general, their resilience had been enhanced by their experiences both in after care. They had been able to make good use of the help they have been offered, often maintaining contact and support from former carers. For many of these young people, "moving on" meant coming to terms with their past difficulties in their birth families, and building on the emotional platform that attachment, stability and continuity of care had given them.

Survivors

I've become more independent, more tough, I know more about the world.

The second group, the "survivors", had experienced more instability, movement and disruption while living in care than the "moving on" group. They were also likely to leave care younger, with few or no qualifications, and often following a breakdown in foster care or a sudden exit from their children's home. They were likely to experience further movement and problems after leaving care, including periods of homelessness, low-paid casual or short-term, unfulfilling work, and unemployment. They were also likely to experience problems in their personal and professional relationships through patterns of detachment and dependency. Many in this group saw themselves as "more tough", as having done things "off my own back" and as "survivors" since leaving care. They believed that the many problems they had faced, and often were still coping with, had made them more grown-up and self-reliant – although their view of themselves as independent was often contradicted by the reality of high degrees of agency dependency for assistance with accommodation, money and personal problems.

There is research evidence that what made the difference to their lives, or promoted their resilience, was the personal and professional support they received after leaving care. Specialist leaving care workers and key workers could assist these young people. Also, mentoring, including mentoring by ex-care young people (or peer mentoring) may assist young people during their journey to independence, and offer them a different type of relationship from professional support or troubled family relationships (Clayden and Stein, 2005). Helping young people in finding and maintaining their accommodation can be critical to their mental health and well-being. Families may also help, but returning to them may prove very problematic for some young people. Overall, some combination of personal and professional support networks could help them overcome their very poor starting points at the time of leaving care.

Strugglers

I hate being like I am. I don't care about myself, so why should I care about other people?

The third group of care leavers was the most disadvantaged. They had the most damaging pre-care family experiences and, in the main, care was unable to compensate them, or to help them overcome their past difficulties. Their lives in care were likely to include many further placement moves, the largest number of moves in the different research studies cited above, and the associated disruption to their lives, especially in relation to their personal relationships and education. They were also likely to have a cluster of difficulties while in care that often began earlier, including emotional and behavioural difficulties, problems at school and getting into trouble. They were the least likely to have a redeeming relationship with a family member or carer, and were likely to leave care younger, following a placement breakdown. At the time of leaving care, their life chances were very poor indeed. After leaving care, they were likely to be unemployed, become homeless and have great difficulties in maintaining their accommodation. They were also highly likely to be lonely, isolated and have mental health problems, often being defined by projects as young people with very complex needs. Aftercare support was unlikely to be able to help them overcome their very poor starting points and they also lacked or alienated personal support. But it was important to these young people that somebody was there for them.

Conclusions

This chapter has shown that young people leaving care, as a group, are likely to be socially excluded. However, the application of a resilience framework also suggests that there are differences in outcomes between young people "moving on", "surviving" and becoming "victims". In general terms, the evidence discussed above shows that these different pathways are associated with the quality of care young people experience, their transitions from care and the support they receive after care.

Improving outcomes for these young people will require more comprehensive responses across their life course: by early interventions and support to young people and their families; by providing better quality care to compensate young people for their damaging pre-care experiences through stability and continuity, as well as assistance to overcome educational deficits; by promoting continuity with birth families and former carers where there is the potential for positive links; by providing young people with opportunities for more gradual transitions from care, more akin to normative transitions; and by providing ongoing support to all those young people who need it, including skilled help for those young people with mental health problems and complex needs.

There are still significant gaps in our research knowledge. There is a need for more outcome research, especially using more experimental and quasi-experimental designs. The use of cohort studies would provide a more sophisticated understanding of "risk" and "protective" factors over time. More ethnographic research would also add to qualitative knowledge. Comparative research is at an early stage although should benefit from the recently established international network (Munro *et al*, 2005; Pinkerton, 2006; Stein and Munro, 2008). There is also a need for more comprehensive government information, not least to measure progress over time. Finally, as I have discussed elsewhere, there is a need to develop far stronger links between empirical and theoretical work (Stein, 2006).

Selected further reading

For current developments in leaving care law, policy and practice, see: National Leaving Care Advisory Service websites, www.nlcas.org, www.leavingcare.org

For research findings, see:

Stein M. (2004) *What Works for Young People Leaving Care*, Barkingside: Barnardo's

Stein M. and Munro E. R. (eds) (2008) *Young People's Transitions from Care to Adulthood*, London: Jessica Kingsley Publishers

References

Ajayi S. and Quigley M. (2006) 'By degrees: Care leavers in higher education', in Chase E., Simon A. and Jackson S. (eds) *Care and After: A positive perspective*, London: Routledge

Barn R., Andrew L. and Mantovani N. (2005) *Life after Care: A study of young people from different ethnic groups*, York: Joseph Rowntree Foundation

Biehal N., Clayden J., Stein M. and Wade J. (1992) *Prepared for Living? A survey of young people leaving the care of three local authorities*, London: National Children's Bureau

Biehal N., Clayden J., Stein M. and Wade J. (1995) *Moving On: Young people and leaving care schemes*, London: HMSO

Biehal N. and Wade J. (1996) 'Looking back, looking forward: Care leavers, families and change', *Children and Youth Services Review*, 18:4/5, pp 425–445

Broad B. (1998) *Young People Leaving Care: Life after the Children Act 1989*, London: Jessica Kingsley Publishers

Broad B. (1999) 'Young people leaving care: Moving towards "joined up" solutions?', *Children and Society*, 13:2, pp 81–93

Broad (2005) *Improving the Health and Well-being of Young People Leaving Care*, Lyme Regis: Russell House Publishing

Chase E. and Knight A. (2006) 'Is early parenthood such a bad thing?', in Chase E., Simon A. and Jackson S. (eds) *Care and After: A positive perspective*, London: Routledge

Clayden J. and Stein M. (2005) *Mentoring Young People Leaving Care: Someone for me*, York: Joseph Rowntree Foundation

Coleman J. C. and Hendry L. (1999) *The Nature of Adolescence*, London: Routledge

Courtney, M. E. and Hughes D. (2003) *The Transition to Adulthood for Youth 'Aging out' of the Foster Care System*, Chicago: Chapin Hall Center for Children at the University of Chicago

Courtney M. E. and Terao S. (2002) *Classification of Independent Living Services*, Chicago, IL: Chapin Hall Center for Children at the University of Chicago

Dixon J., Lee J., Wade J., Byford S. and Weatherly H. (2004) *Young People Leaving Care: An evaluation of costs and outcomes*, York: Report to the DfES, University of York

Dixon J. and Stein M. (2005) *Leaving Care, Through Care and Aftercare in Scotland*, London: Jessica Kingsley Publishers

Downes C. (1992) *Separation Revisited*, Ashgate: Aldershot

Dumaret A. C., Coppel-Batsch M. and Courand S. (1997) 'Adult outcome of children reared for long term periods in foster families', *Child Abuse and Neglect*, 20, pp 911–927

Gilligan R. (2001) *Promoting Resilience: A resource guide on working with children in the care system*, London: BAAF

Hai N. and Williams A. (2004) *Implementing the Children (Leaving Care) Act 2000: The experience of eight London boroughs*, London: National Children's Bureau

Hobcraft J. and Kiernan K. (1999) *Childhood Poverty, Early Motherhood and Adult Social Exclusion*, Case Paper 28, London: London School of Economics

Horrocks C. (2002) 'Using life course theory to explore the social and developmental pathways of young people leaving care', *Journal of Youth Studies*, 5:3, pp 325–335

Howe D. (1995) *Attachment Theory for Social Work Practice*, London: Macmillan

Jackson S., Ajayi S. and Quigley M. (2003) *By Degrees: The first year, from care to university*, London: The Frank Buttle Trust

Jackson S. and Simon A. (2006) 'The costs and benefits of educating children in care', in Chase E., Simon A. and Jackson S. (eds) *Care and After: A positive perspective*, London: Routledge

Marsh P. and Peel M. (1999) *Leaving Care in Partnership: Family involvement with care leavers*, London: The Stationery Office

Masten A. S. (2001) 'Ordinary magic: Resilience processes in development', *American Psychologist*, 56, pp 227–238

Masten A. S. (2006) 'Promoting resilience in development: A general framework for systems of care', in Flynn R. J., Dudding P. M. and Barber J. G. (eds), *Promoting Resilience in Child Welfare*, Ottawa: University of Ottawa Press

Masten A. S. and Powell J. L. (2003) 'A resilience framework for research, policy and practice', in Luthar S. S. (ed.) *Resilience and Vulnerabilities: Adaptation in the context of childhood adversities*, New York: Cambridge University Press, pp 1–25

Munro E. R., Stein M. and Ward H. (2005) 'Comparing how different social, political and legal frameworks support or inhibit transitions from public care to independence in Europe, Israel, Canada and the United States', *International Journal of Child and Family Welfare*, 8:4, pp 191–201

Newman T. (2004) *What Works in Building Resilience?* Barkingside: Barnardo's

Newman T. and Blackburn S. (2002a) *Transitions in the Lives of Children and Young People: Resilience factors*, Interchange 78. Edinburgh: Scottish Executive

Newman T. and Blackburn S. (2002b) *Transitions in the Lives of Children and Young People: Resilience factors*, Report for the Scottish Executive Education and Young People Research Unit, Edinburgh (www.scotland.gov.uk /library5/education/ic78-00.asp)

Pecora P. J., Williams J., Kessler R. J., Downs A., O'Brien K., Hiripi E. and Moorello S. (2004) *Assessing the Effects of Foster Care: Early results from the Casey national alumni study*, Casey Family Programs, Seattle, WA (http://www.casey.org)

Pecora P. J., Williams J., Kessler A., Hiripi E., O'Brien K., Emerson J., Herrick M. and Torres M. P. A. (2006) 'Assessing the educational achievements of adults who formerly were placed in family foster care', *Child and Family Social Work*, Special Issue, Young people leaving care, 11:3, pp 220–231

Pinkerton J. (2006) 'Developing a global approach to the practice of young people leaving state care', *Child and Family Social Work*, Special Issue, Young people leaving care, 11:3, pp 191–198

Pinkerton J. and Dolan P. (2007) 'Family support, social capital, resilience and adolescence coping', *Child and Family Social Work*, 13, pp 219–228

Pinkerton J. and McCrea J. (1999) *Meeting the Challenge? Young people leaving care in Northern Ireland*, Aldershot: Ashgate.

Priestley M., Rabiee P. and Harris J (2003) 'Young disabled people and the "new arrangements" for leaving care in England and Wales', *Children and Youth Services Review*, 25:11, pp 863–890

Rutter M. (1999) 'Resilience concepts and findings: Implications for family therapy', *Journal of Family Therapy*, 21, pp 119–144

Rutter M., Giller H. and Hagell A. (1998) *Antisocial Behaviour by Young People*, Cambridge: Cambridge University Press

Schofield G. (2001) 'Resilience and family placement: A lifespan perspective', *Adoption & Fostering*, 25:3, pp 6–19

Schofield G. and Beek M. (2005) 'Risk and resilience in long-term foster care', *British Journal of Social Work*, 35:8, pp 1283–1301

Schofield G. and Beek M. (2006) *Attachment Handbook for Foster Care and Adoption*, London: BAAF

Simon A. and Owen C. (2006) 'Outcomes for children in care: What do we know?', in Chase E., Simon A. and Jackson S. (eds) *In Care and After: A positive perspective*, London: Routledge

Sinclair I., Baker C., Wilson K. and Gibbs I. (2005) *Foster Children: Where they go and how they get on*, London: Jessica Kingsley Publishers

Stein M. (1990) *Living Out of Care*, Ilford: Barnardo's

Stein M. (2004) *What Works for Young People Leaving Care?* Barkingside: Barnardo's

Stein M. (2005) *Resilience and Young People Leaving Care*, www.jrf.org.uk/bookshop/details.asp?pubID=732, Joseph Rowntree Foundation

Stein M. (2006) 'Young people aging out of care: The poverty of theory', *Children and Youth Services Review*, 28, pp 422–435

Stein M. and Carey K. (1986) *Leaving Care*, Oxford: Blackwell

Stein M. and Dixon J. (2006) (eds) *Child and Family Social Work, Special Issue, Young People Leaving Care*, 11:3

Stein M. and Munro E. (eds) (2008) *Young People's Transitions from Care to Adulthood: International Research and Practice*, London: Jessica Kingsley Publishers

Stein M., Pinkerton J. and Kelleher J. (2000) 'Young people leaving care in England, Northern Ireland, and Ireland', *European Journal of Social Work*, 3:3, pp 235–46

Stein M. and Wade J. (2000) *Helping Care Leavers: Problems and strategic responses*, London: Department of Health

Wade J. and Dixon J. (2006) 'Making a home, finding a job: Investigating early housing and employment outcomes for young people leaving care', *Child and Family Social Work, Special Issue, Young People Leaving Care*, 11:3, pp 199–201

Wade J., Mitchell F. and Baylis G. (2005) *Unaccompanied Asylum Seeking Children: The response of social work services*, London: BAAF

Identity and continuity: Adults' access to and need for information about their history and origins

Julia Feast

Introduction

People of all cultures share a universal fascination about their ancestry and heritage. This is evident in mythology and literature and also from the large number of personal stories that appear in the media about people tracing and reuniting with family members. Researching family history has become a popular pastime and attracted much media attention and, with the availability of public records and other tools on the internet, it has become much more accessible and within the grasp of most people.

Understanding where we come from and who our forebears were can provide us with a real sense of history and continuity. It can help us to develop our own personal identity. For most people, the starting point is within their own families where they can gather together all the facts and details that have been handed down over the years and which can help them build a picture of their family and personal heritage. However, there are certain groups of people who have not grown up in the family they were born to. This chapter focuses on those who were brought up in care or were adopted. For them, accessing information and tracing their families of origin is often not straightforward although the urgency and necessity to do so extends well beyond the "simply curious".

The role of identity and belonging

Much has been written about the importance of people having a secure sense of identity and what we mean by it. Triseliotis (1983, pp 23–31) suggests that people develop a personal identity 'as a result of multiple psychological, social and cultural influences which combine towards the building of an integrated self'. In order to develop a secure sense of identity, children need to grow up in an environment feeling loved and secure, where they are perceived by others as being a valued and worthwhile person, and where they have knowledge about their family background and personal history. They need to have a sense that they belong. Within a secure family environment, the celebrations and specific events that mark transitions such as festivals, marriage and the birth of a child become the source of shared memories, opportunities for story telling, and can become part of the specific cultural history of the family. They can help provide a sense of belonging and togetherness.

For children who, for whatever reason, are not able to live with their family of origin, and particularly those where there is no contact with birth family members, developing a clear sense of who they are and where they come from can be a more difficult and fractured process. They may have many unanswered questions and live with the feeling that there are missing pieces that stir both curiosity and create a sense of longing to enable the person to achieve a fuller sense of who they are and where they come from.

Over the years, there has been a growing body of knowledge about the psychological benefits for adopted people of knowing the truth about their origins and receiving background information about it (Triseliotis, 1973; Sorosky *et al*, 1974, Sobal and Cardiff, 1983; Kowal and Schilling, 1985; Haimes and Timms, 1985; Sachdev, 1989; Bertocci and Schecter, 1991; Campbell *et al*, 1991; Brodzinsky *et al*, 1992; Ryburn, 1995). These studies have been important in identifying the emotional and psychological issues that have been core to the opening of previously closed adoption records and the part that accessing information can play in helping individuals develop a more coherent history with links between the past, present and future.

As one adopted person describes:

It just makes you feel that you belong to something because I used to very much feel as I was growing up, especially when I was going through traumatic times, like I'd just been plonked on the earth – a mystery – no past at all that you can relate to – I'd constantly think, 'why do I think this way, surely there is something else, someone who understands about this or that?' So you feel isolated and cut off. I'm sure that's one of the reasons why wanting to find birth parents is so important, because it makes you feel you have a beginning, a middle and an end. (Adopted person, Howe and Feast, 2000, p 140)

Accessing information can also be important for other reasons. It can help people to make informed decisions which could have a profound effect on their life, particularly medical information. Jane discovered that she was adopted at the age of 48. When she married, she made a decision, based on her family medical history, never to have children, as there was a genetically inherited disease that could be passed down. Jane's decision not to have children was based on false information and she felt very sad and distressed when the truth emerged.

If the opportunity for adopted people to access information has become well established, it is equally important for adults who were formerly in the care of local authorities. This was recognised by the Association of Directors of Social Services (England and Wales) in relation to the children brought up in care.

Few of us depend upon official records for our identity or history. We may throw away old papers about ourselves but that is our choice. Unlike children who have been in public care, we do not depend on the often fragmented and formal records of others.

Yet, for many adults, such information can be critical in fully understanding the past. What records contain or can be found can be vital . . . (ADSS, 2000, p 1)

Although adopted people and post care adults may share the same quest for information and questions about their origins, the legislative framework and processes for accessing information for these two groups are different and therefore these are addressed separately in this chapter.

Adopted people

The legislation

Adoption was first legalised in England and Wales in 1926 (The Adoption of Children Act, 1926). The general principle underlying the concept of adoption was that the child would be legally and emotionally severed from their family of origin. The belief at that time was that the adopted child would become such a complete member of their new family, and have no specific memories of their birth family, that they would have no need or wish to find out information or have contact with their original family. But the experience of adopted people did not bear this out. For many adopted people there was a real need for information about their original family background and reasons they were adopted. This was eventually acknowledged in England and Wales in the Children Act 1975. This gave adopted people aged 18 and over the right to apply to the Registrar General for the information which would enable them to apply for a copy of their original birth certificate and also to find out which agency had arranged their adoption. In Northern Ireland this right was brought in on 8 December 1987. Adopted people in Scotland have always had the right to obtain a copy of their original birth certificate when they reach 16 years of age

The 1975 Act was retrospective, opening the door for thousands of adopted people who wanted to have access to information about their origins and to embark on a search for birth family members. It was an explicit recognition of the importance for adopted people of having information about their origins in order to gain a fuller sense of identity. The access to birth records provisions later formed Section 51 of the 1976 Adoption Act, which was fully implemented on 1 January 1988. The primary legislation has been carried forward for pre-commencement adoptions as Schedule 2 of the Adoption and Children Act 2002, which was implemented on 30 December 2005.

People adopted before 12 November 1975 in England and Wales and before 8 December 1987 in Northern Ireland who want information about their birth records and who do not already know their birth name (but only their adopted name) have to apply to the Registrar General for access to birth records. An appointment is made for them to meet with an adoption social worker (counsellor), at which they will receive the information they need to enable them to apply for their birth certificate. This work can take place at offices of the local authority or the voluntary agency which arranged the adoption, or an adoption support agency or at the General Register Office. For people who were adopted on or after 12 November 1975, counselling is available but not compulsory.

There are also different arrangements for people who have been adopted after 30 December 2005, following the implementation of the Adoption and Children Act 2002. People adopted after this date do not need to apply to the Registrar General for the information they need to obtain a copy of their original birth certificate but to the agency which arranged the adoption.

Access to agency records

The changes made in 1975 have had a significant impact on adoption practice and attitudes about the rights and needs of adopted people accessing information from the adoption records. There is now a greater understanding of the importance for adopted people of having answers to basic but fundamental questions such as 'Who am I?', 'Where do I come from?' and 'Who do I look like?' (Triseliotis, 1973, Howe and Feast 2000, Triseliotis *et al*, 2005). Many adoption agencies have the legal discretion and will share their agency's records, including identifying information, in order to help the adopted person obtain background information and/or to begin a search for birth family members, if they so wish. However, given the emotional impact of this information for many people, it is not simply handed over. People need to be prepared for information they may not be aware of and supported through their decision-making process and the possible outcomes they may have to confront. An assessment would be made as to whether or not releasing identifying information would put anyone at risk of harm. For example, if the adopted person had mental health problems and a history of violence, the decision may be that in such a case it would not be appropriate to disclose identifying information. However, non-identifying information should be shared to help the adopted person build a fuller sense of their identity. Sometimes, there will be information in the adoption records which raises particular moral and ethical dilemmas about whether certain information about a birth family member can be shared. When these situations arise, the adoption social worker needs to make an assessment and use professional judgement in consultation with their manager and the agency's policies to reach a decision about the best way forward.

What we know from research

The *Adoption, Search and Reunion Study* (Howe and Feast, 2000) was the first major British investigation to compare the characteristics and experiences of adopted people who search for information about their background (*searchers*), and those who have shown no apparent interest in accessing information from the adoption records or searching for a birth relative (*non-searchers*). The findings reported the widespread need of many adopted people to find out about, and in many cases meet, their birth relatives. The study identified the importance people gave to the need to answer questions about identity, difference and belonging. It also explored the outcome of the search and reunion process and the particular implications it has for the self-esteem of the adopted person and the continuing relationships they have with their adoptive and birth relatives.

Information was gathered from 394 searchers and 78 non-searchers using a postal questionnaire. In-depth interviews were also carried out with 74 of the 472 adopted people who completed the detailed questionnaire, including 13 of the 32 transracially placed adopted adults. The majority of people in the study had been adopted as babies between 1950 and 1975, mostly through The Children's Society, one of the largest voluntary adoption agencies when adoption was at its peak in the 1960s.

Motivation for accessing information

The study showed that the mean age at which female searchers first contacted the agency for information was 29.8 years, while that for men was 32.3 years, and that women were twice as likely as men to initiate a search.

It also identified that adopted people do not seek information about their background and origins out of idle curiosity but out of a long-standing desire to know more about their background. The strongest of these by far is the question of identity, origins and background (roots) with 82 per cent of adopted people saying that they had 'a longstanding curiosity about their origins', 77 per cent that they 'needed to know more about themselves', and 69 per cent that they wanted 'background information'. Over 90 per cent of adopted people in the survey (searchers and non-searchers) had thought about one or more of their birth relatives when growing up. Indeed, half said they had thought about them 'a lot'. One of the things thought about 'most frequently' by over 80 per cent of people was wondering what their birth relatives looked like, and whether they might look like their birth relative. This need to find and connect with people who might look and behave like them was a strong theme throughout much of the research.

I think that everybody who is adopted, it always crosses their mind: 'I wonder if this bit is like her, or I wonder if that bit is like her?' I was about five or six months when I was adopted and I wanted to know what happened in that part of my life that nobody knew. Or just to ask the question, 'Why did you have me adopted? Why didn't you struggle?' (From original material Howe and Feast, 2000)

It was when I was a teenager that I became very aware of being adopted. Particularly not looking like anyone in my family. I wish I looked like somebody. (From original material, Howe and Feast, 2000)

However, although adopted people in the study thought about their birth parents while growing up, sharing and talking to their adoptive parents about these thoughts and the questions they had about their origins was not easy: 70 per cent of searchers and 74 per cent of non-searchers said they did not feel comfortable asking their adoptive parents for information about their birth families and their origins. In some cases, adopted people said they felt uncomfortable because they were concerned that their adoptive parents might interpret being interested in their background as an indication that they had not been good enough parents, or that the adopted person was being disloyal even to think about their birth relatives and origins. Others felt that their adoptive parents were not comfortable discussing their family of origin.

This is not to say that the adoptive parents did not want to talk to their son or daughter, as a subsequent study revealed (Triseliotis *et al*, 2005). Many adoptive parents said they felt comfortable talking to their child about his or her adoption and background, although they would often wait for their son or daughter to take the initiative to bring up the subject for discussion. This could mean that the subject, although thought about by both parties, was not discussed.

> *I always knew I was adopted. My parents were open that I was adopted but they never told me the details, but then I didn't like to ask. I just felt it was in the past and that's where it had to stay.* (Howe and Feast, 2000, p 79.)

Accessing information – the outcome

Adopted people reported many benefits from accessing information from their adoption records and 80 per cent said that it had been a positive experience. Seventy per cent said that looking at their records meant that they learnt more about their birth mother, had a better understanding of why they were adopted, and that it filled the gaps, improved their sense of identity, and for some, enabled them to learn more about their birth father. Often, the original birth certificate of the adopted person did not include the name of their birth father. As today, if a child was born outside wedlock, the father had to be present to register his name on the birth certificate. However, some adoption records did contain detailed information about the father, including his name, a description of what he looked like, his occupation and interests. Receiving information about the birth father enabled adopted people to identify with the other half of their genetic identity.

> *It may seem odd but my birth father never really featured in my thoughts when thinking about my birth family. On my original birth certificate it was just a blank where the father's name should be, so he felt non-existent. So it was a complete shock to me when I went to the adoption agency to get more information to be confronted with so much information about him. I found out his name, was given a physical description and information about his interests. For the first time he became a real person and I wanted to know more and find him as much as my birth mother.* (From original research material, Howe and Feast, 2000)

Seventy-one per cent said that receiving information had answered important questions about their background.

Added a new depth and a sense of perspective to my sense of identity.
Feel more confident about myself.
I felt I existed and finally had a history.
I really understand why I was adopted and how lucky I was to be with my family.
(Howe and Feast, 2000, p 48 and 49)

However, 28 per cent felt disappointed that the records did not hold as much information as they had hoped, and some found the experience had a negative impact on their self and identity.

Made me more curious but also confused.

Once I found more information I felt more hurt and rejected.
(Howe and Feast, 2000, p 49)

Within a month of accessing their adoption records, 88 per cent of people had begun to search for one of their birth relatives. For the majority (91%), the knowledge gained about the birth mother's circumstances spurred them on to begin to look for her. The search varied in length and complexity, but within three months, 60 per cent of those who had embarked on their quest to find their birth mother had found her and made contact. In many cases, finding the birth mother led to unexpected meetings with other birth relatives, including full and half-siblings, grandparents, and sometimes other members of the extended birth family.

Only in a few cases did the birth parent, when found, refuse to have contact. Nineteen (7%) of the 274 people who had searched for and found their birth relative suffered an outright rejection. Of these nineteen, 17 were rejected by their birth mother and two by their birth father. For these people, the experience was painful, but even in these cases, most individuals (90%), when asked to review events, expressed no regrets about searching, although they did feel frustrated by the outcome.

However, not everyone decided to search for a birth relative after they had received information from their adoption records: 15 per cent of the 394 people who sought information from adoption records said that they did not want to begin a search for and make contact with a birth relative at this point in time. The majority of this number (49%) said one of the main reasons for not searching and making contact with a birth relative was that they 'wanted to wait until the time is right'. Other reasons included 'interested but afraid of rejection by the birth family' (44%), 'interested but don't wish to upset adoptive parents' (42%), 'interested but afraid contact might upset birth family' (42%). So, in these cases, although the desire to search for birth relatives seemed to be present, the timing and the potential impact on the self and others put an emotional brake on the process.

Over 80 per cent of searchers and non-searchers from the original sample reported that access to information and or contact with birth relatives had answered important questions about their origins and identity. Adopted people described feeling more at ease, experiencing a more complete sense of self: 'felt at peace', 'feel more content as an individual', 'understand why I tick better and feel more complete', 'fulfilled now that pieces of the jigsaw are in place' (Howe and Feast, 2000, p 141).

Deciding whether to make enquiries about origins and/or begin a search for birth relatives is a complex business. Some adopted people will have no desire to make this journey in their lifetime, others will feel ambivalent, and some will be very keen to find out all that they can. What is important is that adopted people have the choice and opportunity from which to make decisions that meets their particular needs.

However, for most people in the study, there seems little doubt that accessing information and subsequent contact with the birth relative was a valuable and enriching experience. The study also showed that the adopted person's relationship with their adoptive parent was rarely affected in a negative way. This was also echoed in Triseliotis *et al*'s study (2005). Both studies reported that the relationships and familial bonds developed in childhood were strong and enduring. In most cases, the adopted person was absolutely clear that their adoptive parents were still 'mum and dad'. Indeed, many people felt that, having met birth relatives and gained further knowledge about their background, this enabled them to appreciate all that their adoptive parents had given them, further cementing the bond.

Post care adults

The legislation

There has been a legislative framework in place for some years to assist adopted people to access information about their origins, family background and the circumstances of their adoption and also an intermediary service to help them contact birth family members. The same opportunities and facilities do not extend to post care adults, although they are just as likely to share the same quest for information about their own personal history and the desire to re-establish contact with family members they have lost touch with. However, the length, complexity and significance of the information may be of a quite different order to that of adopted people. Their care arrangements may have changed frequently, with a very large number of people having played a significant part in the person's care and upbringing. Abuse and mistreatment may also have played a part for a significant number of people and some of this may have been at the hands of previous carers.

Prior to the Data Protection Act 1998 (DPA), the governing legislation that enabled people brought up in care to access information came under the Access to Personal Files Act 1987 and the associated Access to Personal Files (Social Services) Regulations 1989. These allowed individuals to see what was recorded about them in local authority paper files. However, this legislation was not retrospective and did not apply to the voluntary sector. This meant that enormous numbers of care leavers – those in care before and during the 1950s, 60s, 70s and 80s, – had no statutory right to see what had been written about them.

The Data Protection Act 1998 which came into effect on 24 October 2001, introduced a new system for the management of personal data, under which any living person who is the subject of personal data held or processed by a social work agency has the right of access to that data. When an application for disclosure of information has been received, the local authority is expected to respond and provide the information within 40 calendar days. Unlike for an adopted person, when a post care adult requests access to information from agency records, there is no expectation and requirement for them to have a personal meeting with a social worker, where the information can be shared in a supportive environment, and where questions and issues can be raised and addressed. The information can simply be sent in the post with no follow-up.

Where the local authority makes a decision to refuse access, then the data subject (the person applying for access to information) may appeal to the courts or to the Office of the Information Commissioner.

The DPA 1998 introduced a single regime to cover both computer-based records (previously dealt with by the Data Protection Act 1984), paper files and also unstructured records of the kinds found within children's homes, such as day books and punishment books. Local authorities are expected to have retention policies that reflect the DPA 1998. The access provisions of the Act only apply to voluntary sector case files when kept, or intended to be kept, on automated equipment or in a 'relevant filing system' (DPA s. 1(1)). Even an archiving system employing microfiche may lack sufficient sophistication to qualify as a 'relevant filing system' within the meaning of the Act.

The Act has two broad purposes: 1) to protect the right of individuals to privacy, and 2) to ensure that those individuals have access to information held about them and can correct it. However, the Act is not an effective way to meet the information needs of post care adults as it does not take into account the particular plight of those adults who mainly want to obtain a family history, including details of their parents and siblings.

Under the Act, a person does not have the right to know what is recorded about someone else. So, for example, one family member is not entitled to see the record of another member. Where information includes details of another person, the agency needs to consider obtaining permission from that person before disclosure. For some post care adults, seeking the written permission of parents or siblings to access certain information may not be in the post care adults' interest. For instance, the post care adult may have had no contact with his or her family since coming into care and have no wish to be in touch now.

The requirements of this Act are such that it can mean that post care adults may be given very little and or disjointed information, because of the restrictions on third party information, as one post care adult has described:

> *I had been in care for 15 years and found out I could apply for my records, but all I got were 10 sheets of paper with lots of information tippexed out – I wondered why I bothered to access the information as what I got did not make a lot of sense.* (Goddard *et al*, 2005)

The post care adult may not receive a coherent history about their family background as in Arthur's case.

> *Arthur had been admitted to local authority care when he was 18 months old where he remained for the next 16 years. He remembers having some contact with his mother early in his childhood but his memory was hazy. He had no contact with any other family member and knew very little about his family background. At the age of 35, he decided that he wanted to access information and particularly to understand why he came into care and remained there for the rest of his childhood. The agency felt that they were able to tell Arthur that he came into care because his mother was admitted to hospital but they decided to withhold the reason why. They considered that disclosing the reasons for his mother's admission to hospital was private and not his information to be had as it was third party information. Arthur was not told that his mother suffered from a long-term severe mental illness.*

Although there are inevitable tensions about whose information it is, the lack of knowledge about the reason for Arthur's mother's admission could have significant implications for his own and his descendents' medical histories. What is more, the information may have helped him think differently about his mother and the reason he came into care. The agency can decide to provide the information where permission has not been given, but they would need to justify the reasons for this.

The current legislative framework for accessing information for post care adults does not make it easy to achieve a coherent and comprehensive picture of family and background. Clarification of legal issues surrounding the implementation of the DPA was given in the Durant Case (Durant v FSA [2003] EWCA Civ 1746 Court of Appeal (Civil Division)). In this case, the Court of Appeal decided that information is only accessible by a data subject (the person making the application for disclosure) if it is both biographical and mainly focused on the data subject. This was not a case of a post care adult, but the judgement has implications for post care adults who are trying to access information. It could mean that access to information could be severely restricted as the records are likely to contain third party information. However, in the case concerning Graham Gaskin, a young man who had been abused during many years in care (MacVeigh, 1982, Gaskin, 2005), who took his complaint to the European Court of Human Rights, the court took a different view. In Gaskin v. UK [12 EHHR 36; 7th July 1989], the European Court found that Gaskin's Article 8 rights under the European Convention (the right to respect for one's private and family life) had been breached by Liverpool City Council's refusal to grant him access to his care records. Gaskin had successfully argued that such information was necessary in order to understand his identity and childhood experiences.

There continues to be a great deal of confusion with different practices surrounding the DPA and access to information for post care adults as discussed later. At the time of writing this chapter, there is a campaign underway that is calling for forthcoming legislation to take account of the lifelong issues of being brought up in care and to ensure that it takes account of the specific information needs of post care adults.

What we know from research

Children and young people who have been brought up in care need as much information about their lives in care as any adopted person. Accessing information about the past can be important in the construction of a 'coherent narrative of their lives that can connect past and present' (Stein and Carey, 1986; Biehal et al, 1995; Lynes and Goddard, 1996; Wheal, 2002; Winter and Cohen, 2005). For children in care today, information and explanation are no less important and it is expected that all children will have their own life story book and ongoing contact with workers who can help them understand their past and information about their family. There is, however, no research study in the UK that confirms whether or not this happens, nor are there any data about the quality and effectiveness of life story books or life story work that helps answer questions that children in care may have about their background and time in care. Additionally, there have been no large scale studies that report on the direct experiences of post care adults who have requested and received access to the information on the childhood records held by the agency they were in the care of.

There have been a few personal accounts written by post care adults (Fever, 1994; Hewitt, 2002; Frampton, 2004; Oldfield, 2004; Gaskin, 2005) which suggest that accessing information and revisiting the care experience can be a valuable, cathartic and important process. Paolo Hewitt, the music journalist and author, used his files to help him to write his account of growing up in care (Hewitt, 2002). He recounts why he needed to access information:

I had had enough of my past dictating my present and future. I had had enough of my past making me feel low, insecure and frightened. I had to face up to it. I was getting close to the point where I had more years behind me than in front of me. It was a time to take on, as best I could, the demons I'd lived with for what seemed like forever.

. . . and what the experience felt like:

I began to read and re-read the story of my life. It was an amazing experience. In those files, you see and hear people talking about your character, your appearance, your demeanour. You see how others view you. Your reactions to events are recorded and so is your world view. Not only is your early life set down forever but also chronicled are the memories that will never fade and the ones that already have. I think it is the closest you can get to attending your own funeral, which makes it a one-off experience, one of the few perks of being a looked after kid . . .'

Phil Frampton also poignantly recounts the experience of developing an autobiographical account of his care experience and the impact this had:

I no longer had a story with no beginning, with half tales and conjecture. It was not the type of shock I had expected. Instead I felt anger. Then came numbness and sadness for all concerned. I'd crammed 18 years of birth, rejection, love, loneliness, guilt and death into four hours. (Phil's story: accessible on www.careleavers.org)

During the past decade there have been a few small scale studies which have looked at the motivation and information needs of post care adults (Pugh, 1999; Kirton *et al*, 2001). Pugh's small scale qualitative study of 12 adults accessing information from Barnardo's records in the late 1990s highlighted a number of themes from their searches:

- the meaning and significance of roots, primarily blood ties;
- the need to know, basic curiosity about one's past;
- the need to create a coherent self-image;
- the intensity of emotion involved in this process.

Kirton *et al*'s analysis of 157 files of post care adults who had requested access to information found that motivation was split between the basic need for information (86%); curiosity about origins (69%); and help to trace birth family members (49%). Post care adults were also interested in seeking medical information (34%). The study also revealed that the age that post care adults access records was much older than their adopted counterparts. The average age for adopted people is 30 years old, whereas post care adults tend to be in their 40s. The level of demand from post care adults to access information from care records also seems to relate to their level of awareness that such information exists, rather than to an intrinsic lack of interest. This was demonstrated by the huge upsurge in demand for access to information following the BBC's screening of *Barnardo's Children* in 1995 (Pugh, 1999). The programme featured former Barnardo's children using their files to revisit their past. Prior to the screening of the programme, enquiries for care records at Barnardo's had been running at about 1,500 per year. After the programmes, there was a huge increase to 4,000 enquiries in the following few weeks alone.

Goddard *et al* (2005) published the findings from a survey of 81 local authorities and how they managed applications for access to information from post care adults under the DPA 1998. They found that one of the main areas agencies struggled with was to do with third party information. Because of the restrictions and constraints of the Data Protection Act 1998, there are tensions created by attempts at making the story meaningful for the post care adult without breaching the Act.

Handling third party information. The former looked after person's rights are not as clearly set out in legislation as in the adoption acts. The DPA was not designed specifically for this group of people's needs.

I think sometimes, as well, I feel there is a huge dilemma. It is all a matter of judgement, at the end of the day, in terms of the confidentiality we owe to third parties and the personal need for an individual to receive information. I sometimes feel you can argue both ways . . . If, say, I was a young person in care and there is information there about my parents, I would want to know that. And yet, as a council employee, I've got to carry forward that duty of confidentiality to the parents.

It is extremely difficult, because you could take out so much that it was meaningless.

When you are looking at bits of paper where, because their information has been with that of their brothers, you have to take out everything about their brother, so every other paragraph is blanked out, or whatever it happens to be, I think that that can cause an additional trauma for people.

The study found that the practices and policies for accessing information under the Data Protection Act varied enormously. Some local authorities believed that it was important for post care adults to be given the opportunity to receive support during the process of accessing information, by offering an appointment to discuss some of the issues this action might raise for them. Others considered that this was not necessary and would compile the information they thought the post care adult should have and send it in the post. The study showed that for many local authorities, services for post care adults are a neglected area in terms of policy, procedure, training and resources. It underlined the gulf between what is available for adopted people and post care adults in terms of support services and resources.

Implications for practice in child placement

This chapter has explored two different groups, adopted people and post care adults, who have been affected by statutory child care provision in terms of both their need to access information about their origins and personal histories, and the opportunities and choices they face. To date, there has been much more recognition and understanding of the importance to adopted people of being able to access the information they need so that they can develop a stronger sense of who they are and where they come from. What has been learnt from both of these groups has significant implications for practice today. The social worker has an important role in ensuring that any child or young person has information that is accurate and of a high quality and which can be accessed at any time in their lifetime. This can only happen if social workers get to know the children and young people on their case load and make meaningful and appropriately lasting relationships with them. Although this is very obvious at one level, changes in social worker have become a serious problem. As Fernando (Fernando, September, 2007), age 11 said, 'Social workers change so often I once had one I never met.' The article goes on to highlight the views of several young people and their dissatisfaction about the relationship they had with their social worker.

The competing demands on social workers' time in the modern day world may also make it more difficult for them to allow sufficient time to get to know and build meaningful relationships with the children on their caseload. For example, whilst important, the need to maintain computerised records and produce information to evaluate and monitor their work, may mean that more of their time is spent on administration rather than building a relationship with the child.

The use of computer databases and electronic records with highly structured formats and extensive use of "tick-box" elements have real advantages in increasing standardisation, efficiency and accessibility when they work well. However, data loss, potential breaches of confidentiality and the speed of technological change may create problems for adults, in even a few years time, who wish to access information about their earlier lives. Tick box and highly structured formats may lack the detailed personal information that people are looking for. It is very unlikely that such record keeping can achieve the core of what people need to gain from access to records – a sense of who they are, their family history, their time in care.

There are now some core messages that have been learnt about these issues that social work practitioners, managers and policy makers need to take note of if we are to ensure that best practice is in place for children and young people who are not able to be brought up within their family of origin.

- The importance of gathering as much information as possible when the child first comes to the notice of the local authority. A comprehensive, accurate chronological family, health, education and social history can provide the foundations for the child to access information and answer the questions they may have across their lifespan.
- Making sure all professionals understand the purposes of gathering information and gaining permission for the information to be shared if and when appropriate. The importance of gathering and recording detailed and accurate information for children who come into care should not be underestimated. Short periods or a childhood in care need to be recorded not just for agency purposes but because they are a part of that child's history.
- Issuing every child with a memory book that accompanies them throughout their time in care. Carers should be encouraged to write down records of important events, including a range of stories that can help the child revisit and recount these events at a later date. For example, the child at the age of two may have used a sound "yoke" instead of "soap", a teacher may have commented on how particularly well the child did in class that day; a story they were particularly fond of at bedtime, names of special friends and notable outings and holidays. The list is endless but the message is that when a person has been brought up in care and has one, two, or several placements, such information can help them achieve a greater sense of their individuality.
- Providing children with the opportunity to ask questions about their family background. This can be done through life story work – but that is not just a one-off task. As children grow up, their understanding and perceptions change and the initial life story work may need to be revisited from time to time to ensure that it is age appropriate.
- Ensuring that legislation and practice take account of the specific needs of post care adults who want to access information about their family background and care history. There will always be tensions about third party information and whose information it is, but information must be meaningful. It should be an expectation that people receive access to the information they would have if they were brought up in their family of origin. For example, that their sibling spent time in a remand home after committing a series of criminal offences.
- Sharing and disclosing information from agency records is a task that needs to be properly resourced. To do the job well, social work practitioners should have access to training, supervision and support, particularly when making decisions about what and how much information should be shared.

A child's identity and personal history are unique and precious. Agencies and practitioners therefore have a prime duty to ensure that they take responsibility for this in the same way

THE CHILD PLACEMENT HANDBOOK

that any parent treasures their child and finds ways of holding that child in their family history and culture.

Selected further reading

Howe D. and Feast J. (2004) *Adoption Search and Reunion: The long-term experience of adopted adults*, London: BAAF
An accessible research study on searchers and non-searchers together with short-term and long-term outcomes.

Trinder L., Feast J. and Howe D. (2004) *The Adoption Reunion Handbook*, Chichester: John Wiley & Sons
This comprehensive and practical "how to" guide is essential for everyone involved in adoption, particularly those considering searching for information on their birth relatives. It is based on a scale research study and draws on real-life experiences of reunions.

Triseliotis J., Feast J. and Kyle F. (2005) *The Adoption Triangle Revisited: A study of adoption, search and reunion experience*, London: BAAF
Another important study of adoption, search and reunion.

References

Association of Directors of Social Services (2000) *Briefing Paper: The Archiving and Destruction of Records for Children in Care/Looked After*, London: ADSS Organisation and Development Committee

Bertocci D. and Schecter M. D. (1991) 'Adopted adults' perception of their need to search: Implications for clinical practice', *Smith Collection of Studies in Social Work*, 61:2, pp 179–96

Biehal N., Clayden J., Stein M. and Wade W. (1995) *Moving On: Young People and Leaving Care Schemes*, London: HMSO

Brodzinsky D. M., Schechter M. D. and Marantz Henig R. (1992) *Being Adopted: The lifelong search for self*, New York: Anchor Books

Campbell L., Silverman P. and Patti P. (1991) 'Reunions between adoptees and birth parents: The adoptees' experience', *Social Work*, 3, pp 329–35

Fernando (2007) 'The trouble with social workers', *Community Care*, 1690, p 21

Fever F. (1994) 'Who cares? Memories of a childhood in Barnardo's', London: Time Warner

Frampton P. (2004) *The Golly in the Cupboard*, Manchester: Tamic Publications

Gaskin G. (2005) *A Boy Called Graham*, London: Blake Publishing

Goddard J., Feast J. and Kirton D. A. (2005) *Childhood on Paper: Accessing the child care files of former looked after children in the UK*, Bradford: University of Bradford

Haimes E. and Timms N. (1985) *Adoption, Identity, and Social Policy: The search for distant relatives*, Aldershot: Gower

Hewitt P. (2002) *The Looked After Kid*, Edinburgh: Mainstream Publishing

Howe D. and Feast J. (2000) *Adoption, Search and Reunion*, London: The Children's Society (now reprinted by BAAF, 2004)

Kirton D., Peltier E. and Webb E. (2001) 'After all these years: Accessing care records', *Adoption & Fostering*, 25:4, pp 39–49

Kowal K. A. and Schilling K. M. (1985) 'Adoption through the eyes of adult adoptees', *American Journal of Orthopsychiatry*, 55, July, pp 354–62

Lynes D. and Goddard J. (1995) *The View from the Front*, Norwich: Norfolk County Council Social Services Department

Oldfield B. (2004), *Rootless: An autobiography*, London: Hutchinson

Pugh G. (1999) *Unlocking the Past: The impact of access to Barnardo's childcare records*, Aldershot: Ashgate

Ryburn M. (1995) 'Adopted children's identity and information needs', *Children and Society*, 9:3, pp 41–6

Sachdev P. (1989) *Unlocking the Adoption Files*, Toronto: Lexington Books

Sobol M. and Cardiff J. (1983) 'A sociopsychological investigation of adult adoptees' search for their birth parents', *Family Relations*, 32, pp 477–83

Sorosky A., Baran A. and Pannor R. (1974) 'The reunion of adoptees and birth relatives', *Journal of Youth and Adolescence*, 3:3, pp 195–206

Stein M. and Carey K. (1986) *Leaving Care*, Oxford : Blackwell

Triseliotis J. (1973) *In Search of Origins: The experiences of adopted people*, London: Routledge and Kegan Paul

Triseliotis J. (1983) 'Identity and security in adoption and long-term fostering', *Adoption & Fostering*, 7:1, pp 22–31

Triseliotis J., Feast J. and Kyle F. (2005) *The Adoption Triangle Revisited: A study of adoption search and reunion experiences*, London: BAAF

Wheal A. (ed.) (2002) *The RHP Companion to Leaving Care*, Lyme Regis: Russell House Publishing

Winter K. and Cohen O. (2005) 'Identity issues for "looked after" children with no knowledge of their origins: Implications for research and practice', *Adoption & Fostering*, 29:2, pp 44–52

Notes about the contributors

David Berridge is Professor of Child and Family Welfare and Head of the Centre for Family Policy and Child Welfare at the School for Policy Studies, University of Bristol. He was formerly Research Director at the National Children's Bureau, Research Fellow at the Dartington Social Research Unit and Director of the Institute of Applied Social Research, University of Luton. David has been a researcher for 25 years and is author/co-author of 12 books and numerous other chapters and articles. He was awarded the OBE in January 2005 for services to children.

Nina Biehal is Research Director of the Children and Young People's Social Work Team at the Social Policy Research Unit at the University of York. She has published on a wide range of child welfare topics including work on looked after children, preventive work with adolescents at risk of entering care, the reunification of children in care with their families and young runaways. Her current work includes a comparative study of adoption and long-term foster care and evaluations of Multi-dimensional Treatment Foster Care programmes working with looked after young people and with young offenders.

Sarah Borthwick is an independent trainer and consultant, specialising in adoption and fostering work. She formerly worked for BAAF as a trainer consultant and regional manager of the Southern region. She then worked as county adoption manager for a local authority. She chairs three local authority adoption panels and has chaired a number of fostering panels. She is the co-author of *Effective Fostering Panels* and the co-author of *Together or Apart? Assessing siblings for permanent placement*.

Roger Bullock began his research work at the Research Centre, King's College, Cambridge on studies into the effects of boarding education. In 1968, he helped establish the Dartington Social Research Unit, retiring in 2003. He is now a fellow of the Centre for Social Policy in the Warren House Group at Dartington, Professor Emeritus of Child Welfare Research at Bristol University and Commissioning Editor of *Adoption & Fostering*. The Unit's work is the subject of *Forty Years of Research, Policy and Practice* (Axford, N., Berry, V., Little, M. and Morpeth, L. eds., 2005).

Jennifer Cousins is consultant to BAAF's *Opening Doors* Disability Project. She has been with BAAF as a child placement consultant and trainer since 1997. Jennifer has extensive practice experience in family placement and children's disability, including a short breaks scheme and a multi-disciplinary child development centre. Since joining

BAAF, her direct contact with practice has been maintained through chairing an adoption and fostering panel. In 2007 she was part of a small international team working with the Romanian government to strengthen their domestic adoption policy and practice. Jennifer has published a number of articles and books on child placement, disability and other social work themes.

Elaine Farmer is Professor of Child and Family Studies in the School for Policy Studies at Bristol University, prior to which she spent several years as a social worker. Her recently completed research on reunification, and her current studies on adoption and on neglect, are funded by the Department for Children, Schools and Families. Her books include *Trials and Tribulations: Returning children from local authority care to their families* (1991), *Child Protection Practice: Private risks and public remedies* (1995), *Sexually Abused and Abusing Children in Substitute Care* (1998), *Fostering Adolescents* (2004) and *Kinship Care: Fostering effective family and friends placements* (2008).

Julia Feast is the Policy, Research and Development Consultant at the British Association for Adoption and Fostering (BAAF). She is an experienced social worker and researcher. She has particular interest in the identity and information rights and needs of adopted people, post care adults and donor conceived people. Her publications include *Adoption Search and Reunion: The long-term experience of adopted adults*, *The Adoption Triangle Revisited: A study of adoption search and reunion experience*, *The Adoption Reunion Handbook* and *A Childhood on Paper: Accessing the child care files of former looked after children in the UK*.

Dr Catherine Hill is a Senior Lecturer in Child Health at the University of Southampton and honorary consultant paediatrician to Southampton City Primary Care Trust. In her clinical role she has worked as designated doctor to a unitary authority and adoption medical advisor to a large shire county. As committee member of the BAAF Health Group since 2000 and now as its Chair she has contributed to the development of standardised statutory health assessment forms, emotional and mental health assessment tools and guidelines for the health assessment of intercountry adoptees. She has published a number of journal articles and chapters about the health of looked after children based on original research.

Malcolm Hill worked as a child care practitioner in London, then moved to Scotland where he has undertaken research and taught social work and social policy students. For several years he was the Commissioning Editor of the journal, *Adoption & Fostering*. He was Director of the Glasgow Centre for the Child & Society and now works part time as a Research Professor at the University of Strathclyde in the Glasgow School of Social Work.

David Howe is Professor of Social Work at the University of East Anglia, Norwich. He has research and teaching interests in attachment, adoption, child abuse and neglect, and emotional development. He is the author of many books including, most recently, *Child Abuse and Neglect: Attachment, development and intervention* (2005) and *The Emotionally Intelligent Social Worker* (2008).

Joan Hunt is Senior Research Fellow in Oxford University's Centre for Family Law and Policy, part of the Department of Social Policy and Social Work. In addition to conducting empirical research on children in kinship care, she is the author of an overview of international research and policy commissioned by the government (*Family and Friends Carers: Scoping paper prepared for the Department of Health*; DH, 2003) and a research and practice briefing paper commissioned by Research in Practice (Briefing Paper 16: *Family and Friends Care*, Research in Practice, 2008). She is guest editor of a forth-coming special issue of the journal *Adoption & Fostering* on kinship care.

Jenifer Lord is a child placement consultant who works in BAAF's Southern region. Before that she worked in a child care team and in an adoption and fostering team in two local authorities. She chairs a local authority adoption and permanence panel and has been a member of a number of others. She is the author of *Adopting a Child: A guide for prospective adopters* and of *The Adoption Process in England: A guide for children's social workers*. She is the principal author of *Effective Panels*, BAAF's guide for adoption panel members; and the co-author of *Effective Fostering Panels* and of *Together or Apart? Assessing siblings for permanent placement*.

Elsbeth Neil is a senior lecturer at the University of East Anglia, Norwich, and a key researcher and author in the field of contact after adoption. She has been carrying out research into this topic since 1996, directing the "Contact after Adoption" study which looked at how direct and indirect contact was working out from the point of view of children, adoptive parents and birth relatives. She is currently directing the DCSF funded "Researching adoption support project" looking at adoption support services for birth parents and post adoption support for direct contact.

Alan Rushton spent many years as a social worker in both child and adult mental health services. Until recently he was Director of the MSc programme in Mental Health Social Work and Reader in Adoption Studies at the Institute of Psychiatry, King's College, London. Since retirement, he continues as a Visiting Professor at the Institute. He has been engaged in follow-up studies of children adopted from care; the outcomes of sibling placements and contact arrangements. He has recently conducted a trial of the effectiveness of parenting programmes for adopters of children late placed from care. He has published many research papers and six books.

Gillian Schofield is Professor of Child and Family Social Work and Co-Director of the Centre for Research on the Child and Family at the University of East Anglia. She was Chair of the BAAF Research Group Advisory Committee from 2001–2006. An experienced social worker, she practised for some years as a Guardian ad Litem. Her research and teaching interests are in attachment theory and family placement practice, the impact of maltreatment on children's development, the role of long-term foster care as a positive permanence option and the experiences of parents of children in long-term foster care.

Hilary Saunders is the Training and Research Officer at the Hadley Centre for Adoption and Foster Care Studies, School for Policy Studies, University of Bristol. Previously she was the Children's Policy Officer at Women's Aid Federation of England, and she worked for Shelter for 16 years as a policy officer, housing aid co-ordinator, trainer and caseworker. Her publications include *Twenty-Nine Child Homicides: Lessons still to be learnt on domestic violence and child protection* (Women's Aid).

Peter Selman is Visiting Fellow in the School of Geography, Politics & Sociology at Newcastle University, UK, where he teaches courses in *Comparative Social Policy and Adoption; a worldwide perspective*. His main areas of research interest are child adoption, teenage pregnancy and demographic change and public policy. He is currently Chair of the Network for Intercountry Adoption (NICA) and a member of the Board of Trustees of the British Association for Adoption & Fostering (BAAF). He is editor of *Intercountry Adoption: Development, trends and perspectives* (BAAF, 2000) and has written many articles and chapters on adoption policy.

Dr. Julie Selwyn is a Senior Lecturer and Director of the Hadley Centre for Adoption and Foster Care Studies in the School for Policy Studies, University of Bristol (www.bristol.ac.uk/hadley). Her previous work includes *Costs and Outcomes of Non-infant Adoptions* (2006, BAAF) and *Finding Adoptive Families for Black, Asian and Ethnic Minority Children*, (2004, NCH).

John Simmonds is Director of Policy, Research and Development at the British Association for Adoption and Fostering. Before coming to BAAF, he was head of the social work programmes at Goldsmiths College, University of London. He is a qualified social worker and has substantial experience in child protection, family placement and residential care settings. He has published widely. He is the adoptive father of two children.

Ian Sinclair worked in secondary teaching, probation, social services, counselling and industrial and social research after completing his first degree in philosophy and ancient history. Since 1989 he has been at the University of York, first as Professor of Social Work, then as Co-director of the Social Work Research and Development Unit and now as a part-time Research Professor at the Social Policy Research Unit. He has published widely in the fields of delinquency and the welfare of old people and children.

Professor Mike Stein is a Research Professor in the Social Policy Research Unit at the University of York. During the last 25 years he has been researching the problems and challenges faced by young people leaving care. He has also researched the experiences of young people running away from home, mentoring for care leavers, and, currently, the maltreatment of adolescents. He is a co-ordinator of the International Research Group, Transitions to Adulthood for Young People Leaving Public Care. He has been involved in the preparation of training materials and guidance, for leaving care legislation in the UK, and has been consulted internationally on the development of services.

Olive Stevenson is Professor Emeritus of Social Work at Nottingham University. She holds honorary degrees from the Universities of East Anglia and Kingston and was awarded the CBE in 1996. Her professional and academic interests include child welfare, especially child protection and the problem of severe neglect, on which she has published extensively, most recently with the second, extensively revised, edition of *Neglected Children and their Families* (Blackwell, 2007). She has been involved in many Serious Case Reviews over the years, beginning with the Maria Colwell Inquiry in 1973, and has chaired five Area Child Protection Committees.

Nigel Thomas is Professor of Childhood and Youth Research at the University of Central Lancashire. He was a social work practitioner and manager in Derbyshire and Oxfordshire for twenty years, after which he taught and researched in child welfare and childhood studies at Swansea University. His publications include *Children, Family and the State: Decision-making and child participation* (Policy Press, 2002) and *Social Work with Young People in Care* (Palgrave, 2005). He is co-editor of the journal, *Children & Society*.

June Thoburn is Professor Emeritus in the School of Social Work and Psychology at the University of East Anglia. A qualified and experienced child and family social worker, she has been teaching on and researching across the field of child welfare since 1978. She is involved in the training of the judiciary and is frequently asked to provide expert evidence and consultation in complex foster care and adoption cases. She is a member of the General Social Care Council and was awarded the CBE in 2000 "for services to social work". She was awarded a Leverhulme Emeritus Fellowship to undertake an international comparison of children in out-of-home care.

Dinithi Wijedasa is a Research Associate at the Hadley Centre. Prior to joining the centre, Dinithi established a culturally sensitive screening tool for assessing development delay for children in Sri Lanka. The centre is currently working on a number of studies including estimating the costs of adoption, evaluating the kinship care services within a local authority and evaluating the effectiveness of a different model of providing domestic adoptions services.

Jim Wade is a Senior Research Fellow in the Social Policy Research Unit, University of York. He has researched and published widely in the area of social work and related services for vulnerable groups of children and young people, including looked after children, care leavers, young runaways and unaccompanied asylum-seeking children. He has been involved in the preparation of best practice guides and official guidance on services for care leavers and young runaways and has acted as consultant to other national and international research initiatives in these areas.

Kate Wilson is a qualified social worker and counsellor whose professional practice includes working as a probation officer in Inner London, as a social worker and team manager on a housing estate in North East England and as a mediator for couples in divorce. Since 2001, she has been at the University of Nottingham, first as Professor of Social Work and more recently as Emeritus Professor. Her teaching and research interests are in child welfare and therapeutic work and the relevance of the study of literature to social work. She is the joint author of *Social Work: An introduction to contemporary practice*, published by Pearson Education.

Julie Young is a Research Associate at the University of East Anglia, Norwich, and an established researcher in the field of contact after adoption. She joined Elsbeth Neil at the UEA in 2001 to work on the "Contact after Adoption" study after several years of experience in the fields of education and counselling. She is currently the main researcher on the DCSF funded "Researching adoption support" project, looking at adoption support services for birth parents and post adoption support for direct contact.

Index

A

preoccupied/insecure attachment 229–33
unresolved attachment 229–33
attachment disorders
adolescents 169
adoptive parents 229
birth parents 195, 197
disinhibited 55, 292
intercountry adoption 292–3
maltreated children 57–9
placement instability 422–3
post-adoption support 270
sibling conflict 403
attachment figure
abusive 50–2
neglectful 55
Australia, intercountry adoption 282, 290

B

BAAF
adoption preparation course 264
Direct Work 77
family finding 346, 349, 351
adoption parties 353–4
sibling groups 412
parental training 342
see also Be My Parent
Barnardo's Children (BBC) 451
Be My Parent (BAAF) 346, 349, 351
outcomes 354, 355
sibling group placement 412
subscriber survey 357
on video-making 358
Be My Parent Online 351, 353
bed and breakfast accommodation 204, 386
behaviour management 271–2
behavioural, emotional and social
difficulties (BESD) 335
behavioural difficulties
adolescents 160, 161–2, 169–70, 171–3
adoption and 227, 234–6, 266–7
asylum seekers 388

comparative care study 225–7
conduct disorder 312
contact and 247
educational attainment 328–9
intercountry adoption 292–3
Kent Family Placement Scheme 15
in kinship care 113, 115
in new placement 57–9
long-term outcomes 434
parenting interventions 270–2
permanence planning 143, 146–8,
234–6
placement disruption 171–2, 227
placement moves 11
placement instability 88
post-reunification 91–2
residential care 125, 204–5, 207–9
in school 335
specialist foster care 166
belonging (sense of)
foster care 122, 151, 153–4
and identity 439–41
kinship care 104, 106
birth families
adolescents, difficult 160, 162–5, 168–9
in adoption 244
composition changes 93, 109, 182
contact
fostered children 127–8, 178–99
legislation on 179
members in 250, 254
post-adoption 263
withdrawal from 190
links with 181–2
long-term placements 141, 150, 155
mixed ethnicity 363–5, 377
permanence plans and 141, 143–5
residential care and 209–10
reunification with 83–96
search and reunion 283–4, 441–6
siblings 401–6
birth family home, contact in 187